RAYMOND LEPPARD ON MUSIC

RAYMOND LEPPARD
ON MUSIC

An Anthology of Critical
and
Personal Writings

EDITED BY

THOMAS P. LEWIS

Pro/Am Music Resources, Inc.
White Plains, New York

Authenticity in Music (Chapter 1) was first published in 1988 by Faber
Music Ltd. (London) in association with Faber & Faber, with distribution
by Amadeus Press (Portland OR) in the U.S.A. and Canada.

Published in the United States of America 1993 by
PRO/AM MUSIC RESOURCES, INC.
63 Prospect Street, White Plains, New York 10606
ISBN 0-912483-96-2

U.S. School & Library Distribution by
PRO/AM MUSIC RESOURCES, INC.

U.S. Trade & Retail Distribution by
THE BOLD STRUMMER, LTD.
20 Turkey Hill Circle, Box 1037, Westport, Connecticut 06880

FIRST EDITION

For Jeffrey

CONTENTS

CONTENTS

LIST OF ILLUSTRATIONS

CONTENTS

[LIST OF ILLUSTRATIONS, *continued*]

ACKNOWLEDGEMENTS

Shirley Fleming's 1979 interview with Raymond Leppard first appeared in *High Fidelity/Musical America* and was republished in the 1979/80 year book of the Scottish Chamber Orchestra.

Tom Aldridge's interview with Raymond Leppard first appeared in *Ovation* for September 1989.

A paperbound edition of *Authenticity in Music* was first published in 1988 by Faber Music Ltd. (London) in association with Faber & Faber, with U.S. and Canadian distribution by Amadeus Press (9999 S.W. Wilshire, Portland Oregon 97225). Please consult publishers for current availability of this edition.

Raymond Leppard's prefaces to and realizations of the baroque operas *La Calisto, L'Egisto, L'Orione* and *L'Ormindo* by Francesco Cavalli and of *L'incoronazione di Poppea, L'Orfeo* and *Il ritorno d'Ulisse in patria* by Claudio Monteverdi and his performing edition of Rameau's opera *Dardanus* are published by Faber Music Ltd., London. For particulars regarding U.S./Canadian distribution please write Faber Music Inc., 50 Cross Street, Winchester MA 01890.

Raymond Leppard's contribution of the article "The Baroque Operas" to *Glyndebourne: A Celebration* edited by John Higgins was first published in 1984 by Jonathan Cape Ltd., London.

The article "The Opera Orchestra" first appeared in David Hamilton, ed., *The Metropolitan Opera Encyclopedia: A Comprehensive Guide to the World of Opera* (Simon & Schuster/Metropolitan Opera Guild, 1987).

The chapter "Unexplored Relationships Between Early 17th-Century Venetian Opera and Contemporary Music in France and England" was read as the 1969 British Academy Italian Lecture and first published in the *Proceedings of the British Academy*, Vol. LV (Oxford University Press, 1969).

Program notes for the Monteverdi *Madrigals* Books 3-4 and 7-10 first appeared with the 1971-1977 Philips recordings (see DISCOGRAPHY for additional information).

"An Overview of Beethoven's Three-Part Career as a Composer" first appeared, in a slightly different form, in the quarterly newsletter of the Indianapolis Symphony Orchestra for Spring 1988.

Joseph Horowitz's review "A Symphony Is Where You Find It" appeared originally in *The New York Times* for 24 April 1992.

The paper/symposium on "Music and the Conductor" was given to The Royal Society for the Encouragement of Arts, Manufacturers and Commerce on 9 May 1973. It is reproduced with permission from the *Journal of the Royal Society of Arts*, Vol. CXXI Nr. 5207, October 1973 (now *RSA Journal*).

The interview with Susan McGregor was conducted for BBC-Radio in 1979, for the series "Conversation Piece" produced by Gillian Hush.

Raymond Leppard's contribution to *My Cambridge* edited by Ronald Hayman was first published in 1977 by Robson Books, London.

Gillian Widdicombe's notes on Raymond Leppard's early career first accompanied Philips' c. 1971 recording 6833 035 featuring music by the Bachs, Handel, Mozart, and Domenico Scarlatti.

Spike Hughes' notes on Glyndebourne productions derive from his *Glyndebourne: A History of the Festival Opera* (David & Charles, 1981).

Notes by Robert Jacobson on the San Francisco Opera production of *L'iincoronazione di Poppea* first appeared in *Opera News*.

Nicholas Kenyon's interviews with Quintin Balardie and Ursula Strebi first appeared in *The English Chamber Orchestra: A Pictorial Review*, published by that organization in 1978. Mr. Kenyon's piece on Raymond Leppard and the "authenticity" question appeared in *The Listener* for 22 November 1984.

Howard Reich's reporting of Raymond Leppard's arrival in Indianapolis appeared in the *Chicago Tribune* for 22 November 1987.

Mark Carrington's review of Raymond Leppard's Washington D.C. Indianapolis Symphony Orchestra concert first appeared in *The Washington Post* for 6 April 1989.

Peter G. Davis's and Otto Friedrich's notes on Raymond Leppard's Mozart Festival performances in New York first appeared in *New York* Magazine for 11 February 1991 and in *Time* Magazine for 11 February 1991, respectively.

Charles Staff's piece on Raymond Leppard and the Indianapolis Symphony Orchestra first appeared in *The Indianapolis News* for 4 October 1991.

Chris Aspin's reporting of Raymond Leppard and the BBC Philharmonic Orchestra first appeared in the *Manchester Evening News* of 23 May 1992.

*

The author and editor wish to thank all of the above-named publishers and other organizations and individuals for permission to use these previously published materials.

In addition, the author's appreciation is expressed to Tom Lewis, whose idea the book was in the first place, and without whose energies it could never have been assembled; and to Mark Grant for his participation in the December 1992 interview sessions. The editor wishes to thank Nicholas Clarke of the Bold Strummer and Mrs. I. Francis Murdock of Quincy, Massachusetts for their support of this and other publications — Carol Ossenfort for typing portions of the manuscript — and Bernette Clark-Obienu for transcribing the interviews.

CREDIT: Lord Snowdon, 1993

INTRODUCTION

FIRST IMPRESSIONS: To players and audiences alike, Raymond Leppard on the podium — fully white-tied and tailed — generally makes an imposing sight. The impression of authority or indeed "charisma" derives, however, not from self-posturing — theatrically stern glances — ecstatic shutting of the eyes — nor from any other baton-wielding histrionics... nor is it linked to the soul of some conductorial demon who means to achieve his or her victories through a breaking-down of the will...

Rather, this particular maestro displays an authority that is based on much more practical (and certainly likeable) skills and traits of character. For instance, he is a leader partly because he knows (and loves) the music itself well enough to have a clear and distinct point of view; and he guides not from feelings of superiority to, but with genuine respect (and often affection) for his (fellow) players.

Any artist must be concerned — surely — with the task of communicating with an audience. The question remains, a communication of what? As children we are, perhaps, mostly concerned with communicating some sense of "me-ness" and indeed our plight, our various strengths and points of vulnerability. Many of us maintain this preoccupation well into adulthood (and, in all fairness, the need to express oneself in such a manner is also *human* enough). At the same time, something else ought to take place... One ought to discover the larger world; life itself; "God" perhaps; that out of which one is made. Somewhere reverence for oneself alone must be (or, at least, ought to be) replaced by a larger reverence for being — and for the accomplishments and rights of others.

One senses that the author of the writings in this book, early on, understood this. It may be impossible in his profession — in the profession of any artist — not to build and secure a firm ego; one's position, in both an economic and a critical sense, seems much too precarious not to. That, perhaps, is a given. But strength of character and esteem for life itself, for art, for the world at large, for people... are not by nature mutually exclusive. The more "at peace" someone is with his or her own self, the more that person *can* communicate with others... communicate, that is to say, not his or her "self" alone, but aspects of the world, the art, the music...

Off the conductor's stand Maestro Leppard is reserved, but usually is smiling in a quiet way; is ready to greet you with interest and civility, as the occasion warrants. He is remarkably accessible for one who doesn't, after all, really know you yet... perhaps he is hoping for the best.

One appreciates his willingness to look one directly in the eyes. And his sense of humor. I think he enjoys some rather down-to-earth, broadly-stroked bits of humor precisely out of a tacit appreciation that, after all — pretensions to "culture" aside — humans *do* remain human, after all: creatures of ordinary flesh and blood. On the one hand, his eyes twinkle at the revelation of some unsuspected innocence — as when a great artist, say, forgets to tie his own shoes... on the other hand, what we laugh at is, perhaps, not very far from what we also are annoyed by: in Raymond's case, he is likely to laugh at (or, be angered by) pompousness and pretension... *presumption*. Thus, among his favorite sorts of jokes seem to be those at the end of which some self-obsessed *poseur* is forced to admit that he, too, must put his trousers on one leg at a time... or whatever.

No one who meets Raymond in person could fail to gain, I should think, the impression that here indeed is a "citizen of the world". He is well educated and — refreshingly, in a day that is often condescending to people of intelligence — proud of it. He is also, by choice and necessity, widely traveled, and his interests go beyond music itself to encompass many other arts, including films and the stage, literature, and the visual arts. He is interested in the history and culture of many different parts of the world... is less taken, perhaps, by the politics of any one country. He is a democrat by nature, who also believes that one is entitled to the fruits of his labors.

Above all he is intellectually curious, which I should like to illustrate with one minor incident. At one of our first meetings we happened to touch on the possible influence which Voltaire's *Candide* and Johnson's *Rasselas* might have had on each other. The question depended, in part, on their dates. Taking nothing for granted, Raymond decided to look it all up, and discovered that, in fact, *both had been published in the same year* (1759). Thus, for the moment, an impasse.

Still, who of us—"learned" or not—would pause to look something up in the dictionary (in this case, Oxford companion to literature)?

LIFE AND CAREER: Let us begin with the bare outline of a distinguished career—adapted indeed from innumerable program sketches which have greeted him, over the years, in countless cities and halls. (I sometimes wonder what it must be like to be met with a *photo* of oneself, everywhere one goes! Seasoned artists like Raymond live a kind of life before the mirror—their likeness in the program book, staring out at one, and their every success or failure returned to them via the pen—or computer stroke—of a critic.)

RAYMOND JOHN LEPPARD was born 11 August 1927 in London. His family moved to Bath (site of the famous Roman baths, and still one of the most charming places in England—with the River Avon running through it), where he had piano and other lessons from boyhood on. After three years in the R.A.F. he entered Trinity College at Cambridge University as a choral scholar and, under the influence of Professor Boris Ord, the early music authority, began to study the harpsichord and immerse himself in baroque and renaissance music. During his undergraduate years in Cambridge he became the director of the local Philharmonic Society, laying the foundation for his later career on the conductor's podium.

Upon graduation in 1952, the young musician went to London and formed the Leppard Ensemble, which he directed from the harpsichord. He appeared at the Edinburgh Festival and made records with Yehudi Menuhin, among many artists. He later joined the New Philharmonia Orchestra as a keyboard player, working under such conductors as Otto Klemperer and Herbert von Karajan. He served as musical director of the Prince's Theatre and the Royal Court Theatre in London, and the Oxford Playhouse and Royal Shakespeare Company in Stratford-upon-Avon—composing instrumental music for the latter, beginning with *A Midsummer Night's Dream* (1959). He also wrote several film scores, among them Peter Brook's *Lord of the Flies* (1963), Tony Richardson's *Laughter in the Dark* (1969), Clive Donner's *Alfred the Great* (1969) and Peter Hall's *Perfect*

Friday (1970); some years later he also scored Tony Richardson's *Hotel New Hampshire* (1984).

Stanley Sadie records (in *The New Grove Dictionary of Music and Musicians*) that RL "made his London debut as a conductor in Wigmore Hall in 1953 and soon became known particularly for his lively interpretations of 17th- and 18th-century music and his inventive continuo playing." He made his Covent Garden debut with *Samson* in 1959 and, in the same year, he was named musical director of the English Chamber Orchestra. He became principal conductor of the BBC Northern Symphony Orchestra in 1972 and, from 1978 on, a principal conductor of the Scottish Chamber Orchestra. In 1984 he undertook his first American post, becoming principal guest conductor of the St. Louis Symphony. His most recent, much enjoyed appointment (from 1987 to the present) has been as musical director of the Indianapolis Symphony Orchestra; like the ECO, BBC Northern Symphony and SCO, he has conducted this fine orchestra both at home and on tour.

Increasingly in demand at music centers in Europe, North and South America, and as far east (or west) as Hong Kong and Tokyo, Maestro Leppard has appeared frequently with the London Philharmonic, London Symphony and Royal Philharmonic Orchestras, in addition to performances with the Israel Philharmonic, Orchestre symphonique de Montréal, Toronto Symphony, National Arts Centre Orchestra (Canada), Scottish National Orchestra, Nouvel Orchestre Philharmonique de Radio-France (Paris), Orchestra sinfonica della Radiotelevisione Italiana (Turin), Radio-Sinfonie-Orchester Frankfurt, Sinfonie-Orchester des Norddeutschen Rundfunks (Stuttgart), Sjaellands Symphony Orchestra (Copenhagen) — and many others.

In the United States alone he has guest conducted the following symphony (or philharmonic) orchestras: Alabama, Atlanta, Baltimore, Boston, Chicago, Cincinnati, Denver, Detroit, Houston, Los Angeles, Milwaukee, Minneapolis, New Mexico, New Orleans, New York, Philadelphia, Pittsburgh, Rochester, San Francisco, and Syracuse.

Opera has always played a central role in Raymond Leppard's musical life — a subject to be treated in some detail throughout this book. In Europe he has appeared at Glyndebourne (where he gave the world premieres of Maw's *Rising of the Moon* and Janacek's *Cunning Little Vixen*, in addition to four Monteverdi and Cavalli operas in his own editions), Sadler's Wells and Covent Garden, as well as at opera houses in Paris, Hamburg, Stockholm, Geneva and Glasgow. Among the operas he has conducted in the United States are Monteverdi's *L'incoronazione di Poppea* for the San Francisco Opera (1975), Cavalli's *L'Egisto* and *L'Orione* at the Santa Fe Opera (1976, 1983), Thomson's *The Mother of Us All* and Mozart's *Così fan tutte* at Santa Fe (1976, 1977), Britten's *Billy Budd* at the Metropolitan Opera (1978, 1980), Rossini's *Il barbiere di Siviglia* and Stravinsky's *The Rake's Progress* at Santa Fe (1981), Gluck's *Alceste* and Handel's *Alcina* at the New York City Opera (1983), and Handel's *Ariodante* in a concert version at Carnegie Hall (1985).

Maestro Leppard has recorded nearly 500 works by more than 100 composers. Among several awards he received, in 1984, a Grammy Award for Best Classical Performance — Instrumental Soloist with Orchestra for a recording featuring Wynton Marsalis. His recordings have also earned the Deutsche Schallplattenpreis, a Grand Prix Mondial du Disque, and the Edison Prize.

In 1969 Maestro Leppard was chosen to deliver the Italian lecture to the British Academy (reprinted below — see Chapter II Section §4), and in 1973 the Republic of Italy conferred upon him the title of *Commendatore* for his services to Italian music, particularly for his restoration of operas by Monteverdi and Cavalli. More recently he was honored with the title of Commander of the British Empire. Among several administrative posts held has been that of successor to Sir John Betjeman, in 1985, as president of the Erin Arts Centre on Britain's Isle of Man.

*

In 1979 an interview appeared in *High Fidelity/Musical America* which begins to flesh out this "who's who"-ish capsule biography. In it Shirley Fleming — *Musical America*'s distinguished editor — gives a lively picture of our subject, leading off with the cheerful announcement that:

> The United States has a new citizen. New York City a new taxpayer, the Metropolitan Opera a new conductor. Raymond Leppard, accompanied by two harpsichords [including a majestic

Thomas Goff instrument], a Bösendorfer, a library of early music manuscripts and good leatherbound books, and an apartment full of handsome mahogany furniture [much of which was moved on later to a permanent home in Connecticut] has come to this country to stay. If the pace of his past career is any gauge, this does not mean that Europe will see less of him but that America will see more...

[Leppard] made his Met debut on the 19th of September last year (1978) conducting the new production of Benjamin Britten's *Billy Budd*, and his appearances in the U.S. during the season included concerts with the Minnesota Orchestra and a series of Rossini *Barbers* with the Miami Opera, as well as his debut with the New York Philharmonic on March 29th of this year. The diversity of these events is in keeping with a career that has compressed an extraordinary amount of activity into the working years of a man who has just turned fifty-two....

[He] was born in London, raised in Bath, and knew from the time he entered Trinity College, Cambridge, that music was to be his life. He studied the harpsichord as an undergraduate and also became the music director of the Philharmonic Society, thus laying the groundwork for two major thrusts of his later career....

He began conducting at Glyndebourne and then in 1958 returned to Cambridge as University Lecturer—a fairly innocent-sounding title that, on closer inspection, appears to have encompassed a formidable array of duties, including instruction in Fugue, Counterpoint, History of Criticism and French Music in the Twentieth Century. His affiliation with the University lasted ten years, but Leppard is not the man to have let himself get lost in the stacks: during these years he was active in London and kept an apartment there which he would often drive to 'through the night'. He became music director of the English Chamber Orchestra [in 1959]. He also took a sabbatical to go to Italy to hunt up Monteverdi material, and there discovered Cavalli. Which, possibly, has led to the rest of the world's discovering Leppard. Although he has made a number of appearances in the United States (San Francisco, Los Angeles, New York), it was his introduction of Cavalli's *L'Egisto* at Santa Fe in 1974 that ignited particular interest in Leppard's doings in this country. He had, in the meantime, become principal conductor of the BBC Northern Symphony in Manchester, but about the time of *L'Egisto* he decided to make the move to the United States....

Leppard hasn't escaped a few brickbats in the process of restoring Venetian and eighteenth-century opera [e.g. Rameau's *Dardanus*] to the twentieth-century stage. His critics accuse him of indulging too richly in orchestral resources, of occasionally overdoing his realizations ('although he's such a damned good conductor it's hard to get mad at him,' remarks a distinguished musicologist). Leppard takes this in stride. 'Academia is inhibiting,' he says cheerfully. 'That's fine — I was an academic myself once. They're interested in the idea of the nineteenth-century *Urtext*.[1] But you take a look at this' — producing a skeletal manuscript displaying an unadorned vocal line and a sparse bass accompaniment — 'and you can see that *that's* no *Urtext!* This music is sensuous, emotional, and passionate. You have to re-create with the composer. You can't stand back from his music like a vestal virgin, you have to be wedded to it, you have to go to bed with it.'

If Leppard is wedded to the scores he has worked on, it is a union brought about by long months in the Marciana Library [in Venice] copying manuscripts by hand — an activity he firmly believes in. 'Microfilm is lethal to scholarship,' he says. 'My music room is full of material I have copied. When you copy you get inside the music, you get a feel for the way the notes move on the page. After all, that's the way painters learn by copying the masters. At Cambridge, for example, all the music students are required to compose, and they spend a year imitating the styles of everybody from Monteverdi to Stravinsky. It's enormously valuable.'

If these remarks betray a mind of marked discipline and control, such an impression is accurate. Leppard, who gets along healthily on four hours's sleep at night, told of one of the

---

1   "Original text" — that which is assumed to be the composer's "version of record" so to speak. (Ed.)

'illuminating' experiences of his life, when, two months before his edition of Monteverdi's *Il ritorno d'Ulisse in patria* was to be produced at Glyndebourne, his London apartment caught fire and eight hundred pages of the manuscript were destroyed. 'I cancelled everything and simply locked myself up with the music for eight weeks. At first I tried to remember what I'd done but that was hopeless, so I rewrote the whole thing. I would work for almost two days at a time—I really compressed two days into one. I'd work around the clock and then bathe, shave, have a drink and go to bed for awhile. The publisher [Faber Music] came by every day and took the sheets I'd done. It wasn't painful. I found it a great experience.'...

At the other end of the [operatic] spectrum stand Virgil Thomson and Benjamin Britten. When the Santa Fe Opera staged *The Mother of Us All* in 1976, this quintessentially American opera was directed by the thoroughly British Mr. Leppard—an irony that did not, of course, escape Virgil Thomson. 'He told me he found it most peculiar that this very American opera was in the hands of an Englishman. I reminded him that if there hadn't been the few Englishmen around there would not have been the opportunity for an "American" opera in the first place. But Virgil was very helpful—he was ill that summer and couldn't come to Santa Fe, so we were in constant touch by phone. I treated *The Mother of Us All* as a piece of theater. Gertrude Stein was no fool. She did know what she wanted to do with words—to explore their meaning and sound in different contexts—and so I took her seriously. The more one listens, the more her meaning emerges. And Virgil Thomson clearly does understand what she means.'[2]

With the Met production of *Billy Budd* which Leppard was conducting for the first time, he had a long friendship with Britten as a point of reference. It was, in fact, Britten who first steered Leppard into Monteverdi in the 1950s—'He came to a performance I was involved in and suggested that I prepare some Monteverdi for Heather Harper to sing at Aldeburgh. It was the first professional realization I'd ever done.' There followed, in

---

2   The Santa Fe production was recorded by New World Records. (Ed.)

due course, productions of *Albert Herring,* and *The Turn of the Screw* with the English Opera Group, and a close association with Peter Pears. 'I have worked with Peter a great deal, and I conducted the *Spring* Symphony performance that Peter sang in just before Ben died....

'Ben was always tremendously concerned with the anatomy of evil. He was obsessed with evil, with the power of evil to destroy good. He was anguished, he had an enormous load of guilt, which he tried to hide. But when Ben was at a party he would simply emanate distress, and soon everybody in the room would be aware of it. [Gérard] Souzay is like that, too. Ben had demons inside him. People think that Peter is the high-strung one, the nervous one, but he is inwardly calm and he always was able to calm Ben. It was a whole activity, an outlet.'

This summer has found Leppard at Glyndebourne (*Ulysses*) and Santa Fe, and the winter will include appearances in San Francisco, Houston, and Toronto. As he showed me out of his apartment with its formal, high-ceilinged living room and flanking fireplace, he glanced at the big piano standing near a window in his music room and remarked that he had it 'very much in mind' to do some more composing, but hadn't the leisure to do it now. 'You're too fussed, there's no time to think,' he said. 'Life just grabs hold of you.' And how.[3]

REPERTORY: Music by eighteenth century masters is by now familiar to so many listeners that it is easy to forget that the "Baroque Revolution", if it may be so termed, is nevertheless a fairly recent event. The "discovery" of Vivaldi *et al.* coincided with the development of the long-playing record in the 1950s and thereafter — and, to feed a suddenly exploding market for such works, which attracted the interest and commitment of a number of musicians and musicologists such as... Raymond Leppard. We have the skills and enthusiasms of Leppard and others like him to thank for the uncovering and revitalizing or "dusting off" if you will of (for instance) so many wonderful "lost" concertos and sonatas by Vival-

---

3   Interview first published in *High Fidelity/Musical America,* 1979; republished in
     1979/80 year book of the Scottish Chamber Orchestra.

di... of splendid instrumental and vocal treasures *other* than *Messiah*, by Handel... for the bringing into the public ear of a near torrent of bright and seductively beautiful compositions by Albinoni, Corelli, Lully, Purcell, Rameau, Sammartini, the Scarlattis, Tartini, Telemann and many others—and, we have not yet mentioned (the) Bach(s)! To peruse Maestro Leppard's own concert listings (in addition to his recordings—for he has become one of the most frequently recorded of all classical music conductors)—is to find such names occurring over and over.[4]

From an article in *Hi-Fi News & Record Review* (May 1973) announcing RL's winning Britain's 1973 Audio Award on May 3:

> During the last decade we have seen a great awakening of interest in the music that is loosely called baroque, and with it an appreciation of the proper styling of the music of the pre-classical era. While most of the big guns of music still thundered away on the battlefields of post-Beethoven German romanticism, it could have been that the baroque revival was left in the hands of that cosy segment of academic music-making that makes little impact beyond the ranks of the dedicated.
>
> It needed somebody like Raymond Leppard, with a vigorous (though not unacademic) approach to making music to add the final impetus to the revival by producing fresh and exciting recordings that would catch the interest of a wider public. Which is precisely what we think he has done. In [his] list of distinguished recordings... we find firstly a series on the Philips label going back to 1963 in which the names of the Bach family and Handel predominate, mainly ranging in time from Monteverdi to Mozart. It is a deliberately confined coverage of music reflecting

---

4   A younger generation of distinguished musicians such as Michael Corboz, John Eliot Gardiner, Christopher Hogwood, Jean-Claude Malgoire and Trevor Pinnock has in part built on the accomplishments of committed players before them such as Harnoncourt, Leonhardt, Leppard, Anthony Lewis, Marriner, I Musici, Roger Norrington, Jean-François Paillard, Brian Priestman, Karl Richter, Helmuth Rilling and Claudio Scimone.

the conductor's chief interests.[5] The achievement is that Leppard has managed to be both a skilled specialist and an entertaining advocate in his chosen field.

To add to the impressive Philips list, mainly recorded with the English Chamber Orchestra, we have equally highly-praised recordings with the London Philharmonic Orchestra, the Bath Festival Orchestra, the New Philharmonia, and the Academy of St Martin-in-the-Fields. These include three interesting, mainly baroque collections for the HMV label, several issues for Decca including two very splendid recordings of Cavalli's *La Calisto* and *L'Ormindo* on the Argo label, and an interesting outsider on Lyrita in Bax's *5th Symphony*. This last admirably illustrates [Leppard's view] that 'experience of one style informs the understanding of another.'

It might have been assumed that Leppard only performed music of the early to mid-eighteenth century. But, in fact, this is far from being the case. His range spans more than four centuries, from the 1500s through the classical period—Haydn, Mozart and Beethoven being among the most often-performed masters in his repertory; into nineteenth century romanticism—Brahms, Dvorak and Tchaikovsky being typical Leppard staples. Finally, twentieth century masters (and some occasional lesser lights) have never been absent from his programs. Among the many present-century British composers whose works he has featured on a regular basis are Arnold, Bax, Berkeley, Britten, Elgar, Finzi, Holst, Maxwell Davies, Rawsthorne, Tippett, Vaughan Williams, and Walton; while Debussy, Rachmaninoff, Ravel, Shostakovich, Sibelius, Strauss, and Stravinsky are among other favorite 20th-century composers. Among the American composers he has programmed with some frequency are Barber, Carter, Copland, Rochberg and Schuman.

APPROACHES TO THE MUSIC (THEORY VS. PRACTICE): More than a little suspicious of theory and abstraction for its own sake, Raymond Lep-

---

5   Of approximately this time—in fact, however, RL's repertory extends to contemporary 20th-century works; see following. (Ed.)

pard is above all a *practicing* musician—be this as instrumental player, conductor, composer, or editor/arranger. In conversation he brings to mind those excellent David Frost interviews with British actors such as Anthony Hopkins and John Gielgud, who seem equally at a loss (and even put off) by questions concerning the "nature of drama" or "the nature of acting"—but, have marvelous tales, and pointed insights, to offer concerning the specifics of an actual performance, or technique. (Laurence Olivier confessed that to achieve the heart-stopping cry of *Oedipus*, upon discovering his true parentage, he would pretend to be an animal with his foot caught in a trap.) Leppard too reveals this preference for "doing not theorizing", not only in the sheer number of his own performances, both live and recorded, over more than forty years, but also in the general tenor of his writings. For example he is more likely to speak about tempos than about the "emotional" aspects of a given passage, or score: for the one (in practical terms) in effect *depends* upon the other. Similarly he tends to believe—on the basis of his own experience, at least—that a full-time academic career and the life of a professional performing artist do not mix; they cannot both be accomplished satisfactorily at the same time. However—as the present work attests—he himself has been at some pains to articulate carefully, in words, his own sense of the music which he plays. There is no contradiction here. What the writing and the playing have in common is... a wish to communicate, not with a scholarly audience (for which, nevertheless, he has sincere regard—indeed, he is extremely proud of his own Cambridge credentials), but with an audience for the music itself. That is to say, when he chooses to put things into words, this is generally meant to support or to amplify his career as a performing musician.

His part in the famous "authenticity" controversy should be viewed in this light. The truth of the matter is that he does not begin with cast-in-stone assumptions concerning the "right" instrumentation of seventeenth-century Italian opera, for instance, but strives instead to craft (project) the materials at hand in such a way that these may truly please, communicate with an audience... in short, "work". This in turn may lead, after all, to certain (written) observations concerning "authentic" performance; however, that was not his original purpose. It was his task (and joy) to entertain modern audiences with certain largely forgotten (and, of course, unperformed) masterpieces by Monteverdi and Cavalli. In essays such as *Authenticity in Music* he has in effect merely enlarged upon his own experience regarding how best this might be accomplished. Contrarily, the interested reader may first examine Leppard's written views on the authenticity question, in this particular book-length essay (which leads off our volume)... one has, then, the unique opportunity to *actually hear a Leppard performance* — on disk, or in the opera house or concert hall.

Other writings may be regarded in this same, practical context of Leppard's wishing to render music in both an *inviting* and *intelligible* fashion. The sampling of program notes for Monteverdi, Cavalli, Vivaldi, Handel, Haydn and Beethoven (Chapter III), for example, not only conveys an accurate sense of some major compositions by these important figures, it also well illustrates our present theme of "working musician": it is significant, and characteristic, that almost all of these miniature essays were written for concerts at which the author was — himself — giving a performance.

Leppard's no-sacred-cows, sometimes playful yet always respectful approach to music is evidenced in a piece written for *Keynote* (October 1982):

> I once said something very rude about an *Urtext*. But it was not so much about the fact of the *Urtext* as the attitude of mind that considers it the crock of gold at the end of a musicological rainbow, the holy grail of the musician's quest: for the notes from which we play, no matter what state they are in, represent only the beginning of the musician's true quest, the journey into performance. Music is, after all, nothing until it sounds.
>
> I find it a fascinating example of how words can, for a time, assume an almost magic, incantation-like aura and power. While it is obviously desirable to have a text that reproduces the composer's manuscript as closely as possible, that is as much as a text can do and is the limit of its value. To use an *Urtext* is certainly no guarantee that you will have a performance, just as the lack of one is no guarantee that you will not.

*

A writer for *The Indianapolis News* (19 May 1989) observed that "Leppard works from the inside out. He does not let the small things fall where they may in striving for some big general effect. He starts with individual notes, their value, their place in the scheme of things, with phrases and lines and how they relate to one another. From such a firm foundation, he builds performances architecturally. On occasion, his classical approach may drain away some of the high drama of high romanticism... but what is gained far outshines what little is lost."

Jay Harvey wrote in *The Indianapolis Star* (22 May 1988) that, however, as the new Music Director of the Indianapolis Symphony Orchestra, "Leppard has concentrated so much on building stylistic and structural awareness into the ISO's performances that it's easy to forget what a knack he has for stirring up dazzling displays of color. [For example,] such an exhibition galvanized [the orchestra's recent performance of Ravel's *Rapsodie Espagnole*]."

*

"Leppard has an exuberant, outgoing personality, a keen intellect and a commanding presence, none of which prevent people from being attracted by his civility and occasionally earthy sense of humor. He holds a very non-pompous view of music, regarding it first as 'entertainment', but always with the potential to bestir the emotions at deeper levels. On top of this he has a distinctly pragmatic view of orchestra finances, programming and audience building. 'Communication' is his watchword; it is seen in his desire always to meet his audiences at least halfway, and in his relationship with the orchestra. Observed one player of Leppard's rehearsal technique: 'He gets what he wants across to us as clearly as anyone we've ever played for, and somehow makes it fun. It's inspired me to give of my best — all the time.'

"[On his becoming the ISO's new Music Director] a difference in the orchestra's playing was immediate and startling. Leppard brought forth from his players a clarity of texture, an exquisite control of dynamics and a level of precision that [compelled attention]. Equally significant was his introduction to Indianapolis of the articulated phrase — meaning that in, say, a Beethoven symphony he separates each phrase from its succeeding one by an obvious break in the line. Leppard argues that this was clearly the intent and practice of Classical period composers, though their works are rarely played that way nowadays." — Tom Aldridge, in *Ovation*, September 1989.

*

"[He has] the shaggy amiability of a cricket-loving schoolmaster," an interviewer wrote, in 1965. "Not at all what you'd expect of an exquisite harpsichordist who has spent years delving into the mind of a seventeenth century composer [i.e. Monteverdi]. Nervy and earnest, you might imagine. Leppard is earnest, but relaxed.

" 'Monteverdi's operas,' he explains, with the kind of loving intensity that some men use to explain their wives, 'were never written down. They used to rehearse for about five months, and the musicians were expected to improvise. A sort of classical jam session — in the end it all crystallized into something coherent.'

"This passion for improvisation means that all that's come down from seventeenth-century composers like Monteverdi is a vocal and a bass line. Nothing in between. Leppard has been working for the past two years on a new edition of Monteverdi's *L'Orfeo* (opening at Sadler's Wells on 5 October) — and in this case 'edition' does not just mean some judicious cutting and a little juggling with musical phrases. It means the creation of an entire, performable score from the sketchiest of outlines.

" 'My version of *Orfeo* will be more elaborate than usual: but Monteverdi was, you see, a Florentine contemporary of Rubens.'

"Leppard doesn't claim that his version of *Orfeo* is better than previous ones — just different. 'It's a version for these times,' he says, sounding disconcertingly like Peter Hall on *Hamlet*. Then, earnestly — 'Well, I mean, people *know* more about Monteverdi than they used to...'

"Which is as near as Raymond Leppard seems likely to get to boasting about his achievements." — Prudence Fay.

CONCERNING LISTS AND CATALOGS: Some people are fond of lists and catalogs—others are not. The present editor has to confess to something of a passion for them... for example, I truly believe that merely to copy out the titles of all the Bach cantatas—remarking also the composition of each (its division into arias, duets, choruses and *sinfonias*)—might well be a useful thing to do. In order to appreciate a particular individual's accomplishments, it seems necessary to know first *what* that person has done; in the case of Bach, in the simple act of listing his two-hundred plus cantatas, one comes to appreciate not only the enormity of his accomplishment, but the characteristic every-day, journeyman's aspect of the music itself— the need which is met for providing a new piece for the churches of Cöthen or Leipzig every Sunday, over so many years... and, how he did it (including his making use of some previously written section or movement... and also his blending some of the movements into some new passion or oratorio, in order to suit a grander occasion). Similarly, is it of no interest to observe that Tchaikovsky—master of the non-verbal orchestral crescendo—composed no fewer than 11 *operas*... apparently driven to express in some passionate, human word-music bonding that which neither, perhaps, can simulate by itself?

In Raymond Leppard's case it is instructive, I think, to take note of *just where he has been,* for instance. Not only are the number of performances (and their geographical range) over the past 40 years rather staggering, but (to a lay-person at least) it is extremely revealing of what constitutes an "authentic" career in music to follow his trail, to see just where every day (or most every day) has taken him...[6]

Discographies have even greater utility: they are often an indispensable guide to what is (or has been) available, at all, and, in some cases, have become the only key to the means by which a given work can be heard. Also, interpretations (and tastes in interpretation) do change, so that, collectively, discographies come to form a kind of perpetual sound-

---

6   See the entries for May-June 1986, for instance: 19 May has him in London, 6-7 June in St. Louis, 17-19 June in Würzburg. Or May 1982, which takes him from Washington DC (4th-7th) to Poitiers and Bordeaux (11th-14th) on to Jerusalem (17th) and Haifa (18th).

archive resource, and, as such, an important element of the cultural store of us all.

Concert diary. From our list (given as APPENDIX I: PARTIAL CHRONOLOGY) it will be seen that concerts both large and small, important and less consequential, fill out the professional working-man's week... Also of potential interest to the historian of musical performances, an attentive reader will come upon, as well, many other artists' appearances alongside Raymond's—then at various stages in their own careers... among them Richard Adeney, Elly Ameling, Sheila Armstrong, Alda Aveling, Janet Baker, Kathleen Battle, Teresa Berganza, James Blades, Judith Blegen, Julian Bream, Carter Brey, Phyllis Bryn-Julson, Norma Burrowes, April Cantelo, John Cheek, Fernando Corena, Ileana Cotrubas, Hugues Cuénod, Thurston Dart, Ryland Davies, Stafford Dean, Jan DeGaetani, Gerald English, Geraint Evans, Maureen Forrester, Rodney Friend, Maurice Gendron, Peter Glossop, George Guest, Ida Haendel, Heather Harper, Lynn Harrell, Heinz Holliger, Marilyn Horne, Martin Isepp, Philip Jones, Patricia Kern, Christopher Keyte, James King, Leonid Kogan, Magda Laszlo, Philip Ledger, Pilar Lorengar, Felicity Lott, Benjamin Luxon, George Malcolm, Neville Marriner, Sylvia McNair, Yehudi Menuhin, Yvonne Minton, James Morris, John Noble, David & Igor Oistrakh, Elmar Oliviera, Felicity Palmer, Geoffrey Parsons, Ian Partridge, Peter Pears, Simon Preston, Jean-Pierre Rampal, Bernard Richards, Leonard Rose, Stanley Sadie (as bassoonist), Irmgard Seefried, John Shirley-Quirk, Derek Simpson, Dmitry Sitkovetsky, Elisabeth Söderström, Isaac Stern, Richard Stilwell, Richard Stoltzman, Joan Sutherland, Hidetaro Suzuki, Henryk Szeryng, Robert Tear, Alan Titus, Paul Tortelier, Barry Tuckwell, Denis Vaughan, Jon Vickers, Frederica Von Stade, Helen Watts, guitarist John Williams, Ransom Wilson, Alexander Young...

The list of featured pianists alone is extensive. It includes Emanuel Ax, Malcolm Binns, Stephen Bishop, Paolo Bordoni, Yefim Bronfman, John Browning, Shura Cherkassky, Aldo Ciccolini, Clifford Curzon, Bella Davidovich, Misha and Cipa Dichter, Barry Douglas, Philippe Entremont, Rudolf Firkusny, Malcolm Frager, Peter Frankl, Bruno Leonardo Gelber, Liv Glaser, Richard Goode, Horacio Gutiérrez, Grant Johannesen, Tedd Joselson, Jeffrey Kahane, Joseph Kalichstein, Louis

Kentner, Walter Klien, Alicia de Larrocha, Radu Lupu, Garrick Ohlsson, Ronan O'Hora, Ursula Oppens, Cécile Ousset, Murray Perahia, Vlado Perlemuter, Maria João Pires, Hans Richter-Haaser, Russell Sherman, Jean-Yves Thibaudet, André Watts, Alexis Weissenberg, Christian Zacharias, Krystian Zimerman...

Discography. Listings are given where possible for cassettes, CDs and LPs. They not only document Leppard's own career, but add to our knowledge of the work of ensembles such as the English Chamber Orchestra. (Not all data for all the recordings have been presented. But one hopes that enough has been assembled here to assist interested collectors and historians of music.)

IN SUM: it is to be hoped that this selection of writings and related materials pertaining to the life and career of a distinguished contemporary musician will be enjoyed and found useful by those who love music, and are concerned with its workings.

CREDIT: Lord Snowdon, 1993

PART ONE

SOME VIEWS OF MUSIC

IN

THEORY AND PRACTICE

I

AUTHENTICITY IN MUSIC

CHAPTER ONE

THE NEW LISTENING

We live at a time when on any day, at any hour, by merely turning a knob we can expect to be able to hear music composed before 1800. Something by Monteverdi or Cavalli; something by Vivaldi, by Handel, by a Scarlatti (either of them) or a Bach (any of them), something by Haydn or Mozart, or almost anything by one of their lesser relations or contemporaries. Nothing is likely any longer to surprise us by its rarity or make us gasp, except for its intrinsic beauty — supposing we have the time to listen to it.

We may not recognize the music we hear but we're likely to be intrigued and curious to know its name. Many of us could have a fairly good shot at placing it in its period and country within the last 400 years. Right or wrong, this guessing game that most of us regularly play has become one of the most widespread of musical diversions; and, it must be emphasized here, a uniquely twentieth-century one. We have come, for the greater part unquestioningly, to regard as normal listening the huge historical span of music that is now so readily available. But it is not so generally realized how recent a phenomenon this is. A few facts, selected at random, may serve to illuminate this development, and point the direction for further discussion as to how it came about and how it has so profoundly affected and conditioned our attitudes to the art of music.

For those who are captivated by the music of early seventeenth-century Italy it is hard to believe that it has only been heard again with any frequency within the last 20 to 30 years.

Monteverdi's opera *L'incoronazione di Poppea* (1642) was given its first professional performance in England at Glyndebourne in 1962; *Il ritorno d'Ulisse* (1641) in 1971. In America, *Poppea* was first heard in 1963, performed by the Dallas Civic Opera; *Il ritorno* in 1974 by the Washington Opera Society.

Even in its skeletal, *Urtext* form the (almost) complete corpus of Monteverdi's music has only been available in print since 1942, when the last volume of Malipiero's great editorial project, begun in 1926, was published.

A recording of some of Monteverdi's madrigals was made in 1937 under the direction of Nadia Boulanger, a result of her new-found enthusiasm for his music. Disregarded when it first came out, it has since become something of a classic, and was almost certainly the first recording of any of the composer's music.

Cavalli's opera *L'Ormindo* (1644) was performed for the first time in over 300 years at Glyndebourne in 1967, as was *La Calisto* (1651) in 1970. *L'Egisto* (1643) and *L'Orione* (1653) saw the light of day again at Santa Fe Opera in 1974 and 1983 respectively.

Virtually nothing by Vivaldi was heard in the nineteenth century or before the First World War. Only one or two violin concertos, made to sound as if composed by Max Bruch, were found to be useful for opening recital programmes, and achieved a certain currency among some of the more adventurous soloists.

Between the wars a few more concertos were exhumed, slowly releasing a crescendo of interest that reached its zenith after the Second World War when Renato Fasano and the Virtuosi di Roma (founded in 1952, the first of several such groups) based their successful careers on the seemingly endless supply of Vivaldi's music that became available in a collected edition begun in 1947. With over 600 instrumental works to be revived, it is scarcely surprising that first performances since the eighteenth century became more the rule than the exception, but this encouragement was hardly necessary in the tidal wave of enthusiasm for his music that has yet to abate.

The case of Handel is somewhat different, particularly in England where the northern choral societies flourished wonderfully during the nineteenth century, satisfying a deep need for spiritual comfort and uplift amid the grimy drabness of the industrial revolution. Apart from specially composed works by Mendelssohn, Dvorák and contemporary English composers, some of Handel's oratorios were regularly performed. However, as Winton Dean points out, "we are apt to over-rate nineteenth century England's knowledge of Handel. Although performances of the oratorios were innumerable, with a few exceptions (mostly at the instance of amateur bodies like the Sacred Harmonic Society) they were confined to the same three or four works."[1] Certainly no opera by Handel was heard at that time, except for a few arias usually adapted to sacred words.

Some did not like Handel at all. In 1907 Ernest Walker denounced "the acres of complacent commonplaces, devoid alike of invention and workmanship."[2] Mr. Cuthbert Harris, writing in *Musical Opinion* in 1900, was not alone in thinking Handel's methods "childlike and lacking variety of resource" and his limitations "more marked than those of perhaps any other composer of equal standing. His music is almost entirely mechanical with its veneer of eighteen century sentiment." Even Sir Hubert Parry considered that "Handel, accepting the conventions of Italian art without hesitation, ruined an enormous number of his works by the emptiest, baldest and most superficial formulae."[3] It is inconceivable that similarly responsible musicians would either venture, or could possibly hold such opinions today. Understanding why this is so, and why such views were possible at the turn of the century, lies at the root of our considerations.

Handel's instrumental music and operas have a much more sharply defined starting point for revival. The sonatas, suites and concertos began to appear between the wars, when the harpsichord was revived for concert use.

After Handel's death, no opera of his was heard anywhere in Europe until 1920, when *Rodelinda* was produced at Göttingen. In 1953 the London Handel Opera Society was founded, and 18 of the operas they have

1 *Handel's Dramatic Oratorios and Masques* (1959), p.144.
2 *The History of Music in England* (1907), p.197.
3 *The Evolution of the Art of Music* (1896), p.165.

produced to date have been first London productions since the eighteenth century. If any more striking example were needed, the first Handel opera ever professionally produced in America was *Giulio Cesare*, performed in 1965 at Kansas City and revived with great success by New York City Opera in 1966.

There is still much of Alessandro Scarlatti's music awaiting twentieth-century performance, but there are few music-lovers now (unlike the great majority of those in our grandparents' day) who can say they have never heard of him, or a note of his music. If any such there be, the admission would be ruefully made, with no implication that they had done very well up to now without the composer or his music — an opinion that would have caused no raised eyebrows at the beginning of the century.

Domenico Scarlatti published only one volume of harpsichord pieces in his lifetime. A number of the more difficult sonatas were known in the nineteenth century, serving as starters or encores at recitals by keyboard virtuosi like Tausig or Scharwenka, who adapted them to suit and show off their own particular technical skills. By 1906 Alessandro Longo had edited and published six volumes containing 300 of Scarlatti's 550-odd sonatas and eventually, with the advent of harpsichordists like Wanda Landowska and Ralph Kirkpatrick, much of the complete opus entered the general listener's experience.

After J.S. Bach died in 1750 his music virtually ceased to exist for the rest of the eighteenth century. In Charles Burney's gigantic four-volume history of music completed in 1789, he is referred to in only four sentences: "In organ-playing and compostion, Handel and Sebastian Bach seem not only to have surpassed their contemporaries, but to have established a style for that instrument which is still respected and imitated by the greatest organists in Germany."[4]

"Among organists of the present century, Handel and Sebastian Bach are the most renowned. Of Handel's performance there are still many

---

4   Burney: *A General History of Music from the Earliest Ages to the Present Period*, Vol. IV (London, 1789), p.590.

living who can remember the grandeur, science and perfection; and Sebastian Bach is said, by Mr. Marpurg, to be many great musicians in one: profound in science, fertile in fancy, and in taste easy and natural."[5]

"The great Sebastian Bach, music-director at Leipzig, no less celebrated for his performance on the organ and compostions for that instrument, than for being the father of four sons, all great musicians in different branches of the art."[6]

"If he had been possessed of the simplicity, clearness, and feeling of Handel, he would have been a greater man."[7]

And that is the sum of attention Bach and all his music merited from the closest of scrutineers towards the end of the eighteenth century.

In fairness it must be said that through the enthusiasm and influence of S.S. Wesley, Burney came, by the end of his long life, to have a slightly deeper knowledge and respect for J.S. Bach. Wesley's enthusiasm, too, accounted for one of the first public manifestations of Bach's music in England, a single concert in 1809 at the New Rooms, Hanover Square. Illustrating the principle that one swallow does not make a summer, it was not well attended and Bach's name scarcely appears again in London until the 1830s. In September 1837, largely due to Mendelssohn's influence, the "St Anne" Prelude and Fugue and a duet from the *St Matthew Passion* were performed at the Birmingham Festival. (In 1829 Mendelssohn had performed the passion in Leipzig for the first time since the composer's death.) A reviewer, with a not unknown lack of perception, found the duet "a laboured production, unvocal and unfit for the words."[8]

The enthusiasm of individuals persisted intermittently, resulting in the first English performance of the *St Matthew Passion* in April 1854, but public apathy and critical antagonism continued. In London, the Bach Choir was formed in 1875 expressly to perform the B Minor Mass, which it did for the first time in 1876. Jenny Lind—whose husband, Otto

---

5   *Ibid.*, p.593.
6   *Ibid.*, p.594.
7   *Ibid.*, p.595.
8   *Birmingham Gazette*, Sept. 1829.

Goldschmidt, conducted — sang in the choir, and remarked afterwards, "to think that an old woman like me, who has lived in music all my life, should have been told of this music by an amateur."[9] North of the border, due perhaps to Scots caution, the Mass had to wait until 1908 for its first performance.

In Germany the Bach Gesellschaft, founded in 1850, began publishing Bach's complete works in 1851: for subscribers only and, for the most part, only in score without performing material. The edition was completed in 1896, providing a solid textual basis for the great revival of Bach's music that has occurred since the First world War. In 1888 the *Musical Times* had observed that "it seems as though the time is coming when it will be still more widely appreciated" and, indeed, Bach now brings audiences into concert halls all over the world.

The music of Bach's sons has taken even longer to reach the public ear. Few people knew their names at the beginning of the century. But now they are more staple listening fare and their differing styles, their personalities and even their places in the family tree are more widely perceived.

Haydn fared almost as badly. In the 1906 *Grove*, C.F. Pohl could write "there is still no complete edition of Haydn's symphonies. Many still remain in manuscript" — and therefore unheard. Now there are complete recordings and, thanks to the scholarship and indefatigable enthusiasm of Robbins Landon, a complete edition with accompanying orchestral material.

When I was at school during the last war I would go anywhere to hear one of the earlier symphonies. "La Chasse", "Mercury", "Passione", "Trauer"; these and their unnamed fellows were known to us as names or numbers only through biographies and dictionaries. Scores were generally unobtainable, there were almost no recordings, and the "London" symphonies arranged for piano duet were our only means of partially discovering what is now so widely heard, the greatest single

---

9   A. D. Coleridge, *Reminiscences*, ed. J. A. Fuller-Maitland (1921).

manifestation of eighteenth-century symphonic thought. And that was only 40 years ago.

Mozart's *Idomeneo* was given its first professional performance in England at Glyndebourne in 1951. It was heard at the Metropolitan Opera for the first time ever in 1982. *Così fan tutte* was first heard there (with very scant success) for a few performances in 1922 and *Il Seraglio* in 1946. *La Clemenza di Tito* was not heard in New York until 1984.

Such rehearsal of facts becomes tedious, and excessive repetition of the point they make blunts its impact. But we can now hear any of this music whenever we will. If concert-hall, opera-house and radio fail us there is always the gramophone, and, finding this very satisfying, we are not prone to question how it was, so short a time ago, when such variety was unknown. Nor do we often consider what our forbears would have made of the present situation. Yet the most significant aspect of any historical period lies in its unquestioned attitudes, and it is in these assumptions that we may see our own period most clearly revealed.

Few question the values that earlier music brings us. Its worth is recognized, but the questions raised about its performance rarely include why this is now so, and why the music is of such profound concern to us. To pause and consider how this passion for older music has come about may bring some focused understanding of its place in our aesthetic—and some resolution to the vexed question of authenticity which has become a blinkered, faddish pursuit among so many performers, listeners and critics, without the understanding of how and in what ways it may be valuable.

CHAPTER TWO

THE OLD LISTENING

We may at first feel some concern, some regret that our grandparents and great-grandparents were deprived of the enormous wealth of pre-1800 music so readily available now for daily listening. But we should be wasting our sympathy. That they would have been amazed by it is certain; that they would have been pleased by it is extremely unlikely. In all probability they would have regarded it as an unwelcome imposition of an eccentric, unsophisticated taste that had no business to occur and which held no real interest for them. The vast corpus of that music we have come to know and love they would have found fustian and quite dislikable, with little or no relevance to the present art of music as they knew and loved it.

Our forebears felt little need to look for values in earlier periods, all of which they believed to be inferior in most ways to their own. Such was the power of the idea of Progress. Life was generally understood to have improved to such an extent that almost any aspect of the past—social, scientific and artistic—was only even remotely interesting to the degree it could be said to have presaged the present. Like old clothes in a wardrobe, it was better discarded for fear of moths.

As far as actually listening to music was concerned, they heard much less than we do and probably listened harder and thought more about what they heard. Gramophones were experimental, concerts were rarer and much more of an event. They mainly heard music of their own time or such as immediately led up to it. Almost everyone subscribed to either the conservative Brahmsian school or the more advanced one of Wagner, and this was regarded as a laudatory example of a liberated society's refusal to accept superficial uniformity.

Each side traced and, with some pleasure, listened to composers who could be said to have made possible the work of those two main upholders of late nineteenth-century excellence. On one side were Schubert, Schumann and Mendelssohn; on the other were Weber and Liszt. Each protagonist had his acceptable contemporaries: Dvořák, Reger and Bruch for the one, Bruckner, Humperdinck and Hugo Wolf for the other. Both sides could trace their lines back to Beethoven as the great original who made it all possible. He was therefore added to their lists of composers worth listening to, but only in works such as the

Seventh Symphony or the "Emperor" Concerto, that could safely be recognized as "influential." And they were generally played in an "influential" manner. In this way was Beethoven regarded by the nineteenth century as an essentially Romantic composer.[10] His more Haydnesque music was ignored. The late quartets, together with the *Missa Solemnis* and the Ninth Symphony, were considered as somewhat hindered, visionary material for a Holy Grail yet to be fashioned at some future time. With Beethoven, the retrospective line of performable composers virtually came to an end.

A few works by Mozart, mostly in minor keys, were heard, though rarely. They were mainly of interest for the way they could be interpreted as precursors of the Romantic movement or identified as being by a composer, neglected in his short lifetime, who suffered and died in penury for his art. Haydn's long, cheerful and successful life did not fit him in any way for such interested concern and his music was largely neglected, except perhaps for *The Creation* which persisted a little, especially in the north of England. Almost nothing of Bach was generally played, except in the organ loft or on the G string. Apart from *Messiah* Handel was best known for a *Largo*, an "Harmonious Blacksmith", and the legend that, as a child, he had had to practise his spinet secretly in an attic by candlelight because of a stern father's injunction against playing it at all.

The rest of music before 1800 was virtually unheard, unknown and unobtainable. There were very many and prolific nineteenth-century composers of every level and sort for salon, church, opera-house or concert-hall, so that our forbears were not short of music to listen to. It did not, in any case, take up anything like the time in daily life that it does now. Everyone was too busy improving themselves and their society to feel very strongly the need to stand, stare and listen to something that would alleviate present cares and doubts. Certainty of man's future and confidence in his ability to reach out and shape it was the prevalent mood of the civilized world in 1900.

The idea of Progress had taken about 300 years to develop into the im-

---

10   The idea is not dead. A recent program note (1986) on Beethoven's *Eroica* observed that "In creating his Third Symphony, Beethoven eroded all the old spatial constraints of the genre, leaving the eighteenth century in the archives of history."

mensely powerful, all-pervading force that dominated the opinions and outlook of our forbears in almost every aspect of living and thought. It was for them virtually beyond questioning. There is hardly space for, or purpose in, tracing at length the stages by which the idea grew into so comprehensive a philosophy. But classical authority had begun to be challenged at the end of the sixteenth century. Copernicus, Galileo and Kepler put an end to Ptolemy's belief that the earth was at the centre of things celestial; Newton discovered gravity; Drake and Champlain, following the lead of Columbus, Pizarro and Magellan, discovered the New World; Descartes discovered himself and came to rely on the discovery. Francis Bacon saw that the "great renovation of knowledge" was not, as the Greeks had held, for the satisfaction of the mind, but enabled man to gain control over nature, the world and, therefore, his own destiny.

This was only the beginning of a chain of continually overthrown authority and an accretion of knowledge in all areas that led the late nineteenth century to believe it had progressed so far that heaven on earth was at least a ponderable possibility: to some, nearly a present reality; to others, ground for untrammelled optimism and a sense of superiority over all times past.

As Herbert Spencer wrote, "It will be seen that as in each event today, so from the beginning, the decomposition of every expended force into several forces has been perpetually producing a higher complication; that the increase of heterogeneity so brought about is still going on and must continue to go on; and that thus progress is not an accident, not a thing within human control, but a beneficent necessity."[11] "The ultimate development of ideal man is logically certain — as certain as any conclusion in which we place the most implicit faith."[12]

Backed by the evidence of the flood of scientific discovery, man clearly was close to complete control of his own future, even to those who regularly attended church or synagogue to thank a benevolent Deity for allowing them to come so far along the path of Progress towards a time when all things would indeed be bright and beautiful. They had, it was

---

11 *Progress, Its Laws and Cause* (1857), Conclusion.

12 *Social Statics (1850), Part 1, Chapter 2.*

reasoned, come a great distance and laboured long and hard for their reward. Music was no less under the sway of this optimistic certainty than the sciences or philosophy, and the idea of Progress when applied to the art produced ways of thinking and systems for writing about it that have persisted, not always consciously, long after the original idea was abandoned.

That sort of certainty always seeks corroboration, and to sustain itself the idea of Progress inevitably needed the supporting evidence of a past from which it came, as well as a future towards which it was going. As far as future progress was concerned, the image of the Romantic composer was ideally suited to the idea. He was a man apart, remote, dreaming dreams, cherishing the public image of mystic incomprehensibility (although it must be said that all the best ones had a shrewd, clear eye to present success as well) and prone to making fairly obscure, seer-like statements about his work and music in general.

Best of all at this was Wagner, who wrote a celebrated book called *The Artwork of the Future* in 1850, part of a gigantic literary smokescreen he created after having deserted in 1848 his fellow revolutionaries in Dresden where they had fought unsuccessfully for a united Germany. A year earlier Marx, under the influence of Comte, had produced his *Communist Manifesto*, and Wagner had become caught up in the egalitarian fervour. Once safely ensconced in Switzerland he began to write about it as far as it affected him, his art, and the part this should play in society.

Taking the ides of Feuerbach (a favourite of Marx)[13] he projected the image of a classical Greece where the drama united poetry, mime and music. In the barbarous Middles Ages, to say nothing of decadent Roman times (the twists and turns the long line of history was forced to follow were many and varied) the unity of the classical drama was shattered and the elements dispersed. The subsequent progress of music's history has been to restore and surpass this classical unity. "It must be born anew, not born again," "Only the great Revolution of mankind can win this Art for us, an art that shall bring back a profound sense of beauty to all."[14]

---

13 The very title of Wagner's book is derived from Feuerbach's *The Philosophy of the Future* (1843).

14 *Gesammelte Schriften* (1872), Vol. III, p.39.

These writings by Wagner were at the heart of a strong force dominating European thought which drove men more and more towards self-reliance, towards learning their own importance, needs and desires so that out of their efforts could come ideal worlds of thought, deed and faith. Christianity and the older faiths became gradually nominal in this view and in man, common man – the *Volk* in Wagner's classification – was where the hope for the world's future lay.

Such woolly views, however passionately he would have defended them, were but supports for Wagner to come to his acts of creation, but they led him not only to folk-legends for inspiration in opera but also to his explanation of the future art-work's development. It would be the apotheosis of man's artistic endeavour and, hopefully, was not so far from being achieved. Certainly it would come within his own lifetime.

Wagner outlined an historical thesis of music, which he developed in *Opera and Drama* (1852), representing the muses sailing through the centuries of history on a sea that divided two continents, those of dancing and of poetry. Somehow the early Christians had lost themselves upon the sea of harmony, as exemplified by Palestrina who showed response neither to the word nor to the dance. In the seventeenth century the rise of secular music and the cultivation of the dance entailed further sailings from shore to shore until Beethoven, "the chosen master who was, in his works, to write the world history of music." Arriving on one shore, with the Sixth Symphony he stops to observe Nature; and then in the Seventh he composes the "apotheosis of the dance". Setting forth again he arrives at the opposite shore where "resolutely he threw out his anchor, and this anchor was the *word*" – so accounting for the Ninth Symphony. "Beyond this lay only the Complete Artwork (*Gesamtkunstwerk*) of the Future, the Universal Drama to which Beethoven has forged for us the artistic key."

It is hard to believe that people would accept such child-like nonsense, but Wagner's writings were widely read and, fitting as they did into the accepted view of man's developing past, optimistic present and shining future, they were not without influence. Nor was his by any means the most fanciful conjecture of music's future. It took many forms, but everyone believed that in all likelihood it would reveal new heights, new splendours as yet unknown, the fruits of a long past and a glorious present, with Brahms and Wagner as bearers of the flame.

Wagner died in 1883, Brahms in 1897. There were no obvious successors to carry the torch forward into the twentieth century, but the philosophical climate and the momentum behind it meant that hopes ran high and there was no immediate doubt that the glorious progress of music would continue alongside that of science and society. Nor would there be until the guns of the First World War had begun to take their toll of optimism, as well as of men and women.

William Rockstro, concluding his very influential *General History of Music* of 1886, laments the death of Wagner. He had only twice mentioned Brahms, relegating him, together with Schumann, Bruch and Dvořák, as part of the "last phase but one of [German music's] development."[15] Music had at this point "fairly reached the threshold of the latest phase of all...which passed its culminating point within the memory of men who have not yet grown old."[16] Wagner is dead. But, "granted that we are without a leader,...does it necessarily follow that no such leader is living among us, even now, unknown; learning his gamut perhaps in a garret in Soho as Beethoven learned his at Bonn? Can we be sure that he is not already at work in London or Paris or Dresden?" "No one can foretell the nature of change that may and in all probability will, take place before the first morning of the twentieth century dawns upon the world. But the signs of the times all point in the direction of solid progress."[17]

Even so dyspeptic an historian as Ernest Walker cannot escape the optimism. "No doubt we have slept the sleep of the dull too often and too long; but now we are awake again. Nearly seven hundred years ago we gave to the world the first artistic music it had ever seen; who knows that we may not be its leaders once more?"[18] Sir Hubert Parry in 1896 gave another slant to the optimism: "The resources are so immense, that none but composers gifted with special vital energy and power to grasp many factors at once, seem likely to use them to the full."[19] "It rests with a very

---

15   *A General History of Music* (1886), p.411.
16   *Ibid.*, p.412.
17   *Ibid.*, pp.471-72.
18   *A History of Music in England* (1907), p.357.
19   *The Evolution of the Art of Music* (1896), p.336.

wide public now to decide what the future of the art shall be. Though a man's life may not be prolonged, it may be widened and deepened by what he puts into it; and any possibility of getting into touch with those highest moments in art in which great ideals have been successfully embodied, is a chance of enriching human experience in the noblest manner: and through such sympathies and interests the humanising influence which mankind will hereafter have at its disposal may be infinitely enlarged."[20]

No one writing about music now would openly venture such optimistic conjecture. But it might be profitable to consider whether we have entirely shed the trappings of the idea that music is progressing towards goals glimpsed by only a few, but more valuable on that account. As representatives of the few such visionaries one might cite those contemporary composers who appear to write more for a discerning future than for a responsive present. The idea that value somehow accrues to music that does not communicate in its own time can prove something of a refuge for lesser lights; as well as a danger not always sufficiently understood or guarded against by the more talented. The system of state-financed music that exists throughout Europe seems to encourage composers to continue this Romantic dream.

Of course, the most significant figures do take present communication seriously and search for ways of transmitting their creative images in recognizable form to establish contact with their own public. But there still exists the critical (and administrative) fallacy that obscurity and technical innovation are themselves talismans of worth. (It is hard, for example, to imagine a conservative composer like J.S. Bach receiving, nowadays, a state subsidy, although with so large a family it is likely that he would have needed one.)

The "glimpsed-at goal" has adversely affected the work of a number of composers, most sadly of all, perhaps, that of Arnold Schoenberg, a seminal influence in twentieth-century music. He considered that his compositions after the invention of his 12-tone system formed not the end of an old era but the beginning of a new one. In some ways he was

---

20   *Ibid.*, p.337.

right; but after 60 years, it is his earlier music that still communicates its fervid, hot-house, *fin de siècle* vitality with striking power, while his 12-tone music remains, for the most part, stubbornly in the head and on the page. The same composer was there all the time, but like one of the *penitentes* he seems to have whipped the emotion out of himself, leaving his influence as a teacher and, at the end, an embittered composer living impecuniously in the Los Angeles smog, while the great communicator, Igor Stravinsky, breathed the more expensive airs at the top of the hill.

This will not, I hope, be interpreted as a sanction, a plea for music that sets out only to divert and appeal with the minimum of effort expected on the part of the listener. High art will never be really easy of access, but it must have an element, a degree of initial communication involving the listener or else we shall not find our way to it. No longer does it count to say "a time will come." If we do not manage it in our time it seems no longer much comfort to say our children's children will understand. Every new work by Beethoven — even as he retreated further and further into his obscure, introverted, deaf world — was eagerly awaited by his contemporaries, whom he still managed to involve despite the handicaps. The C sharp minor quartet was difficult to approach in 1826, and still is; but his contemporaries knew it, as we know it now, to be a most remarkable manifestation of the human spirit.

CHAPTER THREE

THE FRUITFUL PAST

Confirmation of music's progress by evidence of its past was a much more certain activity than by conjecture about its future improvement. As a consequence, research into music's origins increasingly occupied our musical predecessors during the nineteenth century. The number of histories of music grew apace with the new enthusiasm, setting out results and putting in place the conclusions derived from their discoveries. And as the idea of Progress formed and came to dominate society, attitudes towards the story of music's past changed because of it.

The earlier histories, strongly influenced by the French encyclopaedists, had been written to demonstrate, by their compendious universality, man's powers of reason more than his continual improvement. Among the earliest in English were those of Dr. Charles Burney and Sir John Hawkins, their first volumes both appearing in the same year, 1776. They set the style for narrative history (which really did not exist before) that persisted until quite recently when the need for things comprehensive declined. The *New* (and surely the last) *Oxford History of Music,* which began publication in 1954, came to be divided into separate volumes dealing with different periods, themselves divided into topics dealt with in segments researched and expounded by various authors, and reflecting no overall view except insofar as co-ordination by a general editor provides one. The need to show the grander scheme of things is past, and not only because the subject matter has become too large. There is no longer a compulsion to consider music history as a long line of connected categories, composers and techniques. Separate subjects examined in detail and collected together to represent certain periods are today sufficient to constitute history.

For Burney things were quite different. The present, especially as it manifested itself in Italian opera, represented the best in music, the epitome of good taste. The past was an interesting and illuminating study rather than proof or even explanation of eighteenth-century excellence. There was, of course, a consciousness of its contrast with the contemporary cult of sensibility, elegance and form which prompted occasional censure and distaste, but in no way did his extensive research suggest a systematic pattern of music's improvement. As we have already observed, Burney ignored J.S. Bach not from dislike, but simply because he didn't know his music. (It wouldn't have made any difference if he had). He did come across some of Monteverdi's music but, not understanding the composer's intentions in the new style nor even the reasons for the way it was written down, thought very little of it. Comparing him to Peri and Caccini, he wrote: "I am unable to discover Monteverdi's superiority...his counterpoint in two parts is more frequently deficient than in the other two composers."[21] Josquin, whose music was available in a more complete form, he praised highly for its contrapuntal skills. He made no attempt to fit any of them into a grander scheme. The scale and scope of his musical curiosity were enormous, but his studies were intended to enhance the knowledge of mankind, not to prove the validity of any single point of view.

After Burney and Hawkins the flow of histories increased to a flood by the later nineteenth century: Forkel (1788-1801), Kalkbrenner (1802), Busby (1819), Muller (1830), Schilling (1830), Stafford (1830), Kiesewetter (1834), Hogarth (1835), Fischer (1835), Higgins (1838), La Fage (1844), Blondeau (1847), Bird, the first in America (1850), Ambros (1862-82), Andries (1862), Hullah (1875), Trambusti (1867), Fétis (1869), Mendel (1870), Grove (1879), to mention only a few of the more important ones. Little by little, through this maze of print, music's past came to be viewed as a long, connected line steadily moving towards some ideal future. The historical evidence was woven, adapted, strengthened, even occasionally amended as the parallel awareness of man's continued progress in medicine, communication and the useful, as well as the purer sciences, seemed to fill the world with optimism. The pressure to make music fit into that general scheme was irresistible. Most historians of the late nineteenth century found themselves in willing accord, and able to justify their view one way or another.

Among the various solutions to the obvious problems of treating music's past in this way, and one of the most influential ones, was Sir Hubert Parry's *The Evolution of the Art of Music*. It reached its tenth edition in 1931 with extra chapters by H.C. Colles, who then published his own version of the same philosophy, designed for schools, under the appropriate title *The Growth of Music* — still found in educational establishments today. Parry was strongly influenced by the writings of Herbert Spencer, whose optimistic views of man's future are quoted above in Chapter II. Darwin had proposed the idea of biological progress in his *Origin of Species* (1889), and the ever-increasing complexity of compositional techniques, size of orchestras, variety and range of instruments

---

21   *A General History of Music from the Earliest Ages to the Present Period*, Vol IV (London, 1789), p.27.

combined to persuade Sir Hubert that Spencer was right even as far as music was concerned. It had, he was sure, developed from simple, separate elements (primitive cries, scales, folk dances and what he calls "incipient harmony") which had become more and more complex and integrated until the resources were now so considerable that only the greatest minds could fully use them. With Wagner and Brahms only lately deceased it was not unthinkable that a new genius would soon come along to bear the torch.

There were problems in the exposition of this view, for along the line of connected development there were those figures whose greatness could not be denied — although at the end of the nineteenth century these were fewer than today. For Parry and his contemporaries they were Palestrina, Bach, Handel, Haydn, Mozart and Beethoven. His solution to the problem was to accord each of them the accolade of qualified greatness, greatness with a "but" generally not of their own making but imposed on them by the conditions of their era. Palestrina's "but" lay in the fact that he lived at a time when he could only cultivate contrapuntal skills (which he did to a degree almost unique in the history of the art) and was deprived of the use of rhythm. In the Spencerian sense, music was still at a time when its elements were separated and the "higher complications" had not yet enough affected him. For believers in Progress it reflected at once the weakness and the strength of Christianity in its tendency towards homogeneity of thought. The vitality of secular music was needed to add the element that would produce Bach and Handel. The "but" of their greatness lies in the general tenets Parry uses for assessing the degrees of music's advancement. The development of principles of design in music must inevitably wait upon the development of technique. Very little can be done with limited means of performance.[22] Each composer, then as now, added his mite to the resources of a growing art when he managed to do something new.[23] Bach and Handel's erstwhile reputations as poor orchestrators spring from this widely-held view. Parry somewhat exonerates the former. "The very loftiness of

---

22   *The Evolution of the Art of Music* (1896), p.157.

23   *Ibid.*, p.158.

Bach's character and artistic aims prevented his condescending to do some of the work which had to be done before modern music could be completely matured."[24] But Handel doesn't get off so lightly. He "did as little as it is possible for a great master to do in adding to the resources of the instrumental side of music. He looked to the present and finished up much as he began."[25] Then there were the "buts" of Bach's excessive contrapuntal complexity where it is not essential, and Handel's crude recitative already referred to in Chapter I.

So remarkable were the achievements of Haydn and Mozart that "if the world could be satisfied with the ideals of perfectly organized simplicity without any great force of expression, instrumental art might well have stopped at the point to which they brought it."[26] But, of course, it couldn't. In opera, "Mozart's instinct for design was too cautious to allow him to venture upon untried methods which might fit more closely to the dialogue and to the progress of the action."[27] As a result "such sorrows as Elvira's are not in any sense capable of being adequately expressed. It is in such situations that the utter inadequacy of the old operatic scheme becomes too conspicuously glaring."[28] It's hard now to believe he meant it.

With Beethoven, Parry came to a figure known by his readers to be great through widespread aural experience, and his "but" in the name of Progress is more muted and more difficult to rationalize. Parry may even have been a little less convinced of it himself. The composer is called the first of the modern masters who became "the interpreter of the innermost joys and sorrows of all human creatures."[29] "It is a palpable fact to everyone that Beethoven's works sound fuller and richer than those of

---

24 *Ibid.*, p.194.
25 *Ibid.*, p.167.
26 *Ibid.*, p.248.
27 *Ibid.*, p.226.
28 *Ibid.*, p.228.
29 *Ibid.*, p.255.

any composers since Bach."[30] The use of the orchestra is better; the use of the piano is better; the coda is better; the scherzo is better; the subtlety of design and expression is better, but... "after him the course of things naturally changed."[31] Sir Hubert goes on to explain, "Beethoven stands just at the turning point of the ways of modern art, and combines the sum of past human effort in the direction of musical design with the first ripe utterance of the modern impulse — made possible by the great accumulation of artistic sources — in the direction of human expression."[32]

Therein lies Parry's "but" for Progress. Beethoven was at once great in his own right and great as a prophet of more wonderful things to come. His ability "to modify the average scheme of the design of instrumental works in accordance with the ideas which he felt he could artistically express was one of the features in his works which indicated the direction in which art was to travel after him."[33] Doubtless referring to Wagner's use of the *Leitmotiv* and Liszt's thematic metamorphoses, Parry notes that Beethoven's "power of presenting the same subject in different aspects has a very important bearing on the nature of recent progress of the art."[34] So strong were Beethoven's personality and achievement that the rest of the generation rebelled. "The instinct of man was impelled to resent the conventions of form which seemed to fetter his imagination and began his wanderings and experiments anew."[35]

Parry saw the development of music after Beethoven as showing itself in the exploration of technical means (Paganini on the violin, Liszt on the piano), and moving "towards variety and closeness of characterisation,"[36] culminating in the two latest and greatest exponents of the art, the one for purely instrumental music, the other for opera. Brahms

---

30   *Ibid.*, p.256.
31   *Ibid.*, p.272.
32   *Ibid.*, p.273.
33   *Ibid.*, p.259.
34   *Ibid.*, p.269.
35   *Ibid.*, p.273.
36   *Ibid.*, p.275.

"for greatness of expression and novelty of treatment stands out absolutely alone."[37] Wagner is throughout as much dramatist and master of theatrical requirements as musician. "Of the method itself it may be said that it is the logical outcome of the efforts of the long line of previous composers, and the most elaborately organised system for the purposes of dramatic musical expression that the world has ever yet seen."[38]

"The long story of the development of music is a continuous and unbroken record of human effort to extend and enhance the possibilities of effects of sound upon human sensibilities, as representing in a formal or a direct manner the expression of man's inner being."[39] At present (that is, at the end of the nineteenth century) "mankind seems finally to have full measure of almost unlimited materials available to illustrate anything he will."[40] High hopes indeed, and on this optimistic note Parry ends his study of music and its progress up to 1893.

Sir Hubert was among the most widely admired and respected musicians of his time. Professor of Music at Oxford and Director of the Royal College of Music, his beliefs had great influence on several generations of musicians and music-lovers. They were, moreover quite in accord with those of his contemporaries in the other arts and sciences, however differently expressed. Parry might have been speaking for any leading figure in any other discipline, substituting the appropriate subjects, when he wrote: "the whole history of the Arts is mainly a continuous effort of artistically-minded human creatures to make the means and the methods for the expression of the inner impulses rich and more perfect."[41] There was, in his day, very little reason for doubting it.

From our standpoint, 90 years later, there are flaws in a system that results in assessing composers by a scale of ten in the Progress chart. The steps by which music progressed, a real *gradus ad Parnassum*, produce a whole series of over-simplified musical sequiturs: *opera seria* and the intermezzi; French overtures and the suite; Italian overtures and the sym-

---

37   *Ibid.*, p.303.
38   *Ibid.*, p.331.
39   *Ibid.*, p.333.
40   *Ibid.*, p.336.
41   *Ibid.*, p.250.

phony; the *da capo* aria and theatrical perdition; Haydn into Beethoven; Weber into Wagner; Schumann into Brahms. Few of these connections feature large in present-day musical thinking or education, but they once did and it is hard for us to believe it, so enormous is the gulf between our forefathers' philosophy of life and ours. *But...it was so.*

CHAPTER FOUR

HIROSHIMA AND AFTER

While Progress was a logical, even demonstrable fact it was accepted by virtually everyone without question or dissent. Various factors have contributed to its decline, but none so powerful or convincing as the two major European wars. It really was not easy to argue that the years between 1914 and 1918 were an improvement on those that went before; and if there were hope that they might eventually be considered and then dismissed as a temporary aberration as man continued his upward path into the twentieth century, the five years after 1939 effectively disposed of any such idea. Those, without doubt, were distinctly worse, especially 1945 with its atomic bomb which on 6 August shattered more than man's hopes of continued improvement.

Progress in science had, for the very first time, produced something that could destroy man and the entire world he lived in. Given his still imperfect moral condition, the likelihood that he would bungle matters, go ahead and do it became a vivid, universal fear, especially for younger people who had no pre-war funds of optimism to bolster disbelief that such a thing could ever come about. They knew that it could. They knew also that this, for sure, was not better in any way. A comfortable copy of the Celestial City on earth was one thing: to rekindle optimism and assuage fears after the blaze and brilliance of Hiroshima was quite another.

Among the older generations may still be heard an occasional faint bleat in support of Progress, but that's all it is. The real beliefs of our time have moved elsewhere. With them, attitudes to life and the living of it have also changed, and much more significantly than the influence of the Beatles or Michael Jackson might suggest, although they were and are manifestations of it. The ideas generated by the concept of Progress have no part in the present generation's attitudes, except they be unwittingly inherited from the past. The future is no longer something of promise, to leave one's mark on, to save for, worth striving for or even planning for, at least not beyond the children. Thereafter it has to be *their* problem.

The present is what mainly matters, for if and while we have it there is reason to be thankful. If right triumphs there is even reason to be hopeful for the next generation. The striving must be to keep it stable, live it as fully as we can and, in the process, search all the time for reassurances that it will go on. There is a new sort of faith possible in all this which much of the present generation is discovering. Without it comes despair, recourse to violence, drugs, crime, sexual excess, protest or almost any escape from the unpalatable lack of foundation for living.

Fear of what he has done has truly changed man's mind; his predicament is not unlike Adam's in the Garden of Eden.

A faith destroyed needs another to replace it, for man is an incurable optimist. Sadly, the established churches have failed to realize this. Where they could have renewed waning interest they squabbled about language and format; where they could have involved through use of the arts they bored by experimenting with worthless trivialities; where they could have won minds by sympathy with contemporary problems like contraception, abortion and homosexuality, they retreated into synods and conventions discussing arid changes in doctrine and thus alienated intelligent interest. Worst of all, where they could have sustained by conviction they have seemed as daunted and amazed as any of us.

No one faith came to replace the older creeds. The single, binding factor was the fear and sense of peril. The search for reassurance took myriad different courses. Cults flourished as never before, all purporting to provide a solution, sustaining faith. Some, perhaps, achieve something along those lines; some use the needs of the young for their own profit. The more emotional, evangelical religions have fared better than the authoritarian ones. Some people, the more politically minded, make do with anti-nuclear marches and campaigns against various social injustices, real and imaginery. *In extremis* some take to terrorism.

More widespread than any of them, and more important because it can be incorporated in all of them, is the rediscovery of past values. This is no longer made with the intention of proving the present's superiority or the future's promise, but to seek confirmation that what has endured for years, maybe for centuries, and can still be counted valuable, would seem to suggest a sort of permanence when all else around shows very little indication of it. Old houses are visited by thousands of people; old things are collected: furniture, silver, paintings, drawings, clocks, cars, cigarette cards, almost anything that bespeaks an older, enduring value.

Among the main enthusiasms has been, and still is, the rediscovery of old music, of music from the centuries before 1800. The realization that it is still able to communicate its vitality in present performance apparently undiminished by the intervening years has put music among the most vivid and potent instruments of hope that all is not and will not be lost, that some values are constant and likely to remain so.

Almost as if by divine intervention, the means to make this possible seemed to appear at the right time. To our forbears the radio was a minor amateur enthusiasm. Now everyone has one. Some countries have a "third" programme, some a number of classical musical stations. The gramophone, invented at the turn of the century, has evolved through 78, 45 and 33 revolutions to the latest compact disc, and everyone has one or another version of it. The sale of records is big business and the collecting of them, to say nothing of cassettes and video-tapes, a widespread passion. Many people collect more than they are likely to re-hear in a lifetime, but the very passion for them may have something in common with the taking of correspondence courses. They cannot themselves guarantee an education or a future but they both represent the wish to have one.

Orchestras, opera-houses and concert-halls flourish, and television, in its own way, has done its part, although it is mainly concerned with expectations of only a very short duration. At the same time as the proliferation of mechanical aids for the dissemination of music, and not unaffected by them, music has become, especially in Europe, a favoured instrument of education of great importance and on an unprecedented scale. The number and excellence of youth orchestras are evidence of much more widespread musical activities, an outward manifestation of the confidence educators now place in the power of music to inculcate moral as well as musical standards. Before 1914 music was not considered in that light. It was a suitable accomplishment for young ladies, perhaps, but hardly a part of serious education or of inherent value.

Ironically, the passion for music's rediscovery had already begun under the aegis of this philosophy. As the output of music histories increased during the nineteenth century, so did the need for accurate research, especially in Germany, a country noted for its enthusiasm for thoroughness. By the end of the century there had developed a breed of scholars who devoted their energies to unearthing the facts and musical texts of certain periods and topics. It was by no means a wide or popular movement, but by their researches men like Schilling, von Winterfeld and Goldschmidt painstakingly laid the foundations for future enthusiasms. They themselves had little interest in making their chosen fields more widely known through performance, and were largely innocent of the later effects their studies were to have.

That sort of impetus came from another type of scholar more commonly found in England: quasi-amateur, well-read, well-educated, often involved in other professions but with leisure and means to indulge their enthusiasms. J.A. Fuller Maitland and William Barclay-Squire rediscovered the *Fitzwilliam Virginal Book* and had it printed in 1899. The Rev. E.H. Fellowes enthusiastically brought the English Madrigal School back to life, to say nothing of Tudor church music. W.H. Cummings founded the Purcell Society with the aim of publishing and performing that composer's music, little of which had been seen or heard since the seventeenth century. Professor E.J. Dent wrote the first biography of Alessandro Scarlatti; F.T. Arnold made a large compilation of sources of instruction on the playing of figured-bass; H.E. Wooldridge wrote about earlier polyphonic music, Dom Anselm Hughes about plainsong. Scholars all, with an almost evangelical passion for sharing their enthusiasms by putting the music they admired back into sound as much as on to paper in histories or academic journals.

In this they were aided by the small, growing band of performers of the earlier music. Arnold Dolmetsch and his family come to mind, but there were many others: Carl Engel, Wanda Landowska, Violet Gordon-Woodhouse, Henry Watson and F.W. Galpin, to say nothing of more recent figures. Apart from their direct influence through teaching, they provided an aural climate and an example for the next generations. Publishers and their presses were not slow or unenthusiastic about joining in; men like Chrysander, Brahms, Saint-Saëns, Arkwright, William Chappell, Edward Rimbault and more anonymous groups like the German Bach and Handel societies, the Musical Antiquarian Society and the Plainsong and Mediaeval Music Society prepared edition after edition. By the years following the Second World War there was scarcely a note of any value left unpublished, and today there is scarcely a minor figure of any period who is not threatened with a complete edition.

The hunger for the discovering of earlier and still earlier music seems to be insatiable; but there is a limit, and we are reaching it. Before the ninth century, oral tradition was the most accurate, almost the only means of keeping music alive in performance. Up to the eleventh century there were only the vaguest symbols for pitch, and little that can be transcribed into usable modern notation was written down before the end of the thirteen century. That, therefore, is as far back as the search for confirmation of artistic values in music can take us in any tangible way. But the need seems to be so strong that, although most of the ground between 1300 and 1800 has been covered (and in a remarkably short time), the search has turned in on itself and, like a toenail reaching the end of a shoe, is in danger of becoming ingrown.

CHAPTER FIVE

THE END OF THE LINE

Before notation there is virtually nothing to research or revive in music. Painting, sculpture, artefacts, architecture and literature can be examined in much earlier periods, and enthusiasts in these fields have by no means come to the end of the line. But music has, and with the basic need for confirmation in no way abated, the searching process has become extremely involuted with a veritable traffic-jam of eager, industrious scholars travelling back and forth along well-worn paths. The result is a number of very nasty accidents, as well as a good deal of spite and bad temper.

The block in music, as far as the general listener's ability to recognize value is concerned, occurs somewhat later than the beginning of notation. It may yet change, but mediaeval music, except where skilfully adapted for present-day audiences by a Noah Greenberg or a David Munrow, has not been widely appreciated. It serves for some, but has not so far elicited anything like so wide or vivid a response as that of music from the sixteenth and later centuries. All the same, scholars keep hunting high and low in the libraries of Europe and America, and the smallest newly-discovered canzona acquires for them an importance and value usually quite unrelated to its content. Many an academic or critical reputation has been made and lost by such discoveries, so intense is the search even in the most minor fields of musicology.

The same sort of intensity can be seen in all the arts. Not just the discovery of a piffling little fugue possibly by Bach, but a dull little poem possibly by Shakespeare has the media of the world in a frenzy of activity. The attribution (and the faking, formerly quite openly accepted as copying) of old masters has become notoriously big business. There are, for example, many more Canalettos adorning the walls of Europe and America than even that industrious painter could possibly have managed in one lifetime. The plethora of these paintings produced to satisfy a ravenous market for old masters reminds one of those pieces of wood sold as reliquaries in the mediaeval church. Put together, they would have built not just one cross, but several houses. Both, in their separate ways, became symbols of a future life.

The insurmountable impasse of notation, or rather the lack of it, before 1300 has caused responsible scholarship to abandon hope of making significant new discoveries. Instead, while lesser lights turn to the *minutiae* of musicology, the main thrust of research has been towards revealing the ways and means of past performance. In this manner would scholarship enable musicians to copy closely and reproduce exactly the way music was first heard in the hope that it will become still more real, still more valuable. It is, on the face of it, a most attractive idea.

There have been two clearly discernible results. On the one hand, research has contributed wonderfully to illuminating and giving greater insight and freedom to the bringing of older music back to present-day, sentient life. On the other, it has sometimes resulted in restriction and a sort of mean-spirited isolationism, promoting the formation of musical cults. Their exclusivity has in some cases seemed wilfully to impede the twentieth-century listener's access to the music, and even the performer's right to perform it, just as religious cults exclude those outside their beliefs from their sort of salvation.

Well before either of these trends could be distinguished, the process of exploring ways and means had begun under the aegis of historical accuracy, of proving origins and establishing a compendium of reliable evidence on which could be based the theory of music's continued development. This evidence proved easily adaptable to the changed needs of more recent years.

About the turn of the century, instruments moldering in houses and museums, known to have been part of earlier music's performance, began to be resuscitated; at first out of curiosity, then out of enthusiasm for the light they threw on the content of the music as well as the way it had been performed.

The clarity and pulse of a Scarlatti sonata played on the harpsichord eventually showed music-lovers that the music contained things different from those suggested by nineteenth-century virtuosi, beginning their recitals with a well-pedalled group of sonatas—played at speeds and in ways dictated more by technical accomplishment than by concern for the music's meaning, riveting as this approach may have been at a different level of comprehension. This is in no way intended to suggest that Scarlatti sonatas should not be played on the piano; only that the music, once heard on the earlier instrument for which it was composed, reveals aspects of itself that must affect its performance, no matter what instrument is eventually used.

The rediscovery of the harpsichord was initially associated with the arts-and-crafts movement in Europe, characterized also by a certain harmless, bizarre eccentricity associated with herbal remedies, country dancing, weaving, pottery and eclectic societies whose members were initially somewhat mocked by their more conventional contemporaries. Nevertheless the "knit-your-own-violin" school achieved remarkable things and survived to take its place among the first of those who showed older values still valuable. Barely a National Trust house is now without a shop showing considerable evidence of their continued vitality and industry. Their particular enthusiasm bred, too, a gentle generosity of spirit that was apparent in their love for early music, on whose performance they had an almost wholly beneficial effect.

In England the Dolmetsch family, if not alone, were certainly the most celebrated of those early protagonists. Stories about them are legion, with a benevolently tyrannical father making all his large family play a great variety of instruments — harpsichords, virginals, spinets, clavichords, viols, recorders, lutes and sackbuts — some, it must be said, more successfully than others. The family began giving concerts of consort music in 1890 and in 1925 finally established themselves at Haslemere, giving an important annual series of concerts devoted to early music.

The inevitably rickety condition of instruments several hundred years old led to their being copied, and Arnold Dolmetsch made harpsichords, lutes and viols from the 1890s until his death in 1940; a similar movement in France had resulted in the first new harpsichord from Erard in 1882. Enthusiasm for the instrument and its fellows gained momentum and, apart from the restoration of such old instruments as were left in resuscitable state, more and more makers began to copy them, reviving old skills, sometimes combining them with modern scientific methods and discoveries. Reasonably enough there were jealousies, and the makers were not always charitable about each other. Dolmetsch was known for his sharp tongue and, a little later on, I never heard Hugh Gough say anything agreeable about his namesake, Tom Goff. Nor were Mr. Hodgson or Mr Goble above an observation or two concerning their contemporaries. However, as a player in the 1950s one may have favoured one or the other, yet there was never any real difficulty about playing any or all of their instruments, either technically or personally — beyond a sorrowful glance or a shake of the head. They were not exclusive.

Led by the work of two Americans, Frank Hubbard and William Dowd, a new sort of harpsichord began to be produced after the Second World War, and the change is significant.

In the name of authenticity they copied selected earlier instruments, and in building them reproduced exactly their narrow keyboards. Each key is only a matter of millimetres less than the standard keys common to all pianos and a large number of other earlier harpsichords. The narrowness makes no difference to the sound and is scarcely perceptible to the hands over small melodic intervals. Over several octaves, however, the smaller scale becomes an impossible obstacle to accuracy and virtually excludes the player accustomed to the larger keyboard from being able to use them.

Harpsichords, especially two-manual ones, have several ranks of strings which by the later eighteenth century were regularly brought in and out of action by the use of pedals, a great boon to the player whose hands tend to be fully occupied in, say, a busy piece by Rameau. Previously he would have had to bring on or release the various ranks of strings, thus changing the dynamics and colour, by using hand-stops on their instruments; a restriction for players tantamount to an infringement of the First Amendment.

In some quarters the practice of making useless "authenticity" an excuse for further exclusivity continued and diversified, with lower-pitch instruments made of "original" materials which virtually precluded them from playing with most other instruments. Mr Dowd and Mr Hubbard, having started their activities in tandem, had a falling-out and their disciples were divided. They in their turn began to produce instruments whose sources tended to become still more narrowly focused. Be they modelled on harpsichords by Ruckers, Taskin, Schudi, Haas or Kirkman, their creators, rather like high priests of a religious cult, seemed to be laying claim to have discovered the real way, the golden road, *le droit chemin* as Loys Bourgeois called an equally pious musical system in 1556, towards enlightenment and resolution of all stylistic problems. The makers had and have very little good to say of one another, which might perhaps cast doubts as to the universality of their solution, but they all have their followers.

Much the same has happened still more recently with almost every instrument that can be said to have been different at some earlier period of its history. Flutes, oboes, clarinets, bassoons, violins, violas, cellos, basses, trumpets, horns, trombones and timpani, all are now being produced in earlier forms, all in the name of authenticity, all showing fascinating technical features which will help renew attitudes to performance of the music for which they were originally used. The techniques for playing them are often radically different from those of their later counterparts, and generally they are played at a lower pitch—all of which tends to render the player less fit to play both sorts of instrument. This exclusivity also ensures less professional competition, and too often the less good players hide their technical and musical deficiencies under the mantle of "authenticity" and sit behind their "original" instruments bristling with insecure dislike of their colleagues in the professional mainstream.

What all these instruments can show when, as now is often the case, they are well played, are aspects of phrasing, articulation, rhythm, accentuation, rubato, speeds and dynamics that are wonderfully illuminating. They raise questions and generate ideas about the music they play that may never have occurred to the player accustomed to the instruments in their twentieth-century state, especially if these ideas, though stemming from the technical aspects of the instruments, are applied to the content of the music. It must be true that just to play a Handel oboe concerto on a Baroque oboe is no guarantee that deeper penetration of the music's significance will result. That can only come about through the mind, and through intuitive understanding; but these can be stimulated, and the understanding enhanced, by these technical differences between "authentic" and twentieth-century instruments.

Another important result of the notational impasse to historical research has been the increased exploration of ways as opposed to means of performance. Books about the ways to perform early music began to be published early in the twentieth century. In 1916 Arnold Dolmetsch published his *Interpretation of the Music of the XVII and XVIII Centuries,* one of the first of many such exercises in stylistic explanation. More useful still has been the publication of original manuals about performance from all periods. In the 1890s Edward Dannreuther had produced what was essentially a two-volume précis of several such texts.[42] Now virtually all the important texts are available, enabling the student performer to come to his own conclusions as to the way his music should go.

---

42 *Musical Ornamentation,* Novello, Ewer & Co. Music Primer (1893-95).

Like a mirage in the desert, these glimpses of the ways certain music was originally performed may deceive one into thinking one has discovered the authentic oasis. But music is very difficult to write about, and the facts of performance almost impossible accurately to describe. Musicians, too, are not and never have been the most literate of beings. Their skills lie more with notes than words. Even so intelligent a man as C.P.E. Bach, in his *Essay on the True Method of Playing the Clavier* (1753), seems to have been incapable of explaining anything in a foolproof manner, and, though what he writes is extremely valuable, he is the first to admit that "for every case covered even by the best rule there will be an exception." François Couperin in *The Art of Playing the Harpsichord* (1716) describes with characteristic French *insouciance* ways of interpreting his own very individual system of ornamentation signs, and has left players tremulous in their uncertainty, or exaggeratedly assertive, ever since. As for fingering his pieces in the way he would seem to propose, this can only confirm the French propensity for being amused at the discomfort of foreigners.

All the same, these and dozens of other texts now readily available allow one to enter the period of the music they describe. Intelligently read with a certain objectivity, intuition, humour and a considerable ability for compromise, they can light as vividly as anything else the way towards informed performance of the music with which they are associated.

A third result of the impasse, and now a *sine qua non* for the renewal of vitality in our twentieth-century view of earlier music, is the publication of what Germans call the *Urtext*, the closest possible reproduction of the composer's manuscript. To have, as a starting-point for performance, the text of a piece of music as it first appeared on paper must be, without exception, the most important element in the complicated procedure that then follows before the music sounds. But this is not so simple as it would appear. Before the music is transformed from manuscript to print, editors, publishers and printers all have to make decisions that can vitally affect the result.

You have only to compare a Mozart manuscript with the latest editions to see questionable interpretations of unclear phrasemarks; decisions about where the *p* of a *sfp* mark should come (see the opening of the "Prague" Symphony); how various editors have interpreted the differences in Mozart's *staccato* marks, a hideously difficult problem as the composer clearly indicates at least two sorts, but not altogether consistently and with confusing implications of how they should be interpreted.

The printed scores of the Schubert symphonies have been available since the late nineteenth century, and in performance many an opening or closing chord has begun loudly and diminished to *piano* because of a long, pointed sign ═══════ .The sign appears in the composer's manuscript, and to interpret it as a *diminuendo* is not at all unreasonable — until you discover in the body of the manuscript many cases of what are irrefutably accents, not *diminuendo*, written in exactly the same way. Berlioz also wrote long accents, with similar falsely contrived interpretative effects resulting from our tendency to believe what we see in print. The pitfalls are endless, and only a little less dangerous if you work solely from facsimiles of the composer's manuscript. You simply take the burden of deciding these matters on your own shoulder.

All this is to say that *Urtext* editions — like W.S. Gilbert's "skimmed milk" — frequently masquerade as "cream", and all too often reflect the foibles of an academic or a printer with little or no real intuitive understanding of the manuscript, the composer or the process and circumstances of performance it represents. These are most reliably gathered by people experienced in performance, capable of intelligent examination of the composer's score backed up by the widest possible knowledge of the rest of his music.

A fourth element contributory to the rejuvenation of the image of earlier music is the historical study of conditions for performance. To read in the *Mercure galant* of March 1683 that "le Manche des Théorbes de l'orchestre cache toujours quelque chose de la vue" not only tells us something about the height of the orchestra pit, but also of the considerable numbers of theorbos still used for the continuo group in Venetian opera at that time. To look at the famous painting of an operatic performance at Eszterháza shows the exact numbers of players Haydn was accustomed to work with there at that time. An engraving (1749) of the Palazzo Reale in Naples by Giuseppe Vasi shows an orchestra three times as large.

The material is endless and fascinating, serving to give an idea of numbers and scope which cannot help but influence the way we perform the music now. But to put performance therefore into rigid, factual straitjackets is fatal. Handel had many more players and singers for his performances of *Acis and Galatea* in London than in the version that was first heard at Cannons. Who, at this point in time, may say which is the better and, for want of first-hand evidence, which Handel preferred? Both may be convincingly argued, and both may serve to reveal the music's content.

Such variables are so common in the history of performance, composers themselves often being among the most adaptable of people, that it is fruitless to make rules and set absolute conditions for performance. There can be no reason why, for example, a Haydn opera composed for Eszterháza should not be performed in a much larger modern theatre. But to insist in such surroundings on the tiny band that Haydn used may so diminish its effect as to cause the venture to fail. Sensitive judgement, rather than dogmatic statement, is called for.

More important still as part of this fourth element is the study of the culture that surrounds a period of music. The fact that Monteverdi must have known Rubens and his work over a period of seven or eight years (they were both at the small, Mantuan court of the Gonzagas between 1600 and 1608) cannot help but colour our attitude to his music. The plunging horses of *The Fall of Phaeton* (1605); the body of the drowning Leander, the falling Hero and the cupids, nymphs and naiads who try to help, a moment of pure theatre, in *Hero and Leander* (1606); the violence of *St George Fighting the Dragon* (1606); this extreme, superbly controlled sensuality must have struck sympathetic vibrations in the composer's mind as he explored the potential of *le nuove musiche*, and it surely must inform our performances of it now.

Purcell knew Dryden well and was painted by Kneller. Handel was a friend of John Gay and Alexander Pope, ate well and had a great collection of paintings, including two Rembrandts. Bach barely knew anybody except the severe Lutheran Church Councils where he worked, whom we, too, would do well to know.

It must surely be true that the closer we come to the literature, painting, theatre and society around the music, the more likely we are to be able to recreate the ethos in which it was written; more likely than through blind pursuit of fact, in the hope of pinning down the authenticity of a style like a butterfly to a board.

CHAPTER SIX

IN PRACTICE

As we have seen, there are four ways that musical scholarship has responded to the impasse in historical discovery: the revival of old instruments, research into the way composers evidently expected their music to be played, the publication of original texts, and the exploration of the society and culture that surrounded them. All of these pose a multitude of questions, both general in the consideration of music's place in our time, and highly specific when it comes to the performance of a single work, especially one of great significance.

Taking this as a cue, I propose to examine the processes by which three important, but very different, problematic pieces of music may be approached and realized in sound. No single way will be proposed, nor any claimed as best or most desirable. There are always too many variables for that, usually starting with the evidence of the earliest performances in the composer's lifetime. The aim must be to show the music's vitality and meaning to a late-twentieth-century audience — there seems no point in preparing it for any other purpose — so that they may find an equivalent sense of value in it, made the more valuable by having persisted for several hundred years.

My approach may illuminate for some, give courage to others, and offend a few. It will raise the eyebrows of those committed to purity and raise the level of venom in those predisposed to strike; but it is based on the actual experience of bringing these works to effective performance, and I stand by the methods and thinking that went into their preparation even if, because time has passed, I might change some details.

Gluck: *Orfeo*

For those seeking to produce an "authentic" performance of Gluck's *Orfeo* there is one obvious course to take. A gift to the unsuspecting and pure at heart, there is an original first version of the opera. A great deal has been written and said in approval of it, mostly by those who have not left their desks or entered the theatre before writing or saying it. They are persuaded of its superiority by the underlying conviction that to be first is to be best, whereas, even if we do not believe the Bible, we know this is not necessarily so. The only certain thing about being first is that that is what you are. This is as true of motor races as it is of Adam and of the first version of *Orfeo*. There is nothing intrinsically or more widely of value to be drawn from the fact.

The truth is that Gluck, already a composer of many successful but rather ordinary Italian operas, was persuaded in Vienna to undertake a somewhat revolutionary concept of the legend of Orpheus by a rather pushy, adventurer librettist, Raniero de'Calzabigi. That was in 1762. Gluck was no fool — he was ambitious, a *bon viveur* (he eventually died of apoplexy from overeating) and always looking for opportunities. He rose to the challenge and produced a remarkable score aimed at startling the Viennese into new appreciation of its author's talents.

Not remarkable enough, however, for the opera had scant success and scarcely produced more than a ripple on the wider European scene. It was put aside until 12 years later when, in 1774, the opportunity came to produce it in Paris. The venture was masterminded by DuRoullet, a clever and ambitious politician, attaché at the French Embassy in Vienna, friend of both Gluck and Calzabigi and the best P.R. man of his time. The idea was to translate, rework and adapt the first version of *Orfeo* for a French audience, and to sell the idea in advance. The link with Marie Antoinette (to whom, as a princess in Vienna, Gluck had taught singing, and who had gone to France in 1770) was an added encouragement.

The project's success enhanced Gluck's reputation as a composer of revolutionary operas that delighted Gluck for as long as there was money in them. A great deal of music was added to the original version, and of a marvellously theatrical quality; for Gluck had, it transpired, great gifts in that direction, even if he did have no more counterpoint than Handel's cook. The central character of *Orfeo*, first written in Vienna for the famous castrato Gaetano Guadagni, was altered, enlarged and transposed in Paris for the *haut-contre* (an extremely high tenor) of Joseph le Gros. This voice was popular with the French, who did not like the castrati for, presumably, Gallic reasons. Like the castrato, the *haut-contre* sound is almost unknown today.

Most of Gluck's adaptation and expansion for Paris of his earlier score can be stated categorically to be an improvement; and almost all of the items he added — the first aria for Amor, the great recitative and aria for Orfeo that ends Act I, the Dance of the Furies, the Dance of the Blessed Spirits, Euridice's ravishing 6/8 aria with chorus, the last trio and the splendid concluding chaconne — have rightly become celebrated and rated as among the best things in the opera. It seems to me, therefore, to come into the category of cutting noses to spite faces to do without them in the name of authenticity, academically interesting as it may be to see what Gluck and Calzabigi's first thoughts about the opera were. Only an opera buff blinded by an arrogant desire for exclusivity could possibly claim that it was better, or even a decently viable alternative to the later version. It must be remembered, causing our purist to wince perhaps, that at Parma in 1769 Gluck himself arranged the first version of the work for a soprano castrato, Giuseppe Millico, and, like all composers of almost any period before 1800, was quite used to making things work in differing situations.

Assuming the intention to produce the larger, later version, there are problems ahead that will cause the academic mind sleepless nights. Berlioz was the first to propound them and to provide a viable solution. The first problem for Berlioz was the *haut-contre*; the second his passion for the singer Pauline Viardot. The latter no longer matters very much but the present lack of *haut-contres* does. A high tenor under extreme pressure to sustain his line and retain intonation at so elevated a tessitura is a less likely personification of Orpheus, that strange, remote, spiritual singer of songs, than a castrato or a mezzo-soprano in travesty — an operatic convention that has played a large and successful part in the form since it started. Gluck himself found even le Gros' voice difficult to accept, and was said to have complained that sometimes it sounded like sawing through bones. Anguish, he is said to have observed, should be felt inwardly as if it came from the heart.

Berlioz' happy combination of passions resulted in a version based faithfully on the French version, with some transpositions — Orfeo's first strophic aria and subsequent recitative, his last aria in Act I (which Berlioz also rescored unnecessarily, including some monstrous cadenzas for his adored diva), the furies' scene, "*Che farò*" (back to the key Gluck first used in Vienna) — and a very few adaptations in the recitatives, something any good professional could have accomplished without difficulty. Certainly nothing to bring blushes to the virginal cheeks of a purist, complicated as the small alterations involved in the transpositions are.

There is nowadays no reason not to reinstate the vivid colours of the two cor anglais, two clarinets (chalumeaux), two cornetti and harpsichord that were used so effectively in the original Viennese scoring, but which were not available to Gluck in the Paris of 1774 or to Berlioz in the Paris of 1866.

Berlioz performed the opera in French, as had Gluck in 1774. If you think the work sounds better in Italian then you may return to the Calzabigi text for the music of the original version and for the rest must choose between the various Italian translations that have been made since the 1774 version; for this was sung all over Europe, and frequently in Italian.

Today we have all this information and must come to our own solutions, our own compromises. To enshrine the solutions of Berlioz without question is simply to cement in ideas and attitudes of another period foreign to both Gluck's and our own. Very little "tampering" is necessary; it is much more a matter of choosing with the 1774 Parisian score always in mind. Sir Charles Mackerras is mistaken in saying that this, Gluck's second version, is "theatrically not viable."[43] On the contrary, in it lies the authentic and most complete vision that Gluck presented to us, impossible as it is to put directly into practice. He is also in error in saying that the bravura aria of Orfeo that ends Act I, "*Addio, miei sospiri*", is "certainly out of keeping with the lofty character of the rest of the opera."[44] It is out of keeping with Berlioz' high-Romantic view

---

43   "Berlioz: The Best of Both Worlds", *Cambridge Opera Handbooks: C. W. von Gluck*, ed. Patricia Howard, p.101.

44   *Ibid.*, p.102.

of the work, but not at all if we consider it in terms of the eighteenth century. It then wonderfully symbolizes Orpheus' new-found determination to conquer Hell in the search for his beloved Euridice, and Gluck, supremely able dramatist that he was, used it to give the end of Act I a powerfully energetic lift before the hero reappears at the beginning of Act II, now facing the dark portals of the underworld.

Lovingly, unafraid of compromise, never losing touch with the vitality that still courses so strongly through the piece, is, in this case *le droit chemin*, the right road to authenticity. There are many choices to be made and there will be many people with little or no idea of them who will be only too ready to adopt stances. These you don't have to believe.

Monteverdi: *L'incoronazione di Poppea*

Since they began to reach a wider public in the 1960s, there has been a great deal of controversy over the way the operas of Monteverdi and his younger contemporaries, such as Cavalli and Cesti, should be brought back to life in our time. Many talk and write about the subject, but very few of those — and still fewer of the people who come to listen — know what the problems are, what part the revivifier actually plays and to what degree he has to enter into the original creative process to reveal the authentic voice.

From the beginning of the seventeenth century until the 1680s, when success and commercialism radically changed its format, opera was always written down in the same way. There was never anything approaching a full score as we know it today. The libretto was set to music mostly on two staves showing the voice part and the bass line. The latter is rarely rhythmic and mainly intended to indicate the harmonies. Occaionally there is a *ritornello* (an instrumental section, usually for strings) in three or five parts, sometimes indicated perhaps by a *segue ritornello* but with no music. Even more occasionally some indication is given of instruments playing with the voices. That is all. Figs. 1 to 3 — from Monteverdi, Cesti and Cavalli — are typical.

The reasons for so skeletal an initial concept were simple and extremely practical. It was an intelligently conceived, almost ideal way of putting drama and music together in a rehearsable way which left options open for ideas to occur during the long period of preparation before the opera finally reached the stage. The method worked especially well in the earlier years of opera when the composer was always present at rehearsals. The two-line format made any reshaping, cutting, transposition or adaptation extremely easy. Imagine trying to take a few bars out of *Tristan*. It would unravel like a piece of knitting sheared off by scissors, so complex is the score on its 40 staves.

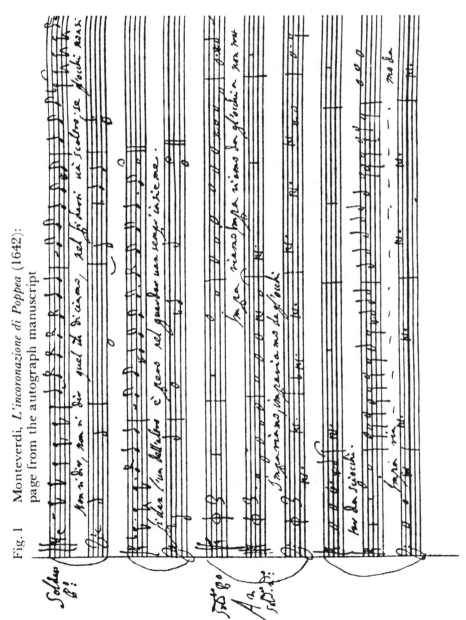

Fig. 1   Monteverdi, *L'incoronazione di Poppea* (1642): page from the autograph manuscript

Fig. 2   Cesti, *L'Argia* (1655): page from the autograph manuscript

Like all the great seventeenth-century painters, the composers of early opera had their pupils and assistants around them to carry out their masters' instructions, fill in a few spaces, add a bar here or there, do transpositions, score others or complete a ritornello, and act as general factotums in the weeks that were always allocated for such preparation. It is touching to think of Cavalli helping Monteverdi in the initial creation of *Poppea*. In the single manuscript left in Venice (there is another, later one in Naples, and that is all) the celebrated last duet is almost certainly in Cavalli's hand and it may be that he even composed it himself. He certainly copied the idea later and wrote several final duets of great beauty in his own operas.

Conjecture as we may, there is clear evidence of collaboration and cooperation in many of these early operas, just as in many paintings of the time. The idea offends or alarms those who, romantically, view the

Fig. 3   Cavalli, *Scipione affricano* (1664): page from the
autograph manuscript

creation of such works as an almost sacred revelation springing complete
from the single author's mind, like soldiers from dragons' teeth.
Academics become very nervous with the idea of collaboration for, apart
from the uncertainty, the ascribing and cataloguing become very
problematic and the footnotes plentiful.

But if we are to accept the responsibility of making these skeletal
scores come alive we must approach the two lines left to us with an
awareness of the theatre that is in them, as well as the fantastically vivid
musical response that opera drew from Monteverdi. We must serve as
his pupils and assistants did, and casting care aside – though not
respect – use every sort of knowledge that scholarship can provide and
participate in the creativity we sense contained within the score. It is like

a love affair. You either give yourself to it wholeheartedly or you should give it up.

In the case of *Poppea* the problems of text are minor. There is the printed libretto of Busenello and the two manuscripts, of which the earlier one in Venice must take precedence. We know the constitution of the orchestra in principle from account books and contemporary observation. Essentially it was divided into two groups which, though able to play at the same time when necessary, fulfilled separate functions. There was a small group of strings which, due to the exigencies of ensemble, usually played when the music was metrical and only very occasionally in rhythmically freer moments of heightened recitative (as at the end of the prison scene in Cavalli's *L'Ormindo*). Fulfilling the major role of accompanying the passionate, expressive recitative which carries most of the drama, and was the most striking innovation of *Le nuove musiche* (as the new operatic style was called), is the continuo.

By continuo is meant something that literally provides a continuum under a solo line, a connecting link above which the voices may unfold the drama, revealing their emotions and characters. It comprised in Monteverdi's time a large group of instruments all separately suited to the accompaniment of freely expressive singing, unconstrained by the rigours of regular metre. We know that the group consisted of one or more of the following: reed and flue portative organs, lutes, guitars, theorbos, chitarrones, harpsichords and harps, sometimes supported by sustaining 'cello lines played by single instruments.

So we may establish the principles of the way the voices were accompanied. For the bulk of the opera the continuo group did it, with the strings added at emotionally heightened moments, when metrical music, incipient arias, tended to appear. (The aria eventually grew in importance while the recitative became increasingly perfunctory and inexpressive.) The strings also played sinfonias and ritornellos where needed. The notes they would be required to play do not always appear in the manuscript.

There is a further principle for the use of the continuo to be deduced. Each of the instruments of which the group is comprised has a special tone-colour of its own. The variety of sound in the harpsichord and the harp are well known; the open pipes of the flue organ make a dulcet sound quite different from the darker, harsher sounds of the reed organ. The lute family varies from the bright, plangent sounds of the smaller instruments to the warm, round sounds of the guitar and the deep sonorities of the chitarrone. In *Orfeo* (1607) Monteverdi indicated in the score (printed not so much for performance as for presentation) how by selecting different instruments for different personages they could be used to enhance characterization. *Caronte canta al suono del regale*— Charon sings to the sound of a reed organ; the Messenger to a flue organ with chitarrone; for Orpheus' echo song two flue organs and two chitarrone placed at opposite sides of the stage. So successful is this use of instrumental colour for characterization in this, Monteverdi's first opera, that there could be no question but that in it he established a principle that continued for as long as recitative played as important a part in the form.

The strings, whenever scored in full, are in three or five parts, and herein lies another source of controversy. There is an enormous difference between the thin three-part texture and the rich, sensuous five-part sound. We are now used to a four-part texture and it is hard to imagine the difference in quality which even the addition of one single line, an inner second viola part, makes. Composers of consort music, madrigals and church music thought most often in five parts. Apart from its richness of sonority, this probably had something to do with complete final chords at cadences. (Following sixteenth-century contrapuntal practice the leading tone could not descend to the fifth of the next chord; this only became acceptable in the four-part writing of Bach's and Handel's time. In five parts these cadential chords can more easily be made complete within the older discipline.)

Therefore, although a three-part texture may possibly have been used from time to time, I believe the most usual one was in five parts. Lully, who learned his operatic trade in seventeenth-century Italy, demonstrated all his life what was probably general practice there in his youth. In virtually all the instrumental music of his operas he wrote down three parts only, leaving two middle staves to be completed (often horribly) by his pupils and assistants. Examples to be found in the scores of Cavalli and Cesti only to serve to confirm this view.

We should next examine what sort of precedent and licence there is in the matter of transposition and cutting. The manuscript of *Poppea*, like almost all the surviving working scores of early seventeenth-century Italian opera, has a number of cuts indicated, and a multitude of directions for transpositions *all'4a, all'5a, come sta, un tuon più alta*, all bespeaking, as one might expect from this method of producing opera, considerable latitude in the treatment of the material first put down on paper.

The last major problem to consider before beginning to bring the work back to musical and theatrical life is that of the bass line. In the manuscript it is rarely figured to indicate the harmony and, unless the vocal line shows some rhythmic cohesion or pattern, it is written almost entirely in white notes that fill the bar. These do not mean necessarily that the notes are to be sustained for their full length, but that a note so indicated is the basis for the harmony for as long as it lasts in the manuscript. Where and when it stops or acquires further pattern to emphasize meaning would have been up to the continuo player, and is now up to the person who "realizes" the work for public performance. The actual harmonies used can only be determined by someone who knows, from the madrigals, church music, ballets and every scrap of more fully-scored music for instruments or voices, what is likely. There is no short cut for the application of this sort of skill or knowledge.

So we return to the manuscript, over 300 years after it was written, and begin our quest for its content. As an example of one approach I will take a single scene, the quarrel between Seneca and Nero, and describe in some detail the thoughts and decisions that went into one way of making it a viable piece of theatre for twentieth-century listeners.

In the opera, Poppea's growing domination over Nero is already established, as is Seneca's sympathy with the neglected empress, Ottavia. Nero encounters the aging philosopher, once his mentor, and, like a truculent pupil, blurts out his intention of banishing his empress and marrying Poppea. Seneca answers respectfully, somewhat at length, but calmly attempting to make his impetuous emperor see reason. To every point Seneca makes Nero gives increasingly heated answers, betraying a wilful immaturity that eventually results in the unworthy accusation that Ottavia is frigid and barren. At this point Seneca himself begins to lose his temper and the interchanges become shorter and more violent until Nero — beaten in all but imperatorial authority — storms out, saying "get out of my sight, you impertinent philosopher, insolent pedagogue". It is a measure of the innate theatrical quality of the libretto and its setting that, in spite of his command, it is Nero who leaves, while Seneca stays to reflect calmly to the audience how power corrupts reason.

Fig. 4 shows how Monteverdi first wrote down the scene in his score.

The manuscript paper Monteverdi used had only ten staves and was expensive. To economize on space, as each character ends a speech the last bar is completed with a final bass-note and a concluding bar-line. The next character is then announced and new clefs are drawn before his phrase is set to music. The process is then repeated. However, in performance to stop and start with each new speech would stultify the dramatic flow and, from the way each voice enters in the key of the previous singer, it is clear that they were intended to follow each other naturally without breaks, depending on the meaning and intention of the words. The phrases are there to be fitted like a jigsaw puzzle into the dramatic scheme of things, emphasizing the *crescendo* of tension that finally erupts into anger on Seneca's part and hysteria on Nero's.

As it stands the scene is a long one, too long if we are to make the entire opera work within the normal span of present-day opera-going. Moreover, it is repetitive once the pattern of exchange between emperor-pupil and philosopher-mentor is established. Once Nero has told Seneca (and us) what he has come for and Seneca urges on him the folly of his wishes and respect for Roman law, there is no need to discuss that law. (Busenello was a lawyer and doubtless found it wonderfully fascinating.) It makes more dramatic sense for Nero immediately to change ground and say:

"We won't discuss it. I will have my way."

Then Seneca can produce other reasons:

"Do not irritate the people or the Senate."

Nero doesn't care about the people or the Senate:

Seneca: "Then care about yourself and your reputation."

Nero: "If anyone dares to say anything I'll tear his tongue out."

Seneca: "The more silent you make them, the more they'll talk."

Nero: "Ottavia is frigid and barren."

Seneca: "Those in the wrong always seek other excuses."

Nero: "Force is law in time and peace..."

Seneca: "Force feeds hatred..."

(Nero) "as the sword is in war..."

(Seneca) "and leads to bloodshed..."

(Nero) "and has no need of reason."

(Seneca) "Reason rules both men and the Gods."

(Pause)

Nero: "You! You risk my displeasure. In spite of you, in spite of the senate, Ottavia, Heaven and Hell, just or unjust, I will have my way today and Poppea shall be my wife."

Seneca: "That a woman should have the power to lead you to such error is a fault worthy neither of an emperor nor a demi-God; it is plebeian."

Nero: "Get out of my sight, you impertinent philosopher, insolent pedagogue." (exits)

Seneca: "Matters will always, always worsen when force contests the claims of reason."

The early part of the encounter must clearly be free, and probably conceived in performance as being in two tempi: Nero rapid, eager and nervous; Seneca, calm by nature and intention, at a slower pace. It seemed to me suitable for Nero to be accompanied by harpsichord and 'cello playing *staccato* chords, Seneca by harp, reed organ and bass playing softly and sustained until he begins to lose his temper. When the music moves into connected, regular metre as tempers rise ("Force is law in time of peace"), the strings can enter and, reflecting the character of the continuo instruments, I used the upper strings for Nero and the lower for Seneca. The rhythms connect and join with a musical logic that brings us up to Nero's major explosion. Seneca regains his self-control, and the quiet of the reed organ and bass emphasize the deadly effectiveness of his final rebuke, which causes the hysterical rage of Nero's last lines. Seneca's final moving, sorrowful observation is metrical, so I again used the lower strings with the reed organ to express the growing calm of the old man as he realizes he will die for his opposition to Nero and for his faith in reason.

Fig. 5 shows the complete realization.

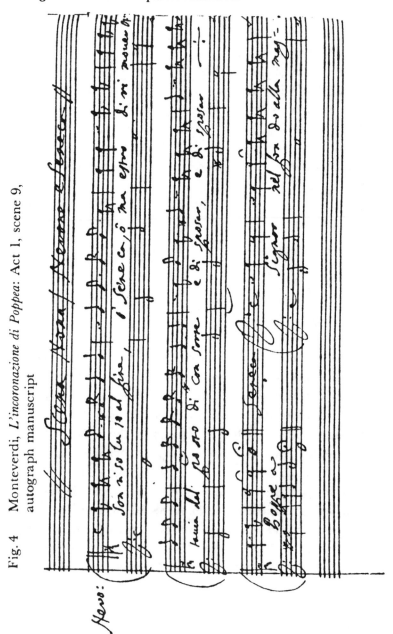

Fig. 4   Monteverdi, *L'incoronazione di Poppea*: Act 1, scene 9, autograph manuscript

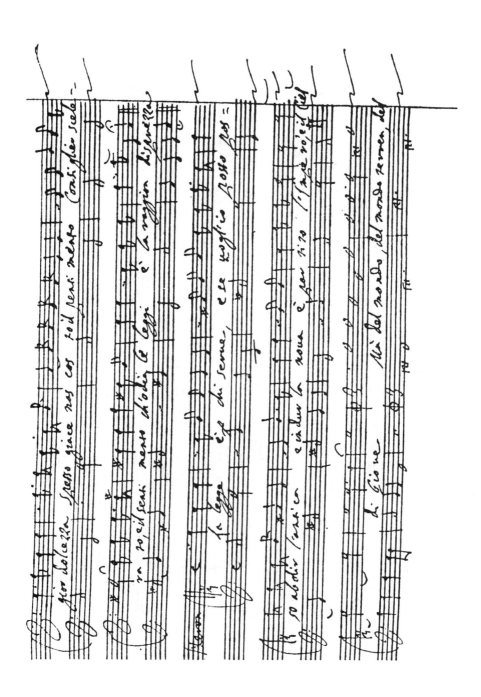

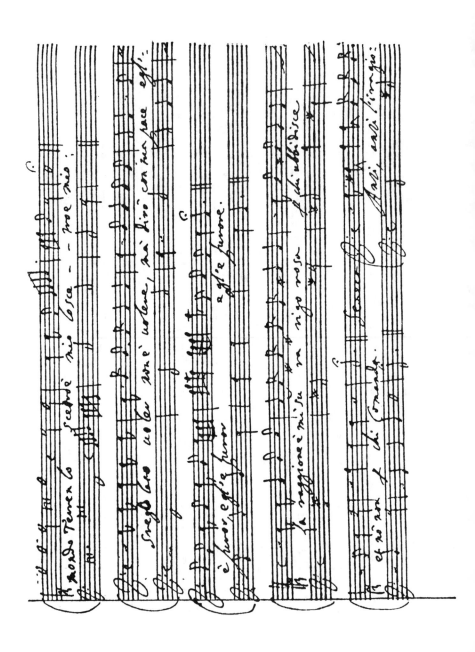

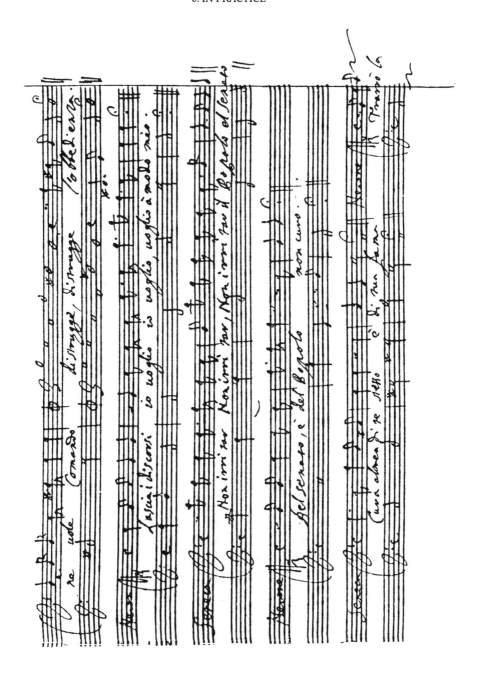

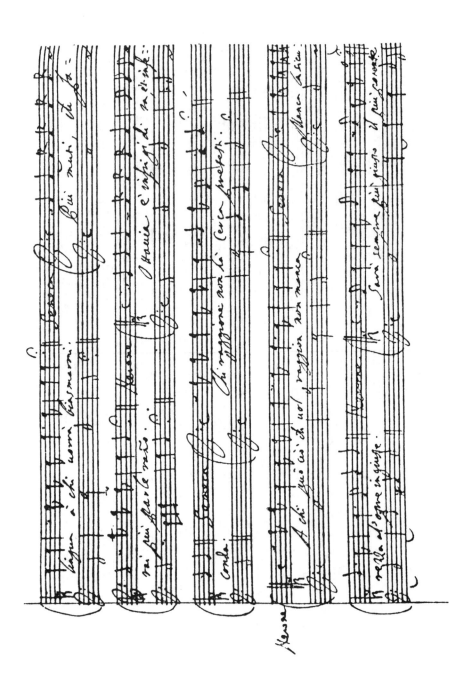

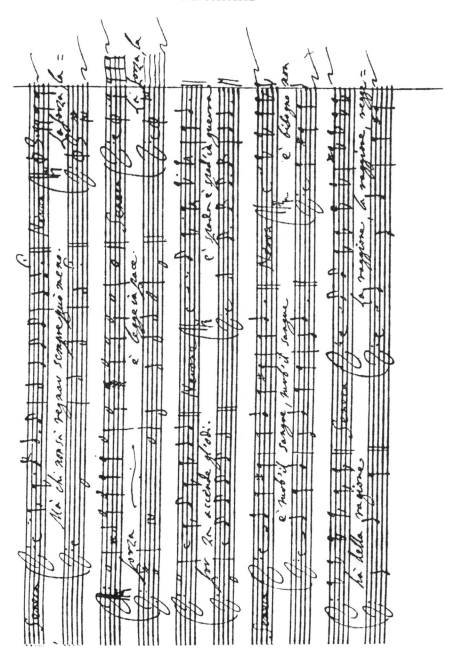

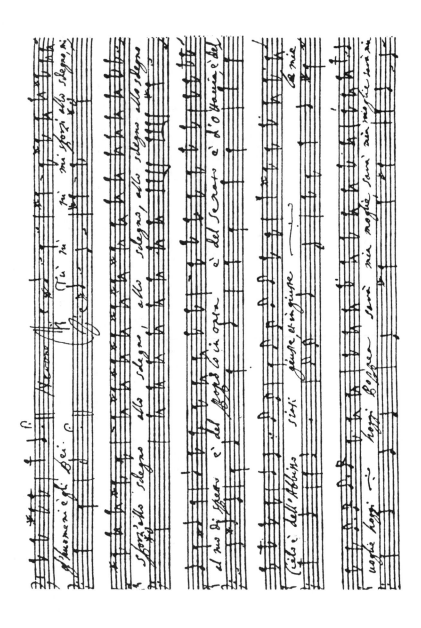

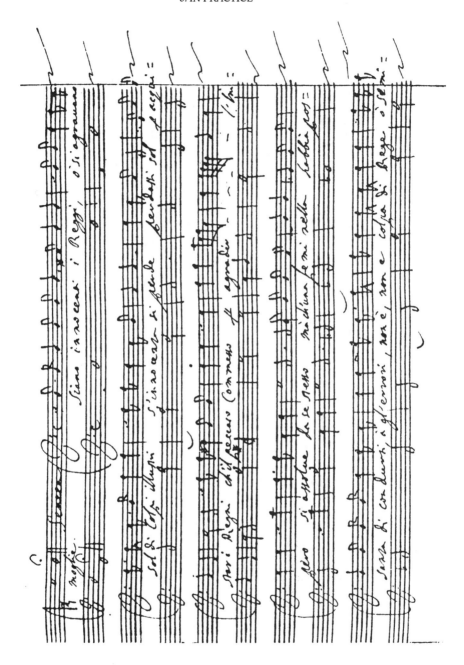

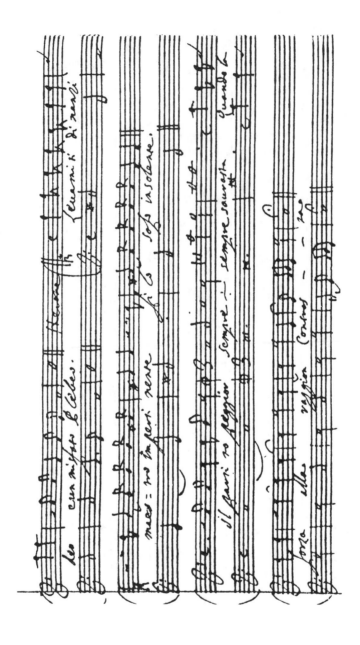

Fig. 5   Monteverdi, *L'incoronazione di Poppea*: Act 1, scene 9,
author's realization

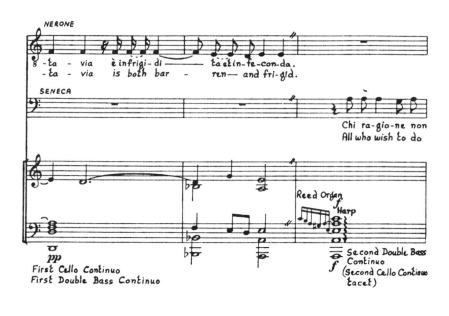

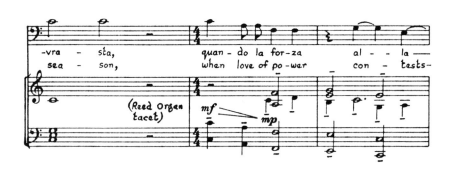

Thus out of two staves of music is a scene recreated, delineating character, furthering the action and involving the listeners in the emotional tensions that grow through it as part of the broader structure of the opera. The notes, sounds and colours all have that in view; and I would urge singers and players always to communicate these tensions to the full so that, as Follino observed at the first performance of Monteverdi's *Arianna* in Mantua, the opera may be performed with so much emotion in so moving a way that no one hearing it is left unmoved.

Handel: *Acis and Galatea*

This is one of the best works Handel composed during his early years in England, and is also one that vexes those who favour the high and narrow road to authenticity, as well as who risk the lower, broader way. The facts are relatively simple, and the difficulties depend on a basic initial choice.

Entitled variously "Serenata", "Pastoral Opera" and "Masque", *Acis* was written in 1718 while Handel was house-composer to the Duke of Chandos at Cannons, a great mansion (alas, no longer standing) by James Gibbs near Edgware just north of London. It was composed for four soloists — soprano, two tenors and a bass — and chorus in the unusual five-part texture of soprano, three tenors and bass. This is the same combination of voices we find in the anthems Handel wrote for the ducal chapel, and we may assume that the choir doffed their cassocks for the occasion. Handel probably used a group of single instruments as accompaniment. Two oboes doubling recorders, probably a bassoon, two violins, 'cello, bass (or second 'cello) and harpsichord: eight or nine players in all.

For those following the high road this is the only way to perform the work, and some critics with but a peripheral knowledge of the facts are only too eager to leap into censorious print when it is otherwise presented. Which is a pity, for Handel himself did so on many occasions and on a much larger scale than at Cannons. These performances came about because the work was becoming popular in other people's hands, notably those of Thomas Arne senior, and Handel had no intention of losing such profits as were to be gained from his own composition.

On the lower road difficulties arise because the composer left very little evidence to show how he transformed the original score into one performable by "a great number". The first of his own performances after Cannons, at the King's Theatre in 1732, was announced as being "now revived by him [Handel] with several additions and to be performed by a *great number of the best voices and instruments*." It was an enormous success, and Handel went on performing it in various large-scale versions for ten years.

At Cannons he had had no option but to write for very small forces, and it is arguable that he himself felt that, performed in that way, the music was inadequately supported, at least in its more robust movements. Moreover, it would nowadays seem regrettably exclusive and certainly questionable to decry in the name of "authenticity" modern performances on a grander scale, depriving larger choruses and orchestras, as well as audiences, the experience of so stunningly beautiful a work.

The history of the different versions that Handel made involving transposition, alterations, cuts, additions and even changes of cast, is daunting in its complexity. Nor is so elaborate a survey worthwhile, for in the end, as with *Messiah*, you only come up with a list of what happened when, with little or no deduced authority for what should happen now. The options are, of course, important; the facts of them are not. We have to survey the possibilities, possess some familiarity with Handel's music and some historical imagination, and make a passionate but modest commitment to the score we eventually come to perform. No small thing to ask. Much more, indeed, than the easier option of the narrow way, accepting the limitations of Cannons and performing the work on a small scale in a small place, something Handel himself never did again.

He left no full score of his later versions, and when *Acis* was printed by Walsh in 1743 the small-scale Cannons score was, basically, the one that the publisher reproduced with almost none of the additions the composer must subsequently have made. It nevertheless probably represents the movements and sequence of movements that Handel preferred.

Preparing a modern performance for larger forces means that we have to face the compromises that Handel himself faced in 1732. Viewed in this way it becomes an exciting challenge. Some of the numbers are so brilliantly scored for the original small combination that they are best left in that form, their special qualities being even enhanced by the larger sounds that surround them. Among these I would include Galatea's "Hush, ye pretty warbling choir" and "As when the dove laments his love". Some numbers might benefit from being accompanied by a medium-sized group, less than the full band but larger than that at Cannons. Even with these one might adopt the practice of contrasting *concertino* and *ripieno*, as Handel often did. All three of Damon's arias would work well in this way, as would Acis's "Where shall I seek the charming fair?", Galatea's "Heart, the beat of soft delight" and Polyphemus's "Ruddier than the cherry" — although this last might sound best (depending on circumstance) with solo instruments, so as to emphasize the humour of Handel's setting. Some numbers benefit greatly from larger-scale accompaniment: Acis's arias "Love in her eyes sits playing" and "Love sounds the alarm," Polyphemus's "Cease to beauty", the duet "Happy we", and the trio "The flocks shall leave the mountains".

The principle, at least, is clear. Each aria has to be presented in the way that will best reveal its character within the larger context, and the three-tier use of the orchestra will help both this and the dynamic contrasts of the drama they unfold.

All the choruses benefit from larger numbers of both voices and instruments, except perhaps the beginning of Act II, "Wretched lovers", which might be more effective with solo voices until the entrance of Polyphemus.

Apart from the allocation of continuo instruments — bassoon, 'cello, bass, harpsichord and organ, judged in the context of the whole — there is the major problem of the violas, an essential part of the larger accompaniment for which there exists virtually no music. We have to do what Handel — or J.C. Smith, or a pupil — did: decide where they are needed and write a part for them. Handel would certainly not have hired players to perform for three minutes in "Happy we" (whose scoring contains the only extant viola part) and sit around twiddling their thumbs for the rest of the evening. In most of the arias they are superfluous, but in all the accompanied recitatives they can add valuable harmonic support. The following example shows how their part might be in Galatea's recitative "Ye verdant plains":

Recitativo

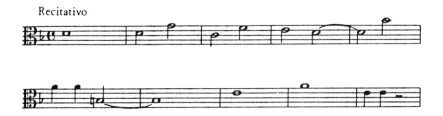

In choruses the viola line can support the tenors to great advantage, as well as fill out the tuttis. They certainly would have played in the brilliant opening Sinfonia (which also benefits from alternating *concertino* and *ripieno*). In such movements Handel generally had them playing an octave above the bass line, occasionally departing from it to provide harmonic support or to avoid rising above the violins. A typical version of the first bars might be as follows:

Sinfonia: **Presto**

Thus may we approach the preparation of *Acis and Galatea* for present-day performance in the form the composer himself most often gave it — and in doing so, hope to realize something of the authentic spirit held within this beautiful work.

There is no one way, no one solution to any of its problems, nor ever was there one. But the indecision stops when you come to performance: then there is only the way you have committed yourself to follow. The difference between the two views of authenticity becomes most clearly apparent in the preparation for that commitment. The one narrows down the possibilities, the other broadens them so that informed choice and compromise can play their part in liberating the vitality of the music.

CHAPTER SEVEN

THE HIGH ROAD, THE LOW ROAD

What, then, is this authenticity that has become so much the concern of all performers of music before 1800 and, equally, the focus of attention for critics and listeners?

It can only mean one thing: the clearest possible revelation of that music so that its intrinsic qualities, vitality and value are presented again as vividly as they may conceivably ever have been. So will the evidence of its power to transcend the years be strengthened, and the delight and elation that communication with things of the spirit brings be confirmed. In these lie the gifts of confidence and joy that encourage us to move more freely about the very dangerous terrain we currently inhabit.

In dispute, or at least confusion, are how and in what ways the revelation may best be achieved. There are those who believe that only as we come closer to the exact conditions, the precisely duplicated ways and means of music's first appearance, can its authentic message and content be revealed.

Then there are those who believe that the closer we come to knowing how and why it was written, why as well as how it was performed, the closer we shall come to the inner vitality of the composer's mind, the revelation of which to present-day audiences is more important than any other aspect of performance.

The two views have much in common, but in the last analysis they diverge greatly, finding themselves often on opposite sides of sometimes vituperative controversy. For the one, scholarship and historical research are the final arbiters; for the other, present communication of perceived vitality is the deciding factor. The one must, perforce, be exclusive and restrictive, as all true academic disciplines are. The other seeks the widest creative freedom within the disciplines that acquired knowledge imposes. The difference of intent is profound.

Authenticity in the first view eventually comes to resemble the mythological bird that flies around in ever-decreasing circles, eventually disappearing into its own feathers. Pursued logically, this concept of authenticity arrives at the dubious but inevitable conclusion that there is only one way perfectly to reveal a piece of earlier music. Yet in the stampede that has accompanied the widespread enthusiasm for things "original" there has, so far, appeared no point at which that sort of authentic practice will deny itself the final absurdity. Sometimes it would seem that the closer people come to it, the louder they are applauded for doing so. Witness Stephen Plaistow in the *Gramophone* of May 1986 on a recent recording of the Mozart Clarinet Concerto: "As R. F. [Roger Fiske] was saying in March, the time must be near when only basset (horn) versions of the Mozart Clarinet Concerto are acceptable at public concerts. For record collectors I think that moment has arrived." How an intelligent person could come to write as absurdly bigoted an opinion as that is hard to imagine, but the example is by no means unique.

If Bach's cantata *Wachet auf* can finally only fully reveal its vitality by being played in St Thomas's Church, Leipzig, with the instruments and voices that the composer had at his disposal, and on the 27th Sunday after Trinity (which occurs very seldom, only twice in Bach's lifetime), we should hear it at its best very rarely indeed. The thesis is not as farfetched as all that, for are there not frequent performances of *Messiah* that claim to reproduce exactly the numbers and conditions of its first appearance in Dublin — and to be superior on that account? Deceive ourselves as we may, the thesis of this first view without qualifications is as absurd as the proposition that a visit to Williamsburg, Virginia — where every house, every buggy, every costume, every aspect of its former life is reproduced quite perfectly — will show in any real sense what early American colonial life was like.

The most important reason why such propositions will eventually prove groundless is always the same. It is we who are different. Not only are time and, for all practical purposes, place dislocated in such narrow-visioned attempts at authenticity, but the very sensibilities by which we have to recognize validity are out of kilter with what people seek to represent in this way. Current speed, noise, media, the stimuli of the world around us, our own backgrounds, to say nothing of our acquired historical awareness have little in common with the original circumstances. None of these factors was present when "early music" was first performed, and the eager search for "authentic purity" along those lines begins to resemble the hoped-for fulfilment of that pathetic nun in Ronald Firbank's *Valmouth*, waiting for her dancing-day that came but once a year and, even so, did not achieve much among the penitential holly-bags, for no one really noticed her.

The nun may have had the gifts of a Fonteyn and danced perfectly: the music may be performed exactly where and as it had been conceived; but only one half, the historical half of the proposition will have been fulfilled. The ignoring of the differences between those who once listened and those who now listen means that the performer has abnegated or at least relegated to secondary importance his first responsibility as a communicator to the present.

Authenticity in the second view must embrace something the other abhors: compromise. This function of the mind, inescapable in almost every aspect of living, symbolizes for some vacillation and weakness of purpose. The nineteenth century, in its preoccupation with man's upward progress, saw compromise as a blemish upon possible perfection and became ashamed of it. It was put aside as if, like original sin, it were best ignored; pretending, if it showed, that it didn't exist. All cults, religious and political as well as musical, tend to reject compromise as an unacceptable failing that mars the ideal, diminishes the particularity and weakens the message. It is the root cause of the fundamental unworkability of socialism, many of whose ideals are quite unexceptionable. Churchill is said once to have advised a fellow politician never to abandon his ideals but, equally, never to try to put them into practice.

Of course, it would have been the most amazing revelation to have heard *Wachet* in Leipzig under Bach's direction on 25 November 1731, but no amount of wishing will make it happen. We can only attempt to understand, from the text that is left to us and the knowledge of it that we can assemble, what it is that he was attempting to do and, subsequently, make as our prime objective a translation of that into our own time; not primarily a reproduction of what actually happened. So viewed, the compromise involved would seem neither impossible nor unprofitable, nor yet unworthy.

Compromise is not as discouraged as it once was. The acceptance that it is an unavoidable part of life has led many to understand that it can also be a productive, stimulating activity worth studying and mastering. In the confrontation between an ideal and its practice there is something illuminating to be found in the realization that it cannot be made fully to work. If, then, we embrace the idea of compromise, for it to be successful there must be nothing of inhibiting regret or guilt, or a sense of second-best or shame that we cannot achieve the "purity" of the first intent, if indeed it was "pure". And, since it plays so precise a part in this second view of authenticity, it would be well to examine in what ways compromise may affect the revelation of music's value that we seek to transmit.

The fact that we live at a difference pace from anything previously known, and are impatient of what we consider the tedium of excessive length, must be one cause for compromise. Occasionally we like extremes and can be persuaded to hear, for example, a Handel opera more complete than Handel probably ever heard it himself. Ordinarily, however, opera-houses cannot mount works that last five hours, nor would the general public be persuaded in the ordinary way to listen for so long. To deprive them of Handel's operas on that account seems a high price to pay when there is a perfectly viable alternative.

The way compromise may be effected can change. There was a time when all manner of snippings were made to keep Handel's operas within bounds. Now that the *da capo* aria is recognised as an inviolable eighteenth-century form, snippings are out and it is whole arias, or even scenes, that have to go. Both methods proved effective for their time, and we should be cautious about stating that one is absolutely better than the other. It may be that our latest solutions, too, will change as a result of the needs and wishes of another time.

Tempi present another variable element in the process of older music's revitalization, one calling for compromises from which purer minds may shrink. But truly there can be no absolute speeds, only ideas of speed which will vary according to numbers, place, acoustics and occasion. This must always have been the case, despite diligent research and strong opinion to the contrary.

A further reason for compromise is that all music before 1800 was created for a restricted public which did not travel much, had national characteristics, local expectations and customs all of which surrounded and influenced it. When the music is played or sung on a world-wide scale today, these elements have to be understood, dealt with and in some way incorporated or deliberately ignored.

But the most important function of compromise as it affects us today lies in the absorption of what the newest manifestation of our quest for the truth has to show us. I speak of "original" instruments.

There can be no question of abandoning the instruments in general use (which will in their turn develop new characteristics and change). It would be pie in the sky to think otherwise, for music would become divided into historical segments, each with its own brand of performer. There is, nevertheless, a world of influence to be absorbed, digested and resolved into modern practice through the work of those who have devoted themselves to the exploration of the particular techniques involved in playing these instruments.

Apart from differently focused sounds, the effects of lower pitch, narrower dynamic range, possibilities of bowing, the quality of vibrato and the generally frailer tone quality, by far the most important revelation, and the one that has and will have the greatest impact on performance, is that of articulation: the infinite variety in degree of separation; the importance of the dynamic structure of the phrases so exposed; and the discovery that, far from splitting the music into pieces, this newly-revealed old element of performance may serve to expound the larger framework in earlier music in a way that the long lines appropriate to Wagner and Brahms cannot do.

It becomes totally absorbing to see what light this can shed on the performance of, say, the Haydn symphonies or the early music of Beethoven, whose players for the *Eroica* symphony (1803) regularly performed for

Haydn and Mozart, and in a style that Beethoven might disrupt but would not have questioned. To conceive his music as if he had already invented Brahms, if not Mahler, is the way whole generations have previously played and thought of it, providing the musical counterpart to the awe-inspiring image the late nineteenth century created for him. Right for them, no doubt, but wrong for us, if still not all of us.

So do our views change, and I would again raise the question as to whether we should consider them better on that account; or if that is not yet another vestige of nineteenth-century philosophy that hangs about our minds.

We rarely hear Casals' playing of the Bach suites or Wanda Landowska's playing of the "48" extolled today. Yet in their time those artists communicated the vitality of that music wonderfully, and we are not so far removed in time that, with a little exercise of musical empathy, we cannot understand why it was so. We would not play in their way today; but it is not that the style of playing was wrong, merely that the circumstances surrounding it have changed, with new influences, new pressures and new thoughts requiring different sets of compromises in bringing the music to life.

For whatever reason, we feel a strong need to get as close as possible to the original sources of music, to separate them out into periods and styles and to be able to sense the difference in our performance of them. Here lies the most significant division between the two views of how it should be done. The one seeks to pin the various periods of music to their sources where they may be exhibited forever, like stuffed animals: for every problem there is one best solution. The other accepts, even enjoys the idea that time changes expectations and needs. The rewards of performance are to be found in constant revision and reinterpretation to keep pace with the present as much as to keep faith with the past. The rewards of the listener are in the new aspects of the music's vitality that these changes continually reveal.

This broader way is complex and difficult. It must embrace the results of research, the conditions of present-day performance and all the compromise that that entails, doing so without losing or betraying the content of the music as we perceive it. The problems will never cease, but they are such that their resolution can bring joy and fulfilment to performer and listener alike. When the inhibitions and restrictions of false authenticity are felt, or even the self-indulgence of undisciplined compromise, then the wrong road has been taken.

Seriousness of purpose combined with the acquisition of knowledge; a never-ending revision of the probabilities and possibilities; a passionate modesty; these are the requisites for allowing the creativity we sense in the music to flourish. In this way we shall, I believe, discover the true meaning and importance of authenticity for our time.

II

OPERA

1

ON PERFORMING BAROQUE OPERAS AT GLYNDEBOURNE[1]

Glyndebourne began with Mozart and for years that composer was regarded, not without reason, as the company's speciality. But it was really the special qualities of the place, the people there and the attitude towards the rehearsal that made things go so well and persuaded public opinion to that conclusion. The house certainly pioneered Mozart in England but, by the time the war was ended, everyone played his operas, standards of ensemble were sometimes nearly as good as in Sussex and the standards of singing sometimes better. What remained to sustain Glyndebourne's particularity was the liberality of spirit, engendered by its founder, which pervaded the whole organisation. John Christie understood that, outside Glyndebourne, changes had come about and gave every encouragement for his company to experiment and find another "speciality" beside Mozart that would maintain Glyndebourne's reputation.

At first, largely due to the enthusiasm of Vittorio Gui, it was Rossini who was chosen to share the course, and he ran a good race. But soon his operas, too, began to be played everywhere. It is tempting to come to the conclusion that there is nothing so contagious as operatic quality, but something closer to "follow my leader" would seem to have been the name of the game. In any case, the Rossini vein continued successfully

---

1 Originally published as a chapter in *Glyndebourne: A Celebration* with contributions by Isaiah Berlin, Asa Briggs, George Christie, John Cox, Bernard Haitink, Sir Peter Hall, Raymond Leppard, John Julius Norwich, Sir John Pritchard, Desmond Shawe-Taylor, Sir Roy Strong and Gillian Widdicombe; ed. by John Higgins (Jonathan Cape, 1984).

for some years until its particularity was dissipated. Other styles had, by this time, been introduced but none had established a new speciality for the company.

Then, far ahead of its time, Glyndebourne struck out again and in 1962 mounted the first fully professional performance of Monteverdi's *L'incoronazione di Poppea* in England, some 280 years after its first performance in Venice.

Only a few days after the first performance John Christie died. His son, George, had already been Chairman of the Board since 1959 and the spirit of confident adventure persisted quite undiminished by the change in leadership. It was, nevertheless, fitting that the founder should have lived until this latest "speciality" was initiated.

It was a risky venture for Glyndebourne and this is how it came about. While I was a student at Cambridge I had become obsessed by the immense power of Monteverdi's music. His name had been accorded traditional respect in music history lectures, but it was not based on any certain knowledge of his work. Believe it or not, even in that august seat of learning, the Pendlebury music library in 1948 boasted, if my memory serves me, only two volumes of the Malipiero complete (at that time, admittedly, incomplete) edition and a few madrigals scattered among some heavily edited collections of German origin. The reality of Monteverdi's music was not readily available either in print or performance.

I was lucky enough to have become a member of the Cambridge University Madrigal Society. Its conductor, Boris Ord, was enthusiastic about the small number of Monteverdi's madrigals that he knew. Having spent part of his early professional life as a repetiteur in Cologne, he clearly sensed the theatricality of them, and we performed them often. For me they were a revelation. I had never heard music like it, let alone taken part in the performing of it. The directness of the music's response to the meaning of the words, even within the somewhat restricting medium of the five-voiced madrigal, was to me astounding and the need to explore this unique world of musical expression became paramount. In succeeding years as I moved out into the professional world (which included two seasons on the music staff at Glyndebourne) I began to put concerts of his music together including, naturally enough, excerpts from his operas. *L'incoronazione di Poppea* especially fascinated me. It seemed the epitome of a style which set out to convey to the listener the emotional import of words with a directness that involved every aspect of their presentation; singing, playing, acting, delivery and accompaniment. No one could sit back uninvolved in this music without betraying it. The highly sensuous plot and the libretto which expounded it gave composer and performers alike every sort of opportunity to develop music's power to reveal the emotion and content within them. I am still convinced that this was Monteverdi's purpose and that, no matter how it is revealed, commitment of this sort must be our first concern in performing his music to twentieth-century audiences. A pallid, cautiously virginal approach does it less than justice.

In 1960 at the Royal Festival Hall I conducted a concert consisting of the first two acts of L'Orfeo and, in the second half, selected scenes from L'incoronazione di Poppea. Moran Caplat was aware of my enthusiasm for Monteverdi and attended with George Christie and various other Glyndebourne colleagues.

The direct outcome was an invitation to prepare a version of the opera for Glyndebourne in 1962. Günther Rennert was to direct and Hugh Casson to create the sets. The costumes were created by Conwy Evans who produced some remarkable designs combining style, color and dramatic purpose to great effect.

Initially it was the series of encounters with Rennert that proved of most value. I greatly admired his sort of theatrical imagination and also liked him very much. He was a "paring-down" director and, although I had had a lot of experience in the theater in Cambridge and in my first professional years, I was, of course, nothing like as experienced or as theatrically certain as he was. His sense of pace and structure stiffened my understanding of the piece and, therefore, the musical realisation of it in terms of performing it at Glyndebourne in 1962.

It must be explained here that Italian opera written between 1600 and 1670 needs considerable attention before it can be performed, due to the way it was conceived, written down and performed at that time. All we have left, for the most part, is a vocal line and a simple bass line. The lack of a "full-score" kept these works on library shelves for three hundred years until the mists surrounding the Valhalla of the unquestionable, unadaptable Urtext were wafted aside and other ways of conceiving and performing opera were revealed. Suffice it to say that an opera from these earlier times in Italy has now to be reconstructed from the skeletal outlines and that my reconstruction was greatly influenced by those meetings with Rennert.

The question was then raised whether I would conduct or play in the performances and, since John Pritchard was keen about the piece, I agreed that it was better that he should conduct and I play the first harpsichord. At that time nobody had worked out how to direct successfully the recitative-music that accounted for about half the opera and was to be accompanied, as in Monteverdi's day, by a large group of free-playing instruments — organs, harp, lutes, chittarones and harpsichords. Their co-ordination with the stage within the limits of twentieth-century rehearsal conditions gave many problems which the normal skills of beating time would not resolve. The memories of that distinguished harpist, Maria Korchinska, who was quite unused to this uncountable music, in frenzied and totally committed lunges at her instrument in order to keep with John or a singer, will remain with me for ever. I sat immediately behind her in the pit. She loved the music and the part I had written had no technical worries for her. It was the controlled freedom of it all that caused the agitation. She wore her hair in a roll around her head and, by the end of each performance, she looked like some handsome Kentucky farmer's wife after a long day plucking turkeys; hair everywhere, but shining with a glow of achievement. Eventually she gave me a beautiful silver box she had brought with her from Russia because she had enjoyed the performances so much.

J.P. was, I think, never very comfortable with the recitative music and, in the last revival, somewhat happily handed the direction to me and, being a demon for punishment, I continued to play first harpsichord as well.

We were extremely fortunate in our cast and Glyndebourne was the ideal place for such a project without precedent. No one really knew how the piece would turn out.

Richard Lewis and Magda Laszlo as Nero and Poppea combined intuition and intelligence with superb musicianship. Rennert used wonderfully the experienced, somewhat contained sensuality of his Poppea to oppose the inner tensions that Richard Lewis's Welsh reserve brought to the part of Nero. They barely touched each other on stage and yet the sense that, in the distance of parting, there was growing an almost intolerable intensity proved immensely effective, even overpowering in the irony of the final scene where, amid the public splendor of Poppea's coronation they stood closest, unable to embrace. Carlo Cava as Seneca was unforgettably impressive and was himself amazingly moved. At the end of the last performance this huge, strong man was found back-stage weeping, inconsolable that he would not inhabit that part again at Glyndebourne. Oralia Dominguez sang Arnalta, Poppea's nurse, the only wholly likeable character in the opera. She sang the famous lullaby as wonderfully as one could ever hope for and the earthy, peasant-like care she showed for her charge, her wiliness and vanity in the last solo scene came to her and us as a wonderful gift of characterisation. Drusilla and Ottone, more simply realised as characters, were perfectly manifested in Lydia Marimpietri and Walter Alberti. Ottavia, a solitary, tragic figure, was beautifully understood and sung by Frances Bible; the two servants by Soo-Bee Lee and Duncan Robertson and, not least, Lucano, Nero's companion in corruption, was sung by Hugues Cuénod. I dare not say what monstrous object Harry Kellard, the propmaker, put instead of a stamen into the exotic flower that Hugues carried during his drunken orgy with Nero. It appeared, evidently, for the first time only on the first night and nearly made Hugues forget his lines. So experienced a horticulturalist, however, was not so easily defeated.

Throughout the rehearsals of this then unknown piece there grew an extraordinary sense of excitement. It occurs always during the best of Glyndebourne's projects. No one talks about it much. Theater people are very superstitious and it might easily go away, but, once recognised, everyone nurtures it, in this case to great effect, for the opening of *Poppea* was an extraordinary evening even in that extraordinary place and the opera was repeated for three years running, something unknown in Glyndebourne's more recent history.

Still more important, as we can see in retrospect, a new vein had been found. Perhaps it was the shock of success, but at first the potential wasn't recognised and it didn't seem possible to follow it up.

In 1965 there was nothing. In 1966, Purcell's *Dido and Aeneas* made half a program with Ravel's *L'Heure espagnole*, and Handel's *Jephtha* was given an evening to itself. Neither did very much to further matters. No great revelation was made by the *Dido* in spite of superb singing by Janet Baker, Sheila Armstrong and Patricia Johnson. The work was already well-known and Franco Enriquez was to do many more interesting productions for the company.

Jephtha must, equally, be considered as something of an unsuccessful by-blow. The oratorio was presented in a singularly static fashion, cruelly chopped about musically and, whatever it did for Hamburg (where it originated) in the way of revealing Handel's genius, it did very little in that way for English audiences. The score seemed to have been prepared by someone who supported the view that Handel was not only a theatrical dolt but also a man who could neither understand nor respond to the words he was setting: an odd verdict on someone who spent most of his highly successful life in the theater. As in *Dido* the cast was unexceptionable with Heather Harper, Patricia Johnson, Margaret Price and Richard Lewis, but Rennert misconceived the piece, Caspar Neher followed suit and Leopold Ludwig's conducting was stolid and dull.

In 1967 Cavalli's *L'Ormindo* represented a return to the freer theatrical airs of *Poppea* and the journey of exploration into early Italian opera was moving forward again.

After *Poppea* I had spent some long time in Venice hoping to discover one of the lost Monteverdi operas. Instead, I discovered the extraordinary lyric talent of Francesco Cavalli. He is to Monteverdi, who taught him, what Schubert was to Beethoven. There was in the Marciana library a large collection of his operas, all in the same skeletal state as *Poppea*, waiting for a process of revivification. Flushed with my discovery of this wonderful and virtually unknown theatrical talent, I proposed *L'Ormindo* to Glyndebourne. They accepted and plans went forward. Rennert once more directed and responded brilliantly to the humor and wit of the piece as well as to the gradual darkening of the plot as it progresses to its near-tragic end. His desire to avoid the conventional led him to propose Erich Kondrak as designer, and some rather strange representations of the Moroccan desert came out of it. Without having much to do with the idea of seventeenth-century Venetian opera they served pretty well.

The cast was superb. The two main male protagonists were sung by Peter-Christoph Runge and John Wakefield, the latter one of the most striking and wonderfully gifted young tenors to appear in England at that time. It was a major tragedy for English music when the voice was irrevocably damaged and he abandoned singing. Peter-Christoph, happily, is still with us and occasionally returns to Glyndebourne. They were a wonderful pair, rivals for the love of the young queen Erisbe, initially miscast but changed during rehearsals and given to the young Anne Howells who rose to the challenge and had her first major success in that part. Jane Berbié as the Queen's maid, Isabel Garcisanz as the page, Nerillo, used their solo scenes (a feature of early Venetian opera) to the greatest effect. It must be told that on the first night Jane, who had no reason at all to be nervous, panicked and had literally to be pushed on the fore-stage after the third unrehearsed repetition of the opening *ritornello* to one of her scenes. In the pit (I was conducting) I couldn't imagine what had happened except that there were distinct flurries off-stage on the prompt side and no Jane on-stage. Once there, however, she brought the house down with her exposition of what lively young wives of impotent grey-beards should do with their time. The jealous, tormented King was played by Federico Davià who looked so magnificent and sang in such a way that the King's impotence became a tragic burden instead of something ridiculous. Irmgard Stadler was the mysterious Sicle out to regain the love of her former suitor, aided and abetted by Maureen Lehane and Hugues Cuénod in drag, another characteristic of early Venetian opera. It would seem that the singing of somewhat crotchety but wise and funny old women by men enabled them, as with our pantomime Dames, to say things that would otherwise be unacceptable. Hugues was incredibly funny but it was all done within the bounds of good taste, probably, like George Robey, the funnier for that. The pathos of Sicle apart, the trio, Stadler, Lehane and Cuénod conspiring about the stage was unforgettable.

The response of Glyndebourne audiences confirmed that we were on the right track again and *L'Ormindo* was repeated with equal success in 1968. We even took it to the Cuvilliès theater in Munich when the Glyndebourne company was invited there in 1969. It takes a long time to prepare one of these early Venetian operas for performance, and, although wheels were in motion and the realisation begun, there was a gap in 1969 before a second Cavalli piece could be fully prepared. This time, in 1970, it was *La Calisto*, a version of Ovid's Metamorphic story of how the little bear (Ursa minor) came to shine in the night sky. The director was to be Peter Hall whom I had known and worked with in London and Stratford since Cambridge days, and the designer was to be John Bury whom I did not know. It proved to be a wonderfully stimulating collaboration with much early concentration given to the problems of translating seventeenth-century Venetian opera on to the twentieth-century stage. It was not just a matter of re-working the idea of machines that would transport the gods from Parnassus to Earth, but also how that resulting immediate and rapid interaction of gods and humans could be made to expose emotions and intentions that would illuminate lively ideas and conditions for us mortals sitting in the stalls at Glyndebourne.

It was, for the three of us, a matter of posing, discussing and resolving questions in the same way, each at once respecting and stimulating the other. Except with *Il ritorno d'Ulisse* where the same company deliberated and resolved still graver problems, I have never felt more fulfilled in the theater.

The plot of *La Calisto* is concerned with the attempts of Jove (Ugo Trama) to seduce Calisto (Ileana Cotrubas), one of the nymphs of the virgin goddess, Diana (Janet Baker). She, more concerned with her mistress than anything else, repulses his first advances until, at the instigation of Mercury (Peter Gottlieb), Jove disguises himself as Diana and is enchanted to find Calisto remarkably responsive. The confusion that results with the real Diana may be imagined. She, in her turn, is loved by Pan (Federico Davià). And Diana, surrounded by her nymphs (including an elderly, crotchety but sexually curious Linfea, played, once more in drag, by Hugues Cuénod), casts longing, amorous glances on Endymion (James Bowman). Juno (Irmgard Stadler), with the chill of cold reality on her lips, descends with her peacocks to put matters to right and change Calisto into a sylvan Ursa minor.

All is sexual ambiguity and, the comedy of the situations apart, quite serious questions are posed by the piece which were truthfully and brilliantly expounded in Peter Hall's direction. The basic design by John Bury was a long A shape that seemed to stretch from here to Olympus.

Forests appeared and vanished in a moment, a fountain sprang water and suddenly was no more. In a whirl of a gorgeous feathered cloak the little bear became Calisto again, transformed through Jove's compassion or conscience, depending on your view of the situation.

In Cavalli's original manuscript at the moment when Jove transforms himself into the image of his daughter, Diana, the music changes from the bass clef to the treble. This gave rise to the attractive idea that Jove should sing falsetto when playing Diana. It was further encouraged by the knowledge that Ugo Trama, always a strong candidate for the part, habitually warmed up his voice an octave or so above its normal tessitura. He bravely agreed to play the double role and we began rehearsals. Every time we came to a Jove-as-Diana scene a general air of hilarity set in which, as it grew, put Peter and myself into deeper and deeper gloom. Funny the piece was, camp and silly it was not. After, perhaps, six days we had a run-through and asked various people so far not connected with the production to come and listen. Danny la Rue would have been delighted at the reception. You could hardly hear the piece for laughter but it was all about one joke and nothing to do with the subtle, intricate opera we were trying to put on. The rehearsal ended and everyone concerned with the production went his own way without even discussing it. At some unearthly hour next morning Peter and I spoke on the telephone and agreed to meet right away in the conductor's room at Glyndebourne. We had both come to the same conclusion: it was Diana who must play the double part of herself and Jove transformed into her own image. After a breakfast consultation with the management we telephoned Janet Baker who had retreated to her home in London for the night and put the proposal to her. Practical as ever, she asked for half an hour to look at the score and think about it, after which she telephoned back to say she would do it. Ugo Trama, whose part was cut more or less in half, behaved better than most would have done and agreed to the change. Janet had taken on a singing and acting challenge which, as it turned out, gave her one of the most memorable parts of her career, and a challenge to which she rose with genius. In the same costume with only a staff to symbolise the difference, she played both parts, the lascivious Jove and the virginal Diana beset by her own love for Endymion, with such skill that there was never a moment's doubt for the audience as to who was on stage even when one followed the other within seconds. She was alternately funny and lecherous, then touching and vulnerable.

La Calisto amused, moved, entertained and even educated the more discerning Glyndebourne audiences for three seasons. It was revived in 1971 and 1974. I used to think sometimes at performances how much old John Christie would have enjoyed it. He might even have wanted to play Sylvano, the earthy woodland creature; after all his granddaughter played the bear.

In between the last two revivals the latest and, until now, the last of the Venetian line, Monteverdi's *Il ritorno d'Ulisse*, was produced in 1972. For some years doubts had been cast upon the authenticity of this, the last of the great man's operas. The gravity of its music, in fitting contrast to the overt sensuality of *Poppea* and the lack of an autograph had left the decision with those who squabbled about it without any certain knowledge or ability to perceive its quality. The work only needed to be imagined creatively and as a piece of musical theater for it to be revealed as an overpowering operatic masterpiece, showing an understanding and response to the human condition comparable only to classical drama or Shakespeare.

During its preparation the sense of excitement at working on so great a piece grew and endured through one complete version of the opera and then another after my house burned down, destroying the entire first manuscript. There were formidable technical and dramatic problems which the three of us, Peter Hall, John Bury and I, discussed and pondered. At least there was an aesthetic for tackling this style of opera already prepared for by *La Calisto*, but the much grander scale of *Ulisse* and the scope of its drama meant that everything had to be re-thought. We had to give the sense of two approaching destinies, one, personified by Ulysses, returning at last from Troy, and the other by Penelope waiting still on Ithaca beset by terrible and increasing dangers, each of them surveyed by the gods, themselves divided into two warring factions. The gods as gods (Minerva, Ulysses' especial protector, becomes at one point a shepherd boy and descends to Ithaca) must stay in the skies and be able to move about. Neptune must rise up there from the seas to play his part in the dispute; the Phoenicians, who help Ulysses to Ithaca, must be transformed, with their departing ship, into a rock; and, worst of all, Ulysses must shoot the suitors with his great bow in a scene of carnage that must convince us as well as provide a fitting theatrical climax to the opera. The final solution for this last, of using real arrows which thudded into wooden tables and flew into the wings, shot from a real bow drawn by Ulysses, initially caused some alarm. But so skilfully was it staged that it was all perfectly safe and yet gave an unforgettable image of revengeful destruction with Penelope (Janet Baker) standing in the midst of it all, quite unharmed, while Minerva, above, guided and protected her beloved Ulysses (Benjamin Luxon).

Technical and scenic matters apart, the hardest question was how to show Penelope, after waiting twenty years for Ulysses to return from Troy, prepared to reject him by refusing recognition even after the holocaust. Peter's great gift for asking the right theatrical questions provided the most wonderful answer. Like a war-widow who has become accustomed to her situation and is suddenly confronted by her lost husband, she would not, could not face the reality of it, for in those years she had nearly become somebody else. So Ulysses, the wily fox who survived Troy and understands, has to woo her all over again. Somehow this last courtship and the final hymn-like duet celebrating love recovered after so long, became one of the greatest moments many of us had experienced in the theater. At the end of the first night Ben Luxon broke down and on the last night so did Janet. On most nights most of us were pretty close to it.

The rest of the cast was superb with Anne Howells a resplendent Minerva, Richard Lewis a vigorously benign Eumete, Virginia Popova as Penelope's wise old nurse, Clifford Grant as Neptune. The three villainous suitors were played by Bernard Dickerson, John Fryatt and Ugo Trama, Iro, the glutton, by Alexander Oliver and the smaller roles were admirably done by members of the company. Each performance was something of an occasion, like setting out on a long, arduous and important journey.

Ulisse was repeated in 1973 and then again in 1979, the latter year with Frederica von Stade and Richard Stilwell as Penelope and Ulysses. Ann Murray replaced Anne Howells with equal flair and virtuosity. With this last cast the opera was recorded for CBS, and filmed as a video.

After that the well of seventeenth-century opera has, for the time being, dried up. Monteverdi is now widely performed and in many differing versions. Cavalli, too, has become a known, accepted composer. His two operas which saw the light of twentieth-century day at Glyndebourne have been played in many other houses and I have realised two more, *L'Egisto* and *L'Orione* which after appearing first at Santa Fe, have been widely performed. Several other of his operas have now been revived in America and Europe. As with Rossini, Glyndebourne's influence has been seminal.

In the most recent years, however, earlier opera has not featured in the season's programs. Perhaps it is a case of *reculer pour mieux sauter* and in due course a different seam, maybe of Handel or Rameau, will be explored and found to be full of silver, or should it be gold? At any rate it will be particular.

A CRITIC REMEMBERS (1992)

"Glyndebourne is no more: long live Glyndebourne! The bulldozers are already in to demolish the old theater, and no one who ever enjoyed opera there is going to feel anything but nostalgic. For me there has never been anything quite like the feeling of expectation as the lights were dimming on the old antler-like lamp-clusters round the walls at Glyndebourne.

"Yet as George Christie pointed out in his farewell speech after the last opera performance, the replacement theater will be the first purpose-built opera house in this country since his father, John Christie, built the old one in 1934. With the foundations for the stage area already laid, it is due to be ready for *The Marriage of Figaro* on May 28, 1994, 60 years to the day since the festival first opened with that same opera....

"Christie [senior] had the genius to see that making the audience take some trouble — paying high prices, venturing into wildest Sussex, putting on evening dress — would only intensify the pleasure of seeing opera of Elysian perfection.

"[On the fairwell occasion] it was good to welcome international stars who early in their careers had Glyndebourne experience — Ruggero

Raimondi (Don Giovanni in 1969) and Montserrat Caballé (a memorable Marschallin in *Rosenkavalier* in 1965, having learned the role in six days).

"It was even better having two of the supreme examples of stars who became Glyndebourne regulars, both introducing their successors in favorite roles. Dame Janet Baker, unforgettable as Penelope in Monteverdi's *Return of Ulysses*, introduced Frederica von Stade, who for the [farewell] concert sang the final duet from the opera with Benjamin Luxon as Ulysses. Equally Elisabeth Söderström—whose first appearance at Glyndebourne was as long ago as 1957—introduced Felicity Lott as the Countess in Strauss's *Capriccio*. The final scene, gloriously sung by Lott with Bernard Haitink taking over from Andrew Davis as the conductor, became the emotional climax of the whole evening.

"[One remembers the 1976 filmed performance of *Capriccio* with Söderström in addition to] the longest serving of all Glyndebourne singers, the Swiss tenor Hugues Cuénod. Looking back through the list of Glyndebourne productions, it is astonishing how many times Cuénod's name reappears in those I enjoyed most of all, the ones that stood out as *echt*-Glyndebourne. He was regularly in Raymond Leppard's sumptuous adaptations of seventeenth-century operas, not just by Monteverdi (*The Coronation of Poppea* as well as *The Return of Ulysses*) but Cavalli too.

"After Cuénod's appearance as the old nurse, Erice, in Cavalli's *L'Ormindo* I remember him telling me with delight that Leppard had found another Cavalli opera with a drag part for him. What emerged a couple of years later was Cavalli's *La Calisto*, and if from nearly 40 years of Glyndebourne going I had to choose one production to cherish above all the others, it would have to be Sir Peter Hall's delectable representation of this classically based piece in Leppard's ultra-romantic realisation. Leppard even introduced two extra arias for the central character, the goddess, Diana, culled from other Cavalli operas, which provided ravishing moments for Dame Janet Baker."—Notes by EDWARD GREENFIELD, *The Guardian*, 27 July 1992.

2

SOME ADDITIONAL NOTES ON EIGHT BAROQUE MASTERWORKS

My passion for seventeenth-century Italian opera was nurtured at Cambridge. Initially I was trained there in the contrapuntal techniques of sixteenth century sacred music as part of my studies for the Music Tripos in the late forties. This led to an enthusiam for their secular manifestation in the English Madrigal School and the great lutenist songs. Further historical studies revealed the Italian connection and led me inevitably to explore *Le nuove musiche* of Monteverdi, his contemporaries and successors.

At that time very little of this music was available, even in libraries, certainly not in general printed circulation, so that each new discovery was a revelation — the facsimile of the Venice *Poppea* manuscript... occasionally-to-be-found volumes of the Malipiero edition of Monteverdi's madrigals... Nadia Boulanger's recording of some of them (with piano continuo)... a small, scratchy recording of Arnalta's lullaby sung by heaven knows who and long since melted... snippets garnered from the publications of the Musical Antiquarians Society, and rare society publications such as those by *I Classici Musicale Italiano* of Milan and the *Istituto Italiana per la Storia Della Musica* of Rome... limited editions published during the war which turned up in rare, single volumes. I wouldn't have missed that time of discovery for anything. They were truly exciting years.

Simultaneously I was fortunate enough to be singing each week in term with the Cambridge University Madrigal Society under Boris Ord (a society I was eventually to conduct myself)[2] where the live experience of the rather few Italian madrigals at that time available brought the reality of it to one's being in a way that no library could provide.

After an initial five years of Cambridge I left for London and the practise of music where I performed at a professional level many of the dis-

---

2   See CHRONOLOGY, below. (Ed.)

coveries I had tried out with my contemporaries at University. There were series of concerts involving singers like Janet Baker, Elsie Morrison, April Cantelo, Heather Harper, Sheila Armstrong, Ilse Wolf, Bob Tear, Gerry English, James Bowman, Sandy Oliver, Alfreda Hodgson, Helen Watts, Anne Howells, Hugues Cuénod, Ryland Davies, Christopher Keyte, Ben Luxon, Stafford Dean – it was a wonderful period for young voices in London, and it led to being invited by Ben Britten to prepare, to "realise" as the process became known (there being generally only a vocal and bass line left for us to imagine how these works might have sounded) Monteverdi's *Il ballo delle Ingrate* for the Aldeburgh Festival of 1958. That was the first one. There followed realisations of:

Monteverdi's *L'incoronazione di Poppea* for Glyndebourne 1962, 1963, 1964, revived 1984
Monteverdi's *L'Orfeo* for Sadler's Wells Opera 1964, 1965, 1966
Cavalli's *L'Ormindo* for Glyndebourne 1967, 1968
Cavalli's *La Calisto* for Glyndebourne 1970, 1971, 1974
Monteverdi's *Il ritorno d'Ulisse in patria* for Glyndebourne 1972, 1973, 1979
Cavalli's *L'Egisto* for Santa Fe 1974, 1976
Cavalli's *L'Orione* for Santa Fe 1983
Rameau's *Dardanus* – a modern edition drawn from the 1739 & 1744 versions, for Paris 1980, 1981

Except for *L'Orfeo* none of the Italian works had been staged professionally for more than 300 years.

All of them were published by Faber Music and for nearly all the editions I wrote an essay or preface dealing with various aspects of the opera's history, my intentions, and the methods I had used in the realisation, as well as some aspects of performance. (The material on Monteverdi and his first great opera, *L'Orfeo*, derives in part from an essay first published in the Sadler's Wells program book, in 1964; that for *Il ritorno* and *L'incoronazione* had similarly helped to launch the Glyndebourne productions, in 1972 and 1962 respectively.)

CLAUDIO MONTEVERDI
L'ORFEO
(1607)

What sort of a man was Monteverdi? There can be few composers of whose private life less is known. We do know that he was born in 1567 at Cremona, the city of violin makers, and that he married when he was twenty-eight. His wife, Claudia, died suddenly thirteen years later. Of his two sons the elder, a priest-musician, died during the plague in Venice in 1630 and the younger, a doctor, was in constant political troubles and caused his father considerable and rather begrudging anxiety.

Only one authentic portrait of him survives and it shows a lean dark face of the sort usually associated with a long thin body. It is ascetic and yet we can be sure that it concealed a deeply passionate nature. The astringent tone of so many of his letters reinforces this dichotomy of outward and inner appearances and it would also account for the impression of aloofness which inspired both respect and occasionally jealousy in his contemporaries.

Being so frank and unrelenting in his musical standards he was not an easy person to get on with, and his constant friend, Alessandro Striggio, the librettist of *Orfeo*, often received the sharp edge of his tongue when proposing some commission for Mantua which he thought unsuitable. Striggio must have found it hard to tone down some of the replies he received to such requests made on behalf of the Duke or Duchess. In truth Monteverdi's pride suffered while he was at Mantua, and when later installed as *Maestro di capella* at St. Mark's in Venice he was invited to return to a similar post at Mantua, he sharply declined saying that he had never suffered greater humiliation than in those early days waiting about in ante-chambers to be paid what was due to him. And he had reason to complain, for when he left Mantua in 1613 after twenty-three years of distinguished service he had only a few scudi in his pocket—and these he lost at the hands of robbers on the way to Venice.

Once installed at St. Mark's he found himself in a position of great authority and considerable social standing—which clearly mattered to him – and he was as happy as such a man could be. A letter of 1620 reveals both these aspects of his character:

> There is no man of good birth who does not honor and respect me. Whenever I perform my music, either ecclesiastical or secular, the whole city comes to listen; this sort of service is sweet indeed.

The very fact that almost all of the surviving letters are about composing or performing is an indication of how small a part personal relationships of an emotional kind played in his life.[3] After the death of his wife we hear of no other claim on his affections and his probable taking of minor orders at the end of his life would only seem to confirm this. There is an almost puritanical devotion to work, and of this we know a great deal. He worked slowly – "I know one can write music quickly but speed and quality do not go together" – and, as with Wagner, intellectual considerations played a large part in the process; he judged a libretto by its power to reflect his own emotions and experience because without this he could not respond and only through this response could he find the proper musical forms with which to clothe the words.

Of performing he wrote that singers must themselves affect the emotions they were expressing, word by word, whether it were war, peace, death or whatever; and he encouraged strongly contrasted expressions because thereby a more powerful image was created.

One can imagine that the decision to give himself completely to music for the greater part of his life must have created terrible inner tensions, making him increasingly difficult as a man. Yet the world would be infinitely the poorer had he not taken this course, and we may hope that he found some consolation in the knowledge that he was in his own time revered and esteemed as the greatest musical figure in all Italy.

When he died (in 1643) he was given a state funeral; according to a contemporary eye-witness "his catafalque was of unforgettable splendor

---

3   These letters are also about thoroughly mundane – and often depressing – questions of money: see Denis Stevens ed. & trans., *The Letters of Claudio Monteverdi* (Cambridge University Press, 1980). (Ed.)

and surrounded by so many candles that the church seemed like a starry night." Now he lies under a new plain and ugly stone set in the floor of the church of the Frari: a bitter comment on three hundred years of neglect which he might, in a wry way, have appreciated.

*

Many people still instinctively tend to put music written before the eighteenth century apart from their everyday musical experience. This attitude shows itself in a sort of cold restraint born partly of respect and partly of a dry, unadventurous scholasticism which is particularly foreign to the music of early seventeenth-century Italy. So much of the music was left to the performer at that time that we need to re-create in our minds the artistic climate as well as the purely technical processes before attempting to bring the music to performing life.

The new music, reacting against the almost impersonal, unemotional music of the church in the previous century, burst out in a flood of sensuous romanticism which echoed a similar change in the literary and visual arts. For example, how interesting and instructive it is to reflect that Rubens, only ten years younger than Monteverdi, was in the service of the same Duke Vincenzo Gonzaga at Mantua for eight years covering the period when *Orfeo* was composed. They could not have helped knowing each other, and it is fascinating to consider the new, exuberant sensuality of Rubens' *Hero and Leander* painted during those years, in relation to the passionate music of Monteverdi's opera.

Music's reaction to its past took at first the form of an almost excessive degree of overt emotionalism not only in vocal writing, but in the keyboard music of, for example, Frescobaldi (1583-1643), whose immensely complex *toccatas* and *canzoni* are built up from a mass of motives developed and expanded with a freedom and virtuosity that is quite breathtaking. This was the new way of playing the harpsichord and we can imagine Monteverdi, who was the most intense man of the age, urging the continuo players to use every technical device of the virtuoso so as to enhance and intensify the new vocal sounds coming from the stage. We are still learning how to do this, but I am quite certain that in Mantua, where the greatest virtuosi of the day were gathered, the accompaniment was not just a matter of simple chords such as an organist might use to accompany a Palestrina Mass.

Over the months of continuous rehearsal for *Orfeo* they must have built up a dazzling web of sound, by a process of trial and error, among the extraordinary variety of continuo instruments which the composer had at his disposal. None of this has survived simply because it was probably never written down, and we have to build it up again using as examples the keyboard and lute music of the day together with the various treatises on continuo playing which only corroborate this tendency to play elaborately expressive accompaniments. In due course this instrumental exuberance became tempered by a melodic lyricism such as we find in Monteverdi's last opera, *Poppea*, and which eventually divided the music into recitative and aria, but while it is there we should enjoy and exploit it to the full.

Similarly in the singing itself the restraint of polyphony was thrown aside and singers were urged to express, with all the means they could devise, the emotions they were enacting in the drama. We have a marvellous example of this in *Orfeo* itself – in the song that Orfeo sings when he is trying to persuade Charon to let him cross over the river Styx into Hades in search of Euridice. Monteverdi's own ornamented version of the original song has survived. It is a fantastic and immensely moving passage which tests present day vocal techniques to their limit and, while Monteverdi clearly meant it to show the *ne plus ultra* of vocal ornamentation, it gives an indication of the sort of decoration which singers were expected to make, more sparingly, elsewhere.

It may, even from this, be surmised that the problems in performing this music are legion. But since we are ourselves still in the midst of a reaction against the Teutonic romanticism of the nineteenth century it is unlikely that we shall go too far: all the same, we must try.

*

Italian composers of the late sixteenth century were very conscious of being the inheritors of a musical style which could be traced back for one hundred and fifty years and which, in their view, had developed into a state of near perfection in the music of Giovanni Pierluigi Palestrina (c.1525-1594), Orlando di Lasso (1532-1594) and Tomás Luis de Victoria (c.1549-1611). It was a style that shunned direct emotional expression and sought to reflect the perfection of God and Ancient Greece (a distinction not always clearly drawn in the late Renaissance mind) in perfectly modulated counterpoint.

Such artistic perfection nearly always carries with it the seeds of its own dissolution, and in the early years of the seventeenth century there was enacted one of the most amazing revolutions in the history of music. We can now see that the elements of it had been amassing for some time but it erupted suddenly and violently. It was at first a largely intellectual revolt on the grounds that, because the contrapuntal style aimed at a purely musical perfection of balance, the words became submerged and their emotional meaning totally obscured. The only way, therefore, to re-store the ancient values ascribed to Greek tragedy was to make music be-come the servant of the words, expressing as vividly as possible their meaning not descriptively but emotionally. The single voice was clearly the most suitable vehicle for this and the stage the most suitable medium. In this way opera was created.

Monteverdi lived and worked through this revolution and became the greatest exponent of the new style rather through his own pro-digious creative energy than through any partisan spirit. Only three full-length operas survive: his first — *Orfeo* — and the last two — *Il ritorno d'Ulisse* and *L'incoronazione di Poppea* — representing the contrasting poles of thirty years operatic endeavor. Before leaping to the conclusion that the first must therefore be an immature work we must remember that in 1607, when *Orfeo* was composed, he was 40 years old and acknowledged as one of Italy's leading composers. And, although the operatic form was for him a new venture, he had already shown himself a master of declamation in the madrigal.[4] This sense of technical security pervades the whole work. We nowhere feel any dramatic or musical uncertainty — except perhaps at the end, where he changed, possibly unwillingly, the librettist's tragic ending for the happy apotheosis with Apollo. The work

---

4   Described below; see Chapter III Section §1. (Ed.)

moves forward through its tragic story with an inevitability and a sense of theatrical timing almost incredible at this period of opera's history.

It is music which, for all its directness of emotional appeal, demands increasingly more involvement from both performers and listeners alike. I am reminded of an incident which took place after some weeks of intensive rehearsal when, after the messenger's narration of Euridice's death, I had reason to complain to the chorus of a lack of intensity in their heart-rending cry *"Ahi! caso acerbo* [Ah bitter sorrow!]". I tried to urge them on by saying "You must let yourselves become more involved in this tragic account of her death." "That is just the trouble," one of them replied, "we get too involved and cannot sing for being so moved."

Little by little we come to realise with what subtlety and power Monteverdi has inflected each syllable of the Italian to get the meaning across with maximum effect. And here we come to one of the most difficult aspects of the work when it is performed outside Italy: out of these separate words, set with such love and intensity, Monteverdi constructs musical lines which, by sequential rhythm and intervals, control of pitch and dissonance and placing of vowel sounds, are integrated into long structures which are primarily musical in effect, and to alter or misplace one part of this (as is inevitable in translation) is to destroy the whole. Paradoxically, the more integrated the music becomes with the meaning of words, the more essentially musical is the final result. This is why [for the Sadler's Wells production] the decision was finally taken to sing the work in Italian with libretto and translations provided for the audience — as at the first performance — so that "every one of the audience might be able to read the story which was being sung."

MONTEVERDI, *L'ORFEO* AND THE FLORENTINE CAMERATA:
MORE ABOUT WORDS AND MUSIC

Monteverdi was the son of a musician and there seems to have been little question but that he would follow the same profession as his father. Like all composers of his day he was trained in the great polyphonic techniques of sixteenth-century Italian church music, publishing his first works, *Sacrae Cantiunculae*, in 1582 when he was only fifteen. Italy was justifiably proud of its music at this time and — as we have noted previously — revering the values of Ancient Greece almost above religion, writers like Glareanus felt that they had equalled Antiquity and achieved "the perfect art to which nothing can be added and after which nothing but decline can be anticipated." There was a complacency in this which was to be rudely shattered by a group of young Florentine dilettanti belonging to an artistic society known as the *Camerata*. This group collected around a certain Count Bardi in whose house the first experiments in what came to be known as *Le nuove musiche* took place. One of their number, Vicento Galilei, the father of the famous astronomer, put the cat among the pigeons by writing in 1581 a pamphlet attacking the very core of the old values.

> For all the height of excellence of the practical music of the moderns[5] there is not heard or seen today the slightest sign of its accomplishing what Ancient music accomplished.

In saying this, Galilei set his face against every musical canon of his day, but he argued his case with great tenacity and fire. Far from being derived from the practice of Ancient Greece, "the present manner of singing several melodies together simultaneously [i.e. the modern church style] is no longer in use than one hundred and fifty years." The rules of counterpoint he calls factitious, too inviolate to savor of the Greek liberal attitude to art. And the root of the trouble lies in the relationship of the words to the music. In contrapuntal music the word is not only distorted as a word, but degraded to an inferior and insignificant function whereas it should be the source, the mistress of the notes. To support his case he began to experiment with settings of Dante and the Lamentations of Jeremiah for one single voice accompanied by a lute or harpsichord in which the music was designed only to support and increase the expressiveness of the words. The experiments continued and in 1589, when Count Bardi was made responsible for the *intermezzi* and other dramatic diversions at the marriage festivals of Ferdinando de Medici and Christine de Lorraine, another of the *Camerata*, Emilio del Cavalieri, composed

---

5   By whom he meant his own contemporaries, exponents of the mature contrapuntal style of men like Palestrina and di Lasso. [RL]

some monodies in the new style which the amateur singer Caccini performed. Such weddings were scarcely private occasions, and among the concourse of Italian nobility was the Duke Vincenzo di Gonzaga from Mantua. It was only a step from the *intermezzi* of Cavalieri to the first complete opera, *Dafne,* with libretto by Rinuccini and music by Peri, also a member of the *Camerata.* Their second opera, *Euridice,* was performed at the wedding festivities of Henry IV of France with Maria de Medici in 1600. Once more, the Duke Vincenzo di Gonzaga was present, and this time among his retinue was most probably the young Claudio Monteverdi, "singer and player of the viola" at the Duke's court in Mantua since 1590.

It may seem curious that Monteverdi's *L'Orfeo* was written as late as 1607 — when he was 40 — but the reasons are not hard to find. He occupied, to begin with, a very junior position at the Mantuan Court and would scarcely have been chosen to compose an opera in preference to his senior colleagues. Morever, it is unlikely that he was very impressed with the music he heard. The *Camerata* attracted a good deal of attention but it was more for the novelty of their ideas than the persuasiveness of their music. Their theories led them to exclude any music which might be thought to rival the words in expressive power, and the result, although interesting as an experiment and attractive as a novelty, tended to a dullness and a monotony which defeated its purpose and would have been unlikely to appeal to someone whose main concern was expressiveness in terms of music. But the principal reason seems to have been that Monteverdi was approaching the form of opera in his own way; working out his own revolution through the madrigal. By the year 1607 he had published five volumes comprising over one hundred madrigals[6] which shows an increasing tendency to change the old polyphonic style into one of choral declamation, treating the five voices as if they were one without losing the potential for expressive counterpoint wherever it would serve the text best. Thus, *L'Orfeo* showed the translation of ideas into the forms of opera which had been arrived at in the madrigal by a

---

6   In 1587, 1590, 1592, 1603, and 1605. Four more books followed, in 1614, 1619, 1638 and — posthumously — 1651; counting miscellaneous numbers published in various anthologies, the total is approx. 250 pieces. (Ed.)

process of gradual musical change rather than abrupt theoretical revolution. The result was a style much less restricted than that of the *Camerata* and infinitely nearer the spirit of affective declamation which they tried so hard to achieve. It must be counted the more valuable because of the short period in which it was practised. In Monteverdi's hands it became more and more expressive as the years passed and at no other time has vocal writing achieved this particular and wonderful fluidity of purpose, slipping from recitative to arioso and even aria without the strict division which later stultified so much seventeenth and eighteenth century opera. Its culmination is to be found in *L'incoronazione di Poppea*.

L'Orfeo was a great success, so much so that in skeletal form it was even printed and then re-printed, a very rare distinction at that time. It was the first of a long succession of full-length operas all of which have been lost save for the last two, *Il ritorno d'Ulisse in patria* and *L'incoronazione di Poppea*.

CLAUDIO MONTEVERDI
L'INCORONAZIONE DI POPPEA
(1642)

[Adapted from an essay for the first performance of the new staged version of *L'incoronazione di Poppea* at Glyndebourne, 1962 — subsequently reworked as a preface to the edition published by Faber Music in 1968.]

It has been said that recitative had great obligations to Monteverdi; for though Emilio del Cavalieri, Jacopo Peri, and Caccini, had attempted that style before him, yet he had so improved it, that he might almost be called its inventor. But being in possession of most of the works of these early dramatic composers, I am unable to discover Monteverdi's superiority. More forms or phrases of musical recitations still in use may be found in Peri and Caccini than in Monteverdi. But what surprised me still more was that his counterpoint in two parts is more frequently deficient than in the other two composers who had never, like him, distinguished themselves in the learned style of masses, motets and madrigals.
— Dr. Charles Burney, *History of Music*, 1789

It may well be doubted if Monteverdi would ever have succeeded in a line of art which required concentration and logical coherence of musical design. He seems to have belonged to that familiar type of artist who regarded expression as the one and only element of importance. The methods of choral art did not provide for dramatic force or the utterence of passionate feeling and under such circumstances it was natural that Monteverdi should misapply his special gifts, which were all in the direction of dramatic expression. His harmonic progressions are for the most part as incoherent as those of his predecessors, and, as might be expected with his peculiar aptitudes, he did very little for design.

— Sir Hubert Parry, *The Art of Music*, 1893

It happened to Bach, it happened to Mozart, and now it is beginning to happen to Monteverdi. The history of musical opinion does not show many consistencies but in one respect it seems to follow a fairly regular pattern. Once a composer has died, his reputation suffers a decline and his works are less and less performed. Sooner or later a revaluation occurs and a very few achieve what would seem to be a permanent place in the hierarchy of the great. Here the consistency ends, since the time taken for the several parts of this process to occur varies greatly from composer to composer. For Bach it took altogether over one hundred and fifty years; he only receives a mention of two lines or so in Burney's *History*, and, although Mendelssohn had performed the *Matthew Passion* in 1828, Sir Hubert Parry, one of the most influential writers on music in the late nineteenth century and a convinced believer in the idea of Progress, could still give as his honest opinion that Bach was

deficient in practical common sense. He worked so much by himself and had so little opportunity of testing his greatest works by the light of experience in performance....

As for Bach, so for Mozart whose revaluation was later than is generally supposed. Of him, Parry could say that he represents the type of man who is contented with the average progress of things and finds no necessity to aim at anything more novel than the doing of what comes to him to be done in the very best manner he can. His best manner was the best of its kind but it was not final.

The idea of Progress is not so widely held today, although it under-lies a considerable amount of our musical thought, and the revaluation of Bach and Mozart is more or less achieved. That of Monteverdi is, by comparison, only beginning as we continue to look further and further back into music's past in search of forgotten values. It is a tendency of our age and one in which we can rejoice for it confirms the durability of some values in a world not much given to permanence. Certain factors affect the process of revaluation, not the least of which is the availability of the music itself. In the case of Monteverdi this has been the most ob-vious cause for delay. Apart from a very few madrigals and an occasional limited publication, there was no complete edition available until, under Malipiero's supervision, such works or portions of works as have sur-vived were published between 1926 and 1942. But even after its publica-tion there were many obstacles to be surmounted before much of the music could be performed. Apart from the early five-part madrigals and some church music in the older sixteenth century style, the texts are so incomplete that their performance requires the sort of reconstruction and improvisation brought about by the imaginative application of what is at present a somewhat specialised knowledge which not all of our prac-tising musicians have the time to acquire. And some of those who have the time have not the imagination. The pedant, failing to realise that Monteverdi was a practising musician for whom music must serve ex-pressive ends or fail, is as much a factor in the delay of revaluation as the well-meaning man who attempts the reconstruction without sufficient knowledge.[7]

For the most part, we do at least have as much as Monteverdi ever put

---

7   Several editions — by RL and others — have appeared since the time of this writing, some of which are cited in Denis Arnold & Nigel Fortune, eds., *The New Monteverdi Companion* (Faber and Faber, 1985) and in *The New Grove Dictionary of Music and Musicians* (1980). Among comprehensive editions are Malipiero's own *Tutte le opere*

down on paper, but in the case of *L'incoronazione di Poppea* even that has been denied to us. Very little in the way of full scores or orchestral parts survived the theater fires and demolitions in seventeenth-century Venice, and *L'incoronazione di Poppea* was no exception. All that we have is a manuscript written in several hands, a sort of rehearsal or continuo copy not unlike a very simple piano-conductor found in some orchestral arrangements, consisting of a single-bass line, very occasional sketches in parts for *ritornelli*, and a vocal line. This manuscript is preserved in Venice and, except for a later copy to be found in Naples, it is the only music we have of the opera: the rest has to be reconstructed.

In 1613 Monteverdi moved from Mantua to Venice to take up his new appointment as *Maestro di capella* of St. Mark's, the most highly coveted musical post in all Italy where, in spite of his church commitments, he continued to accept commissions for operas in Mantua and the private theaters in Venice. But the event which perhaps influenced his last operas more than anything else was the opening of the first public opera-house not only in Venice but in the world, San Cassiano, in 1637. So popular did opera become that before the mid-century was reached five more houses were opened. Their fundamental design was very similar: each auditorium consisted principally of boxes arranged in tiers (in SS. Giovanni and Paolo for which *L'incoronazione di Poppea* was written, there

---

di *Claudio Monteverdi* in a 2nd edition (1954-1968), with supplementary volume xvii (1966); *Monteverdi: 12 composizioni vocali profane e sacre (inedite)* ed. by Wolfgang Osthoff (Milan, 1958); and *Claudio Monteverdi: Opera Omnia* ed. by Fondazione Claudio Monteverdi, Instituta et monumenta, *Monumenta*, v, (Cremona, 1970-). Individual works include *Ballo: Movete al mio bel suon* ed. by Denis Stevens, 1967; *Combattimento di Tancredi e Clorinda* ed. by Denis Stevens, 1962, also by Luciano Berio, 1968; *Christmas Vespers* ed. by Denis Stevens, 1979; *Madrigali a 5 voci, libro primo* ed. by Bernard Bailly de Surcy, 1972; *10 Madrigals* ed. by Denis Stevens, 1978; *Magnificat a sei voci* ed. by Denis Arnold, 1967; *Messa a 4 voci da capella* ed. by Rudolf Walter, 1972; *L'Orfeo* ed. by Bruno Maderna, 1967, also by Denis Stevens, 1967, and Edward H. Tarr, 1974, with a version in preparation by John Eliot Gardiner; *Selva morale: Magnificat I* ed. by Denis Stevens & John Steele, 1969; *Tirsi e Clori* ed. by Kenneth Cooper, 1968; and *Vespro della Beata Vergine* ed. by Denis Stevens, 1961, also by Jürgen Jürgens, 1977. A new ed. of the complete 1641 *Selva morale e spirituale* (ed. Stevens) is also in progress, 1993. (Ed.)

were five tiers of twenty-nine boxes). Each box had a small withdraw-ing-room where conversation could be made and refreshment taken in private. This arrangement contributed not a little to the early success of opera for the boxes were rented annually and much coveted by all the distinguished Venetian families and foreign Embassies. The opera house became a center of Venetian social and political life.

Apart from providing regular employment for singers, the running of a season's performances imposed certain restrictions on the form of opera among the most important of which was the standardisation of the orchestra. If we look at the score of *L'Orfeo* we see a list of instruments which reads like the catalogue of a sale at Sotheby's. It is not evidence of Monteverdi's original or bizarre taste in orchestration, but of his practicality, for it represents all the instruments available in Mantua at the time of performance. The originality comes in the use he made of them. The practice of scoring for whatever instruments were available persisted as long as opera was essentially a festival occasion; but now that a repertoire of several operas was played for a season there had to be consistency. It is important to realise that all of these early seventeenth century scores were based on the continuo instruments: harpsichord, harp, lute and organ. The aim of the setting of words in musical drama was to achieve a malleable line which would give the singer complete freedom for expressive intensity. And even now, with the vastly improved conducting and instrumental techniques it would be impossible to accompany such a line by an orchestra without forcing the singer into rhythmic patterns totally obfuscating the original expressive intention of the music. Herein lies the essential difference between the *prima e seconda prattica*, terms devised by Monteverdi himself to distinguish between the two styles of his own music. The first was the traditional church style in which music was the master of the words, metrical music where an orchestra of instruments could very easily be employed throughout; and the second in which the expression of the dramatic import of the words was the first concern, where the main burden of the accompaniment was borne by the continuo instruments joined by others only in moments of heightened passion where the music moved into a more regular meter. At first the only instruments added to those of the continuo were strings. Of course wind players existed in Venice but there was a strong tendency at this time to departmentalise music—and not without good reason. The brass and certain blending wood-wind instruments belonged properly to the church where their sound would be softened by the great spaces and yet be entirely suited to the dignity of the locale. Wind players' duties lay there and out of doors for ceremonial and festive occasions, their tone being considered too strident for an enclosed space such as an opera house. The first use of wind instruments in opera seems to have been entirely for representational purposes; trumpets and drums for a battle or horns for a hunting scene where they probably played on the stage as members of the cast. Taking this as license, trumpets appear in the Coronation scene of L'incoronazione di Poppea but for the rest it is scored for continuo and strings. If the continuo consisted only of one harpsichord, this might prove monotonous but we know from various letters that Monteverdi took for granted a large number of continuo instruments, even in the later operas, so as to give a wide tonal variety for characterisation and dramatic effect. This reconstruction uses a characteristic group of two harpsichords, a reed and flue organ, lute, chitarrone, guitar and a harp.

L'incoronazione di Poppea was Monteverdi's last work, written in 1642, when he was seventy-five, an achievement paralleled only by another Italian over two centuries later. Compared with L'Orfeo, it shows a narrowing of focus. The earlier opera reflects the formal splendors of the Mantuan court, splendors in which personality is over-shadowed by elaborate surroundings. Now, in the much simpler setting of the Venetian opera house, the focus turns from situation to the characters themselves, probing the innermost aspects of human drama in a quite unprecedented manner. The opera's libretto is by Francesco Busenello, a Venetian lawyer, at one time ambassador to the Court of Mantua, whom Monteverdi met through his pupil Cavalli. A comparison between the full libretto and the libretto actually set to music is a separate study, but it reveals a care for dramatic effect and balance we do not ordinarily associate with the period. Perhaps the most striking single change occurs at the very end. Busenello concluded with the great Coronation scene, but Monteverdi, after a sinfonia for the exit of the Tribunes and Consuls, added an ecstatic love-duet for Nero and his new Empress, left together on a darkening stage. If this was his very last piece of composition, it is a noble ending to a great creative life.

The plot is, perhaps, the least moral in all opera; wrong triumphs in the name of love and we are not expected to mind. Nor indeed is this the real point of the piece for, while retelling the story of Poppea's rise to the power of the throne, it is concerned with the interaction and development of the characters themselves with a realism and intensity totally surprising to the general preconception of early opera.

Every character has a sharply-defined musical personality: Poppea, the beautiful courtesan, shrewd, ambitious, an expert in love but showing only real affection for Arnalta, her old nurse who, like her counterpart in *Romeo and Juliet,* chides but is blind to her charge's faults; Nero, hysterical and wilful, besotted alike with his own power and Poppea's body; Ottavia his Empress, a great and noble soul driven to ignominious crime and banishment by the force of her despair; Seneca, a former-day Gurnemanz, wise, courageous but doomed to self-destruction before his Emperor's will; Ottone, whose hopeless adoration for Poppea brings him to ruin his life and that of Drusilla, companion of the Empress, who, in her turn, loves him. All these work out their destiny in music which exploits every variety of form known at the time with uncanny appropriateness.

There remains something to be said about the voices. In the original, Nero was sung by a male soprano, Ottone, and probably Arnalta by a male alto, voices which no longer exist. It is not to be imagined, if we believe contemporary accounts, that their present-day ecclesiastical counterparts, although ideally suited to the modern *prima prattica*, could possibly achieve the emotional intensity of their secular forbears in the seventeenth century *seconda prattica*. Therefore — for this modern, twentieth-century edition of the work — Nero is cast as a tenor, Arnalta a contralto and Ottone as a baritone. This has involved certain transpositions, but fortunately for the practical musician and unfortunately for the pedant, the manuscript is littered with directions in the composer's hands such as *"un tuon più alto"*, *"alla quarta"*, *"alla quinta"*. With such precedents, the transpositions have not given any qualms to the conscience.

For the most part the manuscript is written on two lines, voice and bass, so that whenever a new character sings, a new stave is drawn, and, apparently, a new start made to the music. It is quite clear (although in the past not generally understood) that, depending on their dramatic relationship, these sections should often interlock, giving a parallel dramatic veracity in dialogue to that found in monologue. Thus, for example, the scene of anger between Seneca and Nero in Act I achieves an emotional intensity when treated in this way which, at first sight, it does not seem to possess [see the appropriage pages in *Authenticity in Music*, Chapter I above]. Once understood as a principle, and the practicality of its application in contemporary rehearsal realised, no doubt remains that such was Monteverdi's intention.

The *basso continuo* line is written mainly in white notes, indicating more often than not merely the harmony underlying the vocal line. While the harmonic implications have been scrupulously observed, the notes themselves have from time to time been shortened, lengthened or elaborated rhythmically in the way that any experienced, imaginative continuo player might have done when entering into the dramatic situation he was accompanying.

For our new performing edition a minimum of ornaments has been added to the vocal line; if a singer can, by devising more, enhance the dramatic effect, he should feel at liberty to do so. The following are to be commended as sources for such elaborations: Giovanni Conforto, *Breve e facile maniera d'essercitarsi a far passagi*, Roma, 1593 (facsimile republished by Pro/Am Music Resources as *The Joy of Ornamentation*, with a preface by Yehudi Menuhin and an introduction by Denis Stevens, 1989); Giovanni Bovicelli, *Regole passagi di musica*, 1594 (Facsimile, Bärenreiter-verlag, Kassel, 1957); Guilio Caccini, *Le nuove musiche*, Florence, 1602.

The continuo parts are already sufficiently elaborate and should only be changed in the way of lengthening or shortening arpeggios or runs in order to accommodate a singer in recitative.

Distinction must be made by all performers between the sections indicated by the time signature C and those by the numerical time signatures $\frac{3}{4}$ $\frac{6}{4}$ $\frac{3}{2}$ etc. The former is intended by the editor to designate those sections in *stile recitativo* in which singers must be free to lengthen or shorten notes as the dramatic situation suggests. It is essential that an underlying rhythm be felt throughout this recitative; the unit of these sections is not the bar but the phrase, and the underlying rhythm from phrase to phrase will and should vary. It has proved useful in practise to conceive such variations by altering the unit of pulse from crochet to minim, or even to semibreve.

An understanding of the difference between rhythm and tempo is essential to the successful performance of this recitative music.

Certain cuts in the original text have been made. Such cutting for a modern performing edition (and, come to that, for a seventeenth-century performing edition, to judge from the manuscripts) is so complex that separate commentary is here impossible. Those wishing to explore this aspect are referred to the full texts given in the following: *Claudio Monteverdi: Opera completa a cura di G.F. Malipiero*, Vol. XIII; Hugo Goldschmidt, *Studien zu Geschichte der italienischen Opera in 17. Jahrh.*; or *Facsimile del Manoscritto It. Cl. 4. N. 439 Della Biblioteca Nazionale di S. Marco in Venezia* (introduzione di Benvenuti), Fratelli Bocca Editori, Milan, 1938.

In planning a performance of this work it is urged that sufficient time be set aside for the separate rehearsal, with and without voices, of the continuo group; to plan in the normal way only for a series of full orchestra rehearsals will prove exasperating and a waste of time and money.

The Prologue, which was not performed at Glyndebourne in 1962, has been added to the Faber edition and performed at Glyndebourne's new production of the opera in 1984. It may be thought to make Act I too long and, if so, this Act should be divided into two. The best place for the division would seem to be either before or after Scene IV.

CLAUDIO MONTEVERDI

IL RITORNO D'ULISSE IN PATRIA

(1641)

[Essay for the first Glyndebourne performance of *Il ritorno d'Ulisse in patria* in 1972.]

Il ritorno d'Ulisse in patria was probably composed in 1640, two years before *L'incoronazione di Poppea* when Monteverdi was 73, was premiered at SS. Giovanni e Paolo and repeated in 1641 at San Cassiano. There has always been a good deal of mystery over the work, indeed so much so that for some time even Monteverdi's authorship was in doubt. This is no longer questioned but whether the single surviving contemporary manuscript, in a copyist's hand, found in Vienna is by Monteverdi or all that Monteverdi wrote is certainly open to doubt. The number of obvious errors it contains is large and the number of dubious points still larger. Moreover, there are three manuscript copies of the libretto (by Giacomo Badoaro) in Venice which differ quite strikingly from one another and from the musical manuscript. Confusingly they ascribe the premiere to different theaters in Venice, all for the same year. It now seems certain that the opera was first performed at the San Cassiano—the oldest theater then in Venice which stood next to the present day *Accademia*.

The Vienna manuscript is similar in layout to all early Venetian opera manuscripts and, one can suppose, was sent as a present or, more likely, for a proposed performance. For the most part there is simply a vocal and a bass line. Every now and then there appears a *sinfonia*, always in five parts, a characteristic number for early Italian instrumental music (stemming, doubtless, from the five-part madrigal) which gives their sound a richness far beyond that which the addition of one part to the nowadays more usual four would seem to promise.

Details of instrumentation are entirely lacking but there are some fascinating points of deduction and speculation which have led me to vary the instrumentation used in *Poppea*. At the first appearance of Giove there is played a *sinfonia alta*—the height presumably relating to Jove in the heavens. This reminded me of the libretto of *Proserpina rapita* which Monteverdi composed for Venice in 1630. The music is lost but there seems no reason why the *sinfonia alta* in that libretto specifically indicated to be played high-up back stage by wind instruments should not have been performed in this way and effectively too. Perhaps the use of a little wind band for celestial appearances was a not infrequent feature of early Italian opera. It may even have come to England later on in the century and been described by Pepys, in 1668, as follows: "But that which did please me beyond anything in the whole world, was the wind-musick when the angel comes down which is so sweet that it ravished me, and indeed, in a word, did wrap up my soul so that it made me really sick, just as I have formerly been when in love with my wife; that neither then, nor all the evening going home, and at home, I was able to think of anything, but remained all night transported."

The instrumental accompaniment of opera began back-stage and the memory of its effectiveness, especially at certain points, may well have persisted long after orchestra pits came to be built.

Il ritorno d'Ulisse, although obviously by the same composer, is a very different opera from *Poppea*. The heroic nature of the story taken directly from the Odyssey has a stark, epic quality which has drawn much more severe music from the composer. There are, it is true, moments of melting beauty especially for the female characters but, Penelope and Minerva apart, the opera is mostly enacted by men and gods intent on revenge and escape from revenge, violence and peace, good and evil. Much of the music is redolent of the heroic solo-lines in the *Madrigali guerrieri* [first part of Monterverdi's *Madrigals*, Book 8], even *L'Orfeo*. In some ways it seems to echo the ideas of the Italian court-operas and, because of this, I have, in certain places, added trombones—especially for the darker characters of Nettuno and Antinoo. It is intriguing that the only copy of *Ulisse* should have been found in Vienna where Ferdinand III (whose mother was Eleanora Gonzaga) was Emperor. In Vienna the opera was still a court affair and conditions of its performance must have been similar to those of Mantua in 1607 when *L'Orfeo* with its varied instrumental score was first performed. A characteristic court-opera score which has in part survived showing this more splendid and varied instrumentation, including trombones, is Cesti's *Il pomo d'oro* composed especially for Vienna in 1668.

Wind instruments apart, the main burden of the accompaniment is still borne by the continuo group with strings playing only when the music moves into regular meter for aria or arioso. That principle remained constant until recitative music gave way to the separate aria and full-scores, roughly in the sense we now know them, became usual.

The opera begins with a prologue whose music and text only exist in the Vienna manuscript. The text is far superior to that found in the Venetian librettos both in quality and in its appositeness to the ensuing opera. The central character, *L'Umana fragiltà*, is clearly a symbol of Penelope's spirit weakening under the three elements to which she is most vulnerable; *Tempo* because time is running out for her; *Fortuna* because that fickle goddess seems to have turned her wheel against her and

Amor who holds her in bondage and also threatens her in the persons of the three suitors. For mortals, they sing at the end, there is no escape and they are pitiless in their exploitation of human weakness.

The libretto of the opera itself gains structural strength from being closely based on Homer—the best storyteller of all time. The divisions into three acts vary in the different sources but the plot is conceived so much in one line that our division into two at the wonderfully moving recognition scene between Ulisse and his son, Telemaco, makes equally good, if not better theatrical sense.

Some of the characters in Homer are merely shadowy figures in an epic story. The libretto makes them consistently more real. The maidservant Melanto and her lover Eurimaco have true purpose in adding pressure to make the Queen submit to the wishes of the suitors, for their own concupiscence cannot prosper in a court devoted to chastity.

The suitors are brilliantly characterised. It is unthinkable that three such ravening creatures with their henchmen should have gone on importuning Penelope for so long without fighting among themselves. Monteverdi and Badoaro resolve this by making them a band of villains in uneasy league with one another. They are given numerous ensembles together which reinforces this idea. It is as if they had agreed amongst themselves jointly to win Penelope and so control Ithaca on the understanding that whoever gains the prize will share it with the others—the bloodshed, we sense, will come afterwards. Yet they are three different characters; Anfimono, sly, mosquito-like, has a sting sharper than his florid music would seem to show; Pisandro is cold and dangerously menacing; Antinoo, the strongest of the three, is bold and openly threatening.

One of the most touching figures in the opera is the old shepherd, Eumete. According to Homer he had been Ulisse's servant at court but, with the arrival of the suitors, he took to the life of a shepherd in the hills where his loyalty causes him to be deeply involved in the final return of his master to the Palace. It is to him Minerva sends the disguised Ulisse for shelter and the joy with which he greets the ardent young Telemaco's return from Sparta makes one of the great lyrical moments of the opera; a marvellous upsurging of hope that all will eventually be well.

Iro, the fat, stuttering glutton presents us with some of the few moments of comic relief. He has treacherously sided with the suitors for the sake of his stomach and eventually pays the price of facing either starvation or self-destruction—a quandary he discusses with the audience in his final comic scene.

Ulisse himself is portrayed as a man possessed of great inner as well as outer strength. In his determination to return to his homeland and the wife he left there, he has withstood twenty years of hardship at the hands of Fate and the angry gods. The nearest he comes to despair is in his opening monologue when he wakes on the misty shore of an island he does not recognise. He has been promised safe passage back to Ithaca by the Feaci and now they have deserted him and he fears one more trick of the implacable gods. In fact the land is Ithaca. The Feaci have paid a terrible price for contravening the command of Nettuno and it is Minerva who has shrouded the coast in mist to prevent Ulisse recognising it and rushing off, unprepared, to his palace and certain death.

Minerva plays a near human role in the drama. She, alone of the gods, wishes Ulisse's safe return and has become his protectress. He is her special care and, as far as a god is able, she loves him. In effect she takes command of the situation and her presence is felt like a shadow over the whole action. She contrives the disguise of Ulisse as an old man, his meeting with Eumete and even, according to Homer, puts the idea of the archery contest into Penelope's mind together with the sweet words she addresses to the suitors at that moment. It is Minerva who finally persuades Giunone to appeal to Giove and Nettuno for clemency towards Ulisse and one cannot doubt that she has some part in the final reconciliation of husband and wife.

The other gods are painted in strong, monochrome colors; Nettuno, implacable in his anger until the last scene; Giove, coldly aloof, barely concerning himself with the plights of men; Giunone, the warm-hearted wife who eventually promotes some concern for Ulisse in her husband's mind.

Badoaro cleverly divides the action in heaven from that on earth. At the beginning of Act I the anger of Nettuno at both the Feaci and Ulisse

The author (center) at a recording session for *Il ritorno d'Ulisse in patria* for CBS Masterworks, 1979 (released as Columbia 35910).

CREDIT: Colin Busby, London

(who blinded his son, Cyclops), together with Giove's compliance with Nettuno's revenge set the menace of the gods clearly before us.

Only Minerva lovingly protects the hero and the implied strife in heaven is echoed by the increasing tension on Ithaca as Ulisse comes nearer and nearer to home under her guidance. And this while Penelope comes nearer and nearer to being forced to the disastrous step of agreeing to marry one of the suitors.

The double growth of tension builds up throughout the opera until the great archery scene when Ulisse, crying out to Minerva (uniting, as it were, the strife of the gods with that of mankind) slays the men who would oppress his land and seize his wife. Even then the opera is not over and Monteverdi and Badoaro grasp the idea, implicit in Homer, that Penelope still does not and will not recognise the returned Ulisse. What in Homer is a reaction to fear on her part becomes, in Monteverdi's hands, a marvellously human statement. Penelope is one of the most fascinat-

The Grammy-nominated CBS recording of *Il ritorno d'Ulisse* featured Frederica von Stade as Penelope – seen above. Other cast members of this distinguished 1979 Glyndebourne Festival production were: Richard Stilwell (Ulisse), Ann Murray (Minerva), Nucci Condo (Ericlea), Patricia Parker (Melanto), Claire Powell (Giunone), Richard Lewis (Eumete), Patrick Power (Telemaco), Roger Bryson (Nettuno), Keith Lewis (Giove) and Ugo Trama (Il Tempo/Antinoo), with the Glyndebourne Festival Chorus and London Philharmonic Orchestra.
CREDIT: Colin Busby, London

ing female characters in all opera. She has waited for twenty years, alone and increasingly under pressure from the suitors. To her the idea of constancy has almost become a way of life. In spite of the yearning love she still has for Ulisse, part of her has become a professional widow and she has begun to take pride in her role. Throughout her great opening monologue we see these two elements unmistakably portrayed. She almost glories in the character of the tragic, lonely woman she has become, yet with the phrase *"torna, o torna"* which recurs three times, she yearns for the love of her husband. She accuses him of insufferable cruelty and immediately excuses him because it is the gods who keep him from her.

This dichotomy is seen in her character until the final resolution. When her maidservant Melanto urges her, in Act I, to fall in love again she angrily repudiates her, although Melanto's magical aria "*Ama dunque*" must surely be intended to penetrate the less resolute side of Penelope's character. In the court scenes of Act II she shows her skill in putting off the suitors as well as outraged, almost virginal outbursts against love. When Telemaco returns from Sparta and tells his mother that Helen, mistress of auguries, promised him that Ulisse was near at hand, Penelope's anger at the mention of the woman who was the root-cause of her troubles gives way in the libretto to a moment of passionate yearning and hope stronger than the image she has created for herself. (This small but crucial moment of revelation is missing from the Vienna manuscript. I have set the words using a bass-line from a madrigal by Monteverdi.)

But the confrontation of her two selves only really happens when Ulisse, disguised as an old beggar, has slain the suitors. Somehow the terror of the slaughter and the simultaneous relief which it brings makes her refuse to accept the word, first of Eumete, then of Telemaco and her faithful nurse Ericlea that her rescuer is in fact Ulisse. Even confronted by Ulisse himself, restored to his own state, she is still unwilling to forsake the image of the tragically heroic woman who waits alone. Only when Ulisse speaks of his knowledge of the counterpane on her bed, which no other man could have seen, does she, with a wonderful eagerness, relinquish her martyrdom. It is a marvellously poignant human study and a great stroke of operatic imagination.

After the tremendous theatrical climax of the archery scene only a genius of Monteverdi's caliber could have capped it with an idea so much more humanly powerful. (He did the same after the Coronation scene in *Poppea*.)

In the midst of Penelope's final struggle for the resurrection of her true, wifely character comes the resolution of the war in heaven. Minerva persuades Giunone to seek the help of Giove and, through it, Nettuno finally agrees to let Ulisse live in peace.

The opera is not a long one so that virtually nothing is cut for the sake of length. The archery scene has been tautened by some small excisions so that the suitors, having addressed Penelope separately once, do not do so again at length before attempting the bow of Ulisse. The storm scene near the beginning of Act I, missing from the musical manuscript but essential to the presentation of the wrath of Nettuno, has been constructed from ideas in the *Madrigali guerrieri*. The *sinfonia* for the disembarkment of the sleeping Ulisse from the ship of the Feaci has been composed according to the direction which Monteverdi gives along with a single bass-note: "*si fa la seguente sinfonia toccata soavemente sempre su una corda*." The *Coro di Naiadi* when, under Minerva's direction, they hide Ulisse's spoils of war is an extension of the preceding duet for Minerva and Ulisse—there being no music for this text. Moments like the disappearance and re-appeareance of Ulisse at the end of Act I in his confrontation with Telemaco cannot take place in silence, nor can the appearance to the suitors of Giove's eagle in Act II. For these appropriate improvisatory bars have been given to the continuo. The *Ballo* in Act II has a text but no music and is essential to the impetus of the scene prior to the entrance of Eumete. This I have set in the manner of the composer's *Scherzi musicali* of 1607 which have many similar texts.

Like so much else in the opera, these and occasional *sinfonie* for exits and entrances would, doubtless, have been left to pupil-collaborators and, in all that I have done for the opera, I count myself no higher.

FOUR OPERAS BY FRANCESCO CAVALLI

[Essay compiled from prefaces to the editions of *L'Egisto* (1643), *L'Ormindo* (1644), *La Calisto* (1651) and *L'Orione* (1653), published by Faber Music Ltd., together with notes for a 28 September 1972 performance of *La Calisto*.]

Opera moved from the private splendors of the princely courts of Italy, where it originated, into the public domain on May 6th, 1637, when the San Cassiano opera house opened its doors in Venice. There, and in the ten opera houses which were to be built before 1690, the new form of *dramma in musica* developed and became the model for all Italy and the rest of Europe to copy. When he granted, in 1669, the first patent for the establishment of an opera in Paris, Louis XIV ordered that they should be *"pareilles et semblables à celles d'Italie"*, and by Italy he meant Venice.

For us the name now mainly associated with Venetian opera of the seventeenth century is that of Claudio Monteverdi; but he died full of years and honor in 1643, so that for fifty years afterwards the standard and distinction he had brought to opera's beginning had to be carried on by his successors. Nor was it possible to rely on memories of that great man, because operas were, at that time, rarely revived: apart from the public demand for novelty, their very method of composition precluded this. In the preface to the libretto of *Ulisse errante*, set to music by Francesco Sacrati, the author, Badovero, observes that he had written *"già molti anni"* a libretto on the same subject entitled *Il ritorno d'Ulisse in patria* which had then been *"decorato dalla musica del Signor Claudio Monteverdi soggetto di tutta famma"* (in fact it was only three years previous), but now it was not considered possible to revive this opera *"poichè è andato il Gran Maestro ad intuonar la Musica degl'angeli à Dio"* — because the Great Master has gone to sound the music of the angels before God — and a new libretto set to new music was the only solution.

Who, then, were the composers who carried on and developed the great tradition maintaining for fifty years Venice as the operatic center of the world? Their names were Cavalli, Cesti, Sacrati, Rovettino, Crivelli, Pallavicino, Boretti, Ziani, Grossi, Legnenzi; names in a history book of men whose music has rarely if ever been heard by anyone reading this, of men who were as well known to their contemporaries as Puccini was to his. Of these the greatest was Francesco Cavalli, whose life spanned nearly the whole period and whose personal fame was unrivalled throughout Europe.

It might reasonably be asked why, if the operas of this time are indeed so valuable, they have not become known and appreciated sooner? The answer is two-fold: the seventeenth century is only now being seen to have a worth-while musical culture of its own and not one merely interesting to music historians because of the way it prepared for and developed into that of the eighteenth century; and, because of the way in which operas were composed, it was thought for a long time that they were unperformable. There is left no such thing as a full score representing in detail the composer's final intentions, nor was there ever such a thing. We have seen that three years after *Il ritorno d'Ulisse in patria*, because the composer was not there to supervise a revival, a new libretto and new music had to be written. In those intervening years all the bits of manuscript paper which had achieved a precarious permanence for the run of performances (as anyone who has had to do with a present-day "musical" will know they can be) had been lost; memories of how things "went" had faded, and the composer who might have put it all together again had died. And only in recent years has this lack of a full score ceased to be interpreted as a factor which marred these seventeenth-century operas for ever, causing them to be fit only for the library shelf.

Since the eighteenth century the tendency has been for composers to become more and more precise in their notation and scoring, to such an extent indeed that in recent years many scores are to be found marked in such detail and with such precision that one might, with advantage, set a collection of computers at them and avoid the element of human interference in performance altogether. The score in which what the composer wrote is all, and all of it sacred, unalterable and only interpretable within those limits, is a conception born of this attitude. Certainly it is one which the seventeenth-century composer simply would not have understood. He composed his operas for the most part on two staves, voice and bass, making in this way the ground plan for the work which eventually reached the stage. All opera scores of the time that have survived are written in this way, and the multitude of directions for cuts, transpositions, instrumentation, changes of all and every sort which they contain, provide sure evidence for this extremely practical attitude to making the opera work in the particular conditions of the particular performances in the particular theater. The fundamental conception is the composer's, the details may be anyone's. It is, for example, not surprising to me to find Cavalli's handwriting in the earlier, contemporary, manuscript of *L'incoronazione di Poppea*; and it would surprise me less to find sure evidence that he had helped to get the work on stage by composing a *ritornello* here and there, if not completing and continuing some of the vocal music as well. Just as painters at this time had pupils to complete their designs, so nothing would have been more natural than for

Monteverdi to enlist the talents of his pupil, friend and by this time colleague, Francesco Cavalli, in the preparation of his last opera for performance. It was a practice we know for certain to have been carried on in the preparation of those operas by Lully, *"pareilles et semblables à celles d'Italie"*, towards the end of the century in France. Much of the middle two or three lines of his five-part string writing can be seen in the manuscripts to have been filled in by assistants not all of whom had a very strong grasp of musical grammar.

This attitude of easy collaboration would, I surmise, have extended to the preparation of the continuo accompaniment rather in the manner of the sessions of improvised music cultivated by jazz musicians. Such sessions are not generally as unrehearsed as their exponents would like us to think, although they may not be written down. Given some ground plan — in Cavalli's case, a voice and bass line — and a sensitive person in charge who controls by look and gesture which players may or may not play, the improvisation, by dint of rehearsal and repetition, gradually assumes a shape; phrases and combinations of instruments are remembered and the whole thing achieves a sort of temporary, unwritten permanency. For Cavalli the principles which guided his control must have been essentially dramatic in the manner indicated in the printed score of Monteverdi's *L'Orfeo* where the continuo instruments are chosen in varying combinations which serve to aid the characterization on the stage. The method of preparation which I have outlined takes a great deal of time, and the failure of it to survive the increasing pressure of theater managers for more productions, and thus shorter rehearsal periods, would account, as much as anything else, for the decline of recitative towards the end of the century and for the decreasing number of continuo instruments used in the orchestra. If there was no time for them to rehearse properly it was better to do without them; and without their vitalising color an essential element of early seventeenth-century recitative was lost.

Today we are also very short of time, and opera managers are quite as importunate, so that if we wish to use large numbers of continuo instruments the parts have to be composed and written out. The difficulty then is to preserve the freedom to mold them to the particular situation on stage if the spirit of the earlier performances is to be revived; given bold creative direction and playing it can and must be done.

Vitally affecting the dramatic presentation of recitative is the convention in these scores of drawing a bar line after one character has sung and then drawing a new set of clefs for the next character — a convention originally adopted to save manuscript paper. If performed as written there would be (and, regrettably, often are) pauses while a cadence is played after one character has made an observation and, after a new chord, another character answers it. The classic example of this is the quarrel between Nero and Seneca in *Poppea*, where, if the sections were not joined, not one spark would fly between them, so interminably should we have to wait between the briefest interjections. The principle implicit in this can also be applied to the joining of *ritornelli* to the ends and beginnings of vocal solos — without it a bar too many may creep in and the rhythm of the whole be upset. Naturally this is not an automatic proceeding. All manner of practical and dramatic considerations have to be taken into account, but, used sensibly and with intuitive understanding, it is an important contributing factor to the successful, taut, presentation of the drama.

One major problem of performance remains to be considered now: the use of the strings. It is manifestly clear that they played considerably more than the surviving scores show. This is hardly to be wondered at if one considers the size of what we now call a full score written out on ten-stave manuscript paper. Certainly no Italian theater manager, then or now, would pay for a group of twenty people to sit in the pit night after night twiddling their thumbs for the best part of four hours. But quite clear principles for the use of strings can be deduced from the scores. Apart from those places where strings are indicated as playing but have no written-out music, there is, taking all the scores into consideration, a large number of arias and duets for which a string accompaniment has either been completed or left unfinished. It is not even uncommon to find four staves drawn in above the vocal and bass lines and left blank. Following these indications of actual practice, there is no reason why other arias and duets should not be given string accompaniments as long as they are added with proper taste, technique, judgment and dramatic sense. There is a further guiding principle involved derived from the practical application of the original ideals of expressive solo singing.

While a group of experienced continuo players can follow the wildest extravagences and *rubati* of a hero dying in recitative, a group of string players, however well directed, will almost certainly get lost, and if not lost they will impose a rigidity of performance upon the singer which will entirely defeat the original purpose.

Thus, in general, the strings would be confined to the more metrical music and even then not indiscriminately for it must be realised that, in adding the string sound, one is not merely making variety but adding a new expressive element, a fresh color and intensity which must be nicely judged if it is not to be a squandered and mis-used effect. With this said, it must be pointed out that there are a few examples in the Cavalli scores of recitative with written-out string accompaniment. But they confirm the underlying principle here outlined, for they occur only at climatic moments as, for example, in the prison scene of *L'Ormindo* when, at the heroine's death, the strings play sostenuto chords (the only practical way of writing such an accompaniment) giving a most telling luster to that moment in the opera.

When all the evidence and conjecture has been brought together it can do no more than prepare us for what must be an intuitive act of re-creation before the operas of this remarkable man, and those of his contemporaries, can be brought to life in the present-day world of professional opera. We must face up to, and adapt to, the conditions which obtain now, just as Cavalli did in his own time. It is foolish — and finally impossible — to adopt a prissily "pure" attitude to these works. It is equally foolish to resent or reject the element of compromise which must play a part in their present-day performance. Only, perhaps, in certain music of the early Renaissance is so much asked of the performer in the way of recognition of the composer's original intention and the re-creation and re-enactment of it. Of course not one solution will ever be right. It never was, for no opera ever achieved that fixed condition, from which present-day rightness could be judged. No half-hearted attempt dampened by academic restraint will do. Performing these works again is like a love affair, you either give and risk all or better leave it alone.

Francesco Cavalli who, after Monteverdi's death, became the acknowledged first musician of Italy, was born at Crema in 1602. His baptismal name was Piero Francesco Caletto Bruno, and his father was an impoverished church musician of no great distinction, whose son, at the age of fourteen, attracted the attention of Federigo Cavalli, Podestà (Venice-appointed governor) of Crema. In 1616, at the end of his term of office, Federigo Cavalli took the young Francesco back with him to Venice where he entered him as a soprano in the choir of St. Mark's under the recently appointed *Maestro di capella*, Claudio Monteverdi. The boy soon adopted his patron's name and stayed at St. Mark's to become successively tenor, second organist, first organist and finally, in his old age, he too became *Maestro di capella*. This last appointment was more a rank of distinction for his retirement than an advancement in career, for while he remained attached to St. Mark's all his life, his main reputation was established in the theaters of Venice where, evidently with the church's approval, he must have spent much of his time.

He produced his first opera, *Le nozze di Teti e di Peleo*, in 1639, the year that Monteverdi revived *L'Arianna* for the opening of the new Teatro San Moisè. Cavalli wrote first for the San Cassiano theater, the oldest of the opera houses which stood near the present-day *Accademia*. He continued to produce new operas there each year until 1646 when he began to write for the newer theaters that were springing up all over Venice. *L'Ormindo* was produced there in 1644, two years after Monteverdi's *Poppea*, and the year following that great man's death. Cavalli's fame spread but, apart from fulfilling occasional commissions in Milan and Florence, he remained in Venice until 1660 when an event took place which was at once the greatest compliment to his genius that he ever received and the greatest disappointment of his professional life.

Cardinal Mazarin, who virtually ruled France during Louis XIV's minority, was anxious to provide the finest possible entertainment for the young King's wedding. Nothing less than a new opera by the great Cavalli would satisfy him, and he went to extraordinary lengths through the person of the French Ambassador in Venice to persuade the ageing composer to undertake the commission. Cavalli, already failing in health, was at first very reluctant to accept, but pressure was put on him both by the French and the Venetians, and at last he agreed to make the long journey to Paris and there compose (and this meant see into performance) an opera entitled *Ercole amante*, in honor of the Royal lover and his bride. Soon after his arrival, Cardinal Mazarin died and Cavalli lost a valuable protector to whom he could have turned in trouble. Trouble came, principally in the person of Jean-Baptiste Lully, then ballet-master at the Court, who as a politic gesture, had been invited to collaborate by composing ballets for the new opera. There was nothing unusual in the idea of such a collaboration, but it seems that in agreeing to it Cavalli was clasping a viper to his bosom. All manner of things began to go wrong over matters like rehearsal time, availability of singers and orchestra, delays in preparation – many directly attributable to Lully who throughout his life showed a similar lack of scruple in dealing with anyone who stood in his way or was a possible rival. As a result, Lully's ballets were acclaimed and Cavalli's work was greeted with respectful but retrained approval – he could not have known, of course, that the French as a race do not greatly care for music, and infinitely prefer spectacle, ballet and scandal, all of which, on this occasion, Lully provided. It was a lesson which the generous-hearted Italian took very hard, and he returned to Venice tired and disillusioned, vowing never to write again for the stage. He believed that the fashions of music had passed him by, and to a certain extent it was true; he could not be expected to know that it was not necessarily for the better. Back in Venice, he accepted the final distinction of being made *Maestro di capella* at St. Mark's, and although he was persuaded to compose three more operas, and they are among his finest, he devoted most of his last years to religious music, even composing a Requiem Mass for his own funeral. He died in January 1676.

The actual amount of music he composed during his life is astounding. Between the years 1639 and 1666 he produced more than forty operas, beginning at the rate of one a year but increasing, as his fame spread, to a record of four operas in 1651. The speed with which he worked is evident in the manuscripts. It is clear that, once having agreed to set a libretto to music, he composed it straight through in vocal line and bass, noting, as he went, *incipits* of sinfonias, indications such as *tutti gl'istrumenti* or *lamento con violini* or a bass-line which would later serve for elaboration into a *ballo*, sometimes even breaking off in the middle of a duet or aria in order to get on, but leaving space for its completion later. This was what served as a basis for the final performances, like the rough-hewn stone of a sculptor which is then ready for detailed completion.

More of this detail we can see in those manuscripts which have clearly been used in the theater where cuts, alterations and transpositions abound.

The middle years of Cavalli's working life were not made easier by a sad decline in public taste. The early ideals of opera representing noble passions and emulating the distinction of classical drama were soon swallowed up in the general desire for more and more vivid spectacle; and, already, the cult of the virtuoso singer had begun to make them more important than the characters they portrayed. It was particularly unfortunate that the *castrato* should have come so soon into general favor, because his ability to play male or female and either impersonating the other was to prove too much of a temptation for the weaker librettists to resist.

The plots of many of these operas are of such a ridiculous complexity that it is doubtful if anybody could ever have known, or cared, what was happening on the stage once the disguises had got under way; it is not exceptional, for instance, to have two pairs of brothers and sisters, all separated since childhood shipwreck, wandering through the operas, all dressed in travesty for no very good reason, and falling in love from time to time in the most unsuitable combinations. Cavalli was forced to set a number of these poor libretti and there is no doubt that these works, although containing much beautiful music, are no longer dramatically viable and will remain so until public taste suffers a similar debasement. But at the beginning and at the end of his career, to comment generally, he was fortunate in his collaboration with men like Francesco Busenello, who also wrote the libretto of L'*incoronazione di Poppea*, Nicolà Minato, who wrote the libretto of his last three operas, and Giovanni Faustini who wrote the libretti of several of the earlier operas, including L'*Ormindo, La Calisto* and L'*Egisto*. The libretto of L'*Orione* was by Francesco Melosio. It is, perhaps, not surprising in view of his teacher and his own evident sense of theater, that he responded to the best libretti with his best music.

He was above all a great melodist with a power to penetrate and respond to a dramatic situation with his tunes that none of his contemporaries possessed. And it was in cultivating this fine lyrical gift that he most clearly developed away from the style of his great predecessor.

Technically the need for violent exploration of new harmonies in a search for an intense expressiveness in the new tonal system was past; that work had been done and it was now a time for consolidation and for expansion within the system that the previous generation had struggled to define. Yet he, of all his contemporaries, never lost sight of the early ideals of recitative as a form of intensely heightened speech which, more than the aria, formed the basis for operatic effectiveness. And at his best, although in a different way from Monteverdi, his arias and ariosos grow out of and emerge into the recitative like jewels set in a crown, but not separate from it. It was a style which was giving way under the public demand for more and more arias and ariettas; recitative was, while Cavalli lived, a rapidly dying art, and with it died the ideals which were at the root of opera's beginning.

The public desire for amusement did encourage one delightful aspect of opera previously thought to have been a feature of opera at Rome, but in fact equally Venetian and greatly cultivated there: the solo comic scene. In it a character, generally a servant, often one in travesty, makes observations pertinent and impertinent upon what has been going on in the drama. They clearly served a practical purpose, as they do today, to enable the scene to be changed, but Cavalli was particularly good at them, turning what was primarily a practical expedient into something more significant. He seemed able to give them an emotional depth which links rather than divorces them from the drama; the characters remain characters and their comments, although often vulgar, are musically as well as verbally apt. The prurient thoughts of the crabby old nymph, Linfea, in *La Calisto*, curious to know if she hasn't missed out on something in her life-long devotion to the virgin goddess, Diana, have a relevance to Diana herself whose resolve is being sorely tested by her growing attraction to Endymion. The page Nerillo's solo scene "*che città*" in *L'Ormindo* reflects his master Amida's attitude to the fair sex, one that will be changed as the drama unfolds. What might have been merely a cynical comment on Venetian society becomes, in this way, integrated with the plot. It is equally true of similar cases in *L'Orione* and *L'Egisto*.

In the principal roles as well as in those of the servants, Cavalli's perception of character and his ability to draw it are shown vividly in these four operas. In *L'Ormindo* it is fascinating to see how the music for the young Queen Erisbe changes as she herself changes from the gay, half-innocent mischievous girl into the lover who is prepared to die for her beloved Ormindo. He, too, develops in a similar way, seeming to mature before our eyes. Very different is the dark coloring which Cavalli gives to the mysterious, passionate figure of Sicle, the disguised Princess from Egypt, and the tense, introspective Amida whom she is pursuing. One of the most interesting figures is that of Ariadeno, the aging King, whose frigidity is a subject for ribald comment by the Queen's irrepressible maid, Mirinda, but whose rage at his wife's elopement with Ormindo is real enough, as is the cruelty with which he orders their deaths by poison. Finally this duality of personality seems to be resolved through the remorse and magnanimity he shows when he realises what he has done.

The opera as a whole is a fascinating experiment in dramatic contrast. It begins as a light-hearted comedy in which the two pairs of lovers seem to be working out their relationships at a very superficial level. Why the colors darken and the atmosphere changes is not obvious; the cause may lie in the gravity of Sicle's anguished outbursts which her disguise as a fortune-teller fails to conceal. Certainly it is when Erisbe realises that Amida has been unfaithful to someone else that she abandons her flirtation with him and thinks only of Ormindo. From this moment the whole pattern of relationships deepens and the opera begins its descent towards tragedy.

The way in which Cavalli's music responds to this change is striking evidence of his originality as an opera composer and a welcome confirmation of his contemporary reputation.

With *La Calisto* we enter a quite different world of sexual ambivalence treated with a sympathy, wit and frankness amazing for its time. The idea for the plot is taken by librettist Giovanni Faustini from Ovid's *Metamorphoses* — those legends of Jove's amorous adventures for which, because of Juno's ever-watchful eye, he had always to disguise himself. Showers of golden rain, a swan, a bull — these are the widely-known disguises. Faustini selected a much less likely one, in which Jove, lusting after one of the goddess Diana's nymphs, Calisto, finds that the only way to achieve his desire is to change himself into his daughter's shape (Diana was his daughter). Assisted by the pimp-like Mercury, he speedily succeeds in his plan. But the plot is a good deal more compicated by the presence of the real Diana, herself falling in love against her will and conscience with the shepherd Endymion. She, in her turn, is loved by the wood-god Pan who, when spurned, proves jealously vindictive and nearly succeeds in killing Endymion.

The possibilities for amusing confrontation are obvious and fully exploited. Calisto enjoys her seduction (albeit innocently, perhaps), and mistakenly approaches the real Diana for a repeat performance. Endymion, having made some headway with the real Diana, makes as if to start where he left off with the disguised Jove. All these goings-on greatly over-excite a sour old nymph in Diana's train, called Linfea. She has kept her virginity too long, but the old desires call and are finally met in an astonishing robust manner by the followers of Pan. Only Juno, when she arrives early in the second act, is not deceived. She has had too much experience of it all and, with pitiless logic, she removes the root cause of the trouble by calling up the Furies to turn Calisto into a little bear. Order is more or less restored and Jove, now returned to his proper shape, takes pity on the little creature and gives her a place in the heavens as a constellation — *Ursa Minor* (the little bear of the night sky) — chilly comfort for her. But already I anticipate the second level of the opera.

The riotous comedy of the plot is set to music which eschews the burlesque. When Jove disguised as Diana seduces Calisto, the music is true, moving love-music. So, unless we turn our ears and eyes away, we are faced with a man disguised as a woman making love to another woman — an ambiguity most of us have been taught from the cradle not even to contemplate. The real Diana — goddess of chastity — falls in love with a young shepherd, sung by a male alto — a further ambiguity we might be too embarrassed to notice. The cross old nymph Linfea (sung by a tenor) is offered, in disarmingly honest fashion, relief from her long-sustained burden of virginity by a young satyr in hot need of experience (sung by a soprano) — another situation which might have brought a blush to a maiden-aunt's (or uncle's) cheek.

The point of these various situations is not to shock — indeed, there is no need for those who do not wish to see them to do so — yet all of them, and the characters, are treated by Cavalli as real. The music is genuine and so directly and honestly expressive that we would be depriving ourselves of valuable experience if we shut our minds to their implications. At this second level the opera is about love and sexuality in some of its varied forms and manifestations. We are, after all, products of both male and female, and psychologists have for years been telling us that our parents are both represented in us in varying degrees. Cavalli and Faustini, it seems, were saying much the same 300 years ago. They take no moralistic view. They just show us, entertain us, and leave us to do our own thinking.

L'Orione is another and more light-hearted imbroglio involving the gods whose focal point is the power of Cupid aided and abetted by his mother Venus, cast here more in the role of trouble-shooter than matchmaker. Together they succeed in disrupting all the gods assembled for Apollo's festival day on Delos including Diana and Aurora who both fall for the handsome hunter, Orion. He, blind, comes to Delos to have his sight restored and arrives with his Leporello-like companion, Filotero, swimming. Diana is eventually tricked by her brother, Apollo, into shooting him with an arrow as he, overly confident in his aquatic prowess, takes part in a swimming race with the other gods.

This time it is Jove who sorts things out, bringing calm to the island by taking Orion to the heavens where he will be seen for ever shining as a constellation.

The music reflects the slighter plot with fast-moving scenes full of spectacular visual effects and witty vocal writing that, although from time to time becoming deeply expressive, mainly suggests the world of revue and musical comedy.

L'Egisto is, perhaps, the grandest and most profound of the four Cavalli operas here reviewed.

The plot has a breadth that recalls the pastoral comedies of Shakespeare.

It concerns two pairs of lovers each divided by Fate and the story is of their relationship as, escaping from bondage, two of them, Climene and Egisto, return to reclaim their old loves, Clori and Lidio, who by now are involved with each other. Jealousy and revenge spurred on by the machinations of Venus and her mischievous son, Cupid, bring near tragedy before resolution and, for Egisto, a distraction that results in a magnificent mad-scene, the first in all opera. The gods, who play a considerable part in the action, finally relent and, as in Shakespeare's *Cymbeline*, alll is resolved in a masque with Egisto restored to sanity and his beloved Clori while Lidio and Climene are also re-united. There is a wonderfully funny comic part for a nurse, sung by a tenor, and throughout the opera some of the most beautifuly melodic and recitative music Cavalli ever penned.

Notes on the realisations and their performance

A. GENERAL PRACTICE

1. In these realisations I have preserved the original note values and would urge anyone performing the operas of early seventeenth-century Italy to make sure the edition they use does the same. There are those in which note values have been halved or quartered with the aim of making some sort of common time unit. Nothing could be more muddling or unhelpful. Such a practise ignores the original conventions of notation, very easily assimilated, that were based on an assumption of a faster speed for white notes than for black and a proportional relationship between the two. It also explains why tempo directions are virtually never seen in scores of the period: they were implicit in the notation.

2. I have, however, devised a notational convention which has proved useful. While not changing note values I have given the time-signature C to the music in recitative whose bars are also often of unequal length. When the music moves into a regular pulse the meter is indicated by the appropriate modern time-signature.

3. Performance of the recitative music should above all be directed towards expressing the true emotional and dramatic context of the words. The recitatives should be not be thought of as being in a regular pulse throughout. Singers should be encouraged to lengthen or shorten the notes, especially at the ends of phrases as the emotional and dramatic situation suggests. In my experience it will prove more convincing if there is, nevertheless, an underlying rhythm within the separate phrases. I have found it very helpful to suggest to singers that they think variously and appropriately in minims or crotchet pulses changing sometimes

smoothly, sometimes abruptly from one to the other within the same sentence. Generally it is best to avoid slowing down at cadences. It tends to stop the opera and either you or someone else has to pick it up and get it moving again.

Good performance of this sort of recitative depends largely on an appreciation of the difference between rhythm and tempo.

4. (This note is primarily intended for the conductor.) Virtually all the recitative music, indicated by the time-signature C, is accompanied only by the continuo groups. I have found that the most efficient method of directing the recitatives is to indicate changes of bass note with the right hand (so that the cello and bass continuo players may easily follow) and with the left hand indicate the entries and embellishments by the rest of the continuo, which also helps to maintain rhythm for the singers. The singers in turn must have been so rehearsed that they can perform the recitative music without being conducted yet with the sort of controlled freedom that will allow them to respond to such gestures as the conductor makes.

A feature of the recitative music is its occasional use of a regular meter for a phrase or two. These passages may be best conducted in the normal way. In general, however, the gentler the hand of the conductor towards both singer and continuo the better the performance.

5. A notational device which appears in the separate continuo parts as well as the vocal scores seeks to differentiate between runs and rolled or spread chords which take up a definite amount of time and those which do not. Both are indicated by cue-size notes in the Faber editions.

The difference occurs when a bar is incomplete without these small notes, in which case the player should allow that specific amount of time for them to be played. Where the bar is already complete, the small notes are to be played freely and generally as fast as possible taking the music on to the next chord or beat. In either case they should be played with appropriate fantasy as if the player himself had thought of them.

6. Opera companies who have not tackled this style of music should pay careful attention to the schedule of orchestral rehearsals.

The main body of strings will need considerably less rehearsal than most operas require. The whole continuo section, however, will only function well if it has rehearsed a great deal with the singers and can enter into the dramatic expression of the music alongside them. The lutes, harp, harpsichords, organ and the cellos and basses who play with them will need much more time than the strings and should, if possible, play for most of the later stage rehearsals long before the normal orchestral rehearsals for a production usually begin.

B. L'ORMINDO

1. The part of Ormindo was originally written in the alto clef, but it lies too low for a twentieth-century male alto (and sometimes too high for a tenor). Seventeenth-century Venetian opera manuscripts provide such extensive evidence for the transposition of parts that no particular details need here to be given of those that have been made in L'Ormindo.

2. I have not included a section in the final scene which shows Ormindo to be, unexpectedly, the son of the King he has cuckolded. As Ariadeno comes to see the bodies of the young lovers he has condemned, a letter is read at great length explaining the peculiar intricacies of affairs and intrigues by which the true father remained ignorant of his son's existence. In my view this ruins the dramatic tension of the scene. It is no less probable and much better theater tacitly to allow the audience to believe it is conscience which moves the King to repent his vindictiveness. I have inserted a *sinfonia,* originally in Act I of the opera, to enable the King to react in this way before singing "*Io sono umano al fine*".

3. In Act I, Scene 5, I have extended the triple-time material of the duet "*Auree trecce inanellate*", which peters out in the original after a few bars.

4. At the end of Act I, where Ormindo and Erisbe elope, a duet begins to the words "*De' nostri abeti*". The manuscript breaks off and I have interpolated a duet from *La Virtu degli Strali d' Amore,* composed by Cavalli in 1642.

5. The spell "*Huat, hanat, Ista, Domiabo damnautra*" is my own invention, designed to enhance the fantastic aspect of the three "fortunetellers". The words of the spell were discovered by Miss Ena Mitchell. They are from the seventeenth century and were originally designed to cure a broken leg.

6. At the end of the opera I have adapted the repeat of Ormindo and Erisbe's duet as a quintet for all the characters left on stage. Many of Cavalli's operas have concluding ensembles, notably *Xerses* (a quartet),

L'Eritrea (a quartet), *L'Orimonte* (a trio), and *La Doriclea* (a quartet). The original duet ending is also included in the vocal score for use if it should be preferred.

7. Cavalli rarely wrote out string accompaniments for arias (he used, initially, manuscript paper with usually only ten staves) but sufficient examples of arias with continuous five-part string accompaniment exist—there are particularly beautiful ones in *L'Egisto* (1642), *La Doriclea* (1645) and *Muzio Scevola* (1665) to warrant adopting the practice occasionally in *L'Ormindo*.

8. The opera was originally in three acts. The printed libretto includes a Prologue, no music for which has survived.

9. Most of the solo comic scenes were clearly designed by Cavalli and Faustini to cover scene changes. (Notably Act I, Scenes 2, 4, and 6 and Act II, Scenes 1 and 3.) No specific scenic directions have been given for these. At the 1967 production in Glyndebourne they were played before dropcloths. The solo scene for Miranda (Act I, Scene 4) was played before a gauze so that Scene 5 could follow without a break.

10. All tempo and dynamic indications are editorial.

11. Distinction must be made by all performers between the sections indicated by the time signature C and those by the numerical time signatures 4/4, 6/2, 4/2 etc. The former is intended by the editor to designate those sections in *stile recitativo* in which singers must be free to lengthen or shorten notes as the drmatic situation suggests. It is essential that an underlying rhythm be felt throughout this recitative; but the unit of these sections is not the bar but the phrase, and the underlying rhythm from phrase to phrase will and should vary. It has proved useful in practice to conceive such variations by altering the unit of pulse from crochet to minim, or even to semibreve. An understanding of the difference between rhythm and tempo is essential to the successful performance of this recitative music.

Rameau's *Dardanus* (1739 & 1744)

[Introduction and preface to the published edition, Faber Music Ltd.]

In 1980 I was invited to prepare and conduct an edition of Rameau's *Dardanus* for the Paris Opéra. I had already recorded and performed in concert extended excerpts from it, and from others of his ballets and operas, finding him unquestionably one of the last truly distinguished eighteenth-century composers whose music for the theater is still largely unknown.

The preparation of the edition provided a most stimulating challenge to creative scholarship. Alas, bringing it to musical life in France proved to be one of the most miserable experiences of my career!

We had a wonderful cast who suffered almost as much as I did, and I have told elsewhere[8] of the ill-prepared flights of pretentious imagination perpetrated by director and designer. The only bonus, apart from spending two months in Paris, was working at the Palais Garnier which with the Colon in Buenos Aires and the Scala in Milan must rank as *the* most beautiful opera houses in the world.

Bernard Lefort was director of the Opéra and seemed to have about as much control of it as the captain of a sinking ship which, as rehearsals proceeded, the institution increasingly resembled. He commanded little respect and was known as "*L'Ombre sans Femme*", a wicked French pun on the Strauss opera *La Femme sans Ombre [Frau ohne Schatten]* which was currently being massacred there.

The whole place was over-staffed, union-ridden and totally devoid of corporate pride or enthusiasm. The threat of *grèves* (strikes) hung around like poison gas in the trenches, and soured almost every activity.

The music staff had little understanding or sympathy for their native eighteenth-century music and resented any attempt to inculcate a sense of style as a slur upon their own abilities. The orchestra had the most elaborate deputy system I have yet encountered. Rarely were more than

---

8   See pp. 165-168, below. (Ed.)

thirty per cent of the players the same at any two consecutive rehearsals or performances, and it was clear they were not about to tackle the problems of playing Rameau in any stylish way at all seriously.

Eventually, some sort of performance took place, and the production was even repeated the following year, and was recorded by Erato. But my own memories are filled with regret at what might have been.

Faber Music published my edition, to which the following is a preface:

*

The preparation of a performing edition of Rameau's *Dardanus* is beset by a multitude of problems. Apart from the many variants and alternative versions of much of the music, the opera was drastically re-written for its second major revival in 1744, and for each of the subsequent revivals considerable changes were made by Rameau in his lifetime and by others after his death, although these do not come into our consideration.

As Professor Girdlestone wrote in his important study of Rameau, "It is deplorable that so much life and beauty should lie unknown and one wonders whether a modern version, based on that of 1744 but incorporating some of the best parts from the earlier score, could not be put together".[9] That, basically, was the premise on which I have based the preparation of this edition.

Dardanus was the third and, arguably, the greatest of Rameau's six *Tragédies en musique*. It was first performed in November 1739.

Operatic audiences in Paris at that time were caught up in the controversy between those who supported what they believed was the traditional opera of France and those who claimed that Italian opera was superior. The argument was a sterile one and little understood by most of those who became involved in it. People abused or praised this or that opera mainly because it was in Italian or French. There were, it is true, two musical styles but they were not at all as separate as people declared them to be. Rameau used both even though his musical language was predominantly French, especially in its ornamentation which is super-

---

9   Cuthbert Girdlestone, *Jean Philippe Rameau: His Life and Work* (Dover Publications, 1969).

imposed upon the melodic line instead of being derived through the Italianate principle of "division".

The following example illustrates the difference between the French and Italian styles:

Dardanus, naturally enough, came in for both the highest praise and the sharpest criticism and, although it was successful enough in its first season to run for twenty-six performances, for the second revival in 1744 Rameau entirely reconstructed the last three of its five acts as well as making his habitual revisions and recomposition of certain parts of the first two. This was, I believe, due less to public criticism than to his own dissatisfaction with the opera's dramatic shape. He abandoned virtually the whole plot of the original after Act II and substituted the capture of Dardanus by his enemies, leading to a wonderful prison scene which

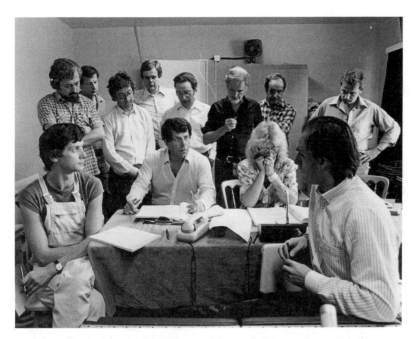

Recording session at Erato's London studios. Rameau's *Dardanus* was recorded by Erato in 1981, with a cast featuring Frederica von Stade, Christiane Eda-Pierre, Georges Gautier, Michaël Devlin, Roger Soyer and José van Dam, with the Chorus and Orchestra of the National Theater of Paris (Erato STU 71416).

CREDIT: Colin Busby, London

makes, so to speak, a low ebb to the hero's fortunes from which, by the magic of Isménor and Vénus, he is able to rise again and by his own heroism not only humble his rival, Anténor, but also gain the hand of his beloved Iphise.

Nevertheless, the reworking was not all pure gain and apart from the magnificent music for the prison scene, the release by Vénus and the slaying of the monster, there are some drab patches. Moreover, in the first 1739 version, there were sections, like the dream scene, containing some of Rameau's greatest music whose exclusion is virtually unthinkable. Professor Girdlestone's conjected mixture of the two versions, it becomes increasingly clear, is the correct method to prepare an edition for our own time.

While I would not claim to have found the only solution, I have found a way to produce a version of the opera with a dramatic structure which makes theatrical sense in terms of the ebb and flow of tension and relaxation, while preserving most of the best music from both versions.

Ballet in the *Tragédies en musique* was for the most part incidental to the drama as opposed to the *Opéra-Ballets* where it was an integral part of the structure and action. It is still highly important, for the visual delights of dancing have always been dear to the French and the divertissement in celebration of Dardanus' capture is a fine example of this important element in French eighteenth-century opera. I have there, and in other places, cut down the quantity of dances as well as the final danced *chaconne* which Rameau himself cut in 1744, and put in its place a chorus of praise for Vénus and Love which seems much more suitable as the conclusion of a predominantly vocal evening.

The prologue has been cut completely following Rameau's own example in the 1744 version.

Separately I hope to publish the best of the instrumental music that has had to be omitted in the interest of keeping the work within lengths acceptable to contemporary audiences. Subsequent performances may then add or substitute as much of it as they see fit.

I have written out all the ornaments (often indicated in the original by a small cross +) except the trills which should always begin on the upper note. All ornaments should be played on the beat unless they are included within a slur when they should precede the beat.

I have adopted the principle of indicating the recitative passages by name and have modernised Rameau's highly individual notation into a constant crochet unit and the number of these is indicated as the bars change by a single figure. The metric music is indicated in the normal way with the original notation.

I have proposed that the orchestra include at least four oboes and four bassoons although nowhere in the score do the bassoons ever play in more than two parts and only once do the oboes play in three. Contemporary engravings show that this doubling was common practice and, apart from saving the players from total exhaustion, when they play all together the sound is most impressive and characteristic.

I have not been consistent in the use of French or Italian tempo indications — but then neither was Rameau!

3

THE OPERA ORCHESTRA[11]

Unless he be born an opera buff, the orchestral musician tends, at least at the beginning of his professional life, to regard the prospect of playing in the pit with apprehension, even scorn. It isn't that there aren't endless interesting and exacting things to play in opera, or a wide spectrum of music to enjoy. It's the thought of being stuck down there out of sight amid the dust and debris beneath the stage, with the added dangerous possibility of things dropping down on you from time to time. It's the knowledge that most people out there in the audience have come mainly to hear the singers and see the production. The orchestra, when noticed at all, comes third in their consideration, and that's no bright prospect for a young, idealistic violinist setting out on a career.

The reality of it is strangely different. If you look at a good, well-established opera orchestra, you will find a group of players who are truly devoted to this somewhat specialized, exclusive form of music-making, and most of them, having come to the sure knowledge that they are happiest and most fulfilled where they are, would do nothing else.

Musicians in opera orchestras share certain characteristics peculiar to their calling. There is a sort of freemasonry among them, probably occasioned by the close proximity and companionship in which they play, closer by far than even the most integrated of symphony orchestras. In the confined space below the stage, they have to learn how to cope with each other on good days and bad; in temper and out of it; through good shows and bad; with each other's family problems and domestic arrangements. They are, too, among the most uxorious of musicians, for tem-

---

11   From David Hamilton, ed., *The Metropolitan Opera Encyclopedia: A Comprehensive Guide to the World of Opera* (Simon & Schuster/ Metropolitan Opera Guild, 1987), pp 262-63.

porary internal inconstancies can be wretched with a whole opera season ahead of you.

The most distinctive characteristic of all is the way they come to know their operas so very well—better, it must be said, than some who conduct them. Collectively, they are much better judges of singing than their audience, because performing with singers gives an element of tangible experience to their judgment. You can't follow a dozen Rodolfos around a dozen *Bohèmes* without learning a good deal about the human voice and the art of singing. In doing this, players also develop a flair for ensemble that is not always so evident among their colleagues in the world of the symphony orchestra. It is wonderful to hear them following the vagaries of a Faust or a Don Giovanni, breathing when the singer does, holding notes, rushing some, cradling the voice with tone and dynamics that anticipate and support without hindering. They may even think nothing of the singing, but pride in their own professional skills will make them follow even to the very brink of their respective abysses.

That skill is properly theirs—not something the conductor, however skillful and sensitive, can accomplish by himself. He can help (he can even get in the way), but he can't really integrate the voices and instruments without the special musical sensitivities of the experienced opera orchestra. It might even be said that sometimes the orchestra makes better, if less spectactular music than those on stage. Top C's are one thing and, though the canary fanciers love them, fairly silly in themselves; but a beautifully executed finale—say, to Act II of *Figaro* or *Falstaff*—by the orchestra is at an altogether different level of music-making, which, complemented by a fine ensemble of distinguished singers in a well-thought, well-rehearsed production, represents the reason why opera is such an irresistible lure to most serious musicians.

Opera orchestras, while not resenting the obscurity of their position in the pit or their third place in the pecking order when it comes to applause, do nevertheless have a constant and perhaps not unwarranted concern that some of the difficulties under which they work are not sufficiently appreciated. It is not a question of salary, for in general they are well and equitably paid. The problem comes from something the general public is scarcely aware of. Opera was never intended for repertory performance. It was conceived as a festival art form, which is to say that each work needs to be rehearsed intensively on its own, played for a number of reasonably consecutive performances, and then abandoned until such time as the process can be repeated. Performing a different opera each night puts a tremendous strain on stage and singers, and especially on the resources of the orchestra.

To rehearse a succession of operas during the day and perform others at night as the schedule dictates, with different singers, different conductors, and no real sequence of concentration, makes terrifying demands. Moreover, in simple terms of hours, there is much more work than one orchestra can encompass. So what the public thinks of as the opera orchestra is in fact at least an orchestra and a half. The organizing of the players' schedule is a horrendously difficult task, approaching the complexity of three-dimensional chess, and the man who does it is usually something of a saint and something of a double-dealer at the same time. The problems seem, and sometimes are, insoluble, and opera orchestras have reason to complain that from time to time the repertory schedule hinders them from giving their best and forces lower standards upon them. They hate it, and resent the fact that they are sometimes unfairly blamed for circumstances out of their control.

In this most dangerous of all art forms, so many elements are involved: acting, dancing, directing, designing, singing, and playing; so many things to go wrong. The miracle is that it succeeds as often as it does. When it does and a masterpiece is brought to vivid, sentient life, to be a part of it, on or behind or under the stage, is an exhilarating experience, the like of which is to be found nowhere else in art.

That's why the opera orchestra is there.

4

UNEXPLORED RELATIONSHIPS
BETWEEN EARLY 17TH-CENTURY VENETIAN OPERA AND CONTEMPORARY MUSIC IN FRANCE AND ENGLAND

I am very sensible to the honour of being asked to deliver the British Academy's forty-first Italian Lecture.[11] But it would be dishonest if I did not at once say that no musician can at present speak of his art in the period that I have chosen without experiencing a profound sense of inadequacy. Compared with parallel studies in the other arts the scant availability of texts and the paucity of worthwhile critical work would be laughable were it not so frustrating and shaming. We have – but only in very recent years – virtually complete editions of Monteverdi, Lully, and Purcell; composers who have been ranked in our art with men like Rubens, Poussin, and Wren. If, however, we look further afield – and not to do so would seem to make our assessments of the three I have mentioned rest mainly on historical hearsay – we find ourselves with a list of composers we know to have been distinguished and successful in their generation but whose work is still but dimly known even to someone who has been passionately involved in the music of the seventeenth century for over twenty years. Of course, the time-scale in musical research holds us back. At least a painting or a building is there to be examined. A single musical manuscript may take weeks of deciphering before any sort of proper assessment of its content can be started. But the fact remains that at present only a few isolated works are generally known of men like Rossi, Landi, Mazzocchi, Cavalli, Cesti, Legrenzi, Pallavicino, Cambert, Charpentier, Campra, Matthew Locke, Pelham Humfrey – to mention but some of the more obvious names. We can for the most part only guess the quality and scope of the main body of their work which still waits in obscurity on library shelves all over Europe.

---

11   1969 British Academy Italian Lecture, read 5 March. From the *Proceedings of the British Academy*, Vol LX (London: Oxford University Press), 1969.

The reason lies in the fact that only in the last sixty years has the seventeenth century been considered a worthwhile subject for musical research. At first, like most of our historical studies, it was viewed as a confirmation of the idea of Progress. And it is significant that Sir Hubert Parry, a man deeply committed to that concept, was invited in 1905 to undertake the third volume of the *Oxford History of Music*, one of the earliest modern studies of the period. For him the seventeenth century could only be regarded as a stepping stone to later and better things. It is perhaps fortunate that he was not asked to prepare an earlier volume where the air of lofty, if compassionate, disdain would have been even more pronounced. As it is the views expressed in his preface to the volume indicate accurately a widely held attitude towards seventeenth-century music.

> The Seventeenth Century is, musically, almost a blank....But this is by no means owing to neglect of the Art, or lack of musical energy and enterprise. There was fully as much activity in musical production throughout the century as at other times: and lovers of the Art were quite under the impression that the music of their time would compare favourably with that of other times, and impress those that came after as much as it impressed themselves; the event proved itself singularly short lived and intrinsically most of it seems to casual observers little better than an archaeological curiosity....
>
> It is interesting to seek for the reasons of its appearing adequate to the people of its time, while it appears so slender and inadequate to those that come after: and it is suggestive of essential but rarely comprehended facts in relation to the very nature of Art...to trace the manner in which the slenderest beginnings manifested during the century, served as the foundations of all the most important and comprehensive forms of Modern Art.

The idea of Progress is now generally discredited and we have come to see that the seventeenth century has something to offer in its own right. Indeed, after the ecclesiastically orientated music of the late Renaissance in which the classical ideas of balance and order were pursued to the exclusion of any attempt at emotive, personal expressiveness, the wave of new music which broke over Italy, and subsequently over Europe, in the early years of the century swept all else aside and brought in a wonderful era, one which the editors of the New Oxford History of Music have aptly called the Age of Humanism.

The desire to make music express the human condition, to reflect man's emotions rather than imitate the order of God's Universe, manifested itself in one particular tendency and one particular fact which are especially relevant to the present subject. The most effective medium for conveying emotion in musical terms is the human voice, and, more specifically the solo human voice allied to expressive poetry. There was therefore a tendency for vocal music to become separated from instrumental music in a way that it had never done before. It assumed a more exalted position and most composers concerned with the new spirit in music wrote almost exclusively for it. The tendency resulted in the fact of opera — one of the few facts about any musical form which have some definite point in time. And opera, especially Venetian opera, became the siege-engine with which the new spirit broke down all musical barriers and influenced all musical styles.

I can say nothing here of the expressive nature of this music save that from the beginning it succeeded in what it set out to do and that we, in our time, can now comprehend this and recognize its effect. But there were certain rapid changes in the form after the first experimental works in Florence and Mantua which are relevant to its later influence in France and England. Opera began as a courtly entertainment both because the facilities in the way of theater, singers, and instrumentalists were all there ready for use and also because the courts tended to be the center of the activities of the various *Accademias*, societies of learning and discussion, somewhat akin to the British Academy, where new ideas would not only flourish but receive intellectual and social backing sufficient, in this case, to see them enacted.

Courtly entertainments of necessity must owe something to the Princely head who foots the bill and even if only by way of a flattering prologue or a general masque-like concluding dance the form will be restricted and inhibited. It is easy to imagine further and more stringent restrictions should the Prince decide to take a large part in the proceedings. (Carl Philip Emmanuel Bach's frustration and irritation at trying to write music for Frederick the Great's somewhat haphazard and erratic flute give a later but none the less vivid illustration of this. A singing Prince might prove a still worse hazard.)

The influence of the classically minded *Accademias* can also be seen in the choice of subject. Pastoral dramas such as Guarini's *Il pastor fido*, or Tasso's *Aminta*, as well as the classical legends of Dafne or Orfeo, were the obvious choice for a new form which, in theory, contrived to claim classical authority for its justification. It was soon found, however, that these subjects are not ideal for the expression of human emotions simply because the characters expressing them are not humanly identifiable. They certainly become involved in deeply moving situations, but this is only half-way towards realizing the intention behind the spirit of the new music. For it to have a chance of making its full effect we must know *who* it is that has become involved in the situation, and one only has to try to describe the character of Orpheus in words to realize that he has none. He is the embodiment of all that is beautiful and good (with, perhaps, the one slight flaw of over-riding curiosity), but he is not a person to be identified in human terms. It is not just for religious reasons that an opera on the life of Christ would be an unthinkable undertaking.

These initially inhibiting influences were overcome in a spectacularly successful way when opera, so to speak, fell on its feet in Venice where state control, combined with liberal-minded aristocratic patronage, enabled it to turn, in the best sense, professional. No other society could, or ever did, provide the freedom and security for such development. Nor could any other society at that time have attracted so great a galaxy of talented men to use the form to such freely expressive ends.

The changes were immediately apparent. Heroes and heroines like Nero and Poppea, Ulysses and Penelope, Dido and Aeneas, Paris and Helen involved listeners in their human dramas to an extent which had never before been conceived. The conditions of performance became standardized and set the pattern for all potential imitators. Theaters were built and equipped to similar design: the orchestra was no longer made up of every available court musician but established as consisting of continuo and strings, and the cast only consisted of those who would contribute in some way to the drama. Within a few years of the opening of the first public opera house in Venice in 1637 the form became famous throughout Europe. Evelyn in 1645 called it "doubtless one of the most magnificent and expensive diversions the wit of man can invent". It would seem reasonable to expect that with that sort of reputation opera could quite simply cross all the international barriers and become part of the musical life of every European country. In a sense it did, but no country, except perhaps Germany, took kindly to a complete foreign importation, and in France it was used as a political instrument becoming the centre of intrigue and controversy at every sort of level. That it strongly influenced French music has always been recognized, but what has never been sufficiently explored is the degree to which the opera in France, when it finally got under way, was in its debt and to what extent French taste changed or blunted its impact.

The political aspect need concern us only marginally. After Louis XIII's death in 1643 Cardinal Mazarin, joint Regent during the minority of Louis XIV with the Queen Mother, Anne of Austria, was active in introducing Italian opera at the French court, partly to keep the Queen happy (for she had become inordinately fond of Italian music) and partly to maintain contact with the Medici and Barberini families at Florence and Rome.

The first work to be imported, in December 1645, was scarcely an opera at all. It was called a *festa teatrale* and entitled *La finta pazza* and was dressed by Giulio Strozzi, the son of Piero Strozzi who was one of the original Florentine Camerata—the group who made the first experiments in *le nuove musiche*. The music was by one Sacrati whose name and music have vanished with the piece itself. It must have been a work close in style to the early Florentine intermezzi with little of the dramatic impact we now associate with early seventeenth-century Italian opera. To judge from contemporary accounts it was notable for its decor and eccentric ballets; one of which was for ostriches attempting to drink at a fountain. Madame de Motteville, that invaluable and indefatigable chronicler of court life, was unimpressed. "Those who know," she wrote, "think highly of the Italians; for me, I find that the length of the spectacle sharply diminishes the pleasure." In the seclusion of the Palais Royal, during the following year a performance, probably of a work unstaged, entitled *L'Egisto* took place. It may possibly have been Cavalli's opera of the same name first produced in Venice in 1643 and then performed in Paris in what we now call a concert version for the Queen's pleasure. However this may be, it incurred Madame de Motteville's displeasure. She records in her diary that "On Shrove Tuesday (1646) the Queen had performed one of her comedies in music in the little room of the Palais Royal. We were but twenty or thirty people and thought we would die of either cold or boredom."

We only know of a few isolated occasions when opera was sung in this intimate domestic setting, but then Madame de Motteville would surely not be invited to every occasion and her somewhat deprecating reference to "one of the Queen's comedies in music" would seem to signify that these musical occasions were fairly numerous, sufficient at any rate to create a climate of opinion about the new music. Mazarin and Anne of Austria were unpopular both at court and in Paris so that nothing they sponsored, even in the artistic field, was likely to meet with much general approval. When Rossi's L'Orfeo was given to a much larger audience in Paris in 1647 the general response can be judged from a malicious little verse which changes the opera's title from Orpheus to Morpheus.

But the enthusiasms of Queens of France are not so easily dampened and troups of Italian actors and singers were often to be seen and heard at court. Their influence on French musicians was very slight, and the French people much preferred the comedy-ballets of Molière for which the young Lully, also imported from Florence, was soon to write dances and to dance himself.

Most of the music performed for the Queen seems to have come from the Roman and Florentine operas, works which persisted in the Pastoral tradition which I spoke of earlier. And it was in this tradition that the first attempt at French opera was made by Pierre Perrin and Robert Cambert in 1659. Indeed the work was called La Pastorale.

Perrin was an immodest and untalented poet who saw and took his chance of success in writing simple verses designed for music. Cambert, a pupil of the great harpsichordist Chambonnières, had a growing reputation as a composer and eventually was appointed "maistre et compositeur de musique de la Reyne Mère."

We are fortunate in having a contemporary account of the first performance by Père Ménestrière in a book he published in 1681 entitled *Des Représentations en musique anciennes et modernes*. He began the section on *La Pastorale* by expounding the problems of setting the French language to music—a point which was argued for another 150 years. "Until this time," he writes, "it was always thought that our language was not capable of furnishing proper subjects for these operas, because in our theaters we had grown used to hearing nothing but Alexandrines which are more suitable for grand declamation than for singing. However, M. Perrin, having often written words for songs which our best composers set, perceived that our language was capable of expressing the most moving passions and tender sentiments, and that if one mixed a little the manner of Italian music with our style of singing one could produce something which was neither one nor the other, and yet more agreeable than both. For there are many people who cannot stand the swaggerings (*rengorgements*) of Italian music."

Ménestrière here puts his finger on what was perhaps the major obstacle to the success of Italian opera in France. French taste in the seventeenth century was as fastidious as it is now and the overt expressiveness of Italian opera was too strong, too direct for comfort. And we shall see that when Lully adapted Venetian opera for Paris the same need to veneer over the emotions was a prime cause for the changes that he made in the form.

Ménestrière goes on the describe *La Pastorale* in terms which remind one of accounts of the early Florentine intermezzi. The cast consisted of a Satyr, three Shepherds, and three Shepherdesses. Their various alarms and excursions during five short acts before finally resolving their amatory problems can have been of only minimal dramatic interest.

But the piece had a considerable success. It was performed ten times at Issy, a suburb of Paris, in the house of a Monsieur de la Haye. The King heard of it and commanded that it should be performed at Vincennes before the court. Ménestrière observes that "the Cardinal Mazarin, who has a taste for these representations...praised the poet, the composer and the actors giving his word that he would call on them to produce other similar works."

This he did, but they were to have a very difficult time of it due to the malicious machinations of Jean-Baptiste Lully whose ambitions lay in the same direction and whose jealous temperament would allow no rival to stand in his way.

Meanwhile, in the following year, 1660, at the announcement of Louis XIV's forthcoming marriage to Maria Theresa, Infanta of Spain and niece to the Queen, Mazarin arranged a visit of Francesco Cavalli, the leading composer of Venetian opera and the man who perhaps above all others was responsible for its international reputation. Cavalli was reluctant to undertake the long, arduous journey to Paris, but considerable pressure was brought to bear on him and finally he agreed. He set out, taking with him the score of *Xerse*, an opera he had already produced in Venice in 1654, and with the agreement to compose a new opera for the wedding festivities on the subject of Hercules in Love. (Hercules, of course, representing the young King.)

This was probably the first occasion that opera in the latest Venetian style would have been heard in Paris, and although it met with little popular success there can be no doubt that it demonstrated to Lully a power and potential in the form which he could not have seen in any of the other Italianate importations.

Lully came to know both *Xerse* and *Ercole amante* intimately, for he directed and provided music for the *entrées de ballets* which were added to each work for the festive occasion. I believe he learned a good deal from each of them. *Xerse* is a characteristically passionate Venetian piece, concerned with jealousy and rivalry. (Incidentally Handel set virtually the whole libretto, by Nicolò Minato, nearly one hundred years later, and it is fascinating to compare the two works, not least the setting of the opening lyric *"Ombra mai fù"*.) Cavalli's opera abundantly demonstrates his particular gifts for expressive recitative and he rarely, if ever, wrote more moving arias and laments. The comic scenes, too, are of an exceptionally high standard. All this Lully must have heard and noted.

Ercole amante is an altogether different piece and quite exceptional even for Cavalli. It is conceived more in the spirit of a court masque than a Venetian opera and, responding to the grandeur of the occasion, the composer wrote large, extended double choruses in almost every scene. They are rhythmically exciting and doubtless served as a vehicle for some of Lully's dances besides giving him ideas for similar effects in his own operas later on.

The dramatic action is slow moving and even Cavalli could not produce much of characterization for the stock Gods and Goddesses who go out of their way to make the course of Hercules' love run smoothly.

One cannot imagine that he felt very happy with this, to him, old-fashioned court opera style and he certainly felt less happy still after its failure to please. His main supporter Mazarin died in the year before its production and the young Lully ran off with all the praise for his ballets when the work was finally performed. To judge from his subsequent behaviour to Perrin and Cambert Lully most probably made life very difficult for Cavalli during the work's preparation and the poor man returned to Italy in a highly depressed state, writing to Venice to say that after that experience he would compose no more operas.

But, failures or not, these two works showed the French, and especially Lully, what opera could be like. Before he could show his paces, however, Lully had to dispose of Perrin and Cambert who were more than one step ahead of him. This he finally did by acts of Machiavellian malice that cause one a shock even at the distance of three hundred years.

Perrin obtained a Royal Licence for opera from Louis XIV in June 1669. The terms of it make interesting reading. Perrin was given the privilege of establishing, throughout France, Academies of Opera, for the presentation of opera in the French language after the model of those in Italy. The activities of the various Italian *Accademias* in Rome, Venice, and other courts of Italy are noted and Perrin is commanded to follow their example with the special purpose of putting on operas. The King hopes that not only will these operas contribute to our diversion and that of the public but that our subjects will become used to the taste of this music and gradually come to perfect themselves in this, "one of the most noble of the liberal arts". Perrin was allowed to charge admission, except to members of the court, and to permit any gentleman or lady to sing without fear of their losing dignity by doing so. (This was of course in direct contrast to the "comédies récitées" of Molière whose actors were not socially *convenable*.)

Perrin set up first in Paris at a converted *Jeu de paume* — Royal tennis court — and produced various works there mostly in the old-fashioned style of *La Pastorale* of 1659. But neither Perrin nor Cambert were adept business men and the Academy soon incurred sizeable debts. Lully's in-

Sante Fe Opera, New Mexico

Summer in Santa Fe, 1976 – RL and production photos for *L'Egisto* featuring Linn Maxwell, Ellen Shade, James Bowman and Jerold Norman; *The Mother of Us All* featuring Mignon Dunn, Ashley Putnam and James Atherton

Recording sessions for *The Mother of Us All* — New World Records

Friends for life... RL, Ashley Putnam – Santa Fe

Glyndebourne from the air (from Spike Hughes' *Glyndebourne: A History of the Festival Opera* — CREDIT: Guy Gravett)

1962 Glyndebourne premiere of *L'incoronazione di Poppea* in RL version – featuring Magda Laszlo (Poppea), Richard Lewis (Nerone), Carlo Cava (Seneca), Oralia Dominguez (Arnalta), John Pritchard cond. (CREDIT: Guy Gravett)

LEFT: Peter Hall (foreground) learns from Benjamin Luxon how to string Ulysses's bow – 1972 Glyndebourne production of *Il ritorno d'Ulisse* in RL vers. (from Spike Hughes' *Glyndebourne: A History of the Festival Opera* – CREDIT: Guy Gravett). *RIGHT:* Hugues Cuénod, from 1964 program book of the Festival of the City of London

Glyndebourne 1975, *The Cunning Little Vixen* in rehearsal.
Left to right: RL, George Christie, Jonathan Miller (from Spike Hughes'
Glyndebourne: A History of the Festival Opera – CREDIT: Guy Gravett)

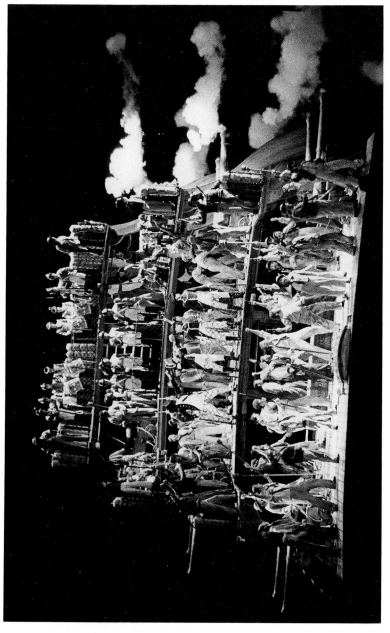

At the Metropolitan Opera, Lincoln Center: *Billy Budd*
CREDIT: Victor Parker, 1978

Geneva, 1978: *Iphegénie en Tauride*
CREDIT: Roland Aeschlimann

terference and scheming did not assist matters, so that by 1672 the King had to shut the theater. Perrin was imprisoned for debt and in March of that year Lully was given the Royal Licence. He had meanwhile to dispose of other rivals, the poet Guichard, and a rich influential amateur composer Jean de Granouilhet who had managed to get an opera entitled *Les amours de Diane et d'Endymion* put on before the King at Versailles in 1671. This he did by accusing Guichard of poisoning him, and he may well have tried to do so from all the evidence that came to light at the trial. Guichard at any rate was convicted and imprisoned. Through his influence with Colbert, Minister of State, Lully managed to get a protest made by Granouilhet in the Paris *Parlement* against Lully's patent quashed and from that moment he was, so to speak, master of all he surveyed. He stayed in charge, without a rival in sight, for fifteen years composing some twenty operas which, without their being much heard in modern times, have come to be regarded as the great classical foundation of French opera.

He certainly produced what the French court wanted, but I wonder if it is not time for a critical reappraisal of his work in the light of the operas of men like Cavalli and Cesti which are only now emerging from an obscurity more dim than those of Lully. I believe that we shall find that he had very little dramatic ability; that his greatly extolled recitatif is nothing much more than a pale imitation of his Italian contemporaries; that his melodies rarely rise above the trivial; and that he was a plagiarist with a nice touch for dance tunes scarcely any of which can compare in vitality or originality with the hundreds of marvellous dances composed by his younger English contemporary, Henry Purcell.

I would like to spend a little time discussing his first opera *Cadmus et Hermione* written in 1673 to a libretto by Quinault. It is difficult to make musical points without illustration, but I can, I hope, convey something of what I mean by analogy and description.

The work begins with a lengthy prologue, in four scenes, taking up a quarter of the opera's length, in which the serpent Python born in the bowels of the earth terrifies the sylvan gods and is finally slain by the Sun who descends on a chariot. It was intended, as were all Lully's subsequent prologues, to be a compliment to the King. A prologue was the

usual curtain-raiser to all Italian operas, but it was always brief and usually, like the good and the bad fairy in pantomime, prepared you in some
measure for the drama ahead. Lully's prologue has virtually no
preparatory dramatic purpose. There is, it is true, a dragon to be slain in
Cadmus, but it cannot be said to be good opera construction to anticipate
the climax of the plot by killing another dragon in the prologue. Of
course, it will be argued that he had to conform to the social pressures of
the court. But this is just what hindered the development of Italian opera
and I do not see that a special case can be made for saying that it improves
Lully's.

The choral writing is homophonic and rhythmic, very similar in style
to that found in Rossi's *L'Orfeo* or Carissimi's oratorios. When Envy
comes to conjure up the serpent she does so in a chirpy C major which
pales into nothing compared to Medea's incantation scene in Cavalli's
Giasone of 1649 or Purcell's witches in *Dido and Aeneas*, written only sixteen years after *Cadmus*. I only give these comparisons by way of illustration. I could equally well say that Envy's incantation could happily be
sung by any shepherdess calling her sheep.

The triple-time melodies have a strong Italianate flavour, using
familiar cadential formulae extended by sequences in a way that is commonly found in Cavalli's melodies of this type. There is, too, the occasional use of the flattened seventh of the scale played in close proximity
to the leading note. This was a device used by Monteverdi for especially expressive moments and later absorbed into the general technical ap-
paratus of the time, giving a certain piquancy to the harmony.

The story of the opera is based on the familiar legend of Cadmus res-
cuing Hermione from the Giant; killing the dragon which guards her,
sowing the dragon's teeth from which spring up armed men. These fight
among themselves, somewhat reducing their number, before coming to
the aid of Cadmus in his fight with the giant. To complicate matters Juno
appears to warn him off and Pallas Athene to encourage him forward.
Amor appears at one point to cheer up Hermione by making a group of
statues dance. And finally Jupiter comes down to sort it all out.

This use of Gods and Goddesses, who do little or nothing to affect the
dramatic action, seems to me frivolous catering to a debased taste. One
only has to think of the visions in Monteverdi's *L'incoronazione di Poppea*

of Pallas to warn Seneca that he must die if he interferes on the part of the Empress Ottavia, or the intervention of Amor to save Poppea from being stabbed by Ottone, to see how such devices can be used to point the drama and heighten the tension. An even better example might be Monteverdi's *Ritorno d'Ulisse* where the hero is caught between two opposing deities: Neptune who wishes to stop him from returning to Penelope and Minerva who wishes to help. Their struggle for power over Ulysses mounts throughout the opera in parallel with the tension of Penelope's increasingly desperate attempts to ward off the attentions of the three false suitors. The tension is only resolved in the last scenes where Ulysses finally returns to Ithaca and destroys his enemies. This it seems to me is a proper dramatic use of such devices. There are two comic characters in *Cadmus* who come straight from the stock of Venetian opera, but they are sadly under-developed; an old nurse who spends a little time admonishing Hermione in characteristic fashion and at one point expresses some disappointed sentiments about the other comic character, Arbas, an African servant of Cadmus. There is little dramatic point in her being there at all; neither does she justify herself by being amusing. Lully provides her with no solo comic scene. The African servant has one amusing scene where he is scared by the corpse of the slain dragon and has a notion to claim the kill for himself. But even this cannot compare with similar moments in Venetian opera. There is in fact an almost identical scene with a dragon, much better done, in Cavalli's *L'Orimonte* (1650). The diversions in Lully's opera are all superimposed from outside the drama and the most trivial excuse is made for a ballet of Africans, Statues, Soldiers, and *Sacrificateurs*.

The main drama has to hobble along in between these moments and sundry irrelevant apparitions, and only at one point, where Cadmus alone laments his lost Hermione — (she has been whisked away by Juno who is irritated by the hero for slaying the giant) — does the music rise to any high level of emotional expressiveness. It is a lament constructed exactly after the Venetian pattern with a beautiful, twice-recurring phrase *"Belle Hermione, hélas puise-je être heureux sans vous"* each time separated by a fine line of expressive recitative. Had Lully managed to maintain this standard my view of the piece would be altogether different. But as a drama revealing in any exalted sense the ideals of using music for expressive, humanistic ends it cannot possibly be regarded as aught but a failure. Were we to hear it again I suspect that like Madame de Motterville *"nous pensâmes y mourir de froid et d'ennui."* As it is, the opera is an uneasy mixture of the masque and early Italian pastoral drama to which, in the name of modernity, a few mannerisms of Venetian opera have been added. The poor dramatic construction is disguised by much incidental and irrelevant dancing—some of it to delightful music.

I have left very little time to say anything about the relationship between English music and Italian opera of the period. And perhaps it is just as well, for I believe that we are on the brink of finding out a hitherto unsuspected closeness and directness of influence.

Only three years ago a copy of Cavalli's *L'Erismena* was discovered in this country decked out with, of all things, a contemporary English translation. The translation of a long opera libretto is not something anyone would undertake without an end in view and yet we have, up to now, no evidence of a performance. There is a manuscript copy of another Cavalli opera *Il Giasone* in the music faculty library at Oxford. In the latest issue of *Music and Letters* the handwriting of the famous large collection of Italian monodies, Add.32.440, has been identified as belonging to Angelo Notari, an Italian musician who spent most of his life in England.

When you begin to assemble the names of Italian musicians to be found in Pepys's diaries you find yourself with a formidable list of men whose work is still for the most part unknown, but who could not but have brought something with them, something of the Italian atmosphere—and that would mean above all else the atmosphere of Italian opera. Two English composers, at least, went to Italy to study. Walter Porter with Monteverdi, Pelham Humfrey mainly with Lully in France, but he was financed by Charles II also to go to Italy. The masque of *Calisto*, performed in the Hall Theatre in 1675 has a libretto which has more than a superficial resemblance to that of Cavalli's *La Calisto* produced in Venice thirty years earlier. Most of the music for the time has now disappeared save for some seven rather paltry little songs by the ubiquitous Nicholas Staggins, later first and least distinguished professor of music at Cambridge.

There is that strange licence written in Italian and given by Charles II, dated 20 October 1660, to Giulio Gentileschi to present in London *"opere musicalic on macchine, mutationi di scene—senza essere da alcuno impedito et molestato."* The licence was to last five years and Gentileschi was to produce in that time only operas. No one yet knows what happened either to the operas or to Gentileschi. The ill-fated Cambert ended up in England and, while not much of a catch, certainly contributes something to the picture with his production of *Ariadne* in 1674 at the New Drury Lane theater, and possibly earlier at Whitehall.

Evelyn saw an Italian opera in music, "the first that has been seen in England of this kind" on 5 January 1673.

Commentators have always havered over the reference by Purcell (or was it Playford?) in the preface to his Sonatas in III Parts in 1683 to the "just imitation of the most famed Italian masters principally to bring the seriousness and gravity of that sort of musik into vogue and reputation among our contrymen whose humour 'tis time now, should begin to loath the levity and balladry of our neighbours." And after apologizing for his own inadequacy (quite unnecessarily) he "thinks he may warrantably affirm that he is not mistaken in the power of the Italian notes or the elegancy of their compositions, which he would recommend to the English Artists."

It has usually been assumed that Purcell was referring to similar sonatas imported from Italy, but a moment's consideration will show that there were scarcely any Italian string sonatas. He may well have known those of Vitali and he certainly knew the work of Lelio Colista, but he speaks in general terms of italian music and that country still produced almost exclusively vocal music in the operatic style. He speaks of the music's seriousness, gravity, and power, all adjectives which apply more to Italian opera than to such instrumental compositions as he would have known.

There is one other fascinating reference to Italian music contained in Purcell's additions to Playford's *Introduction to the Skill of Music,* written in 1694, where, on the subject of ground basses, he commends the Dividing Ground, that is the bass with divisions and transpositions, an elaboration of which he was especially fond, and observes that the Italians were the first inventors of it to "single songs or songs of two parts which to do neatly requires considerable pains, and the best way to be acquainted with them is to score much and chuse the best Authors." It should be stressed that this time vocal music is specified.

This sort of ground bass, of which Monteverdi was perhaps the first expondent, was developed by Cavalli into a major musical form. Every opera contains several examples of it encompassing all sorts of emotions and characterized not by a short pattern of notes repeated constantly but by a long melodic bass which serves to support on each repetition a new vocal melodic line. The resemblance between Cavalli and Purcell's methods in the use of this type of bass is most striking.

This must be, for the present, mostly conjecture. But I am convinced that as more and more texts of Italian opera, and especially of those originating in Venice, come to be more widely known we shall see how greatly all European styles of the later seventeenth century are in their debt and how direct was the influence of this remarkable music of the Age of Humanism.

5

OPERA PERFORMANCE AND REPERTORY:
A RECONSIDERATION (1993)

I don't think I would be very interested any more in accepting an invitation to conduct opera unless I were involved in the whole project from the beginning, long before the period of production and music calls begins. It's too chancy. Preparing and performing opera takes a huge chunk out of one's life and you have to be sure it's likely to be one of the more rewarding and not one of the more frustrating of activities before you begin.

Even after months of deliberations, planning meetings, casting and auditions, the rehearsals take at least four or five weeks intensive work with singers who should already know their notes; with sets and props sufficiently far along to be used and the general style and approach to be agreed by all those responsible for the end result. Without all of this, I, at least, might just as well stay at home, for the weeks ahead are almost certain to be fraught with tensions and conflicting opinions over matters that should have been settled already. There's quite enough to do other-wise, getting everyone to focus on what the opera's really about.

— I Suppose Glyndebourne (with Which
the Present Chapter Began) Spoiled Me —

I remember in the early preparation of Monteverdi's *Il ritorno d'Ulisse*, the last of the seventeenth-century Italian operas I realized for them there, the seemingly endless discussions John Bury, Peter Hall and I had about the archery scene where the returned Ulysses, disguised as a beg-gar, proves to be the only one able to draw the hero's great bow with which he then slays the suitors who have nearly overwhelmed Penelope's constancy and taken her and his island kingdom, Ithaca, for themselves.

Drawing the bow was easy enough but how to shoot the suitors and their followers was another matter. For weeks various solutions were ex-amined, tried out and rejected; arrows on wires, pop-up arrows on the targets, human or otherwise, projections of shadows, flashing beams of light, smoke and screams — there were many others.

I can't remember who it was, probably one of the Bury children during a coffee-break, but someone said, "Why don't you teach Ben (Luxon, who sang Ulysses) archery?"

Well, of course. But imagine coming to rehearsals without that having been decided. The tensions and time wasted have by now absorbed so much energy which should have been focused on shaping the overall performance.

Sad to relate, this sort of thing happens all too often in the ordinary run of opera productions, especially in America where there is a breed of opera managers who like to play, variously, surrogate stage-director, conductor, scene designer and casting director with the result that the entire company frequently meets for the first time only at the beginning of the final run of rehearsals. Four weeks full of surprises.

Why, you may ask, should the music director be involved in such things as stage design and direction?

There are always technical problems for both the stage and the musicians (not all concerned with archery) that have to be agreed or you court later disaster. A Café Momus designed only for Musetta's entrance with the main part of the café, so to speak, in the audience may be a nice idea, but it leads to impossible problems for the chorus who then have to spend their time in the street outside peering in—which isn't at all what they sing about. Sad to relate this actually happened in Glyndebourne when Michael Redgrave was directing *Bohème* and, for once, whoever was conducting wasn't included in the early discussions, or didn't notice.

The finale to Act II of Figaro present such rigorous problems of musical ensemble that a director with original intentions as to plotting it has to be most carefully watched or things will become too perilous, musically speaking.

There are in many operas possibilities of cuts or repetitions that make them more telling in a particular theater, but it would be no good for a director to count on them if the music won't allow.

Of far greater importance is the presence from the beginning of another concerned, informed voice in the discussions of style and meaning that are crucial to the way things eventually turn out.

As for that archery scene, Ben proved an apt and accurate toxophilite. With carefully choreographed arrows whizzing across the stage all around the motionless figure of Janet Baker, our first Penelope, lit from above by a single shaft of light amid all the carnage, it turned out to be one of the most powerful moments I've ever witnessed in the theater. So well directed and rehearsed was it that no one in two seasons of performances was ever hurt. There is, I'm glad to say, a commercial video of it all but nothing could substitute for the reality of the theater.

It's worth while examining why this sort of approach to opera is so exceptional. Almost all the reasons reflect to some extent the perennial struggle in this world between God and Mammon, but there are human factors that make them more interesting than that and, perhaps, more amenable to correction.

Singers are sometimes reluctant to spend the sort of time necessary to achieve great musical theater. Instant opera put together in two or three days in old sets with your own costumes is more lucrative and you reach a larger, more frequent public that way. Even established Repertory opera is sometimes little better than the instant variety especially where revivals of old productions are concerned. I remember a dress-rehearsal, possibly the only dress rehearsal of a *Rigoletto* at San Francisco in grim, futuristic scenery with a black rubber floor onto which stepped Joan Sutherland as Gilda holding a pink muff and dressed in a crinoline that would have done very well in *Quality Street.* It brought the house down at the rehearsal but the performances were sold out and all was left unchanged. I rather think there was even some approving critical talk about theater of alienation.

Some singers are clearly dominated by vanity, greed and self-concern. The worst of them come to see their rôles only as a means of creating an impression that will further their careers, regardless of those around them or the opera they are supposed to be interpreting.

Of course the very best do *not* behave in this way and usually show an impressive awareness of the power of their voices when combined with intelligent direction. That's when the miracle of opera can leave you breathless. The fusion of words, movement and music at that level has a power that almost no other art form can equal.

Audiences must also accept some responsibility for the undermining of operatic standards. A certain percentage will always show more concern for the quality of the voices they hear than the overall performance and effect of the work they are listening to.

At their worst they resemble nothing so much as a collection of canary-fanciers screaming themselves hoarse over the latest song-birds whom they are only too ready to consign to the bottom of the cage once the best of their trilling is over. They talk of old records, old divas, rare operas, present operatic scandals, past disasters, every thing that is peripheral and they make wearisome intermission companions. Because of the amount of noise they make, the tickets and recordings they buy have a sadly corroding effect. It's hard for managers to resist pandering to their enthusiasms and harder still for singers to resist the adulation. The real danger comes when both sides come to believe it. All the same, opera would not flourish as well without them, the darling Dodos of music.

Far more insidious is the influence of certain designers and directors, those, usually, whose talents have been found insufficient for success in the straight theater. What they lack in integrity and real theatrical skills they make up for in nerve and ego which can sometimes con the world of opera into thinking they have something valuable and visionary to contribute. Manon played as a bisexual motel-owner; the *Magic Flute* on a race track; *Fidelio* in a space ship. If you go far enough out you really don't have to bother about the original text of the opera at all: and some idiots will believe you.

While not ill-disposed towards experiment, for wild ideas are often the beginning of something wonderful, I find the best people abandon them when they don't work. Not everyone has that degree of self-discipline.

I remember Jean-Pierre Ponnelle came up with an interesting thesis about the *Flying Dutchman*. He conjectured that the whole story after the arrival of Daland's ship, in the opening scene, takes place as part of the steersman's dream.

The steersman, a nice small part for an up-and-coming tenor, is, in Wagner, ordered by his captain to keep watch while the crew are sent below to rest after their storm-ridden journey. He has no name, is of no evident importance and plays virtually no further part in the rest of the opera. But he does fall asleep at the wheel while the ghostly ship of the Dutchman sails in unseen out of the storm. That's where the idea comes from. Of course he could have dreamt it all and it gave Ponnelle the basis for his production; on the face of it a highly imaginative conception.

It even works for the encounter between the Dutchman and Daland who comes up on deck and invites the sinister stranger to his home where his daughter, Senta, awaits him.

From this point on however we get into much deeper water, for in the next scene Senta, her old nurse and the village maidens are singing a chorus at home while they spin, a fine activity for the women-folk when their men are at sea.

Ponnelle could simply have abandoned the steersman by his wheel at this point, changed the set to that of a suitable room and continued on from there. But in order to make a point and pursue the concept of the dream, he put all the ladies on the deck of Daland's ship where symbolic steering wheels made to resemble the spinning variety sprang up all over the place and the spinners, looking like a coven of witches, used their cheerful music to weave yarn until the stage began to resemble a spider's web in a horror movie.

From then on things became very tangled indeed, for everything was bound to happen within the narrow confines of the ship and its strange little cabin in the poop which glowed red as the Dutchman came closer to his fate. There was no redemption, no cliff from which Senta could make the ultimate sacrifice, no final vision of the Dutchman free at last from his earthly torment; only the snores of the steersman who found himself with one of the longest and dullest parts in operatic history.

A wise director would have abandoned things before they had gone too far to turn back from an idea that was poetic to begin with, but which could finally only distort the opera's intentions.

The dogged adherence to half-thought-out decorative ideas which only damage the work they are meant to serve is characteristic of a certain breed. There was one *Falstaff* (at Glyndebourne, I regret to say—nowhere is perfect) where an irritating little boy popped up at every turn through the floorboards, in the garden and from out the branches in Hermes' oak, making it very difficult to concentrate on what else was going on. The boy it seems was intended to reveal that Falstaff was obsessed with his own youth—"*Quando erà paggio*"—"when I was a page"—and this became the main theme of the opera, which it most certainly is not.

When I hear at early discussions about a new production such phrases as "I see the work as Tiepolo" or "We should do it all in bathing costumes to reveal..." a chill takes hold of my heart. It may lead to good things but, like as not, it is the director lapsing into decorative whimsey and to be avoided like the plague.

One of the worst experiences of my conducting life was with Rameau's *Dardanus* at the Paris Opera, a wonderful work whose music I had edited with great care and enthusiasm.[12]

Jorge Lavelli, a celebrated French director, arrived with supporting entourage having scarcely given the work a moment's detailed thought,

---

12   See pp. 138-143, above. (Ed.)

or so it seemed. I suppose he must have discussed some ideas with Max Bignens, the designer, but what they were remained forever arcane. The result was a collection of set designs and costumes that had no more to do with eighteenth century French music than Marilyn Monroe with Mother Theresa. They appeared to be the product of subconscious artistic meanderings. Whatever their merits in abstract, in reality they were impractical, ludicrous to those who came to see a representation of Rameau and impossible for the singers to relate to the text they were singing or the actions of the plot. The stage direction was of the same order.

I had not been invited to any earlier discussions and was foolish enough not to have protested. I was even more foolish to have stayed on for four weeks of rehearsal knowing all the time we were heading for disaster. Such is the conflict of commitment and principle. An excellent cast was involved including Frederica von Stade, Christiane Eda-Pierre, Eric Tappy, José Van Dam, all friends whom it was difficult to abandon. All the same I wish principle had won, for it was an agonizing experience to witness a work you believed in being so irresponsibly destroyed.

One set resembled a night club, literally a *boîte de nuit*, a huge, black, canvas-lined box lit by thousands of electric light bulbs implanted in the walls and ceiling. Those that fused were infrequently replaced by idle stage-hands so that it always looked a fairly shoddy sort of place, hardly suited to the interaction of royal personages in heroic drama.

Then there were the flying *songes* — dreams — imperfectly designed and inadequately rehearsed technically so that there were frequent mid-air collisions and squeaks of terror punctuating the delectable music Rameau had written, as well as scaring the poor singers (and conductor) to death.

The organization of the Paris Opera was fraught with internal and Union disputes which hampered preparation at every turn. One quite incompetent *répéteur* was appointed to play the chamber organ which he proved incapable of doing. There was no changing him without provoking a general strike (I should have left at that point but, once more, commitment proved stronger than principle) and we arrived at a late dress rehearsal with a beautifully simple aria sung by Frederica von Stade which had been consistently underminded by fumbled wrong notes and inept registration wrecked once again. It was the last straw and, uncharacteristically, I lost my temper and shotued. "*Arrêtez!* Stop! *Monsieur* (to the organist) *vous êtes un con*" — which is about as rude as one can get. *Grand silence.* But as the shock waves subsided there was heard the gently considered opinion of a double-bass continuo player to his cello continuo neighbor: "*C'est vrai ce qu'il a dit*" (it's quite right, what he said). General collapse. It was a lost cause thereafter; the organ played on and never got it right.

The orchestra replaced itself continually for rehearsals and performances. Deputising in France is a custom that has obtained since professional orchestras began there in the early nineteenth century. Berlioz complained of it as have all subsequent conductors. It shows, I suppose, a certain *indépendence d'esprit* but does little for musical standards in that otherwise quite wonderful country.

There is always a clown in a French orchestra and ours was a tall viola player who had an unassailable confidence in his power over women and his instrument, both evidently misplaced but, in a way, endearing until you had to deal with it. He discovered in one aria that an accompanying figure for the violas would translate into a rhumba rhythm, amusing enough at rehearsal. When he employed this effect at every performance with attendant shuffles of approval from his colleagues in the section (and an occasional modest bow of acknowledgement from the perpetrator), the joke wore thin. I felt sad that so chauvinistic a people should take such little trouble over their own music. Rameau was too simple, too ingenuous for them to take seriously and his directness of expression was, somehow, an affront to their sophistication.

The climax of *Dardanus* comes towards the end when the hero saves his rival, Anténor, from destruction by killing the marauding sea-monster which has ravished his country's shores and, in doing so, becomes the undisputed winner of the heroine's hand in marriage.

The monster was represented by a huge, black plastic bag which when inflated by air-machines, would billow out from the back of the stage in menacing fashion. It wasn't a stupid idea, given the abstract look of the whole, but nobody had seen to it that it would work in any consistent fashion. The music was drowned by the air-machines and the billowing was most uncertain. The hero, sword in hand, would occasionally disappear from sight as the monster advanced downstage and had to slash his way out in order to sing. The valiant thrusts of his blade naturally enough frequently pierced the plastic which held up fairly well for a single performance but had to be patched before the next. The plastic strips used for the reparation were usually of a different color so that the monster soon came to look like an advertisement for band-aid and caused great merriment in the audience. The director and designer had left by this time and were presumably wreaking havoc elsewhere.

At least it provided some light-hearted moments in a run of performances that were otherwise extremely distressing. It should have been a wonderful evening in the theater and a proper tribute to a great French composer, but, through the efforts of an absurdly pretentious designer and director, it did more harm than good and left a scar on my psyche that can be seen to this day.

Most of my other experiences in opera have been much more agreeable and rewarding even if not always in an unqualified way or at the level of those at Glyndebourne. As I now realize, it has always depended on the people with whom I worked and, generally, I've been blessed with good fortune.

Even my first major opera at Covent Garden, Handel's *Samson* produced for the Handel bi-centenary in 1959 with Herbert Graf directing, was a joyful time. The style of production belonged to an earlier era when stage oratorio was popular (an early edition of Grove's dictionary contains a delightful cartoon of robust northern choristers with checked trousers and black boots showing under white flowing garments cheerfully impersonating Israelites awaiting rain in *Elijah*). Out of date *Samson* may have been, but with sumptuous sets by Oliver Messel in which the choristers could both take part in the action and act as a Greek chorus, the production conveyed with great visual strength the power of Handel's work. Jon Vickers was a remarkable Samson and Joan Carlyle, looking wonderfully seductive, sang Dalilah beautifully only losing out at the end to Joan Sutherland as a nameless Israelite woman singing "Let the bright seraphim" with a stunning cadenza ending in a high "d" that brought the house down every night.

I was still fairly young and have to thank David Webster, then manager of the Garden, for giving me the opportunity. It worked well because all three responsible for the final production met often and were in agreement as to how it should be done before we started rehearsing.

Covent Garden asked me back to do revivals of *Figaro, Così* and *Giovanni* but soon the return to Cambridge as a University lecturer broke the link. I seemed to everyone at that time to have opted for an academic career and to have turned my back on the profession whereas I had really hoped to show that the two ways of life were not incompatible, indeed that they could benefit and support each other.

It was a hope that I do not now believe possible to be realized. The academic way is one of caution and restraint for fear of error, while the performance of music demands total commitment, a disciplined, fearless abandonment to its content once understood. The two are in direct opposition to each other beyond hope of reconciliation.

By the time I had accepted this disappointment and left once more the academic groves where I had wandered happily in my undergraduate days, I was labelled as an old-music specialist and unsuited for Grand Opera. The fact that I had already come to some adverse conclusions about the worth-whileness of operatic revivals and was already enjoying the beginnings of my involvement with Glyndebourne made me realize I was not missing so much. Grand Opera as it was practiced in the Repertory houses was not for me, a view reinforced by my links with the Royal Shakespeare Theatre at Stratford during Peter Hall's directorship.

Peter was a contemporary of mine at Cambridge and I wrote music for several of his productions there as well as for his first ventures into the Bard's own theater on the banks of the Avon. When he took over Stratford he asked me to help him reorganize the theater's music which previously had been provided by a small salon orchestra in the pit from whence songs in the plays were mysteriously accompanied as if by magic sprites equally adept at providing fanfares and music for the necessary cues as well as pretty tunes for the interval tea-trays.

We removed the pit and made all the music come from the new, apron stage as part of the play with the musicians often appearing on it in costume; something that seems so obvious now but was then quite revolutionary and caused a good deal of consternation and upset. The tea-trays were unaccompanied and the National Anthem sounded rather strange on a combination of instruments made up of such as might have been called for at the Globe Theatre in 1590. As for musicians acting, well, eventually they did it, were good at it and enjoyed it. But they grumbled at first.

I stayed on as music advisor during Peter Hall's years there (and mine back at Cambridge—which wasn't far, cross country) appointing good music directors and selecting composers for the various plays. I bless those years: for working with people like Peter Brook, Peter Wood, Glen Byam Shaw, to say nothing of actors like Dottie Tutin, Peggy Ashcroft, Edith Evans, Olivier and Gielgud—indeed almost everyone in the British Theater—gave me invaluable insight into how theater could be made more effective and powerful by seeking out the meaning of a text without the intrusion of individual egos pursuing only their own satisfaction, tho' we all had them and not always in perfect control.

There is an inner truth in any artistic creation worth bringing to life which, once discovered, will illuminate the whole endeavor of performing a given piece within the circumstances, place and time that happen to present themselves. You may seek out such a truth only by the most intense concentration on the work itself, by the application of all your skills of analysis, training and education until you know (for that time) what it is. The illumination comes from within not from without and it can never be feigned, not to yourself. Once it is clear (and from that moment only) should you proceed to work out how to realize the perception with any certainty and authority.

This is, I discovered, as true of music as of theater.

Another rewarding operatic experience was in Geneva with Gluck's *Iphigénie en Tauride*. It has always been surprising to me that a composer who had such tremendous success in his life-time and was so much admired by his peers has now such a limited public appeal, particularly when he still commands the greatest respect from present-day practitioners of music theater. Apart from *Orpheus*, none of Gluck's operas is likely to engage the box-office in overtime. In my early days at Glyndebourne I rehearsed but did not conduct an *Alceste* which Ebert directed extremely well in suitably classical sets by Hugh Casson. Magda Laszlo played the heroine and Richard Lewis her expiring husband brought back to life by the miraculous power of sacrificial love. More recently I conducted it at City Opera, New York, with Heather Harper singing Alceste wonderfully well in a somewhat abstract but not untrue or dishonest production, all of it under-rehearsed.

The *Iphigénie* at Geneva had beautiful sets by Roland Aeschlimann, a good cast, adequate direction and one very funny moment in rehearsal.

There is in the opera the very small part of the Goddess Diana who, *dea ex machina*, appears at the end to save the lives of Orestes, Pylades and Iphigénie from the marauding Scythians — in French, *Scythes*. There was no need for her to move from her pilastser to utter her few phrases that bring a timely resolution to the plot, so I agreed that a Rumanian (or was it Bulgarian?) soprano with attested voice (who was also an intimate friend of the general manager) should come in at the last minute from whichever of those beyond-the-iron-curtain countries she inhabited. After all, what could go wrong with a few lines sung by a dramatic soprano on the top of a column?

She arrived later than planned and only just in time for the final dress rehearsal for which she had not yet even had a costume fitting. I saw to it that she was rehearsed separately by one of the music staff and was assured that she knew the notes, no French but was musically secure.

The rehearsal went extremely well and in the last moments of the opera Diana duly appeared on her plinth dressed in a severely cut, rather tight travelling suit and sang quite incomprehensibly her first phrase "*Arrêtez...* etc.", admonishing the invaders to cease their agression. The next word, however, *Scythes*, she pronounced in a way that was universally understandable, "*Sch..tt*," and very loudly. The Scythian invasion of Tauris ceased forthwith and a whole stage-full of people, not to speak of the orchestra, conductor and all those present in the house collapsed with a shriek of laughter the like of which I've never heard before nor since. Of course the rehearsal stopped and we called it a day since we were only two or three pages from the end. Every performance perceptibly quivered when we arrived at that moment.

There were two other operatic ventures associated with my Monteverdi/Cavalli years in England, apart from Glyndebourne.

Ben Britten in 1958 invited me to realise Monteverdi's one-act *Il ballo delle Ingrate*, a rather precious little work whose moral that women should give their favors to men instead of forever making themselves look more and more beautiful was rather wasted on the Aldeburgh audiences of the time. Pluto's lengthy strophic address on the subject didn't help much, savoring as it did more of an Anglican sermon than an encouragement to licentiousness. There is at the end, however, a wonderful farewell of one of the ungrateful ladies consigned by him for her lack of generosity to everlasting torment and a ballet which Johnny Cranko choreographed most beautifully. There were attractive sets by John Piper but the work received scant attention from Aldeburgh, its audience or the press, perhaps quite understandably. It was, nevertheless, good experience and the people whose opinions I respected liked it and were encouraging.

Of much greater moment was the preparation of Monteverdi's *L'Orfeo* for Sadler's Wells in 1964 at the Cambridge Festival, a task I greatly enjoyed. It may not be the most overtly involving of his stage-works but it was the first truly successful opera ever written, with deeply expressive declamation of the Italian language, a synthesis of music and words, notes and syllables that has, perhaps, never been surpassed. Later the composer evidently found it didn't have to be that perfectly arranged to be effective but it's a joy to sense the detail of it in the earlier piece much as Stravinsky's setting of Auden's English in *The Rake's Progress* makes the language more vivid and the meaning more acute in our own time.

Consideration of the intimate response of the music to the words made for a precedent at Sadler's Wells. We played it in Italian whereas previously, I think even by charter, they had sung everything in English. The Board made an exception for *L'Orfeo* when we demonstrated to them that the text is virtually untranslatable without adding or cutting notes, changing vocal rhythms and altering the music whose strength depends on its perfect welding to the Italian.

The sets and costumes by Yolande Sonnabend kept the work in a sort of pastoral No Man's Land and Frank Hauser directed it well and simply.

The stars of the evening, apart from Monteverdi and his librettist Alessandro Striggio, were John Wakefield and Patricia Kern. Johnny was a natural singer (and had too brief a career on that account) with a rare and wonderful gift for the stage. It's very hard to make Orpheus an interesting character; he's too good with no faults. Like Parsifal he can easily turn out to be a fool, a saintly bore. John had a beauty and magnetism on stage that made your heart go out to him in his quest for Euridice. Pat Kern, one of the unsung great artists of English opera at the end of the war, was amazing in the great scene of the messenger. Her description of Euridice's encounter with the snake, the slow fading into death and her own loving compassion for Orfeo's loss was utterly mesmerising. No one I've heard since, no matter how "authoritative", has come near the controlled power of that narration unless it be, perhaps, Janet Baker's soliloquy at the beginning of *Ulisse*.

— Santa Fe Opera[13] —

Of all the opera houses in America, Santa Fe comes closest to the Glyndebourne ideal. If John Crosby, its founder and artistic director, did not actually model his *modus operandi* on the Sussex system he must surely have been thinking from the start along the lines of the man whose in initials he shares (Glyndebourne's John Christie).

He asked me to prepare a Cavalli opera for him in 1974. I knew there were two more that I felt confident would come to life again three hundred years after they had first appeared. I chose *L'Egisto* but, sensing an obligation to Glyndebourne for whom I had already produced realizations of two Monteverdi and two Cavalli operas, first offered it to them. They felt the vein of early seventeenth-century Italian opera had been sufficiently mined so I felt free to offer it to Crosby.

It turned out to be the most successful opera, certainly one of the best of Cavalli's I'd resurrected. There was an excellent collaboration with director John Cox and a splendid cast who absorbed the style of the music like blotting paper. It sold out and was repeated with equal success two seasons later. I found it heart-warming to have this early music that I loved so much appreciated in a new place and to know that it connected so vividly with American audiences in the New World after three centuries of neglect in the old.

Santa Fe is in one of the most magical parts of America. Already at seven thousand feet it is surrounded by mountains that rise another four

---

13   See also photos following page 154. (Ed.)

or five above that. The climate is wonderful, if a little breathless until you get used to it. Singers can't manage such long phrases as in other places but are otherwise less prone to minor ailments. The beauty of the skies, the amazingly dramatic weather, violent storms interspersed with long periods of dry sun make it a desert paradise. The fact that it is an hour's drive from the nearest main airport protects it from the casual tripper and the tourists who do come tend to go round and round the central Plaza or take bus trips to Taos and leave the rest unspoiled. The opera is a few miles north of Santa Fe where the opera company lives round about in rented houses creating its own small society amid the local inhabitants in much the same way as at Glyndebourne.

In some ways it is less satisfactory. The opera house itself, being half open to the skies, loses perhaps more than it gains on that account. It can be expremely cold at night and the bugs and the rain are hazards not infrequently encountered. The sound tends to escape at the edges into the dusk in spite of an ingeniously designed roof over the stage and another reaching out to it from the back of the auditorium. There are no stage wings and the openness of it all restricts rather than unleashes the designer although operas that can end with a night sky as back-cloth have an incredible advantage, for out of the unencumbered back of the stage there is a vista of over eighty miles where electric storms in the distant mountains can enhance a final curtain in spectacular fashion. Storms that come close drive the orchestra to the back of the pit while the audience huddles at the back of the auditorium but, all the same, Crosby has created a very particular place which he oversees brilliantly in every detail. Over several years I've had some very good times there conducting *The Rake's Progress*, *Mother of Us All*, *Così*, the *Flute* and another Cavalli, *L'Orione*, prepared as a sequel to *L'Egisto*.

— The Met / Britten and Pears —

My single experience of conducting at the Met was a new production of Britten's *Billy Budd* which was taken on tour and then repeated the following season. It entered the repertoire but by the time of its third year the whole question of repertory opera was becoming a matter of great concern to me. The edges of *Billy Budd* were already becoming frayed and I had had enough.

The production was to me memorable for several things, not least the direction of John Dexter, a social misfit if ever there was one. We had known each other for a very long time, in fact since the days at the Royal Court Theatre, Sloane Square in London where he was one of the very bright, leftist theater people who gathered around John Osborne and William Devlin. I wrote music for a few of those productions; the best was for Middleton's *The Changeling* directed by Tony Richardson, another old friend whose life was sadly cut short recently by AIDS.

John paid great attention in the *Budd* rehearsals and his startling manners were soon generally understood to conceal a tender soul easily hurt and damaged. The opera he understood very well and, like Britten, could identify with all three main characters to a remarkable extent; Vere, Claggart and Billy. There were the amazing sets by Bill Dudley that moved up and down like an expanding telescope revealing at their greatest stretch four layers of deck which, peopled by cast and chorus, looked and sounded awesome. The cast was first-rate: Richard Stilwell as Billy, handsome and vulnerable; James Morris was Claggert, dark and sinister; Peter Pears played Captain Vere, the part written for him, a man who had to make the dreadful decision to have someone hanged whom he knew to be, at heart, innocent; someone who bore him no ill-will as he bowed to the dictates of naval law instead of the instincts of his own heart.

It was during the rehearsals and performances of *Budd* that, for the first time, I got to know Peter very well, Ben had died and he was terribly alone. He stayed with the very first Billy, now more or less retired, whose wife fought all the time a rear-guard action for her husband's fading career which wearied Peter, fond as he was of them both.

My relationship with both Ben and Peter had begun very well in the early fifties. That was for the *Ballo delle Ingrate* in 1958, but my turning to Glyndebourne was in Ben's mind a betrayal, an idea that it took years to dispel. Eventually we were all friends again, but together they were self-contained, as lovers should be, and even their visits to my rooms in Cambridge on the way from Aldeburgh to London didn't do much to break through the barriers between friendship and intimacy. Nor did I

mind for, much as I admired Ben as a musician, I felt ambivalent about
him as a person. I had picked up the pieces of a number of abandoned
friends who had given themselves unreservedly to a relationship that
turned out to be ruthlessly discarded; fine people who, in some obscure
way, he appeared to think had betrayed him. Peter, at his side, may have
seemed to others an untrustworthy *éminence grise* and may have taken a
good deal of the opprobrium directed at Ben; Peter probably was that,
but I believe he saw himself as the protector of a phenomenal talent in
someone he deeply loved. He was pained at times by Ben's behavior to
others, but could be equally ruthless in defending him from hurt.

At any rate, Peter alone was quite different. It was he, this time, who
seemed in need of protection and, for all his fastidious ways, he evidently preferred eating large hamburgers with me at Marell's, an old speak-
easy on Lexington Avenue to *fois-gras* at the Four Seasons. He came often
to my apartment on Park Avenue at 86th Street where we had long long,
quiet talks which I remember with real affection. There was in them much
that was trivial and nostalgic and Ben was, of course, a recurring theme,
for Peter's sense of loss was great. He spoke touchingly about how difficult it had been for them to live openly as a couple in the days during
and immediately after the war. For protection they had run to certain
corners of society where they knew they would find sympathy and support, led by people like Morgan Forster, Ackerly and, most powerfully,
by Auden and Isherwood who influenced their decision to go to America
in 1939. Those enclaves had their own ways and manners which ensured
their safety but kept them from being part of the rest of society. They
literally made their own exclusive camps and you had to subscribe to
belong, something they found increasingly constricting. It took some
years for them to realize that if they just lived their lives together with
discretion and care for the well-being of the society around them, therre
was no need for them to make any sort of public statement about their
relationship. They came to that and were thereafter accepted in every
sphere and at every level of society.

Peter's portrayal of Captain Vere seemd to reflect the restraint he and
Ben used to live their lives. He made it clear that it was containment of
emotion in public that let Vere to make his appallingly wrong decision.
When Jon Vickers, for example, sang the part you could only believe that

such an ox of a man was either a sadist or else unspeakably conformist to let naval law override his own sense of justice. With Pears it all became perfectly understandable and Billy's forgiveness part of unspoken love in the face of weakness. The epilogue in this way was heart-rending and the regret of the old man dreadful in its poignancy. The tremendous B-flat climax at the end speaks of this as only Ben could.

— Festival, Repertory and *Stagione* Systems for Presenting Opera —

Watching carefully nurtured standards decline in the second year revival of *Billy Budd* through lack of rehearsal and the general assumption that what had been first-rate a year before could be so again without much preparation, raised still more seriously the vexed questions which had long troubled me about the relative merits of Repertory as opposed to Festival opera or its first cousin, *Stagione* opera. I was made to concentrate on it the more soon afterwards when asked by Beverly Sills if I would consider becoming music director of City Opera in New York. I simply had then to face the problem, for my future professional happiness would depend on its resolution.

I made a survey of the main opera houses in America and discovered that over a period of six months, the Met performed an average of three and a half different operas a week, San Francisco a little less, Chicago Lyric below two and a half and Santa Fe, three. City Opera performed an average of more than six carrying the repertory idea to its furthest limits. While not terribly exact, the survey exposed the impossible strain Repertory opera imposes on artistic standards.

In most large cities public and economic pressure to have a Repertory system in opera is almost irresistible. The houses open between autumn and early summer and the repertoire is as large as the system will stand so as to attract the largest possible audience. In the Repertory system between three and six different works will be performed each week once the season is under way. In the *Stagione* system, one opera is prepared at a time and then run for as many performances as can be sold but, whereas in Repertory they are spread over the whole season, in *Stagione* they are run as closely together as possible in, maybe, two or three weeks while the next opera is in rehearsal which then, in due course, takes its place for its own run.

Festival opera works on much the same principal but, since the season is limited to the period of the Festival, the number of operas is smaller and there is usually some interleaving of performances and rehearsals giving singers more breathing space and the public more variety within the shorter period.

The differences may be most clearly illustrated by following the fortunes of a new production in the Repertory system.

For its first year it will take precedence in its four weeks of rehearsal and, in a good house, there will be adequate time for technical and lighting preparation. It will have first call on rehearsal rooms with director and conductor usually present and there will be the necessary costume fittings and parades while the sets and props are being made elsewhere and gradually incorporated into the daily schedule of rehearsals. Music-calls for singers and chorus reinforce the progress of the production and slowly the work and its interpretation begin to take shape. As soon as possible the stage is used with piano accompanying in the pit. The orchestra rehearses separately in its own rehearsal room prior to joining the cast in, first, one or two *Sitzprobe*, literally sitting rehearsals, of voices with orchestra to put the piece musically together before amalgamating the action and the technical aspects of the production. Finally it all comes together in a series of dress rehearsals where, if all goes well and things fit into place, everyone gets to sense the results of this frenetic month of varied activities. Miraculously, out of it all comes an opera.

That is how it is supposed to happen, and it takes all those people all that time focusing on one work in their different ways to achieve something which can be greater than the sum of its parts. It is one of the reasons why opera is such a risky business. When the rival claims of other operas being prepared and revived at the same time threaten the concentration and energies of those concerned, the risk factor grows exponentially depending on the number of operas involved.

To follow our opera, supposing it to have been a success, into its revival the next season is to witness something Gibbon noticed about the Roman Empire.

Not to deny the importance with which it is considered in a well-run

Repertory house, it will, nevertheless, not take precedence any more. That must now be accorded the season's novelties and our last year's prize-winner must this year become an also-ran. There will, probably, no longer be four weeks of rehearsal available in the schedule, so that any changes of cast (and they always occur) will be hard-pressed to learn even their moves on stage let alone achieve any real ensemble with their colleagues. Directors and conductors are frequently committed to pastures new and delegate at least the first rehearsals to their assistants who have been assisting in other things meanwhile and can hardly remember how it all went. It may be also that they are less talented and will not rehearse with the same intensity as the original people in charge. They certainly will not have the same vision.

Throughout the theater there is an underlying assumption tha the music and the production are somehow still in place after the intervening silence and months of other mind-engaging activities for most of the people concerned. The opera has been put carefully together once and, like a well-made suit, will surely fit the next time it is brought out of the closet. Those of us accustomed to diets and the need for them know this is not necessarily the case. As a result, revivals in Repertory have often an air of hasty alteration and adaptation to accommodate the new elements which removes them further and further from the thrust and dynamism of the first year. Even supposing all concerned are highly professional, gifted and experienced, standards are bound to slide and the theatrical vision become dimmed.

At this point, too, the factor of the number of performances becomes important. Given the extreme case of six different operas each week, a series of twelve *Figaros* will take all of three months to run its course. Few singers will commit themselves (few singers, that is, whom one wants to hear) to a contract that binds them to one place for one day each week over so long a period, making any other engagements in between virtually impossible to accept since most of them take more than a few days to complete. Inevitably, after the first two or three performances, the changes begin and individual parts are replaced, usually without any rehearsal at all beyond a costume fitting, a walk-through of the moves and perhaps a run-through with the conductor. It is certainly a measure of professionalism that all concerned manage, without mishap, to produce something out of the hat even if it does sometimes resemble a march hare more than a white rabbit.

Conductors may also be unwilling to commit themselves to so long an engagement and their place in Repertory opera is often taken after one or two performances by one of the music staff with aspirations to a conducting career. It can be a wonderful opportunity if the youngster has been working on the opera from the start, indeed it is the time-honored route for most of my colleagues and there is no better schooling. However too frequently in Repertory the assistant who takes over does so at the last minute with only his native wit to sustain him in conducting the performance of a production with which he has had very little previous acquaintance. Properly planned, as at Glyndebourne, to include orchestral rehearsal and music-calls with the cast, the transition from one conductor to another makes an ideal training ground and may indeed inject new vitality into a series of performances. In Repertory it usually lowers the general standard and warps any ideals the new man (or woman) may have had about this great art form and its execution. He or she may even come to believe it is the best way to learn and practice the art. It is not.

At yet another level of focus, imagine an orchestra coming into the pit to play *Figaro* on Monday, *Werther* on Tuesday, *Carmen* on Wednesday, *Wozzeck* on Thursday, *Tannhäuser* on Friday and a newly commissioned piece on Saturday. There may also be a matinee of one or another of those at some point during the week. There will certainly be rehearsals during the day of the other operas in production.

To expect any degree of stylistic variety or awareness in the playing is like trying to purchase the moon, for the players become musically schizoid by the middle of the season and, hard as they try, incapable of changing focus rapidly enough to recapture the vitality that each one of those operas achieved at its première. Such as schedule is, in any case, contractually impossible for one orchestra to play, so that Repertory operas use one and a half orchestras with a great deal of to-ing and fro-ing organized by the orchestra manager who soon becomes an expert in musical acrostics. There is no way it will work out exactly with the result that whoever plays *Werther* on the Tuesday of one week may well not be playing it on Thursday of the next.

The same sort of traumatic state is induced after a while in the chorus who begin to associate helmets with *Tannhäuser* and, if the sopranos look like cigarette girls, then it must be *Carmen*. The costume becomes the clue and (it is supposed) the music will follow — automatically.

That the best Repertory opera is as good as it is testifies to the skills of all those taking part. They live and work on a knife-edge of strained devotion and commitment to their art and to the company they serve. It is, nevertheless, as a system, second best. After the first performances, standards must inevitably decline. There may be an occasional evening when the original inspiration flares up again and a superb performance results, but these only serve to highlight the gradual falling off becauses of changes of cast, last minute substitutions, weary playing in the pit, ill-disciplined singing in the chorus, uncertain direction by surrogate conductors and general lack of oversight that must accompany so cruel a schedule.

Since its inception at the end of the sixteenth century, opera has always been the *poule de luxe* of the Arts. Combining music, theater and design all at the same time, it exercises in almost equal degree the talents of designers, stage directors, conductors, instrumental musicians and singing actors; a veritable army of talent which has to be brought together, paid for and organized into functioning with a single purpose. Small wonder great opera managers are not thick upon the ground. The time it takes to assemble the company, not to speak of the constant overseeing of its various parts, militates against its successful deployment especially within the Repertory system. The expense has to be reflected in the cost of tickets which makes it all the more suited to a Fetival situation or, in a lesser degree, to its first cousin in the *Stagione,* one at a time, opera theater.

— More Glyndebourne Anecdotes —

Glyndebourne, beginning as a rich man's dream, was lucky enough to involve two people, Adolph Busch and Carl Ebert, who saw there the possibility of realizing their own dreams of producing opera in almost ideal conditions with the means to impose upon it the highest standards without compromise. If there were tentative elements in the beginning they were very soon corrected and the standards have been vigilantly kept into the second generation and it still flourishes without State intervention in a country where virtually all the arts are subsidized and to some greater or lesser extent controlled by the government-appointed Arts Council. It's something of a miracle that it continues and a welcome re-affirmation that artistic values can be made to shine through the darkest gloom of bureaucratic society.

For those of us who, at one time or another, have been part of Glyndebourne the very name evokes particular memories and affections. The place is always evolving, and, since we as artists are as well, our ways may diverge perhaps never to coincide again, but when the contact was close and successful, there was the opportunity to make wonderful things happen in our various fields which have cast an unforgettable aura about our recollections of it.

The people who make up Glyndebourne at any one time are inextricably interwoven with the images.

When I was there first, old John Christie, the founder, was still alive. *Vecchio John*, that comfortable phrase in Verdi's *Falstaff*, brings him to mind, although he was only Falstaffian in an amiable rotundity. Gentle, sensitive with a great inner strength and determination, he had an obsession with pug-dogs and a habit of teasing people in very eccentric ways not always understood by the recipient of the tease. Around in his time—of which I only saw the end—were Jock the carpenter, in whom John had absolute faith—either Jock, or one of the pugs, had a solution to any problem that might arise; there was Rhona Byron, a gentle sustainer; Jani Strasser, a head coach to end them all; Irene, a head coach's wife to end them all; Moran Caplat who juggled everything and kept the ping-pong balls afloat on top of the fountain. He had served his apprenticeship as General Manager under Rudolf Bing who had preceded him there before going to the Met in New York.

More recently George and Mary Christie have inherited the mantle and moved with the times, both superbly well. There is even now to be a new opera-house, something the founder would certainly have approved of, for the first had served its purpose and seen its best days.

Still in my time there was Brian Dickie who succeeded Moran Caplat with the ping-pong balls; Jani who stayed on and pretty well saw me out;

June, Geoffrey, Janet, names that would mean a lot to those who were there at that time, and there were many more.

Directors Günther Rennert and Peter Hall were hard to beat as collaborators in my conducting years there. Carl Ebert overshadowed my apprentice time but I was too young to do more than admire the talent and dislike the character.

The place has a lot to do with it, or rather how you yourselve fit in there. Lewes, the nearest town with a station, is too far from London for comfortable commuting so that, at least during the four or five weeks of intensive rehearsal, most people take cottages or apartments close enough to ensure untrammeled journeys to and from rehearsal, a separate private life with room and time enough for a familiar sense to grow within a cast and all those associated with a particular opera. The benefits of this to standards and performances are intangible but very great. The countryside and fresh air aren't bad either. The house and gardens together with the feeling of being made welcome in them provide the focal point for the whole endeavor.

I count my years at Glyndebourne as almost total gain to which, as a bonus, must be added some of my most valued friendships, not to speak of an excellent Godson. They have ensured love for the place and what it stands for in opera.

All this by way of preface to some anecdotes that I doubt but would disappear if not recounted here. I can vouch for all except the first one and I include that only because it illustrates the benevolent teasing of Old John that was sometimes misunderstood.

After the war Glyndebourne, which had started in 1934, re-opened in 1947 with Gluck's *Orpheus* and the first performance of Britten's *Rape of Lucretia,* both featuring Kathleen Ferrier. John Christie saw the point of encouraging a young British composer but didn't care much for modern music and didn't at all mind being thought a stick-in-the-mud. One day it appears he came across Britten alone on a garden seat and sat down next to him. "Who are you then?" "Why, I'm Benjamin Britten, Mr. Christie." "And what do you do?" "I'm a composer, I wrote the music of the *Rape of Lucretia.*" "Oh! did you?... (long wait)... you know you shouldn't't've."

Of course Christie knew perfectly well who Britten was; Ben would have understood nothing of this and it may well have formed a background to the litany against Glyndebourne that continued for the rest of his life.

The same story is also told of W. H. Auden and John Christie at the time of *Elegy for Young Lovers* (1961), Henze's opera for which Auden wrote the excellent libretto. Perhaps it occurred twice. It's quite possible that Old John, delighted with the effect of his remark on the first occasion, remembered it and tried it out a second time.

Of my apprentice years I mostly remember domestic incidents. We were paid so little and had so small an amount of free time that eight pounds a week and free board was quite sufficient but somewhat restricting as to travel and outside adventures. I stayed in the house and, for one season, had the small bedroom at the top of the main staircase. It was a delightful room, presently George Christie's dressing room, but susceptible to surveillance and interruptions since you could see a light on under the door as you walked up the stairs.

I've always been an avid reader and Old John, apart from loving pugs and teasing, hated wasting electricity. At the height of the season he would make several late journeys in his nightgown and slippers to see that the back-stage lights, the ones in the covered way, green-room and other extravagant places were extinguished. Night after night, the summer I slept in that room, there would come a creaking up the staircase, a moment of hesitation, and then a knock at the door. "Ah, Raymond, just thought I would see if you were alright." "Yes, thank you, I'm fine." "Oh, good... er, goodnight." "Goodnight."

Maybe twenty minutes later the same tread from a different direction, his bedroom or maybe up the stairs by a different route for the perambulations went on until there was total darkness; another tap. "Just thought I would see... very bad for the eyes, you now, reading by electric light." Sometimes I gave in after two or three visits, sometimes I went on just to see how many times he would manage. He usually won.

Then there was Margaret Bellamy. Soon after John Christie became a widower he appointed a lady to run his house and Miss Bellamy, who had held some high serving rank in the Royal Navy during the war, was more than qualified.

Every morning tea was brought to your room in traditional English countryside fashion and all else in the house worked like clockwork from that hour onward.

John Pritchard had a room in the house that year, my first, along the corridor past mine at the head of the stairs and, after conducting a late dress-rehearsal, stayed there on one occasion with his boy-friend, Basil.

The next morning began as usual and in the second wave of tea-trays, mine having been brought before, I could hear Margaret Bellamy's heels clicking down the corridor to J.P.'s room. As their door opened they halted in their tracks, something was said followed by a dramatic silence. Improperly curious, I opened my door a crack as the heels came close on their return journey just in time to see Margaret's vexed face as she passed by muttering, "No, no! It won't do, it simply won't do, it won't. We had a lot of this in the WRENS[14] you know" and so on out of earshot. I never found out if J.P. got his second cup of tea but "a lot of this in the WRENS" became a catch phrase for the rest of the season.

—   Then There Were the Things That Happened in the Operas   —

In Cavalli's *La Calisto* which appeared for the first time at Glyndebourne in 1970, the part of the crusty old nymph, Linfea, servant of the goddess Diana, was played in travesty by Hugues Cuénod, a tall bean-pole of a man whose dress was a parody of that worn by the goddess she served. Her somewhat meager bosoms were cleverly represented by a loose brassière stuffed with bird seed.

Naturally enough the outfit had often to be cleaned for Opera is an energetic business and the bra was frequently to be seen in the enclosed artists' courtyard at the back of the opera-house hanging out to dry. Hugues complained after the second or third time of washing that he had a prickly sensation wearing it not unlike crumbs in bed and that his bosoms were getting smaller. Closer inspection revealed that the Sussex bird population had discovered the clothes line and were tucking in with a will causing leakage and diminution.

---

14   The women's branch of the Royal Navy.

At the opening of *L'Ormindo* in 1967, the first of the Cavalli operas I reconstructed, one of those moments a conductor dreads occurred. Mirinda, maid-servant and confidante of the beautiful Queen Erisbe, a sort of seventeenth-century Despina, had several comic solo scenes which commented on the plot as well as the sexual powers of the main charactars. Jane Berbié was wonderful in the part, a charming colleague and quite a catalyst for others in the cast. What we didn't know, for it was her first time at Glyndebourne, was that she suffered sometimes from stage fright, something that has afflicted some of the greatest stage performers from Olivier to Marie Lloyd. Come the première and Jane's first solo scene played before a drop curtain while the set changed behind, there was first a brief opening *sinfonia* from the orchestra lasting about forty-five seconds before Mirinda was to begin a recitative to the audience along the lines of "Do you know what...?"

All had gone well and better than well at rehearsals. Everyone loved the character and the way she played it. But on this first night the *sinfonia* ended and there was no Mirinda, nothing but the shaking of the curtain and the swirl of a skirt in retreat. Stage fright had taken over and she wouldn't go on.

There was nothing to do but play the *sinfonia* again and the London Philharmonic, reading my astonished gestures, did so, with exactly the same sequence of events as before.

We must have played the wretched thing three times, it may have been four and the audience was becoming perceptibly restive when, with a shriek, Mirinda flew on to the stage as if propelled by jet power. It was, I discovered afterwards, the stage manager, Geoffrey Gilbertson, who had given her an almighty shove so that we could all get on with the opera. She gave, I'm glad to say, a superb performance and brought the house down.

— Then There was the Problem of the Bath That Didn't Fit —

In 1984, at the last revival of *L'incoronazione di Poppea* in a new production by Peter Hall with Maria Ewing in the title role, there was a bath scene in which Poppea declares to her nurse, Arnalta, that, since the God of Love is on her side, she will risk all to oust Nero's wife, Ottavia, and become Empress herself. Naked ambition, her sexuality, her vulnerability, her pride in the power of her own physical attractiveness all added up to Peter's decision to make it a bath scene. Maria, a beautiful woman, had no reservations about appearing naked, although all was managed decorously between Arnalta and the towels. Once in the bath everything was so judged that the sight-lines in all parts of the theater would only allow a view of a low décollage. Maria sang standing in the bath which was built for her height.

One day she was unwell and her understudy, an excellent, attractive young singer well prepared and rehearsed had to go on in her place. A single detail had been overlooked. She was several inches taller than Maria, enough to give the audience a quite remarkable view of this well-endowed lady who, for most of the scene, was quite unaware of being *exposé à tous les vents*. As the French also say, *Il y avait du monde dans le balcon* and that evening the entire theater including the stalls was made well aware of the fact.

Nostalgia for me is neither a very profitable nor even a particularly pleasurable activity, but in contemplating why so much that is good in my experience of opera happened at Glyndebourne, there have come a series of flash-backs of happenings and moments affectionately and even sentimentally remembered that would otherwise hardly deserve lengthy, separate exposition. They need little space to describe but they were, all the same, clear manifestations of the good things that can come about given the attitude, distinction, time and method that are to be found there.

This is not to say they couldn't have happened elsewhere but they did happen at Glyndebourne and, of their kind, more frequently: moments worth recalling.

For example, the beginning of Act II of Mozart's *Figaro* in Peter Hall's production. The long orchestral introduction defeats most people and there have been as many solutions to the problem as there have been performances, most of them unsatisfactory. We have seen the Countess in dress wig and full crinoline seated before a looking glass adjusting her beauty spots (at seven in the morning?); we have seen another Countess being painted by an artist who packs up his easel and leves just before she sings, or, worse, stays the course to hear without embarrassment her passionate utterances about lost love; there have been servants serving breakfast either very slowly or very fast as in a silent film (imagine hot chocolate and toast before she says those things); there have been cowardly late curtains that make a noise; slow curtains that distract; early curtains then nothing; processions of servants carrying heaven knows what to heaven knows where. All these devised by directors none of whom seem to have asked the question "what is true about those wonderful three or four minutes of music that Mozart composed to preface the first appearance of his greatest heroine, in her grief for a relationship that had promised so well in the *Barber*, but has turned out so badly by the time of Figaro's marriage to her maid Susanna?"

In Peter's solution at Glyndebourne the curtain rose gently before the music began and there was her dressing room with the shutters still closed from the night before and the morning light gradually filtering in so that soon you could see, down a little corridor to stage left, a boudoir and the edge of a bed. On it more and more clearly could be seen the figure of a woman sobbing. But the day must begin, there are meals to be ordered, guests to be seen to and arrangements to be made for the Figaro wedding, no matter how painful the heartache over her lost Almaviva who hasn't been seen since the previous evening. If the Countess doesn't make it all work no one will; it is what she was bred to. Dishevelled (and of course she will need her maid and hairdresser before she is seen), beautiful and terribly alone she sings "*Porgi Amor*" by herself and we know that Mozart understood it perfectly.

Figaro, by the way, was the occasion of a charming and characteristic Royal story.

The Queen on the 50th anniversary of Glyndebourne's opening asked if she might come to a performance, a typically thoughtful gesture especially when you consider that listening to music is not first among her most pleasurable activities. Glyndebourne was flattered and delighted and asked which opera Her Majesty would like to attend, perhaps *Figaro* since the house began with it and was famous for its Mozart. The answer soon came back as a question. "Isn't that the one with the pin?" (The Queen has an incredible memory and no detail ever escapes her.) "Yes,

Ma'am, that's the one." "Thank you so much, but I'd rather *not* that one, I've seen it."

While on the subject of tricky problems in Mozart operas I must recall one very good solution that Peter Wood, another Cambridge contemporary with whom I've always enormously enjoyed working, found for the end of *Così*.

Neither Mozart nor da Ponte left any clear indication about who ends up with whom. What is clear, especially from Mozart, is that the two girls, only sociably involved with their young men at the beginning of the opera, fall deeply in love with each other's beau-in-disguise by the end.

When the deception is revealed and the ladies' fickleness exposed, there is a problem. Do they go back to their first relationships or admit the power of love and stay with the new? Peter devised a staging of it in such a way that, in making their return to the original pairing (and good manners, which counted so much in eighteenth century *mores*, would have insisted on that no matter what happened afterwards), each lover passed significantly close to his new love so that the wrench of parting from someone so wonderful was made painfully clear to the audience and, suitably delayed, the suspense of their grown-up decision held everyone breathless until the last moment. It also made the music so much easier to perform.

In that production, too, I remember Patricia Kern playing Despina as an older nanny figure left in charge of her wards, not as their contemporary and rival in amatory adventures. It makes so much more sense, not only with the girls but also in her bantering relationship with Don Alfonso with whom familiarity of every sort has long ago bred amused contempt — on both sides and on every subject except for her charges of whom she takes very good care.

Another Mozart figure who made more sense at Glyndebourne than in most other places was Don Ottavio. He was played in Peter Hall's production as an aging, substitute father-figure for Donna Anna who, though intrigued by men of Don Giovanni's age, was easily upset by them.

Graziella Sciutti's "*ma*" in Rosina's first aria in the *Barber* was something to remember, as was the accuracy and theatrical purpose of her coloratura even if she wasn't a mezzo-soprano. *A bas les puristes.* I'm sure Rossini would have loved her.

There was the night after Mattiwilda Dobb's husband died, tragically young, in a London hospital. She turned up, nevertheless, to sing Zerbinetta in *Ariadne auf Naxos* (I was playing keyboard in the pit), and sang it impeccably as if contained in ice, the result not only of her own self-control but probably also of disciplined coaching and long rehearsal. She seemed in another world which, I'm sure, is where she was. The effect on the rest of us was amazing. Everyone wanted to help, to be of comfort, for she was a much loved colleague, but *noli me tangere* was clearly the way it had to be, and the tension this built up was electrifying. Sena Jurinac singing the Composer's finale to the Prologue with tears coursing down her face was unforgettable as was the dreadful heartlessness of the words Zerbinetta had to sing about love and men.

In the same opera the part of Brighetta, one of the four *Commedia dell'-Arte* followers of Zerbinetta, was played by a lascivious young Scot who, it came to be known, always sang flat for some hours after having made a conquest. The smiles and nods of comprehension in the orchestra whenever this happened were a regular and enjoyable part of that season's performances (he wasn't re-engaged). Opera theater is like that; a pit joke and I don't think the stage ever got it.

Singers naturally have resonant speaking voices which can sometimes make for awkward moments. An Italian Don Basilio with strong sensual appetites was heard by approximately sixty people leaving a *Barber* morning rehearsal saying to a young chorister he fancied in what he also fancied was a whisper. "Queek, before lunch." This, too, became a catch phrase for the season. No one is known to have heard the reply or whether there *was indeed* an apertif.

A beautiful, vivacious mezzo-soprano from Spain came for several seasons: Marina de Gabarain whose looks and theatrical talents far surpassed her musical ones, though she has a seductive voice and a commitment in her singing which commanded attention. She sang *Cenerentola* with Gui, a master of the Rossinian style, and troubled him greatly with her musical inaccuracy.

The next year she sang Baba the Turk in *Rake's Progress* when Paul Sacker was conducting. If the simple rhythms of Rossini gave her problems, it can be imagined how she fared in Stravinsky's complicated auction scene to the distraction of the gentle, but not very dynamic conductor.

Sitting next to Gui in a dress rehearsal — which stopped several times on her account — I heard him permit a deep Italian chuckle to escape (from what was normally a rather patrician, dignified person) while this was going on. "Ah hah! you hear, Raymond, Spanish rhythms."

All the same, I'll never forget her appearance as she peered out of her sedan chair. "My love, am I to remain in here forever?" Tom Rakewell didn't stand a chance after that.

Gui was considered a worthy successor to Busch as music director at Glyndebourne, quite different from his predecessor by all accounts but, in his own way, very distinguished. He had been a contemporary of Toscanini (whom he disliked and thought an aggressive poseur in many things musical and social), had known Debussy and had studied hard and well several styles of music about which he expounded in a somewhat autocratic way. He was apt to produce counterfeit impatience and become, as he disarmingly described the process, "red like a *pomo d'oro*", but he was a good friend and, fortunately, both he and his warm-hearted wife, Elda, took to me and encouraged me greatly. His style in Rossini had great distinction, never indulging in exaggeration, for the most part eschewing cuts and other traditional emendations and vulgarities which had crept in through second-rate Italian opera houses. You were always aware that Rossini was a contemporary of Beethoven, essentially a classical composer and a superbly accomplished one who knew what he was writing and could commit it accurately to paper.

Gui occasionally said very striking things. Talking about *Don Giovanni* he volunteered the surprising information that he had never conducted it and, when asked why, said "It will not play", a remark that made me think.

He was very polite but did not always understand spoken English very well. A young assistant producer was introduced to him, shook his hand and in reply to Gui saying his own name "Vittorio Gui" said "Richard Day" to which Gui, without pausing, said "Yes isn't it": another catch-phrase for the season.

I'll never forget the faces of Ugo Trama, Bernard Dickinson and John Fryalt (who played the three suitors in Monteverdi's *Ulisse*) on the day when the way the archery scene would be played was revealed. Actors, especially singing ones, aren't terribly curious about scenes until they themselves are involved in them, so the problem of how the characters they played were to be slaughtered by the returning Ulysses hadn't as yet featured large in their thoughts or conversation. The fact that Ben Luxon had been having archery lessons was kept a secret.

On the morning when the scene was being first set, Peter Hall cleverly spent most of the rehearsal with the three suitors attempting to draw the great bow and finding their differing reactions when each in turn fails.

At the end of the rehearsal, just before lunch, a target was set up and held closely by stage hands who were in on the scheme. Ben arrived with his arrows and, standing at one end of the rehearsal stage, let fly six of them in quick succession, all bull's-eyes. There was a dreadful silence as the three suitors realised the implications of all this and then some subdued talk about contracts and insurance and resignations.

I began to wonder if the scene would ever be achieved in this way, but drinks at lunch and the information that Janet Baker had quite calmly agreed to be in the middle of it all, and much more vulnerable, helped a good deal and, eventually, they joined in with a will and made a great scene of it.

I've already mentioned Janet's soliloquy which opens the opera and it's worth mentioning again to show something of the amazing way it grew in rehearsal and in those circumstances. There would not have been the calm or the time in most other places. It lasts about sixteen minutes wiht only two very brief interruptions by Penelope's old nurse, Ericlea, but, during it, the image grows from that of just a sad, lonely woman to one who is often angry at being left for twenty years while Ulysses went off to Troy. Hope is a deceiver and almost gone, her youth has passed away, her son is in foreign lands searching for news of his father and she is in danger of losing all before he returns. She herself has been changed, beseiged by the suitors and her own constancy, into becoming someone chaste and cold; someone within whom the fires burn more fiercely than ever but without their being allowed to be seen. She prays for calm... but if only Ulysses would come back: the recurring "*Torna, torna Ulisse!*"". So in this huge, uncompromising beginning she lays the foundation for the whole opera. It's a formidable responsibility for both singer and the director, not to speak of everyone else involved.

Janet wore a long cloak and at the beginning Peter persuaded her to keep her hands hidden. Hands are the singer's alter-egos and with so many performers they flail about in time to the voice in meaningless gestures as if to say "the fox went that way", or to demonstrate attempting a cross-channel record.

Penelope, standing stock still contained by the cloak for her first phrases, showed her isolation and the tensions of waiting as powerfully as the music and the text. Gradually, as her women dressed her, she became more mobile, the movement punctuated by the moments of stillness with the recurring "*torna*", and, by the end, she is ready to face the dangers once more, the final assault of the suitors who have driven her so hard to decide which one she will accept. The resolution brings not a huge climax but a soft, ravishing arioso about everything returning to its source, the rivers, the winds, winter, the earth and man himself. Only Ulysses has not come, but, survive another day and perhaps...

All this developed during hours and hours of rehearsal, admittedly with a group of highly gifted people focusing intently, deeply committed and backed up by an entire opera house. It is how it should be done and rarely is so.

Another moment which used to make me gulp during performances occurred well into the opera when Penelope's son, Telemachus, is brought to Ithaca by the goddess Minerva bearing news that Ulysses is indeed alive, wending his way back home. (The gods all flew at Glyndebourne, making a wonderful distinction between the drama in the heavens and that on earth). Penelope does not believe him but loves him for trying to help and sings an aria about a little seed of hope she nurtures in her heart, "*Debole fil di sperme...*"

The words are in the libretto but there was no music in the manuscript. Feeling the opera couldn't be without them, I composed the vocal line above a Monteverdi bass I remembered from somewhere else. I'm most certainly not excusing myself or apologising for it; in fact I'm rather proud of the moment and its effect. It was, rather, an example of "authentic" seventeenth century practise, no more than Cavalli did for *Poppea* and, God knows I've written a lot of Cavalli in my time.

I do think *Ulisse* (in no matter whose version, as long as it comes across the footlights) is one of the truly great operas ever to have been written and feel privileged to have been one of those allowed to bring it to life for my time and in such grand company as we had then at Glyndebourne. Conducting it was like going on a long journey; daunting in prospect but infinitely worthwhile and rewarding at its end.

Since Glyndebourne has been the source for remembering so much that is good in opera, it seems only just to make a brief attempt at describing the circumstances that bring about such a sort of approbation.

Pleasant conditions for work and the concentration that its comparatively isolated country situation induces are important factors, but the causes lie deeper than that. They begin with the care with which management put together the initial group of people who will see the opera on to the stage as one piece, director, designer and conductor, making sure they are compatible and able to come to decisions about style and purpose in the production. Management is, of course, generally involved in the discussions but sees its rôle as one of co-ordinator and supporter, encouraging the three principal thinkers in their efforts while keeping an eye on budget and the policies that obtain and are part of the place. High among these is the encouragement of young, talented singers who are likely to develop in the atmosphere and circumstances at Glyndebourne and become, for a few years, part of the company. This is a long-established intent which has repaid a million times over the care and effort of seeking them out and looking after them once found.

The list of names of those who came early on in their careers and returned often to a place where only the best was expected of them and every encouragement given to help them achieve it is staggering.

Sena Jurinac, Louis Hellergruber, Geraint Evans, Gesto Bruscantini, Irene Isenger, Hugues Cuénod, Roy Henderson, Ina Souez, Richard Lewis, Juan Oncina, Graziella Sciutto, Joan Sutherland, Elizabeth Söderstrom, John Shirley-Quirk, Michael Roux, Tom Allen, Janet Baker, Ileana Cotrubas, Federico Javia, Ryland Davies, Stafford Dean, Leo Gocke, Haken Hagegard, Anne Howells, Ben Luxon, Felicity Hoff, Karstin Meyer, Anthony Rolf-Johnson, Frederica von Stade, Richard Stilwell, Willard White... the list goes on and on.

At a still earlier stage in their careers they may be recruited for the chorus where they gain invaluable theatrical experience and an opportunity for well-coached understanding with the models before them every day in rehearsal.

The likelihood that they may have to go on is much greater than in a city where replacements, who have already sung the part, are more readily available and generally of a lower quality. This weakens the understudy system in Repertory opera where, in any case, there is rarely time to prepare covers from within the company.

At Glyndebourne, apart from the possibilities of actually performing, there are periodic understudy showings, better than any ordinary auditions, and there is the real possibility that they may be given the rôle they have studied in the Touring Opera which takes productions around England outside the season.

All this adds up to a remarkable training ground for young singers, unparalleled. to my knowledge, in the world.

Each production's triumvirate begins meetings and exchange of ideas at least two years before the intended season. Management is all the time vigilantly searching out talent and ready with suggestions when it comes to casting, a matter for all concerned to agree upon.

A robustly healthy-looking soprano would be an unlikely candidate for *La Traviata;* a Tosca who can't jump; a Sieglinde and Siegmund whose only point of contact standing up would be their belly-buttons; an Ariadne as big as the island on which she is stranded; Romeos half the height of Juliets; a Japanese Pinkerton: the improbabilities are unending and frequently encountered in other places. There is a truth to be told in operatic theater and the lies will not prosper. No social slur should possibly be construed by saying that you cannot in all honesty have a black Countess, unless, that is, you move *Figaro* to the twenty-first century, or play it in Harlem and I don't know why you would or how you would make it work.

All plans laid, preparations made, casting done, the style and intent determined, the main rehearsals begin with a week of music calls so that the cast has a chance to establish an ensemble before the rigors of staging begin. Throughout the production there are further music coaching with one or another of the *répétiteurs* and separate ensemble calls to ensure the music develops alongside the growing theater of the piece. That way, too, any problems of positioning or movement can be tackled as they arise and not stored up for explosive tensions in final rehearsals. Daily reports at meetings of junior music and directing staff ensure that watchful eyes are kept on the general progress.

Apart from a number of small studios, Glyndebourne has made sure it has enough larger spaces to accomodate the process. A separate chorus room can, like the organ room (a large room in the house originally built to accomodate both an organ and the earliest operatic ventures of Old John), be used for ensemble calls, as well as more intimate production work. There is, of course, the main stage and contiguous to it, but soundproofed, is a rehearsal stage identical in size so that rehearsals and even performances can go on at the same time. It has in the past lacked a separate orchestral rehearsal room, necessary when the pit is unavailable during technical work on stage. Perhaps the new theater will remedy this.

The process continues for the allotted weeks, no matter if it be a new production or revival. Casts get to know each other socially and in the interaction add much to their own performances as well as to the production itself.

Finally the orchestral, *Sitzprobe* and dress rehearsals arrive including, always, a free public one so as to give the cast a chance to judge audience reaction. When things have gone well there is a sense that whatever potential there was in the cast, the director, the setting, the conducting, the playing, the work itself has a fair chance of being realized.

You don't avoid the nervous tension that accompanies every performance, especially the first, but the risk factor has been minimalized, the work has been thought through, and everyone should be able to give of their best: and that is why Glyndebourne is the source for remembering so much that is really good in opera.

It was, from the beginning, well placed to succeed and not every opera company can boast such good resources; nor it is possible to reproduce, detail by detail, Glyndebourne's structure and *modus operandi*. But there are principles involved which can be translated into the Repertory system with, I believe, great advantage to the people concerned and the standards of their performance. That translation might resolve itself into these more specific proposals:

The number of different operas performed each week should not, in general, exceed three. This, in turn, will tend and should be allowed to restrict the number of different operas performed during the season.

The pivotal main investment and focus should be in a first-rate understudy system alongside which would be developed an associate *répétiteur*-conductor scheme.

The season's repertoire would be divided into two streams, the first of which should consist only of some of the best-known popular operas like *Barber, Figaro, Carmen, Traviata, Magic Flute*. These would regularly be put on with the minimum of stage and orchestra rehearsal and the maximum of coaching for a cast largely chosen from the understudies who would, of course, also cover the other operas of the season. It would be the same cast for each performance always conducted by the associate conductor who has been in charge of its preparation.

This intensive focusing on young singers and *répétiteur*-conductors with the comparative neglect of stage and orchestra in much repeated, well-run, older productions may appear to be promoting something less than first-rate and, in terms of orchestral playing and staging it may be so. But, apart from the realistic price you have to pay for a Repertory opera, it has considerable merit in offering a well-rehearsed vocal ensemble contained within the company in performances which can be sold for less and allow Marketing (who, in any case, always believe they run everything) to give the series a special public image of a spawning ground for young, native singers indended for young, native opera-goers.

This, so to speak, junior stream of performances would allow much more time for the new productions and the revivals of new productions by already established singers, directors and conductors. Every so often one of the "popular" operas would be withdrawn from the junior system and given a new production, re-entering the adult league for as many years as it does well and until it is deemed time to return it to the juniors once more.

The highest level of intelligent planning would be needed but, if the priorities are right and the ideals in place, there would then be no more of that chasing after one's own tail that dogs virtually all the Repertory opera companies I've ever encountered.

Once started, it would take a few seasons before the virtues of the system became apparent. In a society where bureaucracy channels public funds into the Arts and wants quick results for its own self-esteem it is hardly likely to happen. In America however everything is still possible and public monies count for mush less. Who knows, one day it may come about and the best operatic values realised in a great city: Glyndebourne in New York, *rus in urbe;* an ideal worth keeping in mind, and a cheerful application of Martial's epigram which would have pleased the author after two thousand years.

III

OTHER (NON-STAGE) WORKS

1

MADRIGALS OF CLAUDIO MONTEVERDI[1]

Claudio Monteverdi (1567-1643): The greatest composers have always tended to appear at the end of a stylistic period when techniques have become established and the musical aesthetic surrounding them more or less stable.

Perhaps the most extraordinary thing about Monteverdi is that he should have proved himself so completely a master while actually forging a new musical style — one which very largely represented a complete break with the past. A contemporary, Benedetto Ferrari, called him *Oracolo della musica.* There can be very few composers who foreshadowed so much of what was to come and yet lived to fulfill their own prophesies.

Born in Cremona in 1567 of a family, it would seem, of some distinction, he probably received a university education (the wide knowledge of the humanities revealed in his excellent letters supports this conjecture).[2] His musical training was in the hands of Marc'Antonio Ingegneri, organist of Cremona Cathedral and a man of progressive ideas, although his teaching must have been based on the long-accepted contrapuntal techniques of the sixteenth century.

In 1590 Monteverdi was appointed to a junior post in the musical establishment of the Gonzaga court at Mantua. Next to that of the Medici in Florence it was, artistically, the most brilliant in Italy. Under the young Duke Vincenzo artists such as Rubens, Porbus, Tasso, Guarini, Rinuccini,

---

1   Notes adapted from the program notes for the author's own recordings (as conductor) on the Philips label, 1971-77 — for which see DISCOGRAPHY, below. (Ed.)

2   In English see Stevens, ed. & transl., *The Letters of Claudio Monteverdi* (1980), of which a selection also appears in Arnold & Fortune, eds., *The New Monteverdi Companion* (1985). For more on Monteverdi's life and career, see Chapter II Section §2, above. (Ed.)

Gastoldi, Pallavicino, da Viadana, and Rossi all worked there for shorter or longer periods. Given the excellence of his fundamental training this was the perfect atmosphere for the young Monteverdi to develop his originality and essential modernity of spirit. Only seven years after opera was invented he composed the first masterpiece in this new dramatic form — *Orfeo*, 1607 — and, one year later, his *Arianna* (now lost) and *Il ballo delle Ingrate* which he published thirty years later in the eighth book of madrigals.

Monteverdi, never a happy man, stayed at Mantua for 23 years, which were for him years of sadness (his young wife died there) and constant resentment over injustices, some real, some doubtless imagined. In 1613 he removed to Venice where he was appointed *Maestro di cappella* at St. Mark's, the most coveted musical post in all Italy. There he flourished for thirty years producing a wealth of music which only in these latter years has come to be valued for what it is: the work of the greatest musical mind of the seventeenth century. It speaks as vividly to us now as it did to those living 300 years ago.

At the heart of all his work lie the nine books of madrigals and the various supplements. They can be equated with the string quartets of Haydn and the piano concertos of Mozart in reflecting the composer's development throughout his life. Starting brilliantly within the accepted form, the madrigal in his hands eventually broke all bounds and rendered its title absurdly inadequate. The books contain solo song, accompanied aria, opera, ballet, popular trios, comic scenes, and, perhaps greatest of all, the duet for voices and continuo in all of which the human emotions are exposed and expressed with an intensity and beauty which has never been surpassed.

Small wonder that when he died all Europe mourned, marvelling at the power of his music over men's minds and emotions. It was said that the multitude of candles surrounding his catafalque in the Church of the Frari resembled the night sky brilliant with stars where the divine Claudio was already making music with the angels. We surely should not doubt it.

— The First and Second Books of Madrigals —

[Not recorded by RL. The individual titles include:]

IL PRIMO LIBRO DE MADRIGALI for 5 voices (1587)
  "*A che tormi il ben mio*" (3)
  "*Amor per tua mercè vatene a quella*" (4)
  "*Amor, s'il tuo ferire*" (17)
  "*Ari o gela a tua voglia*" *(Riposta)* (Tasso)(20)
  "*Ardo, sì, ma non t'amo*" (Guarini) (19)
  "*Arsi e alsi a mia voglia*" *(Contra-riposta)* (Tasso) (21)
  "*Baci soavi e cari*" (Guarini) (5)
  "*Ch'io ami la mia vita*" (1)
  "*Donna, s'io miro voi, giaccio divengo*" (18)
  "*Filli cara e amata*" (A. Parma) (7)
  "*Fumia la pastorella*" (part 1); "*Almo divino raggio*" (part 2);
      "*All'bora i pastor tutti*" (part 3)(A. Allegretti)(9-11)
  "*Poi che del mio dolore*" (8)
  "*Questa ordì il laccio*" (Strozzi) (15)
  "*Se nel partir da voi, vita mia*" (12)
  "*Se per havervi oimè*" (2)
  "*Se pur non mi consenti*" (6)
  "*Tra mille fiamme e tra mille cathene*" (13)
  "*Usciam, ninfe, homai fuor di questi boschi*" (14)
  "*La vaga pastorella sen va tra fiori*" (16)

IL SECONDO LIBRO DE MADRIGALI for 5 voices (1590)
  "*Bevea Fillide mia*" (G. Cassoni) (3)
  "*La bocc'onde l'asprissime parole solean uscir*" (E. Bentivoglio) (15)
  "*Cantai un tempo, e se fu dolc'il canto*" (P. Bembo) (21)
  "*Crudel, perchè mi fuggi?*" (Tasso) (17)
  "*Dolcemente dormiva la mia Clori*" (Tasso) (16)
  "*Dolcissimi legami di parole amorose*" (Tasso) (4)
  "*Donna, nel mio ritorno*" (Tasso) (9)
  "*Ecco mormorar l'onde*" (Tasso) (14)

"Intorno a due vermiglie e vaghe labra" (6)
"Mentre io miravo fiso de la mia donna gl'occh'ardenti e belli" (Tasso) (12)
"Non giacinti o narcisi" (Casoni) (5)
"Non m'è grave'l morire" (19)
"Non si levav'ancor l'alba novella" (part 1)(Tasso); *"E dicea l'una
    sospirando"* (Tasso) (1-2)
"Non sono in queste rive fiori così vermigli" (Tasso) (7)
"Quel'ombra esser vorrei" (Casoni) (10)
"Questo specchio ti dono, Rosa" (18)
"S'andasse amor a caccia" (Tasso) (11)
"Se tu mi lassi, perfida" (Tasso) (13)
"Ti spontò l'ali amor, la donna mia" (F. Alberti) (20)
"Tutte le bocche belle in questo nero volto" (Alberti) (8)

— The Third and Fourth Books of Madrigals —

The third and fourth books of Monteverdi's great series of publications under the general title of "madrigals" show the transition from complete mastery of an accepted form to the threshold of a totally new world
of musical expression: from the secular manifestation of a great contrapuntal art to the discovery of a new, outgoing, dramatic expressiveness accomplished not by revolution but by evolution.

The third book was published in 1592, the fourth 11 years later in 1603.
Both contain 20 madrigals, some joined in sequence where the length of
text exceeds the limits of the single madrigal.

Perhaps the most striking aspect of the earlier book is the way Monteverdi adapts and uses existing madrigalian techniques toward the
deeper penetration of the texts' emotional content. Coupled with this is
the increased attention to making the words more clearly audible to the
listener. The madrigal began as a secular version of the ecclesiastical
motet in which imitative contrapuntal points caused most of the text to
sound confused and obscure. In the case of the motet this mattered little
since everyone knew the Bible and the *incipit* [text beginning] was
enough to jog the memory. Applied to secular words, these musical techniques forced the madrigal to become a form principally to be enjoyed
by the performers themselves, a private music for the cultured few. For

it to become public, that is sung to a comprehending audience, the clear presentation of the words became essential. From the beginning we can trace concern for this in some of the madrigals of Arcadelt and Verdelot, but until the end of the century it was the exception rather than the rule.

Monteverdi had already published two volumes of madrigals before his appointment, at first as a string player, to the court of the Gonzagas in Mantua in 1590. There he worked under the aging Giaches de Wert who had been *Maestro di capella* in Mantua since1565. De Wert, a consummate craftsman of the older polyphonic techniques, showed some awareness of the problem of textural inaudibility. In the three last of his ten books of madrigals he occasionally set the more important lines to a sort of static declamation for all the five voices together. The motive for this seems directed more towards clarity than dramatic expression but the young Monteverdi must have noted the effect, for it appears quite often in the third book and even more so in the fourth, always to some significantly expressive purpose. De Wert also showed how the five-part madrigalian texture could be varied. In the older style contrapuntal points tended to be observed by all the voices so that by the end of each section all five parts were singing together. De Wert broke away from this and often divided the five-part group into two of three parts, one or other part serving in both groups. Once more it was left to Monteverdi to show the emotive possibilities of this sort of grouping (which also helped the clarity of the words) and the way in which, for example, three higher voices could contrast not only in pitch but in meaning with another group in lower register.

Throughout the third book of madrigals (they were not published in order of composition) we can see Monteverdi trying out these newfound techniques as well as enlarging his harmonic and contrapuntal vocabulary. Some, like "*O come è gran martire*" and"*Ch'io non t'ami*" are far in advance of their time; others like "*Sovra tenere herbette*" belong to the earlier style. The extraordinary thing is that, within the limits imposed by a five-voiced combination, they are so marvelously distinct from one another and in their separate ways, so deeply concerned with the text.

All these elements came to fruition in the fourth book, arguably the greatest book of madrigals (in the true sense of the word) ever to have been published.

As a collecton they are on a knife-edge where the technical and ex-pressive possibilities of the five-voiced texture nearly give way to what was inevitably going to come—the liberation of voices above an in-strumental *basso continuo* and the attendant variation in numbers of voices. But they are still madrigals and the range and intensity of their content is something approaching a musical miracle.

As if to fit the changing musical scene, the texts which attracted Mon-teverdi in the fourth book are much more overtly emotional than before. All but four of the poems are in the first person so that the singers can bareluy help but sing with a united purpose. Most of the poems are by Giovanni Battista Guarini, the principal author of Book III. His pastoral comedy *Il pastor fido* dominated the literary-musical scene for many years to come—even Handel set it as an opera. Two new names appear among the poets: Boccaccio who lived in the fourteenth century and Rinuccini who was associated with the Florentine *Camerata* and was to write the libretto for Monteverdi's opera (now lost) *Arianna* five years later.

There is one further element to be found in the fourth book which calls for observation—a more or less unprecedented concern with over-all musical form. Whether this came about because of the structures of some of the poems or because Monteverdi was stretching out towards this new musical element with an ear to the future is a matter for discus-sion, but the importance of such things as the idea of recapitulation in "*Sì, ch'io vorrei morire*" and "*Non più guerra*"; the integrating use of the melodic line to the words "*O bellezza mortale*" in "*Cor mio, mentre vi miro*"; the binary structure of "*Io mi son giovninetta*" and the motivic use of the opening two-note phrase in "*Ohimè, se tanto amate*" is too great to be over-looked. It is as if the composer were anticipating and partly solving in advance some of the formal problems he would encounter when he was to write for the solo voice in opera. It was always his way to progress slowly, resolving aspects of future problems while securely exercising es-tablished techniques, and this fourth book, while supremely ac-complished and satisfying in itself, yet shows promise of so much that was to come.

Note: Monteverdi normally labels the voices of his five-part madri-gals: *Canto, Quinto, Alto, Tenore, Basso*. But the range of each part does not always correspond to the voices available today. For example, the *Quinto* part is occasionally for soprano rather than for mezzo-soprano, and the *Alto* part often has to be divided between a contralto and a tenor.

Notes for *LIBRO III: MADRIGALI A CINQUE VOCI* (1592)

1. "La giovinetta pianta [A blossoming flower]". Monteverdi takes a gentle view of both the young plant and the young virgin; the sun does not burn so hotly or love's fire so strongly as to disturb the smooth, immaculate word setting and counterpoint. The different groupings of the voices are beautifully managed especially at the words "*Così la verginella* [So, too, a maiden]", first on three high voices to present the young girl and then on the lower three voices as if to represent the lover who looks on her. Although there are several pages of elaborate part-writing in the older madrigalian style Monteverdi always takes care that the lines of the poem set in this way are clearly heard at the outset.

2. "O come è gran martire [Oh, how great a suffering it is]" (Giovanni Battista Guarini). The second madrigal of Book III inhabits a different world from the first. The three ladies who sing of their anguish in the opening may have their origins in Ferrara (where the singing of three particular ladies became a celebrated phenomenon at the end of the sixteenth century) but they can rarely have been given such intensely personal phrases to sing as here. The marvelous effect of introducing all five voices together at the words "*O soave mio ardore* [O my sweet ardor]" is one Monteverdi was to use often again. This sort of homophonic setting has its dangers for the music could easily end up in little disconnected sections which would fragment the whole. It is fascinating to see how Monteverdi avoids the danger by anticipating the next entry or letting the declamation dissolve into counterpoint.

3. "Sovra tenere herbette e bianchi fiori [On the young grass among white flowers]". This poem shows family likeness to *La giovinetta pianta*" (Nr. 1) and the musical setting is also similar in style. Within the somewhat conservative techniques there are some touchingly beautiful moments. The falling phrase to "*Cara Filli, io moro* [Dear Phyllis, I am dying]" perfectly represents the sentiment and it is interesting to notice how the most personal lines of the poem — the final couplet in direct speech — call forth the most personal utterance from the composer.

4. "*O dolce anima mia* [O sweet my love]" (Guarini). The contrasting use of differing groupings of the voices is a strong element in this madrigal. The opening, however, is set to fluent and subtle counterpoint. The first two lines are set to virtually the same phrase which is itself divided into two and the parts used for the elaborately composed texture. At the word "*abbandoni* [leaving (me)]" the music breaks off and the three lower voices, singing homophonically, vividly portray the love-sick young man who pleads his cause in vain — and we never lose sight of him, for that vocal color returns several times, punctuating the more elaborate outbursts for all five voices.

5. "*Stracciami pur il core!* [Go on then, tear my heart!]". It may be that in this madrigal we can see one of Monteverdi's first attempts to develop the new declamatory style, for the opening pages are somewhat less successful than usual. The vigor of the first two lines is beautifully contrasted with the soft regret of the third and fourth, but the re-introduction of the opening in the solo top line after ten bars seems insufficiently supported and too brief to make its effect. The madrigal gets gloriously under way at the words '*ma perchè* [but why torture me for my fidelity etc]" and only at the end does the reversion to contrapuntal elaboration seem to outstay its welcome and show, perhaps, the experimental nature of the setting.

6. "*O rossignuol* [O nightingale]" (Pietro Bembo). The nightingale is delightfully characterised in the extended opening for three voices and as her mate joins in the song so do all five voices join in the madrigal. The sudden slowing of pace as the poet reveals his own misery is most affecting and perfectly judged. We should notice, too, how Monteverdi imposes a structure upon quite a lengthy setting by breaking off before the last quatrain.

7. "*Se per estremo ardore* [If the great heat of passion]" (Guarini). The beginning of this madrigal shows Monteverdi's understanding of the power of the human voice to declaim effectively even upon one note. Moreover the phrase is always perfectly audible throughout the increasingly elaborate texture he builds to the first couplet and seems to gain in intensity as the other parts move through and around it. The music lights

up at the lover's intention to be happy in his love and is beautifully contrasted with the contented sweetness of the words *per dolcezza io mora* [if I sometimes die for very sweetness]". As so often in the third book, the last pages resort to quite elaborate counterpoint. Monteverdi clearly intended (and succeeded) in giving, in this way, a climactic intensity to the setting. Later on he sought other ways to achieve this, possibly finding that this much-used technique of ending a madrigal tended to de-personalise the effect of the whole.

8. *Prima parte* [First part]: *'Vattene pur, crudel, con quella pace* [Go cruel, go; go with such Peace]." 9. *Seconda parte* [Second part]: "*Là tra'l sangu'e le morti egro giacente* [There lying wounded, 'mongst the hurt and slain]". 10. *Terza e ultima parte* [Third and final part] "*Poi ch'ella in sè tornò, deserto e muto* [Wak'd from her trance, forsaken, speechless, sad]" (Torquato Tasso, from *Gerusalemme Liberata* (Canto XVI; transl. by Edward Fairfax from *Godfrey of Bulloigne* or *The Recovery of Jerusalem*, 1600). Three stanzas from Torquato Tasso's *Gerusalemme Liberata* make up the text of this fine group of madrigals. Tasso spent a year at Mantua in 1586 where his eccentricities as well as his poetry must have been remembered well into Monteverdi's time there.

The stanzas are taken from the point where the sorceress Armida, no longer able to hold the Christian knight Rinaldo under her spell, curses him as he leaves her, vowing to haunt the rest of his days. It is a highly charged, almost theatrical moment for, at the end of the second part, Armida faints and wakes in anguish at her failed love and her failed pagan powers. Monteverdi sets the poem with an unprecedented intensity in the manner of a choral declamation. He makes no compromise to popular taste but parallels the ferocity of the text with stark aggressive music using violent rhythms and wide vocal leaps which alternate with closely written intense *parlando*. There is no relaxation until half-way through the second part where Armida faints. Suddenly the music changes and a chilly, descending chromatic phrase, which appears in all the voices in turn, vividly portrays the sinking, exhausted woman. The effect is almost physical, even to the point at the end of the second part where her eyes close.

Her return to consciousness (part three) is set with an equal vividness. In beguiling him she has herself been beguiled and we can hear this in the music. Even the lacerating frustration of the last two lines, which give Monteverdi the opportunity for musical climax, do not dispel the anguish of the final collapse. It is a masterly setting which must have astonished those who heard it first – as indeed it still does us now.

11. *O primavera* [Spring]" (Guarini, from *Il pastor fido;* transl. by Sir Richard Fanshawe, 1647). Note: Monteverdi substitutes the words "*Sì car'a gl'occhi altrui* [the sight of others]" for Guarini's slightly different original (in Fanshaw transl., "her sight / Who is Heaven's master-piece, and Earth's delight").

In complete contrast to the preceding three-part madrigal comes this setting of Guarini's poem to the spring, which, while it brings new life to the world of nature, cannot refesh a faded love.

The music's air of gentle, almost sentimental regret makes no intense demands on the listener, but we should not, therefore, fail to appreciate Monteverdi's skill in composing it – for it is the most perfectly written of all the madrigals in Book III. The three opening lines of the poem are set to phrases which ideally (if unpretentiously) convey the literal meaning and, at the same time, combine in delectable counterpoint. A similarly apt pair of phrases cover the next two lines and contrast touchingly with the opening. They lead on to the more lively phrases which describe the erstwhile beloved. This liveliness lifts the music to exactly the right degree of intensity to make the lyrical sadness of the last couplet a perfect conclusion to a madrigal whose skill and content are ideally matched.

12. "*Perfidissimo volto* [Most treacherous face!]" (Guarini). The uncertain mood of this poem with the lover raging agaisnt the beloved and yet unable to cure the sickness is beautifully conveyed by Monteverdi. The contrasted opening phrases are elaborated into a complete texture which breaks up at the words "*Già mi parevi dir* [Once you seemed to say]", set simply in three parts. The other two voices enter most effectively at the heart-sick cry "*Ahi, ch'è spent'il desio* [Alas, that desire has vanished]", which grows in complexity before becoming simple again as the words *O volto troppo vago* [O face too lovely and too wicked]" change the lover's mood once more.

13. "*Ch'io non t'ami, cor mio* [If ever I should cease to love you]" (Guarini). This touching avowal of love, untroubled by jealousy or anguish, might well have been written by Monteverdi to his wife, so in-

timate and confidential is the mood of the music. If this was so, the sweet invocation to death becomes the more moving for in only four years' time his beloved Claudia was to die, leaving him inconsolable. Not a word is obscured by the setting and yet with consummate skill he avoids any feeling of episode, so perfectly are phrases blended one into the other. It is the least demonstrative and yet among the most moving madrigals in the book.

14. "*Occhi un tempo mia vita* [Eyes that once were my life]" (Guarini). A somewhat conventional poem by Guarini gets more than it deserves in this setting. The brilliant constructional device which binds the first section together shows Monteverdi extending his technical repertoire towards a time when writing for solo voice was to force different formal problems upon him. The bass of the first bars is repeated in the tenor underneath a more florid second phrase which then takes flight on its own in the lower three voices and is taken up by all five, so giving an extended section of 18 bars a tautness of construction while still allowing the maximum expressive freedom. The remainder of the madrigal uses already established techniques with, possibly, less than usual inspiration.

15. *Prima parte* [First part]: "*Vivrò fra i miei tormenti e le mie cure* [Still must I live in Anguish, Grief, and Care]". 16. *Seconda parte* [Second part]: "*Ma dove, o lasso me! dove restaro* [But where, alas! where be those Relics sweet]". 17. *Terza e ultima parte* [Third and final part]: "*Io pur verrò là dove sete; e voi* [But where you be, if still you be, I wend]" (Torquato Tasso, from *Gerusalemme Liberata,* transl. by Edward Fairfax). These three stanzas from *Gerusalemme Liberata* come shortly after the passage which Monteverdi later set as *Il combattimento di Tancredi e Clorinda* (Book VIII Nr. 8). Tancredi has slain his beloved who, disguised as a knight in armor, had challenged him to mortal combat. Now comes his lament as, raising her visor, he realises whom he has killed.

The desperation of his grief in the opening is entrusted by the composer in an extraordinary way to the declamatory power of the human voice, for the parts move very little away from repeated notes. As a result the leap of a fifth in the beginning of the second part comes almost as a shock, making the cry "*dove* [where]" sound truly heartfelt. Even a quite normal descending phrase to the words "*Ahi, sfortunato!* [Ah, hapless (nymph)]" gains enormously in intensity by contrast with the melodically static declamation which precedes it. The three linked madrigals show an extraordinary restraint, depending for their effect not on melodic invention but on declamatory and harmonic power. They follow uncompromisingly the theory current in Monteverdi's time that music must serve the text, the one gaining power from the other. To listen to it without following, word by word, what is being said is to lose the whole point.

18. "*Lumi miei, cari lumi* [My lights, dear eyes]" (Guarini). The gently sensuous melodic lines and harmonies of this setting of Guarini's lyric comes as something of a relief after the stark intensity of the preceding Tasso madrigals. The opening for the three female voices may recall the ladies of Ferrara once more, as in "*O come è gran martire* (Nr. 2 above – see also Book IV Nr. 14 and Book IX Nr 12), but the musical style is altogether earlier with its fluent counterpoint which flows from each newly stated point.

19. *Prima parte* [First part]: "*Rimanti in pace—a la dolente e bella / Fillida Tirsi sospirando disse* ['Stay here in peace,' said Thyrsis, sighing, to the sad and beautiful Phyllis]". 20. *Seconda parte* [Second part]: "*Ond'ei di morte la sua faccia impressa* [And he, with death imprinted on his face]" (Livio Celiano). The parting of Thyrsis and Phyllis which ends the third book takes two madrigals to set. Among the most advanced of the collection, the music is ineffably moving and, technically speaking, amazingly accomplished. It would take many pages to expound the felicities of its composition in any detail but, luckily, Monteverdi at his technical best is always at his most expressive, so that much can be left to sound for itself. One should note the strongly integrating effect of the repeated music for the repetition of the word "*rimanti* [stay here]"; the effect of motionless, silent grief of the descending chromatic phrase as Phyllis weeps; the parallel deathly pallor on Thyrsis's face so effectively evoked at the beginning of the second part; the agitated rocking subject to the words "*di martir in martire* [from suffering to suffering]" and the incredible moment before Phyllis finally speaks. Faced with music like this it is best to be silent and just listen.

Notes for *LIBRO IV: MADRIGALI A CINQUE VOCI* (1603)

1. "*Ah, dolente partita, / Ah, fin de la mia vita, / Da te part'e non moro? e pur i' provo / La pena de la morte / E sento nel partire / Un vivace morire, / Che dà vita al dolore / Per far che moia immortalmenti'il core* [O woeful parting! / O end of my days! From thee how can I go, / and yet not die? The pangs of death I'm sure / I feel, and all that parting souls endure. / For mine, 'tis past into my griefs: Hence I / have ceased to live, those live immortally]" (Giovanni Battista Guarini, from *Il pastor fido;* transl. Sir Richard Fanshawe, 1647, from Act III Scene 3, The parting of Mirtillo from Amarillis). The quality of the fourth book of madrigals is established at the outset by this magnificent madrigal and, it must at once be said, the standard is never lowered.

The noble poem of Guarini is about parting lovers and, with the passionate opening note which splits into a chain of agonised dissonances and resolutions, Monteverdi embarks on a setting of even greater nobility. This is parting on the grand scale.

The music is integrated as never before and shows that inevitability which is characteristic of most great art and virtually beyond the powers of description. Notice how the words "*e pur i' provo*" [I'm sure I feel the pangs of death...] are introduced so subtly at the very cadence of "*Ah, fin de la mia vita* [O end of my days]". The two ideas run concurrently for some bars but the new phrase, with the increased intensity of its syncopated rhythm, takes over until the first quatrain is set. A brief moment of silence and Monteverdi translates the self-contradictory image of "*un vivace morire* [a living death]" into almost tangible sounds. This breeds a new excitement through which, little by little, creeps in the idea of the heart's eternal death and the music sinks to its amazingly beautiful end.

2. "*Cor mio, mentre vi miro* [My beloved! gazing on you, / I am visibly transformed into your likeness, / and so transformed / sigh out my spirit in a single breath. / O beauty giving death, / O beauty giving life, / since the heart / reborn for you must straightway die]" (Guarini). Monteverdi once wrote about training singers for an opera of his. Persuade them, he urged, to concentrate upon the meaning of the actual word they are singing irrespective of its relationship to the overall mood of the scene. Thus in the middle of a lament for lost love, if the text refers to past happiness

then the singer must portray it as vividly as possible. In this way the pathos and sadness of the whole is made the more effective.

This attitude translated in terms of composition enables him to set with complete success the extraordinarily involved literary images of this poem by Guarini. Of course the overall understanding and conception is there but the vivid portrayal of the ideas as they pass by makes a parallel musical image to the complicated verbal one and enhances rather than dulls the ambiguities which are the strengh of the poem.

3. "*Cor mio, non mori? e mori* [My heart, will you not die? Die, die]". The iamge of dying which recurs so often in the love lyrics of the seventeenth century was understood to have an ambiguous meaning. It could be literal, as in this lyric, or have a sexual significance as in the previous one. In the distinction between the two lies the difference of response both from composer and listener in what otherwise might seem to be similar madrigals. In "*Cor mio, mentre vi miro*" the lovers are making love, in "*Cor mio, non mori?*" they are parted and the one who is left alone longs for death as a resolution to his sorrow.

4. "*Sfogava con le stelle / Un infermo d'amore / Sotto notturno ciel il suo dolore* [One tormented by love / cried out his sadness / to the stars / under the night sky]" (Ottavio Rinuccini). The marvelous image contained in this poem by Rinuccini of the lover, love-sick, crying out his passion alone under the night sky has called forth some extraordinary effects from Monteverdi. Several lines of the poem are set as a free declamation for the five singers who are each given one note and the freedom to perform the words as they think best. These moments of improvised performance flow without break each time into composed measures. The extraordinary harmonies and use of dissonance (how the academics must have frowned at the words "*pietosa, sì*" — in the phrase "With your semblance of gold you would make her / full of pity, as you make me full of love") make this among the most original of his compositions at this time.

5. "*Volgea l'anima mia soavemente* [My soul sweetly turned]" (Guarini). Many of these madrigals seem to convey their meaning in almost physical terms, so close is the union between the words and their enhancing music. In the first guatrain of "*Volgea l'anima mea*" we can almost see the slow turn of the head as the beloved turns her glance on her lover and feel the mounting excitement of desire in his response. The tormented

uncertainty which follows is no less clear; neither is her calmly loving acceptance.

6. *Prima parte* [First part]: *(Et tu, Mirtillo)*[3] / *Anima mia, perdona* / *A chi t'è cryda sol* [Pardon, dear (Mirtillo), her that's only cruel when / she must not pity; Pardon thy fierce foe". 7. *Seconda parte* [Second part]: *"Che se tu se'il cor mio* [For if thou be my heart]" (Guarini, from *Il pastor fido;* transl. by Sir Richard Fanshawe, 1647, from Act IV Scene 4). The lover addresses the beloved and seeks forgiveness for her cruelty. As if uncertainly plead- ing the case, the music of the first part constantly breaks off and starts again with the singers declaiming the broken phrases as of one voice. Only in the last couplet of the second part, where the lover takes the suf- fering to herself — and, in a sense, accepts it — does Monteverdi illustrate this resolution in beautifully sustained counterpoint.

8. *"Luci serene e chiare, voi m'incendete* / *Ma prove'il core* / *Nell'incendio diletto, non dolore* [Serene, bright eyes / you set my heart on fire but in the flames / it feels pleasure, not pain]". Once more Monteverdi achieves a near physical realisation of the text. The incredibly beautiful opening presents the beloved's eyes as if she were palpably present. No less vivid is the fire they cause in the lover's breast. This contrast demonstrates clearly the composer's masterly control of his material. The clear stillness of the eyes is set in long sustained notes with all voices moving together; the fire is shown by closely placed separate entries of the voices using the explosive *"v"* of *"voi"* to give a cumulative excitement not unlike sparks rising from the flames.

The poem is in three three-line stanzas and from this Monteverdi takes the structure of his madrigal. *"Dolce parole e care, voi mi ferite* [Sweet, pre- cious words / You wound me]", beginning stanza 2, is set to a heightened version of the opening triplet. The last triplet apostrophising love and its miracle *"O miracol d'amore* / *Alma ch'è tutta foco e tutta sangue* / *Si strugg'e non si duol, mor'e non langue* [O miracle of love, / that a soul so burning and bleeding / can be consumed without anguish, can die and not lan- guish]") is set to music lasting over twice the length and this itself paral- lels the music of the opening triplets by being divided in two with the

---

3   Omitted by Monteverdi.

repetition of the marvellouslly exalted cry "O miracol d'amore". There can be little doubt in what sense Monteverdi understood the reference to dying contained in the last line.

9. *La piaga c'ho nel core* [The wound I have in my heart]". Monteverdi never seems to tire of or fail in his response to the somewhat artificial conceits of these early Italian love-lyrics. Each is treated with a grave sensuality that raises them to a world of real feeling and passion. There is certainly no artificiality in this madrigal's opening image of a wounded heart; the extraordinary harmonies seem to ache with the pain of it. To contemporary ears they must indeed have sounded strange. He passes by the central two lines of the poem in simple unstressed declamation allowing the music to blossom wonderfully in the thrice-repeated final couplet.

10. *"Voi pur da me partite* [Yet you leave me]" (Guarini). The bitter outburst of the opening of this nine-line madrigal persists until the last couplet (the final three lines being "*O meraviglia di durezz'estrema / Esser alma d'un core / E separarsi e non sentir dolore* [A marvel of the utmost hardness, / to be the very soul of a heart / and separating not to feel sadness]"), whose setting takes up over half the piece. The mood changes to one of sad wonder that a lover could part without feeling pain. After the harsh "*meraviglia di durezza*" Monteverdi composes in a series of repeated, fragmented contrapuntal points superbly appropriate to the text. Notice the recurring phrase to "*e separarsi*" where two voices start together in unison and move apart from one another.

11. "*A un giro solo de'begl'occhi lucenti / Ride l'aria d'intorno / E'l mar s'acquet'e i venti / E si fa il ciel d'un altro lum'adorno* [One glance from her fair bright eyes / makes the air laugh with joy, / hushes the winds and the sea, / and graces the heavens with another light]" (Guarini). The music of the first of the two quatrains in the poem illustrates the text phrase by phrase; the rapid glance of the eyes; the laughing air; the silenced wind and sea and the marvelously brilliant new light that is given to the heavens. There is a delectable artificiality in this which is planned in superb contrast to the highly charged setting of the last four lines.

12. "*Ohimè, se tanto amate / Di sentire dir 'ohimè', / Deh, perchè fate / Chi dice 'ohimè' morire?* [Ah me! If you so much love / to hear me say 'Ah me,' / then why do you kill / the one who says it]" (Guarini). This must count

as one of the greatest madrigals ever composed. The elaboration of the word "*ohimè*" in the poem is seized on by Monteverdi as the focal point of his setting. Using the falling interval of a third in two parallel voices (which even sounds like a sigh), he repeatedly works it into the texture with an intensity which would have done credit to Beethoven, contrives to lay bare the heart of its meaning with an incredible directness and apparent simplicity. The chain of the thousand, thousand sighs ("*mill'e mille dolc' 'ohimè*") and the very end of the madrigal are byond comment.

13. "*— Io mi son giovinetta / E rido e canto alla stagion novella —/ Cantava la mia dolce pastorella* ['I am a young girl / and I laugh and sing in springtime.' / So sang my sweet shepherdess]" (Giovanni Boccaccio). It is something of a relief to come to this amusing bitter-sweet poem by Boccaccio brilliantly set by Monteverdi to music which illustrates and illuminates each phrase as it goes by. Yet all is of a piece and belongs together.

14. "*Quel augellin che canta* [That little bird which sings]" (Guarini, from *Il pastor fido*, Act I Scene 1). The idea of the three ladies of Ferrara seems to be present in this enchanting, light-hearted madrigal about the little bird in love. With an art which conceals art, Monteverdi creates a delightful piece of music, subtle in rhythm, graceful in melody.

15. "*Non più guerra! pietate!* [No more battles! Have pity!]" (Guarini). With this madrigal we are back to sterner things. Using the war-like rhythm he was to exploit so much in the *Madrigali guerrieri* (Book VIII, below), the opening creates a vivid picture of strife and battle. So often the last two lines form the crux of the poem and Monteverdi's setting of it, and here the beautiful way he elaborates the descending phrase to "*e del morir*" leads up to a noble climax of heroic despair.

16. *Sì, ch'io vorrei morire* [Yes, I should like to die]". In this book we go from one great madrigal to the next which seems even greater. This amazingly sensual poem is matched by a sensuality of music we rarely find again in Monteverdi until his opera *L'incoronazione di Poppea*. After the opening desperate declamation the interweaving dissonances bring the idea of the tongues of lovers meeting in a kiss with a reality which is at the least surprising even to us today. The eagerness for sexual death mounts through the piece until the final restatement of the opening which has now gained a new meaning.

17. "*Anima dolorosa che vivendo / Tanto peni e tormenti* [Sorrowful soul,

that living finds / such pain and torment]". An anguished soul giving voice to its suffering is the subject of this poem. The music, with violently changing moods, seems to match it perfectly. Once again the principle of responding immediately and directly to the meaning of the words as they come rather than as part of a general mood gives great strength to the image. The languor of the opening bars is broken by the setting of "*che vivendo*" which in its turn relapses into "*tanto peni e tormenti*". The quick changes give a vivid impression of the distracted lover. The points of climax are perfectly judged so as to give maximum point to the twice-repeated final couplet in simple, despairing declamation.

18. "*Animal del cor mio / Poi che da me, misera me, ti parti* [Soul of my heart, / since you have left me, unhappy me]". The "*anima*" of the first line seems to float in mid-air above the lower three voices and the resulting atmosphere of elegiac resignation persists throughout this madrigal in spite of the passing illustration of phrases like "*non isdegnar* [at least allow me to follow you...]" and "*vivrò d'amor* [I shall live an example of love...]". We should, nevertheless, be wrong to undervalue this short madrigal because of its restraint. It is as skilfully written as the rest in Book IV but yields up its content less readily.

19. "*Longe da te, cor mio, struggomi di dolroe* [Far from you, my heart, I die of grief]". The elaborate counterpoint of the opening section with its unusually stressed pont to the word "*struggomi*" makes for a fine contrast with the urgently homophonic request for the beloved's return. The music moves towards its climax as the brilliance of her eyes is recalled and makes a dying fall in the contrapuntal setting of the last two lines.

20. "*Piagn'e sospira, e quand'i caldi raggio* [He wept and sighed, and when the flocks]". Many composers experimented with the idea of a rising or falling chromatic phrase used in the manner of a *cantus firmus* to illustrate the idea of tears falling or weeping. There is nothing, therefore, particularly new in Monteverdi's use of the same device, though few used it as well. The most original part comes with the setting of the last two lines ("*E in rilegendo poi le proprie note / Spargea di pianto le vermiglie gote* [And then, re-reading his own words, / blushed, while tears flowed down his cheeks") where the lover stands back from the tree in whose bark he has carved the beloved's name. Now all the voices sing together

and the sadness as the lover thinks on what he has done come to us with much greater force for the sudden change in style.

— Monteverdi's Fifth and Sixth Books of Madrigals —

[Not recorded by RL. Individual numbers include:]

IL QUINTO LIBRO DE MADRIGALI for 5 voices (1605)
"*Ahi, com'a un vago sol cortese giro*" (14)
"*Amor, se giusto sei*" (16)
"*Che dar più vi poss'io?*" (12)
"*Ch'io t'ami e t'ami più de la mia vita*" (part 1); "*Deh, bella e cara*" (part 2); "*Ma tu più che mai dura*" (part 3)(Guarini, from *Il pastor fido*) (9-11)
"*Cruda Amarilli*" (Guarini, from *Il pastor fido*) (1)
"*Eco, Silvio, colei ch'in odio hai tanto*" (part 1); "*Ma se con la pietà non è in te spenta*" (part 2); "*Dorinda, ah dirò mia, se mia non sei*" (part 3); "*Ecco piegando le ginocchie a terra*" (part 4); "*Ferir quel petto, Silvio*" (part 5)(Guarini, from *Il pastor fido*) (4-8)
"*E cosi a poc'a poco torno farfall*" (Guarini) (18)
"*Era l'anima mia già presso a l'ultim' hore*" (Guarini) (3)
"*M'è piu dolce il penar per Amarilli*" (Guarini, from *Il pastor fido*) (13)
"*O Mirtillo, Mirtill'anima mia*" (Guarini, from *Il pastor fido*) (2)
"*Questi vaghi concenti*" (*a nove voci*) (19)
"*T'amo, mia vita*" (Guarini) (17)
"*Troppo ben può questo tiranno amore*" (Guarini) (15)

IL SESTO LIBRO DE MADRIGALI for 5 voices, with a dialogue for 7 voices (1614)
"*A Dio, Florida bella*" (*concertato*) (G. B. Marini) (7)
"*Batto qui pianse Ergasto*" (*concertato nel clavicembalo*) (Marini) (8)
Lamento d'Arianna: "*Lasciatemi morire*" (part 1); "*O Tseo, Teseo mio*" (part 2); "*Dove, dove è la fede*" (part 3); "*Ahi, ch'ei non pur risponde*" (part 4) (Rinuccini) (1-4)
"*Misero Alceo*" (*concertato*) (18)
"*Ohimè, il bell viso*" (Petrarch) (16)

"*Presso un fiume tranquillo*" *(dialogo a 7, concertato)* for 7 voices (Marini) (9)

"*Qui rise, O Tirsi*" *(concertato)* (Marini) (17)

Sestina ("*Lagrime d'amante al sepolcro dell'amata*"): "*Incenerite spoglie, avara tomba*" (part 1); "*Ditelo, o fiumi e voi ch'udiste*" (part 2); "*Darà la notte il so*" (part 3); "*Ma te raccoglie, o ninfa*" (part 4); "*O chiome d'or, neve gentil del seno*" (part 5); "*Dunque amate reliquie* (part 6) (S. Agnelli) (10-15)

"*Una donna fra l'altre honesta e bella vidi*" *(concertato nel clavicembalo)* (6)

"*Zefiro torna e'l bel tempo rimena*" (Petrarch) (5)

— Monteverdi's Seventh Book of Madrigals —

In 1619, after a gap of five years, Monteverdi published his seventh book of madrigals and, with it, finally abandoned the last vestige of his ties with the older five-voiced madrigal form. Even the title, "*Concerto*", was new and, as if to make the point more clearly, five is the one number not included in the title list of voices employed: "*Concerto. / Settimo Libro / de Madrigali / A 1. 2. 3. 4. & Sei Voci, con altri / generi de Canti.*"

The shedding of his earlier style had been a gradual process for, although well aware of the experiment in monody orginating from the *Camerata* group in Florence, he had virtually disregarded them and gone his own way.

Monteverdi showed first his skills in the older madrigalian techniques (though unmistakably himself from the beginning) and then gradually, from within those techniques, he increased the declamatory power of the combination by distilling the five-voiced textures into what was esssentially two- and three-part music with the extra voices giving greater harmonic potential for expression. The next step was to introduce an instrumental bass, the continuo, to support and finally liberate all five voices. At this point, since the continuo now provided the harmonies, it was not necessary to use all the voices at the same time.

Meanwhile, too, he had turned to opera and been able to explore the different dramatic and expressive possibilities of voices alone and in combination with instruments. It seemed as if, with the confirmation of this accumulated experience, he at last felt himself equipped and mature and free enough to shed for ever the old ties in Book VII of his madrigals.

There are only four solo numbers in what is a very large collection of music. The greater part in quantity and quality is taken up by duet and trio madrigals with continuo—the true distillation of the process of madrigalian development that had been going on in his work for 32 years since the publication of his first book in 1587.

The eighth book, which appeared in 1638, contains a vast and dazzling variety of music, but it is in the seventh that the quintessential genius of Monteverdi is most clearly and consistently exposed.

The overall title, "*Concerto*", has been the subject of a good deal of conjecture as to meaning and intent. It clearly does not imply that the book was intended to be sung in one evening for, apart from length, the numbers are in no meaningful sequence.

A clue, perhaps, lies in the dedication to Catherine Medici who had married Francesco Gonzaga and became Duchess of Mantua. Amid the fulsome phrases there is reference to a concert of the "Muse Concertate" of Apollo who, like the composer, would show "*divoto affetto verso la Serenissima Casa Gonzaga*": Monteverdi had only left Mantua in 1613 to take up his appointment as *Maestro di capella* at St. Mark's in Venice and by paying homage in this way to his former patrons he could at once celebrate the duty of the Muses to the Gonzagas and his own liberation, under their aegis, into the new *concertato* style.

Sinfonia. 1. "*Tempro la cetra* [I temper my lyre]". Placed appropriately at the beginning, "*Tempro la cetra*" is very similar in structure to the prologue of *L'Orfeo*. It begins with a sinfonia for strings whose last six measures punctuate the series of verses for solo tenor and continuo which are all composed above variants of the same bass-line. A dance-like interlude is added at the end before the whole opening sinfonia is repeated.

The text, by Marini, tells of the power of music to celebrate the cause of love—make love not war—and, while it serves splendidly as an introduction to a volume of madrigals exclusively concerned with love, it is tempting to think it might also have been the prologue to a now lost opera.

2. "*Non è di gentile core* [There is no gentle heart]". While the vocal writ-

ing in "*Tempro la cetra*" with its elaborate *gorgie* bears all the hall-marks of the overtly declamatory style of Monteverdi used in his operatic prologues, the two voices in *Non è di gentil core*" speak with an intimate personal warmth that is of quite a different order.

Degl'Atti's poem tells of the pleasing flames of love's fires and the joy the beloved takes in them. All this is winningly depicted in the music and, as the poem returns to its first line, so Monteverdi, with some magical variants, returns to his opening music. The augmentation of the intertwining phrases at the end have a physical sensuality about them that seem to conjure up in sound an actual embrace.

3. "*A quest'olmo* [To this elm]," for six voice *concertato*, at first seems as if it might have come from an earlier period. The imitations of the opening section follow one another with smooth simplicity which, however, soon reveals a control of declamation that could only have come from the composer's maturity. Then enter the instruments other than continuo (violins and flutes) and the point of the opening is made clear. They surround the solo voices as it comes to the heart of Marini's poem; the expression of a bitter-sweet regret at seeing once more Nature's beauty in a place which had been witness to the past fires of the singer's love for Clori. Returning there provides only sad, shadowy memories.

4. "*O come sei gentile* [How pretty you are]". This poem by Guarini was set, in English translation, by Orlando Gibbons as a five-voiced madrigal. But, fine as that is, the comparison of the condition of the caged singing bird with the song of the captivated lover seems more apt as a duet. In Monteverdi's setting there is no mere obvious answering of one voice to the other. Each new inflection of the single or double line is marvellously integrated with the deeper meaning of the text. Especially remarkable is the stillness in the music as we realise the essential difference between the two; the bird singing lives, the lover, singing dies for love. As with all great settings of words to music the meaning takes on a new significance, more profound than before.

5. "*Io son pur vezzosetta pastorella* [I am a beautiful shepherdess]". Monteverdi seems always to have been attracted to lyrics that at some point have an abrupt change of mood in them. A situation is described only to be shown false and illusory; the poet is in love, but there is a flaw; the place where great happiness was experienced is revisited, but the hap-

piness is gone; a bird sings, a lover sings, but there is a fatal difference. Now it is the shepherdess, the prettiest girl at the fair, sought after by everyone – everyone, that is, except Lidio, the one she loves. The opportunities for musical contrast inherent in these lyrics are obvious and, in Monteverdi's hands, capable of infinite variety.

6. *"O viva fiamma* [O living flame]". In the first part of this madrigal Monteverdi uses the two voices singing alternate lines dovetailed with one another to build up a remarkable degree of excitement in the invocation of all things natural and supernatural to witness the poet's anguish in this beautiful place where once such happiness had been but is no more. Then, together, the voices, as if worn out in their pain and no longer able to vie with one another, invoke, in a great curve of sound, the spirits to take pity on their bitter weeping.

7. *"Vorrei baciarti* [I want to kiss you]". Monteverdi chose a combination, unique in this book, of two contraltos for the setting of this poem by Marini. It presents special problems for there is no point of contrast, only a list of the beloved's particularly notable features and the effects they have on the poet. The onus of providing shape and variety is on the composer and the problem is beautifully resolved. Particularly notable are the different ways Monteverdi begins each new paragraph of music. Sometimes the voices answer one another and then join together; sometimes a line is set for one voice and the other picks up the end of it to set off an imitative point which in turn leads to another; sometimes they sing alternate lines skilfully molded as if into one. Length and pace of the paragraphs were also clearly matters for conscious control. This madrigal builds gradually and gently in excitement to a cadence at the words "*onor del bel viso*" [does honor to a beautiful face]. Then comes the final section with the lovely, warm phrase describing the effect of the beloved's smile.

8. *"Dice la mia bellissima Licori* [My most beautiful Licori says]". The two tenor voices begin this deliciously romantic duet, a setting of a poem by Guarini, by moving gently together through the first two lines. Then comes the image of love as a little spirit who flies hither and thither but can never be caught. Immediately the voices separate – the musical imagery is quite clear – and with the interplay of the new figure create a charming picture of the god of love. Indeed he almost seems to disappear

into thin air as the music suddenly breaks off and the beautiful romantic end of the duet begins, leaving no doubt as to the singers' intentions.

9. "*Ah, che non si conviene* [It is not right]". This is among the most consciously adventurous of the duet madrigals in Book VII. The wide range of the opening phrase describing the anguish of the betrayed lover makes this immediately clear. It is almost physical in its quick burst of tension, like a sudden pain in the heart. Equally apt is the sense of distance in the setting of the words "*lontan da voi*" [far from you] and the extraordinary unison of the two voices above a treading bass line describing the rock as immovable in the sea as the poet is in his love.

10. "*Non vedrò mai le stelle* [I shall never see the stars]". Another madrigal of betrayed love, "*Non vedò mai le stelle*" demonstrates still further the infinite flexibility of Monteverdi's use of two voices in setting and expressing the meaning of words. It seems often as if the intent behind the poem is completely master of the way it is set, whereas it is, of course, the composer who does the responding and, by his skills, exposes the meaning of the words and enhances it. In this madrigal the two voices interact to keep the music up in the air, even with some daring gaps over which it seems to soar, until the solo phrase begins the main intent of the poem, the memory of the beloved's eyes as the lover looks up at the night sky and sees them reflected there in the stars. This memorable phrase and the beautiful contrasting triple-meter section take us to the final peroration "*ch'anzi a tanti occhi*" [who before so many eyes].

11. "*Ecco vicine, o bella Tigre* [Now is the time, o beautiful Tiger]". The somewhat exaggerated sentiments of this poem are perfectly echoed in Monteverdi's setting for two tenors. The dotted rhythm of the opening phrase shows us what to expect — you can scarcely perform it without putting your hand on your heart — and we are not disappointed. He follows and amplifies the meaning of each successive phrase so that the singers seem to compete with each other in their fervor. Even the romantic ending has the same slightly tongue-in-cheek touch of exaggeration.

12. "*Perché fuggi* [Why do you run away]". With uncanny sensitivity Monteverdi catches the tone of every poem he sets in this great collection of madrigals. "*Perché fuggi*", in contrast to the posturing of the previous madrigal, is a gentle pastoral poem whose emotional content is caught within the elegant sophistication of Marini's imagery. The musi-

cal picture of the fleeing shepherdess is enchantingly done and the degree of seriousness of the shepherd's involvement is beautifully gauged by the slip into triple meter as he remembers the kiss that did the damage.

13. "*Tornate, o cari baci* [Return, o dear kisses]". Pursuing the topic of kisses with the same degree of seriousness and sophistication, "*Tornate*," to another poem by Marini, celebrates their life-restoring power; their power to refresh fading passings. Musically it is in three sections; the middle section uses one of Monteverdi's favorite harmonic effects, answering one phrase abruptly in a tonality a major third lower and then back again with a delectable chromatic melodic slide of a semitone that is inherent in the change. The third section acts as a sort of recapitulation, based as it is on the little syncopated setting of "*baci, baci*" [kisses, kisses] which concluded the first part.

14. "*Soave libertate* [Sweet freedom]". At an altogether different level of commitment, "*Soave libertate*", a setting of a poem by Chiabrera, is one of the most beautiful madrigals in a volume that sets an amazingly high standard for comparison. The sweet regret (which is at once no regret) for erstwhile liberty, is the memory of freedom of a man happily bound by the chains of love. So tender is the beginning that it seems almost as if the composer might have been recalling the love he had for his own young wife, Claudia, who died many years before in Mantua. The whole duet is suffused with an exceptional warmth; the lyrical phrases intertwine with each other as gently as the lover is held by the bonds of his love. The final "*addio per sempre*" [goodbye for ever] is wonderfully expressive. Perhaps it had special connotations; it certainly can acquire them.

15. "*S'el vostro cor, madonna* [If your heart, madonna]". This is the only madrigal in the volume set for tenor, bass, and continuo. Presumably Monteverdi sought the darker vocal colors for this gloomy poem by Guarini about unhappy love. He certainly exploits the greater range now at his disposal and works the music elaborately with close imitation between the voices and fewer lyrical phrases than usual.

16. "*Interrotte speranze*" [Hopes cut short]". If the quality and maturity of Monteverdi's genius as shown in this volume were ever in doubt, this amazing piece of music would convince the most sceptical of listeners. It takes the somewhat formal poem of Guarini and transforms it, in musi-

cal terms, into a human document of the greatest power. The two voices begin in unison. One slowly rises from the other which then slowly rises to a unison once more, the whole texture gradually moving above a pedal note in the bass, through the range of an octave. The tension in performance becomes almost unbearable. Every new entry of the voices in the first part begins in unison, as if it were one person breaking into two under the strain of the "*interrotte speranze*". And, at the end, after the anger of "*saranno i trofei vostri e'l rogo mio*" [your trophies will be my martyrdom] the voices return once more to a final unison as at the opening. The superficial similarity of this madrigal to Florentine experiments have been over-stated by commentators with eyes not ears; for it shows more clearly than any other the fruits of the slow, individual quest for true expressive declamation of words. The *Camerata* produced nothing comparable.

17. "*Augellin* [Little bird]". This charming trio-madrigal for two tenors, bass, and continuo about the little bird sent to plead in song the lover's cause, is among the most light-hearted of the entire collection. The tenors begin, describing the bird and her singing; then the bass enters contrasting her happy lot with the lover's sadness. All three join together urging her to take flight and plead their cause, giving her the message which takes up the second half of the madrigal. The lady surely could hardly have failed to respond.

18. "*Vaga su spina ascosa* [Beautiful on its hidden thorn]" might have been composed as a companion piece to "*Augellin*" so like it is it in spirit. This time Nature provides the reflected images of the beloved's beauty, and comes off second best. The voices are treated equally and the sequence that introduces them one by one is beautifully contrived. Throughout, the music moves with smooth sophistication which makes the gradual unwinding of tension at the end a perfect resolution of the whole piece.

19. "*Eccomi pronta ai baci* [Here I am ready for your kisses]". Monteverdi seems sometimes to have been strangely unconcerned about men singing a poem intended for women and vice-versa. Perhaps this comic one by Marini, set for two tenors, bass, and continuo, and about the marks that too ardent kissing may leave for others to notice, was considered indelicate and only suitable for male company. All the first part is a preparation for the bite itself — the second tenor ends it alone in tender anticipa-

tion. The outburst when the damage is done needs no remarking; neither does the rebuttal and the sharp refusal ever to try again such an uncomfortable experience.

20. "Parlo, misero, o taccio? [Unhappy me, shall I speak or keep silent?]" This madrigal for two sopranos, bass, and continuo might be subtitled "The Lover's Dilemma". Uncertain what best to do,[4] the lover's options, as they are considered, are first presented to us in clear declamation by the three voices. The conjectured effects develop these points often with a solo voice leading imitative entries for the other two. It makes for a very clear structure that might, perhaps, be thought to divide the piece into too many segments. The tendency, however, is endemic in Guarini's poem.

21. "Tu dormi? [You are asleep?]" In the beginning of this, the first of three madrigals for four voices (soprano, alto, tenor, bass), and continuo it is as if Monteverdi would disguise the number of singers taking part. The upper three voices have the first two pages of music for themselves, gradually integrating their disjointed opening phrases into a touchingly sad cadence. The bass then enters with a lovely, rising chromatic phrase clearly indicating the weeping lover. And, as the others take it up, he adds a strong, downward arpeggio expressing the frustration at the lack of response his tears have brought. The music comes to a cadence and all four voices express their despair together in homophony before beginning the final point of imitation which dies away, as it seems their love must do also.

22. "Al lume delle stelle [Under the lights of the stars]". This wonderfully exalted madrigal, the second of those for four voices, begins with a phrase for solo tenor covering an octave and a half. In its great arch of sound we may imagine the lover, Tirsi, scanning the night sky and seeing in the stars the image of the eyes of his beloved. As he invokes them, the

4   "If I am silent, what help shall I receive as I die?
If I speak, what forgiveness will my daring receive?
Be silent, for the flame which is hidden
is well known to the one who kindles it.
Pity speaks in me,
beauty in her,
and the beautiful hard-hearted face says:
who can look on me and not languish in love."

music turns into a duet madrigal, first for the men and then the women. Love certainly causes suffering they say, but we listeners know from the ravishingly beautiful last section, where all four voices come together again, that it is a welcome pain.

23. "*Con che soavità* [With what sweetness]" *(concertato a una voce e 9 instrumenti).* Unique in Monteverdi's output, "*Con che soavità*" is a love song for solo voice accompanied by three small instrumental groups. The first is made up of continuo instruments only; the second has the three higher strings with continuo; the third uses the lower strings including double-bass — a rare specification for Monteverdi to make. Each group is used separately, as well as together, to color and enhance the single vocal line, rather as if they themselves were making commentary in dialogue on the sentiments of Guarini's beautiful lyric. It is worth noting how the composer saves his third, most sonorous group for the words *che soave armonia fareste*" [what sweet harmony you would make] and the joyous outburst of all three that follows. It is one of the sweetest, most untroubled of all Monteverdi's songs about love.

24. "*Ohimè dov'è il mio ben* [Alas, where is my beloved]". The placing apart of this duet madrigal in the sequence of the seventh book at once suggests there is something very particular about it. The poem, by Bernardo Tasso, is one of deserted love and the questions, accusations, indignation, and despair of the lover are set by Monteverdi in four short sections all composed above variants of a single bass-line, which was widely known in the seventeenth century and used by many composers. It is called the *Romanesca.* But what may have set out as a technical exercise became, in Monteverdi's hands, one of the supreme duet madrigals. The grinding dissonance of the opening sets, as with all great music, the scale and intensity of the whole. The fours sections follow each other without a break and prepare for each other with wonderful skill in dynamic control. Each has its own character: the anguish of the first, the indignation of the second, the accusation of the third, and the cry against cruel fate in the fourth with its final hope for death's release. All are expressed with a freedom that completely belies the technical restrictions of the ground bass above which they are composed.

25. "*Se i languidi miei sguardi (Lettera amorosa a voce sola in genere rappresentativo e si canta senza battuta)* [If my languishing glances — A love

letter]. 26. "*Partenza amorosa: Se pur destina e vole il Cielo* [If it is destined and wished by heaven]". The two love-letters set to music in Book VII are exercises in the art of recitative writing which at first sight might seem to be throw-backs to the earlier experiments by the Florentine *Camerata*. The description "*in genera rappresentativo*" would imply something close to theatrical presentation and the other instruction, that they be sung without a regular beat or pulse, aligns them with the much greater recitative scenes to be found in Monteverdi's operas. Although they do not have such an exalted purpose, the letters are, nevertheless, most skilfully written declamations that use every sort of technical device for integrating the single vocal line short of lyrical melody in regular rhythm. The meticulous control of pitch, imitation and sequence, repetition, and occasional melisma are wonderfully fone, though the length of each of them may prove a stumbling block at first hearing. It is, nevertheless, worthwhile persevering with close attention to the text as the voice takes us through the pages the lover has written.

27. "*Chiome d'oro* [Golden tresses]". This must be among the most infectiously happy pieces of music ever composed. It was very well known in Monteverdi's day and, for anyone listening now, it surely must bring a smile and that tremor of excitement when something so full of life and joy sounds. It is composed for two voices, two violins, and continuo above a ground bass which is deliciously amended from time to time.

28. "*Amor che deggio far* [Love what must I do]". For four voices, but otherwise expressly for the same combination of instruments and to be performed in the same way as "*chiome d'oro*," "*Amor che deggio far*" is another piece full of the springy rhythms that Monteverdi loved to write in his joyful music. The structure, however, is slightly different. All the instrumental *ritornelli* this time are composed above the same bass-line, while the vocal sections have their own repeated bass, with which the instruments only join at the very end.

29. "*Tirsi e Clori (ballo)* [Thyrsis and Cloris—ballet]". The last work in the seventh book of madrigals is a *ballo*: one of those strange mixtures of opera and dance which formed a regular part of seventeenth-century Italian court entertainment. A scene is set, characters introduce and enact a situation which is then resolved in dancing—which also probably enables the court to join in.

"*Tirsi e Clori* is a setting of words by Alessandro Striggio, Monteverdi's old friend in Mantua who also composed the libretto of *Orfeo*. It was written for Mantua in 1615 and probably included in the seventh book of madrigals both as a suitably large ending piece to counterbalance the opening "*Tempo la cetra*", and as a fitting tribute to the Mantuan court. The plot is exceedingly simple. Tirsi observes to Clori that the nymphs and shepherds are gathering to dance together. She is not at first overly keen to join in but allows herself, finally, to be persuaded and a chain of delightful choral and instrumental dances ensue.

— Monteverdi's Eighth Book of Madrigals —

MADRIGALI GUERRIERI, ET AMOROSI, con alcuni opuscoli in genere rapprsentatio, che raanso per breur Epicdi frà a cantilenza gesto. Libro Ottavo... Dedicati Alla Sacra Cesarea Maestà dell'Imperator Ferdinando III con privilegio. In Venetia.

Monteverdi published his eighth book of madrigals in 1638 when he was 71 years old. It appeared after a gap of 19 years in madrigal publication (if we except the small volume of *Scherzi musicali* of 1632) and may, with one major exception, be thought of as a compendium of his secular composition during those years arranged in two volumes, one called "*Madrigali guerrieri*" (Madrigals of War) and the other "*Madrigali amorosi*" (Madrigals of Love). Monteverdi explains this division in a long and somewhat confused general preface. He takes the classical idea that rhythmic patterns (especially in poetry) reflect emotions they should be used to represent. In music he discerns three principal passions, *concitato, molle,* and *temperato* (agitated, sweet, and restrained). The *molle* and *temperato* he commonly finds in music but nowhere the *concitato* which he further defines, after Plato, as that which would properly imitate the words and accents of a brave man in battle. With further elaboration upon the use of the Pyrrhic meter he tells us that he discovered in the use of repeated semiquavers the exact musical representation of this emotion.

Although prone to theorising, Monteverdi was the last composer to allow theory to interfere with his music. It is true that in the first part, the "*Madrigali Guerrieri*", there is a good deal of music in which the idea of repeated notes can be seen as a starting-point for composition — at its simplest in *Il combattimento di Tancredi e Clorinda* (Nr. 8) — but nowhere does it seem the principal concern. The main distinction between the two volumes is one of subject. All the madrigals of the first part use the imagery of war, mostly illustrating the strife of love, while those of the second part are to do with the joys and sadness of love, culminating in a one-act opera (*Il ballo delle ingrate*, Nr. 22) dating from his early years in Mantua, in which the fate of those who will have nothing to do with love is dramatically represented. Monteverdi's response to words was always extremely vivid so that it is to the texts and not to theories that we must look to find the real reason for the division into two parts of this large collection.

The two parts are to a certain extent inter-related. "*Altri canti d'Amor*" which opens the first part is a parody of "*Altri canti di Marte*" which opens the second. The "*Lamento della ninfa*" (from "*Non havea Febo ancora*", Nr. 18) may be thought to be paralleled by "*Gira il nemico insidioso*" (Nr. 3), *Il combattimento* by the *Il ballo delle ingrate*, and "*Ninfa che scalza il piede*" (Nr. 15) by "*Ogni amante è guerrier*" (Nr. 6). But it would be vain to search for a more detailed relationship — this would imply a long-term plan of composition which belongs to the aesthetic of nineteenth-century German Romanticism and not to that of seventeenth-century Venice.

What is, perhaps, most suprising is that this collection of works, which ranges from the solo song to opera and the heroic cantata, should have been published under the title "*Madrigali*". Not one of them bears any resemblance to the typical unaccompanied, five-voiced pieces of the earlier years of the century, and all of them have instrumental accompaniment of one sort or another. If anything the use of the title "*Madrigali*" supports the theory that Monteverdi did not just take up the idea of the solo voice as a medium liberating music fromthe shackles of sixteenth-century counterpoint, somewhat feebly demonstrated by the group of amateurs in Florence called the *Camerata*. Surveying all eight books we can see that he took his time, gradually evolving a declamatory style of his own using the traditional madrigal form as a starting point. By the time of the fifth book a harpsichord has been introduced to relieve the voices from having to provide their own *continuum* — their continuity —

by means of counterpoint. Not that he wishes to abandon the expressive pwoers of counterpoint — that would be like throwing out the baby with the bath-water — but having an instrumental bass together with an instrument like a harpsichord which can fill in harmony, lierates all the voices for us in the more important purpose of declamation. After this the number of voices could safely be varied since the harmony and the continuity are secure. For a long time he had been experimenting with the division of his five voices into two groups, one answering or contrasting with the other as if in dialogue. By the seventh book this seems to have been rationalised out as most of the pieces are for two solo voices and continuo — a combination for which he showed a special predilection (above even that of the solo voice) to the end of his life. In this way he combined the best of both worlds — the expressive power of the solo voice without losing the force of contrapuntal interplay.

The process was gradual and at no point is it possible to say that the madrigal stopped and whatever else one is to call it, began. This is surely why Monteverdi did not change the title even in Book VIII which contains some large-scale pieces. And even these do not represent a return to the earlier style but rather a development, an expansion of the achievement of the seventh book.

A. *CANTI GUERRIERI* [SONGS OF WAR].

Sinfonia. 1. "Altri canti' d'Amor [Let others sing of Love]" (Giovanni Battista Marino). Monteverdi begins his eighth book of madrigals with a short sinfonia followed by a cantata in honor of the Emperor Ferdinand. (It was probably Ferdinand II because the poem is a parody of Giovanni Battista Marino's "*Altri canti di Marte*"," which must have been written before 1625 when the poet died.)

Scored for six voices and strings it is on a grand scale and illustrates the double intent of the collection's grouping. Monteverdi wrote in one of his letters that music and its performers should always try to express the meaning of the words being sung, irrespective of the total intent of the text: thus, although the poem is in praise of the war-like passions, the music begins by illustrating the songs of love which are to be renounced. The advent of Mars ("*Di Marte io canto furibondo e fiero* [I sing of Mars, proud and angry]") is announced by a solo bass who subsequently launches into somewhat sycophantic praise of the great Ferdinand (*"Tu, cui tessuta han di Cesare alloro / La corona immortal* [You, whose immortal crown is woven from the laurels of Caesar]") which the chorus then takes up and expands.

2. *"Hor che'l ciel e la terra e'l vento tace* [Now that in earth and sky the wind is hushed]" (Francesco Petrarca). This is one of the great madrigals. The magnificent Petrarch sonnet, describing the lover awake in the night while all the world sleeps, inspired Monteverdi to rarely equalled heights of expression. The sitllness of the opening is wonderfully conceived. The lover, his passion burning, breaks into the quiet with a marvellous moment of declamation. The music is agitated and languishing by turns until the war within the wakeful poet allows Monteverdi to use his *concitato* rhythms with great effect.

A gleam of hope begins the second part (*"Così sol d'una chiara fonte viva* [So from one bright sparkling fountain]"), but the intense rising chromatic texture maintains the feeling of unrest. The greatest moment comes at the end; after a most striking solo tenor line describing, almost physically, the distance he is from any comfort, all the voices enter and from a simple triad spread out to three and a half octaves in another version of the same phrase. It is one of those rare moments in music about which there is nothing to do but listen in wonder.

3. *"Gira il nemico, insidioso amore* [Love, the insidious enemy, encircles]" (Strozzi). This comic madrigal compares love to an enemy encircling the fortress of the heart. The battle is delightfully described by the three male voices who must enter into all the forays with uninhibited enthusiasm as well as admit their final defeat with suitable lugubriousness. It is a superbly judged piece of composition.

4. *"Se vittorie sì belle* [If such fine victories]". 5. *"Armato il cor* [My heart armed]" (Ottavio Rinuccini). *"Se vittorie sì belle"*, a duet for two tenors and continuo, was an obvious candidate for inclusion in the eighth book of madrigals. Together with its companion piece, *"Armato il cor"*, it uses the flourishes of battle to great effect without becoming arid or losing a delightful underlying sense of wit and humor.

6. *"Ogni amante è guerrier* [Every lover is a warrior]". This obscure and lengthy prose passage must have been set by Monteverdi for some masque or celebration in honor of the Emperor Ferdinand III whose name

features in the text. It begins as a madrigal for two tenors and continuo and is followed by a long section for solo bass in recitative style (in which the *concitato* idea of repeated semiquavers makes another appearance). A brief section of solo tenor separates this from the final trio for three male voices. As an example of occasional music it is interesting but can scarcely rank among the most important compositions of Book VIII.

7. "*Ardo, avvampo* [I burn, I am on fire]". In some ways "*Ardo, avvampo*" might be considered as an extension of "*Gira il nemico insidioso*" (Nr. 3). The charming conceit of the lover in flames crying out to his neighbors for help might well follow on from the sack of his heart's citadel in the earlier piece. Written for eight voices and strings, the opening cries of anguish build up to a stunning climax with some amusing word setting on the way. As the choir sings of the two beautiful, thieving eyes the music becomes lyrical, even ecstatic as the pain of love changes into delight. The music fades into a quiet unison as the lover resolves to bear his lot in silence.

8. *Il combattimento di Tancredi e Clorinda* [The battle between Tancredi and Clorinda]: "*Tancredi che Clorinda un uomo stima* [Tancredi deem'd Clorinda man of might]" (Torquato Tasso, from *Gerusalemme Liberata*, 1581). The first performance of *Il combattimento di Trancredi e Clorinda* took place at the Palazzo Mazzenigo during the carnival in Venice in 1624.

For his text Monteverdi returned to the vast narrative poem of Tasso, *Gerusalemme liberata* (The Recovery of Jerusalem), which he had not used for musical setting since the time of the third book of madrigals in 1593. Now in his maturity he took the stanzas telling of Tancredi's battle with the disguised Clorinda, and set them *in genere rappresentativo* — a term which implied a dramatic attitude to performance, if not necessarily for the stage (although he envisaged such a performance for this work). In it he applied some of his ideas about the use of rhythms to express various emotions, especially the use of repeated semiquavers to represent *ira* (anger), an emotion much to the fore in *Il combattimento*.

Monteverdi's directions for performance are unusually explicit and his string-writing full of subtle imitative strokes, but the work's great strength lies in the vocal lines with the narrator linking the utterances of Tancredi and Clordinda as they enact their battle — as much a sexual symbol as one of war.

9. *Il Ballo (per l'Imperatore Ferdinando)* [Ballet]: *Entrata*. Poet: "*Volgendo il ciel per l'immortal sentiero* [Heaven's wheeling light, serene and gentle]." *Balletto:* Chorus: "*Ei l'armi cinse, e su destrier alato* [He girt on his armor and on his winged steed]". This occasional piece written in honor of Ferdinand III was clearly enacted at its first performance. The Poet, apart from celebrating a martial victory, calls for his lute and then for the water nymphs who sing and dance for their Emperor. The sycophantic text is illustrated at every phrase with wit and humor.

B. *CANTI AMOROSI* [SONGS OF LOVE].

10. "*Altri canti di Marte* [Let others sing of Mars]" (Giovanni Battista Marino). The text of the opening madrigal of the second part, the *Canti Amorosi*, of the eighth book is by Marino. It was parodied (imitated in parallel meter and rhyming scheme) in *Altri canti d'Amor*" (Nr. 1), which opened the *Canti Guerri*.

Now it is time to renounce war-like feelings and to sing of love and of the effect of two lovely eyes. Monteverdi sets it for the same combination of six voices and strings. The music reflects the reversal of sentiment, beginning with martial rhythms and, in the fifth line of the poem, turning to softer, more romantic phrases. As before, the bass soloist, presumably addressing the Emperor Ferdinand, sings lines which obliquely compliment His Royal Highness on his equal prowess in war and love. The chorus (presumably the same *orgoglioso coro* of *Altri canti d'Amor*) repeats and expands the sentiments.[5]

11. "*Vago augelletto* [Pretty little bird]" (Francesco Petrarca). Scored for seven voices and strings this madrigal exploits the contrast between solo and concerted singing. The delightful opening melody breaks off to suggest the little bird flying away and this idea recurs, rather like a rondo theme, throughout the piece, sung by various solo voices as well as by the choir. It even seems to contradict in its last appearance the main message of the poem — the similar condition of the poet and the love-sick bird — whereas in effect it enhances the idea of his loneliness.

---

5   The final lines of Nr. 1 are: "*O Gran Ferdinando, l'orgoglioso coro / Del tuo sommo valor canta e ragiona* [Oh great Ferdinand, the proud choir / sings and tells of your surpassing valor]."

12. "*Mentre vaga angioletta* [Whilst a lovely little angel]" (Giovanni Battista Guarini). Monteverdi uses the tempting imagery of Guarini's poem to make his most virtuoso duet for two tenors. It is a veritable textook of seventeenth-century vocal technique, making great demands on the singers as they imitate the changing aspects of the *angioletta's* voice. In the last quatrain a more lyrical style prevails.

13. "*Ardo, e scoprir, ahi lasso, non aridsco* [I burn and do not dare, alas, to tell]". "*Ardo*" is one of the great duet-madrigals. With a perfect economy of means the emotional significance of the text is marvelously expressed. As the feelings of the lover ebb and flow the music grows and falls in harmonic and rhythmic intensity, reserving a master-stroke for the end where the tongue-tied lover seems physically present.

14. "*O sia tranquillo il mare, o pien d'orgoglio* [Whether the sea be calm or full of pride]". Like "*Ardo*" this madrigal must rank among the best. Monteverdi creates a sense of stillness in the beginning which can be compared with "*Hor che'l ciel*" (Nr. 2). Out of this bursts the lover's anguish and despair. In the middle there is a wonderful lyric section in the triple meter which leads back to a re-creation of the opening stillness as he waits, hopeless, for his beloved's return.

15. "*Ninfa che scalza il piede* [Nymph, who with foot unshod]". Monteverdi divides the poem into three parts, the first quatrain for solo tenor, the second for two tenors, and the last octave for two tenors and bass. It gives a cumulative effect to the sound but is otherwise a somewhat arbitrary scheme. Possibly it is a scene from some larger work for the stage where the visual addition of characters would seem to give the scheme more point. However this may be, the music is delightful, full of subtle rhythms and witty illustration of the words. At the words "*Che ti posso veder* [May I see]" there is a rare tempo markng of *presto*.

16. "*Dolcissimo uscignuolo* [Sweetest nightingale]". 17. "*Chi vol haver felice e lieto il core* [Who would have a happy and carefree heart]" (Giovanni Battista Guarini). There is an unusual sub-title to both madrigals — *A 5 voci, cantando a voce piena, alla francese* (for five voices, sung in full voice in the French manner). The exact implication of this has been much discussed and still remains obscure. What they have in common is a simple brevity of phrase which alternates between solo and *tutti*. This may perhaps be thought of as characteristic of a French chanson but Montever-

di when in lighter vein quite often used this device without labelling it in this way.

18. "*Non havea Febo ancora* [Phoebus had not yet].... *Lamento della ninfa: 'Amor (dicea, il ciel / Mirando il piè fermò)* [The nymph's lament: "Love (she said, stopping and gazing at the skies)]'" (Ottavio Rinuccini). The nymph's lament with its prelude and postlude make up one of the loveliest of all Monteverdi's madrigals. The three male voices set the scene in marvellously sensitive writing. The first streaks of dawn seem to appear before us; the deep sighs of the young girl as she wanders over the fields in her anguish have an uncannily evocative effect. Then, over a ground bass, she begins her lament with the three men, bystanders as it were, showing us their own pity for her sad condition. As she bids herself be silent, the men turn to the audience and sing of the perils of love.

The piece is specifically entitled *rappresentativo* which, apart from reflecting the *temperato* passion, generally implied some quasi-theatrical presentation. The three men should be placed apart for they must sing in good ensemble (*al tempo de la mano*) while the nymph must be free to follow the *affeto del animo* as she expresses her anguish.

19. "*Perchè t'en fuggi, o Fillide?* [Phyllis, why do you flee?]". Using constant changes of rhythm and broken fragments of phrase, Monteverdi creates the image of the distracted lover Aminta. The three male voices are in continual conflict, coming together only when Phyllis runs away.

20. "*Non partir, ritrosetta* [Do not leave me, reluctant maiden]". The combination of three male voices singing in a near-homophonic style must have greatly appealed to Monteverdi and to his Venetian public, for there are many delightful examples in the last books of madrigals. What could easily have been a trivial form of seventeenth-century barber-shop harmony becomes in his hands a touchingly expressive lyrical song, whose very restraint enables the singers to inflect each verse with its own particular meaning.

21. "*Su pastorelli vezzosi* [Rise, sweet shepherds]". Monteverdi set this poem three times. In the eighth book it is for three female voices and in the ninth book for three male voices (see below). In another publication (*Arie de' diversi raccolte* — see below) it is for solo voice. None is an arrangement of another, although the light-hearted spirit of the settings is very similar.

22. *Il ballo delle Ingrate* [Ballet of the ungrateful ones]*: Sinfonia. "De l'implacabil Dio / Eccone giunti al regno* [See, we are close by the Kingdom of the implacable God, Pluto]. The one-act opera *Il ballo delle Ingrate* was composed at Mantua in 1608, one year after *L'Orfeo*. We know that it was performed again at Vienna in 1628 and may assume that the work maintained sufficient currency for it to be published in the eighth book of madrigals. In any case it is a fine example of Monteverdi's early dramatic music and the more to be treasured because so many of his operas have been lost.

It is a satire on being overly virtuous. The *"ingrate"* are the souls of women who are condemned to everlasting torment in Hell for having refused to give themselves to their lovers. Venus and Cupid, dismayed at their lack of success, come to the mouth of Hell in order to ask Pluto's help. As Cupid descends into the abyss, Venus rounds on the ladies in the audience, denouncing them for not offering their beauty in the service of love. Cupid returns with Pluto whose hard heart is melted by Venus's appeal to the love he bears his own wife, Proserpine. He summons up the spirit of the *"ingrate"* who appear through the flames to dance before them.

Pluto gives warning that all may suffer a similar fate before he orders the spirits back to their imprisonment. As they slowly descend, one of them sings a moving farewell to the light of day which is echoed from the depths by those already returned.

— Monteverdi's Ninth Book of Madrigals and
1632 *Scherzi musicali* —

The ninth book of madrigals was published in Venice by Alessandro Vincenti in 1651, eight years after Monteverdi's death. It is a compilation of music for two and three voices in various styles and from various periods — in effect a posthumous collection of pieces which, for the main part, had never before been published. We must be grateful that they have, in this way, been preserved for the quality of the music is very high.

The *Scherzi Musicali Cioè Arie, & Madrigali in stil recitativo, con una Cioaccona a 1 & 2 voci* were published during the composer's lifetime in 1632. He seems to have had nothing to do with the editing of the publication which was left to Bartholomeo Magni. There is no more order apparent in this collection than in the arbitrarily chosen ninth book. The title *Scherzi musicali* had been used by Monteverdi at Mantua in 1607 as the title of a collection of three-voiced pieces which he wrote in collaboration with his brother. Presumably he approved its use again 25 years later.

Since an overall plan is lacking in both these small but important collections, the order of the pieces has been re-arranged for the Philips recordings in order to give the maximum variety for the listener. A small number of pieces for solo, duet, and trio which were printed in various collections are also included, for the sake of completeness. The sequence in which they are performed on the Philips recordings is indicated by the bracketed numbers.

BOOK IX [MADRIGALI E CANZONETTE A DUE E TRE VOCI... dedicate all'illustrissimo Signor mio Patron Colendissimo Il Sigr Gereolamo Orologio. Libro None. Con privilegio. In Venetia.]

[5] "Bel pastor [Fair shepherd]" (Ottavio Rinuccini). This delightful little seduction scene between a shepherd and shepherdess calls so strongly for a stage setting that one is tempted to think it an excerpt from one of the lost pastoral operas — perhaps *La finta pazza Licori* or *Gl'amori di Diana e d'Endiminone* of 1627. It has many of the characteristics of the *buffo* scene which became so popular in Venetian opera. There are similar scenes to be found in Monteverdi's own *Ritorno d'Ulisse* and *L'incoronazione di Poppea*.

[7] "Zefiro torna [Zephyr returns]" (Ottavio Rinuccini). This duet for two tenors and continuo, among the most famous of Monteverdi's compositions, both now and during his lifetime, is based on a two-bar recurring bass which is repeated 56 times in succession and then five times more at the end of the madrigal — hence the sub-title *ciaccona*. It is perhaps more notable for virtuosity than for expressiveness of composition. The invention in the two voices above the recurring bass is quite breathtaking and in fairness it does all and more than the somewhat trivial poem by Rinuccini could demand. There is one heart-sinking moment when the chaconne-bass breaks off and the lamenting lover makes a per-

sonal appearance. The whole work breathes a mastery and a perfect balance of intent and realisation rarely found in any music.

[6] "Alcun non mi consigli [Let no one counsel me]". Each verse of this madrigal for three voices and continuo is set above the same bass line. The last line is treated as a refrain for the trio; the rest of each verse is given to each of them in turn.

[18] "Di far sempre gioire [Love gives hope]". Monteverdi uses the same compositional technique as in "*Alcun non mi consigli*" (Nr. 6, preceding) — three verses above the same bass line with each verse given to one of the three voices and the refrain treated as an ensemble. Within this simple and somewhat restricted form he finds great variety and wit, attempting no more than the form can contain but exploiting it to its limits.

[10] "Quando dentro al tuo seno [When into your breast]". Set entirely in homophony this little, unaffectedly sentimental song for three male voices and continuo charmingly portrays the alternating joy and sadness of the uncertain lover.

[3] "Non voglio amare [I will not love]". This trio-madrigal for three male voices and continuo is like a scherzo, witty and brilliant, with one moment in each verse when the rhythm changes and another, deeper expression fleetingly appears.

[12] "Come dolce hoggi l'auretta [How sweet today the little breeze]". When a young man at Mantua Monteverdi must often have heard three ladies at the neighboring court of Ferrara who became celebrated for their ensemble singing. There is much evidence of their influence in the earlier madrigals and this delightful trio may have been inspired by their memory (for it is certainly not an early work). It creates an untroubled pastoral atmosphere of great sensual charm.

[1] "Alle danze [To dancing]". The virtuosity of this brilliant madrigal for three male voices and continuo creates a dazzling impression of vivacious gaiety. The three verses are set to the same music save for the varied solo phrase which appears in the middle of each of them.

[14] "Perchè se m'odiavi [Why, if you hated me]" (see also Nr. 13 below, 1634 *Arie de'diversi raccolte*). This music appears in two forms which differ sufficiently to warrant both versions being included in the Philips recording. The one for three male voices and continuo (Nr. 14) was printed in the ninth book of madrigals and is an excellent example of the

lyrical stropic song of which so many appear in this collection. In the 1634 collection *Arie de'diversi raccolte* [Arias from diverse collections] the same publisher, Alessandro Vincenti, published it again, this time as a solo song. Whether the variants are Monteverdi's own or the emendations of another composer is unknown.

[16] "*Sì, sì ch'io v'amo* [Yes, yes I love you]". This characteristic trio for male voices and continuo is notable for its rhythmic subtlety. The buoyancy which the syncopations and occasional changes from triple to duple rhythm create give a wonderful lightness to this exuberant outburst in praise of the beloved.

[22] "*Su, pastorelli vezzosi* [Rise sweet shepherds]" (see also Nr. 21, in 1634 *Arie de'diversi raccolte* below). This is a setting for three male voices of the poem which appeared in Book VIII (Nr. 21 – see above) in a version for female voices. Although the spirit of the setting is similar the music is different. It is stronger, more masculine, and more brilliant; shepherds calling to shepherds rather than shepherdesses more modestly summoning their swains. In *Arie de'diversi raccolte* it appears once more as a two-verse solo song – by Monteverdi and with a different melodic line.

[19] "*O mio bene, o mia vita* [O my love, o my life]". This is somewhat more elaborate and more overtly expressive than most of the trio-madrigals for male voices and continuo. The reference to *guerra* in the phrases "*Non più guerra d'amore, no, no mio core!* [Let there be no more war of love, no, no my heart!]", "*Non più guerra di pene, no, no mio bene!* [Let there be no more war of sufferings, no, no my love!]" and *Non più guerra di noia, no, no mia gioia!* [Let there be no more war of weariness, no, no my joy!]" in the second part of each of the three stanzas enables Monteverdi to introduce the "warlike" style of some of the *Madrigali Guerrieri* in Book VIII.

SCHERZI MUSICALI Cioè Arie, & Madrigali in stil recitativo, con una Ciaccona a 1 & 2 voci... Raccolti da Bartholomeo Magni (1632)

[9] "*Quel sguardo sdegnosetto* [That glance, disdainful]". Although on a smaller scale than "*Et è pur dunque vero*" (see Nr. 8 below), this strophic song, composed in the same way with a varied vocal line above a repeated bass, is no less remarkable. The vocal writing is more florid and full of

delightful illustrative touches. Notice how the meaning of the refrain, *feriscami quel sguardo, ma sanimi quel riso* [Let that look wound me, but that smile restore me]", is changed in the third stanza by dropping the final phrase an octave and extending its conclusion.

[26] "*Eri già tutta mia* [You were once all mine]". Even in such small-scale solo songs as this Monteverdi creates an entirely personal atmosphere. The sentiments of the poem are perfectly judged in a melodic line of great subtlety enabling the singer to preserve the sophisticated level of the text without impeding the touching melancholy which underlies it.

[23] "*Ecco di dolci raggi il Solo armato* [See the sun armed with soft beams]". *[24] "Io che armato sin hor d'un duro gelo / Degli assalti d'amor potei difendermi* [I, who was armored with hard ice could defend myself from love's attack]". This strophic song, Nr. 23, had, originally, five verses, the first four to the same melody. The last verse – Nr. 24 – is strikingly different in that the first seven lines are set in a recitative style and only for the last line (line eight) does Monteverdi resume his original bass line and *arioso* melody.

[8] "*Et è pur dunque vero* [And is it then true]" is one of Monteverdi's most important composition for the solo voice. Apart from continuo cello and harpsichord he adds *sinfonie* to each verse for which he gives a single instrumental line (filled out, in the version recorded by Philips, into a five-part string ensemble).

The composer's virtuosity can be appreciated if one realises that each of the six strophes is composed above the same bass line. Yet each *sinfonia* and verse setting is quite different, springing freshly from the text without any sense of limitation.

MADRIGALI DEL SIGNOR CAVALIERE ANSELMI... posti in musica da diversi eccellentissimi spiriti (1624)

[4] "*O come vaghi* [O how charming]". This duet-madrigal was clearly written after Monteverdi's seventh book of madrigals (published in 1619) and, presumably, begged by the publisher Anselmi for his own 1624 collection. It is a love song of great tenderness and lightness.

[25] "*Taci, Armelin* [Be silent, Armelin]". This little trio for male voices

is a charming tongue-in-cheek joke. The beloved's dog, Armelin, will persist in making a disturbance when the lover is trying to declare his passion. Presumably so as not to give the wrong impression he pleads with the dog as tenderly as he might his lady until, all patience spent, he ends up by roundly cursing it, likening it to the hound of hell. This, like "*O come vaghi*" (Nr. 4, preceding), was printed in Anselmi's collection of 1624.

QUARTO SCHERZO DELLE ARIOSE VAGHEZZE, commode da cantarsi a voce sola... di Carlo Milanuzzi con una cantata & altre arie del Signor Monteverde, e del Sig. Francesco suo figliolo [by Carlo Milanuzzi with a cantata and other arias by Signor Monteverdi, and by Signor Francesco his son] (1624)

[2] "*Ohimè ch'io cado* [Alas, I am falling]". In 1624 Carlo Milanuzzi published *Quarto Scherzo... con una cantata....* The cantata was, in fact, an extended strophic song with *ritornelli* which in the Philips recording have been realised for a characteristic group of five strings. Above a repeated bass line Monteverdi writes a wonderfully varied vocal line which intimately reflects the text and its changing meaning. Particularly beautiful is the way the ending is extended as the lover sees heaven in the beloved's glance.

[17] "*La mia Turca, che d'amor / Non ha fè* [My Turkish love, who in love has no faith]". The solo song "*La mia Turca*" is found in Milanuzzi's 1624 collection.

[15] "*Sì dolce è il tormento* [So sweet is the torment]". This beautiful solo song (to which a consort acompaniment has been added for the Philips recording) is found in the collection of madrigals published under Milanuzzi's editorship in 1624.

[11] "*Maledetto / Sia l'aspetto / Che m'arde, / Tristo me* [Curses on that face which burns me, poor me]". Monteverdi must have written many of these witty, lyrical songs of which very few have survived. Thanks, then, to Carlo Milanuzzi for having preserved three of them in his 1624 collection.

ARIE DE'DIVERSI RACCOLTE da Alessandro Vincenti [Arias from diverse collections, selected by Alessandro Vincenti] (1634)

[20] "*Più lieto il guardo / Ver me non tiri* [You no longer turn your smiling glance towards me]". This solo song, with its somewhat eccentric *ritornelli* for strings, was published in Alessandro Vincenti's 1634 collection.

[13] "*Perchè se m'odiavi* [Why, if you hated me]". Solo song version of Nr. 14 — see Book IX, above.

[21] "*Su pastorelli vezzosi* [Rise, sweet shepherds]". Two-verse solo song; see also Nr. 22, Book IX above.

2

FRANCESCO CAVALLI (1602-1676)
SELECTIONS FROM THE *MUSICHE SACRE* (1656)

— *Messa Concertata* —

As noted previously,[6] Francesco Cavalli (1602-1676) when still a boy was taken up by a Venetian patrician and brought to Venice, where, having adopted his patron's name, he was first a chorister at St. Mark's and then second organist under the *Maestro di capella*, Claudio Monteverdi, whose pupil, friend and probable collaborator he became. His name has survived almost solely through histories of music. We read that he was, after Monteverdi's death, the foremost composer of opera in Italy, celebrated throughout Europe — so much so that, towards the end of his life, he was summoned, much against his will, to Paris by no less a person than Cardinal Mazarin to show the French how opera should be written. Partly due to the death of Mazarin soon after his arrival and partly due to the

---

6   For other biographical notes see pp. 126-128, above. The present text derives from the author's preface to his realization of the *Messa concertata* published in 1966 by Faber Music Ltd. The work in this edition was first performed by the Schütz Choir and the English Chamber Orchestra, conducted by RL, in Westminster Abbey 13 May 1966 — see CHRONOLOGY, below. (Ed.)

evil machinations of the jealous Lully, he suffered the most ignominious failure of his career and returned to Venice ill and disillusioned, resolving never to write opera again. Fashion had passed him by, and he spent his last years in comparative retirement, surrounded by his family in his home on the Grand Canal.

This much most students learn in differing versions, but of his many operas and the two great collections of church music virtually nothing is ever seen or heard. Yet this was the man who succeeded Monteverdi as the leading figure in Italian music.

But Cavalli did publish two major collections of church music; the *Musiche sacre* of 1656 and the *Vesperi* of 1675. Throughout his life he maintained his post at St. Mark's and eventually became *Maestro di capella*. The *Musiche sacre* was published at the height of his operatic career in twelve separate part-books. Apart from six sonatas or *canzoni* for three to twelve parts, five elaborate hymns, fifteen motets for three to eight voices and a Magnificat for double choir, the jewel of the collection is the great Mass for double choir, "*Concertata con due violini e violoncino, Ripieni e altri instrumenti se piace*".

The word *concertata* is a stylistic indication. Two sorts of ecclesiastical music were current in Italy at this time. One was a descendant of the polyphonic music of the late sixteenth century, somewhat in the manner of Vittoria and Orlando di Lassus; the other, often associated with separate instrumental parts, sprang from the operatic innovations at the beginning of the century and became known as the "*stile concertata*". (The two styles correspond to Monteverdi's definition of the "*prima e seconda prattica*".) The more elaborate writing of the second style resulted from its main purpose which was to reflect and express the emotional import of the words, and in practice this music became associated with the more important festive ecclesiastical occasions.

The occasion for which the Mass of this collection was written is unknown, although a few years later there is an account of a great performance of a Mass by Cavalli at the Arsenal in Venice and it may well be that it was this Mass that was repeated there. However this may be, it must be accounted the largest single *concerato* ecclesiastical composition to have survived from the first half of the seventeenth century, and it is certainly one of the most important. Apart from the double choir of eight voices, and eight solo voices, there are parts for two violins and violon-cino with indications that it was originally composed for five-part strings, the normal disposition at this time and one which gives a par-ticularly rich dark colour to the string sound. The *basso continuo* part is clearly for organ, very probably for two organs, placed antiphonally with the two choirs, The *violoncino* part is figured and clearly intended for a further harmonizing instrument. In the printer's preface we are told that it may (apart from being used as a string bass) also serve for chitarrone (more suitable for the smaller scale pieces in the collection), bassoon or any other instrument which can move about with "*velocita*" – such as a harpsichord. In Cavalli's own preface, apart from the usual disclaimer of merit, there are interesting explanations of the "*altri instrumenti*". He writes that in some of the vocal parts he was inserted "*sinfonie*" for three trombones or similar instruments, which can be left out or played at will. The trombones may also play when the whole choir is singing, but not with the soloists.

These imprecise instructions are absolutely characteristic of music of this period. The essential parts are there, the rest one adapts and com-poses for the circumstances surrounding the performance – the continuo players improvising and the "orchestra" playing from vocal parts or manuscript, elaborating them as they go along under the control of the *Maestro di capella*. It is very far removed from the elaborate and precise scoring of our time. The main part of the Mass is certainly there for the performing, and in it the splendours of Venetian devotions are recalled in a quite exceptionally vivid and affecting manner. It would not be in-appropriate to use that over-worked word masterpiece to describe it.

– *Magnificat* –

The *Magnificat* is, next to the *Messa concertata*, the longest single work in the 1656 *Musiche sacre* collection. The occasion of its composition, sure-ly for some great festivity in Venice, is at present unknown.

The text, the Virgin Mary's song of rejoicing at the conception of Jesus, is treated sectionally with each line or group of lines put to music which directly reflects their separate meaning. Thus the opening line "My soul doth magnify the Lord (*Magnificat anima mea Dominum*)" is set three times, exploring different inflexions of the individual words, until all voices and instruments come together in a great statement of the whole. There follows a joyous *sinfonia* in dance rhythms changing the mood for the soloists to expound "and my spirit hath rejoiced in God my Savior (*Et exsultavit spiritus meus in Deo salutari meo)*".

This direct and highly emotional response to the words, which continues throughout the work, is a manifestation of the new attitude towards music that came about in the early seventeenth century and gave rise to opera. It makes it essential for the listener to follow the text, line by line, so as not to miss the many subtle and moving points of illustration as the music proceeds. Notice, for example, how Cavalli seems to encompass all mankind in his varied antiphonal setting of the phrase "all generations (*omnes generationes)*". *(Notes for 19 August 1970 concert.)*

—   *"Laetatus Sum"*   —

Monteverdi's better-known setting of Psalm CXXI (122 in the Authorised Version) — one of his most remarkable compositions — is based almost entirely on a four-note ground-bass which he uses in different rhythms: first, seemingly, to suggest the tribes of Israel walking steadfastly to the temple in Jerusalem and then in joyful triple-time as the Psalm speaks of human relationships and the desire for peace. Only at the beginning of the Gloria does the bass change. After so long a time in G major the effect of the sudden E major chord is overwhelming as also is the return to the original bass and tonality at the end. It is such a simple device but it needs someone of Monteverdi's genius to use it so effectively.

Cavalli's setting reveals a different interpretation of the words from that of Monteverdi. Set for three voices and five-part strings (one of the few sacred works with instruments of this time in which all the parts have survived), it is more intimate and probably intended for use in one of the smaller chapels or even for domestic worship in one of the great Venetian houses. Cavalli does not attempt to show the steady tread of the entry into Jerusalem but rather the joy of the opening words ("*Laetatus sum in his quae dicta sunt mihi* [I was glad when they said unto me]"). The duple-time at "*in domum Domini* [in the house of the Lord]") seems to represent the unmoving temple and the recurring triple-time at the word "*ibimus* [let us go]", the movement towards it. So, as each phrase of the Psalm occurs, does Cavalli respond to it. The standing within the gates "*stantes erant pedes nostri in atriis tuis* (our feet shall stand in thy gates)", gazing in wonder at them, the gathering of the tribes with its march-like *ritornelli*, the moment of calm at "*fiat pax* (peace be within thy walls)" and the joy of reunion there, "*propter fratres* (for my brethren and companions' sakes)" — all these he illustrates and, finally, the emphasis by repetition of the words "*semper et in saecula saeculorum* (now and forever — world without end)" set to a flowing triple-measure line.

It is not to be compared in grandeur with Monteverdi's setting but the music speaks in its own intimate way with equal validity. *(Notes for 17-18 December 1970 concerts.)*

— *Canzona a 8* —

The canzona in eight parts exploits the, by then (1656), traditional device of using two groups of instruments playing antiphonally. The music is in alternating sections, some fugal, some homophonic. This form, which had served instrumental composition for over a hundred years was being superseded by the time this example was written, and the rich sonorities which Cavalli uses so expressively have an autumnal feeling about them. *(Notes for 17-18 December 1970 concerts.)*

— Two Hymns: "*Ave Maris Stella*", "*Deus Tuorum Militum*" —

The Latin hymn was very popular in the seventeenth century. Monteverdi composed a number of them as did Cavalli; they were not intended for congregational use. Fundamentally strophic there were usually variants of voice and line for each verse and intermittent *ritornelli*.

"*Ave maris stella* (Hail, O star of ocean)", a hymn to the Virgin, was set by Monteverdi but not more beautifully than by Cavalli whose highly emotional melodies seem to evoke even more powerfully the mother-image of the poem with just the right degree of sentiment and severity. "*Deus tuorum militum / Sors et corona, premium* (O Thou, of all Thy warriors, Lord, Thyself the crown, and sure reward)" is redolent of a seventeenth century Salvation Army with its extrovert call to battle and its almost ingenuous music. *(Notes for 17-18 December 1970 concerts.)*

— *"Salve Regina"* —

On quite another plane is "*Salve, Regina misericordiae* (Hail, Queen, Mother of Mercy)", a marvelously intimate and expressive setting of the prayer for the Virgin's intercession with Christ. Cavalli uses the first notes of a plainsong setting which pervade the opening section. The music becomes more agitated at the words "*Ad te clamamus* (We call to Thee)" and illustrates most beautifully the idea of "*suspiramus* (we sigh [to thee])". The finest moment comes towards the end — while the three lower parts sing quietly "*Et Jesum, benedictum* (and display to us... Jesus, the blessed fruit of our womb...)" the top line repeats the word "*ostende* (display)" and then the line "*O clemens, o pia, / O dulcis Virgo Maria* (O merciful, devout, O sweet Virgin Mary)" with near theatrical effect. And as all the voices become drawn into singing these words we seem almost to kneel before the Virgin in supplication. *(Notes for 17-18 December 1970 concerts.)*

— *"Laudate Dominum"* —

With the short Psalm "*Laudate Dominum omnes gentes laudate / eum omnes populi* (O praise the Lord, all ye heathen: praise him all ye nations)" CXVI (117 in the Authorised Version) we are back in the great nave of San Marco, surely on some high Feast Day. Scored for double chorus with groups of soli, brass, strings and continuo it seems to reflect the gilt splendor of the chapel for which it was written. The opening exhortation for all the nations to praise the Lord is magnificently realised with soli and choirs echoing one another. There follows a moment of quietness at the words "for his merciful kindness is ever more towards us (*Quoiniam confirmatur est super nos misercordia eius*)" but the excitement revives and culminates in the Gloria. *(Notes for 17-18 December 1970 concerts.)*

3

ANTONIO VIVALDI (1678-1741)
SELECTED COMPOSITIONS

Antonio Vivaldi, *Il Prete roso* — the red priest — as he was known to his contemporaries (a nickname denoting not his political sympathies but his shock of red hair) is one of the most perplexing figures in eighteenth century music. His output in sheer aggregate of notes must bid fair to being the largest of any composer of any time — 75 sonatas, 23 sinfonias, 454 concertos as well as over 50 full-length operas and oratorios. His speed in composition was legendary even in his own day — he is reported as having boasted that he could compose a concerto faster than a copyist could copy it. And, while the extent of the boast depends on the copyist's dexterity, it is not surprising that some of his music seems perfunctory to us now. No composer could possibly sustain quality through such a large output. But those were refreshing days when a composer regarded himself first and foremost as a practitioner with a duty to fulfill the demands made upon him. There was not much time to spare waiting for a visitation from the muses and if a concerto pleased once that was as much as it was expected to do.

We know that Vivaldi's contemporaries thought the best of his music unsurpassable in its sphere and that even Bach, in a very different musical milieu, admired his music so much that he adapted nine concertos for his own use, showing also a very proper discrimination in their selection. Hitherto, however, Vivaldi has usually been compared to Bach and Handel to his disadvantage; but just as we would not expect Wagner and Verdi, Beethoven and Bellini to write in the same style or be judged by the same critical standards, so, at last, we seem to be sufficiently at ease in the musical language of the early eighteenth century to see Vivaldi as a true original, working within similar techniques towards very different ends.

One of his most individual traits is the delight in the use of sonorities. More than any of his contemporaries in Germany he writes performers' music. What on paper often seems no more than a pattern of notes repeated above a controlled harmonic plan but without thematic reference or contrapuntal interest, becomes in performance an expression of the instrument's sonorities for their own sake, forward moving because of the strong rhythmic and harmonic impulse that underlies them. It is just one more example of the Italian characteristic of valuing music for its sound at least as much as for its content. In this lies one of the main points of divergence from the music of Bach and Handel. We have long accepted this characteristic in nineteenth century Italian music but are only now beginning to recognise this earlier manifestation of the same trait.

Closely allied to this is Vivaldi's vivid sense of color in instrumental combinations. There are frequent and precise directions for phrasing, muting, bowing and pizzicato of which the slow movement of the F Major Concerto for three violins provides an excellent example of the unprecedented use of instruments such as piccolo, bassoon, horn, trumpet and cello as soloist in concertos.

It is in the programmatic concertos that we find the most striking scoring, as certain as it is original. In the *Concerto Funebre*, for a solo group of oboe, salmoè (chalumeau), violin, three viole all'Inglese (either viols or types of viola d'amore) accompanied by strings and continuo, every instrument except for the solo violin is muted. The first three bars, made up of the simplest one bar, melodic sequence of a descending ninth, cause us, because of their very naiveté, to focus our attention on the enormous tonal gulf that the interval of a ninth makes in terms of instrumental timbres. Seven bars later the oboe and salmoè have a long trill in octaves. Melodically it comes from nowhere and goes nowhere but the coloring that it gives to these bars is worthy of Debussy. And, as if to confirm its significance, it reappears several times throughout the concerto.

Harmonic and rhythmic elements are closely connected in Vivaldi's mind. Whereas in other music of the period a duple meter is usually underlined by either the harmony or the rhythm or both, Vivaldi constantly inserts clauses in triple meter across the bar-line, harmonizing them accordingly, irrespective of the time signature. This unpredictability of the bar-line gives his music a wonderful buoyancy in performance.

There remains one aspect of Vivaldi's originality which, although less obvious, largely accounts for his pre-emindence among Italian composers of his time — the structure on which he builds his movements. The problems of extension in a style which was fast abandoning the techniques of counterpoint were considerable. Vivaldi was among the first to grasp fully the idea that a successful solution lay in the dramatic use of contrasting tonalities; that a musical phrase may be given new inflexions of meaning and possibilities for continuation by being put into another key. In the concerto, though it was not his invention, he found an admirable way to compose movements of adequate, organised length in the homophonic style. The tuttis are the mainstay of the structure; the first and last hold the movement to one key while the rest are free to exploit other tonalities. The intervening solo passages are not then left to be mere flights of virtuoso figuration, but have an underlying purpose of modulating from the key of the last tutti to that of the next.

Vivaldi spent most of his life in Venice as director of music at the *Seminario musicale dell'Ospitale della Pietà*, one of the four musical conservatoires established there as part of charitable institutions for the education of impoverished young ladies — something akin to the Foundlings Hospital in eighteenth century London. They became celebrated for their music and many of the girls became famous virtuosi.

There must have been many concerts at the Pietà similar in spirit to tonight's at the Royal Festival Hall [9 May 1963], with Vivaldi (tonight impersonated by Yehudi Menuhin) now playing a solo concerto, now standing aside, now joining the orchestra to play a concerto with some of his more talented pupils, inspiring them by his great talent to excel themselves in the music he had composed especially for them. *(Notes for 9 May 1963 concert.)*

¶*Concerto* in B Minor for violin, strings and continuo
Andante molto-Allegro non molto; Largo; Allegro
This is just the sort of concerto Vivaldi wrote for himself to play and it probably dates from the last years of his life. It is a serious piece in the grand manner with solo writing of a formidable, but never empty, virtuosity. A short, impressive slow introduction prepares the way for the allegro whose opening tutti reappears to punctuate the movement and define both the tonalities and the four solo sections. The third of these is a striking example of the idea of recapitulation which became a recur-

rent feature of Vivaldi's solution to the problem of formal balance in a homophonic style.

The slow movement, a freely used ground bass, belongs rightly to an older style, but it is one of the most simply beautiful he ever wrote. The finale returns to the serious mood of the first and, more than that, contains several ideas which seem to have been derived from the earlier movement—a fact which shows an unusual degree of extended concentration in composition and, to those analysts who delight in note-grubbing, it will doubtless prove of even greater significance. *(Notes for 9 May 1963 concert.)*

¶*Concerto Funebre* in B Flat *"con hautbois sordini e Salmoe—e Viole all'-Inglese—Tutti li violini e violette sordini—non pero il violino principale"*

Largo; Allegro poco poco-Adagio; Allegro

The peculiar instrumentation of this concerto (here performed by violin, oboe, clarinet, 2 violas, and cello—that is, with clarinet substituting for salmoe, and two violas and cello in place of the viole all'inglese) has been mentioned above. The composer directs that every instrument shall be muted except for the principal violin.

The circumstances of its compositon are, beyond the implication of the title, quite obscure. The music has a remote, spiritual quality evident at the very opening and persisting throughout the mysterious allegro and the very fine fugue which concludes the work. The long octave trills in the wind instruments which appear in each movement have also been noted above; one wonders if they have any programmatic significance. *(Notes for 9 May 1963 concert.)*

¶*Concerto* in D Major for violin, strings and continuo

(*L'Estro Armonico*, Opus 3 Nr 7)

Allegro; Larghetto; Allegro

L'Estro Armonico (the Harmonious Inspiration), a collection of twelve concertos published in 1712, became Vivaldi's most celebrated work and the one which founded his European reputation. This concerto is extremely well known in the arrangement Bach made of it for solo harpsichord. No parts of the original version seem to have been published since the eighteenth century so that [Menuhin's 9 May 1963] performance must be one of the few times that it can have been played since that time. Nothing is needed by way of explanation for this is unpretentious music of unbounded felicity; not a note out of place and a slow movement of magical simplicity. *(Notes for 9 May 1963 concert.)*

¶*Concerto* in D Minor for 2 violins, 'cello, strings and continuo
(*L'Estro Armonico*, Opus 3 Nr. 11)
Allegro; Adagio spiccato e tutti; Allegro; Largo e spiccato; Allegro
This eleventh number in the *L'Estro Armonico* set was arranged by Bach for the organ and subsequently was for many years thought to be an original composition by his son W. Friedemann—so much for the nineteenth century's understanding of eighteenth century style! Some of the other concertos survived in "arrangements" thought suitable for young virtuosi to play in conservatoires. But there is no need to tamper with this music for it to come vividly alive in the form which Vivaldi originally gave it. By any standards this is music of the highest caliber. *(Notes for 9 May 1963 concert.)*

¶*Concerto* in F Major for 3 vioins, strings and continuo
Allegro; Andante; Allegro
Concertos for two, three and four violins with orchestra seem particularly to have appealed to Vivaldi. They were virtually all written for performance at the oratorio of the Pietà where Vivaldi could play one of the solo parts and, at the same time, give opportunities for some of his more talented young ladies to show their paces. The F major concerto is one of the very best and deserves to rank with the much more famous one in B minor for four violins. Superlative violin writing, great rhythmic vitality and a slow movement not unlike that of the B minor concerto with one soloist muted, playing arpeggiando, another playing pizzicato while the third sings a slow melody above them characterize the piece—an outstanding example of the music of this great musical craftsman. *(Notes for 9 May 1963 concert.)*

¶*Concerto* in G Minor for violins, strings and continuo
Largo-Presto ("*Fantasmi*")-Largo; Presto; Largo ("*Il sonno*"); Allegro
Vivaldi composed two programme concertos on the subject of night;

one for bassoon and one for flute and bassoon in which the latter, apart from a few solo passages, acts mainly as a continuo instrument. Descriptive music seems to have brought out the more eccentric side of Vivaldi's musical character and this concerto is no exception. He dares much more in the way of strange harmonies, sonorities and rhythms than usual in order to create the desired impression. The opening largo is astonishly bold in its use of sheer sound to evoke an impression of darkness and the feeling of suspense which can attend it. Suddenly the ghosts appear and then as suddenly fade into the night. Once more they appear in the ensuing presto before the largo with muted strings and slow flute melody describes an ominous and uneasy sleep. Quite what the last movement portrays is difficult to say; there are bars of soft repeated quavers which might be interpreted as momentary noddings but for the most part the ghosts seem to be in control and even at the end when they fade away there does not seem to be much hope for a peaceful awakening. *(Notes for 9 May 1963 concert.)*

¶*Concerto* in C Minor for cello, strings and continuo
Allegro con molto; Adagio; Allegro
The 'cello concertos remain among the least explored of Vivaldi's prodigious output. It is difficult to understand why, for they are very fine and tend to show a graver, more solemn aspect of his personality which contrasts well with the major-keyed brilliance of the concertos more usually found in concert programs. As always Vivaldi's extraordinary response to instrumental colors is in evidence. He thinks in terms of the 'cello's dark, rich sound and the music changes character accordingly.

The structure of the C minor concerto belongs to the characteristic pattern. In all three movements the opening *tuttis* are used to punctuate the music and define the keys through which it passes. In between the soloist goes his own way, elaborating his phrases with an expressive virtuosity of a high order. *(Notes for 10 February 1973 concert.)*

¶*Sonata ("Al Santo Sepolcro")* in E Flat for strings and continuo
Largo molto; Allegro ma poco
This sonata or sinfonia was probably intended for use at some Easter

service at the conservatoire of the Pietà. Composed in the more contrapuntal church style, the opening largo serves as prelude to the allegro which is a double fugue (a fugue on two subjects). For all their complexity, the melodic lines maintain a beautiful cantabile showing more clearly than anything else the country of their origin. *(Notes for 9 May 1963 concert.)*

4

GEORGE FRIDERIC HANDEL (1685-1785)
VOCAL & INSTRUMENTAL SELECTIONS

¶*Trio-Sonata* in D for flute, oboe & continuo
Adagio; Allegro; Affettuoso; Vivace
In his account of the Handel commemoration festival of 1784, Burney recounts a charming anecdote of the composer being shown a copy of the set of early (c. 1696) trio-sonatas of which this is the sixth. Handel was evidently pleased for he laughed and said "I used to write like the devil in those days, but chiefly for the oboe, which was my favourite instrument." In fact "those days" referred to his childhood in Halle for these sonatas — if by Handel at all (though cited as his earliest surviving music, their attribution remains in doubt) — would have been written when Handel was only eleven years old. They reveal a maturity of style that can be compared in achievement to that of the young Mozart. Composed in imitation of the then popular Italian sonatas, their personal style seems authentically "Handelian" and without certain knowledge of the circumstances of their composition might well be included among Handel's maturer works. They were published in England during Handel's lifetime to be played by violin, flute or oboe.

Although composed a generation later than the three- and four-part sonatas of the English composer Henry Purcell (1659-1695), the form is very much the same. The first and third movements are slow and full of beautiful melodic invention. The second movement, although simply entitled Allegro, is clearly a descendant of the fugal Canzona. The sonata ends with a carefree, dance-like movement in triple time. *(After notes for 8 September 1959 concert.)*

¶*Trio-Sonata* in G Minor for 2 violins and harpsichord
Andante; Allegro; Arioso; Allegro
The authenticity of this work too remains in doubt, though it was published by Walsh in 1733 as number 7 of a second set of trio sonatas by Handel.

The trio-sonata was the favorite chamber combination of the eighteenth century. It originated in Italy and developed its own formal characteristics. It was usually in four movements of alternating slow and fast speed. The instrumentation was not always the same; two soprano instruments, either violins, flutes or oboes, with a cello bass part from which the harpsichordist, sitting in the middle and directing proceedings, improvised a keyboard part. Often, too, the other instruments would improvise around their written parts making a sort of eighteenth-century "jam session" of the occasion.

The slower movements were usually either of the "French", dotted variety, or, as in this sonata, made up of those beautiful "Italianate" melodic lines which Handel particularly loved to write. The first of the two allegros was usually "fugued" — a type of writing especially well suited to the three solo voices. The last movement was often a dance — in this case a gigue. *(Notes for 10 September 1959 concert.)*

¶Cantata, "*Delirio Amoroso*" for soprano & continuo
The chamber cantata for solo voice and instruments became a favorite form in Italy and later throughout Europe during the seventeenth and eighteenth centuries. All composers wrote them as a matter of course, just as in the later eighteenth century they wrote sonatas. Alessandro Scarlatti left over 600 of them and Handel wrote enough to fill four large volumes of the Handel Society's collected edition. One can only imagine that they are so little known because so few have been printed in performing editions, for they contain much of Handel's finest music dating from all periods of his life.

Delirio Amoroso probably dates from his first visit to Italy in 1706-1709 and is typical of the Italian cantata of the period. Cloris is sent mad by the death of her lover Thyrsis. In her first aria she declares her intention of following him either to heaven or hell, both locations illustrated delightfully by Handel (*"Un pensiero voli in ciel* [Let my my mind soar to heaven]"). She decides, in somewhat uncomplimentary vein, that he has gone to hell and she makes her way there only to find him more elusive than she expected. In a charming, lilting aria she evidently succeeds in persuading him to leave with her (*"Lascia omai le brune vele* [Cast aside those dark vestments]") and a short *sinfonia* describes their arrival at the Elysian fields, where the cantata ends with Cloris singing of the delights to be gained for her courage (*"In queste amene / Piaggie serene* [On these quiet gentle shores]"). *(Notes for 20 March 1966 concert.)*

¶Cantata, "*Tra le fiamme*" for soprano & instruments
"*Tra le fiamme tu scherzi per gioco* (In your search for happiness, my dear)" was written for flute, oboe, two violins, viola and continuo of 'cello and harpsichord. The occasion for the composition is unknown.

The cantata tells an allegory. The opening aria (*"Tra le fiamme"*) apostrophizes a young man who laughs his way through the flames of love while one thousand butterflies (delightfully illustrated in the accompaniment) fall into the fire. Only the phoenix could survive such flames. The soprano then goes on to tell the story of Daedalus and Icarus. Daedalus, who has conquered the secret of flying, is imitated by his less experienced son Icarus. In the aria "*Pien di nuove e bel diletto* (Full of new and ravishing delights)" his joy at his first flight is described; but he flies too near the sun and his wings, made of feathers and wax, melt in the heat. The following recitative ("*Si, si, per troppo* [Indeed, it is only too true]") points out that there are many human butterflies like Icarus who fly into the flames but only one Daedalus who can emulate the phoenix and survive them. In the varia "*Voli per l'aria è vero chi può volare* (Let those who may fly through the air)" and the following recitative ("*L'uomo che nacque per salire al Cielo* [The man who is born to leap into the heavens]"), the soprano tells the young man to fly through the air if he can without melting his wings but also warns him that he would be better off on the ground. The cantata ends with a repeat of the opening aria, the words of which have by now gained a new significance. *(Notes for 8 September 1959 concert.)*

¶Cantata, "*Lucrezia*" for soprano & continuo
This cantata too belongs to Handel's earliest years and it is all the more

astonishing for that. The direct, passionate declamation may well have been influenced by the dramatic *scenas* of Alessandro Scarlatti's operas which he heard in Italy during his stay there in 1702-09, but he already speaks with a recognisably personal voice. The cantata became very widely known in Germany and the many striking harmonies and modulation were noted by Matheson in his *Exemplarische Organisten-Probe* published in Hamburg in 1719, where the work is said to be owned in manuscript by very many people.

The changing moods of the ravished Lucretia as she curses Tarquinius, remembers her husband Collatinus and prepares herself for death all lead up to the final recitative in which she plunges the sword into her breast. *(Notes for 6 March 1966 concert.)*

¶Cantata, "*Armida Abbandonata*" for soprano & instruments

"*Armida Abbandonata*" dates from his early years in Italy and the accompaniment is for strings and continuo. The opening recitative describing Armida's distress is an early example of Handel's adventurous use of instruments, since the voice is accompanied only by violins playing *arpeggiando*, giving the music an extraordinary sense of agitation. Armida's lovely aria which follows ("*Ah! crudele, e pur ten vai* [Ah, cruel one, in spite of all]") is, by contrast, accompanied only by continuo. The orchestra plays first in the *furioso* recitative in which Armida calls on the winds and seas to destroy her departing love, and also in the following aria in which she recants her curses (*Venti, fermate sì* [Yes, stay, ye winds]"). The cantata ends with a beautiful aria in the rhythm of a *Siciliana*, in which Armida prays that she may cease to love her betrayer [("*In tanti affani miei* [In so much affliction]"). *(Notes for 24 February 1963 concert.)*

¶*Cantata a due*, "*Arresta il Passo*" for 2 sopranos, strings and continuo

As observed above the majority of Handel's many chamber cantatas date from the years 1706-09, which he spent in Italy. Doubtless he had hoped to gain experience in Italian opera but, as luck would have it, his arrival in Rome coincided with a Papal ban on all operatic entertainment. The Italian aristocracy were not so easily to be dissuaded from enjoying their favorite music and gave, instead, parties at which the chief entertainment was the performance of chamber cantatas in the form established by Carrissimi and perfected by Alessandro Scarlatti. They were to all intents and purposes small-scale operas, although not intended for stage performance.

Handel, as always, made good use of his opportunities by composing a large number of cantatas for various combinations of voices and instruments of which "*Arresta il Passo*" is one of the finest and most elaborate.

The libretto is quite conventional. Aminta, the shepherd, tries every means of persuasion to melt the heart of the Nymph, Fillide (Phyllis) — a project in which he is finally successful. Into this stock situation Handel pours out some marvelous music within a framework of an overture and eight arias — three of which he subsequently adapted for the operas *Agrippina* (Venice 1709) and *Rinaldo* (London 1711). The work concludes with a brilliant, joyful duet. *(Notes for 10 February 1973 concert.)*

¶*Sonata* in B Flat for violin, strings & continuo
Andante; Adagio; Allegro

It is generally considered that Handel composed no violin concertos, but a different name cannot disguise the fact that this "sonata" is one. It was first discovered by Chrysander in a Handel manuscript dating from 1709 and has remained virtually unknown ever since. Handel was in Venice in that year and, doubtless, we owe the work to the popularity of the virtuoso concerto in that city although "*il caro Sassone*", as he was affectionately known, was primarily concerned with writing operas there.

The first movement is based on a lovely melody which he used again at various times in his life in opera, oratorio and sonata. One can only say that he had every reason to wish that it should not be wasted on a single performance. The slow movement is really only a chain of chords harmonising a rising and falling scale on which the soloist was expected to improvise. Composers gave performers a marvelous liberty in such movements which we are only now beginning once more to enjoy. The final allegro is a stunning virtuoso piece and the one most in the style of the Italian violin concertos which Handel must have heard in Venice. Except for the fact that it is very difficult one cannot understand why violinists have left this music unplayed for so long. *(Notes for 16 February 1964 concert.)*

¶Overture to "*Il Pastor Fido*"

Il Pastor Fido (The Faithful Shepherd) was the second opera Handel composed for the English theater. The libretto, by Rossi, was based on the celebrated pastoral comedy by Guarini, a source of lyrics for composers of madrigals, cantatas and operas for two hundred years. When it first appeared in 1713 the opera seems to have had only a moderate success, but, twenty-one years later, Handel revived and re-wrote much of it in a vain attempt to save his failing partnership with Heidegger at the King's Theatre, a venture doomed to succumb beneath the rivalry of George II and the Prince of Wales, who maliciously sponsored his own opera company at the Lincoln's Fields Theatre.

Nevertheless it is to this revival that we owe the new overture being performed today. One of the few in which Handel uses horns, it is in the French style with a slow introduction, a fugue and a concluding *bouree*. (*Notes for 24 February 1963 concert.*)

¶*Motetto*, "*Silete venti*" for soprano & orchestra

Handel composed very little church music to Latin words and almost all of it belongs to his early years in Italy, that is to say before his twenty-fifth birthday in 1710. He evidently continued to think well of "*Silete venti*" for he used the three arias again in *Esther*, his first English oratorio.

The work begins with a *sinfonia* consisting of a slow introduction and a *fugato* intended to represent the rustling of wind through the trees. The soprano breaks into this in striking manner bidding them to cease ("*Silete venti* ["Be silent winds]"). From the beginning Handel showed a vivid sense of this essentially theatrical effect, using a musical device which has visual and dramatic associations. Arias and recitatives follow alternately, the second aria ("*Date serta, date flores* [Give garlands, give flowers]") having a particularly striking middle section where the winds rise again and all showing that marvellous gift for affecting melody which, fortunately, never deserted him. The motet concludes with a brilliant *allelujah*. (*Notes for 16 February 1964 concert.*)

¶*Trio Sonata* in F Major, Op 2 Nr 3
Andante; Allegro; Adagio; Allegro
Opus 2 was the title given by the English publisher Walsh to distin-

guish this set of nine trio sonatas from an earlier publication he had made of solo sonatas. They were first published in 1733 and even if, as seems probable, some of the melodies belong to Handel's most youthful period, the sheer craftsmanship alone clearly indicates that they are, as we have them now, works of his maturity composed about the time of *Acis and Galatea.*

They reveal a never-failing fount of melodic inspiration of the highest quality. Cast in the traditional form of *sonata da camera* with alternating slow and fast movements, they have endlessly varying mood and texture. The F major trio sonata begins rather as the G minor (below) does, with the two violins playing melodies which twist about each other above a steadily moving bass. The second movement, as in the G Minor, also a fugue, is on a syncopated subject and altogether lighter in character. It suddenly breaks off in full flight and the movement ends in a brief *adagio.* The *adagio* proper, also in three-four, is sadder and more elegiac in quality than before. The gaiety is resumed in the final *allegro* which sets its bouncy subject against chains of suspensions whose appeal has not diminished with the years or the frequency of their use.

These two sonatas — Op 2 Nrs 3 and 7 — considered together make an interesting example of the way in which convention in art can be the means of providing quite different worlds of experience. *(Notes for 6 March 1966 concert.)*

¶*Trio Sonata* in G Minor, Op 2 Nr 7
Andante; Allegro; Arioso; Allegro
The sixth sonata in G minor opens with a beautiful melody above a characteristic treading bass. It is followed by a virile *fugato* with all the instruments very busy. The *arioso* in three-four has one of Handel's best melting tunes and the sonata ends with a lively *gigue. (Notes for 6 March 1966 concert.)*

¶*Water Music* (Suite 1 in F)
Overture (Grave-Allegro-Arioso); Allegro-Andante-Allegro; Passepied; Air; Bourrée; Allegro; Hornpipe; Menuet
Queen Anne died in 1714 and, so tradition has it, Handel was put in a difficult, not to say uncomfortable, situation by the succession of King

George I. In 1710 he had accepted a sizeable pension from the Elector of Hanover, who generously allowed him to continue his European Tour, and especially to visit England, on condition that he would return before long to take up his duties in Germany. Now the Elector had become King of England, the country which had seduced Handel from his duties for four years.

Charles Burney in his *Account of the Handel Commemoration* (1785) continues the story:

> Handel, conscious of his deficiency in respect and gratitude to a prince who honoured him with such flattering marks of approbation and bounty, durst not approach the court, till by the ingenuity and friendly interposition of Baron Kilmansegge, he was restored to favour in the following manner. The King, soon after his arrival in these kingdoms, having been prevailed on to form a party on the water, the design was communicated to Handel who was advised to compose some pieces expressly for the occasion; the performance of which he secretly conducted in a boat that accompanied the royal barge. Upon hearing these compositions, which have since been so well known and so justly celebrated under the title of the *Water-Music*, his majesty, equally surprised and pleased by their excellence, eagerly enquired who was the author of them; when the Baron acquainted the King that they were the production of a faithful servant of his majesty, who, conscious of the cause of displeasure which he had given so gracious a protector, durst not presume to approach his royal presence, till he had assurances that by every possible demonstration of duty and gratitude in future, he might hope to obtain a pardon. This intercession having been graciously accepted, Handel was restored to favour....

Whether or not the story was as romantic as this account implies, there was certainly a water party on 17th July 1717 for which Handel composed special music. The Royal Barge travelled from Whitehall to Chelsea with music playing all the way. During supper at Chelsea another "consort of music" was performed and yet a third concert accompanied the return journey, which was begun after two o'clock in the morning.

It is not surprising therefore that the *Water Music* divides into three suites: two of them brilliant and vivacious, in F and D major, clearly intended for the journeys by water, and the third in G major, much more intimate and appropriate for the Royal supper.

The F major suite begins with a French Overture; a slow introduction in sharply dotted rhythms followed by a contrapuntal movement with parts for solo oboe and violins rather in the manner of a *concerto grosso*. This leads into a brief but beautiful *Arioso* for oboe and strings. At this point the horns are heard for the first time in an Allegro in triple time, which everyone will have heard in one arrangement or another. As a middle section Handel wrote an Andante in which oboes and bassoons are used antiphonally with strings. The Allegro is then repeated. The horns maintain their soloistic role in the next movement, a *Passepied*, which has a trio for strings in the minor key. Then follows the famous *Air*, one of the most beautiful melodies Handel ever wrote, which, with its wonderfully romantic use of the horns, must have sounded ravishing over the waters of the Thames on that first summer evening.

In the *Bourrée* Handel gives precise instructions for its threefold performance, first by strings, then oboes and lastly all together. The following Allegro, one of the longest movements in the suite, returns in similar style to the earlier antiphonal Andante with oboes and basson echoing and alternating with the strings. The *Hornpipe,* a dance which Handel inherited from composers like Purcell, is played in the manner of the *Bourrée,* and the first suite ends with a Menuet in which the horns play a prominent part. Do not fail to notice the beautiful scoring of the middle section in which second violins, violas and bassoon have the main melody with first violins and bass making a counterpoint round it. *(Notes for 19 August 1970 concert.)*

¶Overture to *"Ottone"*

There were two sorts of operatic overture in the late 17th and early 18th centuries which became subsequently distinguished by the labels French and Italian.

The Italian overture, first regularly used by Alessandro Scarlatti, was a three-movement form. It opened and ended with an allegro, and in between there was a short adagio. The French version was essentially a two-movement form beginning with a pompous slow section in dotted rhythms which was followed by an allegro in fugal style. Sometimes a lighter dance movement was added at the end.

Handel consistently used this grander form for his operas. The one composed for *Ottone* in 1723 is particularly good and, apart from a delightful *gavotte* after the fugal movement, he added, as a bonus, a further movement in fugal style much less serious in intent and full of delectable suspensions. *(Notes for 5 November 1972 concert.)*

¶*Concerto Grosso* in B Flat, Op 3 Nr 1
Allegro; Largo; Allegro
The collection of concerti grossi which Walsh published in 1734 as Handel's Opus 3 has a confused history. It seems to have been put together from a number of different sources and not composed as a set like the great string concertos published as Opus 6 (see below). Their scheme of orchestration is particularly interesting and even more varied than the Brandenburg Concertos of Bach.

In the slow movement of this particular concerto two solo instruments, oboe and violin, weave a delicate web of counterpoint against a double *ripieno* orchestra, one of flutes and bassoon, the other consisting of the full strings. The last movement, somewhat suprisingly in G minor, has also one particularly delightful example of Handel's extraordinary feeling for instrumental color. It begins in the manner of a normally scored dance movement, but, towards the end, two bassoons suddenly take over and, against a diaphonous string accompaniment, carefully scored and with direction for the harpsichord not to play, it provides an enchanting tonal contrast to the rest of the movement. The opening allegro is a brilliant show-piece for the oboe and violin soloists. *(Notes for 16 February 1964 concert.)*

¶*Concerto Grosso* in B Flat, Op 3 Nr 2
Vivace; Largo; Allegro; Andante; Gavotte
The second in the Opus 3 set is the finest of them all and the best planned as a single work. It opens brilliantly in chaconne rhythm as a counterpoint to which the *concertino* violins play *arpeggio* figurations. A modulation to G minor introduces a *largo* of extraordinary beauty. It

makes one realise how grossly underestimated is Handel's sense of instrumental color. Above an accompaniment of two solo cellos and soft
string chords a solo violin plays one of those long, sustained melodies
that Handel could write as no other. The central movement is a double
figure making a strong, solid focal point for the whole work. After it
comes two dances: first a minuet with some deightful antiphonal writing between the soloists and the main orchestra, and, to end, a gavotte
with two variations of irresistible vitality. *(Notes for 10 March 1963 concert.)*

¶*Concerto* in F for organ, Op 4 Nr 4
Allegro; Andante; Adagio; Allegro
Handel's fame as an organist dated from his early years in Venice
where he is said to have taken the laurels at that instrument from
Domenico Scarlatti. Be that as it may, he certainly used his reputation
later in England to encourage audiences for his oratorio performances
by advertising newly composed concertos to be played between the acts.
In 1738 the publishers, John Walsh, collected six of them together and
printed them as Opus 4.

It cannot be supposed that Handel took much part in their publication for the manuscript seems to have been left in much the same state as
they must have been at their original performance. Since he himself
played them, the solo part is often incomplete and the frequent indications "*ad libitum*" nearly always imply an improvisation which he had not
troubled to write out fully. Moreoever, as they were each used on several
occasions there exist several versions of various movements.

The fourth concerto in F is among the most carefully written-out of
the set. The jaunty opening Allegro is composed in the Italian concerto
style with the first *tutti* serving as a punctuating element between the
elaborte solo sections. The Andante starts off as if it will be either a
ground-bass or a set of variations but turns out to be neither. After two
varied statements of the opening four bars the organ begins an enchanting line of its own which involves the orchestra only in interjectory
phrases. At the end the opening bars reappear once more on both organ
and orchestra.

There follows a short *ad libitum* Adagio which leads into an elaborate concertato fugal movement. *(Notes for 5 November 1972 concert.)*

¶*Concerto* in B^b for organ, Op 4 Nr 6
Andate-Allegro; Larghetto; Allegro moderato
The sixth concerto of Handel's Opus 4 is optionally for harp or organ. The whole set was published for either harpsichord or organ and the 18th century historian Hawkins specifies the fifth concerto as having been composed especially for the harp. Nevertheless the sixth does seem to be the most likely candidate if performances with harp were envisaged because the strings are muted throughout and with the use of the flutes and pizzicato bass-line in the first movement a particularly delicate sound is given to the orchestral accompaniments — as delightful, of course, with organ as with harp.

The three movements are all short and set out to delight the ear rather than to instruct the mind. We should not on that account under-estimate the skill and vitality of a composer who can, in so short a space, provide such lively, delectable music. *(Notes for 5 November 1972 concert.)*

¶*Concerto Grosso ("Alexander's Feast")* in C
Allegro; Largo; Allegro; Andante non presto
"That celebrated Concerto in Alexander's Feast", as it was called at its first publication by Walsh in 1740 and so identified ever since, was composed as a prelude to Act II of Handel's wonderful setting of Dryden's *Ode to St. Cecilia*. The success of this masterpiece in 1736 stands out like a beacon in an otherwise bleak and depressing period of his life. His health was poor, quite beyond the powers of Tunbridge Wells to cure; two operatic ventures had failed and a third at Covent Garden was going very badly — so much so that in the autum of 1735 he announced that he would give no more operas in the following season, only oratorios and concerts. At one of these "Alexander's Feast" was first performed, giving Handel his only success of the season.

The practice of playing concertos between the acts of oratorios was one used by Handel to attract audiences and for this purpose he wrote most of his organ concertos. It was much less usual for him to compose as entr'acte music a concerto in the older form of the concerto grosso in which the main body of the orchestra, oboes and strings, is contrasted with a solo *concertino* of two violins and a cello. Perhaps the reason why he did so in the case of "Alexander's Feast" may have had something to do with the early symptoms of the terrible paralysis which was to strike him down the following year.

There is certainly no trace of dolor to be found in the concerto, which is very true to its key of C major: a splendid opening *tutti* alternates in the first *allegro* with charming interludes for the *concertino;* a short languorous *largo* separates this from a brilliant *fugato,* and the concerto ends with Handel in winsome mood dancing a gavotte. *(Notes for 24 February 1963 concert.)*

¶*Concerto Grosso* in A Major, Op 6 Nr 11

Andante larghetto e staccato; Allegro; Largo e staccato; Andante; Allegro

The twelve concerti grossi of Opus 6 are among the great miracles of Handel's musical career. He composed them between 29 September and 30 October 1739, which allows just two days for each concerto. They are all scored for the same solo *concertino* of two violins and cello contrasted with the full *ripieno* string orchestra. Although published together as a set they were not intended to be played in this way. It was customary, and good box-office, for Handel to play an organ concerto or a concerto grosso between the acts of his oratorios and it was for this purpose that they were written.

They vary enormously in mood, the eleventh being perhaps the most sunny and vigorous. The pompous opening *tutti* of the first movement is contrasted with the lyrical phrases of the *concertino* with charming effect. The second movement is a double fugue of great brilliance. The brief *largo* leads into the long *andante* in which the opening *tutti* punctuates the increasingly virtuoso sections for the soloists. The work ends with a delightful dance-like *allegro. (Notes for 20 March 1966 concert.)*

¶*Samson* (dramatic oratorio in three parts)

Libretto by Newburgh Hamilton from Milton's *Samson Agonistes*

Samson, written in 1742, was one of the most popular of Handel's oratorios and performed constantly during his lifetime. In the preparation of the score for Covent Garden's bi-cententary production, the first consideration has been to preserve the over-all plan of the work. Apart from the textual evidence, it is easy to discover, from the various editions published during Handel's lifetime, which of the music he regarded as inessential, and, following Handel's precedent, we have felt free to omit these occasional pieces for this production.

The dramatic movement of the work is like an extraordinarily controlled *crescendo*. The first of the three acts opens with a Philistine procession to the temple of their god, Dagon. This is intended to throw into sharp relief Samson's loneliness and degradation with which the rest of the act is concerned. His thoughts and emotions move in a striking parabola. At first he is passively sorrowful, lamenting his blindness ("Total eclipse"). With the arrival of his father, Manoah, and his devoted Israelite friends led by Micah, his mood changes to angry frustration ("Why does the God of Israel sleep?"). He calls on God to strike down His enemies although he has, as yet, no thought that he might be called to achieve it himself. He falls down in a state of collapse and complete despair, wishing only for death.

The second act is planned to show the rousing of Samson by the taunts of his enemies. It opens in the same mood of despair that ended the first act. Micah and the chorus pray for help ("Return O God of Hosts"), but as if in cruel answer comes the treacherous Dalila, who has sold herself and Samson to the Philistines. She tries to reawaken Samson's affections ("With plaintive notes"), but he rouses himself and angrily spurns her ("Traitor to love"). Immediately she has gone, Harapha, the Philistine champion, comes to jeer at the foe who can no longer fight him ("Honour and arms"). Samson, forgetting his despair, dismisses him ("Go, baffled coward") and challenges the Philistine god, Dagon, to prove his strength against the God of Israel. This challenge is taken up in a splendid double chorus between the two opposing forces ("Fixed in his everlasting seat").

The third act moves swiftly towards its climax. Harapha summons Samson to the feast of Dagon ("Presuming slave"). At first he refuses to go, but in a wonderfully quiet, visionary aria ("Thus when the sun"), the idea comes to him that God might intend him to go. He walks along to the feast which engulfs him. But with his new-found strength he pulls down the temple, so destroying his enemies and himself. Then follows a vast Israelite funeral procession, bearing Samson's body away from the scene of his final victory (*Dead march*). The mood changes from one of sorrow to great joy and thankfulness at the Israelites' liberation from slavery with the words "Let the bright Seraphim in burning row Their loud uplifted trumpets blow".

The whole conception — the action takes place in one day, the last of Samson's life — is startlingly modern. The more obvious aspects of the story are omitted and everything is concentrated in making a study of recovery from adversity. The plan is initially Milton's, but Handel and his librettist, Newburgh Hamilton, have most marvellously realised it in terms of music and drama. *(Notes for October 1958 performances.)*

¶*Concerto a due cori* in B^b Major

Overture; Allegro ma non troppo; Allegro; Largo; A tempo ordinario; Alla breve; Menuet

Handel wrote three *Concerti a due cori* and there remains a mystery about them. They are, perhaps, the grandest and most ambitious of Handel's compositions for orchestra, yet we cannot be certain they were ever performed in his lifetime and the manuscripts have come down to us in an unusually chaotic condition. It is reasonable, from the similarity of the concept, unusual in Handel, of two choruses of wind instruments treated as solo groups divided from each other by the *ripieno* orchestra of strings, to suppose that they were all written at the same period and, from internal evidence, it would seem most likely to have been about the time that he was composing the Fireworks Music to celebrate the peace of Aix la Chapelle in 1749. The Fireworks Music was written for an outdoor celebration in Green Park. Possibly these concertos were written for indoor concerts given to celebrate the same event. Handel did not often write music for double choir of either voices or instruments and the fact that *Solomon*, whose choruss are almost all laid out in this way, was written in 1748 may provide a clue to the dating, at least by analogy.

But the concertos, impressive as they are, could not have reached a wide public if they were in fact performed at all. Burney, a devoted Handel historiographer, makes no mention of them. Deutsch's more recent and meticulously careful researches reveal no documents relating to them and most other historians have, for want of evidence, chosen, more or less, to ignore them. And this is a pity for they are at the pinnacle of Handel's instrumental writing; nothing quite like them in grandeur or virtuosity of scoring exists and their re-assessment in Handel's overall output is badly needed.

This concerto without horns has some suprising features. Instead of a fugue after the *grave* introduction Handel arranges the chorus "And the glory of the Lord shall be revealed" from the *Messiah* of 1742, curtailing it very cleverly to avoid certain repetitions in the middle which the words in the Oratorio sustain but which would become tedious played instrumentally. The *Messiah* was already well known in London by 1749 and there may be some, as yet unknown, significance in this arrangement. Handel was never averse to re-setting his own (and other people's) music but it was generally music that was likely to be known to the people for whom he was arranging it. The instrumental version gives what may be a very interesting clue to the speed at which Handel expected his chorus to be sung. Performed as an instrumental piece and without hind-sight knowledge of the chorus, it falls naturally into a light dance rhythm approaching the beat of one in a bar; anything else would make the pulse drag and the music ponderous. This, translated into choral terms, makes the Glory of the Lord a very joyous thing far removed from Victorian visions of large choirs of angels moving slowly in white. The following Allegro has some octave melodic doubling which gives momentarily a sonority altogether exceptional in Handel, but very lovely none the less. The manuscript of the Largo, the ordinario and most of the *Alla breve* was thought to be incomplete but recently an original copy has re-appeared so that they can now be played as Handel wrote them. *(Notes for 5 November 1972 concert.)*

¶*Music for the Royal Fireworks*
Overture (Larghetto-Allegro); Bourrée; Siciliano ("*La Paix*"); Minuets I & II; Allegro ("*La Réjouissance*")

After the signing of the peace of Aix la Chapelle in October 1748 George II decided to celebrate the event in England with a firework display in Green Park, by St James's. This took place on the 17th April 1749 and for it Handel was commissioned to compose suitable music for the occasion.

Against George II's wishes, Handel appears to have insisted that strings be included in the orchestra for the Fireworks Celebration. Since the numbers of wind instruments were specified for outdoor performance (amounting to some 60 players) and we know that a hundred musicians took part, it would seem probable that Handel had his way and used some 40 string players. Certainly the autograph includes strings although they are always doubled by wind.

It is curious that the music composed for the occasion lasts something under 30 minutes, yet the band began to play at 6 pm and the celebration was over only shortly before 11. There must have been a lot of fireworks, or long gaps in the celebrations, or perhaps Handel used other music as well.

Be that as it may, the *Music for Royal Fireworks* is magnificent and among the best pieces of ceremonial music that Handel ever wrote.

It begins with an overture in dotted rhythms, apt for the Royal Progress across St James's Park but also superb music, superbly controlled. Not for a moment are we aware of the limitation of horns and trumpets restricted to the notes of their harmonic series. The following Allegro begins with fanfares on trumpets and drums answered by the rest of the orchestra in jaunty rhythms. A passage with sustained brass and rhythmically ambiguous quavers in strings and oboes breaks the pattern. It ends with a series of plunging scales which usher in a triumphant new tune for the whole orchestra together. The middle section relaxes the tension and turns towards the key of B minor (one sees here why Handel wanted to keep his strings). The music returns to the splendid D major tune and before the opening section is repeated there is a solemn section of 11 bars in a slow duple-time.

The central part of the Fireworks music is less grandiose – perhaps accompanying some Royal refreshment. A *Bourrée* for strings and woodwind is followed by a *Siciliana* called *"La Paix"*, delightfully eighteenth century in its view of peace as a country pastorale. We return to a more august atmosphere in the pair of minuets, alternating major and minor with differing scorings prescribed by the composer. The music ends (although we do not really know what the original order was on that day in April 1749) with the brilliant *"Réjouissance'*, once more with varied scoring. It is tempting to see it as an accompaniment to a brilliant set-piece, perhaps a figure of George II growing brighter and brighter on each repeat. At any rate the music does not lack spark. *(Notes for 5 November 1972 concert.)*

¶Cantata, *"Ah! crudel, nel pianto mio"* for soprano & instruments
The date of the chamber cantata *"Ah! crudel, nel pianto mio"* is uncertain but it was probably composed in England towards the end of Handel's life. It begins with a *sinfonia* in three sections in which the oboes play a very prominent part. The plot of the cantata is very light — the changing emotions of unrequited love — but it gives Handel an opportunity to write three vividly contrasted arias. The first, accompanied by unison strings, in tragic vein (*"Ah! crudel, nel pianto mio* [Ah, cruel one, your lovely eyes]"), the second spiritedly angry (*"Di quel bel che il ciel ti diede, / Non men vaga è la mia fede* [My constancy is no less fair than the beauty that heaven gave to you]"), and the last, prefaced by a striking accompanied recitative describing the change from storm to sunshine, in joyfully optimistic mood (*"Per trofei di mia constanza* [As a reward for my constancy]") with a beautiful middle section in which the voice and oboe sadly sympathise with each other. *(Notes for 10 March 1963 concert.)*

5

FRANZ JOSEPH HAYDN (1732-1809)
VOCAL & INSTRUMENTAL SELECTIONS

¶*Symphony 6 (Le Matin* [Morning]*)* in D Major
Adagio-Allegro; Adagio-Andante-Adagio; Menuetto e trio; Finale
Haydn's sixth symphony, composed in 1761, is the first of a trilogy whose other two parts are entitled *Le Midi* (Afternoon) and *Le Soir* (Evening). They were the first symphonies to appear after his appointment as assistant *Capellmeister* to the court of Prince Anton Esterházy, and Haydn clearly set out to impress his new patron. They already show the promise of greatness and stand apart from the rest of his early symphonies by virtue of their quality, and their elaborate scoring and large number of movements.

These factors were doubtless influenced by the number of brilliant instrumentalists appointed with Haydn and in whose company he must have come to know the elaborate solo concerti of Vivaldi and Albinoni as well as the concerti grossi of Bonporti and Corelli.

Haydn left no programme to explain his titles although the beginning of Le Matin obviously represents the sunrise. For the rest we can enjoy the music for its own sake or add whatever descriptions we like. *(Notes for 20 March 1966 concert.)*

¶*Cantilena pro Adventu ("Ein' Magd, ein' Dienerin")*

During his early years at Eisenstadt Haydn composed several small-scale works for the church which have only recently been re-discovered during the admirable researches of Mr. Robbins-Landon. This Advent aria was probably composed in 1765 and is scored for two horns, strings and organ continuo. The unpretentiousness and sincerity of its style gives a touching innocence to this song of the young Mary chosen by God to be the mother of Christ. Impractical it may be for a church to raise a small band for such an aria but it is difficult to see why the Catholic church should have chosen to exclude music of this caliber from its services. *(Notes for 22 September 1961 concert.)*

¶*Symphony 34* in D Minor
Adagio; Allegro; Menuetto; Presto assai

The removal of Prince Nikolaus Esterházy's court from Eisenstadt to the new castle of Eszterháza in 1766 coincided with Haydn's promotion to the post of *Capellmeister*. His responsibilities were now so much increased in the chapel and the new theater (for the Prince was passionate about opera) that his output of symphonies decreased very suddenly. Even more striking, although difficult to connect conclusively with the worries of his responsbilities, is the deepening of emotional expression which is from now on more and more frequently to be found in his music. The easy charm and grace of his earlier symphonies is now often abandoned in movements, generally in the minor key, which seem to reflect the spirit found in the contemporary literary movement which we now call "*Sturm und Drang*".

Probably the first symphony to be written for Eszterháza is the 34th which begins with just such a movement. Never before had he attempted anything of such poignancy — it is as if he had discovered an entirely new world of experience in music.

Perhaps because of his audience, or because he himself was not yet ready to complete a symphony in this serious vein, the remaining three movements are in complete contrast. The *allegro* is brilliant and intense, the *menuetto* relaxed with charming music for the oboes and horns and the finale rounds the work off in an atmosphere of irrepressible high spirits. *(Notes for 10 March 1963 concert.)*

¶*Symphony 49 ("La Passione")* in F Minor

Adagio; Allegro di molto; Menuetto; Finale: Presto

Written in the same year as the 39th symphony and subsequently misnumbered, this symphony is the first whole and undisputed masterpiece of Haydn's first maturity. It sparked off a wonderful series of symphonies during the 1770s most of which are still much too little known and appreciated. Quite why it was called "*La Passione*" is not clear. Many of the early titles with religious connotations refer to a piece of plainsong which Haydn incorporates in the music and this may well be another example of the same procedure but as yet the original melody, if it exists, has not been identified. In any case it was only a means to an end and is of largely academic interest.

The symphony begins with a slow movement, a feature common to quite a large number of the more serious early symphonies. But whereas Haydn generally relaxed the intensity in the subsequent movements in this symphony it grows continuously with a brief but enchantingly appropriate respite in the trio of the minuet. The two *allegro* movements are, in a sense, daringly similar; both in duple time; both in the same form using the same tonal scheme. Yet they contrive to convey quite different sorts of tragic vitality. The first is overt, almost hectoring in its aggressiveness while the last is faster and more tense because more held in. Over half the movement is marked *piano*, but the outbursts when they come are the more effective and striking because of it. *(Notes for 16 February 1964 concert.)*

¶*Symphony 44 ("Trauer")* in E Minor

Allegro con brio; Menuetto; Adagio; Presto

During the years 1771 and 1772 Haydn composed something over a dozen symphonies of superb quality. We no longer have to regret that the rest of a symphony is not up to the inspired single movement; these symphonies achieve a completeness and a level of inspiration which he was not to find again so consistently until the last set of twelve which he wrote for London. And even among these the "*Trauer*" — mourning — symphony must rank very high.

The naming of Haydn's symphonies is a useful, if sometimes misleading, means of identification. The name "*Trauer*" seems to have come about from a legend that Haydn, particularly affected by one performance of the beautiful slow movement, asked that it should be played at his funeral. Apart from this possible connection there is nothing funereal about the symphony at all; the mood is rather one of intense emotional conflict whose austerity relaxes only in the trio of the minuet and the slow movement. This intensity is reflected in the very methods of composition, for the first movement grows entirely out of the stark unison opening motive, and all its music is either antithesis to or elaboration of it. Similarly, a unison opening theme serves as the basis for the whole of the last movement where elaborate contrapuntal textures raise the music to an extraordinary pitch of grim intensity. The slow movement, by contrast, is one of the most serenely beautiful he ever wrote, quite beyond the power of words to evoke. *(Notes for 24 February 1963 concert.)*

¶*Aria di Donna Stella* for soprano & instruments

For nearly twenty years Haydn was responsible for producing his own and other composers' operas in the court theater at Eszterháza. It has long been known that, as he matured, Haydn became increasingly critical of the imported operas and took to substituting re-set or interpolated arias of his own composition into their scores. Recently, due largely to the admirable work of Mr. Robbins-Landon, a number of previously unknown arias have been re-discovered, of which this is one intended for the first act of Paisiello's opera *La Frascatana*.

Apart from the intrinsic quality, it is interesting because it is in a style that is more consciously Italianate than Haydn usually liked to affect, presumably to be more in keeping with the rest of the opera—but how good he was at it!

The dramatic situation has to be inferred from the words; the deserted Donna Stella begs pity and help in her distress ("*D'una sposa meschinella* [Have pity, for pity's sake]") and, in spirited fashion, ends by promising dire consequences of her betrayal. *(Notes for 24 February 1963 concert.)*

¶*Concerto* in D for harpsichord and orchestra
Vivace; Un poco adagio; Rondo all'ungharese (Allegro assai)

This work was composed some time before 1784 and is scored for oboes, horns and strings. It draws its effect principally from its unexpectedly sombre depths. The title page of the first edition (1784) describes it as for *clavicembalo o forte piano,* and it is The Haydn D major concerto... equally for piano as for harpsichord.

The opening theme is typical of Haydn at his most *sportif.* The second subject, still in D major, is given by solo violin and oboes. The cadenza of this movement is Haydn's own, and the coda has brisk alternations of *piano* and *forte.*

The second movement is of austere simplicity and is largely a dialogue between soloist and strings, the very graceful coda having some expressive phrases in the oboes.

The sparkling last movement gives a vigorous, dance-like quality to the music, as one would expect from its marking as a (albeit formalised) "gypsy" rondo. *(Notes for 7 February 1976 concert.)*

¶*Symphony 77* in B Flat
Vivace; Andante sostenuto; Menuetto; Finale: Allegro spirituoso

Within the last fifty years several attempts have been made to publish the complete works of Haydn. The need for such an edition is felt most in the sphere of the symphony where there are still nearly twenty symphonies virtually unknown and unplayed simply because the scores and parts are not available. The most serious gap lies between numbers 70 and 80;[7] a particularly interesting period in Haydn's development. After

---

7   Since the time of this writing the complete symphonies have been recorded by Antal Dorati, in addition to other important Haydn projects. (Ed.)

the amazing series of symphonies of his first maturity there seems to have been a falling off: the enthusiasm for the intensity of *Sturm und Drang* faded leaving often somewhat vacuously diverting works without a great deal of content. We can now see that this was only a stage in Haydn's progress towards the great maturity of his later works which shows first in these very symphonies whose scores are nearly impossible to find. The former overt intensity has now become integrated into the sheer processes of composition so that even the gay, brilliant works have an inner strength which render them of far greater stature than their appearance would seem to indicate. Number 77 is just such a symphony: except for the development of the last movement the mood is all brightness and light. But the virtuosity of composition is not only breathtaking to the musician but gives it the durability and importance of a work of much greater pretension.

Who could have predicted the adventures which the unpretentious opening theme would have to undergo as the movement develops? — and, even more surprising is the way the gentle second theme is made to assume first a new expressiveness and then, wittily, to whisk us on to the movement's brilliant conclusion. The slow movement has one of the loveliest tunes that Haydn wrote, and lovely things happen to it, not least the magical change of key which momentarily occurs towards the end. After the amusing minuet and trio we come to the most obviously intense movement. From an historical point of view it is particularly distinguished as it is the first example of sonata-rondo, the form which mixed elements of the simple rondo with the idea of development inherent in the more serious first movement, or sonata form. It begins innocently enough with a gay rondo tune but instead of continuing in this vein it suddenly bursts out into a *fugato* of the greatest virtuosity as if Haydn could be modest about his new mastery no longer. But it all evaporates as quickly as it appeared and the movement ends with the wit and charm which is his most engaging and most misleading characteristic. *(Notes for a concert.)*

¶*Symphony 85 (La Reine)* in B Flat
Adagio-vivace; Romanze-allegretto; Menuetto; Finale-presto
In 1786 Haydn was commissioned to write six symphonies for "*Les con-*

certs de la loge Olympique" in Paris, a concert-promoting society whose patrons included Queen Marie-Antoinette. The present symphony was her favorite and now bears her name. It is the first of the set and the first of the final chain of great masterpieces of symphonic form which crowned Haydn's career. There is an innate sophistication in the music born of complete assurance and technical mastery, and also a new lyrical vein which some have attributed to Haydn's hearing the six quartets which Mozart had composed and dedicated to him in the previous year.

The opening slow introduction presages the scales of the first *tutti* of the *allegro* whose main theme, quiet and subtle, serves for both first and second subject. It is used with amazing ingenuity throughout the movement, welding the whole together with deceptively simple effect. The *Romanze* must have particularly endeared itself to the Queen with its charming tune and variations which nevertheless speak of deeper matters from time to time. The minuet begins conventionally enough but the trio abandons its bucolic mood halfway through and develops a brief phrase in a surprising way. The *finale*, like the first movement, is based on one subject which is made to serve more adventurous purposes than its innocent beginning might lead one to suppose. *(Notes for 20 March 1966 concert.)*

¶*Symphony 90* in C Major
Adagio-Allegro assai; Andante; Menuet; Finale: Allegro assai

In 1788, before embarking upon the last great set of twelve symphonies for Salomon in London, Haydn composed three new symphonies (numbers 90, 91 and 92) at the commission of Le Comte d'Ogny, a man of whom little is known except that he supervised the postal service between Paris and Marseilles. A year later through a regrettable, if profitable, "over-sight" he sold them again to Prince Octtingen-Wallerstein. Perhaps the Fates took a rather more serious view of the "oversight" for these three symphonies have had a peculiarly obscure career sandwiched as they are between the "Paris" and "London" sets. The physical reason for their neglect has been lack of availability. It was only in 1951 that the score was republished, and it was only printed once before that in a nineteenth century collection which has long since been unavailable. It is sad to reflect that there is still [1961] no complete edition of the symphonies. Three attempts have been made of which two failed and we can only hope that the third will fare better.

These three symphonies for Le Comte d'Ogny show Haydn at the very summit of his creative powers. There is no longer the striving for effect which mars some of the early works, or the very lack of it which makes some of them rather conventional. From the "Paris" symphonies onwards we see Haydn in full command of his material; a great creative mind working in complete freedom — a freedom whose signs are concision and economy of material.

Symphony 90 begins with a slow introduction in which, innocently enough, the main theme of the *allegro assai* appears for the first time. This pattern of six repeated notes pervades the movement even appearing in rhythm as an accompaniment to the flute's second subject. Another sign of Haydn's intensification of form is found at the end of the exposition where, formerly, it was common practice to introduce some new musical ideas; now he already begins to develop the main theme. The development section itself is much longer than before and the recapitulation correspondingly shorter and more varied ending in a brief but pertinent coda. It is this sort of approach to the craft of composition which makes Beethoven the true heir of Haydn rather than of Mozart. Yet Haydn, unlike his successor, disguises its very seriousness by the brightness and gaiety of his music.

The slow movement is a set of double variations, a form of Haydn's own devising. Two melodies, the first in the major, the second, more violent, in the minor, are varied alternately. The violent section is used principally as a contrast to the more gentle variations of the major theme, the first of which is given over to the flute and the second to the 'cellos of the orchestra decorated by an enchanting counterpoint on the violins. This variation leads directly into an extended coda in which the wind take precedence passing the opening phrase one to the other. There is one quite magical moment when the music suddenly and softly moves into the remote key of D flat — it is the breath of purest inspiration.

One can never cease to marvel that Haydn in composing thousands of minuets can still find something new to say. This one begins conventionally enough but in the second half the music suddenly finds a greater depth when the flute and oboe answer each other with a phrase from the menuet tune. The trio is a solo for the first oboe.

Perhaps the greatest glory of this symphony is the last movement. Like many of his later finales it is in sonata form and it has only one subject. This was a particular aspect of Haydn's intensification of musical structure which virtually no-one else ever attempted. The tonal relationships of the form are preserved but the fact that the opening fugue appears both as first and second subjects gives the music a feeling of continuous development and for all the vivacity and humor it is by far the most serious of the four movements, full of fire and invention. Towards the end of it, Haydn's love of practical jokes proves irresistible and he plays one on the audience which would spoil in the telling. *(Notes for 22 September 1961 concert.)*

¶*Scena "Arianna a Naxos"* for soprano & harpsichord

Throughout the seventeenth and eighteenth centuries the solo cantata, for voice, continuo, and sometimes instrumental obligati, was one of the most popular vocal forms in Europe. It originated in Italy during the early years of the seventeenth century as an off-shoot of the Florentine opera. Every composer wrote them, sometimes by the hundred. By the end of the eighteenth century its popularity was on the decline but it is very surprising that Haydn only composed three. Perhaps instrumental music was cultivated at Eisenstadt at the expense of music for the solo voice.

"Arianna a Naxos" was composed in 1789. After its first performance in London in 1791, the *Morning Chronicle* critic wrote:

Nothing is talked of — nothing sought after but Haydn's Cantata — or, as it is called in the Italian School — his Scena.... It abounds with such a variety of dramatic modulation — and is so exquisitely captivating in its larmoyant passages, that it touched and dissolved the audience. They speak of it with rapturous recollection, and Haydn's Cantata will accordingly be the musical desideratum for the winter.

And so it was, being sung many times during that and subsequent seasons. Haydn himself was very fond of it and refers to it several times in his letters as his "dear Arianna".

The scene of the cantata is set on the island of Naxos where Ariadne waits alone for Theseus to come for her. In the first recitative she looks forward with happiness to their meeting. The following aria, "*Dove sei mio bel tesoro* (Where are you beloved?)", is a prayer to the Gods for his speedy return colored by the fear that he may have found someone else. She climbs to the top of a rocky cliff (charmingly illustrated in the music) from which she sees the Greek ship, with Theseus on the prow, sailing away past the island. Ariadne cries out in anguish and the cantata ends with an impassioned prayer for death to relieve her of her misery ("*Ah che morir vorrei* [Would I could die]"). *(Notes for 6 March 1966 concert.)*

¶*Scena di Berenice* ("*Berenice, che fai?*") for soprano & orchestra

In his diary for 4th May 1795 Haydn wrote: "I gave my benefit concert at the Haymarket Theatre. The Room was full of a select company (details of the programme follow, including...) Scena nuova by me, Madame Banti – she song *(sic)* very scanty." This was the first performance of the *Scena di Berenice*. The text is taken from Metastasio's libretto for *Antigone* and describes Berenice's anguish as she sees her lover slain.

It is the last and most powerful of Haydn's concert arias, quite breathtaking in its harmonic audacity and a wonderful example of that lyrical melodic vein which Haydn particularly cultivated in his old age. *(Notes for 16 February 1964 concert.)*

¶*Trio* in E Minor for violin, cello & harpsichord

Allegro moderato; Andante; Rondo, presto

Haydn composed thirty-one trios for strings and keyboard, yet there can be no other collection of any master's music that has been so consistently neglected. Even the amateur musician, the last hope of neglected composers, has almost totally abandoned them at the back of the music shelf. The reason is not hard to find. The keyboard part of these trios was written for the harpsichord or the forte-piano whose bass register tends to weakness. The cello parts often make or decoratively reinforce the bass of the music. Played with a harpsichord the cello emerges with a role no less important than in a string quartet. With a modern piano, however, the highly resonant bass almost completely smothers the cello, leading to a not unreasonable resentment and a refusal by the player to perform the Haydn trios at all! Their neglect is the more to be regretted since only four of the trios were written before 1780 when Haydn was entering his maturest years and was at the height of his creative powers. The trio in E minor was composed in 1795, the year he began work on the *Creation*.

The first movement is in a tense and dramatic sonata form whose second subject is derived from the first. The intensity is rarely relaxed and even the brief sunny spell in G major early on in the movement is later turned into a grim E minor. By contrast the slow movement is lyrical and warm with lovely counterpoint between the right hand of the harpsichord and the violin. The final rondo begins cheerfully enough but the grim mood of the first movement returns in a *minore* section and the subject is, even in the major, worked out with an intensity which weights the movement sufficiently to balance the trio. *(Notes for 6 March 1966 concert.)*

¶*Trio* in E^b Major for violin, cello and harpsichord
Allegro moderato; Andanta con moto; Presto
This trio too was composed in 1795 when Haydn was sixty-three, the year he began work on the *Creation*. The serene but serious first movement is a fine example of Haydn's late use of sonata form. The originality of his approach to form, always seeking to make it more closely knit together, has been too little appreciated. In this movement the careful preparation of the dominant tonality leads not to a new subject but to a new version of the first, which in its turn moves on without break to a beautiful new idea in the dominant minor. It is one of the finest examples of Haydn's attempt to break down the sectional aspects of sonata form. The slow movement in C major is a solemn Andante con moto with a most striking bridge passage leading back through A flat and C minor to the original tonic and the brilliant finale. *(Notes for 8 September 1959 concert.)*

¶*Trio* in C Major for violin, cello and harpsichord
Allegro; Andante; Presto
Also composed in 1795. The first movement is an elaborate sonata form

whose vivacity and high spirits belie the intricacies of construction and development that lie within it. The slow movement is in ternary form in which a delightfully treated lilting tune is contrasted with a dramatic middle section. The last movement shows Haydn at his gayest and at his most economical, for it is entirely based on the opening rondo tune and various fragmentary pieces derived from it. *(Notes for 10 September 1959 concert.)*

6

AN OVERVIEW OF BEETHOVEN'S THREE-PART CAREER AS A COMPOSER

The single most important factor in Beethoven's life was an obsessive desire to compose. It overrode matters of the heart, friendship, professional relationships, even family. He was not a sociable man. He was, all the same, constantly assailed by truly potent forces within and without and these vitally affected that obsession.

To the extent they did so can be traced the source of the idea that his creative life fell into three periods. It is not a perfect, unassailable view, but it serves pretty well, especially if you consider the periods historically and in relation to the circumstances that surrounded his life during them.

He began as a firebrand and the first period, *the early years*, is one of arrival from unknown to known, from Bonn to Vienna, from apprenticeship to mastery, from a variety of styles to a consistent musical personality that had infinite variety of its own. It covered, approximately, the years up to 1805, by which time he was thirty-five years old. Haydn was an old man; Mozart was dead. There was no one to rival his growing reputation in Europe save, perhaps, Rossini in opera.

That was the first period. The third one, *the late years*, was one of retreat as far as most wordly matters were concerned. It was also one of defeat, for his deafness isolated him from professional and most social contact, causing him great frustration and anger. But it also released him from much that had trammeled his life in the intervening years so that he was free to create the great spiritual world he inhabited musically, in those last years. He died in 1827 at the age of fifty-seven, with the last thirteen years virtually excluded from the normal world of a musician.

The middle years, the second period, were at once those of the mature composer and those in which he was most beset by trials and tribulations and yet was most able and willing to do battle against them.

He knew his deafness was growing and that the various idiotic treatments he was undergoing were only causing him pain and irritation without bringing any real signs of improvement.

As a pianist he was celebrated for his somewhat wild, eccentric playing which, nevertheless, evidently communicated his fiery, insistent personality wonderfully well. He now had to face the increasing inability to know if he was playing the right notes or not. As a result he never played the "Emperor" Concerto, written in 1809. All the previous concertos had been written for himself to perform. None appeared after that.

His conducting was never, perhaps, counted among his greatest skills, but he knew better than anyone else how his lastest compositions should go and these were the years when the frustration of not being able to hear mistakes made him very irascible. His relationship with the professional musicians in Vienna deteriorated to the extent that rehearsals became fiascos and performances even worse.

There was also the growing concern about the health of his brother, Karl, who was to die of tuerculosis in 1814. He had acted *in loco parentis* for both his younger brothers and was excessively possessive of them, trying to stop their marriages which he considered unsuitable and, eventually, nearly breaking himself over the adoption of Karl's son, pushing the matter into the sordid limelight of the Viennese courts and so tormenting the boy that he eventually put two pistols to his own head and tried to do away with himself. He failed, but the whole process threatened Beethoven's ability to compose with near extinction for some five or six years.

Hovering over all the middle years was the shadow of Napoleon. Like most artists, Beethoven had always had a somewhat simplistic view of politics and the legend of his early admiration and subsequent disillusionment with the Frenchman is well known. Now, ironically, his former hero gave Beethoven as much success as pain, for the symphony,

Wellington's Victory, celebrating Napoleon's downfall, always attracted large audiences and made the composer a small fortune in concert receipts.

Nevertheless, through those middle years the French threat was never far from Vienna. The city was twice beseiged and invaded and, whatever the political situation, there was always the noise of war and the physical danger for Beethoven to contend with.

All these we can see reflected in the works he composed at this time.

You can see the aggressive response in the Fifth Symphony and anticipated in the earlier C minor Piano Concerto; the relief he found in Nature in the "Pastoral" Symphony and the Fourth Piano Concerto; the sense and hope of triumphing over adversity in the "Emperor" Concerto; the dignity of his own tragedy in *Coriolanus;* the progress and death of a hero in *Egmont;* liberation from oppression in the opera *Fidelio.*

All these too, circumstances and music, found reverberant echoes in the growing Romantic spirit of the nineteenth century. But however well we understand and respond to the stresses and strains of his creative life, we must never forget that he was not a Romantic; that the musicians he performed with for as long as he was able and for whom he always wrote, were those who had regularly played for Haydn. That was the sound and style he grew up with and took with him as he retreated into the exclusive world of his last, deaf years. What he did with them has amazed the world ever since.

His was a towering mind and it served as an example, sometimes even as a threat to most composers who came after him in the nineteenth century, just as Shakespeare did to his successors. But at this distance and at this very point in time it seems important to stress that he was not, as some would have us believe, writers and performers alike, the inventor of Brahms who, fifty years later, composed in a completely different style; nor was he the musical bed-fellow of Mendelssohn, Schubert, Weber or Schumann and certainly not the musical progenitor of Siegfried, whose author claimed that he was.

He may have given his great successors courage to be themselves in their own time but his own background and kinship was with the late eighteenth century whose intellectual and musical climate proved ideal for him to achieve the wonders that he did which now even appear more wonderful viewed through Classical eyes.

Beethoven's compositions have never left the music scene and each generation, as with Shakespeare, has interpreted them differently. Lately he was seen as a sort of musical Zeus on an Olympian high altar before which all must kneel respectfully and slowly. Now we are coming to see his genius through the eyes of his own time finding him no less wonderful, no less Olympian but dressed differently, revealing his greatness from within the musical style he inherited and made his own.

The middle years show this most clearly. It was a time of great achievement. *(Notes for Indianapolis Symphony Orchestra quarterly newsletter, Spring 1988.)*

7

AN ORCHESTRATION OF SCHUBERT'S
GRAND DUO, D. 812

In the summer of 1824, Schubert went to stay with the Esterházys at Zseliz in Hungary. The two sisters, Countess Marie and Countess Karoline, were old friends of his and very good pianists for whom he had already written a number of fine piano duets.

In a letter from the painter Schwind to another member of the Schubertians (as the group of admiring friends around the composer called themselves), Schober, dated August 20th we read that "Schubert has written... he is quite well and busy, I believe, with a symphony..."

There are various other references to a new symphony at this time but no full score has survived.

It was a great year for Schubert, one of considerable optimism and creative energy. The song-cycle *Die schöne Müllerin* was being published; by March he had completed the Octet; the A minor and *Death and the Maiden* quartets came a little later and, during the summer at Zseliz, the *Divertissement à la hongroise* and the magnificent set of variations in A-flat, both for piano-duet, intended for performance there by his two gifted friends. Then, in June, came what was eventually published by

Diabelli after his death as the *Grand Duo*, opus 140 (a meaningless, arbitrary sort of number), a major work which has survived only as a piano-duet.

Schumann was among the first to express the opinion that it was either an arrangement of a symphony, possibly a transcription made so that his young ladies could try it out at Zseliz, or the first version of a work that he was to score later.

This latter possibility is the less likely since there is no other example of Schubert following this method of composition, while there are several of his arranging orchestral scores for keyboard for various purposes. It becomes the more probable when the scope of the *Grand Duo* is considered, for it is on a far larger scale than any other of his original piano-duets.

Most convincing of all is the experience of those who have played for many years the extraordinary piano-duet repertory that Schubert left for posterity. He was himself a fine pianist and wrote with great sensitivity and idiomatic mastery of the instrument be it two or four-handed in execution.

You have only to play at one sitting the variations in A-flat, magically imagined for the instrument, and then the *Grand Duo* to feel sure they were not conceived for the same medium even though they were written at the same time.

Joachim, for whom Brahms wrote his Violin Concerto, was the first to orchestrate it in 1855. Stylistic accuracy was not his main concern. He responded to the beauties of the music and made a Brahmsian symphony out of it using the chromatic horns and trumpets of his time, doubling and blending textures into one another in the thicker, more opaque style and sound of his own time. Schubert rarely doubles except (and often) at the octave; the textures are clear with the upper extremes of the strings rarely exploited; the horns and trumpets were limited in their chromatic possibilities while the trombones played a larger role in his scoring and he used them with great flexibility.

This, then, is a version which aspires to sound as it might have done had it been performed as a symphony in 1824 when the work was first conceived.

The music really speaks for itself. It came after the "Unfinished" Symphony and before the "Great" C major whose key it shares. All four movements [Allegro moderato, Andante, Scherzo (Allegro vivace), Finale (Allegro vivace)] are full of those wonderful melodies that poured out of Schubert in his maturity, if 1824 with four more years to go out of thirty-one can count as that. The incredible fluency with tonalities is in full flow as is the sense of timing and space needed for his best music to be put into its right perspective and shape. The lyricism is everything in Schubert no matter how he frames it with the sterner notes, redolent of Beethoven, or the wit he derived from Rossini. At his best, as he certainly is here, he integrates all into a single style and speaks to us in a unique way that is deeply involving and touching. [In 1991 I recorded this orchestration of the *Grand Duo* with the Indianapolis Symphony Orchestra, for Koss Classics, KC-2221.].

From the reviews: "A Symphony Is Where You Find It"
by Joseph Horowitz, *The New York Times*, 24 April 1992

"Schubert was the most prolific and remarkable of piano duet composers. In fact, his output for one piano, four hands, may be the most bewilderingly varied body of music in a single genre by any major composer. And yet this repertory — rarely heard in concert, rarely recorded — is well known only to those who perform it at home.[8]

"The four-movement, 45-minute *Grand Duo* (D. 812) is a case in point. Composed in 1824, two years after the "Unfinished" Symphony, it might have become one of Schubert's most popular and 'characteristic' works had it been conceived for orchestra. In fact, a new, newly recorded version of the *Grand Duo* by the conductor Raymond Leppard achieves precisely this transformation, and with impressive results.

"As absolute music, the *Grand Duo* beggars description. Its huge first movement has plausibly been called one of Schubert's most consummate formal achievements. The poetic opening stiffens, dreamily relaxes, then mightily reclenches: an instability of mood and texture both sympto-

---

8   For a comprehensive survey-analysis of the complete works in this form, see
Schubert's Music for Piano Four-Hands by Dallas A. Weekley and Nancy Arganbright
(Pro/Am Music Resources, Inc., 1990). (Ed.)

matic of the mature Schubert and disorienting to generations of frustrated admirers, beginning with Robert Schumann. The development builds to a pounding climax — also typically Schubertian, although it violates nineteenth-century images of the composer. And this is nothing compared with the convulsive violence of the coda, which alternates, as Beethoven's climaxes never do, with passages of reverie.

"The duo's slow movement is obviously indebted to the slow movement of Beethoven's Second Symphony. Yet the 27-year-old Schubert's Andante transcends the 31-year-old Beethoven's Larghetto — in originality, dramatic impact, lyric bliss. The Scherzo is a motoric tour de force, its Trio an eerie masterpiece of harmonic clairvoyance.

"Schubert, who so often seems to compose extemporaneously, runs out of steam in many a finale. In the *Grand Duo*, the finale never flags. From one perspective, it is a Hungarian dance full of color and charm. But the tempo marking, Allegro vivace, conveys urgency. The humor is obstinate. The argument grows violent. In other words, like Mahler (who revered him), and more than Brahms (who based the finale of the Piano Quintet on this movement), Schubert utterly transfigures the vernacular elements he appropriates.

"In truth, the infrequency of piano duet performances is not the only reason the *Grand Duo* is little known. With its dense textures and 'orchestral' sonorities, it is a hard work to put across in concert. Decades of Schubertians speculated that it was a symphony in disguise. This was Schumann's opinion. Schumann's friend Brahms urged Joseph Joachim to orchestrate the *Grand Duo*, which Joachim did in 1855. More recent orchestral transcriptions were undertaken, I am told, by Felix Weingartner and René Leibowitz. Modern scholarship insists that Schubert wrote the *Grand Duo* for two of his piano pupils. Yet its length, scope and weight remain symphonic.

"Enter the English conductor Raymond Leppard. He believes that the duo may be the first version of a work Schubert intended to orchestrate. Mr. Leppard's own orchestration, which he has recorded with his Indianapolis Symphony, attempts to supplant Joachim's Brahmsian version with something more Schubertian. And Mr. Leppard's Schubert-scaled orchestra does sound remarkably plausible in this music. The prominent trombone parts, in particular, perfectly imitate a Schubert signature.

"Significantly, the movement most readily suited to the piano is the least persuasive. Redistributing the parts, [in this critic's view] the Leppard orchestration unfortunately relieves the intentional strain of the Scherzo's breakneck skips and manic velocity. But in the whirlwind C-major finale, Mr. Leppard's trumpets and drums heighten stirring intimations of the 'Great C major' Symphony, begun a year later. Here, too, the instrumentation clarifies midrange textures that clot on the keyboard.

"[Leppard's version is thus an impressive] achievement. This, in short, is a 'symphony' surpassing Schubert's previous eight, not to mention the symphonies of Mendelssohn and Schumann to come."

From a review by Tom Aldridge, *Arts Indiana*, May 1991

"Leppard's orchestration is a remarkable recreation of the sounds and textures of the mature Schubert — the Schubert of the 'Unfinished' Symphony, the B-minor 'Entr'acte' from *Rosamunde*, and, most of all, the 'Great' C-Major Symphony. Especially characteristic are the prominent trombone parts, which blend with Schubert's harmonization to produce a sonic palette unduplicated by subsequent romantic-era symphonists and not earlier realized in Schubert's youthful first six symphonies. Employing a delicate interweaving of the wind and brass ensembles with the mainly predominant strings and an occasional solo foray (such as the brief bassoon line in the second movement), Leppard *has* reproduced Schubert's sonic palette — and for his effort has made the *Duo* a greater piece."

8

SCHUMANN RE-MET; OR A
TRIBUTE BETTER LATE THAN NEVER (1993)

Anything that happens in the world affects me; politics, for example, literature, people; and I reflect about all these things in my own way — and these reflections then seek to find an outlet in music.

Have an open eye for life as well as the other arts and sciences.

Highly honor the old, but also meet the new with a warm heart. Cherish no prejudice against unknown names.

Nature would burst should she attempt to produce nothing save Beethovens.

— ROBERT SCHUMANN[9]

I came to Schumann rather late.... Of course, as a youngster studying piano with unresolved questions in mind about pursuing that as a career, you played works like the *Etudes symphoniques, Carnaval*, the G minor Sonata. Later I opted in favor of Cambridge and, taken up with baroque enthusiasms, developed an overly severe critical attitude to most music.

At that point I turned my back on Schumann; those endless and invariable four-bar phrases; the feeble (as I thought them) attempts at thematic development, clearly and incompetently aping the great sonata structures of Beethoven (who also came in for his share of knocks at about this time); the orchestration that seemed hardly worth mentioning because everyone already knew how bad it was (even Mahler had failed to do anything effective about that, as we discovered in the Cambridge University Musical Society playing the "Rhenish" Symphony with his re-

---

9   Transl. Paul Rosenfeld; in Konrad Wolff, ed., *Robert Schumann: On Music and Musicians* (Pantheon Books, 1946; reprinted W. W. Norton & Co.), 260, 37, 35, 70.

orchestrations, which only seemed to make things worse... at least from the vantage point of the principal viola chair).

Then, too, there were all those critical effusions we had to read for Tripos [honors music degree] which in their flat-footed enthusiasms seemed, at that distance in time, to be by someone quite unable to distinguish between the masterly and the journeyman composer.

But that has all changed as I have grown older and become a little less opinionated, a little less pretentious in my understanding of what is really valuable and what is not. I have come to realise why Schumann has long been loved by audiences and players and now, rather lately, by me.

It is, I see, the sheer quality of ideas that sets him apart: and it is this simple, intuitive understanding that sets at nought the stupid observation of the regular phrase-lengths which any idiot can see and of which he must certainly have been aware; it is the invention and the very ingenuousness of his constructions which far outshine the obvious struggles with development; and the problems of orchestration were, it becomes clear, not his but ours. Given proper rehearsal and scrupulous attention to balance and the differing qualities of sound at the various levels of scoring, the salient lines can be made clear. The blurred sound of which he is accused only occurs if sustained notes are played too loudly or accompanying figures played with uniform tone-color and, in the strings, as if they had been devised for Max Bruch's G minor Violin Concerto. The transparency of the sound should and can be Mendelssohnian.

As for the critical writings, I realise on more mature re-examination that, when enthusiastic, he was writing with discrimination about music that was successful in his own time, not making pretence always to be predicting future masterpieces. We will never be without the Henselts, the Salieris and the Spohrs. They fulfil a most valuable function, serving as a worthy background to the greater creative talents, and there are never very many of those. The others accompany and should be praised in their lives as Schumann intended them to be.

Then I have come, in more recent years, better to understand the man. The old image was of a rather stuffy, proper German kept in order, perhaps even under a very gifted but very bossy wife who seemed always to be pregnant. The strain of it all made the weakling male jump in the Rhine and, after being ignominiously fished out, end his days in a lunatic asylum. She suffered for him, supported in the last years of his life on the arm, some said in the arms of Brahms. It was, we were led to understand, a fine example of woman's suffrage, courage and final artistic triumph.

Recent research, particularly in a most sympathetic psychological study by Peter Oswald, has shown quite a different picture of a man aware very early on of a divided mind which, Florestan and Eusebius apart, led him into bouts of heavy drinking, loutish, violent behavior, homosexual episodes with the threatening shadow of madness growing like a great thunderstorm over his life.

He was deeply attracted to the strength as well as the musical talent of Clara and saw in his marriage the hope of stability that might keep him anchored while his burning creative gifts could find expression.

It was a vision that was bound to fade and end in disaster but, while it was vivid, the music poured out of him at an amazing rate and level of inspiration. The quality that shines so brightly at the beginning continued to do so more and more fitfully as his mind clouded over until his wretched, lonely death at the age of 45. Clara did not see him for the last two and a half years of his life, save, briefly, on the day before he died.

He was a vulnerable creature easily daunted by the flamboyance of Liszt and Wagner whom he disliked, but he knew about everything that was going on in Europe. There was the discovery of Schubert, the magical playing of Paganini, the waywardness of Meyerbeer, the eccentric talent of Berlioz, the loving admiration of Mendelssohn, Weber and Hummel and, above all finally, the discovery of the young Brahms with whom he was as much in love as was Clara and who loved him, quite platonically.

This was the musical company he liked to keep and they made together a world worth celebrating.

IV

MUSIC AND THE CONDUCTOR

A SYMPOSIUM[1]

THE CHAIRMAN: I need hardly remind you that Mr. Leppard is a very versatile musician who has had an extraordinarily varied and adventurous career in music. I suppose he is best known to the public today for his wonderful contribution to the Glyndebourne repertoire and for his work with the English Chamber Orchestra. Not satisfied with that, he has just accepted the appointment of Chief Conductor of the BBC Northern Orchestra—in which we wish him every success. So your topic tonight is in very safe hands and I have great pleasure in introducing Mr. Leppard.

The following paper was then given.

The conductor, like the director in the theater, is reckoned now to be a significant figure in music, his role as interpreter having far exceeded in importance his more obvious duties as co-ordinator. But the somewhat starry isolation which his raised-up position in front of an orchestra seems to symbolize is a comparatively recent phenomenon.

Of course, wherever music has been performed by a group of people someone has had to take charge. Music demonstrates more clearly than most human activities that there is nothing less able to organize itself effectively than a group of intelligent people, especially one attempting to agree on artistic matters. The old adage of a camel being the result of a committee's attempt to design a horse contains a good deal of hard truth. Nevertheless it was only with the advent of larger orchestras in the early nineteenth century that the conductor began to assume something of his present spectacular singularity. Before that, with smaller forces to direct, he was little more than *primus inter pares* as far as the public's gaze was

---

1   A paper given to The Royal Society for the Encouragement of Arts, Manufactures and Commerce on Wednesday 9th May 1973, with Sir Anthony Lewis, CBE, MA, MusD, Principal, Royal Academy of Music, in the Chair.

concerned. As far as the performing musicians are concerned his domination of the scene goes much further back.

In the sense of being someone actually directing and manipulating a performance, the conductor's career began in the opera house because of the special problems that opera creates. Prior to this virtually all music of any importance which involved more than a very few people was heard only in Church, where the regularity and tradition of performance, as well as the conventions within which the music was composed, enabled it to be performed without obvious direction. Choir practices were sufficient preparation for satisfactory performance in which the *Maestro di capella* remained out of sight in the organ loft and the choir kept together by the merest wag of a forefinger or a roll of paper by a suitably reliable singing priest from his choir-stall. With opera things changed.

It is one of the very few musical forms which may be said to have had a fairly definite beginning, being the first and most enduring fruit of a revolution in musical style which had been brewing since the mid-sixteenth century. A date, 1600, can even be ascribed to the first of its line and, although this represents a gross over-simplification of a separate historical topic, it makes a convenient starting point from which to view the changing image of the conductor. Certainly the problems of operatic performance were new in the field of music and new solutions had to be found. Nor have the problems or their solutions changed very significantly in the ensuing three hundred and fifty years.

Opera is at once the most marvellous and the most ridiculously impractical of artistic forms. A band is secreted out of sight where it does not particularly like to be and where it can get up to all manner of mischief. On the stage is ranged a collection of beings generally noted more for the beauty of their voices than the quickness of their wits. On the grounds of sheer distance from one another the difficulties of being able to perform together with any exactitude must be immediately apparent. But when the people on stage are, in addition to singing, called on to move about and enact the whole gamut of human passions, pick up things and put things down, fight fights, pray prayers, die deaths and make love, it can be imagined that the difficulties are increased a thousandfold. Without someone visibly in charge — visible that is to the orchestra and the singers—the venture could only end in disastrous chaos.

A combination of circumstance and intelligence soon produced the idea of the orchestra in an orchestra pit at a lower level than the singers on the stage with the man in charge so to speak on the mezzanine floor visible to both.

There were some curious variants of this arrangement before it was generally accepted. Raguenet in his *Parallèle des Italiens et des Français en ce qui regard la musique et les opéras*, published in 1702, describes how "some years since the Master of the Musick in the opera at Paris had an elbow-chair and desk placed on the stage where, with the score in one hand and a stick in the other, he beat time on a table put there for that purpose, so loud that he made a greater noise than the whole band on purpose to be heard by the performers. By degrees they removed this abuse from the stage to the music room [pit] where the composer beats time in the same manner and as loud as ever."[2]

We must remember, however, that Raguenet was an ardent admirer of the Italian opera and describes what was, in all probability, an extreme case in order to denigrate the French. Engravings as early as the 1670s show the generally accepted arrangement of pit and stage with the conductor in his now accustomed place.

The first figure in this position of whom we have any significant detail is Jean-Baptiste Lully. He was a Florentine who made his way to Paris in the mid seventeenth century. At the Court of Louis XIV he dominated first the ballet and then the opera with a ruthless ambition which brought him virtual monopoly. First and foremost a ballet master, he was a talented composer of dance tunes and only began his career as an opera composer in the 1660s when Cardinal Mazarin decided to import from Venice the glamorous new artistic form which had become celebrated throughout Europe. Poor Francesco Cavalli was brought all the way to Paris to show the French how it was done. But he received short shrift from Lully, who thereafter composed and directed virtually all the operas at the French Court until his death twenty years later.

---

2   From Galliard's translation of Raguenet, published in London, 1709.

The ballet-master's symbol of authority was the long silver-knobbed cane used to beat time in ballet classes. We can still see such a cane being used by the great ballet-master Perrot in the paintings of Degas at the end of the nineteenth century. Clearly, if the regular tapping of this cane on the floor could keep ballet dancers in step with each other (they are a notoriously un-rhythmical race), it would prove a formidably effective instrument for co-ordination in the opera house. A wooden rostrum to act as a sounding board, two or three good thumps in the time of the music and at least everyone should get off to a good start. And, moreover, if things later on begin to come adrift a few more thumps should, with any luck, bring them together again.

We know this to have been Lully's practise from contemporary descriptions, engravings and a number of complaints about the noise to be found in letters and journals of the time. Ironically Lully died of it. At some particularly exasperating moment of disunity it seems he hit his foot with the cane so severely that it became poisoned. Medical science being what it was in 1687 he died of gangrene within eight weeks.

After Lully's death the long cane, understandably, fell into disuse; not so much on account of its lethal potential but in response to complaints about the noise it made. With that curious logic which lies behind near-ly all changes in musical style and performance it was found that the conductor could manage perfectly well with his staff cut in half so that it would not reach the ground. It was held in exactly the same way, upright with fingers grasped around its substantial circumference and thumb extended upwards on the inner surface. The motion was, as before, large-ly up and down but, in default of thumps, a new lateral motion was introduced — difficult to achieve with a long cane but now perfectly possible — so that units of both two and three could be clearly indicated in silence. This covered all time signatures then in general use.

It was not, I dare say, a very subtle method of conducting but an abatement of noise must have been very welcome and, if the worst came to the worst, the conductor could without much shifting of the hand give the music stand, or even a recalcitrant player a tap or two to compel attention.

In fact we may still see this method of holding the baton in military bands on the march although it is to be doubted that in the eighteenth

"Spy" 's cartoon drawing of Michael Costa,
published in *Vanity Fair* for 6 July 1872

century opera house conductors were in the habit of twirling their batons
between their fingers or hurling them into the air. It was a method which
persisted in the opera house and, later on, the concert hall until the latter half of the nineteenth century.

The batons themselves were thick and heavy, often made of ebony or
mahogany, silver or ivory topped at either end. Their weight alone must
have made conducting a tiring business and the upright position allows
only restricted movement so that niceties of rubato would have been virtually impossible to control in performance. I have, as a matter of interest, brought with me such a baton which once belonged to Sir Michael
Costa, the most celebrated conductor in England at the middle of the
nineteenth century; as admired as Beecham and twice the tyrant. There
is a famous cartoon which shows him using it, or one like it, at one of the
famous Crystal Palace concerts at Sydenham around 1860.

There is too much conflicting evidence to decide exactly when this baton gave way to the type in general use now, made of pliable light wood and held in front of the body between thumb and the first two fingers. Various people have been accredited with the change; Von Bülow, Richter, Mottl, Levi and even Mahler, but I suspect that the process was, in fact, a gradual one and that no individual can be said to have invented it. From photographs and drawings it is clear that the old, thick baton was gradually shortened and held at one end so that the point could be used out from the body rather than the whole length of it held against the body. Berlioz and Wagner, both famous conductors, held their batons in this way. Once the change of hold and position was established the sensible thing was to lighten the wood and lengthen the stick again so that the point could be clearly visible and pliable enough to show a tiny flick as it transmitted the energy of the hand giving the beat.

With the newly adopted hold a series of universally accepted patterns of movement were developed, based on the old ones, which could indicate not only the usual duple and triple metres in all their various manifestations, but also those more eccentric rhythmic patterns which composers like Stravinsky were beginning to use in their compositions.

As the century has progressed the tendency has been to shorten the baton again. This reflects more a change in musical taste and composition than any fundamental change in technique. Style in performance has veered away from the great washes of sound so much loved by the late Romantic composers towards sharper definition of textures and precision of ensemble. The long stick (Sir Henry Wood used one about 2-1/2 feet long) bends as it moves through the air so that the tip describes arcs of movement which have few incidental points of definition. As an indication of a flowing pulse to which every player can adjust the complication of the part he is playing it is admirable, but there is no doubt that with the tendency of performance towards more sharply controlled precision of detail, the shorter stick produces the better results.

That, then, is a brief history of the conductor's equipment, less interesting in itself than for what it tells us of his changing function and purpose. These changes are inextricably bound up with those of musical style and practice. Of course his fundamental concern was, and always

With the BBC Northern Symphony Orchestra
1975 King's Lynn Festival

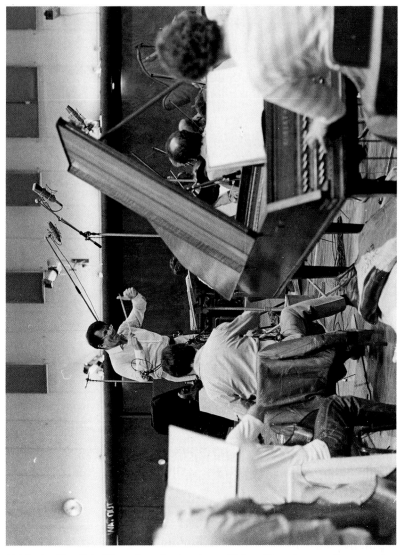

With the English Chamber Orchestra – Abbey Road recording session
CREDIT: Colin Busby, London

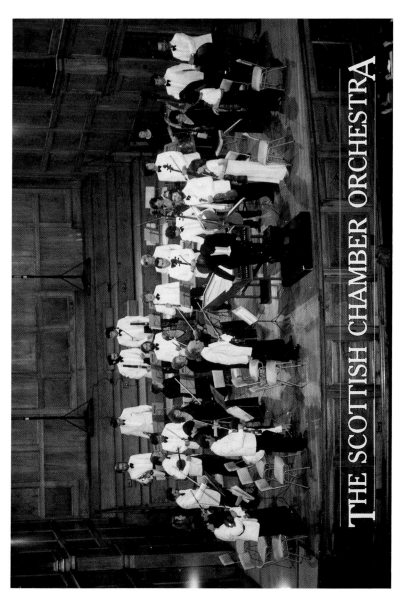

With the Scottish Chamber Orchestra, Glasgow

With James Bowman, Margherita Rinaldi,
Radiotelevisione Italiana orchestra & chorus – Turin, 1973

Recording *Il ritorno d'Ulisse* with the
London Philharmonic Orchestra, 1979
CREDIT: Colin Busby, London

In the pit at Greater Miami Opera, 1979: *The Barber of Seville*
(RL conducting from the harpsichord)

Members of the brass section, BBC Philharmonic
1985 Mananan Festival on the Isle of Man
CREDIT: Manx Star, Isle of Man

With the Indianapolis Symphony Orchestra

will be, for the co-ordination of performance, but as the demands of the music performed altered so did his relationship both with musicians and the public.

It is important to remember that, until the last years of the seventeenth century, composer and conductor were usually one and the same person. In opera so little was written down beyond the vocal line and a bass line that the composer virtually had to be in charge for the work to come to performance at all. Moreover, there was no such thing as a permanent repertoire. Operas were performed for only one season, or even just one occasion, and rarely revived. The exceptions demonstrate the point. We know that some thirty years after Monteverdi's *Arianna* was first performed in Mantua he revived it to open a new opera house, the San Moisè in Venice. He re-wrote the opera, not just because he had second thoughts but because much of it was lost. Similarly Cavalli's *Xerxes*, originally composed for Venice, was taken by him to Paris at the request of Cardinal Mazarin (that was the time when he had such trouble with Lully) and the score he himself used for both occasions has survived, presenting enormously difficult textual problems in the sorting out of the two versions which are superimposed one on the other.

This incompleteness of text, characteristic of all seventeenth-century music in the new style, has previously been a barrier to its performance precisely because it was not understood that the composer almost always conducted its performance, and was able to complete, to clothe the skeleton using the forces available to him. The practicality of this method is admirable, given the prevailing conditions, but is rarely understood sympathetically by critical minds used to the engraved full score of nineteenth century operas which can scarcely ever be made to bend to particular circumstances. Although this belongs to a separate study, it is relevant to our consideration of the position and function of the conductor, for at this time there could be no such thing as comparative interpretation. The reputation of men like Monteverdi and Cavalli was based on their compositions, not only their directing abilities, considerable as they must have been.

The staggering popularity of opera which, by the end of the seventeenth century, resulted in the demand for performances of the same work in different places, eventually forced composers to abandon their early method of composition in favour of more detailed, definitive scores which could be transported and performed by others elsewhere. There was a sad loss of flexibility in this but also a new interpretative element in the conductor's function.

Coincidentally came a change of venue in secular music. Opera had begun in Italy, was copied and to a considerable extent changed, one might say ossified, in France, but the new music of the early eighteenth century was to be found in Germany where, although opera maintained its popularity, the teutonic predilection of instrumental music — they are not primarily a singing race — manifested itself in the establishment of court orchestras, and the widespread composition of purely instrumental music, overtures and suites, symphonies and concertos, laid the foundations of what is now thought of as the classical repertoire.

The courts of Germany with their own musical establishments, which varied a great deal in size and quality, were, as far as day to day activity was concerned, cut off from one another. The possibility of communication betwen musicians was nevertheless somewhat greater than before. Difficulties of travel made the links between Venice and the rest of Europe extremely tenuous. Now, at least, contact between the centers of musical activity could be made, if uncomfortably, by carriage.

There was still nothing approaching the peripatetic life we lead today. Princes might take their *maestro di capella* with them on visits to neighbouring courts either to show him off as a prized possession, or so that he might profit from his experience, but the majority of musicians tended to stay in one place for the whole of their musical lives.

The idea of comparative interpretation, which lies at the root of present-day conductors' separate reputations, did not often arise. There was great rivalry between the various establishments, but it was a rivalry that tended to enclose the conductors within the court structure where his talents could redound to its greater honour and glory. Moreover, the concept of interpretation scarcely existed. In the smaller courts, the head musician was usually the leader of the orchestra or the organist and in either case led his orchestra from his chosen instrument. His daily routine of producing music for chapel, ceremonial occasions, opera and evening entertainments can scarcely have given him much spare time for anything beyond the sheer practicalities of getting things in some sort of order.

Nevertheless some of the greater establishments became celebrated and with them their directors of music; Johann Stamitz at Mannheim, Carl Graun and Carl Philipp Emanuel Bach in Berlin, Johann Adolph Hasse at Dresden and, of course, Joseph Haydn at Esterhazy. They controlled quite large orchestras of between thirty-five and fifty players and, although some still played their instruments, the tendency was for them to relinquish leading their orchestras in favour of directing them by gesture.

A factor which, from the middle of the eighteenth century, played a large part in the conductor's career was the newly viable market in music printing. For the first time scores and parts of the latest symphonies and concertos could be circulated round Europe and, as their composers' reputations grew, they themselves were able to seek leave from their main employment in order to perform their music in other places. Johann Stamitz's son, Carl, provides an excellent example. Born at Mannheim he, like his brother Anton, played in his father's orchestra, which was perhaps the most famous in Europe. Next in line as director of the orchestra, he had become, by the time of his father's death in 1757, a celebrated composer and we hear of him in Paris in 1770 and London in 1778. Haydn too, only with more difficulty, managed to take leave from the Esterhazy family, finally breaking away altogether in the last years of his life. But these men were still known first and foremost as composers. The fact that they were able performers and directors of performance was of secondary importance.

The factor which changed the conductor's status more than anything else was the removal of music from the private sphere of the court to the public one of the concert hall. It was of course a gradual process more advanced in some areas than in others. Public concerts were given in London sporadically from the early years of the eighteenth century, but when orchestras played they tended to be *ad hoc* bodies gathered together for the occasion. It still needed the foundation outside the private sphere of orchestras playing regularly together before the conductor as opposed to the composer could have a career.

This happened first in Germany, where the idea and eventual fact of a united Germany rendered the separate principalities powerless and impoverished. Their musicians were often taken over by neighbouring cities and the long and distingushed tradition of civic music began. Among the first was Leipzig, whose Gewandhaus orchestra began its history as one of the great European orchestras with Mendelssohn's appointment as resident conductor in 1835.

The image of composer-conductor still persists in the first wave of these new, public musicians; Weber, Berlioz, Spohr, Liszt and Wagner are among the most celebrated. But their reputations were two-fold and they did not by any means confine their performances to their own works.[3] It might even be reasonably said that Berlioz was more famous in his day as a conductor than he was as a composer, and his books like *Soirées de L'Orchestre* show a concern and understanding of the orchestral musician's attitude and temperament which is an essential part of the virtuoso conductor's trade. They were soon followed by men like Von Bülow, Hallé, Costa, Habeneck, Richter and Mottl whose reputations lay solely on their abilities to conduct an orchestra and produce performances of distinction.

With the invention of the railway and, eventually, the motor car and the airplane, conductors could travel widely and rapidly so that within weeks the public could hear and compare Weingartner's *Eroica* with that of Richter. With the invention of radio, the gramophone and television, assessment of compared interpretations has become almost a mania with critics and public alike. And with it the conductor reached stardom.

But even in the hundred years or so that he has been a public figure the conductor has changed. Those mid-nineteenth century figures, although they may have travelled widely nevertheless were generally attached to one orchestra with whom they spent most of their time and for whom they became, in some respects, father-figures. Their players were ill-educated apart from the playing of their instruments, so that enforcement of discipline, sometimes of the harshest nature, played a large part in their conductor's relationship with them. It encouraged conductors to become tyrants, and the legends of their tyranny have become famous.

---

3   More recent examples would include Benjamin Britten, Peter Maxwell Davies and Oliver Knussen.

Amusing as they are to recount they could not have made for congenial music-making.

With the more egalitarian social structure that has come about in Europe during this century, and the enormously improved standard of general education, this sort of relationship can no longer persist. A conductor may well find himself facing an orchestra many of whose members are much more intelligent than he is. The players do not find themselves in orchestras because they had an aptitude for an instrument and for nothing else. The majority of our players now choose their way of life and are out to enjoy it and make the best of it. Problems of discipline therefore rarely arise, and a conductor who attempts the old barn-storming technique of tearing up scores and ranting is liable, good manners apart, to find himself in receipt of wittily placed deflationary remarks or, in extreme cases, total revolution. Nowadays he has only himself to blame.[4]

The modern conductor is once more seen by his players as *primus inter pares*. Of course he must be in charge of his orchestra and finally decide one way or the other what is to happen, but the end result is achieved by collaboration rather than by dictatorial methods. He must, of course, dominate but in such a way that the orchestra will welcome the domination. In effect he must be as good a psychologist as a musician. If he succeeds in his more subtle role then the modern orchestra will play for him not as a trained circus but as a group of people fulfilling themselves in the individual contributions they make to the whole performance.

I'm glad to be able to say that England, above all other European countries, seems most effectively to have found the way of making this newer, more subtle relationship between orchestra and conductor work, and the resulting concern and vitality which comes from within our or-

---

4   The story is told, in Shostakovich's "memoirs" entitled *Testimony*, that R.C.A. Victor's gift of a set of recordings of the Shostakovich 7th Symphony by Toscanini and the NBC Symphony orchestra was received coolly by the composer because he could not approve of Toscanini's reputation as a podium despot. (Ed.)

chestras has made their achievements and general musical standard the envy of all.[5]

So much then for the evolving status, equipment and techniques of the conductor. There remains one, finally the most important, aspect of his work to be considered – his function *vis-à-vis* the music he causes to be performed. With it we enter a much less easily defined realm of speculation and on that account best treated here most briefly.

First and foremost it is his job to form an overall view of the work to be played. It may, especially within our changing relationship between conductor and orchestra, be affected in detail during rehearsal but the conception of the whole must be there as a yard-stick against which all details have to be judged, accepted or rejected. The formation of this is a matter for the conductor and his score long before he meets the orchestra. I can here speak most accurately from personal experience, but I suspect the process is fairly general.

You take the score and with it all the evidence it contains – notes, dynamic marks, tempi and metronome indications and so on. In this age of stylistic emphasis all manner of historical evidence can and must be sought, not just with a view to realizing accurately ornaments and all the innumerable elaborations and quirks of notation that composers over the centuries have invented, but, even more important, in order to re-create in the mind the ethos in which the music was composed.

The difficulty at this stage is to keep the mind sufficiently open to allow all these elements to play their part in what is eventually an intuitive, irrational act of understanding of the work's content.

That this sudden intuitive act of comprehension takes place I can only testify to – it is not provable. I see it rather like the act of composition in reverse and we have much evidence that composition of anything worthwhile does involve such a concept of the whole before the details of composition are begun.

Stravinsky, famous for his acute observations on music, when asked how he knew whether or not a piece he had completed was any good,

---

5   Something that in the present days of world recession can no longer be so confident-
     ly claimed. As there is less and less money for music there is less and less time for re-
     hearsal which must cause a decline in standards. [1993]

answered "I recognize it", implying that, if it had worked out well, he could see in its final form the image of the work he had set out to compose.

Hindemith, another highly literate composer, described the intuitive grasp of a composition before working on it as a flash of lightning which can illuminate a scene and so impress it on the mind that every blade of grass is suddenly made apparent. The composer's job is then, in the ensuing darkness, to reconstruct the scene he momentarily saw. Perhaps less lurid, though relevant to the conductor's view, was Mendelssohn's response to a composition sent to him by a contemporary, Henselt. He did not think much of the work and wrote back "You know perfectly well that the composing is not nearly as good as the composition".

It seems to me that in making that judgment he was showing the same sort of intuitive understanding of the music that a conductor should achieve before he faces the orchestra. But his homework is not even then completed, for he must next go into the endless detail of relating the separate elements to the concept of the whole. Phrasing (not bowing, for the orchestral player will amost certainly play his instrument better than you and know how best to achieve what you ask of him), dynamics, execution of ornaments, etc., should all be decided in advance and related to the musical style of the composition. The regular concert repertoire extends over 350 years and unstylistic performance is no longer tolerated. One can no longer play Bach like Brahms, or even Handel like Ebenezer Prout. Some, it is true, still do, but they are of the older generation and their performances are, perhaps, to be valued for the echo they give of passing values. But no one younger should or would, simply because it is not of our time to do so. But, I hasten to add, no amount of knowledge of Bach's ornamentation will of its own accord show you the life that is contained in the music. It has just become an indispensable part of the interpreter's equipment.

The contemplation and decision over detail is an integral part of the modern conductor's technique. He would be a rash man who stood up in front of an orchestra, given present pressure of rehearsal schedules, without it. Another is the care he must take in preparing the orchestral material in advance. A large part of the detail he has decided upon can, with the expenditure of much midnight oil, be indicated in the orchestral parts the players are to use. Only with experience can he tell that such and such a mark will produce such and such an effect but as much as he can put down he should, for it saves hours and hours of rehearsal time and enables players the more quickly to penetrate the content of the music.

You will see, if you had any illusions to the contrary, that the modern conductor's job is not just a matter of getting up on the box, gesticulating more or less clearly in order to produce a performance. There are hours to be spend understanding and learning a score, more hours making decisions and still more in marking the music. You do all this — and then you have to persuade your orchestra. The mysteries of that are, in our scientific age, fortunately still largely occult and, for today, best left at that.

Discussion

THE CHAIRMAN (ANTHONY LEWIS): I think that it is clear by the volume of applause how much that fascinating talk has been appreciated. I listened with the greatest of interest. I liked Mr. Leppard's very lucid description of the earlier development of the mechanical aspects of conducting. I do feel that musicians can congratulate themselves on having evolved this technique. If a Guards sergeant-major were asked to be silent and to convey by persuasive gesture to his battalion how precisely they should carry out their movements on the parade ground, would he be able to achieve an equally disciplined effect, I wonder. I was pleased also to hear the attention paid to psychology, because as head of a teaching institution it is very often necessary for me to point out to young conductors the absolute importance of this quality. They acquire every kind of technical virtue and are very good musicians, and they come in front of a really experienced orchestra and make just one tactless or mistaken remark, and their career as conductors is more or less over from that point.

The real wizard, both as interpreter and as psychologist, was the late Sir Thomas Beecham. He knew how to deal with this situation very well. One of the many stories about him that I enjoy concerns his lateness, which was of course proverbial. Eventually the orchestra with which he was then associated decided that the next time he was more than half an hour late they would not stand up when he arrived. They did not have to wait long for their opportunity. They sat firmly and solidly in their seats while the great man, three-quarters of an hour late, took his place gradually on the rostrum. He looked slowly round and then said, "Very well, gentlemen, then let us pray." An expert psychologist can always be relied upon to restore morale at a critical moment.

I should like to invite Mr. Leppard to say a bit more about the rigors of the practical side of orchestral preparation nowadays. I like to tease my dramatic colleagues about the relatively endless expanse of rehearsal time which they enjoy in the theater — "impossible to put anything on in a month" — whereas we have to make do with two hours, forty minutes perhaps, if we are lucky. A conductor has to wrestle for every half minute of his rehearsal time.

RAYMOND LEPPARD: It is a matter of economics, is it not? I don't think there is a public concert in the world now that pays for itself. Because of the expense, great pressure is put on conductors and orchestras to prepare concerts in the shortest possible time. This must condition the conductor's function. It is up to him — the players themselves are working all the time and cannot mentally prepare new works in advance. So it is for the conductor to make their work as little difficult as possible. He has, for example, to co-ordinate the orchestral parts. Those who are not musicians would simply not believe the condition of some of the parts coming from publishers. I can think of a set of parts of a work by Sir Michael Tippett, one of our most distinguished composers. They render it unperformable. The copyist's work, photographed in several sets, is so appalling that the orchestra cannot read it. Even if the conductor spent a month trying to mark those parts, he could not improve them.

Publishers have a very great responsibility towards musicians, and not always will they accept that responsibility. They often put new works out to youngsters because it is cheaper to get them copied that way, but they are then copied very badly and the work is forced out of circulation. It is not played, therefore no demand is created for it, therefore it will not be copied again.

THE CHAIRMAN: Mr. Leppard has reminded me of Stravinsky's *Persephone*. When last I directed this work I found the copyist had given up the (to him) unequal struggle of putting in the different bar lengths of the rests in the woodwind parts, and has just written "43 *mésures diverses*"!

FELIX APRAHAMIAN: Mr. Leppard said that in Britain there is perhaps a greater *rapport* between the conductor and his players than in some other countries. Can he tell us why he thinks that is so? Could it be due to the wonderful spirit of enthusiasm amongst the amateur group of musicians in this country?

RL: I think it is largely because we are the people in the world who know best how to compromise. No other country, I would say, has taken more readily to the *via media*, in any situation, than England — and somehow it has paid off, has it not? I have conducted in virtually every European country, and I really do think we have the finest relationships between conductors and orchestras, and also that we have the finest orchestral standard in the world, bar none. We should be very proud of the fact. It is partly due to education. Since the war public money has been poured into musical education. Youth orchestras, for example, flourish to an amazing degree. If you hear a youth orchestra in some remote European country you would hardly believe how bad it is; whereas you can listen to almost any youth orchestra in any county in England and it will provide you with a perfectly good evening's music, and in some cases a distinguished evening's music. A very small percentage of those people go into the profession. The rest simply help to create a very healthy musical climate in this country.

THE CHAIRMAN: The Government may have poured money into musical education. If only they would turn the spout towards Marylebone Road I should be very pleased!

A. FREEDMAN: I should like to ask about the relationship between conductor and soloist. Does a conductor control the soloist as part of the ensemble, or can (or does) the soloist, perhaps carried away by his own virtuosity, tend to control or at least inhibit his conductor?

RL: The conductor aims for an amicable collaboration. I personally would always finally give way to a soloist's point of view about a work because he or she is playing it, and I think it is the conductor's job in a concerto to accompany. With almost all the good soloists I know one can generally discuss points quite freely and eventually come to some sort of compromise. I have never known it to be a battle, but then I have never known any good artist to be really difficult about *music*.

D. HADDON-REECE, B.E.N.G.: Mr. Leppard has indicated the difficulties presented by some orchestral scores as published. At what stage of the conductor's rise to stardom can he cut back on his expenditure of midnight oil and rely on the devoted services of an amanuensis in correcting his scores?

RL: Musical notation is a very inexact means of marking. What does "forte" mean? In an enormously detailed Mahler score, the composer may say, for example, "play this more loudly". Well, it depends on how loud you were to begin with! This is why music needs the conductor. Somebody has to stand up in front of a big orchestra and say "That is too loud, the composer did not mean that" — right or wrong, that is what you have done your homework for. I don't think there will ever be a secure means of musical notation. People have tried and tried to reach one, but the more detailed it gets the more obscure it seems to become. Somehow, you are safer with a Handel score, where the composer didn't write much down apart from the notes, and even those are often wrong in the way of rhythm! He just expected everybody to understand.

EDWARD DE RIVERA: I remember once having a very interesting discussion with Sir Adrian Boult about conducting. He said Nikisch was in the habit of using a very long baton, because musical vibration could travel up and down the arm to and from the brain. I thought Sir Adrian was having me on, but I think he was perfectly serious.

RL: Sir Adrian is a man whom I admire and like enormously. He has written a wise and very helpful book for students about conducting. In it he advocates the modern way of holding the baton. I think all conductors now hold it between the thumb and the first two fingers, sometimes using the little finger for balancing. Costa's method of holding it in the middle must have been very hard for the orchestra to follow. But then the stick was shortened and held at the bottom. Cut short, it could point to people, and indicate more easily. The conductor had a form of motion which was much clearer because it focused out from the body instead of upwards into the flies. Subsequently it was lengthened again, and the hold became much more subtle. It allowed the use of the wrist and the arm and the fingers alone. These three sorts of motion extended the range tremendously. The only thing in which I would perhaps differ from Sir Adrian is in the use of a very long stick. Because of the speed of modern rehearsals and the elaborate detail in many modern scores, you have got to be able to indicate very precisely, and so the tendency now is to make the baton smaller than the one Sir Adrian uses. But his beat with the longer baton does have the most marvellous rhythm in it.

R. KINLOCH ANDERSON, MUS.BAC, A.R.C.M., HON.FTCL.: Mr. Leppard hasn't spoken about something which I think quite a large section of the public finds attractive in certain celebrated conductors, namely the exhibitionist gestures, the shut eyes, the swooning. Could he tell us what difference that makes to a performance?

RL: I think you have answered yourself by implication. I do, however, remember a story. A conductor who had left his country in some haste was conducting one of his own compositions in London. He was very serious and very European about rehearsals, but he didn't understand about getting on with the orchestra, and so he didn't get on with it. The piece began with the side-drum player having to play a seemingly interminable drum roll traversing the whole side of the side-drum, very slowly. The orchestra became hysterical in rehearsal, and the Leader had to tell them to behave when it came to the actual concert. On the night this conductor, who conducted throughout with his eyes shut as I remember, raised a very indefinite baton, which vaguely indicated a little silence, and then the side drum player started very, very softly and slowly. The principal double bass, as the sound gradually increased, put his hand up as if to feel whether it was raining.

NORMAN DEL MAR: Mr. Leppard said that he would not put bowings in the orchestral parts. I would suggest that it might be worthwhile, even if they were all changed, inasmuch as it saves time, and we all have short rehearsal schedules. Might it not be a good idea especially in Mozart to put in what you think is right with such experience as you can muster, even if you are not a string player—such bowings as you think would be practical? Then the cooperative Leader may say "Do you mind if you change this?" But of course there are Leaders who will say, "This is entirely my province. You do your job and I will do mine."

RL: The best solution is to possess your own set of parts for everything. You can mark them up to a point, and then ideally you should have the

Leader alone for an hour to do the bowings. Alas, this is not always possible. I used to put bowings in because I am a string player, but I found that with most orchestras they eventually got rubbed out, so it now seems to be a waste of time. What I would suggest is that you should put every sort of phrasing in and then, when it comes to the bowing, rely on your Leader. If you have a good Leader it will be done very quickly. String sections are accustomed now to rehearsing while the inside players mark the parts as they go along. I think a conductor should care enormously about the bowings, but I belief he should leave the actual details of string playing to the players themselves. Whenever I have tried to interfere with bowings I have soon found myself technically out of my depth.

GERALD McDONALD, M.A. (New Philharmonia Orchestra): How do you view a situation when you are undertaking, say, a Brahms or a Beethoven symphony, and you are confronted with sets of the parts marked by some idiosyncratic conductor?

RL: It is the very devil, and hard to know what to do. I have worked mostly in early music and have learned a little in the way of the classical repertoire. This in practical terms means that for everything I do with the English Chamber Orchestra I have sets of parts which are mine. They are marked by me and bowed by the orchestra, and nobody else touches them on pain of death. With the bigger works ideally, of course, I would also have my own parts, but the price of music is very high. I bought a score of Tchaikovsky's Sixth Symphony, a standard work, from a standard publisher, and I think it cost eighteen pounds. It is not even a very good score, but is the only one available. If I bought a set of parts for that work it would cost three hundred to four hundred pounds. As you get into the big orchestra range, however, there is, generally speaking, less necessity for marking. I would never, for example, mark the parts of an Elgar work. He took care of every sort of detail himself and was fortunate in his publisher and proof reader. Britten takes the same sort of care in the details of his scores.

DOUGLAS CAMERON, F.R.A.M.: As a conductor I always had my parts bowed, fingered, etc., in conjunction with my Leader. I have the same parts now, they are all my own. If I were to give a concert now and in ten years time, and had the same players, I could trust the bowings to be just the same as they were. I would save hours and hours of headache, heart-ache, time and money.

PETER GELLHORN: I should like to ask our speaker what his feelings are about the probable role of the conductor in the future? The way that the music of our century is developing suggests a very different kind of music making. Will the element of personal interpretation in conducting become less important so that we come back to the function of the conductor in the early days, when the main concern was to keep things together and keep them going, and to become part and not necessarily a very conspicuous part of an ensemble effort?

RL: Mr. Gellhorn has an important point. I think we shall go on for a time at least with music as we know it; that is to say with composers who wish their music to be emotionally expressive within the disciplines of composition. But there is another use for musical instruments, which is becoming more and more fashionable — that is to create a sort of instrumental mathematics. There is a joy, for some, to be had in the improvised manufacture of sound for its own sake. I don't myself believe that a totally improvised piece actually works. That sort of improvisation soon becomes chaos. Nor do I see any merit in a piece of music if it can never sound remotely the same twice. It doesn't interest me, but it does interest a lot of other people. In this sort of music-making the conductor's role is certainly quite insignificant.

THE CHAIRMAN: We have had a very interesting and stimulating discussion, and it is quite obvious that Mr. Leppard's paper has set us all thinking hard about many aspects of his topic. It just remains for me to thank him on your behalf most warmly.

PART TWO

REFLECTIONS,

EPISODES AND ANECDOTES

V

Interviews

1

INTERVIEW OF NOVEMBER 1965 [1]

Leppard is enormously busy; he divides his life into many parts, all of them musical, and lives in many places; he lectures in music at Cambridge — mostly at Trinity — he conducts — he performs — he composes; he is very happy. "I'm lucky to be doing exactly what I want to do. Music is a way of life. It's not a specialised activity; as one gets older one loses particular enthusiasms and it becomes a complete part of oneself, and one has the same zest for it as for living."

He spends a lot of time in Trinity and when in London lives in a beautiful flat in Kensington which he grandly calls his *pied à terre*. Many people would consider it an ideal home: the windows open onto a terrace shaddowed by the long branches of trees; the flat below is occupied by Peter Shaffer the playwright. 'I remember I had just finished reconstructing an opera for Glyndebourne — I had literally just posted the score — when the phone rang. It was Peter Brook in Paris asking me to come there the next day to do the music for his film *Lord of the Flies*. I knew a lot about the film because Peter Shaffer had been working on the script for Sam Siegel for over a year; but it became totally imposible. Brook brought the rights from him and I went over at the weekend, to a dreary little studio in the suburbs of Paris where Peter was literally surrounded by enough footage to make eighteen films; I saw what had been put together, made lots of notes and flew back here and did a short piano score. Then I went back and saw how it went with the film, synchronized the times exactly and we recorded it in the Aldwych Theatre. It was difficult because the film wasn't quite finished and we hadn't a choir which sounded like boys should after they'd spent some time on that island. Eventually the wives

---

1   Excerpted from an interview with Polly Devlin, published November 1965.

of the English Chamber Orchestra musicians brought their sons along and they marched around the Aldwych singing loudly."

Leppard is thirty-eight and looks a lot younger: he seems lazy and sensual until he starts to move or when he talks about his work when he suddenly becomes very taut and tense. He was born in London but his parents moved to Bath when he was very young. "I don't think they were very convinced that a musical career *was* a career. But they have been very good to me, even if they don't see the point. I started to play the piano when I was very young. I rarely play it now. My interest in the harpsichord started when some friends near Bath who had a splendid one, let me play theirs." He read music at Cambridge for five years and then began research on "The Idea of Progress in Music" which he intends to finish someday. When? "When I'm old. I'll probably never get it done but I want to think I will."[2]

He plays the harpsichord more than any other instrument but hates solo recitals, giving them or going to them. "I much prefer working with other people; it's far more stimulating and exciting. Before a concert, whether I'm conducting or performing I'm nervous. I'm not paralytic but the nervousness doesn't decrease as one does it more often. The gap between conducting and performing isn't anything as big as people imagine. It's a different activity but a similar experience. You've got to persuade the orchestra to play the music in the way you think it should be played which is fundamentally what one is doing for oneself when performing....

"[New projects?] I'm reconstructing Cavalli's Mass for the nine hundredth anniversary of Westminster Abbey for May 1966—a huge thing with double choirs and eight solo voices; I'm reconstructing another Cavalli opera for Glyndebourne 1967, and I'm doing a Mass for Coventry. This is an original piece, I've started it already; they want to build up a whole repertoire of original pieces for their services and have asked a lot of people to write for them. It's a marvellous idea and

2   Portions did get done, informing his essay *Authenticity in Music*—see Chapter I, above. (Ed.)

: 316 :

Coventry has a great choir. One doesn't think about when all this is going to be done. I just go ahead and do it. And enjoy it."[3]

2
INTERVIEW OF 1979[4]

SUE McGREGOR: You say your parents didn't really approve of your becoming a musician, that means presumably that there was nothing musical in your background.

RAYMOND: No, none of my family have been musical in any real sense. My parents were wonderfully helpful in encouraging me to learn music. My father thought it was safe as long as I was in a place like Cambridge; that I wouldn't go too far astray. But I believe he had profound suspicions about the moral rectitude of music as a profession!

SUE: Did you ever persuade him otherwise that you've made the right decision, do you think?

RAYMOND: I don't know that I did, no. (laugh) But we've certainly made up for any tensions that were there.

SUE: There was a time in your life when you seemed to be doing a little bit of everything. You were performing as a harpsichordist. You were composing film scores. You were composing for the theater. You were also conducting. Then you decided perhaps, or perhaps you didn't decide, perhaps you can tell me how it happened, that the seventeenth and eighteenth centuries were going to be your speciality, the area in music you were going to concentrate on. How did this happen?

RAYMOND: As you say, I don't think I chose it, it chose me. It came about that I was constantly being employed in performing earlier music, and, more and more, I became curious about the seventeenth-century Italian music... we learned about Monteverdi and all those people, but we had very little chance of actually seeing any music by them. Copies weren't there, they just didn't exist in 1948. I used to sing in the Madrigal

---

3   The "Mass for Coventry" didn't get done, after all... the organist died, and with him a worthy project. (Ed.)

4   Excerpted from an interview with Sue McGregor, produced for the BBC series "Conversation Piece" produced by Gillian Hush and recorded in London.

Society which Boris Ord ran and conducted marvelously, of course – he was a great figure in my time at Cambridge – he didn't really know much of Monteverdi but he did know some of the madrigals and was tremendously attracted to them and we sang them. They just knocked me for six. I thought, well, if *that's* what that man can do with a five-voice madrigal – which my schooling told me was only an intermediary, passing phase – he eventually came to opera and the smaller-voice madrigals, for two voices and single voice – I thought this really had to be gone into. They represented some form of emotional musical expression which I hadn't been aware of. It really was something like a bright light shining suddenly, and I gradually went into it – in a rather silly dilettante way, if you like, to begin with – but then it became much more serious, and I decided that this was what I wanted to explore most in music for quite a long time.

SUE: Why'd he been neglected, Monteverdi? Was it because the music didn't exist or did the music not exist for you to look at because he'd been neglected and ignored?

RAYMOND: The really interesting works, that is to say the later works of Monteverdi, have come down to us in a very skeletal fashion, even, for example, the two-voice madrigal. You merely have two voices and a bass line which look simple and yet, in content, they are huge pieces. The operas are huge in length as well as in content. Only two of the late ones are left. I began to look at *Poppea* and a great friend of mine found a photostat, a printed photostat of the earliest manuscript of *Poppea* – there are only two in any case, and this, again, knocked me for six. I remember sitting in my rooms in Cambridge, reading through this and thinking my hat, this is fantastic! They set out to express human emotions in terms of the voice, and I really hadn't realized that they did it as well as that. I mean, so over-poweringly as *Poppea* – the last love duet, for example. The first time I looked at that, it just took my breath away. So little was written down that if you just played what was there, it would sound like some awful nursery game, with some nanny playing the bass line, and the care singing the top line. It just wouldn't sound at all... there's simply not enough left. People hadn't really, I think, cast their minds imaginatively as to what you would do in a theater if actually you had only those two lines – and what *would* you do? Imagine you are Monteverdi – that's obviously what survived, therefore it's fairly logical to assume that's what he began with. So you go into a theater, and you know from accounts and engravings and so on the sort of orchestra he had there. Imagine, then, how it came about. And, I'm sure I'm right—I'm absolutely convinced that he had this group of continuo instruments. They each had a copy of the vocal line, the bass line and they were clever at improvising. You can't do much damage to it. It's like Shakespeare really: even if a girl's school plays *Hamlet*, it works. That's the amazing thing.

SUE: We mustn't give the impression that you are only involved in the seventeenth- and eighteenth-century operatic works of Monteverdi and Cavalli and people like that. You are also the principal conductor of the BBC Northern Symphony Orchestra, of course. Now that presumably gives you a chance to be familiar with quite a different kind of repertoire, the more popular works of Beethoven, etc.

RAYMOND: Absolutely! I've never believed that one should be a specialist in music. I think if you should play Bartók well, you're liable to play Bach better. Or Bach well, you'll play Bartók better. One informs the other. Music must never be a narrowing of experience. It must be a widening experience all the time.

I've enjoyed my time with the BBC Northern enormously. Personally, I love the Northern mind. I think it is a wonderful one. I must tell you a little story. We did a whole series of half-hour television things with the Northern and it was fun to do. They all had names, topics like "Ghosts" etc., and having done that, I'd come up to Manchester from London I guess. It was absolutely pouring down. I'd just finished a rehearsal and was walking around with a heavy suitcase up Peter Street and somebody grabbed hold of me. It was pelting down and this guy, I'm not very good with Northern accents (my mother was a Northerner), he said something like "Are you not that fellow that was on the box last night and doing that lovely program about ghosts or whatever it is?" It was pouring and dripping off my hair and everything, I said yes, yes, I supposed I was, and he looked at me. He obviously thought I was a friend. He grabbed hold of me as if I was. He didn't know what to say.

SUE: Well, you'd been in his living room.

RAYMOND: Well right! Two-second pause, he said, "Cor—bloody 'ell!" and rushed off down the street. But it was very sweet because he turned back—I couldn't stop laughing—and just said—"Look after yourself." It was very nice.

SUE: How much of your time do you manage to spend in this country now that America is your home?

RAYMOND: Well, I am allowed ninety days. I guess I spend about that. If they say ninety days, I'm jolly well going to spend ninety days.

SUE: Is music making in America a mixture of all of your enthusiasms? Monteverdi and Cavalli? Nineteenth-century music?

RAYMOND: Yes, it's pretty well everything. Their tradition is nineteenth-century romantic. It's a very sort of romantic view of Beethoven, and post-Beethoven up through Rachmaninoff, and not much else.

SUE: One other difference might be that the money that comes to fund these big orchestras is on the whole private money, isn't it, not state money?

RAYMOND: Almost all. I love the idea that there's a rule about state money. Nothing in the arts can be financed with more than 50% state money. I think that's a marvelous rule. It means that the people who have given the money are going to be tremendously involved in the success of the venture. Of course you'll occasionally get Mrs. Hackenbacker, Jr., who is going to be an interfering old baggage and tiresome, but on the whole rich Americans have made their own money, because you do it generation by generation, and they therefore, to have made their money, have had to be successful themselves. To have been successful means that they are interesting, interested, and probably very intelligent... and rather odd. And I love that combination, it's very exciting to deal with.

SUE: Does it actually give you more freedom as a music maker there?

RAYMOND: It causes you to think more of yourself as an entertainer. If you rely on state money you tend to encourage composers to write self-indulgent rubbish. The more it sounds new and odd, the more money, the more commissions you are likely to get. I think many composers, in a state funded system, do not accept what is their prime function, and that is to be entertainers; actually to involve an audience. And that an American composer has to do. Of course there are pros and cons in the system. There could be very serious side effects—cheap and nasty stuff being written in the name of entertainment. That's not what I am urging at all.

SUE: Do you think of yourself primarily as an entertainer then?

RAYMOND: Oh, yes! Well, if I don't please the customers, where am I? I must be a failure. Yes, surely! Absolutely!

SUE: Would you like to be offered an absolutely permanent musical post, either in this country or perhaps more likely now in America?

RAYMOND: No, not now, I've been offered some posts, three posts, well, three and a half posts since being in America, and I don't want to settle anywhere til I'm done travelling.[5] I'm too much enjoying this time. It's strange, you see, coming from the sort of family I suppose I came from. I've been very aware of security and very attracted to places like Cambridge which was a place that was also extremely generous to me. Security is an attractive thing to a person of my background. But also I know — I'm sure — it is a very dangerous thing too, for an artist. It's why I hope we never in this country have tenure in orchestras, for example. I certainly don't have any security now at all. I depend entirely on my next engagements. Of course it's lovely that your diary is full. I'm cheating a bit and I guess I'm *not* being very brave, it must be said. When your diary is full you don't have to worry too much about it. But equally well I suppose, if I did a lot of lulus and bad shows, at the end of these engagements, there would be no more in the diary. I wouldn't get hired.

SUE: Does music go on being interesting to you after all the years you've devoted to it?

RAYMOND: Yes, absolutely. Complete involvement. I don't think of anything else much. It's why we musicians are so bad with relationships. Music always seems to have prior claim and although you may be tremendously involved with people, the pressure of preparation of music, or the writing of something so abstracts you that it takes five saints rolled into one to cope with that. It isn't your objection to anyone necessarily, you're just not there. I know that that happens and I can't stop it. Music is so totally satisfying. I think that's what it is. It's even physically satisfying. I mean strangely, for example, you're not liable to be very

---

5   RL joined the Indianapolis Symphony Orchestra eight years later, in 1987. (Ed.)

demonstrative even to someone you love very much — immediately after or immediately before a concert — you know you can hug them and hold them and kiss them and all of that, but it's not really 100% and they know it of course. You just haven't got it. It so debilitating that... for example, after *Ulysses* which I have on my mind all the time because we're recording as well as performing it, I go out and I'm in a daze at the end of that show. You are not fit for anybody, really, except to a sort of gentle person around the place. You are nothing but a load of flesh and blood and bones, and that's about all there is. You come around eventually. I think I'm making it sound more glamorous than it is. It's rather tiresome. You're hot and sweaty and rather nasty.

SUE: But there must surely be times when you feel that you can't possibly conduct one more performance of the opera you mentioned, Monteverdi's *Ulysses* or the Beethoven Fifth or something, and still bring something fresh to it. Are there times when music bores just a little bit?

RAYMOND: Well, I don't think you bring something fresh to it, I think it brings something fresh to you each time. I do really believe that — you can translate it into human terms: you don't actually ever get bored with seeing somebody you love, do you? I mean they look different each time you see them — or even people you are just fond of. Now you can translate that into musical terms if it is a piece of great vitality like the Beethoven Fifth — that will never wear out. You could not wear it out. It will always do something for you, if you let it. It is possible to be stale yourself, to be absolutely out of sorts, then you are not receptive and you just use your technique to get through it. But, thank God, that rarely happens — almost never in my experience as yet.

I was thinking about it the other day as I was doing the G minor of Mozart with the English Chamber Orchestra, which I must have done, with them alone, oh, hundreds of times, because it's a work that fits into that sort of setup. We did it in the Festival Room, we did in Düsseldorf, we did it in Paris, and each time it was different, and each time it was a wonder. An absolutely marvelous experience, each time.

SUE: Will music still have all this excitement for you when you are in your 60's or 70's, do you think?

RAYMOND: Well, I am 52 now — I can't see that it will change. I think the excitement has got greater rather than less, and life has got more wonderful. I do find that life improves day by day. Each day seems to be really more interesting and more thrilling and more exciting than the last.

SUE: Do you feel lucky then?

RAYMOND: Absolutely! Oh and how! I think I am one of the luckiest people there is.

SUE: Raymond Leppard — thank you.

3
INTERVIEW OF DECEMBER 1992 [6]

PEOPLE

ADRIAN BOULT, MALCOLM SARGENT

TOM LEWIS: Would you recommend that anyone who is going to be a conductor play first in an orchestra?

RAYMOND: Yes — they all have done, you know. Colin Davis was a clarinetist. Giulini was an oboist. Bernstein was a marvelous pianist.

TOM: And Toscanini played the cello — in the orchestra. Verdi remarked once that the second cellist (Toscanini) was playing a *piano* passage too softly... dynamic markings are always relative.

RAYMOND: I hadn't heard that... he was a very mean man.

TOM: He was mean!

RAYMOND: Partly because he (Toscanini) was a relic of that nine-teenth-century system of conducting when you had to be a *Führer*. You had to be the father, the father figure who ruled his children with an iron hand and kept them all in order. That isn't necessary anymore because players are much better educated.

TOM: How can you maintain discipline without being tyrannical?

RAYMOND: You don't have to be.... Boult was a terribly nice man. I knew him quite well. Great tall bean pole. Stooped. When he walked, he walked like *that*. Used to come and have lunch with me. I knew Sargent

---

6   Interviews held in New York and Connecticut with the editor and composer Mark Grant. The interviewee *is*, now, in his sixties... and every bit as energetic, as open to life as apparently he was before. (Ed.)

too. Apart from from my earning my living playing, I got taken up by EMI and a man called David Bicknell got me to supervise, musically that is, recording sessions. And I did for about six months. It was rather well paid. One or two of the records were with Malcolm Sargent; the *Gondoliers*, I remember. He grew up with all that G&S world. That he knew very well. Malcolm was known as Flash Harry. He found it very difficult to commit himself either to people or to music. He had a sort of tragic family life: an invalid wife and a boy who it was said went to prison. He really had a wretched time, but he was a snob. He went to parties endlessly. He had a marvelous figure. He was a rather little man, but tremendously smart. Wore his hair down; always wore the smartest suits. Was really a very elegant person. The professionals didn't take to him because he was known to be such a social person, and that is why he was called Flash Harry. It was in a way unjustified. He came from a poor background, I think, and lived extravagantly by way of proof that he had succeeded. It's a perfectly understandable equation.

TOM: Stokowski could get away with all of that.

RAYMOND: Well, Malcolm got away with it too. He was always employed and very, very busy. There was a great kindness in him and after these sessions at EMI, he would take me back to his apartment in Albert Hall Mansions, a great big apartment he had there. He would feed me sometimes and give me drinks and that sort of thing. These were the days when I had left my family support so to speak. I really was on my own in London. When I first quit Cambridge, right against my parents' wishes and so forth, I was honestly quite hungry. I didn't know where my money was coming from sometimes, to pay the rent. Sargent never gave me money, but he was very affectionate in a paternalistic sort of way. He sometimes came to concerts. He had an amazing technique. It was carefully studied and he was as clear as a bell. That nobody would ever deny. He wouldn't bother usually to learn scores, and he certainly never got inside scores, or very rarely. But he was as clear as you could imagine. I asked him if he would give me some lessons and he said, "I never had a lesson in my life and I am not about to start telling anybody else how to do it." He said, "Just do. You'll learn by doing it."

TOM: How do you just do it?

RAYMOND: You just do it. Stand up in front of people and conduct! If it works you're doing it right. If not, not. Of course by then I was doing much more, and we were just about to start the English Chamber Orchestra and that sort of thing. So, um...

MYRA HESS, HARRIET COHEN, RALPH VAUGHAN WILLIAMS

MARK GRANT: Did you ever see Dame Myra Hess, for instance during the Blitz?

RAYMOND: Yes. I saw her when I was a school boy. I heard her play at the National Gallery, and later on in Bath. She was getting old and rather frail — well, she never was exactly frail.

MARK: She always was a big woman.

RAYMOND: She was a big woman and a pretty tough one. She was a very remarkable pianist. I remember hearing her almost at the very end of her life when she played Beethoven's Opus 110. I knew the piece because I was learning it myself for a pianist called Solomon.

MARK: The one that had a stroke.

RAYMOND: Yes, in 1956. Paralyzed his right arm. I had lessons from him and then went to Franz Reizenstein who taught for him after. But I was learning this for a solo and she was playing it somewhere. She was very famous for these late Beethoven Sonatas and she played almost nothing else. She loved Beethoven's music, but by that time she had almost recomposed them! There were funny extra notes, and different tempi. It was strange, but lovely and beautiful playing. She was very courageous and did those concerts in the National Gallery during the war, with the bombs coming down and all that.

There was Irene Scharrer, and Harriet Cohen. I even got a Harriet Cohen medal. She drank a lot... she was Bax's mistress for many, many years. All in all about thirty years I guess.

TOM: You did a recording of Bax's Fifth Symphony.

RAYMOND: Yes, that's right. I did the Fifth and Seventh, I think.[7] There was a party, a concert at Leo de Rothschild's house in Thurloe Square, a smart party with little gold chairs. I played the Debussy Violin Sonata, I remember that was one of the pieces, and we must have played a Bax

---

7   See DISCOGRAPHY. (Ed.)

piece. Anyway, Harriet was there and she was absolutely pie-eyed, but she could focus in on me like that. She came very, very close until I backed off and so we continued going around. She kept on saying "I must look into your eyes, I must look in your eyes." Then, "you can never say *no* — can you?" I didn't know what that meant! I began to fear the worst, that I was going to be whisked off to her apartment to know whether I would say yes, or what I could do about saying no. But she took off after a time, and became very quiet.

MARK: She was very attractive looking.

RAYMOND: Yes, she was very handsome. Oh, she was beautiful. When she lived with Bax, he wrote *Tintagel* for her. Later, alone, she used to live a fantasy life. Whenever you talked about Arnold Bax, 'oh, such a great friend of my mother's you know,' she would say.

TOM: And wasn't.

RAYMOND: Well, I don't know... but she was *his* mistress.

MARK: You also met Bax?

RAYMOND: No, Bax I never met. I met most of the composers of that time. Walton I knew quite well.

MARK: What kind of a man was Vaughan Williams?

RAYMOND: Oh, terribly nice. Absolutely genuine. He came from a very distinguished intellectual Cambridge background. He was a Darwin and a Wedgewood, a Cornford — all that. They all intermarried, and he was one of them. He was at my college, Trinity; a terribly nice man who absolutely spurned sophistication. He hated smart talk. It always brought the worst out in him. He used to get crotchety. He and Harriet Cohen could never have got on, and he and Sargent never did get on, for that reason. He liked old Adrian (Boult) who was also a simple, genuine person. He was a lovely man — V.W.

CONSTANT LAMBERT, ADRIAN BOULT, THOMAS BEECHAM

TOM: Who are some of the people whom you have admired the most... have influenced you the most and that you have good feelings about?

RAYMOND: The people I have grown up with. Just all of them.

TOM: I know Janet Baker was one of them.

RAYMOND: Yes, Janet was.... anybody with whom you spend a lot of emotional time is bound to influence you.

TOM: Who are some of these people?

RAYMOND: Janet is certainly one.

MARK: Various British conductors? Beecham, Boult? Did you ever see Constant Lambert?

RAYMOND: Yes, I met Constant Lambert... but by then he was a drunk. Great fun though, a fascinating guy. He was in Cambridge for a while conducting something there and was always asking me out for drinks. Fascinating, and very stimulating. He came from the sort of background that produced Walton, the Sitwells, but there was a sort of despair about him.

Boult was a friend. I played piano for Beecham, twice, and met him socially once or twice. I didn't know him. He was quick, very funny and a kind man. Beecham had been severely criticized by the press for playing *Brandenburg 3* with all the strings of the Royal Philharmonic, or whichever one it was (he kept founding orchestras all his life). Anyway, what did he do, he kept all the strings... and added another harpsichord, and wrote a continuo part the like of which you've never seen. I was dashing around all over the place. It was so funny... He didn't much like the harpsichord, but he wasn't going to be criticized by the critics for playing *Brandenburg 3* with a huge body of strings.

TOM: Without a harpsichord?

RAYMOND: Well, he had one, and I think the critics said, "what's more, you can't hear the harpsichord." So now he had two, amplified.

There was another time which shows the good, the touching side of Beecham. I was playing the piano for him for something, and at the end he said oh, I'll put this in... one of his lollipops. It was a piece of Grétry and he had written in a difficult, elaborate piano part, which I had to sight-read in the rehearsal. The orchestra of course had played it a million times. I thought well, I'll have to practice that — I was sweating a bit. It was really quite hard. I must have seemed nervous because Beecham looked over and said, "well done," or something like that. Then, "Would you like to play it again?" I said, "Oh — would I!" And he said to the orchestra, "Come on, chaps, it's difficult you know." That was nice because I was a youngster starting off, and he knew I was scared sh-tless really. It was very thoughtful. His orchestras adored him.

TOM: I have the feeling that you care about your own musicians. When

I asked what you thought of the New York Philharmonic, you said they were a nice of bunch of people, that you really like them. People are generally pretty hard on New York Philharmonic players.

RAYMOND: Well I do — yes.

HERBERT VON KARAJAN

MARK: I understand that when you were a keyboard player in the Philharmonia, you played under Karajan.

RAYMOND: Sure.

MARK: I am very fascinated to hear what the man must have been like on a personal level as a player working with him.

RAYMOND: Wonderful musician. Extraordinary. He played games and must have been one of the last examples of the old *Führer* type. His game with an orchestra was largely psychological. He used to do terrible things. The Philharmonia was made up of the most distinguished people.

MARK: Stars, great artists.

RAYMOND: Almost everybody you can think of, a marvelous collection, extraordinary. He would call rehearsal at 10:00 for the whole orchestra, and rehearse a Mozart divertimento for 40 people, and insisted they all stayed there until ten to one. Then he would do ten minutes of Respighi. He did that on purpose. Just to keep them there. Just to tell them who's boss. That was a disciplinary thing from his point of view, and he thought it was necessary. The English hated that, and they finally revolted. The English are a very patient people, but, there are limits. The Germans took it, the English couldn't. He took a shine to me and was very amusing privately.

TOM: Very intense eyes, I think, that he had.

RAYMOND: Very attractive person. He had attractive people around him, women and men. It was a very interesting world that he surrounded himself with. He travelled with a small entourage. There was a man called Matoni who was a fat, gay person who tended to put his hands where he shouldn't put his hands. But Karajan also had a gay side too. There was a certain, strange ambivalence to his life. Very good looking, very handsome man. I was young and flattered to be in his company, I suppose. I was fairly bright and certainly not nervous of him as a person. Why should I be?

MARK: You did not play the viola in this orchestra?

RAYMOND: No, I played the piano. I played all the piano parts in the Philharmonia, like *Petrouchka*, Bartók, *Firebird;* works they wouldn't engage a concerto pianist for. I wasn't really up to that level but — yes, I was decent. That was the reason why they took me.

Karajan really was very friendly. Years later he invited me to do *L'Orfeo* in Salzburg, he remembered. But he really was a sh-t, he couldn't help himself.

NADIA BOULANGER

RAYMOND: I knew Nadia Boulanger fairly well; an interesting, remarkable woman. She was conducting the English Chamber Orchestra, at one time rehearsing the Stravinsky Violin Concerto and Yehudi (Menuhin) was playing, remarkably well. She could sing every line of that piece, which isn't that difficult perhaps, but in solfège, which is. She would rattle incomprehensible things off to the ECO, but she couldn't conduct it, she didn't know how the parts moved.... It was very interesting. She could read the lines in exact rhythm, with exactly the right syllables, but together....

TOM: How did she happen to be conducting? I never knew that she did.

RAYMOND: Because she liked to from time to time.

MARK: Didn't she conduct the Monteverdi on that recording?

RAYMOND: The first set of Monteverdi pieces ever to be recorded, I think, were with Nadia. She played them with the piano, with a little group, and they are wonderful, really extraordinary. She had a great understanding of music. It was all tinged with a tremendous social sense. She had to be intellectually *La princesse...* she had to be in the vanguard of every movement there was.

TOM: What made her so effective?

RAYMOND: She kept afloat. She was like a ping-pong ball. Rather strange, long grey-haired ping-pong ball on the top of the musical fountain. She had that great French talent for staying on the top of the fountain.

TOM: But why was she able to bring out all those qualities in people?

RAYMOND: She was so enormously gifted and impressive that she could dazzle any American that came near her. She was extremely intelligent and very musical. She was extremely musical.

TOM: Was she accessible? Did she welcome people?

RAYMOND: No, she wasn't. If she thought you were worth while welcoming, then she would welcome you. But she wasn't really a very openhearted person. A very skillful one. Loved music in a sort of way that... if you think of it, it's strange because she has a reputation for being almost the greatest teacher in our time. But whom did she teach?

MARK: The greatest pupils?

RAYMOND: Who?

MARK: Well, the American composers who studied with her.

MARK: Copland, Virgil Thompson.

RAYMOND: Copland used to deny that he studied with her. She would never tell a lie, but she would say "ah, Aaron showed me the organ symphony... I remember I spent time, a little time with him."

TOM: As if she imparted this magical...

RAYMOND: I once asked him. It was at the time when I was adjuticating with Nadia on the Leeds piano competition.

The only person I know who really studied with her was Lennox Berkeley.

MARK: I know that Elliot Carter took some lessons with her and sort of went back to square one when he did—as she put everybody, you know, in that position.

RAYMOND: I don't know, somehow she managed to perpetuate this idea.... She did a wonderful French job on me, too, and I was very amused.

PETER MAXWELL DAVIES, MICHAEL TIPPETT, BENJAMIN BRITTEN, OLIVE ZORIAN

MARK: I'd like to ask you about Peter Maxwell Davies. Have you conducted some of his work?

RAYMOND: Yes.

MARK: I want to ask you about him and about Tippett.

RAYMOND: In a way, not dissimilar—both are their own worst enemies, musically not personally. Michael is very bright, very intelligent, of course. But I always compare him adversely, I'm afraid, with Britten who was the prime communicator. Britten never mucked up one piece he wrote. That probably is an exaggeration, but if anybody ever knew how to make a piece work it was Ben — even if he was short on imagination, short on inspiration, short on energy, short on anything, it would in some way be effective and would work. Michael has so rarely achieved that effectiveness. For all his imagination and all his great cerebral qualities, he almost always wrecks everything he does. He over complicates.

TOM: He goes too far maybe. The music gets dense.

RAYMOND: I tell you what, the first thing you should hear is Michael lecture. He is an enchanting person, tall and thin as a rake. Good looking, rather handsome in a strange way. Has that strange look of someone who is a wanderer... not a very physical person, but you listen to him and he has great personal charm. Terrific personal charm, and you listen to him in a lecture. I can remember doing this as an undergraduate before I knew him. You sit and these words would come out, chain after chain of them, phrase after phrase, well done, well said. But then you think after a few sentences or few minutes of this, what on earth is he talking about? This doesn't actually mean anything! It never did. And it never does. He talks in strange phrases, and he thinks in strange phrases that don't add up to anything. You read what he has written. It's incomprehensible. And it's affected his music as well. He has a wonderful idea, and something always complicates it. It all becomes abstracted until it removes itself from personal contact. He's always led a strange, removed existence.

Now, Ben's not my hero as a person, gifted as he was. I disliked much about Ben, he behaved worse to some of my friends than any human being. Michael never behaves badly.

TOM: Immature (Britten)?

RAYMOND: No! Vicious. He had a sadistic, cruel, destructive.. awful. I mean, Ben could do terrible things to people. He would lash out as if he had some hidden hatred.... In the early days, the English Opera Group played at Aldeburgh, Ben's home, his festival there. The concert master was a woman, Olive Zorian, marvelous person, sweet, much loved. Very, very good fiddler. Had the Zorian Quartet... Michael Tippett wrote his second quartet for them. Ben adored Olive, to such an extent that Olive would go and spend Christmas with Ben and Peter (Pears), and she always gave a party before going up to Aldeburgh. She was divorced by then, she'd been married to someone called John Amis... she gave always a Christmas party in Earl's Court. I lived nearby at one time. There was a man named Basil Douglas, who was manager of the English Opera Group. He was a funny old thing whom everyone knew as Dazzle Bugless. He just died but was a very funny man, sweet man — well, Ben had taken one of his hates to Dazzle, and Dazzle was fired, and Ben told Olive Dazzle was fired, and he also told Dazzle that Olive was fired.... that Olive was no longer going to lead the English Opera Group. But she was due to go to Aldeburgh that same Christmas. This was two days before Christmas, at Olive's party. We were all there. It's really hair-raising that somebody could do this. In the middle of the evening Olive, a certain amount of alcohol around — lovely party going frightfully well — Olive went up to Dazzle (Basil), and said "Basil, I am so sorry to hear about that — I really am. We've had such wonderful times together." So Basil said, "Olive, I'm so sorry." "Why?" They both told each other. Olive was struck dumb, because she'd devoted her life to the English Opera Group. Dazzle was upset, but he could manage. Olive was a woman alone, husband gone, beautiful, marvelous player and a wonderful person, lovable woman. Was completely stunned, as if somebody hit her over the head. I knew her very well: played a lot with her. She took me into her bedroom and said "Oh Ray, what am I going to do?" She said, "I can't go up to Aldeburgh. Do you think this is true?" I said I had no idea. "Olive darling, what you have to do is to ring up the Red House [Britten's house] now." "Oh, they'll be in bed." I said that doesn't matter, their being in bed. Do you think that you are putting *them* out? I mean, Jesus Christ. And I said, "come on, we'll ring them up now." And we rang. They were absolutely shattered at being faced with this conversation. Olive behaved impeccably. She said "Well, look darlings, I think perhaps it's just as well if I don't come up this Christmas. I'll be fine, absolutely. Have a wonderful time, I love you both, and you're wonderful. But perhaps I won't come up." Of course great sighs of relief went up in Aldeburgh, you could hear them all the way to London. In two years, Olive was dead of cancer. Ben's treatment... it didn't help at all.

TOM: They seem related in some way, not cause and effect of course, just a way of treating people....

RAYMOND: Ben did that to people, I'm afraid. He couldn't face things.

MARK: Sorry to hear that.

RAYMOND: But he *was* this phenomenal composer.

TOM: Well, yes—indeed.

RAYMOND: Michael never would have done anything like that.

TOM: If you think about it, there is an essential demonic element in almost every one of Britten's operas. *Billy Budd,* the Claggert character. *Peter Grimes.* I mean, there's a demonic side of this.

RAYMOND: Well, good and evil was an obsession of Ben's.

TOM: The Henry James story, it has Peter Quint or whatever his name is.

RAYMOND: Innocence and guilt, good and evil were the two things that... Love never figured very largely in Ben's music, but good and evil.... His best music was conceived in terms of good and evil.

TOM: You're suggesting that both of those were in *him.*

RAYMOND: Yes, sure. I really do believe that.

TOM: Even the solo settings are not love poems, or love scenes, are they..

RAYMOND: Not always.

MARK: What about Maxwell Davies?

RAYMOND: Max, not dissimilar from Michael. A man who tends to wreck... immensely gifted. Very nice man, who is slightly crazy! I think they both lack—if I am being really objective, they both lack, from the scholastic point of view, they both lack technique. Their concepts of music tend to override the technical aspects of what they.... Max has great difficulty in writing down anything that... for example, I did a piece of his with the Chicago Symphony called *Runes*... I agreed to do it because Chicago wanted me to do something by him.... (goes to his desk) I had to rewrite pages of this score.... I wrote exactly what he put down, but I wrote it out in such a way that the Chicago Symphony could play it. And we did play it, and Max came over and said it was the best performance he'd ever heard. I don't think he meant it!

TOM: You probably articulated things.

RAYMOND: If you have a look at the score, it has syncopated lines in five (which needn't have been in five) played against syncopated lines in three (which needn't have been written in three) against syncopated lines in four or two which are hardly even in either—eye music. You can do it with solo instruments but, when the lines are each played by 16 players, you would spend a month and it would all sound like mud.

MARK: There's a book on rhythm by the American composer Paul Creston, where he takes the *Rite of Spring* and rebars it. Without really displacing any of the rhythmic accents or the phrasing...

RAYMOND: Didn't Stravinsky agree to such a version?

MARK: This is another version even apart from that. Yes, he does that with some other music, just to demonstrate that it isn't necessary.

RAYMOND: But that is from a very practical man. This is from a man who isn't, but has a tremendous reputation. He has a publicity lady who pushes his works very hard. But he himself lives in a cloud cuckoo land, just like Michael Tippett.

MARK: (looking at Maxwell Davies' score) I'm just fascinated how he pitches the wine glass. He places it on a small timpani... rubs with finger and the pedal moves slowly up and down... This is a marvelous effect.— This is not barred at all.

RAYMOND: You can't put that in front of a symphony, it would take so many words of explanation, and you shouldn't have to explain things.

MARK: I wonder what the composer is thinking by writing an *x* and just leaving it! He's probably thinking something creatively in his head, but he's not translating it correctly.

RAYMOND: Well, I'll never bother to do it again, but I did insist on that, copying it out. I said otherwise I'd have to cancel it.

ON CONDUCTING

SOME ESSENTIALS

TOM: When I'm writing something, one of the things that guides me is that I want to see what I was thinking.... Very often, I don't know what I was thinking until I experiment with it.

RAYMOND: Uh-huh.

TOM: How does experimentation, curiosity as to what a given interpretation is going to sound like, enter into your musicianship, your life— do you hear it before-hand, up here, and then you try to bring it about?

RAYMOND: You are talking about conducting, I think now.

TOM: Well, any way you want to interpret the question.

RAYMOND: I find it is a very definite process that goes on with me. You come to a score and first of all it just looks like ink on paper. But then you gradually hear it. You hear bits, you hear lines. You gradually put them together, it takes time — this is why I have the music always around me. All the scores I may be doing for the next six months, have been around me for the past six months, and I'm *always* picking them up... and looking at them.

TOM: Raymond sometimes memorizes while he is cooking. You have the score up on the side.

RAYMOND: Yes, that can help a bit — just my kink I suppose — but... this morning for example, I was looking at *Mazeppa*, it's an opera I might be doing.

TOM: Tchaikovsky?

RAYMOND: Yes. I looked at it — about six o'clock this morning. I'm also doing Tchaikovsky's *Manfred* — but that's not til after Christmas — and *Romeo and Juliet*, the Prokofiev ballet. I looked at one or two numbers to try and get an idea of a sequence. Anyway, slowly the score... I listen to the lines — I put them together in my head, I sometimes go to the piano and play a bit. Play just a line maybe, or then score-read a bit. The practice is extremely varied, and it's very gradual. Then there always comes a moment — usually close to getting to rehearsal time, that is to say getting towards marking-of-parts time — when I suddenly in my mind say, *I know this piece.* Now, I have an overall... it's like a click of a camera. It's hard to explain but I get an absolute certainty of it. Then I can work fast. When I mark the score and mark the parts and so forth.

TOM: Would the word "coherence" be relevant...

RAYMOND: Cohesion.

TOM: Cohesion be relevant to this click you are describing? Does it somehow come together? Is that what you think it is?

RAYMOND: You know how — you know how it is with people when you, when you don't even sometimes have to speak them. But you look at them and you say, well — I *know* you; I know exactly what you're like. I understand you quite well, and I don't think anything you say or do will actually surprise me terribly.

At home in Connecticut, December 1992
CREDIT: Les Wollam, New York

TOM: That's actually different from cohesion. There's something more.

RAYMOND: I think it is intuitive. I *think* it's intuition... but one uses these words... and I am not philosophically qualified to be very exact with them.

TOM: Have you been very surprised with a piece of music that you thought you knew. and it turned out you didn't?

RAYMOND: I suppose I have, but that would be a disaster! (laugh) It would be awful. I can't think of an example at the moment, but I suppose it's happened. I would be very reluctant to do a piece unless I believed I was certain of it. And now I am old enough to be coming round a num-

ber of times to the same piece. Like Beethoven's Fifth... but it really has to happen *every* time. And the process doesn't necessarily get quicker. That's what's so strange. The conviction of the piece, this certainty about the piece...

TOM: Perhaps it gets back to this business about "now" — because you are not living in the past. You are doing... you are having an encounter now.

RAYMOND: Well, you've got to play it now.... So, each time, it is new for you. That was one of the reasons why I decided to come to America and very largely abandoned doing earlier music. I was working flat out all the time with the English Chamber Orchestra, which I loved — they're a marvelous crowd, and I'm going to work with them again. We did a

particular repertory, and I worked very hard at it, but the treadmill became so much that I was actually—the *Brandenberg Concertos* or Handel
Concerti grossi—just turning the parts out onto the stand, and doing it
without this process. That got to be wearing, very dispiriting. I really got
sick of playing that music. Not because it isn't absolutely stunning as
music but because I wasn't any more experiencing this certainty—it's one
of the great joys...

TOM: As a listener, if I hear the bloody *Four Seasons* one more time, I'm
going to call up the weather....

RAYMOND: As a performer, I would love to do the *Four Seasons*. How
many times have I played the G Minor Symphony [Mozart]? It must be
calculable, but more times than you've heard the *Seasons*, and I don't ever
find it a dud... provided I've got time to learn it again, each time. If, for
example, you're doing an opera and you do fifteen or twenty performances, not exactly in a row because the singers cannot stand it, but over a
period, then as long as the vision of it, as long as the understanding of
it, as long as the belief in it is alive, you can reproduce it with tremendous enthusiasm fifteen times. Six months later, forget it.

*

RAYMOND: You must know how to rehearse. What you see on a concert platform is only the end product of what's been going on for quite
a long time. No concert can be better than its rehearsals, it simply cannot. The rehearsals are meant to move everything forward, so that just
at the right time it will come to fruition.... It's like making love with somebody. If you don't arrive at the same time, it isn't so much fun. It's terribly important that you come together in music. That's part of the art of the
conductor, to woo the orchestra, rehearse the piece in such a way that
the excitement and the interest builds. But don't ever expect them to *perform* at rehearsals. That's fatal, and that's why you don't use emotive
terms in rehearsals. You use technical terms. You say this should be more
legato... what about that *sforzato* piano here... take two bows over this,
why take two bows over that?, articulate this more, or balance with the
flute.... A million things to attend to, but in *your* brain, you're actually
building it up towards the great love act which comes with the show.

*

TOM: How did you get started as a conductor? What was the enthusiasm that drew you in the first place?

RAYMOND: Oh, I never had any wish to be a conductor.

TOM: How did it happen?

RAYMOND: Um—just by being involved with other people. It began, I guess, when I was an undergraduate...

TOM: In college.

RAYMOND: In college at Cambridge, getting involved with works that needed some direction, and I suppose being bossy by nature. I was gradually shoved into taking charge of things. Then I went on to the Cambridge Philharmonic, and that sort of thing. Of course, I got to be known for doing this, but all the time I was playing piano and harpsichord, and viola, etc., etc. But quite seriously, I was studying hard all of those, all those three.

TOM: You played the viola?

RAYMOND: Yes.

TOM: And keyboard?

RAYMOND: Piano and harpsichord. I never liked the organ—couldn't manage it. Too mechanical.

*

RAYMOND: Conducting involves an intuitive awareness of people— we talked about this before. When you stand up in front of an orchestra for the first time, you have quickly to assess what a hundred or so people are like. There's not only an overall atmosphere, but you can find the people who are going to be difficult, and those who are going to be helpful—you have probably ten or fifteen minutes to do it in. Every relationship with every orchestra is different. Once you've started, and you go back and back, then you establish a rapport which you can build on each time. With a new orchestra, you have to be very quick. A conductor must develop this, this intuitive response to people. There are certain orchestras that you may never get on with.

TOM: Based on mutual respect, or what's it based on? I mean with an orchestra, this would be so daunting to the average person. They might have dreams of glory standing up in front of an orchestra.

RAYMOND: That's actually one of the rewards, I think—the mutual respect.

It's based on understanding. Musicianship alone won't do. You see, the conductor's job is to persuade all those people to play one piece of music in one way, and you don't have that much time to do it in. You want to make that piece sound in the way that you've come to believe it should sound, for that moment, for that concert. And then you have to persuade all those different points of view to act as one. That's what you must do, and if you don't, you will only get a disparate performance with the different elements cancelling out the others.

*

RAYMOND: I should say something about the very special bonds that develop between professional musicians generally.

You know, I'm not very good at remembering stories. But I suddenly do think of incidents with people. I was thinking, a few minutes ago, about Hans Geiger, he was a violinist, about what he looked like and how he was always around with this one other violinist in the Philharmonia, Jesse Hinchliff. Marvelous character, used to be married to Alan Rawsthorne. No—that's all—I just remember them together all the time. They were inseparable on tours. Hans would always look after Jesse... they were a pair without being a pair. They were just tremendous friends. But that's the point you see. The friendships you make in our business are rather wonderful. But they are different. They are not relationships in the sense of becoming lovers. That very rarely happens. There is surprisingly little screwing in our business. You—don't—do that, but you do get to know people rather well. Emotional entanglements are rare.

TOM: Because of music, itself—for some strange reason?

RAYMOND: It's because when you are playing next to somebody, or you are standing up in front of somebody who is playing, you are at once so intimate with them that you could never achieve that beyond six months' acquaintance in ordinary life. You are far, far too intimate to begin with.

You can't turn that into a sexual thing, or even really a deeply emotional thing. All it becomes is a friendship thing, because you've shared the same emotion. You've shared the loss of a Beethoven symphony, or you've shared the loss of whatever it is, or you've shared the experience of something, you've been through the war together. You've done all those things together, like play Mahler, or anything you can think of that the orchestra is playing. You've shared that. You haven't actually done it to each other, so it doesn't become an intimate relationship. It just becomes a friendship. I think very valuable for that reason

TOM: I think that's very interesting.

MARK: I'm not sure the same thing is true of the theater.

TOM: That must be a little different.

RAYMOND: Well, don't forget theatrical players usually have a limited engagement, so a quick relationship is possible and usual in the theater, among theater people I mean. They do screw a lot, from my experience. Theater people screw. Orchestra players don't screw. (laughter) On the whole, it's true. Of course, there are exceptions.

A CONDUCTOR'S WEEK

TOM: What's a typical week for you?

RAYMOND: You mean a week in Indianapolis. Mondays... an orchestra always has at least one day off—with us it's Monday. Monday I would usually spend revising scores for the week—reminding myself, because I will have come to the conclusion about the music some weeks before. That's necessary because you have to mark parts and get the library to arrange it all so...

MARK: You've said that ideally you should have a set of your own parts of everything.

RAYMOND: Yes. Which have to be revised every time you do it. So Monday is used to bring it back and make it more vivid. Usually we have four rehearsals for a week's concerts, sometimes five. They have eight sessions in the week, by union rule. Eight two-and-a-half-hour sessions of which three will be concerts. So there may be just four... the other one may be a run out... but it could be five rehearsals. Then we have concerts on Thursday, morning or evening, Friday evening, Saturday evening. I've already planned next year's schedules, they are all done. I know the programs and I have to imagine (part of a music director's job) what works will need more, what will need less rehearsal.

TOM: Can you elaborate on that a little?

RAYMOND: Even if I haven't come to a certainty about performing them, I know the pieces. I've learned enough about them to know how long it will take to rehearse them; how difficult they are. Numbers of players come into it, a lot of factors, so you'll schedule accordingly. That's a matter of experience and you juggle the available time. As I said, Monday is spent getting back into making the music vivid again. Tuesdays you rehearse morning and afternoon. Then I generally go to bed exhausted. I don't socialize. Wednesdays the same. We often have a Thursday morning concert, a coffee concert.

TOM: Do you have open rehearsals?

RAYMOND: No, I don't like open rehearsals because orchestras tend to play to the audience instead of rehearse. But we have coffee concerts on some Thursday mornings, otherwise some Thursday evenings, and we have also so-called Studio concerts when we analyze things. This has been a very successful venture which we began the year before last with a flyer of four programs... I take one work and write a script analyzing it in whatever way seems appropriate, writing out examples for the orchestra to play. The first one we did was on Beethoven's Fifth, we thought it was a good round choice to make, and I scored some of Beethoven's sketches to show what might have happened, and then played what did happen, and all that.

TOM: That is fascinating — it's wonderful.

RAYMOND: Another one we did was Ravel's *Daphnis and Chloé*, and I took the Dawn Scene apart, and did it in layers, and then gradually put them together — to show how he made the colors. We did four of those in the first year, and we are doing six this year. I think we are even going to do eight next year because they have been so popular with the young people.

---

8   See CHRONOLOGY for 3 October 1991 and accompanying news feature. (Ed.)

TOM: You'd think students would like to come.

RAYMOND: Well, not so much—students don't come to things you know! They're too busy doing their own thing. It's youngsters, young marrieds, they are the people who are really enthusiastic about the idea. That way the week is pretty well written off until Saturday when we don't have rehearsals. Then, perhaps, I write some letters.

TOM: It's an easier day.

RAYMOND: Well sort of, I am beginning to think of next week or future projects to get into, all that sort of thing, planning, letters, afternoon bed always—it *has* to be—and then concerts and then party a little bit afterward.

TOM: An afternoon nap?

RAYMOND: I usually take the scores to bed in the afternoon and read them through. Sleep for maybe half an hour. Read something else, read a book. It's a sort of nun's life, I'm sorry to say.

TOM: Then you have various ways of getting mentally and physically ready for a concert.

RAYMOND: It's a major undertaking I find.

TOM: I had a conversation with Yehudi Menuhin once, in the Green Room at Symphony Hall in Boston, which he spent flat on his back across the piano bench, doing his Yoga exercises.

MARK: I gather you're able to study scores in the air.

RAYMOND: I don't find that a problem at all. I never talk to anybody on a plane. I find that just awful. There is nothing to say and the noise is dreadful. I would rather turn myself off and learn a score.

*

MARK: Do you conduct from memory?

RAYMOND: I do but I always have a score. One simple reason is that if somebody goes wrong, you don't know which way they've gone, or *how* they've gone. And it's a tremendous help, even if my eyesight isn't terribly good.... it's all right, I can see enough from the score to know that it's the first clarinet and which way he's gone. You can't always tell, because the first thing is a shock that somebody's got out. Anybody can get out for heaven's sake and it's the conductor's prime job to keep everybody in order.

TOM: What's the musical advantage of conducting from memory?

RAYMOND: Absolutely none because ...

TOM: For show? It looks so impressive to have someone appear to have it all in his head?

RAYMOND: When you have rehearsed well enough, frankly, you're only enhancing something that is already there. For some of the time, at any rate, you're superfluous. All you're doing is saying, "Come on chaps, now we're going to do it. We're going to make it." The turning of pages doesn't really matter. It even keeps the left hand from too much movement and focuses on the right.

TOM: I should think the conductor has an important ceremonial function in the sense that the conductor is a kind of go-between between the players and the audience. You almost represent the audience as much as you do the musicians.... You represent us to the orchestra — do you think? If there's no conductor there, the performance can still be wonderful, like the American Symphony Orchestra.... but it's not quite the same experience for the audience.

RAYMOND: In some strange way, you become the focal point.

TOM: You represent us in a way.

RAYMOND: You're saying we have a sort of dual purpose.

TOM: Well, in a way I think you do.

RAYMOND: But our purpose is the music... yet, at a performance, you do partly represent the audience. Interesting idea... hadn't much thought about that.

RECORDING SESSION

TOM: What about recording? You are among the more prolific recording artists there are. What do you do? You arrive... do you have a rehearsal in the hall?

RAYMOND: You would have had to have prepared it all before. You have come to these certainties, otherwise you are not going to make anything; the material has to be prepared which involves a good deal of marking and bowing and that sort of thing. Let's say that's all done, and you're prepared. You tend to record two sessions a day because the equipment is so expensive to move around – you can't do more than two.

TOM: Two three-hour sessions.

RAYMOND: Two three-hour sessions. Six hours of really intensive work. By which time, I must say, you are no good to man or beast. Honestly, you're nobody's after that, not even your own. There is just *nothing* you can do except have a drink and fall down. You see a concert is a very... just like a race, you gear yourself up to a performance for a short time. In a recording you may have to make that "short time" last for six hours.

TOM: With the same degree of freshness.

RAYMOND: You have constantly to renew this image of the piece that you had at the beginning... in spite of them saying, "that won't do, we got the microphones wrong, we twisted the wrong knob, we made a muddle here, you made a muddle there, they made a muddle somewhere else."

TOM: Do you hear the playbacks and say no, we've got to redo this?

RAYMOND: If you're working with people that you trust, no. All you do is to settle the sound at the beginning.... You must hear the sound. You must be satisfied with what you're hearing.

TOM: Which is what, a question of balances...?

RAYMOND: The quality of sound, and balancing. If it's what you've rehearsed when you go into this little room, where they have their listening speakers. You do some takes, I mean, you play a bit, and they take a bit. You go in and say, well, the violins are too present, or too far away, this and this isn't what I'm hearing in the hall.

TOM: Then what... you go back and record again.

RAYMOND: You go back and re-record it. It can take quite a long time at the beginning, but usually you work with the same recording engineers and you get to know them. They know the sort of .... They should come and listen to you in the hall, which is what the best do. Then they go back and try and reproduce it themselves.

TOM: And your players have also got experience, so they know how to ...

RAYMOND: Oh sure. They know when to give and when not to give. If they give all the time, for three hours, they are going to be pooped.

MARK: Your recent Koss disc, of the Schubert pieces... the symphony and the *Grand Duo*... I thought it was extremely well-balanced and a natural sound.

RAYMOND: Yes, I was very pleased.

MARK: I favor as my personal taste recordings that most nearly simulate the actual sound environment, rather than having a zillion microphones all mixed together. You know Stokowski was famous for doing all sorts of weird things in the recording studio with a microphone. Stokowski was one of those who discovered the gramophone as this great medium, and also kind of hopelessly corrupted it because he fell in love with the dials and did all sorts of funny things. And you hear things on his records, it's more like a film music sort of effect where certain instruments are boosted in a way that has no relationship to the actual balance in the live acoustic environment. A lot of people like recordings that are more nearly natural and conform to the natural...

RAYMOND: Isn't that the modern fashion now?

MARK: It's becoming that, yes.

RAYMOND: It's certainly mine. I think a record should represent what the orchestra does.

TOM: Okay, so naturally that brings us to Glenn Gould. Couldn't you say there are two schools of thought about recording, one that it's to provide a document—literally to make a record of something, whatever the event was, as it was, except of course to get certain things right. The other which might be called the Glenn Gould school is, to put on a production, however you arrived at it.

RAYMOND: For me, I only like the recording of a performance. Of what is actually there. The other makes it never-never land. I don't approve of that.

TOM: A lot of people admire Glenn Gould — and certainly I do as a performer—but I must admit that without knowing anything about it, there's something that makes me very uneasy about the whole thing... of, in effect, creating a bogus performance in the studio.

RAYMOND: I think it represents the sort of lunacy that he himself had.

TOM: Yeah.

RAYMOND: It's a manifestation of an extraordinary talent that went peculiar. I guess he will always have a sort of cult following but it doesn't belong to the real world of music. It's exactly what Vaughan Williams would have disapproved of.

TOM: It also raises the question of what is "music". If there isn't an actual performance, but just the illusion of one?

RAYMOND: I don't think it matters. If it's music to some then it's music. But it means nothing to me. What I hear is an exaggerated, eccentric musician.

MARK: For instance, he made a piano transcription of the *Meistersinger* prelude — I think it's one of his greatest recordings, but he superimposed a couple of extra notes that he couldn't play.

RAYMOND: Well, if you are going to do it that way, why not? It's like so many Lady Macbeths have the final D flat sung by somebody off stage.

TOM: *That* bothers me.

RAYMOND: If it's a real person singing it, then I suppose who cares? But this (Glenn Gould's record) is done electronically. But I suppose that's fine too — it's just become something else. I wouldn't put it down... I don't see there is any need to condemn it. But I don't care for it myself. I prefer a real performance. You know, we haven't really mentioned this at all, in the last event a recording is only a poor substitute for a live performance.

TOM: I'm not sure Gould would agree... he might say that a recording *is* something else again.... but there we go, we're off again. You know, I must say that recordings in general don't excite me as much as they once did. They still excite me, but I really do want to hear the live performance. Even with one of those fabulous recordings, the Callas-Di Stefano-Gobbi *Tosca*, I truly do love it, but it's so predictable by now. It is not fresh any more. I love it, but I don't want to hear it very often. Anyway, I bought records originally to learn the music. There was — is so much to hear.

RAYMOND: That's an admirable reason. If I can't get a hold of the score of something, and there's a disc of it...

TOM: You can hear it.

RAYMOND: You can at least hear it and say, I think that's worth playing and that isn't worth playing. It is very important to have a library of records, it's a great bonus. But then people also like collecting. Most people who collect records collect more records than they could ever possibly be alive long enough to listen to!

TOM: I hate to tell you but I had 6,000 before I got divorced. They were all over the house. I was tremendously proud.

RAYMOND: That's 3,000 hours!

TOM: Forty minutes each.

RAYMOND: That's pretty well 5,000 hours.

TOM: I would tend to listen to things I liked the best, anyway. I would hear the Phillips Verdi recordings over and over, *I lombardi, Masnadieri, Attila*. Some of yours, too!

RAYMOND: Well that's fine.... if you can collect more records than you will ever really hear, fine. I'm not putting records down. In the last event I suppose we're in agreement... you can't have Callas live, now — so, the recording becomes an historical document.

HUMAN RELATIONS

TOM: Let's talk about human relations... Toscanini, for example.

RAYMOND: Oh he was a bully. He was even a musical bully.

TOM: Yes.

RAYMOND: At his best he was stunning. Of course he very much suited the American taste of his time.

TOM: He is still one of my favorites — *La Bohème, Otello*, Beethoven's Ninth with Robert Hupka's remarkable photos on the album cover, the set face and white hair stamped against the black background — they meant a lot to me, But, for example, something of his I really don't much like, any more — I came in on the Brahms Second not too long ago, on the radio, I didn't know who was doing it. But it was so awfully fast, and I was wondering who was playing it. It was Toscanini — and I used to love that. But now it made me ill. It was so fast, it began to make me sick. My own taste, tolerance or whatever, I guess that's changed a bit. I have to be in the mood for something quite that fast.

RAYMOND: When we play Brahms, we really are consciously trying to recreate not how Brahms would have played it, we're trying to recreate the vitality of that piece within the framework of how we now view Brahms' time. Therefore, I think we approach it in a different way, every time.

TOM: That's very tricky.

RAYMOND: But it's a fascinating problem. We are much more aware of history now. Much more stylistically aware. Toscanini was only aware of Toscanini. The brilliant New York world was really the only one in which he ever succeeded. I think he reflects not so much Italian but a New York temperament.

TOM: Even the radio—having to get on with things, before the hour is out.

RAYMOND: And possibly the radio. He bought all that and they puffed him up and he was a little squit of a creature, he was a Perrot-type person who loved all that, and threw his weight around, and threw scores. The more he threw scores, the more they loved him. And he was an extraordinarily gifted musician, beginning to believe his own publicity. Now that's one of the dangers for us all.

TOM: To believe your own handouts.

RAYMOND: People gradually come to do so—they don't mean to, but they want to, and then it begins. They then become impossible, and you can't work with them any more.

TOM: It's a delicate issue, the whole question of talent having to be supported by a fairly strong ego. I suppose you have to have a fairly strong ego because, quite frankly, a lot of people can do you harm. They can either ignore you or they can upset you in some way or another.

RAYMOND: But it depends where the ego shows. We all have egos, but some people wear their egos like a coat and some people wear their egos inside and you can't see them.

MARK: You're not saying that Toscanini was a less great conductor because of his ego....

RAYMOND: No, not at all, because he also was a great conductor. But his method was openly egotistical. I'm not putting him down, I'm only trying to describe him. He did some stunning things. But he must have been a pain to work with.

*

TOM: As a conductor, when is tolerance or patience appropriate, and when is tolerance and patience inappropriate?

RAYMOND: They are quite different things. Tolerance is not possible. Patience is everything. You must not tolerate anything. But you have to have endless patience.

*

TOM: How do you deal with someone you are having difficulty with in the band?

RAYMOND: I usually sleep on it, or brood about it for maybe a week or two. But eventually, I am quite good at facing it and I meet them to tell them and I don't have a problem about telling the truth.

TOM: Have you ever had to fire somebody?

RAYMOND: Oh, absolutely. It goes with the territory. In Indianapolis, we've changed about twelve musicians since I've been there. On the whole amicably.

TOM: Do you think they hold it against you personally?

RAYMOND: No, I don't think so because... ought I to be more tactful now? I wouldn't have fired them if they'd still been good. Also, on the whole, the organization in Indianapolis is such that people are actually looked after and seen safely into retirement, or perhaps even helped into other jobs and that sort of thing, or translated into another sort of career. We are blessed with a very good general manager who agrees with me about this. That the orchestra's standard has risen and bypassed someone who has been with the orchestra for twenty-five years is very important. You have to look after them. You can't throw them on the dust heap.

TOM: There's a loyalty...

RAYMOND: Of course there is. I think we are responsible. But there's no point in being sentimental about someone who can't play anymore.

TOM: Conversely, have you ever personally sought out players for an orchestra, say the English Chamber Orchestra, or Indianapolis?

RAYMOND: No. I may have advised people to go in for an audition. Infrequently.

TOM: What part do you play in the audition?

RAYMOND: That's prescribed by the union. The orchestra itself has an audition committee. The process is extremely well run. There's an application list which is generally wildly in excess of the openings. It would take the orchestra a year to hear. So that's reduced on paper to a manageable number, then a committee elected by the orchestra will hold the auditions. I'm only allowed in at the finals and we all vote upon it. I have a slightly exaggerated vote, which I...

TOM: It sounds a little like the Vienna Philharmonic, the voting.

RAYMOND: Yes, probably. They play behind the screen until the finals. Everybody: which answers this terrible, vexing problem about minorities.

TOM: Oh, sure, because they don't know one way or the other.

RAYMOND: They don't know who's playing. Male, female, color, race.

CRITICS

TOM: What rôle should reviewers and critics play, ideally?

RAYMOND: Ernest Newman was a great critic who wrote about music not performances. I don't think reviewers matter. Everything you are going to write about happened last night. And it will never happen like that again—even if you do three performances. It will never happen again.

TOM: Shouldn't you talk about yesterday's event in a way that it kindles enthusiasm for the art?

RAYMOND: Then you would talk about the *music*, wouldn't you? Then you would say—"to hear a Beethoven symphony as well played as it was last night is to remember what a stunning composer Beethoven really was, which the routine performance may not reveal" and so on. Harold Schoenberg of the *Times* could do that—he would make you want to go to concerts to hear the music.

TOM: Let me pursue this. You would exclude talking about the particular interpretation or the performance itself.

RAYMOND: Not exactly. I only think it doesn't matter. It's a stunt. *En passant*, you may make some remark that is derogatory, or appreciative, but what a critic really should be saying—if there is another performance in the offing—is that this music is worth hearing, and say why it is worth hearing. Or critics should write in advance of the concert, saying "I have heard these people before—you should go and hear them." And then say why you should hear that particular music.

: 351 :

TOM: It differs from book reviewing because, obviously, you can buy the book the reviewer is talking about, you can read it yourself.

RAYMOND: Books and plays are fair game, because you can go to, read them yourself. You can't go to last night's concert.

TOM: Still, music critics are important? Yes, no?

RAYMOND: Yes—but it doesn't really matter if they are important—they are there.

MARK: Critics are important to soloists who need the publicity, or quotes they can extract for their careers.

RAYMOND: Yes, absolutely, they are terribly important from the point of view of publicity. But, you know, who would care if you made some up? Who would even know? You don't have to use real names.... "Martin Spokespan of the Baltimore *Wind* says... 'Miss Loggs has never been *surpassed* in her execution.' "

TOM: " 'Although I forget what it was that she was singing.' " Right.

RAYMOND: Yes. She was so wonderful. I was quite transported.

ELEMENTS OF MUSIC

TOM: What do you think are the basic elements of music, and what weight do they have? I'm thinking of things like rhythm. I should think that rhythm itself is very difficult to define. As a matter of fact, we are doing a book about rhythm—a source guide to different historical interpretations. But what are some of the elements that are important to you... obviously melody, harmony.... Do you want to comment on that?

RAYMOND: I don't think I could, no—it's a philosophical matter, isn't it, the question of how much time music occupies, and what its place is in time? Rhythm is one of the symptoms that music actually takes time.

TOM: Are there certain composers whom you feel are relatively simpler to play...

RAYMOND: No...

TOM: ...is there a reason that has to do with the *musical* structure or elements or a particular piece?

RAYMOND: No—nothing to do with simplicity of texture or anything of that nature. A folk song can be as difficult to play as a complex Schoenberg piece.

TOM: Why? Why would a folk song be just as difficult as, say, some classical form?

RAYMOND: Because it presents its own, different problems... the narrower the focus (in a folk song) doesn't mean it is less problematic to bring to life. You have to adjust your mind to it, the simplexity of the texture you are trying to realize.

MARK: Tom, you used to say that, from your perspective as a listener, Beethoven seemed to play itself—you almost never heard a really unbearable performance. Whereas Mozart, almost never a really good one.

TOM: I didn't mean that Beethoven is simple, all I meant was that I've heard lots of amateurs play Beethoven where I felt I got something out of it, but with Mozart in particular, I think I have heard relatively few really good performances, even when they were played by the very best people. That was all I meant by that. I just wondered if there is something about Mozart's rhythms, for example (I don't know), which are somehow difficult to bring off.

MARK: I once heard a Brahms Third played by a good regional orchestra, and it was such a lousy performance that I thought Brahms would never have come very far if that's the way his music was always played.

RAYMOND: It's certainly a matter of who's performing it... and also of who's listening... and at what time you're listening. Too many variables.

TOM: Still, Boult could play Vaughan Williams beautifully, and I have never, ever heard Monteverdi sound the way you make it sound. Or, you know, those truly beautiful, melting, poetic phrases in the *St. Matthew Passion* recording that you did.... the alto's recitative before her aria about the tears on her cheeks....

RAYMOND: Yes, well.

*

TOM: Quick technical question—do you compose using the piano?

RAYMOND: No, usually, I hear it, then I sometimes go to the piano because the reality of sounds is different. It's like learning scores. I learn a score sitting down and then I go and cook a meal and listen to it in my head. But eventually, I go to the piano, I don't have to but I do go to the keyboard to see what I have been hearing. I don't mean that it's right or wrong as far as notes are concerned, but there is a reality in actual sound.

MARK: Basically his ear is developed enough so that he can read a score and hear it, which is what he is saying. One of the things that is wrong I think pedagogically speaking with these synthesizer programs that can transpose for you is that it obviates the need to develop that as a musical skill, which has been the basis for score reading because instruments are transposing instruments, so a conductor automatically has to be able to translate as it were the pitches at sight in order to read a score. Except for those scores that are all written in concert pitch, which some 20th-century composers....

RAYMOND: Prokofiev's scores drive me potty.

MARK: Does it confuse you? Is it like dyslexia?

RAYMOND: I'm always transposing the horns wrong, for example. Written out at pitch they always look too low to someone who's used to transposing them. There was a fashion at one time for writing everything out at pitch and I think it's a bore. Why should we decrease people's skills? They aren't great skills anyway. There is nothing to them. It's only a matter of knowing....

MARK: Just out of my own personal curiosity, I mean, obviously a conductor of your years of experience will do all these things automatically, but when you were in the beginning stage did you learn by clef reading to transpose, or did you just do it by intervals or...?

RAYMOND: Mostly by clef, I think. I think I still do automatically, I'm not quite sure... playing viola helped because it was in a C clef. Reading it was a norm for me, so I had no problem with the rest of the C clefs. At Cambridge I learned to score-read with every sort of soprano and bass clef as well.

MARK: Mezzo-soprano clef, baritone clef, and all those strange clefs.

RAYMOND: It's a very good discipline. And very intriguing. The skills of someone like Palestrina become really vivid that way. It isn't particularly thrilling music but the skill of writing it is terrific. In the process of reading it, you have to hear all the G, C and F clefs.

MARK: I don't know about conservatories in Europe but I don't really think that composers in this country necessarily are subjected to that kind of a stern discipline where they have to read the clefs.

RAYMOND: Universities do. Cambridge does at least.

MARK: They should.

RAYMOND: As long as I was teaching there we did.

MARK: Did you do tonic solfège?

RAYMOND: No. The French do that. The English were never taught to. I've never believed in it. I still don't. It's a particular form of musical training which is non-productive. It's not necessary — rather like masturbating, it's self-congratulatory.

MARK: You don't think it's something that can help develop the skill of interval recognition?

RAYMOND: If you don't have that anyway, why start? If you don't know what a fifth is, forget it.

REPERTORY

PROGRAMMING FOR THE INDIANAPOLIS SYMPHONY ORCHESTRA

MARK: I have a question about the audience in Indianapolis. I'm curious about their response to music. Is there anything more parochial about your situation there compared with other American orchestras you've conducted, and if so how does that affect your work?

RAYMOND: Doesn't every symphony orchestra reflect the audience it plays to? — it must do. New York is a quite different audience from Boston and so on. So Indianapolis in its turn reflects on the whole a fairly well-educated, restrained, conservative midwest society which has an amazingly good record about supporting its orchestra financially. I think — I am sorry to say — that of the fourteen or fifteen symphony orchestras that play 52 weeks a year, we were the only one last year that played in the black — maybe one of two. In my time we have raised the endowment from.... I think when I went in it was $25 million, to something close to $60 million.

MARK: Are you a part of the fund raising?

RAYMOND: Yes, I'm used — I'm available through it all.

TOM: I saw some of the printed literature and some of it is very good.

RAYMOND: Well, all the staff are very much behind their orchestra. We have a marvelous theater to play in now. We play right downtown in the

Circle in an old Vaudeville theater which has been reconditioned – and it's beautiful. Its acoustic has been doctored so that it's equal all over the theater. It's very cleverly done. And, miracle of miracles, the people of Indianapolis have taken us to their hearts and, apart from the endowment, we raise about $4.5 million a year from subscribers. It's called the annual fund – it's always over $4 million.

TOM: Lots of orchestras are shutting down.

RAYMOND: Of course, each situation is different. We have a stunningly good manager who is also a schooled economist as well as being a musician, a very bright and shrewd man. Also, we are smaller than some orchestras, we are 87 players. This represents a saving if you think in terms of an orchestra of 110. Also, I've tailored our programs to have a minimum of extra players to pay for. For example we don't play the *Sacre du Printemps* and *Ein Heldenleben,* which can take fifteen extra players. Leonard Slatkin is on his way to Europe with the St. Louis Orchestra – I work with them and am very fond of both the orchestra and Leonard – but the orchestra has a deficit and they are planning to take the *Sacre* and *Heldenleben,* both of which require eight horns and I don't know, fifteen extra players. I find that a bit lunatic. See now I get into trouble because I say these things out loud!

*

MARK: I'd still like to ask you about the tastes of the audiences in Indiana. Must you give them the hit parade of the classics, or are they tolerant of post-Bartók music and so on?

RAYMOND: I can't accurately answer that. We do a lot of 20th-century music, but I know that the attention span is limited so I wouldn't do an hour and a half of Schoenberg. I wouldn't program the Schoenberg Piano Concerto. I think they would leave. I think also it is a wretched work. I'm rather of their point of view. I like music that communicates. I don't like music that is theoretically interesting, boring and unlistenable to in spite of being fascinating to examine on paper. I feel very strongly, as I have said many times, that music is for *now....* it's central to everything I believe in. Especially in Schoenberg's case – I really do believe he has had his whack. At his best, what a phenomenal talent that was. The *Gurre-Lieder*, *Verklärte Nacht*, that sort of thing. But he blew it.

MARK: Do you feel that way about the whole Second Viennese School?

RAYMOND: No. I would exclude Berg. I don't find much of Webern communicates very well.

MARK: Just out of a hat, has the ISO done anything by, say, John Adams?

RAYMOND: Yes. We've done the *Chairman Dances*. That communicates.

TOM: You commission pieces too, I know.

RAYMOND: Oh, yes. We do. And we have a composer in residence, David Ott. He wrote a two-cello concerto for Washington for Slava [Mstislav Rostropovich] — he's being recorded all over the place now. We've commissioned one piece from him called *Music for the Canvas* which was for a new gallery in the Indianapolis Art Museum. Very good piece. He's writing another for us called the *Indianapolis Concerto*, a concerto for orchestra.

*

TOM: Erich Leinsdorf at the Boston Symphony Orchestra, for all his critics, introduced a lot of unfamiliar works by living composers and got away with it. And he did a beautiful job with them.

RAYMOND: With the new works, it's still difficult. Leonard Slatkin, who is a good friend, has got a reputation in Saint Louis for turning to that type of music. Fine. But most symphony orchestras are hurting badly. Of course, doing some new music is the right thing. One should, but you should choose what you do, it seems to me, for the place you are doing it in. Leonard has a great gift for sorting out. Some extremely difficult and perhaps not very responsive scores — but he is very good at it. I would absolutely accept more from William Bolcom, an extremely populist composer. We are doing his clarinet concerto next year. Marvelous piece I think, I am all for Bolcom.... I think he's first class. But Leonard will put in something by Claude Baker for example — a very nice person, a pupil of Rochberg — from the university world. It's really so cerebral, so weird. It doesn't actually function, I'm afraid.

MARK: As a composer myself, I am more ambivalent on this point than others... I think a conductor who brings new music to the public is brave and courageous. He is losing money, probably, but the composers want their works played, and how are they going to get played?

RAYMOND: But you don't necessarily start with the expensive level of the symphony orchestra. You have to start at the level which will actually take you, and that's the level which will not only take you (play your music) but school you. So many composers expect to go immediately to the symphony level, and that's a mistake. Nobody's ever done that. You have to start where you can actually get yourself performed, learn your rules of acceptance and rebuttal and all those things. Then gradually, if you are clever enough, you are going to be Mozart, Beethoven or whatever it is, in your own time. You'll mount to the top level orchestras. I don't think the unknown ... I really do search through about a dozen scores a week, and I don't find more than one a month that will play. Then to do even twelve a year...

TOM: The stakes are so high, I know. I remember hearing a gifted local conductor, a friend, Richard Kapp, tell us how much putting on a new piece actually cost his orchestra. Phenomenal! But, still, isn't there a problem here? The stakes are so high—but why? Because people don't come to hear them... but—it's a vicious circle, if they aren't played in the first place.

RAYMOND: The problem isn't quite as new as you might think.

THE RIGHT LENGTH

RAYMOND: I was speaking before of William Bolcom. I think he has a great talent, but he doesn't always have a self-awareness of when to stop. I've heard quite a lot of his music on record, and it's almost all either too short or too long. When you look at Britten's works, they are always the right length. That was a part of his genius. It's like Beethoven. Beethoven is always the right length. You always know, which you never know quite from Bolcom and always do know from Ben, you know in the first twelve bars the size of the composition. You listen to the beginning of the Eighth Symphony (of Beethoven), you know that's going to be a short piece. It has to be a short piece. (Hums the opening measures.) It can't be anything but a short piece. Now you listen to the Ninth. Baaa.. *ba*-ba.

TOM: Yes, the whole proportion is different.

RAYMOND: You know that's going to last an hour.

TOM: It's going to have to, yes.

RAYMOND: That's one of the rarely considered measures of a great composer. If whatever it says in the beginning—the first twenty bars— if the piece lives up to that, then it has a chance.

MARK: Then where do you put Sorabji?

RAYMOND: Well you don't, alas. He's a fascinating character, but he's a dead loss as a composer.

This can be illustrated in the films, too. Take *Hook*. It's absolutely stunning. The control, the dynamic control, right through it, is quite wonderful, and what's marvelous about it he, Spielberg, doesn't cheat on one single detail. You know it's about Pan (Robin Williams) who is a grown up man, with young children of his own. Wendy is now a grandmother. What is so wonderful is the construction of it. It's so elaborate and so wonderfully conceived at different levels but he doesn't—whoever wrote it, and it's a very original idea—he doesn't cheat for one second. There's not a contrived cheat in the whole thing. Now in your one-hour mysteries on television, they arrange circumstances. It's all cooked. It's fun, but a contrived cheat from the first few minutes. Whereas *Hook* is a complete work of art in its own way of being a film comedy. Shakespeare's plays have it, exactly the same but on a different scale.

MARK: Well, Macbeth is the shortest play, shortest tragedy, so you're saying that....

RAYMOND: And it doesn't need to be longer.

MARK: You know with the weird sisters in the beginning, that's it's going to be bum—bum—bum (claps his hands sharply).

RAYMOND: Yes, like *Romeo and Juliet*, another short play. You know from the beginning how short that play's going to be. The lack of intrusion of other characters. The speed with which it all happens. You know *Hamlet* is going to be terribly long when it starts so slowly with the ghost and the tedious night watch.

OPERA

TOM: In opera, do you have any particular favorites?

RAYMOND: No. Well, I do like things that are well integrated theatrically within their own conventions.

TOM: Would you like, say, a *Boris Godonov* as much as you would a Mozart?

RAYMOND: I don't think *Boris* works, though it's got some staggering things in it. Some of the much-vaunted ones really don't work, either. I don't think *Don Carlos* does. Doesn't matter whether you put in the various extra scenes or not.

TOM: It makes a long evening.

RAYMOND: And a boring one, too. It's hard to enjoy or to subscribe totally to works that are not theatrically convincing, no matter how good the music. When they come together, it's wonderful, like *Traviata* or *Bohème*.

TOM: One of my favorites is *Hansel and Gretel*. I think it's one of the great operas.

RAYMOND: It certainly works. It's a charming piece. Doesn't prove anything. I mean it's not a great moral statement about anything. But it *is* complete — oh, I suppose it's about innocence destroying evil, if you need a message.

MARK: Do you like *Pelléas?*

TOM: I get a little bit bored by it. Also, I have trouble with operas when you play drop the needle, and I don't know where I am. I like to know where I am. Of course, the language has something to do with it... if it's in French, and the music all sounds the same...

RAYMOND: Now, I don't think that is such a fair criticism, sorry to say. A piece is a piece.

TOM: Well, it certainly is gorgeous... beautiful.

RAYMOND: If you enter into it, it's a long mystic journey... it works as a whole, but it's a very strange world, a misty sort of world. It's also a matter of conventions. With Mozart you have to get used to the recitative and aria of eighteenth-century operas. Same thing for the Handel operas, and so on. But it takes a long time — it's the stylistic thing we were talking about. You come to an awareness that not all operas are written in the same way. They are not all *durch componiert*.

TOM: Do you think opera has burned itself out?

RAYMOND: Not at all.

TOM: Good. But there are only going to be a few that do survive, anyway.

RAYMOND: At any one time.

TOM: I like some of the Douglas Moore pieces... I think *Showboat* is maybe the greatest American "opera", if you'll allow that...

RAYMOND: *Mother of Us All, Rake's Progress....*

TOM: *Porgy*... and all those wonderful Broadway musicals, which I guess people used to take for granted, the way people might have taken Rossini for granted once, because there was so much of it — *Kiss Me Kate, Guys and Dolls, South Pacific, West Side Story.*

RAYMOND: Well, yes. But you don't have to make a comparative list. I don't think it proves anything, and it doesn't enlighten. It merely confuses. Nobody can knock the best tunes in *Porgy and Bess*, but what you can knock are the recitatives. They don't work. They are too long and too slow for that sort of speech. But the tunes will hold it for a long time. Much of the music is wonderful.

*

TOM: You have had so much theater in your career, Raymond. Opera, films, incidental music. Do you feel some special relationship between theater and music generally? Do you see something of each in the other?

RAYMOND: Sure. Opera especially is such a stunningly good form for music when it succeeds. The chances of its succeeding, I think, are about one in a hundred. Perhaps that's a little pessimistic but....

TOM: Why do you like theater?

RAYMOND: Because it's such a... it's like a consummation. I don't share Wagner's romantic view that the best art is always a joined art of every sort. But I must say that some of the really extraordinary experiences I have had have had to do with music in the theater. But it's always had to do with a combination of excellences. That is to say the excellence in performer, excellence in direction, excellence in stage design, excellence in text. There are so many variables when you do opera, or when you do musical theater at all — I find myself increasingly less willing to do it in fact out of fear that some part may fail.

TOM: In theater of course human beings are very much in evidence. Does that relate to your interest in music-theater?

RAYMOND: I'll tell you what it is. You can examine in theater—you can not only examine, but actually experience definite emotions that you actually never can experience in real life... you can experience them with a degree of veracity that is overwhelming. Tremendously heightened, but at the same time it's not going to kill you. An obvious example is *Otello*, where you experience the jealousy of a man to the extent that he would actually kill a woman. We all know what jealousy is, but you can witness it at such a height and degree and with such stunning—I mean, given the right singing, the right orchestra, the right staging, all those things— it will tell you more about the world of jealousy, the world of that aspect of possessive love, than you could ever experience in your life... nor would you ever wish to experience it in life. There's an illumination of life, which is what art is about.

TOM: That's in the play of course. But is something brought out specially by the musical qualities?

RAYMOND: You mean, is opera a heightened version of theater? I don't think so. The music hasn't added in the sense of value, it's just changed it if only by taking longer to say things. It may strike in you some more potent, clangerous sounds and reverberations but *Otello* is not better than Shakespeare's play, it's different.

There was a very clever, purely orchestral work on Othello, Dvorak's overture, but it doesn't do anything like...

TOM: It could be on another subject.

RAYMOND: It could be on another subject. It's very hard for abstract music to be specific about jealousy. You have to have something of words, and also of movement. I would have to strangle Desdemona, but probably not on the platform. I couldn't strangle the first violin either by way of illustration—it would be misinterpreted.

INTERPRETATION... MUSIC FOR NOW

MARK: In the case of your transcription of the Schubert *Grand Duo* for piano four hands, did you mean to suggest how Schubert himself might have arranged it for orchestra, back in 1824?

RAYMOND: No, that wasn't really the point... The true authenticity is the revelation, is the method by which you reveal the composer's vitality that's in the music *for the time in which you reveal it.*

TOM: In other words, now.

RAYMOND: Now — it's all about now. It's not about any other time. And it seems to me that so often in early music — and that is what I was writing about in my little essay on authenticity[9] — all I was doing with the realizations of Monteverdi and Cavalli pieces, for example, was to try and reveal what I sensed of their vitality for our time, or back in the 1960s and 70s as it was then. Perhaps the 80s and 90s will need something different too. It's very possible. I would always cross swords with anybody who suggested that there is only one way; that authenticity is only one thing. It is not one thing. There are two elements in it. One is the vitality of the composer, and the other is you — now — in your present time. That's where I think the real bond of authenticity lies.

TOM: And I think that ties in with two important things about you, first your affinity with, your love of theater — presenting something that's dramatic, that's going to *engage* an audience. And, second, your being very now-oriented temperamentally anyway... you take singularly small delight in extolling the virtues of the good old days.

RAYMOND: You're right... I have no nostalgia. I have no affection for my past at all. I'm only interested in now. I always have been. It's very odd.

TOM: So the year 1710, say, for Bach, or 1640 for Monteverdi, is not sacrosanct for you.

RAYMOND: No, absolutely not. But to return to your point, Mark, of why you might think it impertinent in a way to rework the Schubert *Grand Duo*, when someone as distinguished as Joachim had already done it. But, you see, I think he did it for *his* time. And it does sound very much of his time. It looks on paper and sounds in reality like Brahms. And that, I think, clouds it for *our* time. Joachim's was the sound almost everybody was making then. But now we've become very much more stylistically conscious. So it would be apposite to try and make (since the music is al-

---

9   Chapter I, above. (Ed.)

ready there) the sort of sounds that Schubert made in his own day—that is, we can study his orchestration at least in a way that Joachim didn't bother to do, or didn't really understand. He didn't *need* to understand, because all he was concerned with was making this wonderful music available for *his* time. And that's also what *I* was concerned with—I thought that Joachim had blurred it for our time by doing it for his...

TOM: And Raymond, isn't the interpreter, the recreator, entitled to his or her interpretation anyway? I mean, Mengelberg will give us one Bach, and then somebody else will give us an entirely different Bach.

RAYMOND: There is a difference even within our time, in the moment, and if you put that down on paper it becomes permanent.... I am all for very eccentric performances every now and then. I think we all do them. And I like that because it stimulates, but...

TOM: You wouldn't want to preserve every one of them.

RAYMOND: Absolutely not! Ideally you should write it out for every performance. But, of course, that's not possible. So you put things down on paper for a certain period of time—and they probably will fade just as—after all—composers fade. I was looking recently into doing a program about music for *Romeo and Juliet*. I looked up an enormous number of scores, including an overture by Raff which MacDowell reorchestrated. Terrible piece of music. Seems that Raff died and left this, this...

TOM: He was MacDowell's teacher.

RAYMOND: Yes, he was. Raff also was involved with Liszt. He orchestrated some of Liszt's *Hungarian Rhapsodies*, until Liszt fired him because he was adding notes. At any rate...

TOM: And Liszt was pretty tolerant.

RAYMOND: Yes.

TOM: He must have been upset.

RAYMOND: Well, Raff went on, became a pedagogue and a well-known composer in his day. And this overture: well, whatever vitality it had... it hasn't anymore. Just a little example of how composers can be valued only in their time. It reinforces this idea that you must do things for now. It is absolutely wonderful that people *can* communicate now and it's only just a little sad, that, when they are dead, perhaps they won't do so anymore. Look at *Les Six* in the 20s, for example. Who would you believe then could survive? Only one has, really, Poulenc. Milhaud is almost gone, dead – one or two little numbers. Tailleferre, never... Honnegger's died – Durey, Auric unknown names....

TOM: I think *that's* too bad... Milhaud, Honnegger especially. It's true, though... I've never heard Auric.

RAYMOND: It's sad, but they did wonderful things in their time, and they were very much alive. People went crazy about them. I think all honor to them for that. You know, to do something in your own time is much more important than to do something for the future. I had a very troublesome lunch, I remember, in San Francisco with a generous, delightful chap. He supports the opera and gives young people recitals, helps composers. Anyway, I sat next to a young composer after a recital who loudly proclaimed that he had absolutely *no* interest in communicating to *anybody*, that he was only interested in communicating to people after he was dead. I said, you are dead already! He didn't like it a bit. He got very angry. Sorabji was one such. He was a rare, rare bird when I was an undergraduate at Cambridge. We used to look at *Opus Clavicembalum*, do you remember that?

TOM: About 36 hours of it.

RAYMOND: God! I've never seen anything so long, and no bar lines in it at all.

TOM: The whole subject of communication is clearly important to you, Raymond – always. When you are doing your own performing edition of Schubert's *Grand Duo*, or a Cavalli opera or whatever, how specific do you get with interpretive remarks?

RAYMOND: Well, it depends. With Schubert I would leave most of the dynamics and articulation as he put them down. They are largely orchestral anyway, for the writing is not pianistic. It feels like an arrangement when you play it, even though, as music, it is one of the greatest pieces in the duet repertoire. At least I think so.

MARK: I think there are some other wrinkles to the question of the validity of a given interpretation at a given point of time. The recording medium makes available to our ears the interpretations of generations ago of the same repertoire. For instance, in your *Authenticity* essay you mention Casals', Landowska's Bach. And we can jump from that to Mengelberg, Toscanini, Nikitsch – they all recorded and you can study these things. Now, sometimes it's hard to tell what it is that makes the sound different. Can we set the metronome and figure out a different tempo? That doesn't really explain it. Or there are certain conventions in string playing, for instance in the violin playing of the 20s and 30s you'll hear more of a portamento than is stylistically acceptable today. Anyway, I may find the interpretation of the Landowska just as valid and enjoyable today as it presumably was 50, 60 or 70 years ago when it was made...

RAYMOND: Yes, but it *is* different, isn't it. In her day all the people who listened to Landowska said "Ah, now that... *that* is how Bach should be played." You know the famous story about... who's the other pianist that played a lot of Bach, an American woman?

TOM: Rosalyn Tureck?

RAYMOND: Yes... poor woman. She and Wanda Landowska quarrelled badly... there is this lovely story — probably apocryphal, but it's so charming — a party was given so that they should be reconciled. All of them music lovers there — one Tureck camp, one Landowska. The hostess said, "now, come along my dears — two great artists really must not be disagreeable to each other! They must make up!" So Landowska said, "I will tell you what, Rosalyn — you play Bach as you like it, and I will play Bach as he liked it."

TOM: Yes — it's the sort of story one hopes really did take place!

RAYMOND: And there are two (and more) valid ways of playing Bach within a lifetime. Each has its following. Tureck's was sort of grotesquely rigid in a way, affected... consciously playing very slowly. Landowska I think was a much wider musician than that; she played Scarlatti, she played everybody — whatever she did, she did it with the whole of her being. I think Tureck's was an applied style, which she found paid off. She was quite convincing at it. Studied it hard, I know — I knew her a little bit when she used to be in London. Not terribly agreeable.

MARK: She was very full of herself.

RAYMOND: Yes, rather. Well, so probably was Landowska, who lived near us in Connecticut as it turns out. Over in Salisbury.

*

MARK: Do you think what makes greatness in a composer is the ability

of his or her music to withstand the greatest number of differing interpretations? Bach being the universal composer—you know, you put it
through a computer, put it through the synthesizer, put it through....

RAYMOND: (laugh) It still turns out not bad.

MARK: Yes.

RAYMOND: You see, I think that street of critical journeying takes you
into the realm of comparative criticism. Because you are going to ask,
"Well, and is so and so greater *because* he lasts longer?" I think that's not
only dangerous, but also worthless. I don't think it matters. I think what
matters is what we conceive of as being great now. Nevertheless, it certainly is true that someone like Beethoven has survived since... he seems
to have been such a towering person mentally that whatever he said in
music, whatever the vitality he put into his music, has seemed apposite
to every generation ever since, for 200 years now. And that's—I mean—
I think that's jolly good. I wouldn't say it's more than that, but it is rather
wonderful.

TOM: There are certain basic emotions or basic somethings, aren't
there, such as... coherence, cohesion, compassion, beauty, something
"universal" (whatever that means) or "right" sometimes, that somehow
comes through in Beethoven or anybody else... the clothing that it's
clothed in doesn't much matter, in a way? Of course it does matter, but
you always...

RAYMOND: But then, Tom, how do you explain why the vitality of one
man will not survive into the next generation? When you look at the
musical theater writers in America.... the durability of Gershwin's tunes
is astonishing...

TOM: Now as much as ever....

RAYMOND: But an awful lot of his contemporaries... most, have written stuff which is faded. And yet, it clearly *was* wonderful (coherent,
cohesive, compassionate, beautiful etc).

TOM: Yes I guess—that's absolutely true. I wouldn't know how to
begin to find "it".

RAYMOND: I don't think it matters. I think all you have to do is observe
it. I don't see that there is anything to be gained by comparison... who is
"greater" and who is not... even when they are all alive.

TOM: This comparison thing...

RAYMOND: "I've got a bigger one than you have."

TOM: That's what it is. And it's collecting... trying to account for every-thing—I've got all the pieces together. I've got all the greatest hits.

RAYMOND: Right! It's a great period for collecting—for doing the "complete" everybody.

MARK: You know part of that is the insatiable need to get product for recordings. It's like an audio version of television. They just have a slot to fill and they turn everything in. I don't think it's entirely good either, because you have a complete cycle of something where the inherent quality and material has got to be uneven.

TOM: I think it's actually quite wonderful, though, to do some of these complete things, like all the Bach cantatas, Haydn symphonies, Verdi operas, and lots and *lots* of Handel... so long as you also do all the other worthwhile stuff, too. I'd like to hear everything at least once.... all of Sibelius, all of Grieg. It's fascinating to discover what a composer has done.

RAYMOND: I don't think there is anything wrong in that—it's all a part of our time. It's also a part of this need we have for reassurance in our time. So many of our mainstays, which our grandparents had, have been knocked from under us. Their religion, even certainty of the world going on...

TOM: Community.

RAYMOND: Community... a totally different moral structure... you could kick against it, but you were there *in* it. The society is very largely disintegrated as far as all that's concerned, and people get so fussed... take all this family-talk in the past [Clinton-Bush] election. It's so stupid when the "family", itself, has become such a different thing. I mean, *we* might be family. We could well be—if we were to like each other tremen-dously, we could become the family. People do.

TOM: For that matter, great plays are written about families in a tradi-tional sense that *don't* quite work... let's see, there was *Agamemnon*.

RAYMOND: Absolutely—sure.

TOM: There was a little problem, as I recall, that Elektra had with her biological mother.

RAYMOND: Certainly, if you knock religion away—and religion has really failed almost everybody, unfortunately—and it's very sad that it has—then you need other things. This is why music has become such an important element, I think.

TOM: It has to do with celebrity, too.

RAYMOND: And the grabbing of it. The amount of it. Anybody who is evangelistic in religion can't stop grabbing the next bit...

TOM: Somebody will collect Bernstein's off-takes or lousy days or something, simply because it's Bernstein. Or stay with Johnny Carson for the worst possible night, because it's "Johnny Carson". Celebrity— the 27th recording of Dvorak's New World Symphony, indifferently performed or not—or, just a snatch of it, for the 53rd time in a week on radio—as giving value of itself. There's something—I mean, I don't know.

RAYMOND: It's anchoring onto a faith of some sort.

TOM: A kind of faith, or faith-substitute.

RAYMOND: It's an element of faith, and there's a need because overshadowing all is the certainty that we *can* destroy ourselves, and the world has been very close to actually blowing itself up. And will be again, and may eventually do it. It's a...

TOM: Orientation, too. If I was on the moon or a different planet or something, and there was nothing there, the first thing I would do would be to plant something on the horizon—a post or something—and another post over here. Then, back away so that I could orient myself against at least those two posts on the horizon. The very first thing I would ask myself is—where am I? I wonder if some of these celebrities— and the complete things—aren't in the way of being landmarks... milestones that you orient yourself to.

RAYMOND: Yes, perhaps they are.

*

TOM: What's a proportion for new scores that you consider, and then the scores that you sort of settle into, and that you actually are going to perform?

RAYMOND: You mean contemporary music. Very small, unfortunately or fortunately. It depends on the quality and not the number of pieces.

America is producing an amazing amount of music, just in sheer quantity. It's staggering, but a lot of it is produced under the aegis of the university world which – and this goes back to something I've said many times before – has very little to do with the expressive world.

TOM: Some would say the universities have a hammerlock on what new music does get performed... or even gets written.

RAYMOND: I don't know whether they have that much real control. When universities had money, then they had an influence – much more than now. It may be that what was originally a benevolent impetus from the universities – to harbor and encourage young composers – has been abused... that the composers have nested like mice in a threshing machine, and are actually abusing the situation by increasing in number and producing less and less good music. Bernstein never had much to do with universities as far as I know.

TOM: Okay, now we get into something... the so-called commercial world as opposed to the non-commerical (academic). What if a conductor or someone who is in charge, Seiji Ozawa in Boston for example – though not him particularly – says, we'll do a certain amount of new music, but we're not going to do very much because audiences won't come to us.

RAYMOND: I think that's not at all a bad thing. I would defend that. I think that's the old process reasserting itself within twentieth century society. It's what Haydn, Beethoven and Mozart had to put up with. I think it's perfectly fair.

TOM: You mean it's the free enterprise system. I'm afraid I'm not entirely sympathetic to that! I think new music almost always needs more help than it gets... what if the "familiar" never gets a chance to become familiar, in the first place? But, you are saying, it's up to the customer – audiences – whether they are going to buy it or not.

RAYMOND: Absolutely. That's why I'm suspicious of the university system, because it's become a closed system. Self-engendering, self-adulatory – I think it atrophies the mind and creativity of the composer. Also, it's a very bitchy world.

COMPOSING

TOM: At one time you might have been, in the main, a composer.

RAYMOND: I'm sure I could have been – professionally, I mean – but I chose not to be. I think to be a composer – like anything else – you have to be at it full-time. You have to have a fluency. It's just sitting down like Trollope and writing every day. You must write every day, it must be your choice of a musical life, to write. I decided early on that that wasn't the way of life that I wanted.

MARK: I heard stories about Britten and his fluency, fantastic things about pages and pages of orchestral score at one sitting.

RAYMOND: Sure, absolutely true. Even slow coaches like Walton wrote in a disciplined way, every morning, and tore it up – but wrote. It is a discipline.

FILM MUSIC

RAYMOND: You are an accessory after the fact. If you are writing an opera, you are in on it from the start, whereas on a film you are only engaged after the film itself is shot.

TOM: Did you work with a movieola or with a screen?

MARK: A click track.

RAYMOND: It's a very scientific business. You have to write within a third of a second. Of course, you know the techniques.

TOM: Cue sheets and so on.

RAYMOND: I did a film of *Alfred the Great* which had about 45 minutes of music in it. That's a hell of a lot. My brief was to write something like Walton's score for *Henry the Fifth*. That was the brief. That's what I did, I churned it out. It was a star-studded thing. It had David Hemmings in it, Michael York and it was just awful – made no sense at all!

TOM: In your writing, do you think in terms of individual moments or scenes or what? What is the unit of composition?

RAYMOND: You have to start with the style and then you just follow, whatever – you go see it a dozen times with the director, and you say "what about here and there?" Usually the director has a pretty clear image of where he wants the music. You are entirely in his hands, really. You can say, what about doing some... and he says, no – oh no. He's the one that really has the control over it. Then of course he can cut another 400 feet of film — and he's lost that bit.

TOM: Was there anything you liked in particular about the process? Something about it that was exciting to you?

RAYMOND: The check. Otherwise I only saw it as an intellectual exercise, as a musical exercise. I bought my house in London with *Alfred the Great*. Did an extension here in Connecticut with *The Hotel New Hampshire*. I still get about $25 a year out of *Lord of the Flies*. That was done on a shoestring.

But there comes a time in your life when you have to decide about all this. The good ones — they are damn good at it. John Williams....

TOM: Danny Elfman.

RAYMOND: ...and Elfman.

MARK: Successful film composers are the most reliably compensated composers of any kind of composer. With the exception perhaps of the commercial jingle writers, if you call that composition. That's all in the hands of synthesizer experts now, anyway.

RAYMOND: I remember I once did some jingles for a sausage maker, pork pie maker called Bowyer in England. I did a series of jingles for them which they recorded. I got paid and I can't even remember how much it was. It was the highest rate per-second of music, the highest paid I've ever been in my life, doing anything. An unbelievable amount of money they paid, because that was the going rate. Ridiculous! I did, I think, five of these things — I think I got about thirty to forty thousand pounds for that.

TOM: In a way, it's not exactly sacrilegious to think of Tchaikovsky doing a Smirnov commercial. It's a question of career choices that you make.

RAYMOND: It really is a question of choice. I love writing music, I enjoy enormously putting notes down on paper. It gives me a really terrific, almost physical pleasure doing it — but I don't think I would have been satisfied with that... I wouldn't have been good enough to make it worth doing, for me that is.

TOM: Shall we take a break? I expect we've covered quite a bit of ground.

RAYMOND: Oh sure, let's... it's been most enjoyable.

VI

EPISODES AND ANECDOTES

1
BY WAY OF INTRODUCTION

My life in music has not followed the traditional patterns of most of those who end up as conductors of orchestras. Almost all of my peers studied instruments in academies, colleges or *conservatoires*, and spent a good deal of their early years in orchestras or opera-houses from whence they were weaned away into the world of directing. I did all of those things but by no means in the usual amounts or in the usual order.

When still a schoolboy I won a scholarship to the Royal Academy of Music and, at the same time, another scholarship to read music at Trinity College, Cambridge. By the time I had spent three years of conscripted military service in the R.A.F. (1945-1948), I had decided to take the latter option. I spent five years as an undergraduate and graduate researcher, and then moved to London, having come to the point when I needed to take part in the real world of professional music. There was no other way to find out if you were good enough or meant for music.

After a few years (1958) I returned to Cambridge (which is only fifty miles from London) as a University Lecturer and Fellow of Trinity, leading a double life of professional musician and academic: this not because I couldn't make up my mind, but because I wanted to prove that the academic life could enrich the professional, and vice-versa.

It took me ten years finally to realize I was wrong—partly because I was so much enjoying both lives, and partly because I was reluctant to face the fact that the two ways of life, in spite of many similarities of purpose, are fundamentally opposed to each other. In the end you have to choose one or the other or do neither well.

All this took longer than would usually be needed to determine a conductor's aptitude and ability. I left Cambridge for good in 1968. I was forty-one and, at last, an enthusiastically full-time professional musician.

Things were further complicated by the fact that by now I played the harpsichord reasonably well, and had developed at Cambridge an en-thusiasm and something of a reputation for seventeenth- and eighteenth-century music which found a professional outlet in, first, my own chamber orchestra and then — as a result of an amalgamation with the Goldsbrough orchestra after its founder's death — with the English Chamber Orchestra.

Directing from the harpsichord became a successful activity which set me somewhat apart from my contemporaries who were finding their con-ducting feet... if such a solecism may be permitted... with the larger or-chestras.

However, the chamber orchestra world and my activities in the field of seventeenth-century opera also type-cast me, which seven years as principal conductor of the BBC Northern Symphony, doing modern opera at Glyndebourne, conducting Mozart at Covent Garden, and even the influence of people like Walter Legge at EMI entirely failed to eradi-cate.

By 1976 the wave of "original instruments" and "authentic" performan-ces, discussed elsewhere, threatened to engulf us all and rendered me old-fashioned in my own time. The critics and those they influenced found new pegs on which to hang their epithets, and making music be-came less enjoyable for me — something I would always count as a per-sonal failure in living, no matter where or what the circumstances which brought it about.

The only way to change matters that I could see was to come to America, which is what — in that year — I did. I have been pleasurably and fruitfully immersed in the symphonic world ever since.

I shouldn't wish, in recounting this sequence of events, to slight some wonderfully enjoyable, important years.

All my activities have dovetailed each other and the main direction, if I can be said to have had one, has always emerged through pursuing companionable if rival occupations, rather than as the result of making purposeful, single-minded decisions.

Thus, while lecturing and teaching in an intellectual climate which I found most stimulating — between 1958 and 1968 — I was also working on seventeenth-century opera at Glyndebourne, writing the music for Peter

Brook's film *The Lord of the Flies* (and, later on, among others, the dreadful *Alfred the Great* for M.G.M.), which helped pay for my house in London. Then there were various other theater productions needing music in London and Stratford (involving, for the latter, many pleasant cross-country drives from Cambridge) and an increasing amount of recordings and concerts with the English Chamber Orchestra, which also involved a good deal of driving to and fro often in the small hours.

There were tours — usually during the Cambridge vacations — to South and North America, Italy, France, Germany, Japan and occasional concerts and broadcasts with artists like Janet Baker, Heather Harper, Yehudi Menuhin, Hugues Cuénod, Richard Adeney, Nadia Boulanger, April Cantelo — the list is endless — all wonderful people to be with and to make music with.[1]

You may well understand why I did not wish to give up either of the two lives.

One of the most rewarding and influential activities between the two Cambridge periods (1952-1958) was playing keyboard parts for the Philharmonia orchestra.

That also helped pay the rent in those impecunious days, for I had quarreled with my family over leaving Cambridge and, out of stubborn pride more than anything else, now had to support myself in the profession.

The Philharmonia was founded by Walter Legge as a recording orchestra for EMI and was probably the finest England had ever seen. Walter was not the easiest of people, but he had unflinching standards and from top to bottom the orchestra was composed of the finest players, mostly but not all British, who had emerged in the years after the war.

Manoug Parikian, Neville Marriner, Sidney Sutcliffe, the Walton brothers, Gareth Morris, Ernest Hall, Dennis Brain, all names to conjur with in those days and the rest were not far below them in standard.

There grew a most remarkable corporate spirit in the orchestra. None of us who were there will ever forget the announcement by Walter Legge

---

1   Specific concerts dates are given in the CHRONOLOGY below. (Ed.)

one chilly August morning before a 10 AM recording session in the Kingsway Hall, that our great first horn Dennis Brain had driven into a tree and been killed coming down by himself from a concert we had all given together the previous evening in Edinburgh. The shock froze us as if we had suddenly heard of the death of a much loved brother. Musicians become very intimate making music together even if, as is usually the case, they lead very separate lives when it comes to family and relationships outside their profession.

My association with the Philharmonia came about by chance. In 1953 my pianist predecessor, whoever he was, couldn't do a concert given under the direction and, I suspect, financing of a Hawaiian conductor of little or no talent. One of the works scheduled to be performed was the extremely difficult Bartók *Music for Strings, Piano and Percussion.* I was telephoned out of the blue at short notice to see if I would do it. I think Ursula Strebi who worked under the formidable Jane, secretary to Walter Legge, may have had something to do with it. (Ursula, now an old and dear friend, was later a co-founder of the English Chamber Orchestra.) At any rate, during rehearsals it became abundantly clear that the conductor couldn't manage the complicated rhythms and, catching Manoug Parikian's eye, we seemed between us to be able to hold the thing together enough, at least, to give a decent performance when the time came.

Such nerve-wracking, if rather thrilling occasions can bear fruit, and I was subsequently asked to play all their keyboard work—piano, harpsichord and celeste.

In that short period, between 1953 and 1958 — for, given my other commitments, conducting especially, I had to give it up when I returned as a lecturer to Cambridge — almost all the most celebrated conductors and composers came to direct us and, sitting at the receiving end of their sticks and their personalities gave me the most valuable insight into what in conducting will work and what will not.

The most effective ones were those who conducted as an extension of their own musical characters and personalities. Most good musicians have a sense of ensemble and can count so that the beating time of the measures, though still important, is the least significant part of it all. What really counts is the ability to project the musical meaning, the content of a piece by gesture and rehearsal and to be able to persuade a hundred musicians to adopt a single view of the work being played.

Composers conducting their own music, you would think, should be the best at it, but it was not so.

Hindemith recorded with us several times. Bald, genial, almost cherubic, he conducted with small, uncommitted gestures which were easy to follow but only conveyed the impression we all had of his music whose reputation was in decline at that time. It seemed as if he was as little interested in it, except as a series of problems to be resolved, as he caused us to be. This was altogether a wrong assessment. He wrote much too much but we can now see the difference between the music he wrote to prove a point and that which he really meant to write. The best of it, like *Mathis*, the 1940 *Cello Concerto* and the *Symphonic Metamorphoses* still carries its vitality like a torch.

He was unaccompanied at the recording sessions unlike Stravinsky who was always surrounded by a sycophantic entourage. Hindemith came and talked with us, Stravinsky was unapproachable. On the podium he set out to please the orchestra who admired his music greatly but in fact he impressed one as a sly, fox-like person conducting with nervous, small gestures that conveyed more uncertainty than authority.

Walton was just like his music, urbane and witty, pretending a lack of commitment to his own scores that was not, in fact, the case... something we knew, and an appearance we took trouble to correct when we played. His amused, sophisticated manner combined with down-to-earth Northern practicality suited us, and the orchestra played very well for him as they always do for Malcolm Arnold who had, himself, been principal trumpet with the London Philharmonic Orchestra and was one of the boys. With him recording sessions usually turned into jolly parties.

Quite different was Carl Orff. We recorded his opera *Die Kluge*. He was a tall, thin streak of misery who soon abandoned the conducting of it to someone else after finding he couldn't manage us or it. He represented, to me at least, the spirit of pre-war Germany. Humorless and arrogant, he made the most awful fuss because certain of the percussion instruments, in which field he was an expert, were not exactly what he wanted and the sessions were held up while someone flew to Germany to find the correct ones which then, having been the cause of a great deal of bad temper, sounded exactly the same. Music-hall music in shiny black boots and grey uniforms was the general verdict, hardly worth the talents of Schwarzkopf and Fischer-Dieskau who were among the cast for the recording.

Guido Cantelli had met his tragic end just before I began playing with the orchestra and the new star in Legge's firmament was Karajan.

I know no musician of his stature who was less mourned at his death. It was almost as if he had never been. Yet, off the rostrum, he was intelligent and could be very good company, at least in those years. Conducting, he appeared to have nothing but disdain for his players and his behavior to them was despicable. A consummate psychologist, he used his skills to manipulate the orchestra without respect for their abilities or their own sense of artistic responsibility. Nietzsche said "A good German is an obedient one" and Karajan believed it to be true of all musicians. He seemed even to get pleasure out of their discomfort.

For example in the beginning of Mozart's D minor piano concerto his technique was to be mystifyingly unclear. No-one could tell where the point of the beat would occur. A mere parting of the hands (he used the stick less and less) and there followed what seemed an interminable, electrifying silence. With lesser players nothing would have happened or, alternatively, it would have resulted in chaos. With the Philharmonia (and Karajan knew well the quality of the orchestra he was using) experience, responsibility to the music and sheer nerve meant that the first desks of cellos and basses eventually began the triplet semi-quavers which was followed, like magnetic dominoes, by the rest of the section a fraction of a second later. The opening sounded like a magic wave breaking on a D minor shore — Mozart would never have recognised it — and audiences marvelled. It was cold calculation on his part and a terrible expenditure of nervous energy on the part of the orchestra.

His quotidianal behavior was no better. He would call the entire orchestra for a ten o'clock rehearsal, take a Mozart Divertimento, which uses only forty players, for all but the last fifteen minutes of the section, and then have the full band called in for a movement from *The Pines of Rome*. This would have been bad-mannered enough with a crowd of students: with the finest players in Europe it was inexcusable.

Nevertheless I owed him my first trip to America.

It was said that he wanted either the New York Philharmonic or the Met and — having failed with the Berlin Philharmonic to play in New York — to win the stakes he rode the best English orchestra across the Atlantic, and seemed to despise us for letting him do so.

He got neither position and by the time we played our last concert in Boston he was in a foul mood, so foul that he had left the stage after the last note in Ann Arbor the previous evening and took no applause; a sort of calculated insult to the orchestra and American audiences for his failure in New York. The reception at Ann Arbor turned from being ecstatic to censorious and the orchestra had by then had enough. The British are a tolerant people, slow to anger, but resolute when aroused.

There was a rehearsal in Boston the following morning and the atmosphere was electric. Karajan came in late, called a rehearsal number at which point one of the first violins, Peter Gibbs, himself a fighter pilot in the R.A.F. during the war, stood up.

His attempts to address Karajan were interrupted by Walter Legge sitting in the hall who ordered him to sit down.

"I will not sit down, and, Mr Karajan, I did not spend four years of my life fighting bastards like you to be insulted before our own Allies as you did last evening."

At this the orchestra to a man stood up, applauded and left the stage. Karajan couldn't get off and, for once, was completely nonplussed.

It says something for his character that he conducted the concert, but it was the last one he ever gave with the orchestra. I believe he vowed he would never again conduct an English orchestra. Just as well. He stayed where he belonged.

Peter Gibbs, apart from his distinguished career as a fighter pilot and the courageous stand in Boston, was an extraordinarily sympathetic, vulnerable character who seemed to have great difficulty in coming to terms with life. A fine violinist, he started a quartet in his Oxford days when I first knew him. They gave some remarkable performances and were much noticed but he soon had a large family and chamber concerts are not very remunerative. Even later on, after the Philharmonia, when concert-master at Covent Garden there was something unresolved, unsettled in him, perhaps due to the war. Finally it seems he could cope no longer and flew his own small plane out alone above the North Sea and never came back. His fate moved me then and still does infinitely more than that of his German adversary.

There was an interim after the Philharmonia's return from America but quite soon Otto Klemperer became the principal helmsman. A monolith of a man who, at the end of a long career, after a series of strokes and a bad burning through setting his bed on fire, seemed indestructible. He was a different sort of German; autocratic, certainly, but paternalistically aware of his players and always urging the best out of them with that wry, lop-sided smile of his. He had *a* little sense of humor and — as if to demonstrate the fact — he played at every opportunity that presented itself a drab little composition of his own called "A Merry Waltz", which it was not, and I used to wonder if he knew it.

In a world that was going faster and faster his music got slower and slower and, in doing so, revealed, especially in the music of Beethoven, things we had never heard before, aspects of the composer's thought that had never occurred to us. It was, of course, not the only way to play Beethoven, nor, on all the evidence, were they anything like the speeds Beethoven intended, but wonderful things happened and we can extrapolate many good thoughts on the subject of authenticity by considering this.

Half-way through Klemperer's régime I returned to Cambridge and my life changed once more (1958). It was time to look for greater responsibilities and to explore other realms of music.

2

STUDENT DAYS AT CAMBRIDGE
— A REMINISCENCE —[2]

From the amount of time that I have spent in Cambridge, it might quite reasonably be deduced that my attachment to the place would prove overly strong for any sort of detached consideration. Not only was I there for five years as a student but, later on, returned for ten more as a don.

---

2   First published in *My Cambridge* ed. by Ronald Hayman (Robson Books, 1977).

Yet both times I left because I knew I had to get away and neither now, nor in the period between my student and more senior days, did I find myself dwelling for any length of time, or in any sentimental way, on the place or the people I knew there. I suspect and dislike nostalgia, so that it is quite an exercise of memory and intellect to recall my student days and put such construction as I can upon them, which is the brief of this memoir.

I failed little-go in 1945 as a result of a wilful refusal to learn Latin, something of which I am now ashamed. In the event it was among the most fortunate things that ever happened to me, as it meant I first had to do National Service before coming up, three years later, to spend my time with as unusual a vintage of undergraduates as Cambridge had ever seen.

While I wouldn't wish the wasted years of service in the armed forces on anybody, I do think it was valuable, at least for me, to have spent time in a totally different world from home and school before entering that of Cambridge. Almost all undergraduates in the late 'forties were in the same boat, and the odd ones out were those who came up directly from school. I think they may have suffered as a result. The majority of us, after the inanities of service life at that time, were intellectually starved, and eager for learning and intelligent company. The fact that we were older meant that many of the tiresome hang-ups, emotional and sexual, had at least been encountered if not resolved, and we were a good deal more experienced in meeting and getting on easy terms with a much wider array of people than school or home could ever have provided. Many of our fellow-students were older and more experienced still in the darker horrors of war, but they never spoke of them and we all surely profited from their deeper maturity.

You might think that such a generation would be lawless and fiercely revolutionary in a Cambridge whose rules for running its own society were still much the same as in 1939. But it was not the case. We were all perfectly happy to be in college by midnight, or to climb in if not. The fines for being late and the rebukes if caught climbing were cheerfully accepted as necessary restrictions of a society designed for the general good. There was very little in the way of love affairs; we all knew, by then, how socially disruptive they could be, and term was so busy there really wasn't time. Those who did fall were generally objects of some sympathy, for it kept them out of general circulation; more their loss, we felt, than ours. There was, too, an amused tolerance of the more idiosyncratic features of Cambridge life — like the wearing of gowns and the attentions of the Proctor and his "bulldogs"[3] — which, of course, we knew were of no actual importance, but acceptable, even enjoyable, because they were symbols of the society we were enjoying and felt fortunate to be part of. Society at large did not then owe us an education. We had to prove ourselves — arrogant as it may sound in these egalitarian days — worthy of it, even to the extent of knuckling down and learning Latin, *quod in tempore perfecti*. Cambridge terms were periods of tremendous and intense high spirits, and the activities that we all managed to cram into those eight weeks were so many and so varied that there seemed little time for sleep. When we weren't involved in concerts, theater, Footlights, meetings, lectures, study or supervisions, we were discussing them and anything else that came to mind in the gradual process of making contact with the friends who were to remain so and become an integral part of life.

The way our society was ordered meant that the colleges led a more separate corporate existence than they do now, and gained, I think, in character as a result. Their particular characteristics and qualities, it was generally agreed, rubbed off on their undergraduates who then had to deal with their foregone reputations as best they were able. Such generalizations were, of course, foolish but amusing to make and sustain. As they reflected the period and have, doubtless, since then changed, it might be worth recounting how the colleges looked to a Trinity man in the late 'forties.

The college I would most like to have belonged to, had I not been a member of Trinity, was King's. It had a special aura about it and King's men always gave the impression of having been, like the twelve, chosen — often, we thought, more for their looks than for intellectual or social talent. Within the college there was a delightfully titillating undercurrent of homosexuality, man-about-townery, café-society sophis-

---

3   *Canis humanus* — trained to catch students climbing in late. (Ed.)

tication that we didn't necessarily want, but envied nevertheless. The high-table—now rendered sadly low—was full of people who remembered Rupert Brooke and knew the Bloomsbury group: Keynes, Lytton Strachey, the Woolfs, a world that has of late been so wearisomely oversung. There was enough glamor in it for returning servicemen to be dazzled. King's was headed by Provost Sheppard, old long before his time but nimble enough at selecting the best-looking undergraduates for his blessing as they left chapel services. He was a confirmed gambler, and I remember seeing him at the beginning of term in London (from the labels on his luggage, just returned from Monte Carlo), fast asleep on the inner circle, presumably going round and round until he had recovered sufficiently to get off at Liverpool Street and catch the train for Cambridge. The literary jewel in King's crown was E.M. Forster who was kind to the better known or bred undergraduates, and used to give parties and occasional readings of chapters from his overtly homosexual novel, *Maurice*, which finally proved disappointing when published in its entirety after his death. I rather think he knew it wasn't very good. He was aware, though, of being one of the figures of Cambridge, and bore it with a charmingly exaggerated modesty that deceived no one.

My experience of King's was largely through music and theater, which were much cultivated there. Boris Ord and Philip Radcliffe, of whom more later, both lectured in the Music Faculty and Boris was in charge of Chapel music. Donald Beves acted well; I remember particularly an excellent Monsieur Jourdain in Molière's *Le Bourgeois Gentilhomme*; better, I thought, than Miles Malleson's more famous interpretation, because more real, and so more touching. He entertained with a distant friendliness in his rooms which housed his very fine collection of glass. He used also to perform a memorable, portly Puritan in the various pageants that "Pop" (Camille) Prior used to direct during long vacation terms, in which we all took part in one way or another at least once. Each pageant set out to illustrate different aspects of history—Queens of England, Cambridge through the ages, Kings of England—but ended up much the same each time, with the celebrated "Prior step", the only one she knew to give a semblance of corporate dancing, much in evidence, as well as the inevitable Cromwellian sequence.

Apart from Boris Ord, perhaps the most influential figure in King's, as far as the university was concerned, was Dadie Rylands, the epitome for many of theatrically-orientated sophistication.[4] He always seemed to know so much and, as we gradually found out, did; much more than we used to give him credit for at those moments of extreme exasperation at his bland, devastating demolition of our more pretentious views. Lovable and maddening at the same time, he was, I think a true educator and the majority of our current theatrical talents owe him something; or would vehemently deny it, which comes to the same thing. I certainly count my life the richer for having continued to meet and, occasionally, collaborate with him.

Architecturally, King's is a misshapen college, but with a chapel immeasurably greater than any other in Cambridge. And, though the majority of choral scholars have subsequently done very little except live on their memories, they represented then the most exclusive musical society in Cambridge; but one I now count myself fortunate in not having belonged to.

If King's was a college we envied, John's, our nearest neighbor, was not. It wasn't as big as ours, and most of the people there came from places we didn't care to talk about. The chapel was a joke, architecturally, and the courts generally had a grim, unfriendly aspect which seemed reflected by the members of the college. Quite a lot of wild parties went on in the Wedding Cake, but it wasn't generally an hospitable place and, I must say, I found it no different when I went back as a Fellow of Trinity. I don't think I ever dined there in fifteen years of Cambridge life, and the small number of people I am fond of who belonged there seemed to prefer to entertain elsewhere rather than risk, I suppose, a collegiate chill on the proceedings.

I didn't know anyone at Christ's, and if I did know someone from Sidney Sussex he never admitted to it. Fitzwilliam House was another place we looked down on, though I came to sympathize with its excluded condition during the two very happy years I spent, out of college, living with

---

4   Among several "entertainments" devised by George Rylands and RL were the "Homage to Purcell" which opened the Purcell Room at the South Bank (perf. 1967, 1968), an evening of "Poetry, Prose and Music" (perf. 1969) and "The World a Stage" (perf. 1970). (Ed.)

Erika and Stefi Bach — he was a senior member of Fitzwilliam — and was glad for his sake when it achieved full collegiate status.

Caius was, for me, dominated by the figure of Paddy Hadley, our Professor of Music who, I suspect, was happier with the chaps in his chapel choir than in his Faculty. He was wonderful with them, composing pieces and arranging the most surprising things, like scenes from *Boris Godunov*, for them to sing at college concerts. So great was the fervor he brought to the music he loved that they came off amazingly well in performance. Something to learn from that. He was not cut out for the chair of music. Something to learn from that, too. Such musical techniques as he had were locked firmly away in his mind, and could not easily be transmitted. His musical tastes were strong and quite irrational, but we were very fond of him. He drank a lot. It was charitably said to be on account of the pain in his wooden leg, whose mechanism occasionally gave out and left him stranded, immobile, in the middle of Cambridge — I saw him once being wheeled home by the Caius porters in a wheelbarrow, wearing full professorial academic dress — but I believe the drinking was much more to hide from his own failure to fulfil in music the creativity within him. There was a lost generation of English composers — Warlock, Lambert, Moeran, Ireland — who, nervous of academicism, eschewed technical training and finally took to drink for lack of it. Paddy was one of them. Thinking about those days, I remember him in his rooms at composition seminars, which frequently came upon him too suddenly for him to be dressed in anything but pajamas, and those often in some disarray of which he was quite oblivious. One day a prissy little virginal Girton miss ventured a know-all musicological point which maddened Paddy by its total disregard for the expressive ends of the music under discussion — "Baroque? Fuck Baroque!" he shouted. It wasn't much of an intellectual point, but I bet she never forgot it.

Magdalene was a stuffy college with a very high social rating; Emmanuel was practically non-conformist, and had an annual free-for-all sing-through of the *Messiah*. I tried it once and left during "And the glory of the Lord". Selwyn was non-conformist, but had a lot of good concerts including quite a few professional ones, which irritated Mrs. Hackforth (who ran the professional Thursday concerts) and those who believed, as, on the whole, I did, that Cambridge should do most of its entertaining itself.

Pembroke, Trinity Hall, Peterhouse and Corpus were my most visited colleges. They all boasted flourishing musical societies and there was a good deal of helping out at each other's concerts, which meant that we got to know each other's societies and, to some extent, were accepted into them. Corpus was the most urbane, in some ways more than King's, to which it felt, but was not, superior. Quite a lot of Footlights people belonged there and gave sophisticated parties, for which we were supposed to dress well and talk intelligently. One of my closest friends, Malcom Burgess, who used to design all that period of Footlights shows, and became a Fellow there and University Lecturer in Russian, I met after one of these, wrapped elegantly round a lampost in King's Parade; he was tall and slender in those days, and apt to wear somewhat exaggerated dress. He also stole umbrellas, especially mine. It became a habit. There was a move to go on somewhere to dinner, probably at the KP, but we had not been introduced at the party. "Gracious," he said, when we were; a remark I took to be predatory, but it was only curiously appreciative, and set the tone for banter that continued for the years of friendship that were left to us. (He died of cancer in 1978.)

We were all jealous of Peterhouse food. In winning the war, it seemed England won the right to starve, and things were worse in the 'forties than at any other time, especially in Cambridge, where a miscalculation in the allocation of rations meant that sometimes we really went hungry. I think the Master of Trinity eventually went to see the Minister of Food about it and, I suppose, though I don't remember, the bad-tempered old harridan who grudgingly doled out our meager rations of butter, bread, and sugar for private consumption in our rooms, gave us a little more as a result. Peterhouse kitchens were subsidized by a handsome bequest, so they ate more and better than any other college.

Pembroke and Trinity Hall were smaller colleges, full of quiet, companionable people. I was a member of a regular string quartet and our leader, Martin Chadwick was at Trinity Hall and our cellist, Ki Bunting, at Pembroke, so we were frequently to be heard rehearsing in either college.

St. Catharine's was a somber place, and the people there seemed to take on the despressed character of the dark red-brick buildings. It was said that the buildings had never stopped blushing for shame over the scandal of a dishonest Mastership election earlier in the century, on which C.P. Snow based his novel *The Masters*. They—the buildings—have subsequently been cleaned. Downing had some pretty eighteenth-century buildings and some horrid ones in twentieth-century bankers' Georgian, which you saw on the way to the railway station. It housed F.R. Leavis, of whom we became heartily sick on behalf of the friends who read English and had all their enthusiasm dampened by his power-ful, ascetic critical theories.

Queens' had a lot of serious-minded theatrical people who knew, or pretended to know, a lot about Ionesco and Genet. People at Clare rowed. Girton and Newnham didn't count very much—especially Newnham. The care that was taken to preserve the girls' virginity was, with a few notable exceptions, far in excess of any threat they were like-ly to encounter. A few of the female dons indulged in a little gentle match-making, but we were, mostly, well past the stage of coy innuen-do and found all that a waste of time. Women in the university were wel-come to join in most activities on an equal basis with us. It was, never-theless, an essentially male society at that time.

Trinity, the largest of the colleges, was far from being the amorphous microcosm of all types and classes it was sometimes accused of being. You had to live in its society to discover that its character was based on the recognition of two important distinctions, more clearly made there than in any other college, largely, I think, because of its size. First and foremost there was the concentration on intellectual matters. Ordinary social levels played no part in this and the appreciation of intellectual achieve-ment and exchange was in no way affected by background or per-sonality. Beyond that point, every sort of distinction was drawn. If you hunted or beagled, you had usually done it before and would surely do it again. If you played badminton, you tended to play it with people who came from places where badminton was played. The same went for all sports: squash, real tennis, rowing, football, hockey, rugger. You played with your type. In various ways and degrees of emphasis this applied to all the societies in the college. They were exclusive, and made no bones about it. Everyone understood, and the larger and smaller distinctions were rigorously maintained. You mixed freely with your intellectual equals when intellectual matters were foremost, and with people who shared your other interests when not. It was a very good way of making a society work, though somewhat unfashionable in these days when every sort of distinction, real and imaginary, is being ironed out.

Crucial to the scheme of things was the participation of the senior members, and my memory is that the Fellows of Trinity were, at that time, a good deal more conscientious about it than in later years. They were almost all readily available, and many of them entertained regularly in their rooms. The most regular meetings were, of course, in the weekly supervisions or seminars, but the extra-curricular meetings were often just as rewarding, and, in retrospect, I think the Fellows I knew were very generous with their time.

Trinity High Table really did have the most distinguished history of any college in virtually all the disciplines and, though it was beginning to fade after the war, the reputation of its intellectual standard was still very high, and deservedly so. G.M. Trevelyan was Master and the shades of G.E. Moore, Bertrand Russell and J.J. Thompson were in evidence everywhere. Bertrand Russell came to dine sometimes, and I remember being invited to meet him after hall by, I think, Harry Holland, who didn't much like him. I can't remember anything he said, only the beak-like nose, the hair, the nasal voice, and the physical movements remarkably agile in one so old.

The point about High Table was that you saw its members constantly about the college, and could very easily see and speak with them more intimately whenever the need arose. They, almost all, felt an obligation to be available and take an interest in the undergraduates with whom, for one reason or another, they came in contact. Nor did they overdo it — they were just there and part of the place.

The ones I saw most of were interested in and involved with college music. Principal among them was Hubert Middleton, a much loved but underestimated man. I owe him and his wife, Dorothy, a very great deal. He directed my studies, but generally, in college, he was in charge of chapel and college music, which he looked after with a wisdom and consistency of practice that taught us much beyond the events themselves, and helped to order and develop our various enthusiasms. He had been organist for many years before I met him, and only lately a Fellow of the College, which we felt did not reflect much credit on the Fellowship, though, it must be said, his modesty was as much reason for this late appointment as any lack of appreciation of his worth in the college. At home he and Dorothy were tireless in entertaining numbers of us to memorable evenings of talk, food and drink with, occasionally, a little music; but not often, for Hubert was a thinker about music with a marvellous ear and a warm enthusiasm for what was valuable. Its practice was something he loved to encourage in us, but was not good at himself. He was one of those people who said unforgettable things which influence you for the rest of your life. As a teacher, he had that greatest gift of all of making you feel that he thought you so much better than you knew you were; and you loved him, so you couldn't let him down by not being so.[5]

College music flourished and the place was large enough for us to undertake quite large ventures. There were chamber concerts each Sunday evening, and the college orchestra met on Sunday mornings. Various Fellows' wives joined in, a few friends as well from colleges that had no orchestra of their own, and there was Nellie Naylor who had been turned out of CUMS (Cambridge University Musical Society) by Boris Ord. She was not, perhaps, very much of a violinist but, together with her sisters, Glad and Doll, daughters of a former mayor of Cambridge, she was in the world class at croquet, and many an eccentric afternoon was spent in their garden with other friends — Neil, Philip, Brian — learning some of the skills and marvelling at the passions aroused in those otherwise gentle maiden-ladies. Doll was small and did the cooking; Glad gardened and was on various local committees; Nellie was the racy one and, apart from playing the violin, taught ballroom dancing in a little studio at the bottom of their garden. It was not much patronized as far as we could see. Her dismissal from the university orchestra was something of a legend. Boris Ord, searching for a clearly audible mistake in a rehearsal of the slow movement of Beethoven's Choral Symphony, narrowed it

---

5   RL will mention Hubert Middleton again, including him in his list of "six most influential persons" in his life. See page 422, below. (Ed.)

down to the second violins and, finally, resolved it altogether by saying firmly, "Miss Naylor, stop playing." CUMS's loss was Trinity's gain.[6]

I was a choral scholar, and this meant regular attendance at two week-day evensongs and one on Sundays—not an intolerable burden, even though it was a dreary business musically. Hubert went on valiantly but unenthusiastically with choir practices at which there was, irregularly, a motley collection of boys bribed in from the highways and byways. Some had been there so long they seemed biological miracles. It was all a sad echo of the days when Stanford and Alan Gray had a choir-school to draw from for a table of services that would have graced a cathedral. When I returned to Trinity some years later, we sacked the boys and established a male-voice choir along the lines of Caius, which has gone from strength to strength ever since.

Congregations were abysmally small, even on Sunday evenings, but occasionally a sermon would lift a service out of its habitual drabness into something memorable. I recall several by Harry Williams, whose concentration on life and the fruitful living of it seemed to me so much more meaningful than the usual dosage of guilt the church seemed to minister. I remember, too, one foggy November evening—Remembrance Sunday—and F.A. Simpson preaching about the gift Trinity men had made of their lives in the First World War.[7]

Finally, of course, it was the undergraduates who counted most, and the foundation of friendships by now too long established, too intimate, and too involved for any public reckoning. The years, in confirming things, also complicate them so that they go beyond powers of description and analysis; they are simply a part of life.

Official university studies were carried on at the University Music School in Downing Place, a converted church hall with bits added on. It was early days of the Music Tripos;[8] I think I must have been on the second or third wave of undergraduates able to read for an honors degree in Music. The importance of this for the status of music in the university was great, if difficult to explain, and it was largely the work of Hubert

---

6   See also page 396, below.
7   Described below, pp. 394-95. (Ed.)
8   Honors degree in Music.

Middleton and R.M. Rattenbury, another Fellow of Trinity and Registrar of the university. The whole Faculty was not much above a hundred, and the music school was just about adequate to house us and the Pendlebury Music Library, which, though not comprehensive, did contain an amazing variety of things, and the voracious exploration of unknown music was a feature of those years.

Lectures varied greatly in quality and the bad ones were less and less well attended as term went on. It could be disastrous to leave it too late before giving up as you might be among the last two or three and forced, out of charity, to complete the course. Henry Moule lectured well and precisely on subjects like fugue and sixteenth-century counterpoint, giving us to understand that music could be observed with a cool intellect as well as with a warm heart. This thesis underlay the whole Tripos, and the aim was a synthesis of intellect, heart and sensibility. I still believe in this as a way of approaching music, but I did not find it possible, as I had hoped, to live the double life of teacher and performer. The rival claims of each were too strong. Hubert Middleton understood this and was very sympathetic when I decided to throw up my Ph.D. thesis and remove to the profession in London.

Boris Ord's time was largely taken up with King's Chapel so that he lectured infrequently and not often well. He was at his best in practical seminars on continuo playing and score-reading at both of which he was superb. We learnt much in watching his work in CUMS rehearsals — I led the violas in the orchestra — and in the University Madrigal Society in which I sang. I first encountered the reality of Monteverdi's madrigals with this small, select choir which met every week in term, gave infrequent concerts during the year and also the celebrated Madrigals on the River which, as an occasion, always had more of sentiment about it than serious musical achievement. It worked, though, as an entertainment, and thousands came each year to see us float down the Cam singing "Draw on, Sweet Night". Boris could occasionally be persuaded to play in the University Music Club, of which I became President, and his sense of standard helped us greatly to become aware of such things. Perhaps best of all were the parties he used to give in his lovely set at the top of Gibbs building, above Jumbo Arch. He had two pianos which could safely be played at all hours. Improvising with him, in between ministrations of drinks and "blotting paper" (biscuits) to his guests into the small hours and, on occasions in May Week, through the night, remains among the most enjoyable of undergraduate memories.

Philip Radcliffe was also a Fellow of King's and had an encyclopaedic knowledge of music. His lectures always carried the implication that we should further explore the unknown territories he was showing us; not that we needed much pushing. The illustrations he gave at the piano were famous for he didn't play well and, quite undaunted, would set out on a most difficult piece — a Scriabin sonata maybe — and after a few bars the brakes would seem to fail and the music increase in speed until the inevitable tumble in a flurry of notes. Hands would fly into the air and the illustration end with a somewhat disdainful "and so on". Example, illustration and illustrator became, in this way, quite memorable.

Robin Orr, who had returned to Cambridge from the war only a short while before we came up, lectured with a dry humor, but we thought of him principally as a composer, and went to hear the new pieces he was writing for the choir at John's. I remember, too, playing some very striking music he wrote for the Greek play — a triennial production at the Arts. The play was *Oedipus at Colonnus* and must have been among the last of their productions in Greek.

There were other major productions, usually under the aegis of CUMS, at either the Arts or the Guildhall, but most of the really interesting theater went on at the ADC where many of the productions needed music composing or playing. Peter Hall, Peter Wood, Toby Robertson were actively directing plays and the current professional stage is peopled with Cambridge actors of that time, too numerous to attempt any sort of list that would not be invidious in its selectivity. It is amazing to consider what a high percentage of the major talent in the entertainment world, to speak of no other, was around in Cambridge and Oxford during those years.

The other society that occupied a fair amount of time was the Footlights. Every generation of that Society thinks its own the best, which probably says more about changes in style of humor than much else. Ours was certainly a very lively vintage. The smokers — social evenings for which, symptom of the times, we used to dress, where new material was tried out — were well attended, and the standard of writing and performance was high. Peter Tranchell was musical director, surely the most original one in the Society's history, and put the music of the May Week revues together with great skill and wit. The intention at that time was to produce a sophisticated, elegant revue rather on the lines of Hermione Gingold's *Sweet and Low* series, though, if anything, ours were more barbed, aimed at a more intelligent audience and, with Peter in charge, far superior musically. Occasionally the Society was invited to perform for a week or two in London. Some thought it a great thing, but in my view it was a mistake, for London management diluted the wit and, eventually, insisted on including women — which changed the style, and the Society lost at least as much as it gained.

If all this was not enough, there were still open lectures to attend, the *Cambridge Review* to read — except for that wretched university sermon which, it was said, could be heard in pulpits all over England the Sunday following its publication. There were *Varsity* and *Granta* to giggle over, college committees to sit on, dinner parties, and occasional walks alone or with friends.

There scarcely seemed time to draw breath and yet, somewhere within the frenetic energy of term, there lay the essence of the paradox that is the strength of the Oxbridge system. While we stretched ourselves to the limit, there was still time to find out about ourselves, our minds, our capabilities and failings — not all but enough, at least, to make a good start. It was not a system for everyone, nor was it designed to be. You had, in due course, to find within you the determination to get down to work on your own, for no one would make you. The time was there for you to do what you had to do with it. A term or two in the wilderness didn't matter; you could go to pieces; you could try out all manner of eccentricities; you could sport your oak and be in undisturbed quiet for as long as you needed, but, eventually, you had to recognize and accept some responsibility for the life that was in you.

I do hope the sadly mean, jealous spirit that seems to pervade much of our present-day society will not prompt Government to standardize university education in the ridiculous name of equality or fairness; two principles which apply at no point in life. People are all manner of things worth caring about but they are not equal, and life is always worth the living, but it is certainly not fair. Cambridge has shown for over five hundred years that it can adapt to almost any social climate; the lack of any serious undergraduate troubles in recent times is present evidence of that; but it could be destroyed by the disenfranchisement of the colleges, and, I'm sure, there are those in power who would do it to catch a vote, or appease their own wretchedly misguided sense of injustice. I pray the university has enough sense to shout very loud if the need arises.

3
IMAGES & IMPRESSIONS

THE TRINITY IMAGE

F. A. Simpson was originally from Oxford. After completing a first volume of a history of Louis Napoleon (note the indefinite articles) he was given a Life Fellowship at Trinity, Cambridge, and, under the Old Statutes, he was indeed elected for life.

After a year or so a second volume appeared which received some adverse reviews at which point Simpson gave up and did nothing for the rest of his long life. He was a cleric and declined to preach or act as Dean of Chapel; he was a scholar and declined to teach or lecture.

By the time I was a first-year undergraduate he was an eccentric old man, object of curiosity and amusement, known for being an interested but harmless observer at the University bathing pool where we swam naked.

He had been known, in the long distant past, to preach but only very occasionally and while he was at Oxford after he had just taken orders; so that when it was announced that he would do so again on Remembrance Sunday 1948 there was quite a stir and the chapel was full. I was an undergraduate singing in the choir and had an assured place.

The November mists from the fens had invaded the chapel which was always dimly lit, mostly from the candles in the choir-stalls. These gave sufficient light for the rows of gilded names of Trinity men, many from the great families of England, who were destroyed in that dreadful war, to glint from the memorial panels that line the chancel. They gave a terrible poignancy to the occasion.

Simpson spoke *ex tempore,* apparently, although it was probably nothing of the sort for it seems he returned to his rooms after Hall and dictated it to someone from Cambridge University Press who published it a few weeks later.

The text was a phrase he had seen on a cross at one of those great burial fields in France: "Not in vain my darling, not in vain". The argument and the sentiment were overpowering, not a little because of the incongruity of this tall, gowned figure, neck swathed in a great grey scarf, swaying as he spoke those words in a cracked, crabby voice. It made the profound emotions he brought before us not only shocking but almost unbearably moving.

It was published under the title "A Last Sermon" and is probably still in print for it became widely celebrated.

Years later I returned to Trinity as a Fellow, elected under the new Statutes, I hasten to add. Simpson was still there. He must have been older, but he looked and behaved the same. Perhaps he seemed a little more benign but he was not. The college has always had a reputation for intellectual rigor which allowed nothing for the frailer emotions of sympathy, friendship or compassion.

The surprising news came that Simpson had agreed to preach once again and had this time chosen the subject of the Good Samaritan.

The chapel was packed. Once more I had an assured seat, this time as a Fellow and responsible for chapel music in the organ loft above the chancel from which there was an uninterrupted view.

Instead of using the pulpit, Simpson chose to deliver his sermon standing, still in the same gown and grey scarf, swaying and stepping to and fro between the Masters' stall and the choir seats. As he paced up and down his gown billowed out and the long scarf followed every movement of his scraggy neck.

It was not a good sermon.

In Hall afterwards it was customary for the week's preacher to sit at the Master's right and, by some lucky chance, I sat that night next to

Simpson. Opposite was a former Dean of Chapel, John Burnaby, who disliked and had suffered from him for years.

Lord Adrian, the Master, once we had settled after Grace did not set things off too well by observing that he thought the Good Samaritan a peculiar choice for Simpson to have made for his text. Simpson was among the most selfish of men. Emboldened by this, Burnaby went on to say that he had remembered the sermon of November 1948 and had it not been published and become known as Simpson's farewell to the pulpit? (The title as published by Cambridge University Press had been, I repeat, "A Last Sermon" by F. A. Simpson.) So, what had possessed him to renege on his originally expressed intention?

With the assurance of an intellectual marksman despatching his shaft to a certain bulls-eye, Simpson replied with the utmost disdain in a voice quivering with anticipated pleasure, "Do you not know yet, Burnaby, the different between the definite and the indefinite article?"

It seemed, for a moment, the traditions of Broad, Wittgenstein and Russell were not lost.

EXPOSURE

I confess to at least one moment of abject moral cowardice. It was when I was an undergraduate at Cambridge playing viola in the Trinity orchestra.

As an orchestra it was a poor thing, but it was also a collegiate activity and loyalties were involved. Attendance at weekly rehearsals was sparse and a constant disappointment to Hubert Middleton who was the college's director, a wonderful man and a great teacher but hardly experienced in matters of orchestral training. He bore his burden like the saint he was, which made it the more certain that as the very occasional concerts came round all the better players felt bound to join in.

Among the regular rehearsers was Nellie Naylor, a late middle-aged instructor of the fox-trot to, as far as one could gather, almost nobody. She played in the first violins. The connection with Trinity was tenuous. Possibly her father, a former Mayor of Cambridge, had been a member of the college but I'm not certain of that. She had been thrown out of more orchestras than most people knew even existed in Cambridge for her playing was not of the highest standard. But there she was with us in Trinity, a cheerful eccentric; more of a darling Dodo than a positive contributor to the tottering standards of the first violin section.

One Sunday afternoon in the Michaelmas term there was a concert and I was close to being late as I parked my bicycle outside Great Gate. Living at Barnabas Road at the time I found a quick dash home to change after a morning rehearsal was cutting it fine. With some relief, however, I noticed Nellie Naylor hurrying on ahead of me. I also noticed that beneath her fur coat there was something unusual about her hem line. We were the last two in the rooms set aside for coat and instrument cases and, as I turned round tightening my bow, I saw why. Nellie's skirt was tucked at the back into a large expanse of shiny pink knicker.

Of course I should have told her, but imagine the sentence. "Miss Naylor, I'm afraid your knickers are showing." It was unthinkable. Perhaps I could have tweaked her skirt out with my bow or pulled it free with a swift, bold grab as I followed her up the steps into the lecture-room where the concert was to be given, but I was inexperienced with knickers or skirts and it might have been misinterpreted. In any case I failed and am ashamed of my pusillanimous behavior.

The room was full with the orchestra at one end and, following Miss Naylor as she edged her way to her place in the first violins, facing front, I witnessed the collapse of all the players *en route*. Hubert Middleton, already in place and anxious to begin, saw nothing, though he was perceptibly confused by the array of shaking shoulders.

I remember we began with the overture to *Titus* of Mozart and those descending scales suggesting the immolation of the Capitol in Rome were made the more vivid by the flashes of pink, glimpsed through tears, as Nellie leaned forward to turn the pages of music for her stand partner.

Only at the interval did Barbara, a violinist sitting directly behind Miss Naylor, tactfully put things to right and some measure of decorum was restored. The only saving grace was that I rather think Nellie never knew the extent of the exposure.

FOR WHOM THE BELL TOLD

Malcolm Bullock used to tell a story which I think it would be a pity to lose.

Immediately following the war a celebrated exponent of an earlier, flamboyant style of acting in France, Marie Bell, had an exuberant last professional fling. No one had heard anything like it for years. She specialised in Racine and, when in London, reminded the pundits there of Henry Irving. When in Paris there was talk of the divine Sarah. Most of us went more for the shock than the pleasure and were not disappointed.

Her popularity was brief but sensational.

Malcolm recounted how, at the beginning of her vogue, he had invited a party of old pre-war Parisian friends, all part of the old, fashionable *haut-monde,* to hear her. They were, of course, of a certain age, mostly getting about with a limp or a cane, and among them was *La Princesse Marthe Bibesco,* a formidable echo of Proustian days, a relic of the Roumanian royal family, a writer, something of a scavenger, not liked by everyone but a character nevertheless.

There was first a dinner at Maxim's and then the performance of *Berenice* which everyone pronounced formidable and, instead of dispersing afterwards, it was determined by Marthe Bibesco that everyone should go back-stage to congratulate Marie Bell, "my oldest friend".

The stage-door keeper was quite unable to check such an advance by the Old Guard though visitors were officially forbidden. Mme. Bell's dressing-room was at the top of a circular iron staircase up which the Old Guard's legs and canes made slow progress. At the top Malcolm tapped on the star's door and a crotchety old dresser appeared. A message was passed and the Princess's name mentioned.

In spite of the door being closed there following something of an audible explosion within and the ringing tones that had been so admired in the theater rang out once more, perfectly clear over all the back-stage. "*Qui? La Princesse Bibesco? Ça, non! Il y a des limites.*"

There was nothing to do but for the whole party to turn round where it stood and, like a slowly unwinding coil, make its way down the staircase in silence and out into the night air.

One should be sure of one's friends, old or new.

"*Il y a des limites*" became quite a catch phrase for a time.

SCYLLA AND CHARYBDIS

When I was at school Diana Dors was the British version of Betty Grable with, perhaps, something of Veronica Lake and Jayne Mansfield included in the same package; an image of vulgar, blonde sexuality whose individuality and likeability lay in her propensity to laugh at herself.

In the event she proved also to be a woman of sterling quality, acting in all manner of styles well past her glamorous days and eventually, through a painful last illness, becoming something of a heroine, a touching, rather common, maternal figure in a TV sit-com series, known for her generosity of spirit and dying before the series ended for real as well as in the play.

While still a blonde bombshell she was asked by the Vicar of Farnham, where she was born Diana Fluck, to open a church fête intended to raise money for the steeple or the organ or both. Of course she agreed. She was like that.

The vicar was young, new and very nervous about having to present the celebrated actress when she arrived. He did so along these lines:

"I hardly need to introduce the famous, beautiful lady who has so graciously consented to come and open our humble fête. Indeed, as a newcomer to the parish I hardly have the right to introduce her at all for she grew up among you and so many of you know her much better than I; know her not as the great actress Diana Dors but as Diana.... " Here he fatally hestitated and, after cavernous seconds spent, one can only assume, in deciding which route he should take between Scylla and Charybdis, he put on a brave face and said — "as Diana Clunt".

She told me this story.

THE ROOF LEAKS?

Orchestral musicians can be merciless — and very funny.

In my early professional years playing keyboard for the Philharmonia we saw many, if not most of the best conductors then practising their art. Some were not so good and I remember a political refugee from Poland conducting us at a concert put on by the Free Poles, so to speak.

There was some dismay at his humorless, pretentious rehearsal manner, not to mention his wayward beat. Matters were not improved by his eccentric ideas about the standard works he had chosen to include in his program. Beethoven's Fourth Symphony began so slowly that the woodwind were quite unable to hold out for so long. Even Gareth Morris, famous for never seeming to have to take a breath, was defeated by it and the mutterings increased.

Amid the familiar works was a *Nocturne* by the great man himself which began with a long, a very long side-drum roll. He was one of those musicians who seem to believe that because something is impressive we should stop the clock, stay around and watch it being so, whereupon, of course, it ceases to be impressive at all. His interpretations were full of such moments.

The long side-drum roll was rehearsed several times, the player directed to begin at one side of the drum and slowly, very slowly traverse the drum head to the other side. It took an age and didn't seem to us as significant an effect as it did to the composer who conducted it every time with eyes closed and an ecstatic expression.

The orchestra was restive after several such rehearsals, so much so that, on the day of the concert, Manoug Parikian, the concertmaster had to admonish us all to behave.

The evening began with us all doing our best, anxious to show support for this exile from Communism before a Festival Hall packed with his free compatriots.

The strains and irritations gradually mounted as one miscue followed the other, but all went reasonably well until the *Nocturne* and the interminable side-drum roll.

After about thirty seconds of it, the principal double-bass slowly extended his left hand and gave a puzzled look up at the Royal Festival Hall ceiling. Could it be that the rain was coming through?

I'm glad to say the composer with rapt expression and eyes closed did not see it and went on conducting.

THE EAR-TRUMPET

Vaughan Williams was among the least pretentious of remarkable men. He seemed to view his extraordinary talents as a master carpenter would his trade. He saw himself, I think, as a journeyman composer, his life devoted to music as a carpenter is to the woods he uses but, "no need to make a fuss about it, my boy." He was a countryman, the sort who wears tweeds even in summer and always likes to have mud on his boots. The lack of pretention reflected his Cambridge days. He had been at Trinity and was part of that extraordinary inter-married intellectual dynasty that comprised the Darwins, Cornfords, Keynes, Adrians, Barlows and Wedgewoods. No room for being grand in their company, it wouldn't wash. Gwen Raverat, a Darwin cousin of V.W.'s, showed it wonderfully in her enchanting book of memoirs *Period Piece—A Cambridge Childhood*, remembering her aunt calling him "a foolish young man" who "would go on working at music when he was so hopelessly bad at it."

By the time I knew him he had become somwhat hard of hearing and, rather than fiddle with wires and contraptions (a necessary part of hearing aids in those days)[9] he carried an ear-trumpet, a curved hunting horn probably a relic from his days in the Trinity Lake Hunt.[10]

Our paths crossed on many occasions but one of the earliest was at a

---

9   There seems to me only one advantage of the old type of hearing aid with the wires and the box you kept in your pocket: you could turn it off.
      There used to be a Fellow of Trinity who always wore his contraption into Hall for dinner. The control box was somehow fixed to his waistcoat and if he sat between two Fellows he found boring or if he strongly disagreed or disapproved of an opinion expressed in a discussion around him he would rather decisively put down his knife and fork, reach for the box with his left hand and with his right ostentatiously switch it off.
      It was a real conversation stopper. You couldn't do that with the little invisible ones without appearing rather unsanitary. I hope I never have to use either.

10   A vacation man-hunt in the Lake District started by V.W.'s generation of select Trinity men like Trevelyan and Moore. At the beginning it lasted for days on end, but when I used to go on it the two hares set off after breakfast and were given a half-hour start before the hounds were sent out to hunt them. The hares (human variety) had to sound their trumpets every so often so as to give a clue to the hounds (also human) in their chase. If not caught before, the hunt was declared to be over around tea-time when everyone repaired to a cottage some miles away which served delicious scones with brandy-butter. It was tougher in V.W.'s day.

concert in 1956 in which we were playing several of his works including *A Lark Ascending*. It was in the St Pancras Town Hall, a dreadful place with tip-up seats.

After the interval the stage manager asked the soloist and myself to hold backstage as our distinguished guest hadn't arrived back at his seat. Peering through the side curtains I saw V.W. who was also by then rather stout, his mid-riff beginning to resemble that of a football, moving into his seat, ear-trumpet in hand.

Of course he had forgotten the tip-up seats and, lowering himself rather heavily without looking, suddenly disappeared from sight. The ear-trumpet flew into the air and from subterranean depths came a very loud "damn."

He was quite unhurt, thank heavens, and, once re-established, said afterwards that he had greatly enjoyed the concert. A nice man.

GHOULIES AND GHOSTIES

Few of my friends will admit to an unqualified belief in the world of specters and banshees; things that go bump in the night. Most of them, however, read ghost stories from time to time, and have a creepy, unexplained incident or two to tell, given the right circumstances for the telling. These are mine; small in number but true, or, at least, I believe them to be.

I used often to visit the Bagots, Netta and Robin, at Levens Hall near Kendal.[11] Robin made harpsichords and they lived in a fine fourteenth-century house with a famous seventeenth-century topiary garden and a number of resident ghosts inside and out. They also had a impressive collection of King Charles' spaniels.

Late one night, after practicing alone for a concert the next day (the family had gone to bed in their wing of the house), I was putting out the lights prior to climbing the staircase to a small gallery that led down a narrow passage to the room I usually occupied, when I saw a little dog that had clearly escaped the nightly lock-in that went on belowstairs. It

---

11   They now live a few miles away in a sort of dower house. Their son Hal and his family occupy Levens.

ran ahead of me down the little passage whose door I quickly shut, pleased that it wouldn't be difficult to catch and restore to its fellows. At the end of this corridor there is a bathroom, Bishop Ken's bedroom to the left — he either died there or wrote there the hymn "Glory to Thee my God this night / for all the blessings of the light" sung to Tallis' famous canon — and a larger one to the right with a lovely carved fireplace. The dog was nowhere to be seen and after a while I gave up and went to bed, leaving Bishop Ken to sort it out.

At breakfast in the morning I apologized to Netta who was surprised to hear that one of her dogs had gone astray. "They were all there when I came to let them out. What did yours look like?" "Oh, like the rest, but black." "That's the ghost dog," was the reply as coffee was being poured, "ours now are all brown."

Come to think of it, there was no noise as it pattered up the wooden staircase.

On another occasion at Levens one wintry night I was playing in the sitting room at the other end of the central hall from the staircase and Bishop Ken. There was a roaring fire, only Robin and Netta were there and the dogs, noses down on the floor, dozing. Suddenly they all raised their heads, looked at something I couldn't see by the window behind the harpsichord, and slowly turned their heads in unison as if following someone across the room to the door. Then they settled down to their doze as if nothing had happened. Robin and Netta didn't even notice: an old friend I supposed, so I didn't mention it either.

My third encounter with such things happened on the Isle of Man.

I took the BBC Northern Symphony Orchestra (now the Philharmonic) there for a concert. We flew from Manchester to Ronaldsway airport and thence by coach to Douglas where there is a charming nineteenth-century theater, the Gaiety, virtually the only possible venue for a symphony orchestra on the island.

All Manx people treat the fairies, the little people, as part of their lives and with great respect. There is a fairy bridge which no one passes without raising their hat or wishing them "good-day".

The orchestra had been forewarned of this by John Bethell, our librarian who happened also to live on the Island, and the coach was to pass over the fairy bridge on the road between the airport and Douglas.

Most people did something polite as we crossed the tiny bridge but the first clarinet, a disgruntled sort of fellow, put his head out and said something rudely alliterative about the fairies.

We arrived at the theater and, as we assembled on the stage for a brief rehearsal, there was a wail from the mocker. "Where's my clarinet?" Where indeed, it was nowhere to be found.

I can't remember what arrangements were made to provide a substitute instrument for the concert but I do know his own clarinet was found in its case on the tarmac at Manchester airport later that afternoon.

LOONY TUNES

On one tour of Canada, in 1970, coming back to London from the World's Fair in Japan we, the English Chamber Orchestra and I, found ourselves committed by an incompetent agent who, presumably, had not been able to find us a more suitable date, to a concert in the middle of that vast country at a university town called Brandon. We drove, I remember, for five hours across flat plains — could it have been from Winnipeg? — before eventually arriving at the campus to discover that not only were we hardly expected but it was the day the academic year began and the Vice-Chancellor was giving an evening reception for the entire university. We were not part of the entertainment.

To make some sort of audience the local old-age homes and, I believe, selected inmates from the Brandon asylum were invited. But the response had been poor and in an auditorium normally seating two thousand we had a public of, maybe, two hundred, mostly over the age of seventy.

There was nothing for it but to play the concert and leave as soon as possible. The first obstacle to this was the tendency of the audience to applaud after every movement, sometimes even in silences within the movements which, of course, slowed things down. At the end of the first half there was to come Britten's *Les Illuminations* and Bob Tear, our soloist, rightly observed that if they applauded after every song we should be there for the night.

**With the ECO
c. 1982**

CREDIT: Clive
Barda, London

I thereupon addressed our small but lively audience, suggesting that they save their plaudits until after the sequence of nine songs was completed. They seemed to understand and we arrived at the half-way point of the cycle uneventfully and uninterrupted. This last song of the first part, "*Marine*", ended with a long-held high A from the tenor and a resounding pizzicato chord from the orchestra; whereupon an old crone, whom some of the orchestra had identified as the ringleader for the applause, leaped to her feet and let out a screech that might have woken Rimbaud (author of Britten's text) himself.

After the song there followed a quiet orchestral interlude but it had never before sounded like this. The orchestra shook, entries were haphazard and notes, hardly seen through tears of hysteria, were certainly not those Ben had written. I had no idea how to get things straight, being no better off than the rest, so we ploughed our way through it getting increasingly out of control.

To make matters worse Bob Tear slipped on a set of toy Dracula's teeth that he must have bought earlier that day for one of his children and, turning to the orchestra, gave us an awesome smile as we wrecked Ben's Interlude. He then turned back to the audience and sang the rest of the cycle with them in.

That kept them quiet.[12]

THE GODS GO A-CAMPING

The plot of *La Calisto*, the seventeenth-century opera by Cavalli which I reconstructed for performances at Glyndebourne in 1970,[13] came from Ovid's *Metamorphoses*, those lively escapades of Jove in search of relief

---

12 RL has another souvenir of this same trip, in the memory of his dining alone in Tokyo one evening after one of the Festival concerts. A waiter brought him a note to the effect that "I was there this evening at your concert, and enjoyed it very much. Won't you join me for a drink? (signed) Marlene Dietrich." He did, and recalls that not only was she entirely mesmerizing, but in person more beautiful than she seemed in any of her films. (Ed.)

13 Musical aspects of the 1970 Glyndebourne production of *La Calisto* have been addressed previously—see Chapter II Section §2, for example. The present memoir adds a few details of a more personal nature. (Ed.)

for an itchy libido wherein he becomes a swan, a bull, a shower of rain... anything that works.

In order to satisfy his lust for Calisto, one of Diana's virtuous nymphs, he even assumes the person of the Moon-Goddess herself, for whom her votive hand-maidens would do anything, however unexpected or surprising.

The story echoes the ambivalence found in most people as to the male or femaleness of their natures, and seemed particularly apposite to these revelatory times. The witty, salacious complications created by the librettist, Faustini, encouraged exploration of the theme, not to speak of the promptings to be found in Cavalli's musical manuscript.

When the part of *Giove* becomes that of *Giove in Diana*, the vocal line which had, naturally, been in the male, bass-clef, changes to soprano, giving rise to the conjecture that whoever performed Jove for the first time in 1651 could sing equally well as a bass-baritone or mezzo-soprano in falsetto.

The idea was not that implausible to anyone who had heard the great counter-tenor, Alfred Deller, sing "There is a green hill far away" starting at the bottom of the bass register and, by omitting to descend a fourth at the beginning of the third line, slowly ascend, verse by verse, through baritone, tenor, counter-tenor and way on up to soprano. It was a trick he was prone to perform at parties.

I had often heard Ugo Trama — an Italian bass-baritone who had appeared in several operas at Glyndebourne — warming up in a good, strong falsetto with quality and flexibility in the sound; an odd quirk but opportune. He was delighted and intrigued by the suggestion that he should play the dual role and appear — for half the performance — in drag.

The rest of the cast was stunning.

Janet Baker agreed to sing the real Diana, and I added two beautiful arias from other Cavalli operas to make the part worthy of her talents. As rehearsals progressed, and the implications of sexual confusion spread through the opera, her performance stood apart shining with a moonlit purity.

Hugues Cuénod was extremely funny as Diana's crusty old attendant nymph, Linfea. The comic servant travesty role was commonly found in early Venetian opera, obviously a popular turn rather in the manner of the Dame in British pantomime or Klinger in *M.A.S.H.*

A little satyr who eventually leads the assault on Linfea's somewhat reluctant virginity was played by a charming, topless little mezzo, Janet Hughes. So was the theme of sexual ambivalence furthered.

Ileana Cotrubas sang the innocent Calisto, one of the few "straight" parts in the opera. On stage she had a natural air of pathos and the lovely purity of her voice suited the part perfectly. Eventually it was all recorded and perhaps, one day, it may be heard again.

Endimione, for whom the real Diana conceived an illicit passion, was sung by James Bowman, the successor to Alfred Deller, whose countertenor voice emanating from a handsome, virile body further added to the confusion.

The wood creatures, Pane and Sylvano, portrayed by Federico Davia and Owen Brannigan, were unmistakeably male.

As we rehearsed we all became caught up in the underlying themes, serious and comic, that developed under the superb guidance of Peter Hall.

Working with Peter has been one of the greatest joys of my professional life and, having known each other since undergraduate days, there was no mistaking, after a couple of weeks, the sense of unrest at the way the opera was shaping.

To allay these apprehensions we decided to have a rough and ready run-through on stage with such scenery and costumes as were available and to open the rehearsal to the entire company who were, in any case, curious about this new three-hundred year old opera.

If laughter were the criterion, it couldn't have been a greater success. You could hardly hear the music at times for the howls of pleasure, especially raucous whenever *Giove in Diana* made a pass at Calisto. Even the serious moments were undermined by sniggers for it became hard to know which was which.

In the pit my heart sank and I slunk away at the end without speaking to anyone. For my money the audience response had nothing to do with the beautiful music I had sensed in Cavalli's score. As *Saturday Night Live* or *That Was the Week That Was* it would have made a million, but as a work of art it wouldn't stand a chance.

Back in the quiet of my rented house I told myself it didn't matter; I was expecting more of the piece that was there. That went on for most of the night until the beginning of a solution began to appear and at 6 a.m. I rang Peter in his rented house to discover that he hadn't slept either and was thinking much along the same lines.

It was clear that *Giove in Diana* couldn't be sung by *Giove*. It had to be sung by the real *Diana* who must assume the character of the lustful Jove within her own body, costume and voice. It also required consummate acting and singing skills but then, as we agreed on the telephone, we did have Janet singing *Diana* and if anyone could...

By 7 a.m. we were both at Glyndebourne talking it over with George Christie and Moran Caplat who were, perhaps, a little reluctant to abandon such a sure-fire laugh-in as they had witnessed the previous day, but saw, nevertheless, the rightness of our conclusions.

The next thing was to ask Janet who had returned to London after the rehearsal. It was now 7:30 a.m. but Janet was up and had also, it appeared, not enjoyed yesterday's run-through. Being a practical North Country girl she asked for half an hour to look at the part and consider the problem. At 8 a.m. she rang back and said she could and would do it.

We now had to tell Ugo Trama and deprive him of half his role and the most obviously successful half at that which he was enormously enjoying. Ugo couldn't have behaved better or more generously and I will always be grateful to him for his understanding of the situation.

From that day forward *Calisto* took off and became one of the most remarkable of Glyndebourne's productions. Janet was incredibly moving as the real *Diana*, tremulously on the brink of giving in to her love for Endimion and, with the single extra prop of a cane, amazingly strong and lustful as the figure of herself impersonated by Jove. The confusion of poor little Calisto wavering between the two Janets worked wonderfully whereas before it had been bawdily distasteful. The plight of Linfea, played with superlative taste by Cuénod, came to have that quality of sadness that is part of all great comedy.

Even *Giove* in the end, and at the end, came out of it for the better as he took Calisto up into the heavens to become *Ursa minor*, the little bear — a hard, chilly price for her to pay for Jove's infidelity to his wife, Juno.

You even felt a little sorry for him as well as for Calisto; the one suffering for his insatiable appetites, the other for her innocence.

It was truly a magical evening in the theater.

UNCERTAINTIES

Talking of Alfred Deller, the first counter-tenor to make an international career since the days of the *castrati* (which Alfred certainly was not): there was the wonderful story of Beecham encountering Alfred for the first time. Not much of a church-goer the renowned conductor was, of course, unaware of the great traditions of the English Cathedrals where male-altos had sung since choirs began to sing.

Beecham had taken over someone else's program at the last minute, which included a Purcell *Welcome Ode* and, with it, Alfred Deller.

The surprise on Sir Thomas's face at the first notes was evident, but good manners prevailed and the rehearsal passed without comment.

At the orchestra break, after a hurried conversation with the concertmaster, Beecham went up to Deller.

"Mr. Deller, it was a most interesting experience to hear you sing."

"Thank you, Sir Thomas."

"Mr. Deller, I understand that you are married."

"Yes, that is so, Sir Thomas."

"Mr. Deller, I understand you have a son."

"That is so, Sir Thomas, and another child is soon expected."

Lengthy pause.

"Mr. Deller, I'm very relieved to hear it."

I was not present at that exchange but, in my student days, sat behind two elderly ladies at a recital Alfred gave in King's Chapel, Cambridge.

They were obviously very impressed musically but curious and uncertain how to express it.

"What a beautiful song...."

"Wasn't it just."

"...and so beautifully sung... rather high."

"Yes, hasn't Mr. Deller such an unusual voice."

"Indeed I thought so. I wondered a little...."

"Yes, well I heard he has a son at St. John's."

"Oh!! ... does he?—he certainly is a fine figure of a man... with that beard and everything."

"Yes, he grew that to conceal the scar."

"Oh."

There was absolute silence between them for at least two minutes.

LONDON, OCTOBER 1972

A great occasion at the Theatre Royal, Haymarket was planned to celebrate the 90th birthday of Sybil Thorndike. Everyone in the theater who was not working that evening seemed to be involved and those that were came on to the party afterwards. By midnight virtually three complete generations of actors were gathered together and, as someone observed, a single bomb would have destroyed the entire British theater.

The first half of the program was a mixture of individual tributes culminating in Margot Fonteyn dancing the Shadow dance from Freddie Ashton's *Ondine*.

The second half was a most engaging pot-pourri of theatrical memorabilia compiled by Dadie Rylands. I was there because Sybil had asked me to play some Bach on the harpsichord. All the actors sat in a semicircle, stepping forward for their various pieces. There was Wendy Hiller, Celia Johnson, Larry Olivier, Rachel Kempson, Paul Scofield, Irene Worth, Alec Guiness, Joan Plowright, Gwen Francon-Davies, Peggy Ashcroft: the odd man out was Edith Evans, nearly as old as Sybil, doing less in the theater now and jealous.

She was to read a marvelous description from Mrs. Siddons' journal of learning the part of Lady Macbeth late one night when on tour at that lovely eighteenth-century theater in Richmond, Yorkshire, lately saved and restored.

In their everyday clothes everyone read their bit at the afternoon run-through and variously well. All, that is, except Edith who was dreadful. She mumbled, confused her pages, stumbled over words and was generally incomprehensible.

As she came back to her seat, just in the neck of the harpschord, she whispered to me in a mournful voice everyone could hear, "They'll never do this for me." It was true, they wouldn't have and the knowledge of it corroded her spirit.

The run-through over, there were drinks and a great deal of gossip, mostly in the wings, until everyone became conscious of a commotion.

Edith's voice, always powerful, could be heard still on stage in a crescendo of agitation. You have to imagine her playing Lady Bracknell for the sound which, in any case, wasn't far from her ordinary speech. As an actress she was a master at varying the inflection; the tonal quality of her speech remained fairly constant.

"It's no good, no good Binkie (Beaumont, the theatrical impresario who had arranged the whole thing), no good at all. I can't do it. I'm too old and I live in the country now. It's no good. I shall go away. I can't do it: you mustn't expect it."

Eyebrows were raised — Edith was at it again — and the noise of the chatter rose once more to cover her complaint.

But Edith did do it.

She must have gone back to her hotel room and rehearsed and rehearsed for, while many of the others, like Wendy Hiller, were only as good as their run-through, or less so, Edith gave a reading that chilled the whole theater.

We were all in Richmond with Mrs. Siddons sitting alone in an upper room at her lodgings learning those frightening lines of Lady Macbeth until they scared her so that she fled down the stairs pursued by the rustle of her skirts, the ghosts of Banquo, Duncan and many others of our own making, to fling herself down beside her sleeping husband, shaking with fear.

It was unforgettable.

GOOD HEALTH

In January 1973 there was an exhibition of Duncan Grant's paintings at the Fermoy Gallery, Kings Lynn, possibly the last in his life for he was 88 that year.[14]

Queen Elizabeth, the Queen Mother, an admirer of his work was to attend the opening and had lent two remarkable paintings of St. Paul's Cathedral from her collection. So it was rather a grand affair.

Ruth Fermoy had a house-party at near-by Hillington where she owned a lovely vicarage and was kind enough to include me in it together with Duncan Grant and one or two friends of his.

At dinner the night before I was asked by Ruth to find out what people would have to drink and was surprised to find that D.G. wanted a dry martini in the American style — straight up. Not only one did he have but three and before we went in to dinner appeared very sprightly indeed. I remember what a beautiful old man he was with flowing pure-white hair and almost transparent skin.

Dinner began and the martinis took their toll, for D.G., after toying with some soup, fell fast asleep sitting motionless, upright in his chair. Our hostess told the butler not to disturb him. D.G.'s place was cleared and we went on with the rest of dinner talking as usual until, towards the end, all attention was suddenly focused on the silent guest.

Without opening his eyes, he stretched out his extraordinarily delicate right hand, reached forward to an imaginary wine glass which he raised to his lips. He drank from it, appearing to savor and swallow the invisible wine and, with infinite care, restored the non-existent glass to its original spot, settling back then into his former position.

At the end of the dinner one of his friends helped him upstairs and the next morning, right as rain, he came to the opening and charmed everybody especially the Royal patron.

It was odd that back in the sitting-room after dinner no-one mentioned the incident. It had seemed the most normal thing in the world.

---

14   RL participated in at least half a dozen Kings Lynn Festivals, in the colorful medieval-Georgian town situated on the northwest Norfolk Coast in off the North Sea. See CHRONOLOGY below. (Ed.)

Of course one would need a glass of wine, however spiritual, sitting with company that long.

INSTANT INDIGNATION

Clifford Curzon was a most remarkable man, a true thinker of musical thoughts which he could translate into effective pianism. Febrile, affectionate and gentle he had, nevertheless, an amazing ability to work himself very quickly into a highly agitated condition. It was rather like pouring hot water on to dried coffee crystals, a sort of instant indignation which dissipated as rapidly as it appeared, accompanied by quite startling color changes.

He was very kind to the young and, in my early days, he gladly came for very little to play Mozart concertos with my newly-formed orchestra and inspiring encounters they were.

Later, when I became Musical Director of the BBC Northern (later Philharmonic) Orchestra in Manchester, I rang Clifford and asked if he would help me start it all by coming up for a well-rehearsed Emperor Concerto at one of our first public concerts together at the Free Trade Hall.[15] He not only agreed but offered to come up at his own expense for an extra rehearsal during the week.

This was duly arranged and on a Wednesday morning he arrived at Piccadilly Station, was met, taken to the Midland Hotel where he rested after a good luncheon at the French restaurant (he cared and knew about good food and wine) before the rehearsal at six.

Needless to say, the orchestra wasn't very pleased to be asked to rehearse in the evening but that was the only possible time. Nor did they much relish spending three hours, even with Clifford, on a concerto they'd played a million times.

Six o'clock on a very grey January evening at the Milton Hall, a dreadfully bleak little place long since abandoned for a smart new studio, there we were but no Clifford. He had, it appeared, refused a BBC ride from

---

15   Given 29 January 1974. (Ed.)

the hotel which was only just at the top of the hill, preferring to walk for the good of his health. He should not have been permitted to do so.

There was nothing to do but start rehearsing the orchestral opening while scouts went out to find him. After an hour, when we had just about run out of *tuttis*, the door of the studio was suddenly flung open and there stood Clifford, scarlet, disheveled and sweating, his indignation at himself, at life, at anyone was at *ristretto* level.

I believe he meant to apologise to me, to the orchestra for his lateness and his stupidity at getting lost between the Midland Hotel and the Milton Hall (only Clifford could have done it) but what he actually said at the top of his voice was, "Ray! What a f--g awful city this is."

Since upwards of seventy per cent of the orchestra came from Manchester and loved it, the remark was not generally interpreted as an apology, so I called a break.

It says a lot for the resiliance of the Northern temperament that the second half of the rehearsal intrigued and involved everyone once the heat had been dissipated, normal color restored and proper explanations made. After a wonderfully intense hour and a half we parted best of friends and all fired-up about the concert to come. So well had it gone that we decided a brush-up on the day would suffice to bring it to life again. This also gave me more time for the other work on the program, the long and difficult choral symphony Number 13 by Shostakovich "Baba Yar".

On the day of the concert it took up the first half of the morning rehearsal, leaving plenty of time for the concert. Clifford had come up the night before and spent several hours with the piano technician perfecting the touch and balance of the Steinway.

"No need to play it all" was the agreed view and we began with the first strong chord on the orchestra, one that because of its unusual scoring and lack of a fifth in the triad can sound wierdly ineffective. We had balanced it carefully in the Wednesday rehearsal; they remembered and the sound of that chord was also something to remember, as were the magnificent arpeggios and figurations that followed from Clifford, at the piano.

We should have stopped but there was no way that we could have done so. The fires had been lit and there was no putting them out.

There followed perhaps the best Emperor concerto I've ever been involved in. No-one heard it except us and the Director of BBC music in the north, Ernest Warburton, and his secretary sitting in the hall in lonely state.

At the end of it no-one said anything and we all went our ways quietly as if not daring to break the spell.

Come the evening after lunch, a walk and a rest we dressed and assembled at the hall but it was all quite different. Clifford was pacing up and down wearing his frayed, fingerless gloves intended to keep his hands warm but usually a sign of nervousness. He was getting redder by the minute and could be heard muttering to anyone who would listen "I can't think why Ray asked me up here to play. It's only a fill-in anyway and they've all come (full-house because of him I should add) to hear the Shostakovich. They don't want to hear me. Quite unimportant. I shouldn't have agreed... f--g awful city; never again."

Eventually we got him on the stage, but a rapturous reception did nothing for him, nor did our first chord which was not only ill-balanced but out of tune. There followed a series of arpeggios half in E flat, half in E major as Clifford's fingers slipped off the keys. There followed the worst performance of the Emperor I've ever been associated with.

In retrospect I felt sorry for all of us and very sad for the audience. They'd missed the good one.

Later on Clifford came on tour with us to Germany and Austria playing the Emperor many times and always to great acclaim. But it was never as good as that morning in the empty Free Trade Hall.

HUGUES CUÉNOD

The English became so fond of him that they liked to think he was mostly theirs. His successful career ranged over all of Europe and America but his blend of urbane sophistication and modest charm seemed particularly to appeal to audiences at the British end of the channel tunnel. The fact that he had an English mother may have had something to do with it, though he is, in fact, Swiss, coming from a distinguished family who owned the *Chateau de Lully* overlooking Lake Leman near Morges where they spent the summer months. There were vineyards which produced a pleasantly undistinguished white wine and a handsome 18th-century house which made an elegantly assured background for Hugues and his painter sister, Ninette, in their formative years.

There was a gentle, amused confidence in everything he did from the earliest years when he was one of the Boys with the Green Carnation in Noël Coward's *Bitter Sweet* to his debut at the Metropolitan Opera aged nearly 90 as Don Curzio in *Figaro*.

The sensitivity and innate musicianship of his singing recommended themselves to Nadia Boulanger who engaged him in 1937 to sing in the remarkable Monterverdi recordings that heralded the revival of interest in that composer's music.

He was the first to admit that his voice was not remarkable for its size or quality, but it was unmistakeable and he learned the art of singing. Possibly the fact that he had to focus so intently on vocal techniques gave an exrtra quality to the master classes he frequently gave in later years. He helped and advised countless young singers.

He was that rare creature, a truly civilized tenor able to go anywhere and mix with every sort of person in or out of music, inspiring respect and affection with his zest for life and the humor he found in the living of it. A true cosmpolitan.

Stravinsky engaged him as the auctioneer, Sellem, in 1951 for the first performance of *The Rake's Progress*, a role he repeated with great success at Glyndebourne where he appeared in more seasons than any other singer. As the reference books remind us, he also sang in Stravinsky's *Threni* (1958) and *A Sermon, a Narrative and a Prayer* (1962); after which he turned almost exclusively to baroque music, founding an *Ensemble baroque* in Lausanne. There were also outstanding recordings of lute-songs, of Couperin, and of the Evangelist in Bach's *St Matthew Passion*.

The funniest Basilio in *Figaro*, he was a wonderfully debauched Liberto in *Poppea* and his impersonation of the crabby old nymph Linfea in *La Calisto* as well as the sorcerer Erice in *L'Ormindo* were miracles of high comedy and good taste.

Everyone will have their own especial memories of him in the theater: the astrologer in *Coq d'Or*, the Captain in *Wozzeck*, the dancing master in

Ariadne, the Cock in *The Cunning Little Vixen,* M. Triquet in *Eugene Onegin.*

Whatever he undertook he sang well, and demonstrated his remarkable power to convey musical and theatrical veracity. It was the same in his concert life, though in England we saw less of him in recital than in opera.

Now in his nineties (he was born in 1902), Hugues Cuénod has lived a fruitful and successful life, giving much joy to his public and still more to the close friends who have loved him.

GOOD MANNERS

William Walton's first symphony ends with an impressive series of very loud, isolated chords.

On one occasion,[16] conducting the work before a packed Newcastle Town Hall with the BBC Northern Symphony Orchestra of which I was then music director, I well remember arriving at those last chords with particular zest and élan for it had been an especially good performance and everyone in the orchestra sensed it.

The excitement was evidently shared by the audience for in the silence following the first of the final crashes a man's voice shouted a loud "bravo". The next crash came quickly upon it, and elicited a rather surprised but very audible "Oh" from the same voice. Another crash and it called out — by way, I suppose, of genial apology — "Sorry!"

There were several chords to go but, as I recall, we could hardly play them.

It was a live broadcast but there's probably a tape of it at Broadcasting House in London.

MY NEW HOME IN INDIANAPOLIS

I moved across from England to the U.S. in 1976. There followed some eight years of immensely enjoyable traveling about America guest-con-

---

16   22 January 1975. (Ed.)

ducting with the intention both of discovering this great country for myself and also of finding out if I had done the right thing in removing from my own country. I had, and my ever-increasing delight in the freshness and skills of the American orchestra has only confirmed this.

Naturally I often fell to thinking about the structure and condition of the symphony in America (so different from that in Europe) with all its great qualities, as well as its less viable ones, given the present trend and the future economic condition of music. There was one odd and strikingly consistent feature: it seemed to me that most American orchestras, even the biggest, aspired to be bigger, as if volume of sound and the capability of performing the most gargantuan repertoire should be the goals of any successful organization. The smaller orchestras seemed to sense themselves restricted, and somehow less good, on that account alone. Their music directors spoke wistfully of one day being able to perform Strauss's *Also Sprach Zarathustra* or Mahler's Second Symphony.

After the wandering years, I was fortunate enough to be invited by Leonard Slatkin to become principal guest conductor of the St. Louis Symphony, an orchestra I had quite often conducted and liked and admired very much. The closeness of contact, the involvement, and the admiration increased so that with these stronger ties came also the desire to accept, once more, some greater responsibility. Apart from the English Chamber Orchestra, I had been for seven years principal conductor of the BBC Philharmonic and had enjoyed every minute of it. Now, after the intervening years, I began, rather like an old hen, to feel broody.

In my travels, I had once been to Indianapolis where I had had a very good experience with the orchestra. There had been some little talk about my being interested in the idea of taking them on. However, without forming any wider assessment of the potential, I declined because the city seemed, outwardly, almost moribund, and the orchestra was playing (but not rehearsing regularly) in a hall some distance outside the city. Fine as the hall was as a building, it had very little of the intimacy needed for music to communicate. An elegant, concrete place for lectures, conventions, and degree presentations was my assessment of it.

Some years later, I was invited back to their new home, the Circle Theatre; a renovation wonderfully done. The orchestra had its very own hall with administrative offices in a connecting building. Furthermore, it was in the very center of the city which, it turned out, had entirely revivified itself. The city was teeming with life, night and day, and abounding with a spirit that the elders of ancient Greece would have admired.

How these miracles came about must be left to the historians of Indianapolis. The place was and is transformed and continues to grow. I dare say a lot of the credit belongs to Senator Richard Lugar during his time as mayor, and to his successors, but also to an onset of what can best be described as public-spiritedness. The latter was graphically described to me by the director of one of Indianapolis' major banks as a distinct, observable phenomenon which had caught up civic leaders, private individuals, commerce, and industry alike, all aided and abetted by the profoundly civic-minded Lilly family and foundation. It was a true renaissance. One felt it in the air and saw it in the streets.

I think the orchestra sensed it too, for they were even more enjoyable to work with than before. I came to the understanding that, apart from being a most attractive group of people, they were exactly the right sort of orchestra in the right place. They were 88 strong: triple woodwind, five horns, three trumpets, three trombones, tuba, timpani, three percussion, harp and keyboard, sixteen first violins, fourteen seconds, ten violas, ten cellos, and eight basses; the exact numbers that Beethoven was used to in the latter half of his life and that persisted through the early, middle, and late Romantics until the inflated days of the later nineteenth century. They had a full-time, 52-week contract as well.

The Circle Theatre seats just under 2,000 — about the capacity of the best European concert halls — with an acoustic well-designed by Chris Jaffé. It is the sort of place that embraces you when you sit listening to music. The decor and color scheme only serve to enhance that feeling of welcome. Here was just the situation that seemed to offer the antidote to the American orchestra's obsessive desire to increase in size. The numbers, the theater, the city, the circumstances, the excellent management under the strong leadership of Bob Jones, and the evident support and involvement of their board all added up to an acceptance of the invitation to become the music director without really having to make a decision.

Also, it required little further analysis to come to the conclusion that all of these factors could combine to establish us as what virtually no other American orchestra claims to be: a first-rate *Classical* orchestra. We are ideally suited to the repertoire that will let us develop into a stylistically conscious ensemble, capable of inhabiting the world of Beethoven as well as responding to the different stylistic demands of Brahms, Mendelssohn, Tchaikovsky, Shostakovich, Lutoslawski – any music from the late-eighteenth century to the present day written for an orchestra of our size, involving disciplines in playing that would develop our classical approach to the fullest extent of the meaning of that word.

Of course it would mean virtually abandoning Mahler, most of Strauss, much of Berg, Messiaen, Scriabin, Respighi; all the self-indulgent, late-nineteenth/early-twentieth century composers who used huge orchestras to paint massive, splashy canvases.[17]

There is, I'm glad to say, a great deal of wonderful music left, and the understanding and interest in these ideas on the part of the orchestra, so far in our collaboration (1989), has been quite extraordinary. They are an extremely gifted body of players, and working with them has made me very glad to be alive. God willing, I've got at least a few more years of music-making still in me. As far as this "artist's life" goes, I really think I have come to my best, happiest years yet.[18]

REFLECTIONS I – SIX OF THE BEST

To be asked to list the six people who have meant most in your life and give the reasons is an impossible request, but, once made and made in the context of preparing an essentially autobiographical volume such as this, then not to respond becomes as difficult as to do so.

---

17 The author's long-term commitment to music of the baroque and classical eras – and to modestly scaled ensembles such as the English Chamber Orchestra – is of course consistent with these views. At the same time it should be noted that RL has not entirely excluded "large-scale" works from his repertory: e.g. Rachmaninoff, Sibelius, Shostakovich. Moreover, however modestly-scaled the orchestra may be, surely *Messiah* and Bach's *Mass* in b and *St John* and *St Matthew Passions* are not works of a small dimension! In the end it may be that this important issue (especially in an economic context) is less about "size" alone than about elephantinism. (Ed.)

18 First published in *Keynote* for April, 1989. In September 1993 the author began his seventh season with the Indianapolis Symphony Orchestra. (Ed.)

I would have to exclude parents and immediate family from consideration as they are clearly so much part of one's make-up as to render their
relationship to it indescribable by the person concerned and their influences only discernible by others.

¶Mentors must rank high in the list, and there have been many whom
I have valued greatly. Of them unquestionably the most important was
a little-known man, Hubert Middleton. He produced nothing significant
except people; a few papers to the Royal Musical Association and a small
number of modest religious compositions. (He does have a distinguished
poet as a son.) He wasn't a great practical musician although a perfectly
able player of the organ—he had been organist of Truro and Ely
Cathedrals before I met him. Perhaps his most important public work was
to be a prime mover in the establishment of a Music Tripos at Cambridge
which raised the dignity of musical studies to that of an Honours Degree, whereas previously it was of minor status, a Bachelor of Music degree, that counted for very little in academic terms. He succeeded with
the University where many more celebrated than he had failed before.

But it was as a promoter of learning and a giver of inspiration to those
he chose to adopt as pupils that he was unsurpassed. I was lucky enough
to be one of those and among the first generations of undergraduates
who read music as a Tripos and could hold up their heads in academic
circles thereafter as having acquired a properly recognized degree
through the disciplines of music.

He once remarked, after patiently listening to a jejune student tirade
of mine either for or against some composer, 'you know, Raymond, as a
professional, it will not be your business to like or dislike any music—it
is enough to be aware and to know about it." I don't know that I believed
him then, but I now realize it to be true. Music eventually becomes a way
of life and a marvellously gratifying one. No-one who enjoys living
would ever think in terms of liking or disliking life, so why do so about
music? Certainly some aspects of it are more or less agreeable, but the
serious consideration of it is removed to altogether less trivial planes. Almost the most gratifying thing about music is that the experience of it
grows more engrossing as time passes. A good work is more satisfying

to perform now than it was twenty years ago, and there is no reason to suppose that the process will come to an end.

For all his distinction and intellect, the fact that Hubert was a musician meant that it took years for him to be offered a Fellowship at Trinity. Sir Charles Villiers Stanford never was (and minded it very much) though he was Professor of Music in the University as well as organist of Trinity and widely celebrated as a composer. (The College was glad enough nevertheless later to hang the great portrait of him by Orpen in Hall.)

Because of music's new status I was offered a Fellowship at Trinity as well as a University lectureship in order to persuade me back to Cambridge as Hubert's successor: something I gladly accepted aware somewhat of justifying his faith in me and the dignity of the subject, and had a wonderfully enjoyable second period at Cambridge as a result.

Hubert taught me so many things: how to work, how to think clearly about music, how to manage with little sleep, how and when to compromise and when not, how to make music part of the larger process of living, how to make mind and heart function at the same time.

He always expected so much of his pupils, much more than we thought we were capable of and we strove not to disappoint for we loved him.

¶Leo de Rothschild has been a friend for over forty-five years, certainly one of the most important people in my life.[19] He is, I suppose, as close to a brother without the psychological or emotional complications that family relationships entail. We have spent a very great deal of time together, have talked and laughed so much together, have occasionally been sad and stern but mostly optimistic, tolerant and enthusiastic about life, always mutually supportive, so much so that it's really past assessing. Leo is there and seems always to have been so.

I've been welcomed into his family as if I were a part of it. I always go to him for advice. I don't always take it, but there's hardly been a move

---

19 Leopold de Rothschild served as Chairman of the English Chamber Orchestra and Music Society, having been closely associated with the organization since its foundation in 1960. (Ed.)

in my life which I haven't discussed with him and greatly valued his response. At the very least it has always helped me make up my mind.

I believe his concern and work for music in England over the years, although brought up, trained and having practised all his professional life as a banker, has been far greater than many others who have received much more public notice. Most of him prefers it that way but his friends who love him and admire what he has done have regrets about it and would have him more widely honored. It is, of course, not too late.

But it is his immensely valued close friendship that makes him unquestionably one of the six.

¶The third on the list is not so much an individual as a generation — of theater directors, all of whom were at University in my time; all of whom became friends; all of whom I've worked with frequently and profited from not just because they are all gifted in their different ways but because being in their company helped me to formulate and confirm my approach and attitude toward the performance of music; one I perceive to be similar to theirs.

Peter Hall, Peter Wood, Peter Brook, Tony Richardson — the generation list is longer but these four have been the most important to me and influenced me the most.

Their personal achievements are not here relevant and are, in any case, well known and highly esteemed. Their significance in my life lies in their approach to theater which may not be so widely understood, at least in this way.

However different their styles and responses to a piece, their concern has always appeared to me to be identical. They ask first the question, what is true about the work, what is the truth about it that can be seen at this point in time and how may this truth be best expressed in terms that are relevant to present-day audiences? As they, the audiences and the times change so will the response but the question remains the same.

The highly acclaimed *Midsummer Night's Dream* that Peter Hall directed at Stratford in 1959 (I composed the music and Lila de Nobili the sets) could never make the same statement again today; neither could Peter Brook's production later on in white light and trapezes. But both were true in their time.

It is one of the reasons why our lives as interpreters are being constantly refreshed.

Aware of their own talents that generation certainly was (the past tense is for Tony who, sadly, is no longer with us), but never, with any of them, did you have the impression that they were making theater as a self-indulgence, as if their egos were more important that the text they were re-presenting. The quest for meaning was paramount and no-one could begin without having discovered it.

So many young directors, particularly opera-directors in America, seem to say as they present images each more startling than the last, "I see *Charley's Aunt* as a Freudian tragedy, or *Macbeth* as a Feydean farce, or *Streetcar* as a Fragonard painting", whereas what they are really saying is, how can I so indulge myself as to startle the public, shock the critics and, by doing so, make my reputation. It becomes a sort of public, theatrical masturbation.

The four of the generation that meant so much to me were very different and all very different from each other.

The more uncertain, weak and inexpert the text, provided the inner content and impulse was strong the more it would involve Peter Brook whose intelligence and creativity was sparked off by that sort of frailty. Peter Wood had always a great ability to shore up weakness and provide a brilliant overall concept making pieces better and more effective than they were. Tony was quixotic and, being a champagne socialist, was drawn to subjects that had a social message whose truth, beyond the politics, he could illuminate better than most. Peter Hall was best at the great texts already formed but needing a strong interpretive intelligence to bring them together, sweep away hoary, inherited traditions and marshall the power that lies within them.

The attitudes I perceive in all four, the quest for truth without intrusion of self, the finding out of what the text means to us now, is something I profoundly believe in and have translated into everything I do in music. I have no time for the pretentious self-indulgence that proclaims "*My* Beethoven, *My* Mozart, *My* Tchaikovsky".

Of course when a good mind and a strong personality interprets any work of art, however modestly, there is an intensity of identification which is bound to cause an imprint, but once it become purposefully self-conscious then count me out.

¶Another collective "most important person" must be the society I found myself in at Cambridge between 1948 and 1952. The magic of that place always works as I saw on many occasions after returning there as a don but my undergraduate years were unusual in that we were all older than the usual student intake because of military service and were eager to bursting point for what Cambridge had to offer.

I had come from a comfortable, middle-class home, blessed with excellent teachers in most subjects but particularly in music in which I had sought out the most varied experiences I could find: piano, viola, singing, composition, harpsichord, conducting, accompanying — all at varying levels, and had received great encouragement and some local success without really focusing or knowing what I wanted to be successful at.

Then came three years in the R.A.F. and my musical and intellectual life was on hold. Those years, however, provided many other experiences and I met a range of people, many of them stunning examples of the human race, whom I would otherwise never have encountered.

Then came Cambridge and the company of people who really educated me and became my life-long companions.

They rank very high in the "most important" stakes.

¶The other collective group that must be considered among those who have meant the most in my life are some/many of the artists I have worked with.

In casting about for reasons why some so strongly qualify, while others do not, I came to the conclusion that it was not directly connected with talent, although that must surely play some part in it all.

There have been some immensely gifted and very celebrated artists who have meant nothing, even less than nothing in my life, and some immensely gifted and very celebrated artists who have meant the world to me and enriched my musical life more than I can say.

You can tell the difference between them primarily by the effect they have. Working with those who mean the most, you come out of the experience uplifted, enlivened, enriched, excited, a full person with your

The author from one to three, 1928 – 1930
(flanked in lower right by brother & other friend)

Ernest Read Summer School, 1940s – RL principal viola
(4th row from top and 7th in from left – bow in hand)

At Cambridge c. 1950

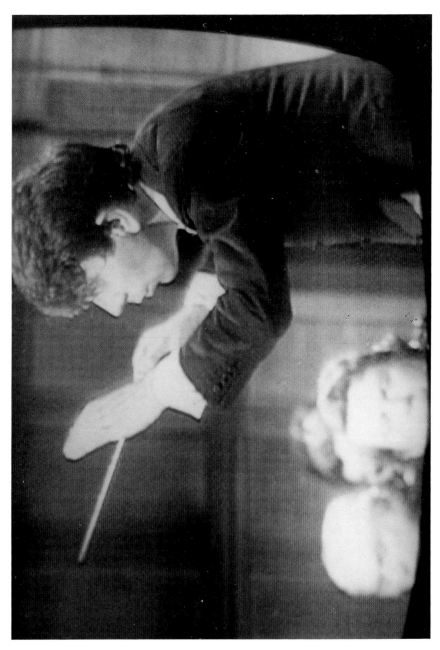

On television, c. 1960

At Hamilton Terrace Garden, c. 1960
CREDIT: Clive Barda, London

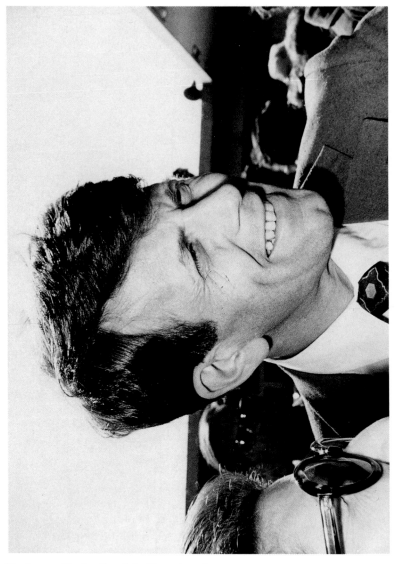

On tour with the English Chamber Orchestra – Buenos Aires, 1968

With Bela Siki, Leeds Piano Competition jury – 1969

Rehearsal, English Chamber Orchestra – Birmingham, 1971
CREDIT: Mike Evans

Rehearsing with the ECO at Birmingham
CREDIT: Mike Evans

With the ECO, 1971   CREDIT: Mike Evans

Upper photo: RL receives 1973 Audio Award – previous winner Neville Marriner looking on at center.
Lower: With Derek Hill painting – Northern Ireland, late 1970s

RL, Ann Murray at Aix en Provence, 1978 (Handel's *Alcina*, also featuring Teresa Berganza & other soloists, chorus, Scottish Chamber Orchestra)

CREDIT: Agence de Presse Bernand, Paris

With the Boston Symphony Orchestra, Tanglewood Festival 1979

Janet Craylin, Lennox Berkeley, RL – 1st perf. Berkeley
oboe concerto, BBC Proms, Albert Hall 1979

Mananan Festival on the Isle of Man – Poet Laureate
Sir John Betjeman (holding papers), April Cantelo,
Richard Adeney (in dinner jacket), RL, Malcolm Binns

Top: Stockholm Opera, 1980s. *Bottom:* Photo Dustin Munoz, 1986

RL at Indianapolis
CREDIT: Les Wollam, New York

Upper photo: RL welcomes visitors to Indianapolis
Lower: Getting around town

**Work, work, work... Georgia Buchanan, Fund-raiser Chairperson, trips
the light fantastic with ISO's new Music Director**
CREDIT: Rob Goebel, The Indianapolis Star

Upper photo: At home in Indianapolis during the concert season
Lower: Three friends at Glyndebourne –
RL, Mrs. Walter Engel, Jeffrey Engel

At home in Northern Connecticut

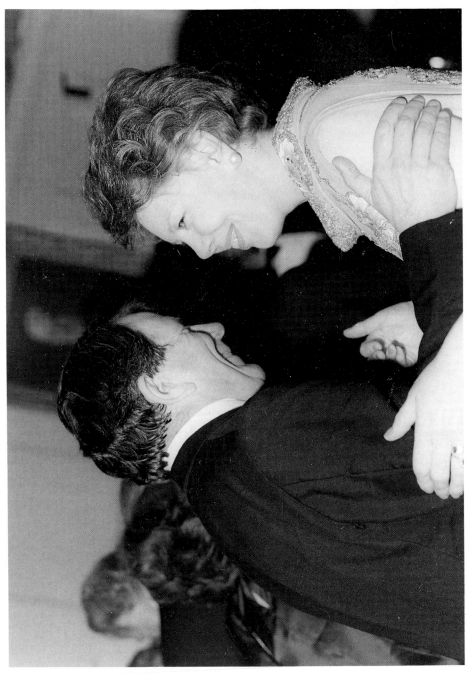

Colleagues and friends of very long standing: RL, Janet Baker
CREDIT: Chris Christodoulou, Middlesex

love of life and music enhanced and your experience and knowledge of both increased. They are the givers.

With the others you sense mainly pretentious self-concern and you emerge drained, tense and tired to the extinction of music within you. They are the takers.

It would be invidious to name names. The takers, the non-givers will never know who they are as far as I'm concerned and the givers know already how much they have meant to me so far in my life.

I should like to remember one of the first of those, Mabel Wilson-Ewer. She was well-off, lived in the Royal Crescent, Bath, came from the Novello family, had been a very good violinist and was the first to teach me the viola.

I was already a good pianist aged thirteen or fourteen, and, over a period of three or four years at weekly meetings, she took me through the entire violin and piano repertoire in her handsome drawing room overlooking the city and Jane Austen's Beechen Cliff, until she died of galloping liver cancer, even up to the last days. I found then that she had left me all her music. She was a giver. I was too young to know if I was giving her anything back but there was certainly a musical accord between us that has characterized all my most valued musical relationships ever since.

¶The sixth most important person in my life, but not at all in that order, is the dedicatée of this volume.

REFLECTIONS II – MY DAY IN CHURCH

I should like to add a next-to-last word regarding my religious beliefs, and background.

My father was a Congregationalist; at some point so deeply committed that he became a lay preacher. My mother was an Anglican not so deeply committed that she would not go to hear my father preach but she preferred Matins and Evensong and on the High side.

I grew up in between, curious but not committed, comfortably enjoying the benefits of both societies without feeling strongly drawn to either. Music provided my visions of Heaven and Hell and most stages in between. So it has continued, but the awe and respect for life have grown and I find myself in a state of wonder at the beauty and vigor of life, natural and human, and increasingly intolerant of attitudes that impose guilt instead of responsibility for behavior.

At Trinity, Cambridge, I was lucky enough to come to know well Harry Williams, a loveably rebellious priest with a great zest for living which, quite understandably, has turned him into being a member of the community at Mirfield, Yorkshire, where guilt at almost anything except intellectual sloth (as far as each individual mind can understand it) is forbidden along with ownership of property and possessions.

He was Dean of Chapel while I was a Fellow of Trinity and his sermons were among the few I have ever listened to with avid attention. I was very surprised when he asked me to preach one day, and very scared when he would not accept refusal.

Since music was the most palpably religious of all my experiences, I used it as the basis of a celebration of life and the living of it, for it has made everything worthwhile for me and there is a sort of high-level Evangelism built into the knowledge of it that spills sometimes over into words.

— Sermon Preached in Trinity College Chapel, Spring 1966[20] —

That which did please me beyond anything in the whole world was the wind-musick when the angel comes down, which is so sweet that it ravished me, and indeed, in a word, did wrap up my soul so that it made me really sick, just as I have formerly been when in love with my wife: that neither then nor all the evening going home, and at home, I was able to think of anything, but remained all night transported.

So Samuel Pepys in 1668 tried to describe the effect of some music he had heard in the theater. He might equally well have been speaking of

---

20 Reprinted as "The Church Boring" in *New Christian* for 5 May 1966, p. 12 (London: Prism Publications). The Pepys quotation which follows also appears on page 114, above. (Ed.)

the experience of a painting, a piece of sculpture, a poem or of the aware-ness of God, or of any other of those unreasonable activities of the human mind which raise the spirit to a condition in which aspects of life, of vitality, are seen with an absorbing clarity and vividness, even wonder, not ordinarily found in day to day existence.

These experiences are not reasonable, they are not to be gained by logic although some of them may prove inaccessible without acquired knowledge: the actual experience of them is intuitive, that is to say im-mediate, it either does or does not happen. Fortunately intuition seems to be a facet of the mind whose greater use provides a wider and more frequent response. And its exercise produces a certainty, a knowledge that has nothing to do with the certainty or knowledge deduced from proved facts, nor does it come into confict with this last sort of knowledge for it is altogether of a different sort.

I could not prove to anyone that Schubert's "Great" C major Sym-phony is great, but I know that it is, and how else than through intuition do I know that Rembrandt's picture of Saul and David conveys infinite-ly more than the delineation of two figures and a harp, how else do I know that I love someone or that I am aware of God?

All these and countless other less striking examples seem to me to be aspects of the same faculty of the mind and, except in their outward forms, I do not believe they differ from each other.

They have come to be regarded as being different and serving dif-ferent functions, one religious, one musical, one emotional, one pictorial, but it was not always the case. Until the seventeenth century all these activities as well as those of everyday life were literally encompassed by the Church—there was virtually no painter, no sculptor, no musician who did not derive all the images of his art from the Church, from religion. Since then there has been a gradual divorce; the church, retrac-ing its boundaries under seventeenth century scrutiny, began to leave a great deal of life outside its doors. The process has continued and the Church has now become a stagnant backwater of artistic endeavor while artists mostly find their inspiration in the life that goes on outside.

But what they are doing is in no way different from their forbears and no less religious, for it is I believe not God that has diminished, but the Church. Almost all the musicians that I know have a profound belief in a spiritual vitality outside themselves, and the more aware they are of it the more responsibility they feel towards it. Almost every great figure in music has left evidence of this — recently Igor Stravinsky described his realization of it as follows:

> At fourteen or fifteen I began to criticise and rebel against the church and before leaving my school I had abandoned it completely — a rupture that was left unrepaired for almost three decades. I cannot now evaluate the events which, at the end of those thirty years, made me discover the necessity of religious belief. I was not reasoned into my disposition. Though I admire the structured thought of theology, it is to religion no more than counterpoint exercises are to music.

And yet he will not go to church, and nor will most of the other musicians and artists that I know. And it is because they are dealing with matters of life while the Church to the outsider seems to talk mainly of sin, repentance, and death. In the past the Church has presented us with a number of images; the Church triumphant, the Church penitent, the Church militant — it seems now to have acquired a new one — the Church boring.

I am not sure that being boring or being bored should not rank among the deadliest of deadly sins — certainly far above covetousness, envy, gluttony or lust, which seem to me to be natural if occasionally unsociable tendencies which usually carry with them their own correctives. To be bored is to have life stopped up for the duration of the boredom; it is a sort of temporary murder. And I do not think I am alone in finding often a mounting impatience and feeling of frustration as I sit out an Evensong. It is a feeling closely akin to that which comes while sitting inside a car in the middle of a traffic-jam — one is powerless to do anything about it and the precious minutes of liveable life tick inexorably by outside.

It seems to me that the Church has become uncomfortably aware of the effect that she sometimes has and spends a good deal of time and energy pushing altars about here and there, beginning with a hymn, or *not* beginning with a hymn, introducing Beatle-like persons with electric guitars, or setting the canticles to footlights tunes. And people may come once to hear all these things but they will come mainly for the titillation; for the true state of affairs you should look in on a Wednesday Evensong — anywhere in the country — and you are likely to find yourself fairly solitary.

These things are enlivenings of the surface only, not unlike the activities of the mortician at the Everglades in Evelyn Waugh's novel *The Loved One* and the Church for the moment assumes the "smile beatnik", the "smile modern", the "smile rogueish" — let us hope it is not the moment before she is trundled off to the incinerator. But the inertia, the boredom, is occasioned not by the order of service, the position of the altar, not by those dreadful hymns, those incomprehensible lessons, or the inanities of the psalms — but by the refusal of people to accept the endless self-recrimination, the denial of life, and the burden of guilt which the Church seems continually to thrust upon us.

In these years when we live under the constant and imminent threat of total destruction — and who is to say how deeply the knowledge of this possibility, even probability, affects our times — one might have thought that people would flock to the churches in search of what they mainly offer — the hope of a life after death (a hope which seems constantly obscured by an apparent denial of life on earth), whereas paradoxically this threat has made people rush eagerly into the living of life and to value it the more.

Why then should I go to my Father and say to him only — I have sinned against heaven and before thee, and am no more worthy to be called thy son — when what I want to say is that I love my Father and am endlessly grateful to him for the joy of life and of living that I feel within me; and to ask to be shown the means of living it more fully so that as a son I may do more credit to my Father.

Why should I say "there is no health in me" when I know there *is* health in me, and that it is the knowledge of this health, of this vitality, which enables me to accept without curiosity or fear that there is also sickness and death in me too. It is the value which I put upon life and the full living of it which makes me know and hate and repent the sins that I commit against life either in myself or in others. I think there has never before been a time when life and the living of it has been so highly prized: and because the love of God can be discerned through the living of the life that emanates from Him I believe that this could be the generation of them that seek him. But they will only do so if they are encouraged to believe that "The Earth is the Lord's and the fulness thereof".

If the Church would but open its arms to life again and show us mainly how best to live it fully, then people would come inside and say, like the father of the epileptic boy, "I believe Lord, help thou my unbelief".

REFLECTIONS III — ENVOI

Being involved in the preparation of this book has meant a great deal of unwonted looking back, something I'm not only reluctant to do but temperamentally unsuited for. My brain shies off the past. Thinking of it leads me to nostalgia and that leads to regret either for what happened or that what happened cannot happen again. I have learned to live life for the present and found it increasingly enjoyable that way. It seems to me to get better and better, so why look back?

All the same, in the past six months I've been urged to write down accounts of things that have happened and some of that has been fun. While doing it there have been frequent ancillary flashes of memory recalling touching, funny, important things that have occurred not presently relevant. Some of these I noted as they darted in and out of the mind, mostly subjects barely worth more than a line or two, if that, and I thought, as a last gesture to what is done with in my life, I would give them their line, in no particular order, in case they should strike a chord, ring a bell reminding others of similar moments over which they might care to smile or shed a tear.

There were a few to do with recordings.

I once owned a very small record (which certainly melted when my house burnt—only one short work, 78 RPM, and you had to turn it over in the middle of the cello recitative)—the *Italian Serenade* by Hugo Wolf played by the Budapest String Quartet heaven knows how long ago. It was such brilliant playing, very fast and very musical. I found I could still play it through in my head twenty-five years later, even to turning it over. Something perhaps for record hunters.

That brought to mind a much older recording someone played to me at school of Dvorak's E^b string quintet, a work I hadn't known, came to love and played quite often in Cambridge days. Alongside the music I remember the amazing slitherings of the strings as they used a portamento on virtually every change of position. Banana-skin Dvorak.

If that was authentic nineteenth-century string playing I didn't like it. It must have started something.

Generally speaking I don't much enjoy listening to recordings. Perhaps it's because I would rather be doing; they seem to be a poor substitute for the real thing.

They can, however, capture moments and one such is Neil Black's playing of that long oboe A (bars 322-333) in the first movement of Mendelssohn's *Italian Symphony* in a recording I made with the ECO for Erato ages ago. Neil's a great player but this note, a perfect arc of sound emerging from the strings, seeming to rise like a rainbow — though it stays the same pitch of course — before descending to continue the movement, was a gift from heaven. And there it is, captured for ever on disc. That'll teach some not to be too dogmatic.

In spite of the fact the production failed, there flashed into my mind the magic of Peter Wood's vision of *The Beggar's Opera* for the Royal Shakespeare Company at the Aldwych (for which I re-set all the tunes so that everything happened on stage, played and sung by the cast). The opera was as if improvised by a group of beggars waiting in jail for transportation to Australia. It was a wonderful idea. Unfortunately, none of the otherwise admirable cast could sing.

At Stratford there was Vanessa Redgrave's adorably gawkey Helena in *Midsummer Night's Dream;* Gerry McEwan's concupiscent "most wonderful" at the end of *Twelfth Night* as she sees the twins, Viola and Sebastian, together for the first time — and another from her (assisted by Tom Stoppard and Peter Wood) more recently at the National Theatre's *Rivals:* Mrs. Malaprop's new last line as she swept out "You are all

Bavarians" (barbarians) of which Sheridan would most certainly have been proud.

One of the first theater jobs I had was to arrange the music for *Alice Through the Looking-Glass* with Margaret Rutherford as the White Queen. Michael Denison, Binnie Hale, Wally Crisham were in it and a charming Alice, Carole Marsh, with whom most of us fell in love.

There was a cherishable moment when Margaret as the sheep, knitting, rowed with Alice across the stage in a boat (pulled by stage-hands) singing the Eton boating song. One day they pulled too hard and it tipped over. Wool and needles went flying, legs in the air and general consternation. Thinking along the lines of helping, for she was a girl-guide at heart, Margaret put her head above the footlights, mob-cap askew, fleece in a muddle and with the inimitable wobble of the jowels, looked hard at the audience and said "splash". Actually it saved the day.[21]

Perhaps the most powerful memory of the theater was the end of the *Orestia* at the National, Peter Hall directing.

After Orestes is acquitted of the murder of Aegisthus by one vote, the anger of the Eumenides — the Furies — has been assuaged by Athene and peace brought to the land the audience stood as they walked among us bringing us the blessing of relief from strife. I hardly think there was one member of the audience that didn't weep.

The trilogy had taken a whole afternoon and evening with the entire cast in masks which they had so inhabited that they came to reflect the characters of their wearers and seemed eventually more expressive than the human face. Yet the masks were all the same. The actors were un-named but between them and Aeschylus I don't remember a greater occasion in the theater.

On the same sort of level I remember being taken in the early summer of 1945, I was seventeen, to the first night of *Peter Grimes*. I remember par-

---

21   Mob-cap: "a large, high cap trimmed with frills and ribbons, worn by women in the eighteenth and early nineteenth centuries." — *American Heritage Dictionary of the English Language* (1969). (Ed.)

ticularly the excitement, the opening woodwind phrases of the prologue and Owen Brannigan singing "Peter Grimes, take the oath after me"; Auntie's "A joke's a joke and fun is fun"; Peter's entrance in the pub at the height of the storm and the dreadful silences between the chorus singing "Peter Grimes" at the end as the man-hunt begins.

Later on, of course, I came to know the opera very well. It may be Ben's most enduring masterpiece as *Bohème* is Puccini's, though he would have hated that analogy.

Thinking of "Peter" and Peter Pears, someone I worked with much more often after Ben had died than before, I shall never forget the last night of *Billy Budd* at the Met which I conducted for two seasons.[22] It was a marvelous production by John Dexter and a great cast with Richard Stilwell as Billy and James Morris as Claggart.

Peter was an unsurpassable Vere but there was one place, after Billy has struck Claggart and caused his death, which he never could get right, a complicated little two-four section beginning "God o' mercy". He came to my dressing room before that last performance and we went through it, he determined to sing it correctly at least once in the run.

Come the moment, of course he got out again and was so cross with himself he came down to the footlights and instead of singing: "Fated boy, what have you done? Go in there, Go! God help us everyone," he looked down at me and sang "Fated boy, what have you done? Bloody fool. Damn. God help us every one." I was the only one who laughed.

It was being broadcast so there's probably a tape of it somewhere.

One year Ruth Fermoy lent me her house at Hillington, Norfolk for a few weeks to finish work on Monteverdi's *L'Orfeo* which I was preparing for Sadler's Wells.[23]

I hired a cook, took over Ruth's cleaning lady, worked hard in peaceful tranquility during the week and each weekend, had close friends to stay, bought eight copies of *Paradise Lost* and we read it together, all

---

22   In 1978 and 1980. (Ed.)

23   Sadly, Ruth — a dear friend — died only recently, as this book was being prepared for publication.

twelve books, each one taking turns to read aloud while the others followed. It was a most worthwhile project for we had all known only bits here and there and the whole poem made the losing of Paradise a great moral saga, a seventeenth-century *Lords of the Ring*, only much better poetry.

The Fall of Satan and his cohorts:

> so numberless were those bad Angels seen
> Hovering on wing under the cope of Hell

— and nameless now —

> blotted out and ras'd by their Rebellion from the books of life.

What a fate!

Their council in Hell; Eden where Man was tested and failed, the beauty of it as pristine as when Milton described it. The moment as evening falls and a quiet descends on the tranquil Garden, save for the nightingale who sings all night so beautifully that "Silence was pleased"; it makes you shiver three hundred years later. The forsaking of Paradise and the descent of the Cherubim to guard it against evil while Adam and Eve wend their solitary way, "the World was all before them."

It seems to me we're still wandering.

Eventually when *L'Orfeo* was produced, there was Pat Kern's Messenger and Johnny Wakefield's Orpheus to look forward to and an operatic world not so far removed from Milton's.

All through this period of reflection flashes of Janet Baker have kept on appearing for we have worked a good deal together, become close friends and shared a host of memorable musical moments—the first soliloquy of Penelope in *Il ritorno d'Ulisse*, Diana and Jove-as-Diana in *La*

Calisto, the Angel in Gerontius, the *Matthew Passion,* recitals, Schubert's *Ständchen* — you begin and it's difficult to stop.[24]

Perhaps one funny one will do it — the wrong key version of Arne's "where the bee sucks there suck I", an encore at an Edinburgh Festival recital.

She had, it appeared, always sung it in E major and wanted to try it a tone higher so, at the last minute, I played the introduction in $F^\#$ major. Old habits die hard and she promptly began back in E major. There followed the strangest performance of the little song anyone could have imagined, oscillating between these two keys. Giggles set in and we could hardly get off the stage — or on again once off.

There was one *Matthew Passion* (Janet was not involved this time) on live TV from Lincoln Cathedral which really tempted Fate. It was an extraordinarily ambitious production with arias coming from all parts of that wonderful building and only the chorus, orchestra and myself (with earphones and monitors when not in view) more or less in one place. It needed one muddle, one wrong cue, one camera to break down, one set of lights to fuse for the whole thing to come to a grinding halt. Miraculously, nothing untoward happened and it went so well that the filmed recording of it was repeated at least twice in the following years. I don't think any of us realized at the time how risky it was. James Morris, our Claggart in *Billy Budd,* came over to sing the bass aria, Jon Garrison the Evangelist and Alan Titus, Jesus; Sheila Armstrong and Alfreda Hodgson were the ladies and all, with nerves of steel, in tremendous form; it was very good television, too, as well as being very good Bach.

In the early seventies my house in London, 16 Hamilton Terrace, near

---

24   In addition to numerous opera and other orchestral recordings, a fine set of four LPs titled simply JANET BAKER — RAYMOND LEPPARD, with Raymond at the piano and harpsichord, has been issued on the Philips label. The program includes a treasury of works by Beethoven, Gluck, Handel, Haydn, Mozart and Schubert. See DISCOGRAPHY, below. (Ed.)

Lord's cricket ground, burned down due to a faulty thermostat sparking on to some old window shutters. Virtually all my music, a new Steinway (uninsured, it was so new) and a good deal of eighteenth-century furniture and silver melted or went up in smoke, Most trying of all, the just completed full-score of *Il ritorno d'Ulisse*, hundreds of pages of manuscript, had been sitting on the piano and was no more. It had to be done all over again in the succeeding weeks so as to be ready for the following summer at Glyndebourne.[25]

Traumatic as it must have been somewhere in my mind, there was no immediate reaction — nor any since that I can tell, which says something about the value of possessions — only concern for a live lunch-hour broadcast the next day from St. John's, Smith Square, a concert the day after that in Westminster Abbey and a Bach flute and harpsichord recital with Richard Adeney, also at St. John's the day after that. A blessing, I suppose, that there was so much to do. There was the added concern that after the early evening flute recital I had been invited to join a party to hear *Showboat* at a theater in the Strand by Princess Margaret. Queen Elizabeth, her mother, was coming too and I was to meet them at the theater.

The timetable was carefully worked out and, with a taxi waiting at Smith Square, I could just do it.

The days after the fire passed in something of a haze but the concerts went well as far as I can recall.

I had only one suit to wear for it all, the one I was wearing when I returned from dinner at a friend's house to find the house a-blaze. Some clothes, sealed in a cupboard, had survived including a dinner jacket and evening shoes which, since I could change at St. John's, Una Marchetti, who was my secretary at the time, took to the cleaners. In fact she kept on taking them to the cleaners over a period of forty-eight hours to get rid of the smell of smoke. At last they seemed clear of it and I hurriedly

---

25 Which he succeeded in doing. Bringing to mind the episode of Thomas Carlyle having left the only copy of his manuscript for *The French Revolution* with his friend, John Stuart Mill, whose housekeeper, apparently, somehow managed to throw it out. Back home in Scotland, Carlyle rewrote the work in its entirety. (Ed.)

changed after the flute recital, dashed into the taxi and just made it as the Royal party was arriving.

I dare say I had become somewhat heated in the race to get there and the warmth of the theater helped, but halfway through Act One Princess Margaret turned to me and whispered, "There's the most awful smell of burning. Do you think the theater's on fire?"

It was me, of course, and I had to confess though she knew about the fire. I took off my coat and shoes, the only victims of the smoke save for my trousers and "*il y a des limites*", stuffed them under my seat and we enjoyed thereafter a smoke-free show. The party was highly amused — and very sympathetic about the reasons, of course — but it must have looked very odd that a guest of the Queen Mother's had to dress to leave the theater.

Writing about Duncan Grant and his last exhibition at King's Lynn gave me several vivid flash-backs of that small group of houses at Firle near Glyndebourne where the Bloomsbury people spent so much of their time.

I particularly remember going to visit Lydia Keynes — Lopokova — for the first time while working at Glyndebourne in the mid-50's. I had met her from time to time at Cambridge but was so glad of the chance to get to know her better for she had a great vitality and an intuitive understanding of things that had not at all dimmed with age.

The house was difficult to find for the first time, but, once there, you breathed another air.

On this occasion I was met at the door by the husband of a couple Lydia had living there to look after her rather simple needs. "Lady Keynes is gardening and asked if you would go out and find her when you came, sir." Through the house and a large sitting room I went, through French windows, making my way down a covered path at the end of which I could see a diminutive stooping figure and a hat.

She heard me, stood up, waved and came to meet me at which moment I realized that, apart from the hat and sandals, she was completely naked, and completely unconcerned about it and so, as a result, was I.

"How nice to see you, Raymond. Come in and have a drink while I go up and put something on for lunch" — which was very sensible for she would have been cold indoors. She must have been seventy and her figure was quite perfect.

Writing about Cambridge triggered off an absurd picture showing how foolish an over-serious group of undergraduates can make themselves appear. They were a left-wing collection outside the Senate House. As I passed by on some sort of official University day I heard them chanting, "Adrian out, intellectuals in."

Lord Adrian, a gentle, delightful man was Master of Trinity, Vice-Chancellor of the University, O.M., President of the Royal Society, one of the most distinguished men of his time.

One hilarious flash came with thinking about Santa Fe. The time when the Queen of the Night making her second entrance through a trap door, center stage, found herself stuck after the elevator had only risen two feet. She had to sing "*Der hölle Rache*" as a disembodied head.

In the spooky blue light it looked like a Charles Addams cartoon and greatly amused the customers. The soprano, like Queen Victoria, was not exactly tickled pink by it.

When I left England for America I was pestered by the Press and learned two lessons. First, only make statements to reporters, never try to explain anything. My reasons for leaving were complicated but the media selected only the bits they thought might be newsworthy; otherwise they weren't interested.

My second lesson came after questions had been asked on two occasions, 8th and 15th November 1976, in the House of Commons as to why I was leaving: "That this House regrets the emigration of the distinguished conductor Mr. Raymond...."

I thought for a moment there was real concern, but it was only politicians trying to score a point off their opposition. Never trust them in that sort of situation. Their desire to score and so improve their chances for re-election will take precedence over any altruistic feelings they may have.[26]

During rehearsals of *Poppea* at San Francisco in 1975 I spent quite some time with Günther Rennert with whom I had worked twice before at Glyndebourne. For all his crusty, Germanic reputation he had an impish curiosity and one afternoon, after we had ended our rehearsal in another building, we sneaked in to the back of a dress-rehearsal of *Rigoletto* where things were not going too well. After the third explosion of bad temper from the conductor, I suggested to Günther that we might leave for an early dinner together.

Through the pass-door to backstage we bumped into Joan Sutherland who was singing Gilda. The fourth row was by this time underway, now with Herbert Adler, the General Manager of the Company, involved, the mounting fervor of it increasingly audible backstage.

I introduced Joan to Günther but we couldn't help but focus on the disturbance in the house. "Oh never mind Ray, after all it's only opera!"

Rather a balanced view, I thought.

Peter Wood directed, Robert Indiana designed the scenery and costumes and I conducted Virgil Thomson and Gertrude Stein's *The Mother of Us All* at Santa Fe, in 1976: we even recorded it.

Just as rehearsals were due to begin I was relieved somewhat to hear that, because of ill-health, the composer would not be able to attend any rehearsals. He had the reputation of being interfering and cantankerous. As it turned out he was neither of those things but, rather, helpful and appreciative.

---

26 One supposes one has to have *been* someone in order for one to have been taken notice of in this way, by the House of Commons. But, to what end! The speakers expressed their "regrets" not in cultural terms, but only in the most unimaginative economic ones, that is, according to crowd-pleasing definitions of loyalty of their own devising. In fact our subject remains an ardent patriot with respect to *both* countries, and only recently (May 1993) brought the Indianapolis Symphony Orchestra to London's Barbican Centre in a program centered on Elgar's *"Enigma"* *Variations.* (Ed.)

Before we got onto correspondence terms (all our contact was by telephone or letter, we never met), there were one or two conversations that, whether on account of his nervousness or mine, tended to confirm his reputation.

There were problems over wrong notes in the score, faulty notation, audibility of text all of which he summarily dismissed saying, "whatever you do, you can't ruin it," and ending testily "I really don't know what Crosby is thinking of handing *Mother of Us All* over to two Englishmen [Wood and myself]."

To which I — equally testily — replied, "Mr. Thomson, I would remind you that without the English there wouldn't have been anything much of a country to be mothered."

He laughed, acknowledged the point and, thereafter, we got on like a house a-fire. He even allowed me to concoct an overture to accompany the parade for Women's Suffrage that began Peter's brilliant production.

He was right, too. We *didn't* ruin it.

In 1942 I was at school in Bath when Hitler decided to perpetrate his infamous Baedecker raids on English cities noted mainly for their cathedrals and architecture.

The two nights of intensive bombing (over four hundred people were killed) have faded from the memory but, a day or so after when the stoicism which sustained was beginning to wane as we realized what a terrible amount of damage had been done, apart from the killing, the visit of King George and Queen Elizabeth stays vividly in the mind.

They came from London, where they had plenty of bombs of their own, and went all around Bath, climbing over rubble, talking to everyone, unguarded and caringly sympathetic. I was serving out meals to the homeless at an improvised soup-kitchen and saw the effect they had. It was magical and powerful. At that moment they were the symbol of the spirit of England and people's contact with it uplifted hearts and the triumph of good was assured.

We don't have air raids, we do have a new generation, and we have the media.

The equation must surely be made to work, it's too good to lose. There are responsibilities to be accepted on all sides but especially by those who control the instruments of communication. They should become the Senate of our generation.

It's hard to make life work in private during these troubled, irreverent times, and in public most saints would show a blemish or two. The sinners seem only to delight in their ability to sell more newspapers or win higher ratings, and by taking notice we encourage them.

Perhaps Tennyson's dying Merlin at the troubled court of Camelot has the answer as he urges the young mariner to pursue his ideals:

> Call your companions,
> launch your vessel
> and crowd your canvas,
> and, ere it vanishes
> over the margin,
> after it, follow it,
> follow the gleam.

Personally I'm blessed with wonderful companions, the vessel still appears to be water-tight and I certainly intend to follow the gleam.

PART THREE

APPENDICES

APPENDICES

Editorial note: Raymond Leppard's very full career is, in some ways, representative of any modern major career in music, given one's ability to cross oceans and continents with relative ease. It is also exceptional — with respect to range of repertory (music of all historical periods, both instrumental and operatic) and his unusually extensive recordings output, for example. Thus, the materials in this section serve the dual purpose of documenting the events and milestones of a unique musical life — and also of enabling readers to glimpse the actual, day-to-day experience of professional music-making in a way that no summary narrative of itself, perhaps, can quite suggest.

APPENDIX I

PARTIAL CHRONOLOGY

NOTE: The Chronology is in two parts—first, a *Curriculum Vita* listing selected biographical events, followed by a *Concert Diary* derived from surviving concert programs, c.1950 to present.

A. Curriculum Vitae

11 Aug 1927	Born—Raymond John Leppard—London
1938-43	Family moved to Bath. Piano studies with Betty Allen. Viola studies with Mabel Wilson-Ewer. Studied singing with Eugene Hanson. Much involved with the various musical societies in Bath: recitals, accompanying, singing, chamber music, etc.
1944-45	Ernest Read Summer Orchestral School, Sherborne. Principal viola; played piano concertos, e.g. Beethoven *Concerto 1* and by Armstrong Gibbs.
1945	Choral scholarship to Trinity College, Cambridge; scholarship to Royal Academy of Music, London.
1945-48	Military service with the R.A.F.
1948-53	Trinity College, Cambridge University.

§A.D.C. Theatre, Arts Theatre Cambridge, Footlights: composed, played and directed music for various productions directed by Peter Hall (e.g. *Love's Labour's Lost*), Peter Wood, Toby Robertson, etc.

§Cambridge University Madrigal Society: tenor— succeeded Boris Ord as conductor in 1958; regular concerts, occasional tours, broadcasts, Aldeburgh Festival 17 Jun 1949, Festival of Britain prod. "An Historical Pageant of British Music" Aug 1951.

§Cambridge University Music Club: regular concerts, became president in 1950. For 1952 May Week Concerts orchestrated Dibdin's Ballad Opera *The Padlock* (6 Jun), perf. as soloist in Mozart piano concerto K 453 (7 Jun), etc. 1951-52: concerts given at Exbury House, Southampton, incl. 2 compositions by RL (*Les Amusements de Marise* and *Nocturne*).

§Cambridge University Musical Society: regular concerts—as principal viola, occasional conductor.

§1950: Elected Senior Scholar.
§1951: 1st Class Honors, Music Tripos.
§1951-53: Cambridge Philharmonic Society. Conducted
Haydn *Seasons* (7 Feb 1952), Handel *Messiah* (11 Apr
1952), Berlioz *Damnation of Faust* (15 May 1952),
Fauré *Requiem* & Verdi *Sacred Pieces* (29 Jan 1953),
Bach *Cantata 4* & Handel *Messiah II-III* (3 Apr 1953).
Soloists incl. April Cantelo, Lorely Dyer, Anne
Keynes, Victoria Sladen (s), Catherine Lawson, Sylvia Rowlands, (cn), Wilfred Brown, Eric Green,
Parry Jones (t), Gordon Clinton, Thomas Hemsley
(bar), George Pizzey, Robert Rowell, Roger Stalman
(b), Hugh Middleton (org), George Guest, Boris
Ord (cont).
§1952: Elected Research Scholar.

1952   Orchestrated & conducted David King musical score,
with additional music by RL, for *Alice Through the
Looking Glass* (Felicity Douglas adaptation of Lewis
Carroll story), Her Majesty's Theatre, Brighton —
later transferred to the Princes' Theatre, London;
dir. Toby Robertson, featuring Carole Marsh, Joyce

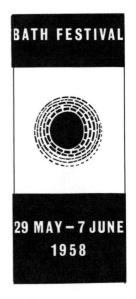

	Graeme, Binnie Hale, Margaret Rutherford, Walter Crisham, Michael Denison.[1]
19 Jan 1952	Arranged & composed music for revue *Light and Variable*, Mitchell Hall, Royal Surrey County Hospital, Surrey — incl. RL lyrics for "Sirens All", "You Can't Be Really Greek Without a Pillar" and "Going Home"; prod. Josephine Bell.
22 Jan 1952	Arranged & played music for Hugh Thomas Venetian Fantasy *Some Talk of Angels*, Amateur Dramatic Club, Cambridge.
7 Feb 1952	Soloist in John Stanley and Alec Rowley piano concertos, Assembly Rooms, Norwich, cond. Cyril Pearce.
1953	Formed Leppard Chamber Orchestra, Leppard Ensemble, known for performances of Baroque music. Typical list of players included Jürgen Hess (vln, with whom RL played many recitals), Raymond Keenleyside (vln), Cecil Aronowitz (vla), Bernard Richards (vc), Adrian Beers (db), Richard Adeney (fl), Janet Craxton (ob), Philip Jones (tpt).
2 May 1953	London debut as a conductor: Leppard Chamber Orchestra at Wigmore Hall, London (see *Concert Diary* for program)

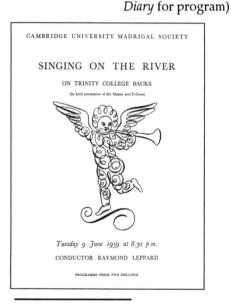

CAMBRIDGE UNIVERSITY MADRIGAL SOCIETY

SINGING ON THE RIVER

ON TRINITY COLLEGE BACKS

(by kind permission of the Master and Fellows)

Tuesday 9 June 1959 at 8.30 p.m.

CONDUCTOR RAYMOND LEPPARD

PROGRAMME PRICE TWO SHILLINGS

LEPPARD

ENSEMBLE

Conductor RAYMOND LEPPARD
Soloist ILSE WOLF
CITY MUSIC SOCIETY
Goldsmiths' Hall
10TH DECEMBER 1959

---

1   For a related commentary see page 434, above.

10 Dec 1953	Orchestrated & conducted Vivian Ellis musical score, with additional music by RL, for Christmas play *Listen to the Wind*, New Theatre, Oxford; dir. Peter Hall.
May 1954– Aug 1955	First seasons at Glyndebourne — as asst conductor & hpsd player.
3 Jul 1956	Provided musical score for *Love's Labour's Lost*, Shakespeare Memorial Theatre, Stratford-upon-Avon, featuring Basil Hoskins, Alan Badel, Clive Revill, Harry Andrews, Prunella Scales, dir. Peter Hall (1st RL score for Statford).
2 Jul 1957	Provided musical score for *Cymbeline*, Shakespeare Memorial Theatre, Stratford-upon-Avon, featuring Peggy Ashcroft, Geoffrey Keen, Cyril Luckham, Donald Eccles, Clive Revill, dir. Peter Hall.
1958-1968	Fellow and University Lecturer in Music, Trinity College, Cambridge University.
1959-1970	Music director, English Chamber Orchestra (1st appt).
Jul 1959	Provided musical score for *A Midsummer Night's Dream*, Shakespeare Memorial Theatre, Stratford-upon-Avon, featuring Mary Ure (Titania), Charles Laughton (Bottom), Robert Hardy, Ian Holm, Roy Dotrice, Stephanie Bidmead, Albert Finney (Lysander), Vanessa Redgrave, Zoe Caldwell, Diana Rigg, dir. Peter Hall.[2]
Jul 1960	Provided musical scores for *Twelfth Night*, Shakespeare Memorial Theatre, Stratford-upon-Avon, featuring Dorothy Tutin, Max Adrian, Eric Porter, Roy Dotrice, Patrick Wymark, Ian Holm, Derek Godfrey, Patrick Allen, Ian Richardson, dir. Peter Hall; and for *The Two Gentlemen of Verona*, featuring Denholm Elliott, Susan Maryott, Frances Cuka, Derek Godfrey, Mavis Edwards, Patrick Wymark, Jack MacGowran, dir. Peter Hall. Named Music Adviser to the Shakespeare Memorial Theatre; orch. & arr. the National Anthem in a vers. based on c.1740 sources — thereafter employed at all Stratford performs.
Jul 1961	Provided musical scores for *Ondine* (Jean Giraudoux),

---

2   Also mentioned on pp. 424, 433 above.

Shakespeare Memorial Theatre, Stratford-upon-Avon. *Left:* Bottom
played by Charles Laughton, *A Midsummer Night's Dream*, 1959.
Right: Ondine played by Leslie Caron (Mrs. Peter Hall), *Ondine,* 1961.
CREDITS: Karsh of Ottawa, Terrence Le Goubin

Stratford's 1959 *A Midsummer Night's Dream:*
Lila de Nobili (scenery & costumes), RL (music), Peter Hall (director)
CREDIT: Alec Murray

	Shakespeare Memorial Theatre, Stratford-upon-Avon, featuring Leslie Caron, Richard Johnson, Gwen Ffrangcon-Davies, Diana Rigg, Ian Holm, Roy Dotrice, Peter Jeffrey, Eric Porter, James Bree, dir. Peter Hall; and for *Romeo and Juliet*, featuring Brian Murray, Dorothy Tutin, Max Adrian, Peter McEnery, Barry Stockwell, Edith Evans, dir. Peter Hall. Music Adviser to the Shakespeare Memorial Theatre.
Jul 1962	Music Adviser to the Shakespeare Memorial Theater, Stratford-upon-Avon. RL's musical score for *A Midsummer Night's Dream* (from 1959 prod.) used for current performs, featuring Judi Dench, Paul Hardwick, Ian Holm, Tony Steedman, Yvonne Bonnamy, Ian Richardson, Brian Murray, Patrick Brake, Diana Rigg, dir. Peter Hall.
1963	Composed film score for *Lord of the Flies*, dir. Peter Brook.
Aug 1962	First performances (12, at Glyndebourne, cond. by John Pritchard) of RL's modern performing edition of Monteverdi's *L'incoronazione di Poppea*.
Summer 1964	Conducting debut at Glyndebourne: Monteverdi's *L'incoronazione di Poppea* — RL vers (12 performs, prod. Günther Rennert).
5 May 1966	Delivered sermon at Trinity College Chapel, Cambridge — later published as "The Church Boring".[3]
Summer 1967	Conducted at Glyndebourne: Cavalli's *L'Ormindo* — RL vers (15 performs, prod. Günther Rennert).
Summer 1968	Conducted at Glyndebourne: Cavalli's *L'Ormindo* — RL vers (prod. Günther Rennert).
1969	Composed film scores for *Alfred the Great*, dir. Clive Donner, *Laughter in the Dark*, dir. Tony Richardson.
5 Mar 1969	Gave Italian Lecture at the British Academy.[4]
Oct 1969	Jury member, Leeds International Piano Competition (with Nadia Boulanger, Ingrid Haebler, Gina Bachauer, Charles Groves, Clifford Curzon, Nikita Magaloff).
4 Nov 1969	Conducted at Lincoln Center, New York (soloists,

---

3 For text see page 428, above.
4 For text see Chapter II Section §4, above.

	chorus, members New York Philharmonic — RL American debut).
1970	Composed film score for *Perfect Friday*, dir. Peter Hall.
Summer 1970	Conducted at Glyndebourne: Cavalli's *La Calisto* — RL vers (9 performs, prod. Peter Hall); Maw's *The Rising of the Moon* (8 performs).
Summer 1971	Conducted at Glyndebourne: Cavalli's *La Calisto* — RL vers (8 performs, prod. Colin Graham).
1972-1980	Principal Conductor, BBC Northern Symphony Orchestra (later BBC Philharmonic), Manchester.
Summer 1972	Conducted at Glyndebourne: Monteverdi's *Il ritorno d'Ulisse in patria* — RL vers (15 performs, prod. Peter Hall).
13 Dec 1972	Received Hon. D.Litt, University of Bath.
3 May 1973	At Royal Festival Hall, London, received 1973 Audio Award (inaugurated in 1967) presented to RL by the Composer's Guild of Great Britain, Mechanical Copyright Protection Society, National Federation of Gramophone Societies, National Music Council, Performing Rights Society, Songwriters' Guild of Great Britain, and *Hi-Fi News & Record Reviews*. Previous winners incl. Neville Marriner (1971) and Sir Adrian Boult (1972).
9 May 1973	Gave paper to The Royal Society for the Encouragement of Arts, Manufactures and Commerce.[5]
Summer 1973	Conducted at Glyndebourne: Monteverdi's *Il ritorno d'Ulisse in patria* — RL vers (11 performs, prod. Peter Hall).
Jul 1973	Received Honorary Doctorate, University of Bath.
May, Jun 1974	Conducted at Glyndebourne: Cavalli's *La Calisto* — RL vers (10 performs, prod. Peter Hall).
Aug 1974	Conducted at Santa Fe Opera: Cavalli's *L'Egisto* — RL vers (3 performs, dir. John Cox).
Summer 1975	Conducted at Glyndebourne: Janácek's *The Cunning Little Vixen* (13 performs, prod. Jonathan Miller).
Summer 1976	Conducted at Santa Fe Opera: Cavalli's *L'Egisto* — RL vers (6 performs).
Summer 1976	Conducted at Santa Fe Opera: Thomson's *The Mother of Us All* (4 performs, dir. Peter Wood).

---

5   For text see Chapter IV, above.

The International Center of Indianapolis
cordially welcomes you to
The 1991 International Citizen of the Year Awards
to honor

Maestro Raymond Leppard
Music Director of the Indianapolis Symphony Orchestra

Thursday, October 3, 1991
Hilton On The Circle

PROGRAM

Welcome and Introductions	K.P. Singh, ICI Board of Directors

Breakfast

International Center	Robert J. Shula, 1st Vice President, ICI Board of Directors

Award

Introduction	Robert C. Jones, President, Indianapolis Symphony Orchestra
Award Presentation	The Honorable William H. Hudnut, III, Mayor, City of Indianapolis

RAYMOND LEPPARD

Closing Remarks	William S. Hogsett, ICI Executive Director

PREVIOUS AWARD WINNERS

1990 - **The Honorable Lee H. Hamilton,** Member of Congress,
Ninth District of Indiana
Sister Marie Pierre Buttell, O.S.F. Professor Emerita,
Marian College
1989 - **The Honorable William H. Hudnut, III,** Mayor of Indianapolis
J. George Mikelsons, CEO & President, American Trans Air
1988 - **The Honorable Robert D. Orr,** Former Governor of Indiana,
U.S. Ambassador to Singapore
1986 - **The Honorable Richard G. Lugar,** U.S. Senator
1985 - **Riad Shaheen,** Past CEO & President, Long Electric Co., Inc.

Summer 1977   Conducted at Santa Fe Opera: Mozart's *Così fan tutte*
(6 performs, dir. Peter Wood).
Jan 1978   Conducted Boston Symphony Orchestra (debut
with BSO).

5 Apr 1978	Received Hon. R.A.M. (Royal Academy of Music).
Sep 1978	Conducted at Metropolitan Opera: Britten's *Billy Budd*.
Summer 1979	Conducted at Glyndebourne: Monteverdi's *Il ritorno d'Ulisse in patria* – RL vers (10 performs, prod. Peter Hall).
1980-1981	Music Director, English Chamber Orchestra (2nd appt).
Apr 1980	Conducted at Metropolitan Opera: Britten's *Billy Budd*.
May 1980	Conducted Chicago Symphony Orchestra (debut with CSO).
Summer 1981	Conducted at Santa Fe Opera: Rossini's *Il barbiere di Siviglia* (6 performs, dir. Lou Galterio); Stravinsky's *The Rake's Progress* (4 performs, dir. Bliss Herbert).
Summer 1982	Conducted at Glyndebourne: Gluck's *Orfeo ed Euridice* (10 performs).
Oct 1992	Conducted at New York City Opera: Gluck's *Alceste* (dir. Brian Macdonald).
Feb 1983	Conducted Indianapolis Symphony Orchestra (debut with ISO).
11 Jun 1983	At Buckingham Palace, London, made C.B.E. (Commander of the British Empire).
Summer 1983	Conducted at Santa Fe Opera: Donizetti's *Don Pasquale* (9 performs, dir. Anthony Besch); Cavalli's *L'Orione* – RL vers (5 performs, dir. Peter Wood).
Sep 1983	Conducted at New York City Opera: Handel's *Alcina*.
Oct 1983	Conducted Philadelphia Orchestra (debut with PO).
1984-1988	Principal guest conductor, St Louis Symphony Orchestra.
	¶1984-1986: Artistic Director, St Louis Symphony Summerfest.
1984	Composed film score for *The Hotel New Hampshire*, dir. Tony Richardson.
Summer 1984	Conducted at Glyndebourne: Monteverdi's *L'incoronazione di Poppea* – RL vers (14 performs, dir. Peter Hall).
25 Nov 1984	Received Hon. F.R.C.M. (Fellow Royal College of Music).
1985	Succeeded Sir John Betjeman as president Erin Arts Centre, the Isle of Man.
1987-	Music Director, Indianapolis Symphony Orchestra.
27 Apr 1991	Received Hon. Mus.D., University of Indianapolis.
3 Oct 1991	Received Citizen of the Year Award, International Center of Indianapolis.
9 May 1992	Received Hon. Doctor of Fine Arts, Purdue University.

B. Concert Diary

† performance conducted by RL
¶ dates of special significance
Abbreviations: audit = auditorium
c, co = chamber, chamber orchestra
coll = college
conc = concerto
fest = festival
p, po = philharmonic, philharmonic orchestra
s, so = symphony, symphony orchestra
schl = school
soc = society
BBC Northern SO = BBC Northern Symphony Orchestra
ECO = English Chamber Orchestra
ISO = Indianapolis Symphony Orchestra
LPO = London Philharmonic Orchestra
LSO = London Symphony Orchestra
RPO = Royal Philharmonic Orchestra
SCO = Scottish Chamber Orchestra

2 May 1953	Wigmore Hall	London

Leppard CO† (London debut as a conductor)
Bach, Gluck, Haydn, Mozart, Stravinsky, Walton

13 Oct 1953	Chelsea Town Hall	London

Cantelo (s), Leppard CO†
Haydn, Milhaud, Mozart, Sauguet

21 Oct 1953	Guildhall, Cambridge Univ	Cambridge

Thurston Dart (hpsd), Leppard CO†
Bach, Handel, Haydn, Walter Leigh, Robin Orr

9 Nov 1953	Wigmore Hall	London

Thurston Dart (hpsd), Leppard CO†
Repeat of 21 Oct program

*

21 Jan 1954	Guildhall, Cambridge Univ	Cambridge

chorus, RL (pno – in *Beethoven* conc 3), Cambridge P

11 Feb 1954	Wigmore Hall	London

Lina Lalandi (hpsd), Christopher Bunting (vc), Leppard CO†
Bach, Berkeley, Willy Burkhard, Mozart

14 May 1954	Wigmore Hall	London

Ilse Wolf (s), Neil Black (ob), Neville Marriner, Norman Nelson (vlns), Joy Hall (vc), RL (hpsd) (Redcliffe Fest of British Music)
Handel, Purcell

14 Oct 1954   Bath
RL (hpsd), members of LSO cond. by Cuthbert Bates (Bath
  Bach Fest — 2 programs)
10 Nov 1954   Tate Gallery   London
Wolf (s), Bunting (vc), Maria Donska (pno), RL (pno — in
  Brahms & Schubert lieder)

*

26 Jan 1955   Wigmore Hall   London
Gervase de Peyer (cl), Leppard CO†
  Copland, Mozart, R Strauss, Tchaikovsky
8 Mar 1955   Wigmore Hall   London
George Malcolm (hpsd), Hess (vln), Geoffrey Gilbert, George
  Crozier (fls), Vivian Joseph (vc), Leppard CO†
  Bach, Frank Martin, Mozart, Stravinsky, Telemann
3 May 1955   Royal Fest Hall   London
Jack Rothstein (vln), Leppard CO†/pno (Orpheus Saturday
  Concerts)
  *Bach, Beethoven, Berkeley (sonatina), Corelli, Paganini, Saint-
  Saëns*
15 May 1955   Guildhall Banqueting Room   Bath
Gioconda de Vito, Yehudi Menuhin (vlns), John Shinebourne
  (vc), RL (hpsd)(Bath Fest — followed at 9:45 p.m. by Hand-
  el *Water Music* played on the River Avon by members of the
  Bournemouth SO†, in costume)
  Handel, Purcell, Spohr, Viotti
5 Dec 1955   Royal Fest Hall   London
Gioconda de Vito, Yehudi Menuhin (vlns), John Shinebourne
  (vc), RL (hpsd) (Internatl Celebrity Recital)
  Repeat of 15 May 1955
7 Dec 1955   St Pancras Town Hall   St Pancras
Ilse Wolf (s), Janet Baker (ms), Gwyn Griffiths (b), Hess (vln),
  Michael Dobson (ob), Morley Coll Choir, Leppard O†
  (Morley Coll Concert Soc)
  Bach, Anthony Milner, Bernard Naylor, Purcell, Vivaldi

*

2 Feb 1956   Wigmore Hall   London
Hess (vln), Aronowitz (vla), Leppard O† (Palladian Concert
  Soc)
  Bach, Couperin, Haydn, Mozart

3 Mar 1956
Desmond Bradley (vln), RL (pno) (Westonbirt & District
Music Club)
Brahms, Mozart, Saint-Saëns, Suk, Szymanowski, Vitali
20 Mar 1956   All Souls' Church   London
Eileen McLoughlin (s), Baker (ms), Edgar Fleet (t), Ian Pater-
son (b), Leonard Brain (Eh), RL (hpsd), cond by Peter
Racine Fricker (Morley Coll Concert Soc)
Bach, Gibbons, Monteverdi, Purcell, Tallis, Taverner, Telemann
10 Apr 1956   Wigmore Hall   London
Adeney (fl, picc), Leppard O† (Palladian Concert Soc)
Arnold, Bartók, Rameau, Vivaldi
11 Apr 1956   Wigmore Hall   London
Helen McKinnon (cn), Adeney (fl), Leppard O† (Palladian
Concert Soc)
Arnold, Bartók, Lully, Pergolesi, Vivaldi
15 May 1956   St Pancras Town Hall   St Pancras
orch – RL, Walter Goehr conds
Peter Racine Fricker, Holst, Monteverdi, Purcell, Tippett
15 May 1956   St Pancras Town Hall   St Pancras
Wolf (s), Patricia Clarke (s), Alexander Young (t), Wilfred
Brown (t), Hess (vln), Morley College Choir, Morley Col-
lege Recorder Consort, Leppard O† (Morley College Con-
cert Soc)
*Peter Racine Fricker, Holst, Monteverdi, Purcell, Tippett,
Vaughan Williams*
5 Aug 1956   Victoria & Albert Museum   London
Dart (hpsd), Boyd Neel O† (Museum Gallery Concerts)
Bach, Handel
6 Sep 1956   Guildhall Banqueting Room   Cambridge
"A concert of vocal and instrumental music given in aid of
the Bath Abbey Restoration Fund by the following former
pupils of the City of Bath Boys' School" – schl orch incl. RL
(pno – in *Bartók* 6 Dances in Bulgarian Rhythm, *Brahms*
trio in a, op 114)
29 Oct; 3, 7, 8 Nov 1956
          Cambridge Arts Theatre   Cambridge
Soloists & chorus, Raymond Leppard O† (The Opera Schl,
The Scala Theatre)
*Mozart (*The Marriage of Figaro*)*
18 Nov 1956   Royal Fest Hall   London
Julian Bream (gtr), Philharmonia O† (Palladian Concert Soc)
Haydn, Prokofiev, Rodrigo (conc), *Weber, Villa-Lobos* (conc)

1 Dec 1956   Farmer Hall   Dauntsey
London Reed Trio: Michael Dobson (ob), Stephen Walters
(cl), Cecil James (bsn), with RL (pno) (Dauntsey's Schl
Subscr Concerts)
Beethoven, Bonneau, Milhaud, Mozart, Poulenc, Schumann,
Tartini, Walton

*

4 Apr 1957   Wigmore Hall   London
Osian Ellis (harp), Leppard O†
Bach, Damase, Debussy, Mozart, Pergolesi, Stravinsky
21 May 1957   Royal Fest Hall   London
Valda Aveling, Dart, Malcolm, Denis Vaughan (hpds),
Philomusica of London† (concs for 2, 3 & 4 hpsds – see also
May 1958, 1959, 1960, 1961 & Nov 1965)
22 May 1957   Great Hall, Bristol Univ   Bristol
RL (hpsd), Bristol Madrigal Soc cond. by Herbert Byard
12 Jun 1957   Cambridge Univ   Cambridge
Cambridge Univ Madrigal Soc†
16 Jun 1957   Kenwood   London
Ilse Wolf (s), RL (pno) (Iveagh Bequest)
Brahms, Schubert, Schumann, Wolf
9 Aug 1957   Dartington Hall   Devon
Summer Schl Choir†; Noel Lee, Paul Jacobs, James Blades
(perc), Elizabeth Odell, Richard Bennett, Cornelius Car-
dew (Summer Schl of Music)[6]
Constant Lambert, Daniel Jones, Stravinsky, Taverner
28 Oct – 2 Nov 1957   Cambridge Arts Theatre   Cambridge
The Opera Schl, English Opera Group O† (The Opera Schl)
¶*Britten (Albert Herring)*
6, 7 Nov 1957   The Scala Theatre   London
As 28 October-2 November
14 Nov 1957   Wigmore Hall   London
McKinnon (c), Leppard O† (Palladian Concert Soc)
JC Bach, JS Bach, Couperin, Handel

*

2 Feb 1958   Victoria & Albert Museum   London
Cantelo (s), Leppard O† (Palladian Concert Soc)
Berkeley (Serenade), Finzi (Dies Natalis), Mozart

---

6   Other conductors for concerts this season incl. Robert Craft, George Malcolm.

"The diary of Raymond Leppard's late twenties bears a superficial resemblance to many another young musician's haphazard series of casual engagements. But it is possible to isolate two categories of work which have since born special fruit. One was his engagement as keyboard player in the Philharmonia Orchestra. This was undoubtedly one of the world's finest orchestras, working with Hindemith, Karajan [and others]; and classical records were being made. Orchestral pianist was an excellent position from which to observe the workings of an orchestra and the tricks of the great conductors: Leppard was inside the band but not too busy. The debts he acknowledges particularly mention Karajan, whose cultivation of beautiful sound quality in the nineteenth-century repertory left a lasting influence. [See also, however, related commentary, Chapter VI Section §1, above. (Ed.)]

"The other influential engagements were in the theater. The first was modest: Raymond Leppard was musical director at the Prince's Theatre for the 1953 Christmas production of *Alice Through the Looking Glass.* Then he was appointed musical adviser to the Royal Shakespeare Company at Stratford, which involved writing incidental music as well as advising on appropriate instrumentation. (One of his Stratford achievements was to persuade Peter Hall to do away with the pit orchestra in favor of a wind band with lute, harpsichord and guitar.) Later he worked at the Oxford Playhouse and the Royal Court Theatre. Another engagement was of even more value: two years as a repetiteur at Glyndebourne, from 1954. The operas on which he worked then have left indelible marks on his tastes today: *Falstaff* (which was conducted by Giulini), *The Rake's Progress, Il barbieri di Siviglia, La nozze di Figaro,* and *Don Giovanni;* all of these he names among his special favorites....

"Working with chamber orchestras, Leppard swears by detailed preparation; and this accounts for much of his success with unknown works by composers such as junior members of the Bach family. During his preliminary preparation of a performance, he is conscious of what might loosely be called a sudden understanding of what the music is about: a sudden feeling of conviction in the content and purpose of the piece,

- which then motivates the resulting dynamics and ornamen-
- tation. Like all scholars, he has a wide knowledge of the long
- lost art of ornamentation; but he refuses to use that
- knowledge as dogma, and may well scrap it altogether if he
- finds the character of a solo line becomes confused....
- "Talking to Leppard about music, one realizes that his ap-
- proach is extremely emotional; that the expressive qualities
- which mark his individuality as a musician are those more
- often associated with the nineteenth century. The paradox
- that his interests have [so often been] channeled to the seven-
- teenth and eighteenth centuries [may be] the secret of his
- success. He admits that he likes the restrictions of the seven-
- teenth and eighteenth century musical languages; but the im-
- portant thing to those who admire and enjoy his work is that
- he constantly proves that emotional conviction was not in-
- vented by the nineteenth century. That, for example, the
- operas of Monteverdi have expressive passions just as
- powerful, in their own idiom, as the most purple passages of
- the so-called Romantic era." —*Gillian Widdicombe, liner*
- *notes for Philips recording 6833 035 (works by CPE Bach,*
- *JC Bach, WF Bach, Handel, Mozart & Domenico Scarlatti).*

9 Feb 1958   Victoria & Albert Museum   London
          Wolf (s), Leppard O† (Palladian Concert Soc)
          Bach, Handel, Haydn, Milhaud
16 Feb 1958   Victoria & Albert Museum   London
          Richard Lewis (t), Leppard O† (Palladian Concert Soc)
          Britten, Dvorak, Mozart, Walton
4 Mar 1958   New Theatre   Oxford
          Forbes Robinson, Jeannette Sinclair, Michael Langdon,
          Josephine Veasey, Geraint Evans (bar), John Lanigan, Una
          Hale, Covent Garden Opera Company†
          ¶*Mozart (*The Marriage of Figaro*)*
20 May 1958   Royal Fest Hall   London
          Aveling, Dart, Malcolm, Vaughan (hpds), Philomusica of
          London† (concs for 2, 3 & 4 hpsds—see also May 1957,
          1959, 1960, 1961 & Nov 1965)
3 Jun 1958   Cambridge Univ   Cambridge
          Cambridge Univ Madrigal Soc†

5 Jun 1958   Guildhall   Bath
Jacqueline Delman (s), Leppard O† (The Bath Fest)
Couperin, Haydn, Mozart, Pergolesi, Sacchini
13, 16 Jun 1958   Jubilee Hall   Aldeburgh
Brian Roberts, Pamela Bowden, Hervey Alan, Margaret
Lensky, Bream (lute), English Opera Group† (Aldeburgh
Fest)
¶*Monteverdi (*Il ballo delle Ingrate*)*[7]
8 Aug 1958   Totnes Parish Church   Totnes, Devon
Peter Pears (t), Malcolm (org), Dartington String Qt, Summer
Schl Choir†
*Bach, Britten (*Saint Nicolas*)*
11-18 Oct 1958   Grand Theatre & Opera House   Leeds
Elisabeth Lindermeier (s), Jon Vickers (t), Lauris Elms,
Joseph Rouleau, James Pease, Joan Sutherland (s), Covent
Garden Opera Company† (Leeds Centenary Music Fest)
¶*Handel (*Samson*)*

*

6 Mar 1959   Wigmore Hall   London
Irma Kolassi (s), Jacques Fevrier (pno), Alex Murray (fl),
Philip Jones (ob), Thomas Kelly (cl), John Harper (bsn),
Barry Tuckwell (hn), Cambridge Univ Madrigal Soc† (Le
Centre de la musique française)
Poulenc ("A 60th Birthday Tribute")
24 Mar 1959   Royal Fest Hall   London
Gioconda de Vito (vln), Leppard O† (Palladian Concert Soc)
Haydn, Mozart, Rossini, R Strauss, Stravinsky
28 Apr 1959   Royal Fest Hall   London
Moura Lympany (pno), Leppard O† (Palladian Concert Soc)
Haydn, Mozart, Rossini, R Strauss, Stravinsky
26 May 1959   Royal Fest Hall   London
Aveling, Dart, Malcolm, Vaughan (hpds), Philomusica of Lon-
don† (concs for 2, 3 & 4 hpsds — see also May 1957, 1958,
1960, 1961 & Nov 1965)
9 Jun 1959   Cambridge Univ   Cambridge
Cambridge Univ Madrigal Soc†

---

7   Program also incl. Poulenc (*Terésias*) featuring David Allen, Jennifer Vyvyan (s),
Peter Pears (t), Francis Poulenc, Benjamin Britten (pnos), others, cond. by Charles
Mackerras.

10 Jun 1959   Walcot Church   Bath
Yehudi Menuhin (vln), RL (hpsd) (Bath Fest)
Handel, Purcell
23 Jun 1959   Aldeburgh
§Cambridge Univ Madirgal Soc† (11:30 AM – Parish Church)
Richard Dering, Dunstable, Holst, Poulenc
§Cambridge Univ Madrigal Soc† (5:00 PM – Thorpeness)
Thomas Bateson, Britten, Farnaby, Weelkes, Wilbye
24 Jun 1959   Parish Church   Aldeburgh
Pears (t), Trevor Anthony (b), Bream (lute), Joy Hall (vla da
    gamba), Cambridge Univ Madrigal Soc†/hpsd
Dowland, Purcell
8, 10 Sep 1959   Freemason's Hall   Edinburgh
Vyvyan (s), RL (cont), Leppard Ens† (Edinburgh Int'l Fest)
Handel, Haydn, Purcell (2 different programs)
Fall 1959   Covent Garden   London
Covent Garden Opera Company†
¶*Handel (Samson)*
10 Dec 1959   Goldsmith's Hall   London
Wolf (s), RL (cont), Leppard Ens† (City Music Soc)
Haydn, Purcell, Vivaldi

*

1960s   Sherborne St John   Hampshire
Clarke (s), Adeney (fl), RL (pno) ("A Musical Afternoon at
    the Vyne, Sherborne" – National Trust House in Hamp-
    shire) – also other concerts
Bach, Bishop, Handel, Purcell, Milhaud, Sullivan
30 Mar 1960   Royal Fest Hall   London
Clifford Curzon (pno), Goldsbrough O†[8] (Palladian Concert
    Soc)
JC Bach, Mozart, Stravinsky
8 Apr 1960   Theatre at Rosehill   Moresby, Whitehaven
Pilar Lorengar (s), Leppard Ens†/hpsd
JC Bach, JS Bach
9 Apr 1960   Theatre at Rosehill   Moresby, Whitehaven
Pilar Lorengar (s), RL (hpsd), Leppard Ens†
Couperin, Handel, Haydn, Vivaldi
27 Apr 1960   Senate House, Cambridge Univ   Cambridge
Dart (hpsd), Cambridge Univ Madrigal Soc†
Lelio Colista, Lotti, Monteverdi, D Scarlatti, Gasparo Zanetti

---

8   Later renamed **English Chamber Orchestra.**

ROYAL FESTIVAL HALL
General Manager: T. E. Bean, C.B.E.

Tuesday, 11th October, 1960, at 8 p.m.

PROGRAMME

L'ORFEO ACTS I and II

INTERVAL

L'INCORONAZIONE DI POPPEA Opening Scene
Octavia's Lament
Drinking Duet
Duet and Lullaby
Duet and Coronation Scene

ELSIE MORISON NORMA PROCTER HUGHES CUENOD
DUNCAN ROBERTSON MAX WORTHLEY JOSEPH WARD

Cambridge University Madrigal Society

ENGLISH CHAMBER ORCHESTRA*
Leader: Emanuel Hurwitz

Thurston Dart (Harpsichord) Ralph Downes (Organ)
Desmond Dupré (Lute) Robert Spencer (Lute and Chitarrone)
'Renata Scheffel-Stein (Harp)

The Music of this evening's concert edited and directed by
RAYMOND LEPPARD

(Harpsichords by Thomas Goff)

Management: IBBS & TILLETT LTD 124 WIGMORE STREET. W.I

The first concert ever given by the newly designated
"English Chamber Orchestra"

20 May 1960 Guildhall Southampton
Tuckwell (hn), Goldsbrough O† (John Lewis Partnership
Concerts)
Haydn, Mozart, Schubert
24 May 1960 Royal Fest Hall London
Aveling, Dart, Malcolm, Vaughan, (hpds), Philomusica of
London† (concs for 2, 3 & 4 hpsds — see also May 1957,
1958, 1959, 1961 & Nov 1965)
7 Jun 1960 Cambridge Univ Cambridge
Cambridge Univ Madrigal Soc†

11 Oct 1960   Royal Fest Hall   London
Elsie Morison, Norma Procter, Hugues Cuënod, Duncan
Robertson, Max Worthley, Joseph Ward, Dart (hpsd),
Cambridge Univ Madrigal Soc, ECO†
Monteverdi (L'Orfeo, L'Incoronazione di Poppea scenes)
23, 26, 28 Oct 1960   The Pavilion   Bath
RL (hpsd), other insts; LSO (Bach Fest)
Bach orchestral concerts (3 programs)
24, 27 Oct 1960   Banqueting Room, Guildhall   Bath
RL (hpsd), other insts (Bach Fest)
Bach, Corelli, Handel, A Scarlatti — chamber works (2 programs)
27 Oct 1960   Bath Abbey   Bath
Soloists; RL (hpsd), other insts; City of Bath Bach Choir; LSO
(Bach Fest)
Bach choral works
3 Nov 1960   Winter Gardens   Bournemouth
Nina Milkina (pno), Bournemouth SO†
JC Bach, Dvorak, Mozart, Schubert
5 Nov 1960   Queen's Theatre   Minehead
As 3 November
6 Nov 1960   Theatre Royal   Exeter
As 3 November
7 Nov 1960   Queen's Hall   Barnstaple
As 3 November
10 Nov 1960   Winter Gardens   Bournemouth
Manoug Parikian (vln), Bournemouth SO†
Mendelssohn (conc), Mozart, Prokofiev, Wagner
12 Nov 1960   Farmer Hall   Dauntsey
RL (hpsd), Leppard Ens† (Dauntsey's Schl Subscription
Series)
JC Bach, Couperin, Pergolesi, Purcell, Vivaldi
26 Nov 1960   Saffron Waldren and District Music Club
at the Training College   Cambridgeshire
Hess (vln), RL (pno)
Bach, Beethoven, Prokofiev, Schubert
21, 22 Dec 1960   Theatre at Rosehill, Univ of Durham
Moresby, Whitehaven
Delman (s), Cuénod (t), RL (cont), Leppard Ens†
Buxtehude, Couperin, Purcell, A Scarlatti, Vivaldi
*

Royal Festival Hall, Feb 1961. The English Chamber Orchestra, conducted by Colin Davis with Raymond Leppard at the harpsichord, plays Bach's *Concerto* for Two Violins with David and Igor Oistrakh, making their joint London debut.

21 Jan 1961   Leeds Town Hall   Leeds

Emanuel Hurwitz (vln), Cecil Aronowitz (vla), ECO†[9]
Arnold (Sinfonietta), *JC Bach, Mozart, Schubert*
Feb 1961   Royal Fest Hall   London
David & Igor Oistrakh (vlns), RL (hpsd), ECO cond.
Colin Davis
Bach
23 Feb 1961   Sheldonian Theatre   Oxford
David & Igor Oistrakh (vlns), ECO† (John Lewis Partnership
Concerts)
Bach

---

9   Formerly The Goldsbrough Orchestra.

7 Mar 1961   Town Hall   Chelsea
Allan Schiller (pno), ECO† (Chelsea Music Club)
Arnold (Sinfonietta), Berkeley (Serenade), Haydn, Mozart
10 Mar 1961   All Saints Church   North Runcton, Norfolk
Cambridge Univ Madrigal Soc†
Bach, Brahms, Kodaly, Purcell
20 Mar 1961   Hampshire
Clarke (s), Hess (vln), RL (pno) (Basingstroke Concert Club)
Bach, Beethoven, Elgar, Fauré, Handel
9 Apr 1961   Levens Hall   Westmorland
Leppard Ens: Hess (vln), Bernard Richards (vc), Adeney (fl),
RL (hpsd)
Bach, Haydn
15 Apr 1961   London
Boyd Neel O† (British Medical Assn)
*Britten (Simple Symphony), Handel, Mozart, Warlock
(Capriol-Suite), Wirèn (Serenade)*
23 May 1961   Royal Fest Hall   London
Aveling, Dart, Malcolm, Parsons (hpds), Philomusica of Lon-
don† (concs for 2, 3 & 4 hpsds — see also May 1957, 1958,
1959, 1960 & Nov 1965)
CPE Bach-Leppard, JS Bach, George Malcolm (Variations on a
Theme of Mozart *for 4 hpsds), Mozart, Vivaldi, Vivaldi-
Bach, Vivaldi-Dart*
9 Jun 1961   Cambridge Univ   Cambridge
Cambridge Univ Madrigal Soc†
9 Sep 1961   Leith Town Hall   Leith
Evans (bar), ECO† (Edinburgh International Fest)
Cimarosa (Il maestro di capella)
22 Sep 1961   Royal Fest Hall   London
Irmgard Seefried (s), ECO†
JC Bach, Beethoven, Haydn, Mahler, Mozart, Schubert
2 Dec 1961   Leeds Town Hall   Leeds
Carmen Prietto, Joseph Ward, RL (hpsd), Boyd Neel O†
Bach, Mozart
6 Dec (1961?)   Victoria & Albert Museum   London
Clarke (s), Gerald English (t), Cambridge Univ Madrigal Soc,
Leppard Ens† (Palladian Concert Soc)
Monteverdi

*

1962   Pavilion, Hemel Hemstead   St Albans
Cambridge Univ Madrigal Soc† (Arts Fest)

6 Jan 1962   Levens Hall   Westmorland
Leppard Ens: Hess (vln), Richards (vc), Adeney (fl),
RL (hpsd)
CPE Bach, Handel, Haydn
9 Jan 1962   Wimbledon Town Hall   Wimbledon
Boyd Neel O†
Bach, Mozart, Warlock (Capriol Suite), Tchaikovsky
11 Feb 1962   Princess Theatre   Torquay
Valerie Tryon (pno), Bournemouth SO†
Beethoven, Stravinsky
12 Jun 1962   Cambridge Univ   Cambridge
Cambridge Univ Madrigal Soc†
17 Jun 1962   Guildhall   Bath
Cuénod (t), RL (pno) with Nadia Boulanger, Yehudi
    Menuhin, Robert Masters, Derek Simpson (Bath Fest Soc)
Haydn, Machaut, Monteverdi, Purcell, Schütz
21 Jul 1962   Charleston Manor   Alfriston
Wolf (s), Cuénod (t), English (t), Christopher Keyte (b),
    Leppard Ens† (Sussex Fest)
Monteverdi
27 Jul 1962   Theatre at Rosehill   Moresby, Whitehaven
Oralia Dominguez, RL (hpsd)(1st half of program featured
    solo pno recital by Alexis Weissenberg)
Falla, Milhaud, Monteverdi
17 Sep 1962   Salle de l'Emulation   Liège
Vyvyan (s), L'orchestre de chambre de la Radio-diffusion-
    Télévision Belge†
JC Bach, Bononcini, Handel, Haydn, Mozart
10 Nov 1962   Leeds Town Hall   Leeds
Paul Tortelier (vc), Boyd Neel O†
Boccherini, Haydn, Schubert, Tchaikovsky
9 Dec 1962   Levens Hall   Westmorland
Leppard Ens: Hess (vln), Richards (vc), Adeney (fl),
RL (hpsd)
Bach, Handel, Haydn, Vivaldi
*

24 Feb 1963   Victoria & Albert Museum   London
Stefania Woytowicz (s), ECO† (Palladian Concert Soc)
Handel, Haydn
9 Mar 1963   Senate House, Cambridge Univ   Cambridge
Cambridge Univ Madrigal Soc†

"The second novelty of the year [1962 at Glyndebourne] was Monteverdi's *L'incoronazione di Poppea* [in Raymond Leppard's new performing edition, produced by Günther Rennert and conducted by John Pritchard], which a Nottingham paper, in a story about a local ex-collier who had joined the Glyndebourne chorus, delighted everybody by calling 'The Coronation of the Pope'....

"To perform *Poppea* at Glyndebourne was in its way a greater challenge to its audience than the [same year's new] production of *Pelléas*. Debussy's opera had at least some idiomatic points of contact with everyday musical life; Monteverdi's, on the other hand, had none. It was unlike anything the great majority of the audience had ever heard in their lives before and I could find only one other critic who had also heard the [1927 Oxford University Opera Club performance, in Sir Jack Westrup's edition], and he was an undergraduate at the time. The odds against *Poppea* making any sort of impact on the non-professional listener ought to have been overwhelming. It didn't even have the snob appeal which we are always told makes people go to Glyndebourne. But once more the instinct which had sensed the quality of *Pelléas* recognized the genius of Monteverdi—to such effect, indeed, that for the first time an opera not by Mozart has been performed in three successive years at the Festival Opera House. Raymond Leppard's arrangement of the music of *Poppea* was most imaginative and dramatically effective. He was criticized for an allegedly anachronistic harp glissando at one point in his score; his reply was that nobody could tell him that in 1642 people didn't run their fingers up and down the strings in a glissando just for the joy of it—just as anybody still does today. This struck me as the best possible answer." —*Spike Hughes,* **Glyndebourne: A History of the Festival Opera,** *New Ed. (London: David & Charles, 1981).*

10 Mar 1963   Victoria & Albert Museum   London
Kerstin Meyer (ms), ECO† (Palladian Concert Soc)
Handel, Haydn
9 May 1963   Royal Fest Hall   London
Yehudi Menuhin, Hurwitz, Kenneth Sillito (vlns), Adeney (fl),
Martin Gatt (bsn), Keith Harvey (ob), Michael Howard
(org cont), ECO†
Vivaldi
27 May 1963   Audley End House, Cambridge Univ   Cambridge
Cambridge Univ Madrigal Soc†
4 Jun 1963   Cambridge Univ   Cambridge
Cambridge Univ Madrigal Soc† ("Singing on the River")
Singers are in punts moving down the River Avon towards
St John's Bridge. "As the procession is the width of seven
punts, ladies and gentlemen in boats on the river are asked
to move out of the way during the short interval before the
last madrigal, so that the procession may pass down the river
unimpeded.
    "Punters: You are requested to make as little noise as pos-
sible, this evening *please,* on the river below Trinity Bridge
and Clare Bridge – in order not to disturb the Trinity Hall
production of *Hamlet* on the terrace."
8 Jun 1963   Pavilion   Bath
Yehudi Menuhin, Alberto Lysey (vlns), Essex Youth O† (Bath
Festival)
*Arnold (*3 Dances*), Bach (*conc 2 vlns in d*), Beethoven, Sibelius
(*sym 2*)*
11 Jun 1963   Assembly Rooms   Bath
Yehudi Menuhin (vln), Johnny Dankworth, Maurice Gendron
(vc), RL, Patrick Smith, David Snell, members of
Dankworth O, William Russo & the Russo O (Bath Fest)
"An evening of new music, improvisation and jazz" (incl. im-
provisation by selected insts prepared by Johnny
Dankworth & RL and a newly commissioned work by Wil-
liam Russo, *Music for Violin and Jazz Orchestra*)
29 Jun 1963   The Vyne   Basingstoke
Susa Longfield (s), Aurèle Nicolet (fl), RL (hpsd) (National
Trust Concert Soc)
CPE Bach, JS Bach, Couperin, Handel, Haydn, Purcell
2 Jul 1963   Town Hall   Oxford
Rita Streich (s), Geoffrey Gilbert (fl), Lionel Salter (cont),
ECO† (English Bach Fest)
CPE Bach, JC Bach, JL Bach, WF Bach

13 Jul 1963   Charleston Manor   Alfriston
Cantelo (s), Lewis (t), RL (hpsd), Leppard Ens† (Sussex Fest)
JC Bach, Handel, Haydn, Purcell
15 Jul 1963   Civic Theatre   Chelmsford
Peter Thomas, Christopher Adey (vlns), Essex Youth O†
(Anglo-Dutch Orchestral Fest)
*Arnold (Malcolm — 3 English Dances), Bach, Beethoven,
Sibelius*
27 Jul 1963   St Nicholas Chapel   King's Lynn
Adeney (fl), ECO† (13th King's Lynn Fest)
Bach
19 Sep 1963   Zaal l'Emulation   Liège
Aimée Van de Wiele (hpsd), Ingrid Häbler, Orchestre de
Chambre de Liège† (Festival de musique de Liège)
Couperin, Haydn, Mozart, Rameau
21 Sep 1963   Conservatoire   Liège
Dart, Malcolm, RL, Charles Koenig (hpsds), L'Orchestre
Symphonique de Liège (Festival de musique de Liège)
CPE Bach, JS Bach, Vivaldi, Vivaldi-Bach
24 Sep 1963   Victoria & Albert Museum   London
Stefania Woytowicz (s), ECO† (Palladian Concert Soc)
Handel, Haydn
4 Oct 1963   Fairfield Hall   Croydon
Eugene List (pno), Northern SO†
Haydn, Liszt, Mozart, Shostakovich (conc 1)
2 Dec 1963   Festsaal des Evangelischen Gemeindehauses
ECO†/hpsd (Städtisches Kulturamt Leverkusen)
JC Bach (conc op 7/5), Couperin, Haydn, Monteverdi
Dec 1963   Musikhalle gr. Saal   Hamburg
Ingird Haebler (pno), ECO†
*Beethoven (conc 2), Britten (Frank Bridge Variations), Haydn,
Schoenberg*
6 Dec 1963   Assembly House   Norwich
RL (pno), Norwich CO cond. by Cyril Pearce
*Byrd, Elgar, Finzi, Holst, Mozart (conc K 414), Purcell, Matyas
Seiber*
9 Dec 1963   Herkules-Saal   Munich
Ingrid Haebler (pno), ECO†
*Britten (Frank Bridge Variations), Haydn, Mozart (conc K
453), Schoenberg*

*

14, 15, 16 Jan 1964   Philharmonic Hall   Liverpool
Cantelo (s), Heinz Massen, Carlos Feller, Alan Stringer, Royal
     Liverpool PO†
Britten, Haydn, Mozart, Pergolesi
16 Feb 1964   Victoria & Albert Museum   London
Heather Harper (s), Hurwitz (vln), ECO† (Palladian Concert
     Soc)
Handel, Haydn
11 Mar 1964   Senate House, Cambridge Univ   Cambridge
Joan Westwood, RL (hpsd) (Cambridge Univ Madrigal Soc –
     for the benefit of the Fitzwilliam Music Library)
Bach
22 Apr 1964   Colston Hall   Bristol
ECO†
Mozart, Tchaikovsky
6 Jun 1964   Dyrham Park   Bath
Baker (s), RL (hpsd)
Arne, Bach, Handel, Haydn
Summer 1964   Glyndebourne Festival Opera   Glyndebourne
Saramae Endich (Poppea), Oralia Dominguez, Elizabeth
     Bainbridge, Annon Lee Silver, Richard Lewis (Nero),
     Walter Alberti, Carlo Cava, Cuénod, Gerald English,
     Stafford Dean, Glyndebourne Fest O†
¶*Monteverdi (L'incoronazione di Poppea – RL vers)(RL*
     Glyndebourne cond. debut: 12 performs)
11 Jun 1964   Cambridge Univ   Cambridge
Cambridge Univ Madrigal Soc†
12 Jun 1964   Dyrham Park   Bath
English (t), Cuénod (t), Derek Simpson (vc), RL (hpsd)
Bach, Monteverdi
15 Jul 1964   Goldsmith's Hall   London
Magda Laszlo (s), Cuénod (t), RL (hpsd) (Fest of the City of
     London)
Cavalli, Cesti, Monteverdi
19 Jul 1964   Guildhall of St George   King's Lynn
Ens† (14th King's Lynn Fest)
"An Evening of Chamber Music in Honor of Dr Charles
     Burney" (arr & dir by RL)
15 Aug 1964   Philharmonic Hall   Liverpool
English (t), Tuckwell (hn), Royal Liverpool PO†
Britten (Serenade), Dvorak, Schubert

12 Sep 1964   Melford Hall   Aldeburgh
Harper (s), Robert Tear (t), Owen Brannigan (b), Adeney (fl),
    RL (hpsd), ECO† (Aldeburgh Fest)
Bach
18 Oct 1964   Odeon Theatre, Swiss Cottage   London
Peter Frankl (pno), RPO†
Beethoven (conc 4), Liszt, Sibelius
22 Oct 1964   Sheldonian Theatre   Oxford
As 18 October

*

20 Jan 1965   Commonwealth Institute   London
Harper (s), Hurwitz (vln), Adeney, Norman Knight (fls),
    Philip Jones (tpt), RL (hpsd), ECO†
Bach
27 Jan 1965   Commonwealth Institute   London
Cantelo (s), Clarke (s), Keith Harvey (vc), ECO†
Handel, Haydn
3 Feb 1965   Commonwealth Institute   London
Wolf (s), English (t), Tear (t), Keyte (b), ECO†
Monteverdi
18 Feb 1965   Victoria Hall   Hanley
Iona Brown (vln), Royal Liverpool PO†
Beethoven, Mendelssohn (conc), Schubert
10 Mar 1965   Senate House, Cambridge Univ   Cambridge
Cambridge Univ Madrigal Soc†
8 Jun 1965   Cambridge Univ   Cambridge
Cambridge Univ Madrigal Soc†
11 Jun 1965   Cambridge Univ   Cambridge
Ens incl. RL (pno), Keith Elcome (pno) (Trinity College
    Music Soc)
Walter Leigh (The Jolly Roger, or The Admiral's Daughter)
22 Jul 1965   Guildhall of St George   King's Lynn
Cantelo (s), Johanna Peters (cn), English (t), John Holmes
    (bar), RL (hpsd), insts† (15th King's Lynn Fest)
"Purcell Cabaret" *(for details, see Appendix II, below).*
6 Sep 1965   London
RL (hpsd), ECO cond. by Charles Mackerras
Bach, Purcell
5 Oct 1965   London Coliseum   London
Patricia Kern (ms), John Wakefield (t), Sadler's Wells Opera†
¶*Monteverdi (L'Orfeo — in RL edition)*

: 473 :

9 Nov 1965   Royal Fest Hall   London
Aveling, Dart, Malcolm, Parsons (hpds), Philomusica of London† (concs for 2, 3 & 4 hpsds – see also May 1957, 1958, 1959, 1960, 1961)
17 Nov 1965   Commonwealth Institute   London
ECO†
Bach, Telemann
5 Dec 1965   Levens Hall   Westmorland
Tear (t), English (t), Richards (vc), RL (hpsd)
Bach (English Suite 2), Monteverdi
9 Dec 1965   Colfox Schl Hall   Dorset
Adeney (fl), RL (pno) (Bridport & West Dorset Music Clubs)
19 Dec 1965   Odeon Theatre, Swiss Cottage   London
Jeannette Sinclair (s), Helen Watts (c), Tear (t), Keyte (b), Heinrich Schütz Choir, RPO†
¶*Handel (*Messiah*)*

*

1966   Norwegian Opera   Oslo
Kari Frisell, Sven Olof Eliasson, Astrid Hellesnes, Marit Isene, Knut Skram, RL, Guttorm Skjerven (hpsds), Norske Opera (Norwegian Opera)†
*Monteverdi (*Poppeas Kroning – The Coronation of Poppea*)*
23 Jan 1966   Selwyn Coll Music Soc   Cambridge
RL (hpsd – solo recital)
CPE Bach, JS Bach, Couperin, Haydn, David Spence-Lyons (5 Preludes)
12 Feb 1966   Leeds Town Hall   Leeds
Ida Haendel (vln), ECO†
Mozart (incl. conc K 219)
6 Mar 1966   Victoria & Albert Museum   London
Baker (ms), Sillito (vln), Raymond Keenlyside (vln), Richards (vc), RL (hpsd) (Palladian Concert Soc)
Handel, Haydn
13 Mar 1966
Hurwitz (vln), Derek Simpson (vc), RL (hpsd)
Handel, Haydn
20 Mar 1966   Victoria & Albert Museum   London
Elizabeth Harwood (s), ECO† (Palladian Concert Soc)
Handel, Haydn
1 Apr 1966   Royal Fest Hall   London
Cantelo (s), Watts (c), English (t), Keyte (b), Heinrich Schütz Choir, ECO†

Haydn *(The Seven Last Words of Our Savior on the Cross)*
10 May 1966   SPA Pavilion   Felixstowe
Marjorie Thomas (cn), Adeney (fl), RL (pno)
Bach, Berkeley (Sonatina fl & pno), Brahms, Giordani, Haydn,
Mozart, Purcell, Schubert
13 May 1966   Westminster Abbey   London
Cantelo (s), Yvonne Minton (ms), Watts (c), Maureen Lehane,
Tear (t), English (t), Keyte (b), Ambrosian Singers, Hein-
rich Schütz Choir, Douglas Guest, Cecil Aronowitz, ECO†
Cavalli (Messa concertata), Rameau, Vaughan Williams
14 Jul 1966   Senate House, Cambridge Univ   Cambridge
Cantelo (s), Watts (c), English (t), Keyte (b), RL (cont),
Cambridge Univ Madrigal Soc, ECO† (Fitzwilliam
Museum 150th Anniversary Concert)
Boyce, Byrd, Charpentier, Fitzwilliam, Handel, Marenzio, Mor-
ley, D Scarlatti, Stradella
27 Jul 1966   Castleacre Priory   King's Lynn
Cambridge Univ Madrigal Soc† (16th King's Lynn Fest)
Farmer, Gibbons, Greaves, Marenzio, Monteverdi, Morley,
Poulenc, Tomkins, Vautor, Wilbye

29 Jul 1966 St Nicholas Chapel King's Lynn
Cantelo (s), Pamela Bowden, Lehane, Watts (c), Bernard
Dickerson, English (t), Stafford Dean (b), Keyte (b),
Ambrosian Singers, Schütz Choir, ECO† (16th King's Lynn
Fest)
Cavalli
30 Jul 1966 Corn Exchange King's Lynn
Fou Ts'ong (pno), ECO† (16th King's Lynn Fest)
Honegger, Milhaud, Mozart (incl. conc K 595), *Schubert*
18 Aug 1966 Baalbeck (Lebanon)
ECO† (11th Festival International de Baalbeck)
Honegger, Haydn, Purcell, Schoenberg
20 Aug 1966 Baalbeck (Lebanon)
Adeney (fl), Aronowitz (vla), Hurwitz (vln), ECO† (11th Fes-
tival International de Baalbeck)
Arnold (fl conc), Bach, Mozart (sinfonia concertante K364*),
Schubert*
26 Aug 1966 Kunsthaus Luzerne
Nicolet (fl), ECO† (Internationale MusikFestwochen)
Arnold (conc), Purcell, Schubert, Schoenberg
5 Sep 1966 Royal Albert Hall London
Cantelo (s), Minton (ms), Dean (b), Keyte (b), Stephen
Bishop, BBC Chorus, ECO† (Henry Wood Promenade
Concerts)
Bach, Cavalli, Handel, Mozart
*

9 Feb 1967 Grande Salle Henry Le Boeuf, Palais des
Beaux-Arts Brussels
Harper (s), ECO†
Cavallil, Cesti, Monteverdi
3 Mar 1967 Purcell Room, South Bank London
Flora Robson, George Rylands, Gary Watson, Cantelo (s),
Tear (t), Richards (vc), RL (hpsd)(Purcell Room inaugural
recitals / Greater London Council)
"Homage to Henry Purcell: His music and the poetry of his
time (by John Milton, John Dryden) in a program devised
by George Rylands & RL" (see also 29 Oct 1967; 23 Jun, 11
Jul, 30 Jul 1968)
5 Mar 1967 Purcell Room, South Bank London
Baker (ms), RL (hpsd, pno) (Purcell Room inaugural recitals
/ Greater London Council)
*Handel, Maw (*The Voice of Love*), Purcell, Schubert, Wolf*

17 Mar 1967   Queen Elizabeth Hall   London
Harper (s), Watts (c), Tear (t), Dean (b), Heinrich Schütz
Chorale, Hurwitz, Sillito (vlns), ECO†
Bach
14 May 1967   Queen Elizabeth Hall   London
Clarke (s), Margaret Curphey (s), Ursula Connors (s), Peta
Bartlett (s), Minton (ms), Maureen Lehane (cn), Tear (t),
Kenneth Bowen (t), Dean (b), Michael Rippon (b), ECO†
(Monteverdi Quartercentenary 1567-1643)
*Monteverdi (*Il ballo delle Ingrate, Madrigali guerrieri et
amorosi)
6 Jun 1967   Cambridge Univ   Cambridge
Cambridge Univ Madrigal Soc†
16, 18, 23, 27 Jun; 4, 9, 13, 15,
17, 20, 22, 24, 26, 28, 30 Jul 1967   Glyndebourne
Isabel Garcisanz, Anne Howells, Irmgard Stadler, Maurene
Lehane, Jane Berbié, Wakefield (Ormindo), Peter-Chris-
toph Runge, Hugues Cuénod, Federico Davià, Richard
Van Allen, Glyndebourne Festival Opera, LPO†
¶*Cavalli (*L'Ormindo— *in RL edition)*
23 Jul 1967   St Nicholas Chapel   King's Lynn
Cantelo (s), Jean Allister (cn), English (t), Richard Angas (b),
BBC Northern Singers, ECO† (17th King's Lynn Fest)
*Haydn (*Maria Theresa Mass*), Milhaud, Mozart*
25 Jul 1967   Guildhall of St George   King's Lynn
Cantelo (s), Tear (t), English (t), Keyte (b), ECO† (17th King's
Lynn Fest)
Monteverdi
4 Aug 1967   Royal Albert Hall   London
Cantelo (s), Kern (ms), Minton (cn), Wakefield (t), John
Noble (bar), Dean (b), Tess Miller (ob), BBC Chorus,
ECO† (Henry Wood Promenade Concerts)
*Handel (*Saul III*), Monteverdi, Mozart*
29 Aug 1967   Palais des Beaux-Arts   Brussels
Cantelo (s), Kern (ms), Watts (cn), Margaret Curphey,
Wakefield (t), Tear (t), English (t), Clifford Grant, Dean
(b), chorus & orchestra† (Fest of Flanders)
¶*Monteverdi (*L'Orfeo)
7 Sep 1967   Leith Town Hall   Leith
Harper (s), Tear (t), insts incl. RL (hpsd) (Edinburgh Inter-
national Fest)
Cavalli, Monteverdi

• "The first known performance anywhere since 1644 of *L'Ormindo* by Cavalli, arranged by Raymond Leppard, proved the [1967 Glyndebourne] season's outstanding experience. This enchanting opera, a remarkable medley of solemn, pathetic, bawdy and comic scenes, was a triumph of music and performance.... What proved to be Günther Rennert's last production for Glyndebourne suffered from a little too mcuh German 'comicity', however, from a musical standpoint a fascinatingly inventive and entertaining score received as satsifying a performance as anything at Glyndebourne for a long time.

"Without exception the cast was first-rate, Anne Howells making such an outstanding success of Erisbe that one critic was convinced that Rennert had obviously built his production 'round the warm, one might almost say sexy, Erisbe of Anne Howells'—which, considering that Miss Howells came into the production as a replacement so late that she didn't even get her name in the program, was pretty fast production-building. It did not seem to occur to the writer that Anne Howells's own individuality might have had something to do with it. But that's a singer's life all over: it's your responsibility if you're bad, somebody else's if you're good. You can't win.

"Perhaps fearing they were in for another *Jephtha*, the public was a little timid about booking for *L'Ormindo* to begin with, but once word got around that it provided an evening of beautiful and unusually entertaining music, the work settled down as one of the most popular operas in the Glyndebourne repertoire." —*Spike Hughes*, **Glyndebourne: A History of the Festival Opera**, *New Ed. (London: David & Charles, 1981).*

9 Sep 1967   Leith Town Hall   Leith
   Harper (s), Tear (t), English (t), Keyte (b), 6 insts incl. RL
   (hpsd) (Edinburgh International Fest)
   Cavalli, Monteverdi
18 Sep 1967   Assembly Hall, Nicolson Inst   Stornoway
   Thomas Ratter (ob), Scottish National O†
   CPE Bach, Françaix, Rossini, Schubert, Stravinsky

19 Sep 1967   Tain
    As 18 September
20 Sep 1967   Kirkwall
    As 18 September
21 Sep 1967   Lerwick
    As 18 September
28 Sep 1967   Koninklijke Opera   Gent
    Cantelo (s), Kern (ms), Watts (ms), English (t), Wakefield (t),
    Tear (t), Clifford Grant, Dean (b), chorus & orch† (Fest of
    Flanders)
    ¶*Monteverdi (L'Orfeo)*
13 Oct 1967   Queen Elizabeth Hall   London
    José-Luis Garcia (vln), Tess Miller (ob), Douglas Whittaker
    (fl), Philomusica of London†/hpsd
    Bach
24 Oct 1967   Music Hall   Aberdeen
    Adeney (fl), Osian Ellis (hp), ECO†
    Debussy, Haydn, Mozart (conc K 299), Orr (String Rhapsody)
29 Oct 1967   Wigmore Hall   London
    Flora Robson, George Rylands, Gary Watson, Cantelo (s),
    Tear (t), Richards (vc), RL (hpsd) (The Apollo Soc)
    "Homage to Henry Purcell: His music and the poetry of his
    time (by John Milton, John Dryden) in a program devised
    by George Rylands & RL" (see also 3 Mar 1967; 23 Jun, 11
    Jul, 30 Jul 1968)
 4 Nov 1967   Leeds Town Hall   Leeds
    Stephen Bishop (pno), ECO†
    Haydn, Mozart (conc K 503), Stravinsky
17 Nov 1967   Queen Elizabeth Hall   London
    Baker (ms), ECO†
    Handel, Haydn, Smalley (Variations)
16 Dec 1967   Theatre at Rosehill   Moresby, Whitehaven
    Baker (ms), Leppard Ens†
    Cavalli, Centi, Corelli, Monteverdi, A Scarlatti
21 Dec 1967   Queen Elizabeth Hall   London
    Harper (s), Watts (c), Tear (t), John Shirley-Quirk (b),
    Ambrosian Singers, ECO†
    ¶*Handel (Messiah)*

*

14 Jan 1968
    Cantelo (s), English (t), Richards (vc), RL (hpsd)

27 Jan 1968   Queen Elizabeth Hall   London
John McCaw (cl), David Mason (tpt), Richard Morgan (ob),
Michael Winfield (ob), New Philharmonia CO†
Boccherini, Mozart, Nielsen (cl conc), Telemann
29 Jan 1968   Théatre municipal   Lausanne
Cantelo (s), Cuénod (t), L'Orchestre de chambre
de Lausanne†
Cavalli, Maw (sym for co), Monteverdi, Purcell
17 Apr 1968   Teatro municipal   Rio de Janeiro
Adeney (fl), Hurwitz (vln), Aronowitz (vla), ECO†
Arnold (flute conc), Haydn, Mozart, Schubert
20 Apr 1968   Teatro municipal   São Paulo
As 17 April
24 Apr 1968   (Brazil)
Adeney (fl), Aronowitz (vla), ECO†
Arnold (Sinfonietta), Haydn, Holst, Pergolesi
26 Apr 1968   S.O.D.R.E. Estudio Auditorio   Montevideo
As 17 April
27 Apr 1968   Teatro Colón   Buenos Aires
As 17 April (Mozarteum Argentino)
30 Apr 1968   Teatro Colón   Buenos Aires
Sillito (vln), ECO† (Mozarteum Argentino)
Handel, Holst (St Paul Suite), Mozart (incl. conc K 216)
2 May 1968   Teatro Argentino   Buenos Aires
As 24 April
4 May 1968   Teatro concepcion   Concepcion (Chile)
Adeney (fl), Aronowitz (vla), ECO†
Arnold (Sinfonietta), Holst, Haydn, Mozart
5 May 1968   Teatro municipal   Viña del mar (Chile)
Sillito (vln), ECO†
Handel, Holst, Mozart
7 May 1968   Teatro municipal   Lima
As 17 April
10 May 1968   Teatro municipal   Caracas
As 17 April
14 May 1968   Instituto nacional de bellas artes   Mexico City
As 17 April
18 May 1968   Instituto nacional de bellas artes   Mexico City
Sillito (vln), ECO†
Handel, Holst, Mozart

11 Jun 1968   Jubilee Hall   Aldeburgh
Vyvyan (s), Tear (t), RL (hpsd), Cremona String Qt, Roger
Smalley (pno), Shirley-Quirk (bar), Britten (pno)
Britten, Cavalli, Cesti, Peter Sculthorpe, Roger Smalley
23 Jun 1968   Theatre Royal   Bath
Peggy Ashcroft, George Rylands, Gary Watson, Cantelo (s),
Tear (t), Richards (vc), RL (hpsd) (Bath Fest)
"Music and poetry of the time of Henry Purcell" (program
devised by George Rylands & RL, orig. given as the in-
augural recital at Purcell Room, South Bank, London on 3
Mar 1967; see also 29 Oct 1967, 11 Jul 1968, 30 Jul 1968)
26 Jun 1968   The Maltings   Aldeburgh
Philip Jones Brass Ens, RL (hpsd) (Aldeburgh Fest)
Anon, Bach, Anthony Bassano, Jerome Bassano, Britten, Bull,
Stephen Dodgson, Frescobaldi, G Gabrieli, Stefan de Haan,
Monteverdi, Leonard Salzedo, Scheidt
28 Jun 1968   Jubilee Hall   Aldeburgh
Vyvyan (s), Mary Wells (s), ECO chamber group†/hpsd (Al-
deburgh Fest)
Couperin (le Grand)
Summer 1968   Glyndebourne Festival Opera   Glyndebourne
Garcisanz, Howells, Wakefield, Runge, Cuénod, Davià, Van
Allan, Glyndebourne Fest Opera, LPO†
¶*Cavalli (L'Ormindo—RL vers)*
11 Jul 1968   Stationers' Hall   London
As 23 Jun 1968 (Gerald English substituting for Robert Tear)
15 Jul (1968?)   Goldsmith's Hall   London
Laszlo (s), Cuénod (t), insts (Humphreys, Ireland, Gerhardt,
Simpson, McGee)†/hpsd (City of Music Soc)
Cavalli, Cesti, Monteverdi
24 Jul 1968   Royal Albert Hall   London
Glyndebourne Fest Opera, LPO† (BBC-Henry Wood
Promenade Concerts)
¶*Cavalli (L'Ormindo—concert vers.)*
30 Jul 1968   Guildhall of St George   King's Lynn
Peggy Ashcroft, Cantelo (s), George Rylands, Tear (t), Gary
Watson, Richards (vc), RL (hpsd) (18th King's Lynn Fest)
"Music and poetry of the time of Henry Purcell" (program
devised by George Rylands & RL, orig. given as the in-
augural recital at Purcell Room, South Bank, London on 3
Mar 1967; see also 29 Oct 1967, 23 Jun, 11 Jul 1968)

1 Aug 1968   Hillington Church   King's Lynn
Simon Preston (org), ECO members† (18th King's Lynn Fest)
Handel, Purcell
30 Aug 1968   Gloucester Cathedral   Gloucester
Sillito (vln), ECO† (Three Choirs Festival, being the 241st an-
nual meeting of the Three Choirs of Gloucester, Worcester
and Hereford)
*Haydn, Mozart (conc K 216), Rawsthorne (Elegiac Rhapsody),
Schubert*
4 Sep 1968   Palais des Beaux-Arts   Brussels
Isabel Garcisanz, Hanneke Van Bork, Jean Allister, Anne
Howells, Jane Berbié, Wakefield (t), Peter-Christoph
Runge, Cuénod (t), Federico Davià, Richard Van Allen,
Martin Isepp (hpsd), Glyndebourne Fest Opera, LPO†
(Fest of Flanders)
¶*Cavalli (L'Ormindo)*
5 Sep 1968   Koninklijke Opera   Gent
Wakefield (t), Runge, Isabel Garcisanz, Hanneke Van Bork,
Jean Allister, Cuénod (t), Anne Howells (ms), Jane Berbié,
Federico Davia, Richard Van Allan, Glyndebourne Fest
Opera, LPO† (Fest of Flanders)
¶*Cavalli (L'Ormindo)*
15 Sep 1968   Galeriegebäde Herrenhausen   Hannover
Harper (s), Annon Lee Silver (s), Angas (b), Hannoverschen
Solistenvereinigung, RL (hpsd), Rundfunkorchester Han-
nover des NDR†
Monteverdi, Purcell, A Scarlatti
16, 17, 18 Oct 1968   Oslo
Liv Glaser (pno), Filharmonisk Selskaps Orkester†
Bach, Beethoven, Walton
25 Oct 1968   Queen Elizabeth Hall   London
Minton (ms), ECO†
Gazzaniga, Maw (Nocturne), Mozart
30 Oct 1968   Rutherford College of Technology   Newcastle
Northern Sinfonia O†
Grieg, Handel, Mozart, Schubert, Vivaldi
31 Oct 1968   Bedworth
As 30 October
1 Nov 1968   Queen Elizabeth Hall   London
As 30 October
2 Nov 1968   Guildhall, Cambridge Univ   Cambridge
As 30 October

6 Dec 1968   Queen Elizabeth Hall   London
Cantelo (s), Watts (c), Tear (t), Shirley-Quirk (b), Ambrosian
Singers, ECO†
Handel (Messiah — chamber vers. ed. RL)

8 Dec 1968   Royal Albert Hall   London
Sheila Armstrong (s), Anna Reynolds, English (t), Raimund
Herincx, London P Choir, LPO†
Handel (Messiah — Mozart vers.)

20 Dec 1968   Queen Elizabeth Hall   London
Harper (s), ECO†
Cavalli, Cesti, Corelli, Monteverdi, A Scarlatti

*

4, 5 Jan 1969
Leppard Ens†
Bach, Eccles, Handel, Monteverdi, Pergolesi, Piccini

16 Jan 1969   Guildhall   Newcastle-upon-Tyne
Cantelo (s), Leppard Ens: Andrew McGee, Margaret Cowen
(vlns), Olga Hegedus (vc), RL (hpsd)
Handel, Haydn, Purcell, A Scarlatti

31 Jan 1969   Exeter Univ   Exeter
As 16 January (Exeter Univ Music Club)

7 Feb 1969   Usher Hall   Edinburgh
Malcolm Binns (pno), ECO†
*JC Bach, Beethoven (conc 2), Mozart, Rawsthorne (Elegiac
Rhapsody)*

8, 10, 11 May 1969   Cuvilliés Theater   Munich
Wakefield (t), Runge, Isabel Garcisanz, Irmgard Stadler/Han-
neke van Bork, Jean Allister, Cuénod (t), Howells (ms),
Jane Berbié, Ugo Trama, Ian Comboy, Glyndebourne Fest
Opera, LPO† (Bavarian State Opera)
¶*Cavalli (L'Ormindo)*

9 Jun 1969   Royal Fest Hall   London
Eilleen Joyce, RL, Parsons, Preston (hpsds), Acad of St Martin-in-the-Fields cond. by Neville Marriner (see also 30 Jul
1969)
Bach, Mozart, Vivaldi — concs for 2, 3, 4 hpsds

11 Jun 1969   St Cuthbert's Church   Wells
RL (hpsd), Philip Jones Brass Ens (St. Cuthbert's Church,
Wells (Bath Fest)
*Aston, Bach, Brade, Byrd, Gabrieli, Holborne, Palestrina,
Tomkins*

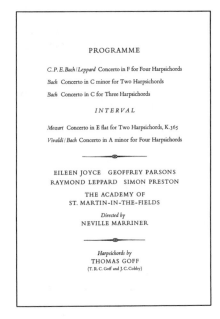

25 Jul 1969   St Nicholas Chapel   King's Lynn
Cantelo (s), Watts (cn), Tear (t), Angas (b), Ambrosian
Singers, Boys Choir of St Joseph's College, ECO† (19th
King's Lynn Fest)
Britten (St Nicholas Cantata), Haydn (St Nicholas Mass)
27 Jul 1969   Guildhall of St George   King's Lynn
C. Day-Lewis, Jill Balcon, George Rylands (rdrs); Ruth
Fermoy, RL (pnos) (19th King's Lynn Fest)
"Poetry, Prose and Music" (incl. *Dvorak, Poulenc, Satie*)
30 Jul 1969   St Nicholas Chapel   King's Lynn
Aveling, Joyce, RL, Henry Ward (hpds); Neville Marriner &
string qt from Academy of St Martin-in-the-Fields (19th
King's Lynn Fest)(see also 9 Jun 1969)
Bach, Vivaldi-Bach, Vivaldi-Thurston Dart
27 Aug 1969   Royal Fest Hall   London
Harper (s), Malcolm (hpsd), Adeney (fl), Sillito (vln), Can-
tores in ecclesia, ECO† (BBC-Henry Wood Promenade
Concerts)
Bach
1969?   Drottningholms Slottsteater   Stockholm
Rolf Jupither, Elisabeth Söderström, Bengt Rundgren, others,
Royal O† (The Royal Opera)
Sacchini (Oidipus i Athen)

7 Sep 1969   Royal Shakespeare Theatre   Stratford-upon-Avon
Paul Rogers, Cantelo (s), Young (t), London Mozart Players†
(Garrick Jubilee Concert)
Arne, Boyce, Dibdin, Mozart, Philidor, Piccinni
4 Nov 1969   Philharmonic Hall, Lincoln Center   New York
Patricia Brooks (s), Kay Creed (ms), John McCollum (t),
Julian Patrick (b-bar), Spiro Malas (b), Robert Carwithen
(org), Westminster Choir, NY PO members† (America
Bible Society Benefit Concert – RL American debut)
¶*Bach (cant 50), Handel (Samson III), Haydn (hpsd conc,
Missa Sancti Nicolai)*

*

1970   Arts Theatre   Cambridge
Alan Bennett, Judi Dench, RL, Prunella Scales, Timothy West
(benefit evening for the Oxford and Cambridge Shake-
speare Company)
"The World a Stage: Illusion, Delusion and Imagination –
an evening's entertainment devised and compiled by
George Rylands and RL" (incl. readings from Beerbohm,
Dickens, Hazlitt, Keats, James, Lamb, Shelley, Yeats etc;
music by *CPE Bach, Berners, Liszt, Purcell*)
1970   Oslo
Den Norske Opera†
Monteverdi (L'incoronazione di Poppea – RL vers)
18 Feb 1970   Queen Elizabeth Hall   London
Armstrong (s), James Bowman (ct), Benjamin Luxon (b),
Ambrosian Singers, ECO†
Rameau
24 Feb 1970   Lounge Hall   Harrogate
Cantelo (s), Leppard Ens: McGee, Cowen (vlns), Hegedus
(vc), RL (hpsd) (Harrogate Concert Soc)
Handel, Haydn, Purcell, A Scarlatti
27 Feb 1970   Usher Hall   Edinburgh
Masuko Ushioda (vln), ECO†
Bartók, Haydn, Mozart, R Strauss
28 Feb 1970   City Hall   Glasgow
Masuko Ushioda (vln), ECO† (City Hall, Glasgow)
Bartók, Haydn, Mozart (conc K 216), R Strauss
28 Mar 1970   Queen Elizabeth Hall   London
Baker (ms), ECO†
Albinoni, Cavalli, Cesti, D Scarlatti

18 Apr 1970   Town Hall   Leeds
Baker (ms), English (t), Shirley-Quirk (bar), Fest Chorus, Leeds Parish Church Choir, ECO† (Leeds Triennial Musical Fest)
Britten (Cantata misericordium), Cavalli (incl. Magnificat), Handel (Lucrezia), Stravinsky (conc in D)

20 Apr 1970   Town Hall   Leeds
Cantelo (s), Alfreda Hodgson (cn), English (t), Keyte (b), Fest Chorus, ECO† with Donald Hunt (Leeds Triennial Musical Fest)
JC Bach, Mozart, Leighton (The Light Invisible)

23 Apr 1970   Town Hall   Leeds
Baker (ms), RL (pno) (Leeds Tirennial Musical Fest)
Arne, Boyce, Parry, Purcell, Rossini, Schubert, Wagner, Warlock

20 May 1970   Queen Elizabeth Hall   London
Binns (pno), ECO†
Britten (Bridge Variations), Poulenc, Rawsthorne (conc 1), Satie

Summer 1970   Glyndebourne Festival Opera   Glyndebourne
Ileana Cotrubas (Calisto), Baker (Diana), Janet Hughes, Bowman, Ugo Trama, Cuénod, Davià, Owen Brannigan, Glyndebourne Fest Opera, LPO†
¶*Cavalli (La Calisto — RL vers)(9 performs, opening 26 May)*
Howells, Kerstin Meyer, Annon Lee Silver, Alexander Oliver, John Gibbs, Van Allan, Peter Gottlieb, Wakefield, Glyndebourne Fest Opera, LPO†
¶*Nicholas Maw (The Rising of the Moon)(8 performs; world prem. 19 July)*

29 Jul 1970   Hillington Church   King's Lynn
Preston (org), instl ens† (20th King's Lynn Fest)
Albinoni, Handel

19 Aug 1970   Royal Albert Hall   London
Harper (s), Watts (c), BBC Chorus, Sillito (vln), Adeney (fl), RL, Leslie Pearson (hpsds), ECO† (BBC-Henry Wood Promenade Concerts)
Bach, Cavalli, Handel, Pergolesi

7 Sep 1970   Festival Hall   Osaka
Tear (t), ECO†
Bach, Britten (Les Illuminations), Haydn, Mozart, Purcell

8 Sep 1970   Festival Hall   Osaka
Tear (t), Ifor James (hn), ECO†
Britten (Serenade), Handel, Haydn, Mozart

"[Glyndebourne's] 1970 five-opera program included three novelties: Cavalli's *La Calisto,* which had not been performed anywhere since its first production in Venice in 1651; Rossini's *Il turco in Italia,* gradually coming back into circulation after a century's neglect; and the world première of *The Rising of the Moon* by Nicholas Maw (b. 1935), commissioned by Glyndebourne.

"The Cavalli, arranged by Raymond Leppard, and produced by Peter Hall with designs by John Bury, proved to be an enchanting evening's entertainment, with a first-rate cast, imaginative use of machines and an atmosphere of baroque fantasy, extravagance and sheer magic, created by original, twentieth-century means without resort to the theatrical equivalent of reproduction furniture to suggest a seventeenth-century Venetian spectacle.

"Janet Baker, who had not sung at Glyndebourne since her Dido in Purcell's opera in 1966, had a magnificent part as Diana, in which she appeared as the gooddess, and as her father, Jove, disguised as the goddess, the one a lyrical role, touching and sad in the scenes with Endymion (a countertenor beautifully sung by James Bowman), the other a thoroughly ambiguous comic part, which Miss Baker played expertly.

"In the title role Ileana Cotrubas was thought by some to have suggested too much of the 'lost and dispirited Mélisande' in her performance; but then Calisto had a rather bewildering time, what with the way Jove treated her when he was disguised as Diana, and Juno turning her into a bear. The closing scene of the opera, where Calisto is taken up to
[CONTINUED NEXT PAGE]

9 Sep 1970   Kosei Kaikan Hall   Tokyo
     Tear (t), ECO†
     Bach, Britten (Les Illuminations), Haydn, Mozart, Purcell
10 Sep 1970   Kagoshima Cultural Center
     Tear (t), Ifor James (hn), ECO†/pno
     Bach, Britten (Serenade tenor, hn), Haydn (pno conc), Mozart
12 Sep 1970   Hibya Public Hall   Tokyo
     As 9 September

heaven by Jove and transformed into the constellation Ursa Minor, had great pathos; but being a true baroque opera. *Calisto* also had its fair Shakespearian share of bawdy comedy. There were thirteen strongly contrasted principal characters, all carefully drawn by Cavalli, and each of them a part worth singing. Hugues Cuénod, *en travesti* as the elderly nymph Linfea, inevitably brought the house down, and there were memorable performances by Ugo Trama as Jove, Peter Gottlieb as Mercury, Federico Davià as Pan and Janet Hughes as the mischievous little satyr. (After the run of *Calisto*, Cotrubas sang Pamina exquisitely in the last seven performances of the revived *Magic Flute.*)...

"The third novelty of 1970 was Nicholas Maw's *The Rising of the Moon* [with a book by Beverley Cross]. It was a brilliant libretto, classical in its strict observance of the Aristotelian unities, witty, with moving and melancholy moments, and making the most of a genuinely comical situation that might have been invented by Boccaccio.

"Musically, apart from a good rowdy English regimental chorus, the most memorable passages were lyrical, particularly a lullaby sung by Anne Howells in Act II.... [Later on] Nicholas Maw toned down some of his orchestral boisterousness, and the opera was revived in the same admirable production by Colin Graham in 1971.

"Why the work has not been heard much more frequently since then, I do not know.... Is caricature a form of bad-light shedding? The Victorian English officers looked and behaved like figures straight out of a cartoon by Osbert Lancaster (not surprisingly, since he did the décor), [but] I would have thought only the most naïve audience could really take their antics seriously.

"However, as the Cross and Maw opera was to the taste of the Glyndebourne public, there should really be nothing to prevent the Welsh or Scottish National, and certainly not Australian or American, opera audiences also enjoying it, since all of them have relished seeing the English in a bad light for centuries." *— Spike Hughes,* **Glyndebourne: A History of the Festival Opera,** *New Ed. (London: David & Charles, 1981).*

Sep 1970		Vancouver, Winnipeg, Brandon (Canada)

Tear (t), ECO†[10]

3 Oct 1970	Queen Elizabeth Hall	London

ECO†
Bach

10 Nov 1970	Teatro Colon	Buenos Aires

Wakefield (t), Angel Masttiello, Carmen Burello, Susana Rouco, Tatiana Zlatar, Eugenio Valori, Myrtha Garbarini, Norma Lerer, Victor de Narke, Gui Gallardo, chorus & orchestra†
¶*Cavalli (L'Ormindo)*

17 Nov 1970	Queen Elizabeth Hall	London

Tear (t), ECO†
CPE Bach, Britten (Les Illuminations), Haydn, Mendelssohn

17 Dec 1970	St Nicholas Chapel	Kings Lynn

Philip Jones Brass Ens, Ambrosian Singers, ECO†
Cavalli, G Gabrieli, Monteverdi

18 Dec 1970	Southwark Cathedral	London

As 17 December

*

7 Jan 1971	Royal Albert Hall	London

Angela Beale (s), Norma Proctor (c), Tear (t), Luxon (b), Royal Choral Soc, RPO†
Handel (Messiah — Mozart orch.)

25 Jan 1971	Théatre municipal	Lausanne

RL (hpsd), L'Orchestre de chambre de Lausanne†
CPE Bach (1740 conc), Britten (Bridge Variations), Handel, Rameau

28 Jan 1971	Pavilion	Hemel Hemstead, St Albans

John McCaw (cl), New Philharmonia O†
Brahms, Mozart

30 Jan 1971	Dorking Halls	Dorking, Surrey

Sillito (vln), Aronowitz (vla), ECO†
Elgar, Handel, Mozart

17 Feb 1971	Queen Elizabeth Hall	London

Baker (ms), ECO†
Handel, Orr (From the Book of Philip Sparrow), Tippett (conc double string orch)

---

10   For a related memoir see page 404 above.

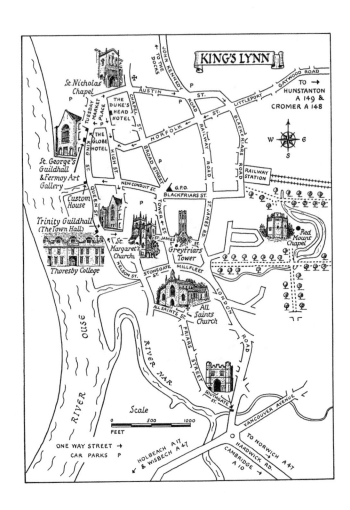

23 Feb 1971   Royal Fest Hall   London
    Henryk Szeryng (vln), LPO†
    Beethoven (conc), *Handel, Sibelius*
18 Mar 1971   Town Hall   Birmingham
    Garcia (vln), Adeney (fl), Norman Knight (fl), Peter Graeme
      (ob), John Wilbraham (tpt), RL (hpsd), ECO†
    Bach

16, 20, 22, 24, 26, 28 Jul; 1, 3 Aug 1971
        Glyndebourne Festival Opera   Glyndebourne
    Cotrubas, Baker, Hughes, Trama, Bowman, Cuénod, Davià,
    Brannigan, Glyndebourne Fest Opera, LPO†
    ¶*Cavalli (La Calisto — RL vers)*
30 Jul 1971   St Nicholas Chapel   King's Lynn
    Harper (s), Gendron (vc), ECO† (21st King's Lynn Fest)
    Berkeley (Dialogue for vc & co), Maconchy (Ariadne), Mozart
31 Jul 1971   St Nicholas Chapel   King's Lynn
    Ambrosian Singers, Philip Jones Brass Ens, ECO† (21st King's
    Lynn Fest)
    Cavalli, G Gabrieli, Monteverdi — program as "The Splendors of
    Venice"

Heinz Holliger, Thomas Igloi, RL, Heather Harper

1 Dec 1971   London Coliseum   London
Baker (ms), Anne Collins, Katherine Pring, Robert Ferguson,
Clifford Grant, Sadler's Wells Opera† (Royal Gala Perfor-
mance)
¶*Monteverdi (*The Coronation of Poppea *— RL realisation)*
5 Dec 1971   Royal Albert Hall   London
Armstrong (s), Watts (c), English (t), Shirley-Quirk (b),
Ambrosian Singers, ECO†
*Handel (*Messiah *— chamb vers ed by RL)*
19 Dec 1971   Queen Elizabeth Hall   London
Armstrong (s), ECO†
Boyce, Haydn, Manfredini, Mozart, A Scarlatti
*

1972   Covent Garden   London
Covent Garden†
¶*Mozart (*The Marriage of Figaro*)*
11 Feb 1972   Queen Elizabeth Hall   London
Harper (s), Heinz Holliger (ob), Thomas Igloi (vc), ECO†
*Berkeley (*Dialogue*), Bennett (*ob conc*), Britten (*Metamor-
phosen*), Maconchy (*Ariadne*), Rawsthorne (*Elegiac Rhap-
sody*)*
18 Feb 1972   Auditorium del centro di produzione RAI   Naples
Orchestra "A. Scarlatti" di Napoli della RAI
(Radiotelevisione Italiana)†
Boccherini, Cavalli, Couperin, Rameau
8 Mar 1972   Royal Fest Hall   London
Armstrong (s), Tear (t), Luxon (bar), Alan Harverson (org
cont), Charles Spinks (hpsd cont), BBC Chorus, BBC SO†
¶*Haydn (*Creation*)*

29 Mar 1972   Royal Hall   Harrogate
Ralph Holmes (vln), RPO†
Brahms, Mendelssohn, Tchaikovsky (conc)
3 May 1972   Chandos House   London
Kern (ms), Leppard Ens† (Royal Soc of Medicine Music Club)
Albinoni, JC Bach, Cavalli, Monteverdi
25, 27, 30 May; 1, 3, 6, 8, 11, 13, 17 Jun; 19, 22, 24, 28, 30 Jul 1972
                    Glyndebourne Festival Opera   Glyndebourne
Baker (Penelope), Hughes, Howells, Trama, Wakefield,
Luxon (Ulisse), Lewis, Oliver, Glyndebourne Fest Opera,
LPO†
¶*Monteverdi (*Il ritorno d'Ulisse in patria—*RL vers)*
25 Jul 1972   Guildhall of St George   King's Lynn
John Betjeman (spkr), Lillian Watson (s), Philip Langridge (t),
Adeney (fl), Binns, RL (pno duet) (22nd King's Lynn Fest)
"Victorian Knights"—program devised by RL (see Appendix
II, below)
26 Jul 1972   St Nicholas Chapel   King's Lynn
Baker (ms), RL (pno) (22nd King's Lynn Fest)
Debussy, Fauré, Pelham Humfrey, Mahler, Monteverdi, Mozart,
Schubert
1 Aug 1972   Guildhall, Cambridge Univ   Cambridge
Baker (ms), RL (pno) (Cambridge Fest)
Debussy, Fauré, Pelham Humphrey, Mahler, Monteverdi,
Mozart, Purcell, Schubert
3 Aug 1972   London
Janet Hughes (s), Baker (ms), Howells (ms), Lewis (t), Ian
Caley (t), Luxon (b), Glynebourne Chorus, LPO† (BBC-
Henry Wood Promenade Concerts / Glyndebourne Fest
Opera)
¶*Monteverdi (*Il ritorno d'Ulisse in patria*)*
10 Aug 1972   Teatro Coliseo   Buenos Aires
Festival de musica barroca y preclasica (orchestra)†
CPE Bach, JC Bach, Boccherini, Grétry, Haydn
16 Aug 1972   Teatro Coliseo   Buenos Aires
Harper (s), Profesores orquesta sinfonica nacional† (Festival
de musica barroca y preclasica)
Albinoni, JC Bach, Handel, Rameau, Telemann
24 Aug 1972   Teatro Coliseo   Buenos Aires
Profesores orquesta sinfonica nacional (chorus & orchestra)†
(Festival de musica barroca y preclasica)
*Purcell (*A Masque in Dioclesian—*RL vers), Schütz*

28 Aug 1972   Brussels
Marjorie Biggar, Annabel Hunt, Penelope MacKay, Trama,
Alan Charles, Jill Gomez, Hughes (s), Cuénod (t), Bowman
(ct), Simon Estes, Glyndebourne Chorus, insts, strings of
B.R.T. CO† (Glyndebourne Fest Opera / Fest of Flanders)
¶*Cavalli (La Calisto)*
31 Aug 1972   Théâtre Royal de la Monnaie   Brussels
As 28 August
28 Sep 1972   Theatre Royal   Nottingham
Glyndebourne Touring Opera (Soloists, Glyndebourne
Chorus, Northern Sinfonia O)†
Cavalli (La Calisto)
30 Sep, 1 Oct 1972   (Sweden)
Radiokören, Sveriges Radios Symfoniorkester†
(Sveriges Radio)
Handel, Jolivet, Mozart, Johan Helmich Roman
19 Oct 1972   Royal Fest Hall   London
Paul Tortelier (vc), LPO†
Elgar (incl. vc conc*), Maw (*Cassation*), Schubert*
28 Oct 1972   Fitzwilliam Museum   London
RL (hpsd)
Bach, Byrd, Gibbons, Haydn, Pierson
29 Oct 1972   Theatre Royal, Haymarket   London
"Sybil": tribute to Dame Sybil Thorndike, featuring Laurence
Olivier, Vanessa Redgrave, Peter Ustinov, Joan Plowright,
Alec Guinness, Joyce Grenfell, Margot Fonteyn, RL (hpsd
in Bach *Partita 4*, Purcell *Entrada)*, Roger Livesey, Wendy
Hiller, Celia Johnson, Edith Evans, Paul Scofied, Irene
Worth, Alec Guinness, George Rylands, Peggy Ashcroft,
Ralph Richardson, others[11]
5 Nov 1972   Queen Elizabeth Hall   London
Daniel Chorzempa (org), ECO†
Handel
13 Nov 1972   White Rock Pavilion   Hastings
Veronica Jochum (pno), LPO†
*Beethoven (*conc 3*), Elgar, Butterworth (*Shropshire Lad*),
Schubert*

---

11   For related memoir see Chapter VI, page 411, above.

FRIENDS OF THE
FITZWILLIAM

RAYMOND
LEPPARD
Honorary Keeper of the Music

HARPSICHORD
RECITAL

IN GALLERY III

Saturday 28 October 1972

PROGRAMME

Sonata in E major *Haydn*
Moderato - Menuetto e trio - Finale : presto

Sonatas in C minor, B major & D major
D. Scarlatti

Partita IV in D major *J. S. Bach*
Overture - Allemande - Courante - Aria -
Sarabande - Menuet - Gigue

Interval *of half an hour during which wine
will be served*

from *The Fitzwilliam Virginal Book*:
Italian Ground, The King's Jewel,
The Lord of Salisbury's Pavane
and Galliard *Gibbons*
The Bells *Byrd*
The Fall of the Leaf *Pierson*

Sonata in F *Haydn*
Allegro moderato - Larghetto - Finale : presto

Harpsichord kindly lent by Malcolm Russell

28 Nov 1972   Auditorium di San Francesco al Corso   Verona
Piero Toso (vln), Clementine Hoogendoorn Scimone (fl), Or-
chestra da camera di Padova†
Handel, Haydn, Stamitz
29 Nov 1972   Palasport   Belluno
As 28 November
1 Dec 1972   Duomo di San Clemente   Valdagno (Italy)
Piero Toso (vln), Clementine Hoogendoorn Scimone (fl), Or-
chestra da camera di Padova [CO of Padua]†
Handel, Haydn, Carl Stamitz
9 Dec 1972   Haberdashers Schl   Elstree
Baker (ms), ECO† (Mill Hill Toc H Music Club Celebrity
Concerts)
Albinoni, Cavalli, Dowland, Handel, Monteverdi
11 Dec 1972   Zaal Koningin Elisabeth   Antwerp
RL (hpsd), ECO†
Boyce, Handel, Haydn (incl. hpsd conc)
12 Dec 1972   Église Saint-Louis des Invalides   Paris
Baker (ms), ECO†
Albinoni, Cavalli, Dowland, Monteverdi, D Scarlatti

13 Dec 1972   Salle Pleyel   Paris
    Baker (ms), RL (hpsd), ECO†
    Handel, Haydn
14 Dec 1972   Théatre Sylvia Montfort   Paris
    Emmanuel Krivine (vln), Neil Black (ob), RL (hpsd), ECO†
    *Boyce, Handel (ob conc), Mozart (con K 216), Stanley (hpsd
    conc)*
15 Dec 1972   Queen Elizabeth Hall   London
    Baker (ms), ECO†
    Albinoni, Cavalli, Dowland, Handel, Monteverdi, Stanley
                              *

10 Feb 1973   Queen Elizabeth Hall   London
    Norma Burrowes (s), Nan Christie (s), Jonathan Williams (vc),
        Douglas Young, ECO†
    Handel, Mozart, Vivaldi, Young (Aubade)
29 Mar 1973   Göteborgs Theater   Göteborg
    Irene Wilhelmi (vln), Göteborg SO†
    Cavalli, Handel, Mozart, R Strauss
 6 Apr 1973   Auditorium della Radiotelevisione Italiana   Torino
    Sesto Bruscantini, Margherita Rinaldi, Kern (ms), Bowman
        (ct), Orchestra sinfonica e Coro di Torino della
        Radiotelevisione Italiana†
    ¶*Handel* (Ariodante)
28 Apr 1973   KGL Teater   (Denmark)
    Biggar, Hunt, MacKay, Trama, Charles, Gomez, Bowman (ct),
        Wallis, Cuénod (t), Hughes, Estes, Glyndebourne Chorus,
        insts† (Glyndebourne Fest Opera)
    ¶*Cavalli* (La Calisto)
 6 May 1973   Queen Elizabeth Hall   London
    Harper (s), Murray Perahia (pno), ECO† (Queen Elizabeth
        Hall, London)
    Maconchy (Ariadne, Genesis), *Mendelssohn (incl. conc 2)*
15, 22, 28, 30 Jun; 2, 4, 6, 8, 15, 17, 19 Jul 1973
                       Glyndebourne Festival Opera   Glyndebourne
    Baker (Penelope), Hughes, Howells, Trama, Wakefield,
        Luxon (Ulisse), Richard Stilwell, Lewis, Oliver, Glyn-
        debourne Fest Opera, LPO†
    ¶*Monteverdi* (Il ritorno d'Ulisse in patria — RL vers)
21 Jul 1973   St Nicholas Chapel   King's Lynn
    Kathleen Jones (pno), Adeney (fl), ECO† (23rd King's Lynn
        Fest)
    Mozart (incl. fl conc K 314, pno conc K 450)

3 Aug 1973   Royal Albert Hall   London
Janet Craxton (ob), BBC Northern SO† (BBC-Henry Wood
Promenade Concerts)
Berkeley (Sinfonia concertante, sym 3), Britten, Tchaikovsky
17, 18 Aug 1973   Philharmonic Hall, Lincoln Center   New York
Florence Kopleff (cn), Fou Ts'ong (pno), Mostly Mozart Fest
O† (Mostly Mozart Fest)
Bach (cant 53), Handel, Mozart (conc 25)
3 Sep 1973   Royal Albert Hall   London
Cantelo (s), Hodgson (cn), English (t), Richard Van Allen (b),
BBC Singers, Amadeus String Qt, BBC SO† (BBC-Henry
Wood Promenade Concerts)
Haydn
7 Sep 1973   Hemel Hempstead Pavilion   London
Erich Gruenburg (vln), RPO†
Bruch (conc), Mendelssohn, Rimsky-Korsakov
6 Oct 1973   Leeds Town Hall   Leeds
Don Garrard (b), Leeds Fest Chorus, BBC Northern SO†
Mozart, Shostakovich
9 Oct 1973   Free Trade Hall   Manchester
Don Garrard (b), Nikita Magaloff (pno), Leeds Fest Chorus,
BBC Northern SO†
Mozart (conc 22), Shostakovich (sym 13)
11 Oct 1973   King George's Hall   Blackburn
Armstrong (s), BBC Northern SO†
Elgar, Mozart, R Strauss, Stravinsky
19 Oct 1973   Københavns Rådhus, Festsalen   Copenhagen
RL (hpsd), Sjaellands SO†
JC Bach (hpsd conc), Boccherini, Handel, Haydn (hpsd conc)
6 Nov 1973   Free Trade Hall   Manchester
Elisabeth Speiser (s), BBC Northern SO†
Bach, Handel
21 Dec 1973   Queen Elizabeth Hall   London
Armstrong (s), Garcia (vln), Wilbraham (tpt), ECO†
Bach, Cavalli, Corelli, Haydn (vln conc), Monteverdi
*

12 Jan 1974   Dorking Halls   Dorking, Surrey
Nicholas Busch (hn), LPO†
Dvorak, Mendelssohn, Mozart

29 Jan 1974	Free Trade Hall	Manchester

Curzon (pno), Ella Lee (s), BBC Northern SO†
Beethoven (conc 5), Tippett (sym 3)[12]

3 Feb 1974	Corn Exchange	Bedford

Horacio Gutiérrez (pno), RPO†
Brahms, Rachmaninoff (conc 3), Smetana

22 Feb 1974	Queen Elizabeth Hall	London

Holliger (ob), ECO†
CPE Bach, Cimarosa, Mozart (incl. ob conc), Young
(3 Regions from Terrain — *cond by composer)*

5 Mar 1974	Watford Town Hall	Watford

Louis Kentner (pno), RPO†
Beethoven, Chopin (conc 1), Smetana

23 Mar 1974	Leeds Town Hall	Leeds

Linda Esther Gray (s), Anne Collins (c), Ryland Davies (t),
Richard Angas (b), Leeds P Chorus, BBC Northern SO†
Dvorak (Saint Ludmila)

26 Mar 1974	Free Trade Hall	Manchester

Cantelo (s), Watts (c), John Mitchinson (t), Noble (b), BBC
Singers, BBC Northern SO†
Beethoven (Missa Solemnis)

9 Apr 1974	Royal Fest Hall	London

Shirley-Quirk (b), London P Choir, LPO†
Bach-Elgar, Bax (sym 7), Walton

27 Apr 1974	Fairfield Hall	Croydon

Miriam Fried (vln), LPO†
Bach-Elgar, Bax (sym 7), Mendelssohn

4 May 1974	Congress Theatre	Eastbourne

Veronica Jochum (pno), LPO†
Bach-Elgar, Bax (sym 7), Mendelssohn

18 May 1974	The Dome	Brighton

Perahia (pno), BBC Northern SO† (Brighton Fest)
Berlioz, Bridge (The Sea), Chopin (conc 1), Handel

23, 25, 29, 31 May; 2, 6, 8, 10, 12, 14 Jun 1974

	Glyndebourne Festival Opera	Glyndebourne

Barbara Hendricks (Calisto), Howells (Diana), Hughes, Bowman, Trama, Cuénod, Glyndebourne Festival Opera, LPO†
¶*Cavalli (La Calisto — RL vers)*

---

12   For related memoir see Chapter VI, page 414 above.

3 Jul 1974   Hollywood Bowl   Los Angeles
William Tim Read, John Steele Ritter, Susanne Shapiro, RL
(hpsds), Los Angeles P†
Bach, Dowland
5 Jul 1974   Hollywood Bowl   Los Angeles
Bishop (pno), Frederica von Stade (ms), Los Angeles P†
Mozart
6 Jul 1974   Hollywood Bowl   Los Angeles
Von Stade (ms), Roger Wagner Chorale, Los Angeles P†
Cavalli, Gabrieli, Monteverdi
1, 9, 21 Aug 1974   Santa Fe Opera   Santa Fe
Judith Forst, Ellen Shade, James Bowman, George Shirley,
   Whitney Burnett, Santa Fe Opera†
¶*Cavalli (L'Egisto)*
9 Sep 1974   Royal Albert Hall   London
Burrowes (s), Gale (s), Baker (ms), Bainbridge (ms), Procter
(cn), Hodgson (cn), Langridge (t), Hagegard (bar), BBC
Singers† (BBC – Henry Wood Promenade Concerts)
Purcell (Dido and Aeneas), Tippett
24 Sep 1974   Free Trade Hall   Manchester
Mstislav Rostropovich (vc), BBC Northern SO†
Brahms, Elgar, Strauss (Don Quixote)
28 Sep 1974   Leeds Town Hall   Leeds
Perahia (pno), BBC Northern SO†
Elgr, Schumann, Tchaikovsky
4 Oct 1974   Eton School Hall   Windsor
Black (ob), Charles Tunnell (vc), ECO†/hpsd (Windsor Fest)
CPE Bach, JC Bach, JS Bach
6 Oct 1974   Cathedral Church of St Nichols
                                      Newcastle-upon-Tyne
Black (ob), Charles Tunnell (vc), RL (hpsd), ECO†
(Newcastle Fest)
CPE Bach, JC Bach, JS Bach
26 Oct 1974   Royal Fest Hall   London
Imogen Cooper (pno), ECO† (Robert Mayer Concerts)
Bach, Dvorak, Mozart (conc K 459: 1st movt), *Satie, Stravinsky*
5 Nov 1974   Free Trade Hall   Manchester
Gyorgy Cziffra (pno), BBC Northern SO†
Dvorak, Rachmaninoff (conc 2), *Tchaikovsky*
8 Nov 1974   Chechester Fest Theatre   Chichester
Garcia (vln), ECO†
Bach

9 Nov 1974   Birmingham Cathedral   Birmingham
Garcia (vln), RL (hpsd), ECO† (Birmingham Bach Soc)
Bach
14 Nov 1974   Dame Alice Harpur Schl
ECO† (Bedford Music Club)
Bach
17 Nov 1974   Queen Elizabeth Hall   London
ECO†
Bach
26 Nov 1974   Royal Albert Hall   London
Sheila Armstrong (s), Shura Cherkassky (pno), Kneller Hall
    Trumpeteers, Royal PO† (St Cecilia Fest / Royal Concert
    1974)
Arnold (Fanfare), *Holst* (The Perfect Fool), *Jacobs* (Fanfare &
    Natl Anthem), *Liszt* (conc 1), *Mozart, Rimsky-Korsakov*
5 Dec 1974   Lancaster Univ   Lancaster
Vlado Perlemuter (pno), BBC Northern SO† (Lancaster Univ
    Concerts)
Beethoven, Chopin (conc 2), *Schumann, Smetana*
*

22 Jan 1975   City Hall   Newcastle-upon-Tyne
Armstrong (s), BBC Northern SO†[13]
Handel, R Strauss, Walton (sym 1)
23 Jan 1975   City Hall   Newcastle-upon-Tyne
BBC Northern SO†
*Delius, Handel, Rimsky-Korsakov — BBC recording session, open
    to public*
26 Jan 1975   Queen Elizabeth Hall   London
Adeney (fl), ECO†
Bach
Feb? 1975   Honk Kong Fest   Hong Kong
ECO†
15 Feb 1975   City Hall   Sheffield
Mincho Mnchev (vln), BBC Northern SO†
Bruch (conc), *Ravel, Walton* (sym 1)
19 Feb 1975   Fairfield   Croydon
Michael Roll (pno), RPO†
Grieg, Mendelssohn, Schumann (conc), *Tchaikovsky*

---

13   A related incident is described in Chapter VI, page 418 above.

26 Feb 1975   St John's   London
Trevor Pinnock (hpsd), BBC Singers† (radio concert)
8 Mar 1975   Philharmonic Hall   Liverpool
Curzon (pno), Royal Liverpool PO†
Mendelssohn, Mozart (conc K 491), *Schubert*
25 Mar 1975   Free Trade Hall   Manchester
Harper (s), Hodgson (c), Tear (t), Stephen Roberts (bar),
Dean (b), BBC Northern Singers, BBC Singers, BBC
Northern SO†
Bach (Mass in b)
27 Apr 1975??   Great Hall, Lancaster Univ   Lancaster
Cécile Ousset (pno), BBC Northern SO† (Lancaster
Univ Concerts)
Bizet, Franck, Méhul, Poulenc, Ravel
22, 24, 28, 30 May; 1, 5, 7, 9, 11, 13, 15, 17, 20 Jun 1975
Glyndebourne Festival Opera   Glyndebourne
Burrowes, Luxon, Alan Watt, Cuénod, Bernard Dickerson,
Glyndebourne Fest Opera, LPO†
¶*Janácek* (The Cunning Little Vixen)
3 Jul 1975   Chichester Cathedral   Chichester
Maurice Hasson (vln), John Birch (org), BBC Northern SO†
Bruch (conc), *Mozart, Saint-Saëns*
25 Jul 1975   St Nicholas' Chapel   King's Lynn, Norfolk
Armstrong (s), Hodgson (c), Tear (t), Luxon (bar), BBC
Singers, BBC Northern SO† (King's Lynn Fest)
Beethoven, Haydn (Nelson Mass), *Saint-Saëns*
5 Aug 1975   Royal Albert Hall   London
Yitkin Seow (pno), BBC Northern SO† (BBC-Henry Wood
Promenade Concerts)
Beethoven (conc 2), *Britten* (Sinfonia da Requiem), *Schubert*
6 Aug 1975   Glyndebourne
Mem concert for Rhona Mary Byron with Donald Bell, George
Christie, John Cox, Hugues Cuénod, Martin Isepp, RL,
John Pritchard, Rex Rogers, Elisabeth Söderström
19 Aug 1975   Hollywood Bowl   Los Angeles
Ellen Shade (s), Susan Todhunter (s), Bonnie Hurwood (ms),
Jonath Mack (t), Stilwell (bar), Roger Wagner Chorale, Los
Angeles P† (Summer Fest)
Bach (Magnificat), *Fauré* (Requiem)
21 Aug 1975   Hollywood Bowl   Los Angeles
Michael Sells (t), Barry Tuckwell (hn), Los Angeles P† (Sum-
mer Fest)
Brahms, Britten (Serenade), *Mozart* (incl. Rondo K 371)

13, 16, 19, 24, 28 Sep 1975
            San Francisco Opera   San Francisco
Tatiana Troyanos (Poppea), Maureen Forrester, Beverly
    Wolff, Carol Malone, Eric Tappy, Peter Meven, Richard
    Stilwell, San Francisco Opera†
    ¶*Monteverdi* (L'incoronazione di Poppea— *RL vers)*
2 Oct 1975   Town Hall   Watford
    Ralph Holmes (vln), LPO†
    Mendelssohn, Sibelius, Tchaikovsky
27 Oct 1975   St John's   Westminster
    Armstrong (s), Wilbraham (tpt), ECO†
    Handel, Purcell, Torelli
30 Oct 1975   Palau de la musica Catalana   Barcelona
    Sheila Armstrong (s), ECO†
    Arnold (Sinfonietta 1), JC Bach, Haydn, Mozart (incl.
        Exsultate, jubilate)
31 Oct 1975   Palau de la musica Catalana   Barcelona
    Sheila Armstrong (s), ECO†
    Boccherini, Cimarosa, Handel (3 arias), Haydn, Mozart (aria K
        217)
6 Nov 1975   Auditorium del centro di produzione RAI   Naples
    Wilbraham (tpt), (ECO† (Associazione "A. Scarlatti")
    Arnold (Sinfonietta), Bach, Haydn, Torelli
7 Nov 1975   Sala di Via dei Greci   (Italy)
    ECO† (Accademia Nazionale di Santa Cecilia)
    Arnold (Sinfonietta), JC Bach, JS Bach, Haydn, Mozart, Tippett
        (Little Music), *Torelli*
25 Nov 1975   Free Trade Hall   Manchester
    Armstrong (s), BBC Northern SO† (BBC Master Concerts)
    Tchaikovsky
13 Dec 1975   Royal Fest Hall   London
    Jennifer Smith (s), Ian Partridge (t), BBC Singers, ECO†
    (Robert Mayer Concerts)
    Bach, Berlioz, Mendelssohn, Mozart, Walton
19 Dec 1975   Queen Elizabeth Hall   London
    Tear (t), Anthony Halstead (hn), ECO†
    Britten (Serenade), Handel, Tchaikovsky, Vaughan Williams
                                    *

12 Jan 1976   London
    BBC Lunchtime Concert† (radio)
    Cavalli

SAN FRANCISCO. "Ah, the ever changing winds of operatic values! Who would have thought that Monteverdi's *Incoronazione di Poppea* would raise the body temperature and have a greater gut impact than Verdi's blood-and-thunder *Trovatore?* But such was the case in the two opening productions of the San Francisco Opera's 53rd season. It was a matter of ideal conducting and directing choices, aligned with perfection throughout the casting — and [in the new *Trovatore* production] just the reverse. The Monteverdi had the advantage of all these elements, beginning with Raymond Leppard, who brilliantly led his familiar 'realization' of the opera. His music-making was lustrous, clear-textured, buoyant and tautly secure, a model of its kind.

"Within Ita Maximowna's burnished, classic semicircular coliseum setting, with portals that changed for the various scenes, Günther Rennert's direction was the essence of concision and simplicity, not only clarifying the action and relationships of this richly moving human drama with swift telling strokes but also filling it with stirring stage pictures. The love scenes, played without a bit of sensationalism, achieved strength and animation purely through the tensions created. Movements, word inflection and character interaction made a magnificent totality that seamlessly blended stylization with realism.

"As the courtesan Poppea, Tatiana Troyanos was vocally and physically ravishing, the embodiment of sensuality. Her voice has an easy, wide range, and she colored it gorgeously, impeccable in scales and ornaments. Physically her impact was enormous, aided by Maximowna's flowing costumes. Together with tenor Eric Tappy as Nero, one felt the presence of cruelly scheming creatures, using sex and passion as weapons. Though the historically unattractive sides of both were stressed, they had the necessary stage glamor and sympathy as well. Tappy's strong characterization and well-controlled voice were ideal, and in his drunken scene he skillfully managed on a pair of stilts. As the wronged Ottavia, Beverly Wolff was magnificent, playing in the style of a great French tragédienne and singing with commanding intensity.
[CONTINUED NEXT PAGE]

Maureen Forrester (Arnalta) mixed high-camp moments with a lusciously sung lullaby. Peter Meven brought strength to Seneca's great scene, and Richard Stilwell offered vocal opulence and dynamic presence as Ottone. Barbara Hendricks lent brightness to Damigella/Amor." — *Robert Jacobson*, **Opera News.**

20 Jan 1976   Free Trade Hall   Manchester
Gyorgy Pauk (vln), Ralph Kirshbaum (vc), BBC Northern SO†
(BBC Master Concerts)
Bartók, Brahms (double conc), *Dvorak*
6 Feb 1976   Newcastle City Hall   Newcastle
Watts (c), RL (hpsd), Northern Sinfonia O†
JC Bach, JS Bach, Cavalli, Haydn, Monteverdi
7 Feb 1976   Billingham Forum Theatre   Billingham
As 6 February
8 Feb 1976   Carlisle Market Hall   Carlisle
As 6 February
12 Feb 1976   Town Hall   Birmingham
City of Birmingham SO†
Arensky, Bach, Handel, Tchaikovsky
17 Feb 1976   Philharmonic Hall   Liverpool
Royal Liverpool SO†
Bach, Haydn, Tchaikovsky
28 Feb 1976   Guildhall, Cambridge Univ   Cambridge
Douglas Cummings (vc), RL (pno)
Beethoven, Brahms, Vivaldi
6 Mar 1976   St John's, Smith Square   London
Elizabeth Gale (s), Collins (c), Alexander Oliver (t), Malcolm
    King (b), ECO Chorus, ECO†
Mendelssohn, Wagner, Weber
10 Mar 1976   Royal Fest Hall   London
Leonard Rose (vc), BBC Singers, BBC SO†
Beethoven, Bloch (Schelomo), *Debussy*
16 Mar 1976   Chapelle du Lycée Henri IV   Poitiers
Anthony Rolfe-Johnson (t), Anthony Halstead (hn), ECO†
    (Printemps Musical de Poitiers [Poitiers Fest])
Arne, Britten (Serenade tenor, hn), *Handel, Purcell*

18 Mar 1976   Chapelle du Lycée Henri IV   Poitiers
Black (ob), ECO† (Printemps Musical de Poitiers [Poitiers Fest])
Arnold, Britten (Bridge Vns), Elgar, Grainger (Molly on the Shore, Irish Tune from County Derry), Rawsthorne (conc)
19 Mar 1976   Eglise de la Madeleine   Paris
Udo Reinemann (bar), Bernard Soustrot (tpt), ECO†
Bach, Handel, Hummel (conc), Telemann
30 Mar 1976   Free Trade Hall   Manchester
Felicity Palmer (s), Norma Procter (c), Pears (t), King (b), BBC Northern Singers, BBC Singers, BBC Northern SO†
Britten (Spring Symphony), Haydn (Harmonienmesse)
21 Apr 1976   Grosser Konzerthaussaal   Cologne
BBC Northern SO†
Beethoven, Haydn, Tippett
22 Apr 1976   Grosses Festspielhaus   Salzburg
Curzon (pno), BBC Northern SO†
Brahms, Britten, Mozart
24 Apr 1976   Grosser Kurhaussaal   Wiesbaden
Curzon (pno), BBC Northern SO†
Britten, Dvorak, Mozart
25 Apr 1976   Theater der Stadt Schweinfurt   Schweinfurt
Curzon (pno), BBC Northern SO†
Berkeley (sym 3), Brahms, Mozart
27 Apr 1976   Stadthalle   Göttingen
Minton (ms), BBC Northern SO†
Elgar, Mahler, Tchaikovsky
28 Apr 1976   Liederhalle Beethovensaal   Stuttgart
Curzon (pno), BBC Northern SO†
Beethoven, Tchaikovsky
29 Apr 1976   Staddtheater Aschaffenburg   Aschaffenburg
Minton (ms), BBC Northern SO†
Berkeley (sym 3), Dvorak, Mahler
2 May 1976   Cultuurcentrum de Oosterpoort   Oosterpoort
Minton (ms), BBC Northern SO†
Beethoven, Elgar, Mahler
4 May 1976   City Hall   Braunwschweig
Hans Richter-Haaser (pno), BBC Northern SO†
Beethoven, Dvorak
5 May 1976   Stadthalle, Festsaal   Oberhausen
Minton (ms), BBC Northern SO† (Städtische Konzerte Oberhausen)
Berkeley (sym 3), Brahms, Mahler

OPERA THEATRE
OF SAINT LOUIS

2nd Season . . . May 20 – June 11, 1977
LORETTO-HILTON THEATRE   Tel. 961-0171

COSI FAN TUTTE (Mozart)   GIANNI SCHICCHI (Puccini)
PYGMALION (Rameau)   COUNT ORY (Rossini)

6 May 1976   Stadsschouwburg Kortrijk   Kortrijk (Belgium)
Minton (ms), BBC Northern SO†
Brahms, Britten, Mahler
?7 May 1976   Stadttheater   Wilhelmshaven
Minton (ms), BBC Northern SO†
Beethoven, Mahler, Tippett
12 May 1976   Free Trade Hall   Manchester
Baker (ms), RL (pno)
Cavalli, Liszt, Schubert, others

2 Jul 1976   Town Hall   Cheltenham
Baker (mz), BBC Northern SO† (Cheltenham Intl Fest)
Bliss (Introduction & Allegro, Metamorphic Variations),
Cavalli, Handel
24, 28 Jul; 6, 10, 19, 27 Aug 1976
          Santa Fe Opera   Santa Fe
Linn Maxwell, Ellen Shade, James Bowman, Jerold Norman,
   Santa Fe Opera†
¶*Cavalli* (L'Egisto— *in RL version*)
7, 11, 20, 25 Aug 1976
          Santa Fe Opera   Santa Fe
Mignon Dunn, Ashley Putnam, James Atherton, Santa Fe
   Opera†
¶*Thomson* (The Mother of Us All)
*

1976/77?   Free Trade Hall   Manchester
Baker (ms), Mitchinson (t), BBC Northern SO†
Mahler (Das Lied von der Erde), *Schubert*
*

22 Mar 1977   Free Trade Hall   Manchester
Felicity Lott (s), Collins (c), Philip Langridge (t), Tear (t), Wil-
   liam Elvin (bar), Ian Caddy (b), BBC Northern Singers,
   BBC Northern SO† (BBC Master Concerts)
¶*Bach* (St. John Passion— *in new [1976] English transl by RL*)
6, 8 Apr 1977   Orchestra Hall   Minneapolis
Robert White (t), Carole Bogard (s), Elaine Bonazzi (a), Gary
   Glaze (t), Ronald Corrado (bar), John Cheek (b-bar), Bach
   Soc Chorus, Minnesota O†
¶*Bach* (St. John Passion— *in RL's English transl*)
9 Apr 1977   O'Shaughnessy Audit   St Paul
As 6, 8 April
21, 25, 27 May; 2, 10 Jun 1977
          Opera Theatre of St Louis   St Louis
Sheri Greenawald, Rebecca Littig, Marguerite Smith, John
   Aler, RL (hpsd), Opera Theatre of St Louis†
¶*Rameau* (Pygmalion— *Engl. transl. by RL*)
28 May; 1, 3, 9, 11 Jun 1977
          Opera Theatre of St Louis   St Louis
Ashley Putnam, Judith Farris, Peggy Cantrell, Vinson Cole,
   Peter Strummer, Opera Theatre of St Louis†
¶*Rossini* (Count Ory)

ST LOUIS. Rossini's *Count Ory,* his penultimate opera, was composed for Paris in 1828 and, perhaps, next to the *Barber of Seville,* is his funniest and finest essay in the comic vein. It was written with the happy confidence of a past-master in the art of opera-buffo but with the extra stimulation of the titillating challenge to make the sophisticated cynical French opera-goers fall once more beneath his charm. The challenge did not go unanswered – like any great entertainer, Rossini was never really arrogant about his audience – and the extra effort needed for the renewed conquest of Paris shows in the quality of invention, the extraordinary subtle instrumentation and in the unusual formal construction of the piece. Much was expected of him and much he gave.

He chose to set a most unusual libretto by Scribe and Delestre-Poirson which connects, within the two acts, a series of quite distinct scenes, each with its own plot and character. The scenes each show attempt (and failure) on the part of the notorious womaniser Count Ory to pursue his lascivious designs. His wicked, lustful intentions range widely over the medieval female population, but there is a constant preoccupation with the seduction of the beautiful Countess Adele de Fourmoutiers who has sworn (somewhat oddly) a proud vow of chastity until her brother returns from his crusades against the infidels; it was, presumably, intended as some sort of Talisman for his safety in foreign parts.

The Count's escapades are beautifully judged so that the tensions build from the first dalliance with village maidens in the guise of a hermit; his discovery and unmasking in an attempt to outwit his own page, Isolier, who is also en-amoured of the Countess; his new attempt, at the beginning of Act II, re-disguised, together with his companions, as a group of wandering nuns seeking shelter with the Countess from the storm; to the remarkable climax in the last scene where the Countess, acknowledging her frailty toward Isolier – the Crusades are by this time over and the Crusaders on their way home, victorious – becomes involved in a trio of mistaken identities, with the Count in nun's habit causing all manner of confusion. It is set to some of the most magically beautiful music that Rossini ever composed, and the suspense of its soft, inter-twining musical lines

is a theatrical master-stroke rarely paralleled and never surpassed in any of his other operas.

At first sight the opera appears to contain all the old,
famous Rossini formulae: the controlled crescendi in the big
ensembles; one of his best storms (in the second scene of
Act II); coloratura *sans pareil* for his hero and heroine and an
ensemble at the end of Act I that rivals the famous end of Act
I of the *Barber of Seville.* Yet the whole work has a quite different flavor from his earlier masterpiece and there are two
main reasons for this.

There is a very noticeable extra care over detail in the composition as well as a new, more adventurous use of harmonies. The old insouciance of his earlier Italian pieces is a
thing of the past. He had often declared his respect and
desire to emulate the skills of Beethoven; he felt himself out-
classed and was determined in his last years to do something
about it. *Count Ory* shows something of that great man's influence — not too much, and, happily it is absorbed without
losing anything of the original great man's wit and vitality.

The second point of distinction lies in the orchestration,
much more subtle and detailed than in most of his earlier
pieces. Apart from the greater variety and delicate invention
of accompanying figuration, particularly noticeable is the
lavish, brilliant use of the wind instruments. Rossini had always been fond of exploiting them for flamboyant, daring
solos, but rarely in the past had he explored their colors in
such original combinations and in subtly blocked-out contrast with the strings.

Finally, of course, the strength of the work lies in the freshness and vitality of its musical invention. It was as if the composer (who had already announced his intention of retiring
from the world of music, and was soon to do so) had discovered at the end a new, last spring of inspiration in this
delightful comedy about the wicked Count Ory. Perhaps he
saw something of what he himself would have liked to have
been in the character of the Count, and it amused him so
much that he gave it his best to do, at least, himself justice.
                    — *RL notes for May-June 1977 production,*
                              Opera Theatre of St Louis.

5 Jun 1977   Opera Theatre of St Louis   St Louis
Richard Stilwell (bar), RL (pno)
Stephen Foster, Mozart, Rodgers, Rossini, Schumann
(Dichterliebe)
28, 30 Jun 1977   Filene Center, Wolf Trap Farm Park
          for the Performing Arts   Vienna VA
Jane Bane (s), Richard Stilwell (bar), Donald Gramm (b-bar),
RL (hpsd), Wolf Trap Bach O†
Bach (2 programs)
30 Jul; 3, 8, 12, 16, 25 Aug 1977
          Santa Fe Opera   Santa Fe
Patricia Kern, Evelyn Petros, Linda Zoghby, Claude Corbeil,
          Stephen Dickson, Jon Garrison (t), Santa Fe Opera†
          ¶*Mozart (Così fan tutte)*
30 Sep 1977   Södra teatern   Stockholm
Soloists, insts†
¶*Cavalli (L'Egisto)*
20 Oct 1977   (Sweden)
Haendel (vln), Göteborg SO†
Delius, Elgar, Wieniawski (conc 1)
29 Oct 1977   Rikssalen, Örebro Slott   (Sweden)
Örebro CO†/hpsd
CPE Bach, WF Bach, Handel, Mozart, Sibelius
3, 4 Nov 1977   Palace of Fine Arts Theater   San Francisco
San Francisco Sym CO†/pno
Boccherini, Cimarosa, Mozart (incl. conc 12)
5 Nov 1977   Zellerbach Audit   CA
As 3, 4 November
18 Nov 1977   Town Hall   Dewsbury
Peter Katin (pno), BBC Northern SO†
Beethoven (conc 2), Elgar, Tchaikovsky
8, 9, 10, 11, 16, 17, 18 Dec 1977
          Orchestra Hall   Minneapolis
Kathryn Bouleyn (s), Rose Taylor/Dana Krueger (ms), Vinson
          Cole (t), Thomas Paul (b), Bach Soc Chorus, Minnesota O
          Chamb Ens†
          ¶*Handel (Messiah)*
15 Dec 1977   St Paul Cathedral   St Paul
As 8-18 December
23 Dec 1977   Ford Audit   Detroit
Robert Williams (bsn), Detroit Sym CO†
Bach, Boyce, Handel, Haydn, Vivaldi

SANTA FE. *Così fan tutte* was long thought to be one of the least successful of Mozart's operas. Surprising as it may now seem it only began to be performed again with any frequency in the late 1930s; the first performance in America, and that without revival, was in New York in 1922.

The problem was that to the critical mind which had inherited traditional nineteenth-century Teutonic views about music it was immediately trivial, even offensive, in subject matter. *The Marriage of Figaro* could be said to present something of social significance in the relationship of servant to master; *The Magic Flute* manifested in some mystical, Masonical way the struggle between good and evil; *Don Giovanni* could be seen as a piece about a characteristically Romantic hero whose exploits had been well attested by that most romantic of poets, Lord Byron. *Così* could present no such extra-musical message or connection. It seemed to be only a flippant skit on women's weakness and inconstancy which did not at all accord with the Romantic view of the fairer sex.

The need to ascribe great messages to art before it can be said to have worthwhile stature is now much less urgent than it was. So that we can now without embarrassment examine the piece on its own terms and see the values of it, so to speak, from within.

In the past, productions of the opera have often militated against this approach. Directors have regularly sought to impose trivialities in the way of parallel twirlings of sunshades, balletic embroidery, formalized patterns of movement, stage jokes — anything that would gild the insubstantial lily. It was almost all applied decoration that obscured much of the real wit and humor of the piece.

Ironically, another element which has militated against the acceptance of the work, arguably Mozart's greatest piece for the stage, was the enthusiasm of potential Dorabellas and Fiordigligis for the wonderfully virtuosic music they have to sing. In the pecking order, the parts inevitably went to the singers of greatest repute who, therefore, were not perhaps in their

[CONTINUED NEXT PAGE]

first youth. Management, initially uncertain of the opera's success at the box office, encouraged this practice. Of course, the parts were generally sung very well, but the near-adolescent behavior of the two girls in the first half of the opera could scarcely be attempted by ladies at the height of their career.

Fiordiligi often became like some artifical Countess from *Figaro* placed in what, for her, seem absurd and highly ridiculous situations, while Dorabella tended to become a sort of hoydenish version of Cherubino.

If we try to look in some unprejudiced way at what actually happens in the opera, we may find another, more truthful, attitude towards the characters which would leave the wit and humor to emerge from within. The plot may lose something of its absurdities (though nothing of its conventions) and show a progression and development of character that accords perfectly with the structure that Da Ponte, the librettist, gave to the piece.

In the beginning, the young men and the girls behave like ardent teenagers. Everything is exaggerated because they have to compensate for their lack of experience. Bets are rushed into with little heed for the consequence; partings are dramatized into tragedies, and vows of constancy and love are too many and too often repeated. The slow realization that there may be weaknesses, other concerns, other considerations gradually affects all four of the young people. Dorabella falls first — but then she is the more open of the two girls, and she would. Fiordiligi, the darker of the two, suffers much more before admitting her frailties — and how wonderfully her music shows this. The young men then have to taste the bitterness of having their male pride shown for what it so often is — vanity of possession.

With the connivance of Don Alfonso and Despina, old allies — and probably a good deal more — they learn the first lessons of love and, by the end of the opera, we see that they will be that much wiser, that much more mature the next time around.

Mozart found in *Così* a subject that reflected his favorite interest, one might almost say hobby, in life: women. He ex-

> amines them lovingly, cynically, wittily, knowingly, affec-
> tionately, and, with the heightened power of his second act
> music, wonderingly. There is no real moral to the opera, but
> there is a great deal to be learned from it.
> *—RL notes for Santa Fe Opera*
> *production, July-August 1977.*

*

14, 17 Jan 1978   Music Hall   Cincinnati
Yong Uck Kim (vln), Cincinnati SO†
Bruch, Glinka, Tchaikovsky
18, 19 Jan 1978   National Arts Center   Ottawa
Isaac Stern (vln), National Arts Centre/L'Orchestre du Centre
national des Arts†
Beethoven (conc), Mozart, Schubert
26, 27, 28, 31 Jan 1978 (open rehearsal 25 Jan)
Symphony Hall   Boston
Doriot Anthony Dwyer (fl), Boston SO†
¶*CPE Bach, JC Bach, JCF Bach, JS Bach, WF Bach*
14, 15 Feb 1978   New Orleans Theater
of the Performing Arts   New Orleans
New Orleans PSO†
Britten, Handel, Schumann
16 Feb 1978   Mobile Municipal Theater   Mobile AL
As 14, 15 February
20 Feb 1978   Ft Lauderdale
Judith Blegen, Fernando Corena, John Brecknock, Dominic
Cossa, Opera Guild of Ft Lauderdale†
Rossini (The Barber of Seville)
21, 23 Feb 1978   New Orleans Theater
of the Performing Arts   New Orleans
Susan Starr (pno), New Orleans PSO†
Liszt, Saint-Saëns, Walton
22 Feb 1978   Ursuline Acad Audit   LA
As 21, 23 February
11 Mar 1978   City Hall   Sheffield
Craig Sheppard (pno), BBC Northern SO†
Brahms, Mendelssohn (conc 1), Rimsky-Korsakov
17 Mar 1978   Town Hall   Huddersfield
Gale (s), Robin Leggate, Thomas Allen (bar), Huddersfield
Choral Soc, BBC Northern SO†
¶*Brahms (German Requiem), Liszt (Psalm 13)*

21 Mar 1978   Free Trade Hall   Manchester
Eiddwen Harrhy (s), Kathleen Livingstone (s), Sarah Walker
(ms), Anthony Rolfe-Johnson (t), King (b-bar), BBC
Singers, BBC Northern Singers, BBC Northern SO† (BBC
Master Concerts)
*Bach (*Magnificat*), Beethoven (sym 9)*
7, 8, 10, 13 Apr 1978
            Grand Théâtre de Genève   Geneva
Rachel Yakar, Erhard Fischer, Roland Aeschllimann, Rudolf
Constantin, Robert Massard, Eric Tappy, choeurs et ballet
du Grand Théâtre, Orchestre de la Suisse Romande†
¶*Gluck (*Iphigénie en Tauride*)*
3 May 1978   Queen Elizabeth Hall   London
Ann Murray (ms), ECO†
Bach, A Scarlatti, D Scarlatti, Telemann, Vivaldi
15, 19, 24, 29 Jul, 3 Aug 1978
            Théatre de l'Archevêche   (France)
Teresa Berganza (s), Christiane Eda-Pierre, Valérie Master-
son, Murray (ms), Christiane Chateau, Langridge (t),
François Loup, chorus, SCO† (Festival Aix en Provence)
¶*Handel (*Alcina*)*
23 Jul 1978   Cathédrale Saint-Sauveur   Aix en Provence
Yasuko Hayashi, Nadine Denize, chorus, Nouvel orchestre
philharmonique de Radio France† (Festival Aix en
Provence)
A Scarlatti, D Scarlatti, Vivaldi
28 Jul 1978   Saint-Germain des-Prés   Paris
P. Bouveret (s), H. Schaer (ms), Nouvel orchestre philhar-
monique de Radio-France† (Paris Summer Fest)
A Scarlatti, D Scarlatti, Vivaldi
16 Aug 1978   Royal Albert Hall   London
Holliger (ob), BBC Northern SO† (BBC-Henry Wood
Promenade Concerts)
*Britten (*Ovid Metamorphoses*), Elgar, Mozart (*conc K 314*),
R Strauss, Walton*
19 Sep 1978   Lincoln Center   New York
Pears (t), Peter Glossop (bar), Stilwell (bar), Cheek (b-bar),
James Morris (b), Metropolitan Opera Chorus & O†
¶*Britten (*Billy Budd*)*
10 Oct 1978   Free Trade Hall   Manchester
Burrowes (s), Allen (bar), Huddersfield Choral Soc, BBC
Northern SO† (BBC Master Concerts)
*Berkeley (sym 4), Brahms (*German Requiem*)*

| 14 Oct 1978 | Leeds Town Hall | Leeds |

Haendel (vln), BBC Northern SO†
Britten, Elgar, Walton

| 24 Nov 1978 | Royal Northern Coll of Music (day) | Manchester |

Valerie Masterson (s), BBC Northern SO†/hpsd
(Midday Proms)
Britten, Mendelssohn, Mozart

| | Tatton Park (evening) | Manchester |

BBC Northern SO†/hpsd (Cheshire County Council)
JC Bach, JS Bach, Debussy, Handel, Mozart, Vivaldi

| 25 Nov 1978 | Leeds Town Hall | Leeds |

Ralphael Wallfisch (vc), BBC Northern SO†
Dvorak, Rossini, Shostakovich

| 5 Dec 1978 | Free Trade Hall | Manchester |

Lott (s), Watts (c), John Elwes (t), Roberts (bar), BBC Northern Singers, BBC Northern SO† (BBC Master Concerts)
Bach (Christmas Oratorio)

*

| 10, 12 Jan 1979 | Orchestra Hall | Minneapolis |

Yefim Bronfman (pno), Minnesota O†
Beethoven, Liszt, Walton (sym 1)

| 11 Jan 1979 | O'Shaughnessy Audit | St Paul |

As 10, 12 January

| 14 Jan 1979 | Orchestra Hall | Minneapolis |

Lea Foli (vln), Robert Jamieson (vc), Sidney Zeitlin (fl), Basil Reeve (ob), John Miller (bsn), RL (hpsd)
Vivaldi

| 24, 26 Jan 1979 | Orchestra Hall | Minneapolis |

Ellen Shade (s), Eugene Levinson (db), Minnesota O†
Cavalli, Handel, Monteverdi, Vivaldi

| 27 Jan 1979 | O'Shaughnessy Audit | St Paul |

As 14, 16 January

| 13 Feb 1979 | Dade County Audit | Miami |

Morris White, James Hoback, Ralph Griffin, Susan Belling, James Billings, Arnold Voketaitis, Greater Miami Opera†
¶*Rossini (*The Barber of Seville*)*

| 18 Feb 1979 | Miami Beach Theater of the Performing Arts | Miami Beach |

As 13 February

| 27 Feb 1979 | Free Trade Hall | Manchester |

Radu Lupu (pno), BBC Northern SO† (BBC Master Concrts)
Grieg (conc), Haydn, Schoenberg, Wagner

"ABOUT THE ENGLISH CHAMBER ORCHESTRA. The English Chamber Orchestra wasn't created: it grew. It had its roots in a chamber orchestra founded after the second world war in order to play the large and varied baroque repertoire under one of the finest scholars and interpreters of that music: the late Arnold Goldsbrough. The Goldsbrough Orchestra, as it was then known, was founded by Goldsbrough and the conductor Lawrence Leonard....

"The Orchestra was soon called upon to expand its activities, and by the mid-1950s it had established a secure place for itself among England's orchestras. 1957, for instance, found it opening the Cheltenham Festival with a program of English music conducted by Charles Mackerras. Highlights of 1958 included a concert with Elisabeth Schwarzkopf at the Festival Hall....

"1959 was a vintage year for the orchestra, for it marked the 200th anniversary of Handel's death, and several concerts were given to celebrate the occasion. In the Purcell-Handel Festival they presented *King Arthur* for the BBC, and at Aldeburgh Emanuel Hurwitz directed the orchestra in a

ECO Leaders Emanuel Hurwitz (left), Kenneth Sillito (right) and José-Luis Garcia (standing)

very successful Handel birthday program.

"A new society was formed to promote the orchestra's activities: the Palladian Concert Society, which launched itself with two concerts at the beginning of 1960 directed by Raymond Leppard, one with Clifford Curzon as soloist. But increasingly there was a problem with the name of the orchestra: 'we wanted to go abroad much more, but people weren't interested because they had never heard of the name: they couldn't even pronounce it!' It was Ian Hunter who proposed the name English Chamber Orchestra, and he became an important force in the ECO's artistic direction during the early years of its existence. On 11 October 1960, the renamed orchestra made its first appearance, at the Festival Hall, in a most adventurous program of excerpts from two Monteverdi operas, edited and directed by Raymond Leppard....

"At the beginning of the ECO's life, it formed a permanent relationship with the young conductor Colin Davis, [who] directed the Bach program at the Royal Festival Hall on 18 February 1961, in which the soloists were David and Igor Oistrakh, who had never appeared together in London before. It was a remarkable success....

"The ECO appeared at the major festivals: Aldeburgh, Cheltenham, Edinburgh – but with the first of these festivals, the brainchild of Benjamin Britten, with whom the orchestra had been associated for some time through the perform-

[CONTINUED NEXT PAGE]

Arnold
Goldsbrough

ances of the English Opera Group, a special connection was developing. Aldeburgh became an important focus of the ECO's life....

"The success of the orchestra's change of name bore fruit in extensive touring during the 1962-63 season. Switzerland was visited with Raymond Leppard.... In December 1963 the orchestra went to Germany and Austria with Raymond Leppard, with programs ranging from Bach to Britten and Schoenberg.... 1967 was rounded off by the recordings of Handel's *Concerti Grossi* Op 6, which was to become a most successful set....

"1973 saw the premiere at Aldeburgh of what was to be Britten's last opera, *Death in Venice*.... The 1973 season ended with a *Christmas Oratorio* in the Festival Hall, for which Karl Richter brought with him his own highly skilled Munich Bach Choir....

"In 1975 an important series of concerts took place at the Hong Kong Festival with Isaac Stern, Raymond Leppard and Alexander Schneider....

"The orchestra's extensive touring commitments extended to Belgarde (with David Atherton) and Spain (with Raymond Leppard) at the end of 1975, and the next year saw two visits to France with Leppard as well as the yearly visit to Aldeburgh for the premiere of the remarkable new work by Britten, his cantata *Phaedra* written for Janet Baker....

An early ECO recording session with RL

> "And so the hectic, rewarding life of the ECO continues apace.In 1977 the ECO gave a total of 133 concerts at home and abroad, and recorded 92 sessions which produced around 40 records." *— Nicholas Kenyon, based on interviews with Quintin Ballardie (ECO director) and Ursula Strebi (general manager until 1974), in* **The English Chamber Orchestra: A Pictorial Review** *(1978).*

2 Mar 1979   Victoria Hall   Hanley
Leonid Kogan (vln), BBC Northern SO†
Elgar, Mozart, R Strauss, Tchaikovsky
13 Mar 1979   Concert Hall, Lancaster Univ   Lancaster
Black (ob), BBC Northern SO†
Saint-Saëns, R Strauss (conc), Tchaikovsky
16 Mar 1979   Royal Northern Coll of Music   Manchester
Vladimir Spivakov (vln), BBC Northern SO† (Midday Proms)
Beethoven, Mozart, Sibelius, Werle (L.J.)
29, 30, 31 Mar, 3 Apr 1979
          Avery Fisher Hall, Lincoln Center   New York
Ellen Shade (s), New York Philharmonic†
¶*Bach, Cavalli, Monteverdi*
27 Apr 1979   Free Trade Hall   Manchester
André Watts (pno), BBC Northern SO†
Berg, Schumann (conc), Tippett (sym 4)
30 Apr 1979   Tonhalle   Düsseldorf
Baker (ms), ECO†
Boccherini, Britten (Phaedra), Cimerosa, Haydn, Mozart
4 May 1979   Royal Fest Hall   London
As 30 April
Summer 1979   Glyndebourne Festival Opera   Glyndebourne
Von Stade (Penelope), Patricia Parker, Murray, Trama, Keith
Lewis, Stilwell (Ulisse), Oliver, Richard Lewis, Glyndebourne Fest Opera, LPO†
¶*Monteverdi (Il ritorno d'Ulisse in patria—RL vers)(10 performs)*
8 Jul 1979   Tanglewood Fest   Lennox MA
Boston SO† (Tanglewood Fest)
Bach
6, 8 Aug 1979   Avery Fisher Hall, Lincoln Center   New York
Claudine Carlson, Phyllis Bryn-Julson (s), Evelyn Petros,

The English Chamber Orchestra & Music Society
presents

The English Chamber Orchestra
Leader: José-Luis Garcia

Raymond Leppard
conductor

Janet Baker
mezzo-soprano

Cimarosa
Overture: 'I traci amanti'
Boccherini
Symphony G506 in D minor
'Della casa del diavolo'
Haydn
Cantata: 'Miseri noi, misera Patria'
Britten
'Phaedra', Op 93
Mozart
Symphony no 40 in G minor K550

Greater London Council
Royal Festival Hall   **Friday 4 May 1979**
Director: George Mann OBE   **8.00pm**

David Kuebler, Kathryn Bouleyn, Cheek (b-bar), RL
(narr), Mostly Mozart Fest O† (Mostly Mozart Fest)
¶*Mozart (La* Clemenza di Tito)

| 24 Sep 1979 | City Hall Concert Hall | Hong Kong |

Michael Roll (pno), BBC Northern SO†
Rachmaninoff (conc 3), Tchaikovsky, Walton (Scapino)

| 25 Sep 1979 | City Hall Concert Hall | Hong Kong |

Pauk (vln), BBC Northern SO†
Dvorak, Elgar, Tchaikovsky (conc)

| 26 Sep 1979 | City Hall | Hong Kong |

Roll (pno), BBC Northern SO†
Holst, Mozart (conc K 482), Sibelius

| 27 Sep 1979 | City Hall Concert Hall | Hong Kong |

Pauk (vln), BBC Northern SO†
Berlioz, Shostakovich, Walton (conc)

| 28 Sep 1979 | City Hall Concert Hall | Hong Kong |

BBC Northern SO†
Bach, Haydn, Stravinsky, Tippet (Ritual Dances)

| 17 Oct 1979 | Zellerbach Audit | Berkeley CA |

Shlomo Mintz (vln), San Francisco S†
JC Bach, JS Bach, Mozart (incl. con K 218)

| 18 Oct 1979 | Flint Center | Cupertino CA |

As 17 October

19, 20 Oct 1979	Herbst Theatre	San Francisco

As 17 October

23, 25, 27 Nov 1979   Jones Hall   Houston
Sunny Joy Langton, Diane Kesling, Maria Ewing, Richard
Vernon, Paolo Montarsolo, Rockwell Blake, Claudio Des-
deri, Houston Grand Opera†
¶*Rossini (La Cenerentola)*

2 Dec 1979   Queen Elizabeth Hall   London
Lott (s), Aydin Önac (pno), Louise Williams (vln), Roger
Chase (vla), ECO†
Brown, Handel, Mozart, Vaughan Williams, Weber

7 Dec 1979   Free Trade Hall   Manchester
John Browning (pno), BBC Northern SO† (BBC Master
Concerts)
Barber (Medea's Meditation & Dance of Vengeance*),
Bernstein* (On the Waterfront: Suite*), Carter* (Variations*),
Gershwin* (conc in F)

19, 21, 22 Dec 1979   Massey Hall   Toronto
Jeannette Zarou (s), Janet Stubbs (ms), Neil Rosenshein (t),
Donald Bell (b-bar), Toronto Mendelssohn Choir, Toron-
to S†
¶*Handel (Messiah)*

＊

1980   Lincoln Cathedral   Lincolnshire
Armstrong, Hodgson, Garrison (t), Titus, Morris (b), BBC
Singers (London), BBC Northern Singers, BBC Northern
SO† (televised; repeated 1981, 1982)
¶*Bach* (St. Matthew Passion)

15 Jan 1980   Free Trade Hall   Manchester
Lott (s), Hodgson (c), Tear (t), Glossop (bar), John Daszak
(treble), BBC Singers, BBC Northern SO† (BBC Master
Concerts)
¶*Mendelssohn (Elijah)*

26 Jan 1980   Ford Audit   Detroit
Detroit Symphony CO†
Albinoni, Bach, Corelli, Pachelbel, Telemann, Vivaldi

5, 6 Feb 1980   New Orleans Theatre
                        of the Performing Arts   New Orleans
Marilyn Horne (s), New Orleans Philharmonic SO†
Elgar (Sea Pictures*), Mozart, Rossini, Tchaikovsky*

: 521 :

9, 10 Feb 1980   Jones Hall   Houston
Misha Dichter (pno), Houston S†
Elgar (sym 1), *Grieg (conc), Liszt*
18 Feb 1980   Younger Hall   St Andrews (Scotland)
Nicolet (fl), Wilbraham (tpt), John Tunnell (vln), Robin Miller
(ob), SCO†
JC Bach, JS Bach (Brandenburg concs 1, 3, 4), *Vivaldi* (fl *conc)*
19 Feb 1980   Queen's Hall   Edinburgh
As 18 February
20 Feb 1980   St Machar's Cathedral   Aberdeen
Nicolet (fl), Wilbraham (tpt), Tunnell (vln), Robin Miller (ob),
SCO†
Boccherini (fl *conc), JC Bach, JS Bach*
21 Feb 1980   Queen's Hall   Edinburgh
As 20 February
23 Feb 1980   Queen's Hall   Edinburgh
Nicolet (fl), Wilbraham (tpt), Tunnell (vln), Robin Miller (ob),
SCO†
Program as 19, 21 February, but substituting *Bach* Branden-
burg concs 2, 3, 5 *for* concs 1, 3, 4
24 Feb 1980   Theatre Royal   Glasgow
As 23 February
15, 19 Apr 1980   Lincoln Center   New York
Stilwell (bar), Cassilly, Glossop (bar), Morris (b), Ward, Rob-
bins, Foldi, Atherton, Velis, Nagy, Darrenkamp, Meredith,
Metropolitan Opera Chorus & O†
¶*Britten (Billy Budd)*
22, 23 Apr 1980   Salle Wilfrid-Pelletier, Place des Arts   Montreal
Martha Agerich (pno), Orchestre symphonique de Montréal†
Beethoven (conc 2), *Handel, Walton* (sym 1)
26 Apr 1980   Kennedy Center   Washington
As 15, 19 April
1 May 1980   National Arts Centre   Ottawa
Louis Lortie (pno), National Arts Centre O†
Britten (Suite on Engl Folk Tunes), *Brahms, Cimarosa, Haydn,*
Mozart (conc 23)
3 May 1980   Public Audit   Cleveland
As 15, 19 April
10 May 1980   Civic Center   Atlanta
As 15, 19 April

15, 16, 17 May 1980   Orchestra Hall   Chicago
Isobel Buchanan (s), Shirley-Quirk (bar), Chicago
Sym Chorus, Chicago SO†
¶*Vaughan Williams (*Serenade to Music, Sea Symphony*)*
24 May 1980   Northrop Memorial Audit   Minneapolis
As 15, 19 April
5, 6 Jun 1980   Orchestra Hall   Chicago
Adolph Herseth (tpt), Chicago SO†/hpsd
¶*Britten, Haydn (concs tpt, hpsd), Stravinsky (*Firebird suite*),
Vivaldi*
2 Jul 1980   Hollywood Bowl   Los Angeles
Sidney Weiss (vln), Heiichiro Ohyama (vla), Los Angeles P†
Mozart (incl. Sinfonia concertante K 364*)*
5 Jul 1980   Hollywood Bowl   Los Angeles
Elly Ameling (s), Los Angeles P†
Bach
17 Jul 1980   Oakland Univ   MI
James Galway (fl), Detroit SO† (Meadow Brook Music Fest)
Bach (fl conc — *transcr from* hpsd conc 5), *Mozart (*fl, hp conc*),
Rimsky-Korsakov, Stravinsky*
19 Jul 1980   Oakland Univ   MI
Claudine Carlson (ms), Frank Little (t), Detroit SO† (Meadow
Brook Music Fest)
25 Jul 1980   Temple Univ   Philadelphia
Beaux Arts Trio (Pressler, Cohen, Greenhouse),
Pittsburgh SO†
*Beethoven (*triple conc*), Elgar, Tchaikovsky*
*Mahler (*Das Lied von der Erde*), Schubert*
31 Jul 1980   St Nicholas' Chapel   King's Lynn
Baker (ms), RL (pno) (30th King's Lynn Fest)
*Caccini, Caldara, Copland, Delius, Durante, Fauré, Martini,
Mendelssohn, Pergolesi, Plumstead, Quilter, Scarlatti*
14 Aug 1980   Queen Elizabeth Hall   London
Yvonne Lea (ms), James Atherton (t), ECO†
Albinoni, Cavalli, Cesti, Monteverdi
19 Aug 1980   Royal Albert Hall   London
David Wilde (pno), BBC Northerm SO† (BBC-Henry
Wood Promenade Concerts)
*Beethoven, Liszt (*conc 1*), Shostakovich (*sym 5*)*
26 Aug 1980   Usher Hall   Edinburgh
Margaret Marshall (s), SCO† (Edinburgh Internatl Fest)
Cimarosa, Mendelssohn, Mozart, R Strauss

17, 20, 25, 28 Oct; 1, 3, 8, 13 Nov 1980   Paris
Eda-Pierre, Von Stade (ms), George Gautier, Michael Devlin
(b-bar), Roger Soyer, José Van Dam, Theatre National
Opera de Paris†
¶*Rameau* (Dardanus — RL *performing ed.*)[14]
30 Nov 1980   Theatre Royal   Glasgow
Baker (ms), SCO†
Handel, Mendelssohn
3 Dec 1980   Usher Hall   Edinburgh
As 30 November
11 Dec 1980   New Broadcasting House   Manchester
BBC Northern SO† (Live broadcast concert to mark opening
of the new Music Studio in New Broadcasting House)
Britten (Building of the House), *Delius, Elgar* (sym 1), *Harty,*
Walton
16 Dec 1980   Free Trade Hall   Manchester
Palmer (s), Watts (cn), Ryland Davies (t), Alan Titus (bar),
BBC Northern Singers, BBC Northern SO† (BBC Master
Concerts)
¶*Handel* (Messiah)

*

15, 16 Jan 1981   Popejoy Hall, Univ of NM   Albuquerque
New Mexico SO†
Britten, Dvorak, Sibelius
17, 18 Jan 1981   Powell Sym Hall   St Louis
John Korman (vln), Joan Korman (vla), Saint Louis SO†
Benjamin (Romantic Fantasy), *Elgar* (Enigma Variations),
Haydn
22 Jan 1981   Browning Center   Ogden UT
Lynn Harrell (vc), Utah S†
Handel, Herbert (conc 2), *Vaughan Williams* (sym 5)
23, 24 Jan 1981   Sym Hall   Salt Lake City
As 22 January
28, 29 Jan 1981   National Arts Centre   Ottawa
National Arts Centre O†
Albinoni, Bach, Corelli, Pachelbel, Telemann, Vivaldi
12 Feb 1981   Palau de la música catalana   Barcelona
SCO†
Handel, Mendelssohn, Mozart

---

14   For a related commentary, see Chapter II §2 above.

13 Feb 1981   Palau de la música catalana   Barcelona
Teresa Berganza (ms), SCO†
Handel (incl. arias), Haydn (incl. arias)
5, 7 Mar 1981   Music Hall   Kansas City MO
Russell Sherman (pno), Kansas City P†
Beethoven (conc 3), *Cimarosa, Haydn, Sibelius*
6 Mar 1981   Plaza Theatre   Kansas City MO
Same as 5, 7 March
12 Mar 1981   Temple Beth Israel   Houston
RL (hpsd), Houston Symphony Chamb O†
Haydn
21, 23, 24 Mar 1981   Vancouver
Aldo Ciccolini (pno), Vancouver SO† (QM-FM Great Com-
posers Programme)
Beethoven (conc 3), *Rimsky-Korsakov, Sibelius*
18, 19 Apr 1981   Uihlein Hall   Milwaukee
Milwaukee SO†
Mozart, Stravinsky
16 May 1981   Arts Centre, Univ of Warwick   Coventry
Graham Sheen (bsn), ECO†
Handel, Mozart (incl. conc K 171)
18 May 1981   Royal Fest Hall   London
Baker (ms), Garcia (vln), ECO†
Beethoven, Berlioz (Réverie and Caprice), Handel,
Mendelssohn, Mozart
4, 8, 10, 17 Jul; 4, 13 Aug 1981
          Santa Fe Opera   Santa Fe
Janice Hall, Jean Kraft, Hakan Hagegard, Morris (b), Rosen-
shein (t), Günter von Kannen, Santa Fe Opera†
¶*Rossini (Il barbiere di Siviglia)*
25 Jul; 7, 15, 19 Aug 1981
          Santa Fe Opera   Santa Fe
Elizabeth Hynes, Carolyne James, Rosalind Elias, Garrison
(t), Joseph McKee, Morris (b), Santa Fe Opera†
¶*Stravinsky (The Rake's Progress)*[15]
31 Jul, 1 Aug 1981   Avery Fisher Hall, Lincoln Center   New York
Bryn-Julson (s), Ruth Welting (s), David Britton (t), Marius
Rintzler (b), Mostly Mozart Fest O† (Mostly Mozart Fest)
Mozart (Bastien und Bastienne, Der Schauspieldirektor),
Salieri

---

15   For a related memoir see Chapter VI Section §3, above.

16? Aug 1981   Edinburgh
Festival Service 1981: Choir of St Giles' Cathedral, SCO,
Thomas Allen (bar), John Wallace (tpt), Equale Brass
(Edinburgh International Fest)
25 Aug 1981   Usher Hall   Edinburgh
Perahia (pno), LPO† (Edinburgh International Fest)
Beethoven (incl. conc 1*), Sibelius*
28 Aug 1981   The Queen's Hall   Edinburgh
Isobel Buchanan (s), SCO† (Edinburgh International Fest)
Bach, Couperin, Haydn, Rameau
16 Oct 1981   Royal Fest Hall   London
Janet Price (s), Margaret Cable (ms), Garcia (vln),
Josef Fröhlich (vln), London Choral Soc, ECO†
Bach, Vivaldi
22 Oct 1981   Royal Fest Hall   London
Söderström (s), Philharmonia O†
*Borodin (*sym 2*), Corelli, R Strauss, Tchaikovsky, Tippett*
(Corelli Fantasia)
30 Oct 1981   Queen Elizabeth Hall   London
Richard Stoltzman (cl), ECO†
Mozart (incl. conc*)*
8 Nov 1981   Queen Elizabeth Hall   London
Lott (s), ECO†
Mozart
13, 14, 15 Nov 1981   Uihlein Hall   Milwaukee
Bella Davidovich (pno), Milwaukee SO†
*Saint-Saëns (*conc 2*), Sibelius, Vaughan Williams*
18, 19, 20 Nov 1981   Orchestra Hall   Minneapolis
Tuckwell (hn), Kendall Betts (hn), Minnesota O†
*Handel, Hindemith, Mozart, Telemann (*conc 2 hns*)*
21 Nov 1981   O'Shaughnessy Audit   St Paul
As 18-20 November
25, 27, 28 Nov, 1 Dec 1981
                    Avery Fisher Hall, Lincoln Center   New York
Christian Blackshaw (pno), New York P†
¶*Britten (incl.* conc, Building of the House, Young Apollo,
      Sinfonia da Requiem*)*
3, 4, 5, 8 Dec 1981   Avery Fisher Hall, Lincoln Center   New York
Hilda Harris (ms), Britton (t), New York P†
Purcell ("A Purcell Cabaret" *— dev. by RL), Shostakovich*
15 Dec 1981   Carnegie Hall   New York
Paul Tobias (vc), National O of New York†
*Barber (*conc*), Liszt, Tchaikovsky, Wolf-Ferrari*

17, 18, 20 Dec 1981   Orchestra Hall   Chicago
Dale Clevenger (hn), Chicago SO†
¶*Debussy, Mozart, William Schuman (3* Colloquies*), R Strauss*

*

16 Jan 1982   Carnegie Hall   New York
New American SO†
4, 6, 7 Feb 1982   Boettcher Hall   Denver
Tedd Joselson (pno), Denver SO†
Mozart, Rachmaninoff (con 2)*, Vaughan Williams* (sym 5)
13 Feb 1982   Ford Audit   Detroit
Eugene Wade (hn), Bobos Mortchikian, Joseph Goldman,
    Gordon Peterson (vlns), Detroit Sym Chamb O†
Mozart, Vivaldi
14 Feb 1982   Leon Mandel Hall   Chicago
Adolph Herseth (tpt), Ray Still (ob), members Chicago SO†
Haydn, Mozart
18, 19 Feb 1982   Ford Audit   Detroit
Cynthia Clarey (ms), Detroit SO†
Falla (El Amor Brujo)*, Holst*
19, 21 Mar 1982   Barbican Centre   London
Lott (s), Garcia (vln), Adeney, Christopher Nicolls (fls), RL
    (hpsd), ECO†
Bach
31 Mar, 2, 3 Apr 1982 Davies Sym Hall   San Francisco
Ameling (s), Delia Wallis (ms), John Aler (t), Garrison (t),
    Stilwell (bar), Shirley-Quirk (b), San Francisco Sym
    Chorus, San Francisco S†
¶*Bach* (St. Matthew Passion)
22, 23, 25 Apr 1982
                         Heinz Hall   Pittsburgh
Kathleen Battle (s), Pittsburgh SO†
Mozart
4, 5, 6, 7 May 1982   Kennedy Center   Washington
Bruno Leonardo Gelber (pno), National SO†
Schumann (conc)*, Sibelius*
11 May 1982   La Salle des Pas Perdus, Palais   Poitiers
SCO† (8th Printemps Musical de Poitiers [Poitiers Fest])
Gluck, Mozart, Schubert, Stravinsky
13 May 1982   La Salle des Pas Perdus, Palais   Poitiers
Lott (s), Neil Jenkins (t), Caddy (b), Scottish P Singers, SCO†
    (8th Printemps Musical de Poitiers [Poitiers Fest])
¶*Haydn* (Creation)

Much that is misleading has been written about the problems of performing Gluck's *Orfeo ed Euridice*. It is at once a simple and a delicately complex problem that needs one major decision, the choice of voice for the main protagonist, and then many lesser but important ones that follow therefrom.

The facts of the case are simple. Gluck composed the work twice: first for Vienna in 1762 with a male castrato as Orfeo, and secondly for Paris in 1774 with an *haute-contre* in the part. The *haut-contre* is a very high tenor voice that the French had favored for many years, not much liking the castrato for, presumably, Gallic reasons.

The Paris version, although in concept the same, necessitated a good deal of transposition and the recomposition of Gluck's recitatives. Gluck also took the opportunity to enlarge the short Vienna score by adding some wonderful new music and, in general, profiting from the earlier experience.

Neither version is really satisfactory for present-day performance.

There are a few male altos who could manage the earlier version. But the version itself is very short, containing many first thoughts of things he did better later. And who would willingly forego Euridice's aria in Act II, the dance of the blessed spirits, the first aria for Amor or the duet scene in Act III, all only to be found in the Paris version? Yet this too is unsatisfactory. *Haut-contres* do exist, but none, in my experience, could bring to the part the stature it needs. Moreover, the high tessitura gives a sense of strain to the role that is quite unsuited to much of the drama. It is very hard to be elegiac on a top C.

What, then, does one do?

Gluck demonstrated that his concern was for present effectiveness in the various revivals in his life-time. In 1769, for example, he remodelled the main part for a distinguished male soprano, and the Paris version contained several numbers adapted from earlier works. Even the sublimely beautiful *'che puro ciel'* was a re-write of an aria from *Ezio* composed some twelve years earlier.

In 1859 Berlioz prepared what has proved to be the most enduring accommodation. Adapted for the celebrated Pauline

Viardot-Garcia, in essence it restored the alto range of Orfeo to the French score. (The part had been sung by a woman as early as 1813, probably earlier.) Where necessary the French version was transposed and the vocal line adapted in recitative to the French accompaniment. The rest he left in the French version. It was sung in French and the Italian translation of it wanders far from the style of Calzabigi, who, in any case, did not adapt his own libretto for Paris.

What are we going to do at Glyndebourne? I hope it may be said that we have followed Gluck's precepts and chosen what is most effective now.

Our intention is to remain true to Gluck's inspired, mature version of the piece, and we are now ready to being work on it.

We shall sing it in Italian. Dame Janet Baker who is our Orfeo, prefers, for the transposed recitatives, as do we, the Italian text that was prepared for Milan in 1884.

Berlioz wanted to return as far as possible to the more varied instrumentation of the Vienna score. Paris had no cors anglais, no cornetti, no chalumeaux and Gluck had to make do with clarinets. We can now go further than Berlioz with both cornetti and a specially prepared chalumeau as well as cor anglais.

*—RL, program notes for Glyndebourne
1982 performances.*

14 May 1982   Basilique Saint-Seurin   Bordeaux
        As 13 May (Mai Musical de Bordeaux [Bordeau Fest])
17 May 1982   Binyenei Ha-Oomah   Jerusalem
        Garcia (vln), ECO†
        *Handel, David Matthews (*Serenade*), Mozart (*conc 5*), Purcell*
18, 19, 20 May 1982   Haifa Audit   Haifa
        Stephen Isserlis (vc), ECO†
        Handel, Haydn (incl. conc in C*), Robin Holloway (*Ode*)*
22, 24 May 1982   Mann Audit   Tel-Aviv
        As 17 May
27, 30 Jun; 2, 4, 6, 8, 10, 12, 15, 17 Jul 1982
                    Glyndebourne Festival Opera   Glyndebourne
        Baker (Orfeo), Gale (Amore), Speiser (Euridice), Jean
            Mallandaine (hpsd), Glyndebourne Chorus, LPO†
        ¶*Gluck (*Orfeo ed Euridice*)*

: 529 :

11 Aug 1982   Royal Albert Hall   London
Speiser (s), Gale (s), Baker (ms), Glyndebourne Chorus,
Mallandaine (hpsd), Glyndebourne Fest Opera†
(BBC-Henry Wood Promenade Concerts)
¶*Gluck (Orfeo ed Euridice)*
27 Aug 1982   Royal Albert Hall   London
Emanuel Ax (pno), Yvonne Kenny (s), ECO† (BBC-Henry
Wood Promenade Concerts)
Beethoven (incl. conc 1*), Berg (7 Early Songs), Stravinsky*
31 Aug 1982   Usher Hall   Edinburgh
Ileana Cotrubas (s), SCO†
Pergolesi, Schubert, Stravinsky
    Oct 1982   State Theater, Lincoln Center   New York
Harper (s), Garrison (t), New York City Opera†
¶*Gluck (Alceste)*
23 Oct 1982   Powell Sym Hall   St Louis
John Sant' Ambrogio (vc), Saint Louis SO†
Mendelssohn, Saint-Saëns (conc 1), Schubert, Wagner
1 Nov 1982   Theatre Royal   Glasgow
Jean-Pierre Rampal (fl), SCO†
Hadyn, Mendelssohn, Mozart (fl conc 2)
4 Nov 1982   Queen's Hall   Edinburgh
As 1 November
5 Nov 1982   Younger Hall   St Andrews
As 1 November
12, 14 Nov 1982   Barbican Centre   London
Linda Finnie (a), Garcia (vln), William Bennett (fl), ECO†
Bach
17 Nov 1982   Queen's Hall   Edinburgh
Mintz (vln), SCO†
Bruch (conc 1), Schubert, Weber
18 Nov 1982   Younger Hall   St Andrews
As 17 November
24 Nov 1982   Royal Fest Hall   London
Philip Ledger, Simon Preston, Melvyn Tan, RL (hpsds), ECO†
CPE Bach-Leppard, JS Bach, Vivaldi-Bach
*

25, 27 Jan 1983   Paramount Theatre of the Arts   Oakland
Kaaren Erickson (s), Clarey (ms), Leo Goeke (t), Jeffrey Gall
(ct), Louis Lebherz (b), Elwood Thornton (b), Oakland
Sym Chorus, Oakland Sym CO†
Handel (Samson)

29 Jan 1983   Zellerbach Audit   Berkeley CA
As 25, 27 January
3, 4 Feb 1983   Clowes Hall   Indianapolis
Hidetaro Suzuki (vln), ISO† (RL's debut appearances with
    ISO)
¶*Elgar* (sym 1), *Mozart, Prokofiev* (conc 2)
19, 20 Feb 1983   Kaufmann Concert Hall   New York
Dmitry Sitkovetsky (vln), Y Chamb S†
Mozart, Prokofiev (incl. conc 2*)*
1, 2 Feb 1983   New Orleans Theatre of the Performing Arts
                                      New Orleans
Dean Miller (fl), Rachel Van Voorhees (hp), New Orleans
    Philharmonic SO†
*Mozart (*conc*), Sibelius, Vaughan Williams*
1 Mar 1983   Queen Elizabeth Hall   London
Black (ob), ECO†
*Albinoni (*ob conc op 9 nr 2*), Corellli, Handel, A Scarlatti*
6 Mar 1983   Queen Elizabeth Hall   London
Murray (s), ECO†
Handel (incl. "Lucrezia" cantata*), Locatelli, A Scarlatti*
13 Mar 1983?   Royal Fest Hall   London
Soloists, chorus, LPO†
¶*Mendelssohn (Elijah)*
19 Mar 1983   Usher Hall   Edinburgh
Baker (s), Male Chorus of Scottish P Singers, SCO†
Brahms (incl. Alto Rhapsody*), Haydn, Mozart*
20 Mar 1983   City Hall   Glasgow
As 19 March
1 Apr 1983   Barbican Centre   London
Soloists, chorus, ECO†
¶*Bach (*St Matthew Passion*)*
23, 25 Apr 1983   Orchestra Hall   Chicago
Krystian Zimerman (pno), Chicago SO†
¶*Dvorak, Handel, Liszt* (conc 2)
28, 29 Apr; 1 May 1983   Orchestra Hall   Chicago
Jan DeGaetani (ms), Chicago SO†
¶*Bax (*Tintagel*), Britten (*Occasional Overture*), Elgar (*sym 1*),*
    *Maxwell Davies (*Runes from a House of the Dead, Stone
    Liturgy*)*
7, 9, 10 May 1983   Vancouver
Gutiérrez (pno), Vancouver SO† (QM-FM Great Composer
    Series)
Rachmaninoff (incl. conc 3, sym 2*)*

14 May 1983   Gesellschaft der Musikfreunde   Vienna
    Berganza (s), SCO† (Musikverein)
    Crosse, Falla, Haydn, Mozart, Rossini, Vivaldi
16, 17 May 1983   Poitiers
    Berganza (s), SCO† (Poitiers Fest)
18 May 1983   Lyons
    Berganza (s), SCO†
23, 24 May 1983   Lisbon
    Berganza (s), SCO† (Lisbon Fest)
26 May 1983   Théâtre musical de Paris-Châtelet   Paris
    As 14 May
27 May 1983   Barbican Centre   London
    Tuckwell (hn), SCO†
    Hadyn (incl. hn conc 1*), Mendelssohn, Mozart (*hn conc 3*)*
29 May 1983   Barbican Centre   London
    Berganza (s), SCO†
    *Brahms, Falla (*7 Popular Spanish Songs*), Haydn, Rossini,
    Vivaldi*
2 Jun 1983   Avery Fisher Hall, Lincoln Center   New York
    Bryn-Julson (s), Ida Kavafian (vln), New York P†
    (Horizons '83[16])
    *Consoli (*afterimages*), Del Tredici (*All in the Golden After-
    noon*), Takemitsu (*Far Calls, Coming Far!*)*
2, 6, 8, 15 Jul; 2, 10, 16, 24, 26 Aug 1983
                    Santa Fe Opera   Santa Fe NM
    Günter von Kannen, Thomas Hampson/Dale Duesing, Robert
        Gambill, Janice Hall, Nico Castel, Sante Fe Opera†
    ¶*Donizetti (*Don Pasquale*)*
23, 27 Jul; 5, 13, 17 Aug 1983
                    Santa Fe Opera   Santa Fe NM
    Cynthia Clarey, Neil Rosenshein (Orione), Richard Owen,
        Evelyn Lear, Thomas Stewart, Sante Fe Opera†
    ¶*Cavalli (*L'Orione — RL ed.*)*
29 Sep 1983   State Theater, Lincoln Center   New York
    Carol Vaness, Mimi Lerner, Erie Mills, D'Anna Fortunato,
        Nadia Pelle, Harry Dworchak, John Stewart, New York
        City Opera†
    ¶*Handel (*Alcina*)*

---

16   Program also incl. New York New Music Ens cond by Robert Black.

21, 22, 25 Oct 1983   Academy of Music   Philadelphia
    Philadelphia O†
    ¶*Borodin, Liadov, Mozart*
10, 11, 12 Nov 1983   Heinz Hall   Pittsburgh
    Rudolf Firkusny (pno), Pittsburgh SO†
    Borodin (sym 2), Liadov (2 Legends), Mozart (conc 15), Wag-
      ner
19, 20, 21 Nov 1983   Commun Center Theater   Sacramento
    Antonio Meneses (vc), Sacramento SO†
    Britten, Dvorak, Haydn, Tchaikovsky
8 Dec 1983   Queen's Hall   Edinburgh
    Berganza (s), Robin Miller (ob), SCO†
    Albinoni, Cavalli, Handel, Monteverdi
10 Dec 1983   Usher Hall   Edinburgh
    Lott (s), Murray (ms), Linda Finnie (c), Glenn Winslade (t),
      Henry Herford (b), Scottish Philharmonic Singers, SCO†
    Handel, Pergolesi
11 Dec 1983   City Hall   Glasgow
    As 10 December

*

7 Jan 1984   Powell Sym Hall   St Louis
    Richard Goode (pno), St Louis Sym CO†
    Beethoven (con 1), Mozart, R Strauss
26, 28, 29 Jan 1984   Denver Center for the Performing Arts   Denver
    Denver SO†
    Britten, Elgar, Vaughan Williams, Walton
7, 8 Feb 1984   Salle Wilfrid-Pelletier   Montreal
    Harper (s), Dale Duesing (bar), Orchestra symphonique de
      Montréal†
    Handel
16, 17 Feb 1984   Civic Center Concert Hall   Birmingham
    Alabama SO†
    Dvorak, Liadov, Tchaikovsky
1, 2, 3 Mar 1984   Woodruff Arts Center   Atlanta GA
    Juliana Markova (pno), Atlanta SO†
    Bax, Dvorak, Handel, Rachmaninoff
9, 10 Mar 1984   Popejoy Hall, Univ of NM   Albuquerque
    New Mexico SO†
    Britten, Brahms
11 Mar 1984   Sweeney Center   Santa Fe
    As 9, 10 March

15, 16 Mar 1984   Davies Sym Hall   San Francisco
Douglas Rioth (hp), San Francisco S† (Mostly Mozart Fest)
Handel, Mozart
20 Mar 1984   Davies Sym Hall   San Francisco
Alexandre Lagoya (gtr), San Francisco S† (Mostly Mozart Fest)
Handel, Haydn, Mozart
13 Apr 1984   Queen Elizabeth Hall   London
Ax (pno), ECO†
Matthews (David — Serenade op 29), *Mozart, Schubert*
15 Apr 1984   City Hall   Glasgow
Perahia (pno), SCO†
Beethoven (incl. conc 5), *Saint-Saëns*
18 Apr 1984   Queen's Hall   Edinburgh
As 15 April
29, 31 May; 2, 7, 9, 11, 15, 17, 19, 21, 23, 29 Jun; 1, 4 Jul 1984
     Glyndebourne Festival Opera   Glyndebourne
Maria Ewing (Poppea), Anne-Marie Owens, Cynthia Clarey,
Gale, Dennis Bailey (Nero), Robert Lloyd/Roderick Ken-
nedy, Keith Lewis, Glyndebourne Chorus, LPO†
¶*Monteverdi* (L'incoronazione di Poppea — *RL vers)*
24 Jul 1984   Royal Albert Hall   London
Alison Hargan (s), Eilene Hannan (ms), Linda Finnie (c), BBC
PO† (BBC-Henry Wood Promenade Concerts)
Bax (sym 5), Delius, Maw (scenes & arias)
1 Sep 1984   Rochester NY
Bronfman (pno), Rochester PO†
Beethoven
20 Sep 1984   Krannert Center, Univ of IL   Urbana
Chicago SO†
Barber, Dvorak, Shostakovich
22 Sep 1984   Hill Audit, Univ of Mich   Ann Arbor
Chicago SO†
Barber, Dvorak, Shostakovich
6, 7 Oct 1984   Powell Sym Hall   St Louis
Jacques Israelievitch (vln), St Louis SO†
Elgar (sym 1), Saint-Saëns (conc 3), Walton
24, 27, 30 Oct; 1, 3 Nov 1984
     Theater Royal   Glasgow
Anne Howells, Ian Caley, Alexander Morrison, Norman
White, Scottish Opera Chorus, Scottish Opera O†
¶*Cavallli* (Orion)

16 Nov 1984   Barbican Centre   London
John Williams (gtr), ECO†
Bach (conc), *Ravel, Respighi, Rodrigo* (Fantasia)
9 Dec 1984   Carnegie Hall   New York
Grant Johannesen (pno), American SO†
Mozart, Rachmaninoff (conc 2), *Schubert*
15, 17, 18, 19, 20 Dec 1984   Mann Audit   Tel-Aviv
Armstrong (s), Britton (t), Alexis Weissenberg (pno),
    Israel PO†
Brahms (conc 1), *Purcell* ("A Purcell Cabaret" *— devised by RL*)
16 Dec 1984   Binyenei Ha-Oomah   Jerusalem
As 15, 17-20 December
22, 23, 24 Dec 1984
                    Mann Audit   Tel-Aviv
Weissenberg (pno), Israel PO†
Elgar, Prokofiev (con 3), *Rachmaninoff* (sym 2)
25, 26, 27 Dec 1984   Haifa Audit   Haifa
As 22-24 December
                           *

1985   Isle of Man
Cantelo, Binns (pno), BBC Philharmonic (Mananan Fest)
1985   Westminster Abbey   London
Holliger (ob), Tallis Choir, ECO† (Handel tricentennial:
    live telecast) — all Handel program
5 Jan 1985   Powell Sym Hall   St Louis
Young Uck Kim (vln), St Louis SO†
Bizet (sym 1), *Boccherini, Mozart* (conc 4)
12, 13 Jan 1985   Jones Hall   Houston
Abbey Simon (pno), Houston SO†
Dvorak, Rachmaninoff (Rhapsody), *Sibelius*
27 Jan 1985   Carnegie Hall   New York
Tatiana Troyanos, June Anderson, Mills, Dimitri Kavrakos,
    Rosenshein (t), Bowman (ct), Frank Lopardo, Orpheon
    Chorale, Orchestra of St Luke's†
¶*Handel* (Ariodante)
7, 8 Feb 1985   Meyerhoff Sym Hall   Baltimore
Minsk (vln), Baltimore SO†
Elgar (sym 1), *Lalo* (Symphonie Espagnole), *Mozart*
14, 15, 16 Feb 1985   Symphony Hall   Boston
Margaret Marshall (s), Michael Myers (t), Britton (t), Willard
    White (b-bar), Tanglewood Fest Chorus, Boston SO†
¶*Handel* (Acis and Galatea)

12 Mar 1985   Free Trade Hall   Manchester
Haendel (vln), BBC Philharmonic O†[17]
Britten (conc), Elgar, Walton (sym 1)
16 Mar 1985   Victoria Hall   Bolton
Takashi Shimizu (vln), BBC Philharmonic O†
Brahms (conc), Dvorak, Mendelssohn
30 Mar 1985   Usher Hall   Edinburgh
Pamela Coburn (s), Baker (ms), Garrison (t), Titus, Keith
Latham, Rosa Mannion, Scottish Philharmonic Singers &
Boys Choir, SCO†
¶*Bach (St* Matthew Passion*)*
31 Mar 1985   City Hall   Glasgow
As 30 March
18, 19, 20, 23 Apr 1985
     Avery Fisher Hall, Lincoln Center   New York
Clarey (s), Carol Webb (vln), New York P†
¶*Handel*
9, 10 May 1985   Popejoy Hall, Univ of NM   Albuquerque
Garrison (t), NM Sym O Chorus, Albuquerque Boy Choir,
New Mexico SO†
Beethoven (sym 3), Berlioz (Te Deum)
17 May 1985   Queen Elizabeth Hall   London
Baker (ms), Crispian Steele-Perkins (tpt), ECO†
Cavalli, Haydn, Monteverdi, Purcell
31 May 1985   Edison Theatre, Washington Univ   St Louis
St Louis SO†
Beethoven, Schubert
7 Jun 1985   Edison Theatre, Washington Univ   St Louis
Sylvia McNair (s), Kallen Esperian (s), Schubertian Qt,
Leonard Slatkin, RL (pnos), George Silfies (cl) (Summer-
fest '85)
Schubert
8 Jun 1985   Edison Theatre, Washington Univ   St Louis
Schubertian Octet, St Louis SO† (Summerfest '85)
Mozart, Rossini, Schubert
26 Jun 1985   Kennedy Center   Washington DC
Janos Starker (vc), Ken Noda (pno), Mostly Mozart Fest O†
Boccherini, Haydn (incl. vc conc*), Mozart (conc K 466)*

---

17   Formerly BBC Northern Symphony Orchestra.

19, 20 Jul 1985   Avery Fisher Hall, Lincoln Center   New York
André Watts (pno), Mostly Mozart Fest O†
¶*Boccherini, Mozart (incl.* conc K 271)
3 Aug 1985   Tanglewood Fest   Lennox MA
Sherman Walt (bsn), Richard Sebring, Daniel Katzen (hns),
Boston SO† (Tanglewood Fest)
¶*Boccherini, Spohr* (sym 7), *Telemann* (conc 2 hns), *Vivaldi*
(bsn conc)
6, 7 Sep 1985   Planting Fields Arboretum   Oyster Bay NY
Sherman (pno), Orchestra of St. Luke's† (Beethoven Fest)
Beethoven (2 programs – concs 1-5)
11, 12 Oct 1985   Crouse-Hinds Concert Theater   Syracuse NY
Syracuse S†
Beethoven, Dvorak, Handel
25 Oct 1985   St Louis
Elmar Oliveira (vln), St Louis SO†
Barber, Lutoslawski, Tchaikovsky
14, 19, 22, 27, 30 Nov; 3, 8 Dec 1985
               San Francisco Opera   San Francisco
Dale Duesing, Morris (b), James King (t), Glossop (bar), San
Francisco Opera†
¶*Britten* (Billy Budd)
23 Dec 1985   Carnegie Hall   New York
Baker (ms), Orchestra of St. Luke's†
Cavalli, Corelli, Haydn, Monteverdi, Mozart

*

9, 10, 11 Jan 1986   Orchestra Hall   Chicago
Anthony & Joseph Paratore (duo pnos), Chicago SO†
¶*Bartók* (conc), *Bizet, Chabrier*
18, 19 Jan 1986   Kaufmann Concert Hall   New York
Joseph Kalichstein (pno), Neil Balm (tpt), Y Chamber S†
Haydn, Saint-Saëns (sym 2), *Shostakovich* (conc 1)
29, 30, 31 Jan 1986
               Roy Thomson Hall   Toronto
Sherman (pno), Toronto S†
CPE Bach, Grieg (conc), *Shostakovich* (sym 15)
8 Feb 1986   Powell Sym Hall   St Louis
Michala Petri (rec), St Louis SO†
Mozart, Sammartini (rec conc), *Vivaldi* (rec conc RV 443)
21, 22, 23 Feb 1986   Powell Sym Hall   St Louis
St Louis SO†
Beethoven, Britten, Elgar

27 Feb 1986 Eastman Theater Rochester NY
Britton (t), John Beck (timp), Rochester PO†
Britten(Nocturne*)*, *Premru (*Celebrations*)*, *Shostakovich*
(sym 9)
4, 5, 6 Mar 1986 Orpheum Theater New Orleans
Jon Klibonoff (pno), New Orleans SO†
Beethoven, Mendelssohn, Schumann (conc)
13, 15 Mar 1986 Ford Audit Detroit
Davidovich (pno), Detroit S†
Mozart (conc 17), Rameau, Vaughan Williams (sym 5)
21 Mar 1986 Orchestra Hall Detroit
Detroit S†
CPE Bach, JCF Bach, JS Bach
23 Mar 1986 Orchestra Hall Detroit
Paul Schaller (cl), Robert Williams (bsn), Detroit S†
*Haydn, R Strauss (*Duet-concertino*)*
27, 28, 29 Mar, 1, 3, 4, Apr 1986
Avery Fisher Hall, Lincoln Center New York
Stanley Drucker (cl), New York P†
¶*Copland (incl. conc), Haydn, Mendelssohn*
1, 2, 3 May 1986 Circle Theatre Indianapolis
Shura Cherkassky (pno), ISO†
*Borodin, Grieg, Tchaikovsky (*conc 1*)(Sibelius* sym 7 *added for 2,*
3 May)
19 May 1986 Barbican Centre London
Cho-Liang Lin (vln), ECO†
Mendelssohn, Mozart, Saint-Saëns, Stravinsky
30 May 1986 Powell Sym Hall St Louis
Lorraine Hunt (s), St Louis SO†
Beethoven
31 May 1986 Powell Sym Hall St Louis
Christopher O'Riley (pno), St Louis SO†
Beethoven
6, 7 Jun 1986 Edison Theatre, Washington Univ St Louis
Ursula Oppens (pno), St Louis SO† (Summerfest '86)
Beethoven (2 programs—incl. Eroica Varns, concs 1, 5*)*,
Mendelssohn, Mozart (conc 5), Saint-Saëns, Stravinsky
17 Jun 1986 Kaisersaal der Residenz Würzburg
Pamela Coburn (s), Radio-Sinfonie-Orchester Frankfurt†
(Mozart Fest)
Mozart

19 Jun 1986   Kaisersaal der Residenz   Würzburg
    Christian Zacharias (pno), Radio-Sinfonie-Orchester
    Frankfurt† (Mozart Fest)
    Mozart (incl. conc K 595*)*
20 Jun 1986   Frankfurt
    Zacharias (pno), Radio-Sinfonie-Orchester Frankfurt†
    Mozart
5 Jul 1986   Caramoor Fest   Katonah NY
    Ameling (s), Elizabeth Mann (fl), Deborah Hoffman (harp),
    O of St. Luke's† (Caramoor Fest)
    Mozart, R Strauss
24 Jul 1986   Mann Music Center   Philadelphia
    Philadelphia O† (Summer Fest)
    Bizet, Chabrier, Ravel
25 Jul 1986   Mann Music Center   Philadelphia
    Armstrong (s), Britton (t), Philadelphia O† (Summer Fest)
    *Beethoven (*sym 3*), Purcell, A Purcell Cabaret (devised by RL)*
10 Sep 1986   Royal Albert Hall   London
    Lott (s), Rodney Friend (vln), BBC SO† (BBC-Henry
    Wood Promenade Concerts)
    Berlioz, Duparc, Brahms
13 Sep 1986   Royal Albert Hall   London
    David Rendall (t), David Wilson-Johnson (bar), Matthew
    Best (b), BBC S Chorus, BBC SO† (BBC-Henry Wood
    Promenade Concerts)
    *Britten (*Soirées musicales*), Elgar, Parry-Elgar, Puccini (incl.*
    Messa di gloria, Preludio sinfonico*), Walton, Wood*
19, 20, 21 Sep 1986   St Louis
    Gutiérrez (pno), St Louis SO†
    *Beethoven, Brahms, William Schuman (*New England
    Triptych*)*
26, 27 Sep 1986   St Louis
    Haendel (vln), St Louis SO†
    Britten, Elgar, Sullivan, Walton
8 Oct 1986   Queen Elizabeth Hall   London
    Frank Peter Zimmermann (vln), ECO†
    Mozart (incl. Adagio K 261, Rondo K 373*), Prokofiev*
    (incl. conc 2*)*
14 Oct 1986   Queen Elizabeth Hall   London
    Cho-Liang Lin (vln), ECO†
    *Mozart (*concs 1, 4*), Stravinsky*

INDIANAPOLIS. "If you're strolling through downtown Indianapolis these days, you can't miss him. His name is plastered on banners hanging from street lamps, his face smiles broadly from posters pasted to the sides of buses.

"There's even a larger-than-life picture of him at the U.S. terminal of Indianapolis International Airport, welcoming visitors to his town.

"But this is not the mayor or the governor — it's Raymond Leppard, the internationally respected maestro who began work a few weeks ago as music director of the Indianapolis Symphony Orchestra.

"The town has yet to recover from the shock.

" 'You haven't seen anything yet,' says Leppard of the hubub his arrival has caused. 'When you come into the airport, it's more embarrassing than I can say. When I first saw it, I had to look away, I was so shattered.

" 'It was a big photograph of me [on a billboard], and it says — oh, I don't know what it says, but it's totally embarrassing. I went very red when I saw it.

" 'I actually did drop my bag, I was so surprised.' "
— *Howard Reich*, **Chicago Tribune,**
22 November 1987.

21 Oct 1986   Queen Elizabeth Hall   London
    Adeney (fl), Bream (gtr), Trumpeters of Roy Military Schl
    of Mus, ECO† (Malcolm Arnold 65th Birthday Concert)[18]
    Arnold (incl. fl conc 2, gtr conc*), Rodrigo (*Fantasia para un gentilhombre*), Rossini*
28, 29, 30 Nov 1986   Teatro Real   Madrid
    Isabelle Van Keulen (vln), Orquesta nacional de España†
    *Beethoven, Bruch (*conc 1*), Rameau*
11, 12 Dec 1986   Grande Auditório   Lisbon
    Thomas Zehetmair (vln), Orquestra Gulbenkian†
    *Beethoven, Rameau, Tchaikovsky (*conc*)*
                        *

---

18   The composer conducted in perf. of his guitar concerto.

8, 10 Jan 1987   Boettcher Concert Hall   Denver
Denver SO†
Dvorak, Elgar, Sibelius
14, 16 Jan 1987   Orchestra Hall   Minneapolis
Malcolm Frager (pno), Minnesota O†
Boccherini, Mozart (incl. conc 17)
15 Jan 1987   Ordway Music Theatre   Minneapolis
As 14, 16 January
14 Feb 1987   Powell Sym Hall   St Louis
Oppens (pno), St Louis Sym CO†
Mendelssohn (incl. Serenade and Allegro gioioso, op 43),
*Schumann, Weber (*Konzertstück, op 79)
7 Mar 1987   Powell Sym Hall   St Louis
Ameling (s), St Louis Sym CO†
*Haydn, Mozart (*arias, Exsultate jubilate)
23, 24 Mar 1987   Gaillard Municipal Audit   Charleston SC
Paolo Bordoni (pno), O of St Luke's† (Spoleto Fest U.S.A.)
Beethoven (incl. conc 3)
27, 28 Mar 1987   Civic Center Concert Hall   Birmingham
William DeRosa (vc), Alabama SO†
*Brahms, Elgar (*conc*), Rossini*
7 Apr 1987   Queen Elizabeth Hall   London
Lott (s), Lorraine McAslan (vln), ECO†
*Mendelssohn (*aria Op 94, sym 4*), Spohr (*conc 8*), Weber*
16, 18 Apr 1987   Powell Sym Hall   St Louis
Peter Orth (pno), St Louis SO†
*Debussy, Liszt (*conc 1*), Mendelssohn*
1, 2, 3 May 1987   Ohio Theatre   Columbus OH
Midori (vln), Columbus SO† (The Columbus Foundation)
*Brahms, Britten, Elgar, Mendelssohn (*conc)
29 May 1987   Powell Sym Hall   St Louis
Daniel Heifetz, Manuel Ramos (vlns), St Louis SO† (Citicorp
     Summerfest '87)
JC Bach, JS Bach
30 May 1987   Powell Sym Hall   St Louis
Soloists, St Louis SO† (Citicorp Summerfest '87)[19]
CPE Bach, JC Bach, JS Bach

---

19   Preceded by Jacques Israelievitch (vln), RL (hpsd) recital of JS Bach *Sonata* 3 for vln
     & hpsd.

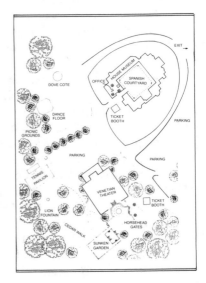

⊗ RESTROOMS
□ TELEPHONE
⊞ FIRST AID

5 Jun 1987   Powell Sym Hall   St Louis
St Louis SO† (Citicorp Summerfest '87)
CPE Bach, JC Bach, WF Bach

6 Jun 1987   Powell Sym Hall   St Louis
Ransom Wilson (fl), St Louis SO† (Citicorp Summerfest '87)
CPE Bach, JL Bach, JS Bach, WF Bach

19 Jun 1987   Powell Sym Hall   St Louis
St Louis SO† (Citicorp Summerfest '87)
Bach

20 Jun 1987   Powell Sym Hall   St Louis
Layton James (hpsd), Jacob Berg (fl), Cara Mia Antonello
(vln), St Louis SO† (Citicorp Summerfest '87)
CPE Bach, JC Bach, JS Bach, WF Bach

11 Jul 1987   Venetian Theater   Katonah NY
Peter Orth (pno), Orchestra of St Luke's† (Caramoor Music
Fest)
Brahms, Dvorak, Schumann, Weber (Konzertstück op 79)

17 Sep 1987   Phoenix Sym Hall   Phoeniz AZ
Werner Klemperer (narr), Loraine Hunt (s), Phoenix S†
(Beethoven Fest)
Beethoven (Egmont, Siegessymphonie, sym 8)

19 Sep 1987   Phoenix Sym Hall   Phoenix AZ
Aaron Rosand (vln), Phoenix S† (Beethoven Fest)
*Beethoven (*Prometheus over, sym 2, vln conc)
9, 10 Oct 1987   Circle Theatre   Indianapolis
ISO†
Beethoven, Brahms, Wagner
15, 16, 17 Oct 1987   Circle Theatre   Indianapolis
Zacharias (pno), ISO†
Elgar, Mozart (conc K 537; overture *added for 16, 17 Oct*)
29, 30, 31 Oct 1987   Circle Theatre   Indianapolis
Susan Starr (pno), ISO†
Falla (Nights), *Mendelssohn, Rochberg* (Night Music), *Sibelius*
5, 6, 7 Nov 1987   Circle Theatre   Indianapolis
Haendel (vln), ISO†
Glazunov (conc), *Schwantner* (A Sudden Rainbow),
    Tchaikovsky
13, 14 Nov 1987   Powell Sym Hall   St Louis
Sergei Edelmann (pno), St Louis SO†
Elgar (sym 1), *Prokofiev* (conc 3), *Rossini*
22, 23, 24 Nov 1987   Arlene Schnitzer Concert Hall   Portland
Davidovich (pno), Oregon SO†
Dvorak, Mendelssohn, Saint-Saëns (con 2)
10, 11, 12 Dec 1987   Kennedy Center   Washington DC
Bruno Leonardo Gelber (pno), National SO†
Birten (Sinfonia da requiem), *Haydn, Ravel (incl.* conc in G)
*

25, 26, 27 Feb 1988   Circle Theatre   Indianapolis
Carter Brey (vc), ISO†
Schumann (conc), *Sibelius (Dvorak added for 26, 27 Feb)*
10, 11, 12 Mar 1988   Circle Theatre   Indianapolis
Alicia de Larrocha (pno), ISO†
Beethoven (incl. conc 4)
17, 18, 19 March 1988 Circle Theatre   Indianapolis
Oppens (pno), ISO†
Beethoven (incl. conc 5)
20 Mar 1988   Circle Theatre   Indianapolis
Nicholas Roth (pno), ISO†
Beethoven (incl. conc 5: Allegro)
24, 25, 26, 27 Mar 1988
    Circle Theatre   Indianapolis
Lee Luvisi (pno), ISO†
Beethoven (incl. conc 3; overture *added for 25, 26 Mar)*

27 Mar 1988   Jasper IN
  As 25, 26 March
1, 2 Apr 1988   Powell Sym Hall   St Louis
  Larrocha (pno), St Louis SO†
  Mozart (conc 23), Ravel, Rochberg (Night Music), *Schubert*
8, 9, 10 Apr 1988   Powell Sym Hall   St Louis
  Sylvia McNair (s), Garrison (t), Devlin (b-bar), St Louis S
    Chorus, St Louis SO†
  Haydn (The Creation)
16 Apr 1988   Powell Sym Hall   St Louis
  Jacques Israelievitch (vln), Thomass Dumm (vla), St Louis
    CO†
  Haydn, Mozart (incl. Sinfonia concertante K 320d [364]*)*
12, 13, 14 May 1988   Circle Theatre   Indianapolis
  ISO†
  *Gluck, Massenet, Meyerbeer, Verdi (Wagner added for 13, 14
    May)*
19, 20, 21 May 1988   Circle Theatre   Indianapolis
  McNair (s), Claudine Carlson (ms), Stanford Olsen (t), Alan
    Titus (bar), Indianapolis Symphonic Choir, ISO†
  Beethoven (sym 9), *Schubert*
8 Jul 1988   Jones Hall   Houston
  Mark Peskanov (vln), Houston SO†
  Mozart (incl. conc 3)
7 Sep 1988   Liederhalle, Beethovensalle   Stuttgart
  Zacharias (pno), NDR SO† (Sinfonieorchester des
    Norddeutschen Rundfunks)
  Dvorak, Mozart (incl. conc KV 488)
23, 24 Sep 1988   Circle Theatre   Indianapolis
  ISO†
  Brahms, Dvorak, Janacek
30 Sep, 1 Oct 1988   Circle Theatre   Indianapolis
  André Watts (pno), ISO†
  Brahms (conc 2), *Haydn, Mendelssohn*
6, 7, 8 Oct 1988   Circle Theatre   Indianapolis
  Ransom Wilson (fl), ISO†
  Glinka, Khachaturian (conc), *Stravinsky*
9 Oct 1988   Circle Theatre   Indianapolis
  ISO† (Donor Appreciation Concert)
27, 28 Oct; 1 Nov 1988
                    Avery Fisher Hall, Lincoln Center   New York
  Haendel (vln), New York P†
  ¶*Britten* (conc), *Dvorak, Handel*

29 Oct 1988   Tilles Center, Long Island Univ   NY
    As 27, 28 October, 1 November
17, 18, 19 Nov 1988   Circle Theatre   Indianapolis
    Cécile Ousset (pno), ISO†
    Ravel (incl. conc for left hand*), Schubert (Adams* Chairman
        Dances, Tromba lontana *added for 18, 19 Nov)*
20 Nov 1988   Circle Theatre   Indianapolis
    ISO† (Donor Appreciation Concert)
                               *

5, 6, 7 Jan 1989   Circle Theatre   Indianapolis
    Cherkassky (pno), ISO†
    *Haydn, Liszt (*conc 1 *— Shostakovich added for 6, 7 Jan)*
26, 27, 28 Jan 1989   Circle Theatre   Indianapolis
    John Wood (spkr), ISO†
    *Sullivan, Tchaikovsky, Walton, Verdi (Shostakovich added
        for 27, 28 Jan) — all music for* Hamlet *&* Macbeth
2, 3, 4 Feb 1989   Circle Theatre   Indianapolis
    Erie Mills (s), ISO†
    *Bellini, Berlioz, Gounod, Prokofiev, Tchaikovsky — all music
        for* Romeo and Juliet
3 Feb 1989   Circle Theatre   Indianapolis
    ISO†
    *Prokofiev (*Romeo and Juliet*), Tchaikovsky (*Hamlet *inc. music,
        Romeo and Juliet)*
5 Feb 1989   Miami Univ   Oxford OH
    As 3, 4 February
16, 17, 18 Feb 1989   Circle Theatre   Indianapolis
    Alan Titus (bar), ISO†
    *Balfe, Elgar, Nicolai, Salieri, Verdi (Vaughan Williams
        added for 17, 18 Feb) — all music for* Falstaff
3, 4, 5 Mar 1989   Powell Sym Hall   St Louis
    Haendel (vln), St Louis SO†
    *Adams (*Chairman Dances *—* foxtrot, Tomba lontana,
        Borodin *(sym 2), Sibelius (*conc)
9, 10, 11 Mar 1989   Circle Theatre   Indianapolis
    Suzuki (vln), ISO†
    *Delius-Beecham, Dvorak (*conc*), Schumann*
18, 19 Mar 1989   Powell Sym Hall   St Louis
    Bronfman (pno), St Louis SO†
    Beethoven, Mozart

WASHINGTON, D.C. "While Raymond Leppard is only in his second season as music director of the Indianapolis Symphony Orchestra, last night's concert at the Kennedy Center's Concert Hall was ample testament to just how far this talented orchestra has come under a most gifted conductor. Everything it touched had verve and sparkle.

"Opening with Elgar's *Cockaigne* overture, Op. 40, Leppard quickly established a tone that was both well modulated and finely detailed. Phrasing was always crisp, and the orchestra made the most of Elgar's brilliant orchestration....

"In Canteloube's famous *Bailèro'*, mezzo-soprano Marianne Rorholm's pianissimos were heart-stopping....

"Choosing to close with Beethoven's *Symphony No. 7* in A, Op. 92, was a masterstroke. There can be few pieces as touchingly simple as the second-movement allegretto of this symphony, yet in the hands of a good conductor and a fine orchestra the music takes on almost sublime dimensions. The orchestra was convincing right from the start. From the opening cello statement to the glorious fugal section and beyond, Leppard guided his artists with grace and style, and they responded with splendid musicianship."

> —*Mark Carrington,* **The Washington Post,** *6 April 1989.*

30, 31 Mar; 1 Apr 1989 Circle Theatre   Indianapolis
        Marianne Rorholm (ms), ISO†
        Beethoven, Canteloube (Chants d'Auvergne I), *Chausson*
            (Elgar added for 31 Mar, 1 Apr)
5 Apr 1989   Kennedy Center   Washington DC
        ¶As 31 March, 1 April
6 Apr 1989   Carnegie Hall   New York
        ¶As 31 March, 1 April
7 Apr 1989   Bucknell Univ   Lewisburg PA
        ISO†
        Beethoven, Delius-Beecham (Walk to the Paradise Garden),
            Elgar, Strauss
27, 28, 29 Apr 1989
            [The following notice appeared in ISO programs: "Indianapolis Symphony Orchestra Music Director Raymond Leppard has had to cancel conducting this weekend's con-

certs in order to continue treatment for an injury he sustained when he fell on the ice in February."]

4, 5, 6 May 1989   Circle Theatre   Indianapolis
Devlin (b-bar), ISO†
Beethoven-Stravinsky, Berlioz, Boito, Gounod, Liszt, Mussorgsky-Rimsky-Korsakov, Saint-Saëns—all works with a Mephistophelean theme

18, 19, 20 May 1989   Circle Theatre   Indianapolis
ISO†
Brahms, Ravel (Haydn added for 19, 20 May)

2 Jun 1989   Powell Sym Hall   St Louis
Susan Slaughter (tpt), St Louis SO† (Citicorp Summerfest '89)
Handel, Haydn (incl. conc in E^b)

3 Jun 1989   Powell Sym Hall   St Louis
St Louis SO† (Citicorp Summerfest '89)
Handel, Haydn

16 Jun 1989   Circle Theatre   Indianapolis
Jeffrey Kahane (pno), ISO† (Sym Promenades)
Beethoven (incl. conc 3)

17 Jun 1989   Circle Theatre   Indianapolis
Kahane (pno), Indianapolis Sym CO†) (Sym Promenades)
Beethoven (incl. conc 2, Rondo WoO6)

22 Jun 1989   Circle Theatre   Indianapolis
Lucy Shelton (s), Robert Broemel (bsn), Kahane (pno), Karen Moratz (fl), Arkady Orlovsky (vc), Philip Palermo, Suzuki, Konstantin Umanski (vlns), Indianapolis Sym CO†) (Sym Promenades)
Beethoven

29 Jun 1989   Circle Theatre   Indianapolis
Rebecca Abram (s), Mark Thomsen (t), Randall Turner (bar), Kahane (pno), Indianapolis Symphonic Choir, ISO† (Sym Promenades)
Beethoven (conc 1, Christ on the Mount of Olives)

30 Jun 1989   Circle Theatre   Indianapolis
Kahane (pno), ISO† (Sym Promenades)
Beethoven (incl. variations, op 35)

12, 15 Jul 1989   Conner Prairie IN
ISO† (Sym on the Prairie concerts)

4 Aug 1989   Deer Creek IN
Philippe Entremont (pno), ISO†

22, 23 Sep 1989   Circle Theatre   Indianapolis
Barry Douglas (pno), ISO†
Mozart, Tchaikovsky (incl. conc 2)

| 24 Sep 1989 | Miami Univ | Oxford OH |

As 22, 23 September
26 Sep 1989   Storm Lake IA
Suzuki (vln), ISO†
5, 6, 7 Oct 1989   Circle Theatre   Indianapolis
Peskanov (vln), ISO†
Hindemith, Schumann, Sibelius (conc)
12, 13, 14 Oct 1989   Circle Theatrer   Indianapolis
Jean-Yves Thibaudet (pno), ISO†
Debussy, Poulenc (conc), Tchaikovsky
15 Oct 1989   Circle Theatre   Indianapolis
Malcolm Smith (), ISO†
26, 28 Oct 1989   Powell Sym Hall   St Louis
Brey (vc), St Louis SO†
Schumann, Shostakovich (conc 1)
3, 4, 5 Nov 1989   Powell Sym Hall   St Louis
Frager (pno), St Louis SO†
*Dohnányi (*Varns on a Nursery Song*), Elgar (sym 2), Ravel*
16, 17, 18 Nov 1989   Circle Theatre   Indianapolis
Oliveira (vln), ISO†
Elgar, Suppé, Wieniawski (conc 2)
30 Nov; 1 Dec 1989   Frankfurt
Gerda Sperlich, Ursula Kepser, John MacDonald, John
    Stobart (hns), Radio-Sinfonie-Orchester Frankfurt†
*Britten (*Sinfonia da requiem*), Schumann (*Konzertstück Op
    86*), Sibelius (sym 1)*

*

4 Jan 1990   Columbus IN
McNair (s), ISO†
*Barber (*Knoxville, Summer of 1915*), Debussy, Glazunov,
    Tchaikovsky*
5, 6 Jan 1990   Circle Theatre   Indianapolis
As 4 January
11, 12, 13 Jan 1990   Circle Theatre   Indianapolis
Suzuki (vln), ISO†
Mozart (incl. conc 5*), Tchaikovsky (incl.* Sérénade
    mélancolique)*
14 Jan 1990   Circle Theatre   Indianapolis
Broemel (bsn), ISO†
17 Jan 1990   Elkhart IN
Philip Myers, ISO†

15 Feb 1990   Beethovensaal der Stuttgarter
                     Liederhalle   Stuttgart
Ulrike-Anima Mathé (vln), Stuttgart PO†
*Dvorak, Prokofiev (conc 2), Schuman (New England
Triptych)*
22, 23, 24 Feb 1990   Circle Theatre   Indianapolis
Walter Klien (pno), ISO†
Mozart (incl. conc 19)
25 Feb 1990   Circle Theatre   Indianapolis
Diane Evans, ISO†
8, 9, 10 Mar 1990   Circle Theatre   Indianapolis
ISO†
*Arensky (Tchaikovsky varns), Hahn (Overture to Mozart),
Reger (Mozart varns, op 132 — Rachmaninoff, Stravinsky
added for 9, 10 Mar)*
11 Mar 1990   Wabash IN
As 8-10 March
15, 16, 17 Mar 1990   Circle Theatre   Indianapolis
Juliana Gondek (s), ISO†
Tchaikovsky
18 Mar 1990   LaPorte IN
ISO†
19, 20, 21 Apr 1990   Circle Theatre   Indianapolis
Julia Bentley (ms), Thomsen (t), David Hamilton (b-bar),
     Indianapolis Symphonic Choir, ISO†
*Dvorak (The American Flag), Michael Runyan (The Age of the
Offered Hand), Rimsky-Korsakov, Tchaikovsky
(Moscow)*
22 Apr 1990   Circle Theatre   Indianapolis
Peter Sepanski, ISO†
6 May 1990   Circle Theatre   Indianapolis
ISO†
10, 11, 12 May 1990   Circle Theatre   Indianapolis
Charles Manning (org), ISO†
*Rochberg (sym 6), Saint-Saëns (sym 3 — Handel added
for 11, 12 May)*
17, 18, 19 May 1990   Circle Theatre   Indianapolis
Dmitri Alexeev (pno), ISO†
Debussy, Dvorak, Tchaikovsky (conc 1)
15 Jun 1990   Circle Theatre   Indianapolis
Angela Cheng (pno), Malcolm Smith (ob), ISO†
Mozart (incl. ob conc, pno conc 17)

16 Jun 1990   Circle Theatre   Indianapolis
Kathryn Selby (pno), Broemel (bsn), ISO†
Mozart (incl. bsn conc, pno conc *9)*
28 Jun 1990   Circle Theatre   Indianapolis
Helene Jeanney, Asaf Zohar (pnos), David Bellman (cl), ISO†
Mozart (incl. cl conc, 2-pno conc)
30 Jun 1990   Circle Theatre   Indianapolis
Zeyda Ruga Suzuki (pno), ISO†
Mozart (incl. conc *27)*
9 Sep 1990   Circle Theatre   Indianapolis
Jean-Pierre Rampal (fl), ISO† (Gala Opening Night)
21, 22 Sep 1990   Circle Theatre   Indianapolis
Murray (s), ISO†
Dvorak, Schubert
23 Sep 1990   Circle Theatre   Indianapolis
Marvin Perry (tpt), ISO†
*Dvorak, Hovhaness (*Prayer to St. Gregory*), Haydn, Schubert*
27, 28, 29 Sep 1990   Circle Theatre   Indianapolis
Leonidas Kavakos (vln), ISO†
*Beethoven (*conc*), Blacher (*Paganini Variations*—Brahms* over
added for *28, 29 Sep)*
30 Sep 1990   Purdue Univ   West Lafayette IN
As 28, 29 Sep
11, 12, 13 Oct 1990   Circle Theatre   Indianapolis
ISO†
*Dvorak, Holst, Ott (*Music of the Canvas*), Schubert*
21 Oct 1990   DePauw Univ   Greencastle IN
ISO†
26, 27, 28 Oct 1990   Powell Sym Hall   St Louis
Zacharias (pno), St Louis SO†
*Britten, Glazunov, Mozart (*conc 18*), Stravinsky (*Capriccio*)*
8, 9, 10 Nov 1990   Circle Theatre   Indianapolis
Gutiérrez (pno), ISO†
*Mozart (*conc 24*), Schubert-Leppard (*Grand Duo*), Stravinsky*
11 Nov 1990   Urbana IL
As 9, 10 March
20, 21 Nov 1990   Circle Theatre   Indianapolis
ISO†
Berlioz, Dvorak, Holst, Pachelbel-Leppard, Rossini, Stravinsky
29, 30 Nov; 1, 2 Dec 1990
Orchestra Hall   Detroit
Emmanuelle Boisvert (vln), Detroit SO†
*Holst, Mendelssohn, Stravinsky (*conc*)*

*

9, 10, 11 Jan 1991   Circle Theatre   Indianapolis
Von Stade (ms), Indianapolis Symphonic Choir, ISO†
Rossini
17, 18, 19 Jan 1991   Circle Theatre   Indianapolis
Maureen Forrester (c), ISO†
Britten-Matthews (A Charm of Lullabies*), Shostakovich,
Sibelius*
22 Jan 1991   Carnegie Hall   New York
¶As 18, 19 January
27 Jan 1991   Avery Fisher Hall, Lincoln Center   New York
Barbara Kilduff (s), Ruth Ann Swenson (s), Dawn Upshaw (s),
Vinson Cole (t), Kahane, Lee Luvisi (pnos), Juilliard O
members, New York P†(Mozart Bicentennial Birthday
Serenade)
¶*Mozart*
28 Feb, 1, 2 Mar 1991 Circle Theatre   Indianapolis
Bruno Leonardo Gelber (pno), ISO†
Brahms (conc 1*), Schubert, Stravinsky*
9 Mar 1991   Theater of Performing Arts   Miami Beach
Gelber (pno), ISO†
*9-17 March concerts incl. Beethoven, Brahms, Dvorak,
Schubert, Shostakovich*
10 Mar 1991   Van Wezel Performing Arts Center   Sarasota FL
Gelber (pno), ISO†
11 Mar 1991   Peabody Audit   Daytona Beach FL
ISO†
12 Mar 1991   Riverside Theater   Vero Beach FL
ISO†
13, 14 Mar 1991   West Palm Beach Audit   West Palm Beach FL
Gelber (pno), ISO†
15 Mar 1991   Branscomb Audit   Lakeland FL
Gelber (pno), ISO†
17 Mar 1991   Carr Performing Arts Centre   Orlando FL
Gelber (pno), ISO†
21, 22, 23 Mar 1991   Circle Theatre   Indianapolis
Richard Stolzman (cl), ISO†
Brahms, Weber (conc 2—*Maw* The World in the Evening
added for 22, 23 Mar)
24 Mar 1991   Indiana Univ   Bloomington IN
As 22, 23 March

NEW YORK. "One of music history's legendary galas, the all-Mozart concert presented by the composer in Vienna on March 23, 1783, [was] faithfully re-created last week in Avery Fisher Hall to inaugurate the Mozart bicentennial.... One could readily appreciate Mozart's cunning as a programmer—the sheer variety of the musical material and its effective juxtaposition—thanks to Leppard's sensitive response to everything that came his way. The 1991 Mozart marathon has been auspiciously launched."

> —*Peter G. Davis,* **New York,** *11 February 1991.*

*

"From his podium at New York City's Lincoln Center last week, Raymond Leppard gave a brisk downbeat and drew forth the majestic D that opens the 'Haffner' Symphony. In doing so, he began the gala observance of Wolfgang Amadeus Mozart's 235th birthday. He also began an unprecedented Lincoln Center extravaganza to celebrate the 200th anniversary of Mozart's death by performing during the next 19 months every note he ever wrote.

"Leppard's lively performance of the 'Haffner', with a scaled-down orchestra assembled from the New York Philharmonic and the Juilliard School Orchestra, was peculiar because it broke off after the minuet. Then came two piano concertos, two piano solos, a serenade, and four individual arias (all admirably performed by such soloists as pianist Jeffrey Kahane and soprano Dawn Upshaw) before the 'Haffner' finale arrived as a kind of farewell.

"This sort of programming was standard in Mozart's day, and Leppard was inaugurating the bicentennial by re-creating a concert that Mozart himself had presented in 1783. 'Suffice it to say that the theater could not have been more crowded, and that every box was full,' the composer proudly wrote to his father Leopold (which is why we know the details of the program). 'But what pleased me most of all was that His Majesty the Emperor was present, and goodness! how delighted he was and how he applauded me!' "

> —*Otto Friedrich,* **Time,** *11 February 1991.*

4, 5, 6 Apr 1991   Circle Theatre   Indianapolis
Charles Webb, Wallace Hornbrook (duo pno),
RL (narr), ISO†
*Coates (*Three Bears*), Quilter (*Children's Overture*),*
Prokofiev, Saint-Saëns— program for children
7 Apr 1991   Honeywell Center   Wabash IN
As 5, 6 April
11, 12, 13 Apr 1991   Circle Theatre   Indianapolis
Indianapolis Children's Choir, ISO†
*Britten (*Children's Crusade, Young Person's Guide*), Dvorak*
*(*Noonday Witch*), Elgar (*Wand of Youth *ste 2), Humper-*
*dinck (*Hansel and Gretel *prelude)*
18, 19, 20 Apr 1991   Circle Theatre   Indianapolis
ISO†
*Bizet (*Jeux d'enfants*), Ravel (*Ma Mere l'Oye*), Respighi (*La
Boutique fantasque*— Dukas *L'Apprenti Sorcier*, Haydn*
Toy Symphony *added for 19, 20 Apr)*
21 Apr 1991   Circle Theatre   Indianapolis
Fu-Chia Yang (pno), ISO†
*Dukas (*L'Apprenti Sorcier*), Elgar (*Nursery Suite, Wand of
Youth *ste 1), Mozart (*conc 23*)*
2, 3, 4 May 1991   Circle Theatre   Indianapolis
Joan Rodgers (s), Susan Quittmayer (ms), Carl Havorson
(bar), Morris (b), Indianapolis Symphonic Choir, In-
dianapolis Children's Choir, ISO†
¶*Mendelssohn (*Elijah*)*
9, 10, 11 May 1991   Circle Theatre   Indianapolis
Ralph Kirshbaum (vc), ISO†
Dvorak (incl. conc — Schubert added for 10, 11 May)
12 May 1991   Columbus IN
As 5, 6 April
17, 19 May 1991   Circle Theatre   Indianapolis
25 May 1991   Powell Sym Hall   St Louis
Thibaudet (pno), St Louis Sym CO†
*Beethoven (*conc 2*), Haydn, R Strauss*
7 Jun 1991   Circle Theatre   Indianapolis
Ernesto Bitetti (gtr), ISO† (Sym Promenades)
Bach, Vivaldi
8 Jun 1991   Circle Theatre   Indianapolis
Suzuki (hpsd), Malcolm Smith, Sharron Possick-Lange,
Paula Engerer (obs), ISO† (Sym Promenades)
Albinoni, Bach, Telemann, Vivaldi

14 Jun 1991   Circle Theatre   Indianapolis
Soloists, ISO† (Sym Promenades)
Vivaldi
15 Jun 1991   Circle Theatre   Indianapolis
Karen Moratz (fl), Dean Franke, David Collins (vlns), ISO†
(Sym Promenades)
Bach
21 Jun 1991   Circle Theatre   Indianapolis
Suzuki (vln), ISO† (Sym Promenades)
Bach-Leppard (Ricercar from Musical Offering*),*
Pachelbel-Leppard (Canon), Vivaldi
22 Jun 1991   Circle Theatre   Indianapolis
Broemel, John Wetherell (bsns), ISO† (Sym Promenades)
Bach, Vivaldi
26 Jun 1991   Erin Arts Centre   Port Erin, Isle of Man
Söderström (s), RL (pno) (Mananan Intl Fest / Fest Gala)
27 Jul 1991   Westchester Community College   Valhalla NY
New York P†
Brahms, Copland, Respighi, Vivaldi
7, 10 Aug 1991   Conner Prairie IN
Rochelle Ellis (s), Jane Bunnell (ms), Louis Gentile (t), Roy
Samuelson (b), Summer Fest Chorus, ISO† (Marsh Sym on
the Prairie)
Bach, Beethoven (sym 9)
15 Sep 1991   Circle Theatre   Indianapolis
Beverly Sills (compere), ISO† (Gala Opening Night)
¶*Beethoven, Herbert (American Fantasia), Mussorgsky-Ravel,*
Rodgers-Bennett (Slaughter on 10th Avenue), R Strauss
27, 28 Sep 1991   Circle Theatre   Indianapolis
Richard Goode (pno), ISO†
Beethoven (incl. conc 4)
29 Sep 1991   Purdue Univ   West Lafayette IN
As 27, 28 September
3 Oct 1991   Circle Theatre   Indianapolis
Pavel Berman (vln), ISO†
Beethoven, Brahms (conc)
4, 5 Oct 1991   Circle Theatre   Indianapolis
Berman (vln), ISO†
Brahms (conc), Hanson (sym 2), Schumann
17, 18, 19 Oct 1991 Circle Theatre   Indianapolis
Barry Douglas (pno), ISO†
Britten (conc 1), Schumann, Vaughan Williams

INDIANAPOLIS. "About the next best thing to music speaking for itself is Raymond Leppard speaking for it — or of it.

"In fact, one woman admitted at Thursday's [3 October's] first Indianapolis Symphony Orchestra Studio Series concert, 'I love to hear him. I don't care what he says.'

"Perhaps his mellifluous, middle-range voice — the English accent aristocratic, but not snobbish — particularly charms those of us with Hoosier twangs. But he's also amusing, quick-witted and though he seems to have read everything, never stuffy or merely academic.

"The Circle Theatre was packed for the opening of the series, which began with Leppard analysing certain aspects of Beethoven's Fifth Symphony and ended with a performance of the work.

"With the orchestra's help, Leppard used 'The Star-Spangled Banner', 'God Save the Queen' and Johann Strauss' 'Blue Danube Waltz' to illustrate how a tune can be recognized instantly with only the first three or four notes.

"Using his own orchestrations of passages from Beethoven's sketchbooks, Leppard traced the famous opening dot-dot-dot-dash motto from its beginnings through the composer's various attempts to develop it over a four-year period.

"Rather than scatter the motto throughout the orchestra horizontally, Beethoven stacked it to create harmonies that allowed him to stay in C minor, the symphony's 'home' key, until he was ready for a second subject in E-flat.

"Though it seemed like 10 and must have lasted about 25 minutes, the talk which concentrated on the first movement and only touched on the [others], ended too soon."
— *Charles Staff*, **The Indianapolis News**,
4 October 1991.

29, 30 Oct 1991   Circle Theatre   Indianapolis
          ISO†
          Dvorak, Grieg, Mussorgsky, Schumann, R Strauss
14, 15, 16 Nov 1991   Circle Theatre   Indianapolis
          Emile Naoumoff (pno), ISO†
          Mozart (conc 23), Schumann (Stravinsky Capriccio,
          Pulcinella suite added for 15, 16 Nov)

21, 22, 23 Nov 1991   Orchestra Hall   Detroit
Arleen Auger (s), Detroit SO†
Mozart
7 Dec 1991   Powell Sym Hall   St Louis
Stephen Hough (pno), St Louis Sym CO†
Beethoven, Mozart (conc 9), Schubert
                                *

9, 10, 11 Jan 1992   Circle Theatre   Indianapolis
Von Stade (ms), Indianapolis Symphonic Choir, ISO†
Rossini
16 Jan 1992   Circle Theatre   Indianapolis
Panayis Lyras (pno), RL (narr), ISO†
Beethoven (conc 3), Ravel (Daphnis et Chloé suite)
17, 18 Jan 1992   Circle Theatre   Indianapolis
Indianapolis Symphonic Choir, RL (narr), ISO†
Heiden (Euphorion), Pain (Oedipus Tyrannus prel),
  Ravel (Daphnis et Chloé)
7, 8 Feb 1992   Sym Hall   Salt Lake City
Konrad Nelson (hp), Utah S†
Handel (incl. hp conc), Tchaikovsky (sym 5)
27, 28, 29 Feb 1992   Circle Theatre   Indianapolis
Brey (vc), Roger Allam (narr), Dominique Labelle (s), In-
dianapolis Symphonic Choir, ISO†
¶*Bax, Elgar (conc), Vaughan Williams (Sinfonia antarctica,*
  with RL narration)
5, 6, 7 Mar 1992   Circle Theatre   Indianapolis
Harvey Phillips (tuba), ISO†
Elgar, Vaughan Williams (conc), Walton
8 Mar 1992   Muncie IN
As 6, 7 March
12, 13, 14 Mar 1992   Circle Theatre   Indianapolis
Ronan O'Hora (pno), ISO†
Ireland (conc), Vaughan Williams (Holst added for 13,
  14 Mar)
2, 3, 4 Apr 1992   Circle Theatre   Indianapolis
Michel Dalberto (pno), ISO†
Barber, Hindemith, Mozart (conc 20)
5 Apr 1992   Frankort IN
As 3, 4 April
9, 10, 11 Apr 1992   Circle Theatre   Indianapolis
Hermann Baumann (hn), ISO†
Dvorak, Janacek, R Strauss (conc 2)

MANCHESTER (ENGLAND). "The BBC Philharmonic Orchestra's final concert of a successful Friday night series took listeners off the beaten track, the main work being the British premiere of the stimulating *Symphony No. 6* by the 74-year-old American George Rochberg, the sort of piece that could easily get modern music a good name. The audience certainly gave it a rousing reception and I would recommend everybody to switch on when the concert is broadcast. The 35-minute symphony is in two parts: A powerful anti-war fantasia, followed by a much lighter movement based on three marches. Fanfares in various guises underline the composer's feelings about what he calls 'the sophisticated barbarism of modern conflict.' He lost a son in Vietnam. The writing is taut and vigorous, broken only by a brooding lento section which adds to the tension. A large percussion section is needed for the march movement which is a remarkable tour de force.... Under the enthusiastic direction of Raymond Leppard the Phil played this symphony with such panache that one would have thought it had been in their repertoire for years."

— Chris Aspin, **Manchester Evening News,** *23 May 1992.*

30 Apr 1992	Royal Northern College of Music	Manchester

Soloists, BBC PO† (Manchester Intl Cello Fest)
Fauré, Tristan Keuris (double conc — world prem), Schumann, Tchaikovsky, Vivaldi

7, 8, 9 May 1992	Circle Theatre	Indianapolis

Suzuki (vln), ISO†
Bach, Stravinsky (Barber added for 8, 9 May)

14, 15, 16 May 1992	Circle Theatre	Indianapolis

Tzimon Barto (pno), ISO†
Bach-Stokowski, Rachmaninoff (conc 2), Shostakovich

22 May 1992	Royal Northern Coll of Music	Manchester

Tasmin Little (vln), BBC P† (RNCM Philharmonic Series)
Delius (conc), Massenet, Rochberg (sym 6)

5 Jun 1992	Circle Theatre	Indianapolis

Panayis Lyras (pno), ISO† (Sym Promenades)
Beethoven, Mendelssohn, Schubert, Schumann (conc)

12 Jun 1992   Circle Theatre   Indianapolis
Suzuki (pno), Suzuki (vln), ISO† (Sym Promenades)
Gretry, Mendelssohn (vln conc), Schumann (op 92), Weber
13 Jun 1992   Circle Theatre   Indianapolis
Lyras (pno), Suzuki (pno), ISO† (Sym Promenades)
Cherubini, Mendelssohn (conc 2 pnos), Schumann (op 46)
19 Jun 1992   Circle Theatre   Indianapolis
James Tocco (pno), ISO† (Sym Promenades)
Hummel (conc), Mendelssohn, Weber (incl. Konzertstück*)*
20 Jun 1992   Circle Theatre   Indianapolis
Lyras, Tocco, Suzuki (pnos), ISO† (Sym Promenades)
Berwald, Donizett, Dussek, Field, Henselt, Litolff, Meyerbeer,
Schubert, Smetana
12, 15 Aug 1992   Conner Prairie IN
Joseph Kalichstein (pno), ISO† (Marsh Sym on the Prairie)
Beethoven (incl. conc 5)
18, 19 Sep 1992   Circle Theatre   Indianapolis
Juliana Gondek (s), Camellia Johnson (ms), Jon Garrison (t),
John Cheek (b), Indianapolis Sym Choir, ISO†
Beethoven (sym 9), *Liszt* (Cantata for the Unveiling of the
Beethoveen Monument in Bonn, 1845 – *U.S. prem)*
1, 2, 3 Oct 1992   Circle Theatre   Indianapolis
Suzuki (vln), ISO†
Sibelius (sym 5), Walton (conc) (Bax Tintagel *added for 2, 3*
Oct)(also 1 Oct: Studio conc with analysis of Sibelius)
8, 9, 10 Oct 1992   Circle Theatre   Indianapolis
Ousset (pno), ISO†
Prokofiev (conc 3, sym 5 – Lt. Kije suite *added for 9, 10 Oct)*
23, 24, 25 Oct 1992   Uihlein Hall   Milwaukee
Suzuki (vln), ISO†
Respighi, Sibelius, Walton (conc)
19, 20, 21 Nov 1992   Circle Theatre   Indianapolis
Emanuel Ax (pno), ISO†
Liszt (conc 1), Respighi (Ott sym 2, R Strauss Burleske *added*
for 20, 21 Nov)(also 19 Nov: Studio conc with analysis of Liszt)
23 Nov 1992   Circle Theatre   Indianapolis
"The portrait of Raymond Leppard, fifth music director of
the Indianapolis Symphony Orchestra, was unveiled at the
Annual Meeting of the Indiana State Symphony Society. It
was painted by Bonnie Sklarski, a member of the faculty of
Indiana University since 1970. Funds for the portrait were
donated by Mrs. Joyce Enkema and Mr. Stephen Enkema
in memory of their husband and father, respectively, Mr.

Lewis A. Enkema. He was, for many years, chief executive of the Universal Flavor Corporation and was involved in the civic and cultural life of the city. The portrait will hang, along with those of previous Indianapois Symphony Orchestra music directors, in the main floor lobby of the Circle Theatre." – ISO quarterly newsletter, Winter 1992.

5 Dec 1992   Powell Sym Hall   St Louis
Roland Pandolfi, Lawrence Strieby, Roger Kaza, James Wehrman (hns), St Louis SO†
Grieg, Mendelssohn, Schumann (Konzerstück op 86)

*

15, 16 Jan 1993   Circle Theatre   Indianapolis
ISO†/narrator
Bernstein (West Side Story Dances), Prokofiev (Romeo and Juliet Act I), Tchaikovsky (Romeo and Juliet) (also 14 Jan: Studio conc with analysis of "Romeo and Juliet" music by Bellini, Berlioz, Bernstein, Gounod, MacDowell, Tchaikovsky)

21, 22, 23 Jan 1993   Circle Theatre   Indianaplis
ISO†
R Strauss (Ariadne auf Naxos excs, Don Quixote; Der Liebe der Danae, Salome excs added for 22, 23 Jan)

29, 30 Jan 1993   Circle Theatre   Indianapolis
Dmitry Sitkovetsky (vln), ISO†
Bruch (conc), Tchaikovsky (Manfred), Wagner (also 28 Jan: Studio conc with analysis of Tchaikovsky)

12 Feb 1993   National Concert Hall   Dublin
Raphael Oleg (vln), Marc Coppy (vc), Philippe Cassard (pno), National SO (of Ireland)†
Beethoven (incl. triple conc)

12, 13 Mar 1993   Circle Theatre   Indianapolis
Cho-Liang Lin (vln), ISO†
Schuman (New England Tripytch), Shostakovich (conc 1), Tchaikovsky (also 11 Mar: Studio conc with analysis of Shostakovich)

25, 26, 27 Mar 1993   Circle Theatre   Indianapolis
Ralph Kirshbaum (vc), ISO†
Beethoven, Hindemith (Sym Metamorphoses), Prokofiev (Sinfonia concertante)

16, 17 Apr 1993   Circle Theatre   Indianapolis
Maria Joao Pires (pno), ISO†
Beethoven (conc 2), Elgar (Enigma Varns), Schubert (also 15 Apr: Studio conc with analysis of Elgar)

LONDON. "The Indianapolis Symphony under Raymond Leppard brought a wide ranging program to the Barbican Centre, paying gracious tribute to their hosts with a warm-hearted interpretation of Elgar's *Enigma Variations,* and reflecting native culture with William Schuman's *New England Triptych,* a sinewy and ebullient example of the modern American mainstream.

"Paying homage to the 18th-century American 'primitive' composer William Billings, Schuman reflects on some of his rugged inventions and produces in *New England Triptych* a work that brings alive the resonances of pioneer thought and feeling. Its endearing vigor and straight talking were wholeheartedly rendered by the orchestra, as were the alternating moments of exuberance and tender inwardness in the Elgar." — *The Independent,* 5 May 1993.

"The Indianapolis Symphony Orchestra is remarkably polished, athletic and precise in its articulation but with a burnished tone which is more resonant of a European than an American sound.... Its approach to Elgar's *Enigma Variations* brought the orchestra's own appreciable credentials to this most British of works, neither reverential nor radical but redefining the portraits with a gleaming palette of colors." — Geoffrey Norris, *The Daily Telegraph,* 8 May 1993.

"Leppard has honed his orchestra's strings to a warm, willing transparency, ready for the cultivated phrasing and buoyant rhythms which are so much his own conducting hallmark. The band, in return, responds with ebullience and sometimes bravado. The wind section is characterful, even fruity, and much enjoyed the skirling finale of the American piece, to say nothing of the witty third variation of the *Enigma.*" — Hilary Finch, *The (London) Times,* 4 May 1993.

22, 23, 24 Apr 1993   Circle Theatre   Indianapolis
    Jon Kimura Parker (pno), ISO†
    Grieg (conc), Prokofiev (Schumann sym 4 added for 23, 24 Apr)
30 Apr 1993   Barbican Centre   London
    Sitkovetsky (vln), ISO†
    ¶*Bruch (conc), Elgar (Engima Varns, Wand exc), Schuman*
    (New England Triptych)
1 May 1993   Symphony Hall   Birmingham
    Pires (pno), ISO†
    Beethoven (conc 2), Elgar (Wand exc), Schubert (sym 8),
    Schumann (sym 4)
3 May 1993   Jahrhunderthalle   Frankfurt
    Pirres (pno), ISO†
    Beethoven (conc 2, sym 7), Schubert
4 May 1993   Alte Oper   Frankfurt
    Sitkovetsky (vln), ISO†
    Bruch, Schubert, Schumann
5 May 1993   Philharmonie   Cologne
    Pires (pno), ISO†
    Beethoven, Hindemith (Sym Metamorphoses), Schumann
6 May 1993   Tonhalle   Dusseldorf
    As 4 May
7 May 1993   Kongresshalle   Stuttgart
    As 5 May
8 May 1993   Kultur-und Kongresszentrum
                       Rosengarten   Mannheim
    Pires (pno), ISO†
    Beethoven, Elgar (Enigma), Schubert
10 May 1993   Musikverein   Vienna
    Pires (pno), ISO†
    Beethoven, Elgar, Schuman
11 May 1993   Philharmonie am Gasteig   Munich
    Sitkovetsky (vln), ISO†
    Beethoven, Bruch, Schubert
12 May 1993   Theatre de Beaulieu   Lausanne
    Sitkovetsky (vln), ISO†
    Elgar, Prokofiev (conc 2), Schubert
13 May 1993   Victoria Hall   Geneva
    As 12 May
14 May 1993   Vaduzen Saal   Vaduz (Lichtenstein)
    As 11 May
15 May 1993   Tonhalle   Zurich
    As 12 May

: 561 :

21, 22 May 1993   Circle Theatre   Indianapolis
Elizabeth Futral (s), David Britton (t), Robert Orth (bar), Indianapolis Sym Choir, ISO†
Orff (Carmina burana), *R Strauss*
9, 11 Jun 1993   Circle Theatre   Indianapolis
Stolzman (cl), ISO†
Mozart
16, 18 Jun 1993   Circle Theatre   Indianapolis
Misha Dichter, Cipa Dichter (pnos), ISO†/pno
Mozart (incl. conc 3 pnos)
23, 24 Jun 1993   Circle Theatre   Indianapolis
Ohlsson (pno), ISO†
Mozart

APPENDIX II
WORKS

Original concert works

Les Amusements de Marise, for Exbury House Chamber Orchestra, 1951.
In 4 movts: *Promenade du matin; Promenade du soir; Pour les enfants —
Chasse au limier; Promenade au bistro*
> Program notes: "This [orchestral] suite was written for performance at two
> concerts given by Cambridge musicians at Exbury in the New Forest, the home
> of Mrs Lionel de Rothschild. Most of the players stayed at Marise Cottage
> which supplied the title for the suite. The titles of the movements are self-ex-
> planatory save perhaps for *'Pour les enfants'* which is based on an old Scottish
> nursery song 'Dance to your Daddy' and whose trio describes an old French
> game *'Chasse au limier'* which was played there."

Nocturne, for Exbury House Chamber Orchestra, 1952.
> Program notes: "This piece is the second to be written specially for the Exbury
> House Chamber Orchestra, and is less frivolous in mood than last year's
> *Amusements de Marise.* Composed in one movement, it describes both the peace
> and the stress of night."

Film scores / incidental music

Alfred the Great, film score, 1969. Recorded by MGM.

Alice Through the Looking Glass, additional music & orchestrations for
Felicity Douglas adaptation of Lewis Carroll story, 1952.

Cymbeline (Shakespeare), for 1957 Shakespeare Memorial Theatre
prod., Stratford-upon-Avon.

The Hotel New Hampshire, film score based on music by Jacques Offenbach, 1984. Recorded by EMI/Capitol.

Laughter in the Dark, film score, 1969.

Light and Variable, The Masque Players revue, 1952, incl. lyrics for
"Going Home", "Sirens All", "You Can't Be Really Greek Without
a Pillar".

Listen to the Wind, orchestrations for Vivial Ellis Christmas Play, 1953.

Lord of the Flies, film score, 1963. Recorded by AVA Records.

Love's Labour's Lost (Shakespeare), for 1956 Shakespeare Memorial
Theatre prod., Statford-upon-Avon.

A Midsummer Night's Dream (Shakespeare), for 1959, 1962 Shakespeare
Memorial Theatre prods., Stratford-upon-Avon.

Ondine (Jean Giraudoux), for 1961 Shakespeare Memorial Theatre
prod., Stratford-upon-Avon.

The Padlock (Charles Dibdin), arr. for Trinity College Music Society prod., 1952.

Perfect Friday, film score, 1970.

Romeo and Juliet (Shakespeare), for 1961 Shakespeare Memorial Theatre prod., Stratford-upon-Avon.

Some Talk of Angels, arrangements for Hugh Thomas Venetian Fantasy, 1952.

Twelfth Night (Shakespeare), for 1960 Shakespeare Memorial Theatre prod., Stratford-upon-Avon.

The Two Gentlemen of Verona (Shakespeare), for 1960 Shakespeare Memorial Theatre prod., Stratford-upon-Avon.

Editions / realizations

BACH (CPE) — *Concerto* in F for 2 harpsichords & strings, W 46: arr. by RL for 4 harpsichords & orchestra, c. 1982. Recorded by Decca.

CAVALLI — *La Calisto:* opera in 2 acts with prologue (1651), performing ed. realized by RL. Libretto by Giovanni Faustini (Italian); English by Geoffrey Dunn; German by Karl Robert Marz. Publ. Faber Music Ltd; recorded by Argo.

"Those who suppose that old operas must be stiff, unmelodious, lacking in vivid humanity, will be thankful that Raymond Leppard has resuscitated *La Calisto.* The libretto by Faustini is cynical, sensual, irreverent, and hilariously amusing.... *La Calisto* gives us one exquisitely beautiful number after another, justifying those experts who have pointed to Cavalli's depth of dramatic characterisation." — William Mann, *The (London) Times.*

CAVALLI — *L'Egisto:* opera in 3 acts with prologue (1643), performing ed. realized by RL. Libretto by Giovanni Fuastini (Italian); English by Geoffrey Dunn and RL; German by Karl Robert Marz. Publ. Faber Music Ltd. 1977; recorded by Argo.

"This is a marvellous work, broad in its range of passions, inspired in its melodic flights, elegant in its multiple fusions of tragedy and whimsy, heroism and intimacy, reality and illusion." — Martin Bernheimer, *Los Angeles Times.*

"The opera is a charmer.... Cavalli is never at a loss for ingratiating tunes, and Mr Leppard has clothed them all in a luscious harmonic framework that is rich in textural variety and full of ingenious theatrical gestures." — Peter G. Davis, *The New York Times.*

CAVALLI — *Messa concertata* for double chorus, 8 solo voices and orchestra: realized by RL (1st perf at Westminster Abbey 13 May 1966). Publ Faber Music Ltd.

CAVALLI — *5 Operatic Arias:* for high voice with keyboard accompaniment, realized by RL. Publ Faber Music Ltd.

CAVALLI — *L'Orione:* opera in 3 acts (1653), performing ed. realized by RL. Libretto by Francesco Melosio (Italian); English by RL. Publ. Faber Music Ltd; recorded by Argo.

"Cavalli, the composer, shines through the centuries with undiminished lyrical and comic brilliance.... This is a charmingly acid study of sexual jealousy that gives the gods feet of clay, hearts of gold and eyes green with envy." — *The Daily Mail.*

"The score is remarkably varied with plenty of humorous touches yet capable of rising to sustained expressiveness.... Mr. Leppard is concerned with recreating the work using contemporary resources. This reconstruction succeeds brilliantly and makes for a wholly delightful evening." — *Glasgow Herald.*

CAVALLI — *L'Ormindo:* opera in 2 acts, realized by RL. Publ Faber Music Ltd. 1967; vocal score with preface 1969; recorded by Argo.

¶Prison Scene from L'Ormindo: duet for soprano & tenor with keyboard accompaniment, realized by RL. Publ by Faber Music Ltd.

MONTEVERDI — *Ballo from "Il Ballo delle ingrate"* suite of dances for 5-part strings & continuo (or 2 guitars), realized by RL. Publ. Faber Music Ltd.

MONTEVERDI — *L'Incoronazione di Poppea:* opera in 2 acts with prologue (1642), performing ed. realized by RL. Libretto by Francesco Busenello (Italian); English by Geoffrey Dunn; German by Reinhold Rudiger & Karl Robert Marz. Publ. Faber Music Ltd. 1966; new & enl. ed. 1968; vocal score 1977.

"My admiration for Raymond Leppard's edition grows at each hearing.... His continuo-based realization alone can allow the freedom of declamation which the work needs — support varied, colorful and always apt, but never dictating to the vividly dramatic utterance of the singers." — Andrew Porter, *The Financial Times.*

"Raymond Leppard's scholarly but far from academic realisation of melody and bass line — all that has survived — is a miracle of empathy and fertility of imagination." — Peter Stradlen, *The Daily Telegraph.*

MONTEVERDI — *L'Orfeo:* opera in 2 acts with prologue (1607), performing ed. realised by RL. Libretto by Alessandro Striggio (Italian); English by Anne Ridler; German by Claus Henneberg. Publ. by Faber Music Ltd.

"The boldness in this performance was wholly justified by the extraordinary beauty and interest of the score in Raymond Leppard's realization. Mr Leppard makes wonderfully imaginative use of harp, flue organ and the lute and chitarrone that lend a distinctive, buoyant yet pensive character to the orchestral palette." — Martin Cooper, *The Daily Telegraph.*

"Throughout, Mr Leppard, without resorting to the inapt orchestrations which bedevil most earlier Monteverdi performing-editions, has enhanced the words, and the song, with beautiful, eloquent sounds." — Andrew Porter, *The Financial Times.*

MONTEVERDI — *Il Ritorno d'Ulisse in patria:* opera in 2 acts with prologue (1641), performing ed. realized by RL. Libretto by Giacomo Badoaro (Italian); English by Geoffrey Dunn; Germany by Horst Goerges and H. Gutheim. Publ. Faber Music Ltd; recorded by CBS.

"A restored masterpiece of opera, spontaneous, instantly communicative, deeply emotional and rich both in melodic invention and in all those ingenuities of design and device that we think of as typically Monteverdian. What is most remarkable in the opera is the freedom and natural ease of the vocal writing as it moves from declamation to formal song. Each character comes to life in musical terms, while for their confrontations Monteverdi draws on his madrigal techniques of half a century... all the potent theatrical magic finally yields to the simplest and deepest emotions of humanity and truth." — Desmond Shawe-Taylor, *The (London) Sunday Times.*

RAMEAU — *Dardanus, tragédie en musique* in 5 acts (1739), performing ed. by Raymond Leppard. Libretto by Le Clerc de la Bruère (French); German by Claus Henneberg. Publ. Faber Music Ltd; recorded by Erato.

Edition based on the second revival of 1744, including elements of exceptional dramatic quality from the earlier (1739) version.

Misc. performing versions & arrangements

Cadmus et Herminoe: Chaconne (Lully): ed. RL, perf. 11 Apr 1956.

"Very little of Lully's music is now heard [1956] apart from a few poorly arranged airs. Perhaps the greatest difficulty lies in the fact that so much of his and other composers' music of this period has come to us in almost skeletal condition with rhythms and ornaments omitted which would have been automatically incorporated in contemporary performances.

"*Cadmus et Hermionne*, produced in 1673, was the first of a new type of 'opera seria' which Lully introduced to France superseding the trivial opera-ballets and seeking a more profound musical and dramatic expression. The story deals with the trials and battles of Cadmus before he can win Hermione the daughter of Mars. The Chaconne occurs towards the end of Act I when Hermione is surrounded by Africans and Giants who dance for her and later sing to the same music their praise of love and their rival claims to her hand.

"The Chaconne is for five-part strings with alternating sections for solo trio." — *Notes for 11 Apr 1956 concert.*

Canon (Pachelbel): arr. by RL for 3 flutes & orch, perf. 20, 21 Nov 1990; for 3 tpts & orch, recorded by CBS; for 3 vlns & orch, perf. 21 Jun 1991.

Concerto in D, P 175; *Concerto* in G Minor, P 392; *Sonata ("Al Santo Sepolcro")* in E Flat, P 441 (Vivaldi): ed. by RL. Recorded by EMI/Music for Pleasure Ltd.

Concerto in F for 2 harpsichords & orch (CPE Bach): arr. for 4 harpsichords & orch. Recorded by Decca.

Concerto Grosso in F (Correlli, Op 6 Nr 9): ed. by RL. Recorded by EMI/Music for Pleasure Ltd.

Daphnis et Chloé (Ravel): with narration prepared by RL, perf. 16-18 Jan 1992.

Grand Duo for piano 4-hands: arr. for orch RL. Perf. 8-10 Nov 1990; recorded by Koss.

A Masque in "Dioclesian" (Purcell): vers. by RL, c. 1972
Messiah (Handel): chamber version, c. 1968.
The Musical Offering: Ricercar (Bach): arr. RL, perf. 21 Jun 1991.
The National Anthem ("God Save Our Gracious Queen"): arr. RL, based
   on c. 1740 sources, for Shakespeare Memorial Theatre, Stratford-
   upon-Avon. Perf. July 1960 & thereafter.
"A Purcell Cabaret": devised by RL & Colin Graham (vers 1); devised
   by RL (vers 2-3).

"The theater took up a great deal of Purcell's life. Apart from the major works like *Dido, The Fairy Queen* and *King Arthur*, he composed incidental music — overtures, songs and dances — for over forty plays none of which is regularly, or even occasionally, given today. A few of the theater songs have found their way into song-recitals but for the most part they are as neglected as the plays; with considerably less justification, however, for they include some of Purcell's most delightful music.

"Apart from their inaccessiblity, the main problem is one of presentation. It is unthinkable that Southerne's tragedy *Oroonoko* or Scott's comedy *The Mock Marriage* should be revived from the few songs they contain. Yet when this music is performed in concerts it lacks an essential element — dramatic presentation. Thus the idea came about to give them in the form of a pasticcio for a group of singers and instrumentalists where the inter-action of personalities and a tenuous dramatic thread give some semblance of the theater for which they were written. [The loose-fitting story-line of the 1981 vers. follows — approximately — the relationship of two lovers, from initial hostility and resistance through consummation]." —*RL notes for July 1965 presentation, King's Lynn Festival.*

¶1959 vers. ("an entertainment devised by RL and Colin Graham, with music by Henry Purcell") for soprano, alto, tenor, baritone, bass, 2 fl, 2 vln, vla, vc, hpsd. Notes by Peter Pears for Aldeburgh prod.: "In this Entertainment we have endeavored to string on to a tenuous thread some Purcellian pearls and to provide sufficient context to give them some of their original sparkle. Not all the music is unfamiliar — some comes from *The Fairy Queen* and *King Arthur*; the catches too may not be unknown.

"It is perfectly clear, if one peruses the pages of 'The Catch Club', not only that Purcell was not an inch behind his contemporaries in the robustness of his humor, but also that he would have been highly delighted that on such an occasion as this [presentation] his music should be accompanied by Wine.

    He that drinks is immortal and can ne'er decay,
    For Wine still supplies what Age wears away.
    How can he be Dust that moistens his Clay?"

¶1965 vers (for soprano, contralto, tenor, baritone, 2 violins, viola, cello & hpsd): (1) Borée from *The Old Bachelor*; (2) "May the God of wit inspire" from *The Fairy Queen*; "Now the maids and the men" from *The Fairy Queen*; (4) "Shepherd, shepherd leave decoying" from *King Arthur*; (5) Slow air from *The Virtuous Wife*; (6) Hornpipe from *Henry II*; (7) "Take not a woman's anger ill" from *The Rival Sisters*; (8) "There's nothing so fatal as woman" from *A Fool's Preferment*; (9) Air from *The Virtuous Wife*; (10) "In all our Cynthia's shining sphere"; (11) Minuet from *The Gordian Knot Untied*; (12) "Dear pretty youth" from *The Tempest*; (13) "Hark how the songsters" from *Timon of Athens*; INTERVAL (14) Hornpipe on a ground from *The Married Beau*; (15) "Celemene, pray tell me" from *Oroonoko*; (16) "Good neighbour why do you look away?" from

"A Purcell Cabaret" at Aldeburgh, 1959

CREDIT: Kurt Hutten

"A Purcell Cabaret", Aldeburgh 1959 — Barry Kay costume

The Canterbury Guest; (17) Rondeau from *The Gordian Knot Untied;* (18) "From silent shades"; (19) Slow air form *The Old Bachelor;* (20) Air from *The Virtuous Wife;* (21) "Ah where are you now?" from *The comical History of Don Quixote;* (22) "Oh how you protest" from *The Mock Marriage;* (23) "The cares of lovers" from *Timon of Athens;* (24) "If love's a sweet passion" from *The Fairy Queen;* (25) "The Danger is over" from *The Fatal Marriage;* (26) "No stars again shall hurt you" from *The Tempest.*

¶1981 vers (for mezzo-soprano, tenor & orchestra; perf. with the New York Philharmonic, Dec 1981 & Philadelphia Orchestra, Jul 1986; materials from 12 plays and 2 semi-operas, mostly dating from 1688-1695): (1) Rondo from *The Old Bachelor* (1693); (2) "Man is for the woman made" (tenor) from *The Mock Marriage* (1695); (3) Hornpipe on a Ground from *The Married Beau* (1694); (4) "Pursuing beauty" (soprano) from *Sir Anthony Love* (1690); (5) "The cares of lovers" (tenor) from *Timon of Athens* (1694); (6) Slow Air from *The Virtuous Wife* (1694?) (7) "O how you protest" (soprano) from *The Mock Marriage* (1695); (8) "Take not a woman's anger ill" (tenor) from *The Rival Sisters* (1695); (9) Air from *The Virtuous Wife* (1694?); (10) "There's nothing so fatal as woman" (tenor) from *A Fool's Preferment* (1688); (11) "What can we poor females do?" (soprano) (1694); (12) Slow Air from *The Old Bachelor* (1693); (13) "If love's a sweet passion" (duet) from *The Fairy Queen* (1692); (14) "Celemene, pray tell me" (duet) from *Oroonoko* (1695); (15) Menuet from *The Gordian Knot Untied* (1691); (16) Hornpipe from *The Double Dealer* (1693); (17) "The danger is over" (duet) from *The Fatal Marriage* (1694); (18) "Hark how the songsters" (duet) from *Timon of Athens* (1694); (19) "No stars again shall hurt you" (duet) from *The Tempest* (1695?) (20) Bourrée from *The Old Bachelor* (1693).

Salve Regina (D. Scarlatti): arr. by RL (recorded by EMI).

Sonata a cinque in A, Op 2 Nr 3; *Sonata a cinque* in G Minor, Op 2 Nr 6 (Albinoni): ed. by RL. Recorded by EMI/Music for Pleasure Ltd.

Symphony 7 ("Sinfonia Antarctica") (Vaughan Williams): vers. with text by RL, incl. excerpts from Scott journals, perf. 27-29 Apr 1992. Recorded by Koss Classics.

"Victorian Knights" — devised by RL, perf. 25 July 1972.

"Queen Victoria was taught singing by Mendelssohn and, encouraged by Prince Albert, himself no mean composer, retained a love of music all her life. Over twenty musicians were honored with a knighthood during her reign — including Sir Arthur Sullivan, Sir Hubert Parry, Sir Charles Villiers Stanford, Sir William Sterndale-Bennett, Sir Alexander Mackenzie, Sir Henry Bishop, Sir George MacFarren and Sir Frederick Cowen — men whose work laid the foundation for the present flowering of music in England. Their labors have for too long remained in obscurity and this program is intended as a tribute to these remarkable men of music." — RL *notes for July 1972 presentation, King's Lynn Festival.*

THE "AUTHENTICITY" CONTROVERSY

Ed. note: into every professional life some rain (disapproval) must fall. With the strengthening of the so-called "authenticity" movement, and cause — which itself might be said to derive from the accomplishments of musicians and scholars such as Leppard himself — certain editions, performances and recordings by our author and others were attacked on the grounds of their being historically unpersuasive, "unfaithful", etc. Leppard himself admits that, from his having been in the 1960s and 1970s something of a favorite of the early music audience in England, with the onset of the new "movement" for authenticity he "became very rapidly the corrupter of purity and aborter of the baroque." (He adds that, by then, he himself had also moved along into several other directions, though continuing to retain his love of baroque music.)

In September 1984, in a gesture rather extraordinary for a music publisher, Sir Donald Mitchell, the chairman of Faber Music Limited, came to Leppard's particular defense. He issued a small collection of articles and reviews relating to the various editions prepared by RL, to which he prefaced a warm letter of support over his own signature.

Two months later, critic Nicholas Kenyon (himself to become editor of the respected publication *Early Music*) reported on all this, remarking on the controvery itself:

> BAROQUE FUN. Possibly the tide is turning against Raymond Leppard. The revival of his version of Monteverdi's *L'Incoronazione di Poppea* at Glyndebourne this summer was not received with unreserved rapture, and [his] treatment of one of Cavalli's liveliest comedies, *L'Orione,* met with an extraordinarily intense degree of critical vilification when it was seen [recently] during the Edinburgh Festival.
>
> So virulent was the outcry against the production — though the objects of scorn seemed to be the music, the performance and the staging in about equal measure — that Faber Music, the publishers of Leppard's score, were stung into producing a reply. 'The clash in opinions about the work has been sharp indeed. We do not complain about that, but that there have been so

many poorly informed adverse opinions has been a legitimate source of concern,' wrote Donald Mitchell, the company's chairman, in a letter [addressed to the public].

The [Faber pamphlet] included a winning and perfectly acceptable defense of the light-heartedness of Venetian opera by Michael Tilmouth, Professor of Music at Edinburgh University, recalling that *Orione* was not written for the public theater but for a wedding celebration, that of Ferdinand IV in Milan in 1653. 'Its function was to entertain rather than to improve an audience perhaps tipsy from the nuptial feast. An audience which, moreover, brought a pretty good knowledge of the ancient myths to bear on their understanding of the work—something we today lack.' Tilmouth suggests that 'the colloquialisms of Raymond Leppard's English version nicely convey the down-to-earth humour.'

Tilmouth argues that 'Leppard's version, with its opulent strings, harp glissandi and harpsichord redolent of Brahms, will have its critics, but it is sure of its aim.' Perhaps it was sure of its aim, but did it misfire? Leppard himself, in his introduction to these Scottish Opera performances, suggests that the work sounds 'as if an Italian-born Offenbach had taken a step backwards of 200 years and made a romp of an opera of it, whose points flash by at the rate of knots; once missed, lost forever... *Orione* was intended to amuse and delight a small, well-educated, warm-hearted Italian audience intent on domestic pleasures and the convivial celebration of a family wedding.'

The controversy would appear to surround not the question of Cavalli's fun but Leppard's realisation of it both in his text and in his musical arrangements, which are lavish. His views on authenticity in performance are well known, and were spelt out in an article for the Glyndebourne program book this year which accompanied his *Poppea* production. Without, I hope, oversimplifying too far, the essential Leppard message about attempts at 'authentic' performance is clear: he's against it. 'As every aspect of successful living is a profitable compromise between what might be and what is, so is successful performance a profitable compromise between what happened once and what happens now.' But it is the balance that counts, and Leppard's sense of faithfulness to the past rarely interferes with his search for an attractive solution in the present. The problem may be that audiences, who are becoming familiar with a different approach to the past, are beginning to find Leppard's solutions less attractive than they did in the early days, when Venetian opera was scarcely known.[1]

Leppard also remarks that the first audience had a different background: 'The family relationships of the gods were as clear to them as their own. We would do well to do a little boning up on them before embarking on our trip to Delos.' The opera begins on Apollo's festal day on the island of Delos, where he was born. Though it starts farcically, the mood gradually darkens and the characters acquire greater depth as the opera proceeds. Orion is the half-mortal, half-god son of Neptune, with whom an interfering Cupid causes both Diana and Aurora (the one a virgin, the other married) to fall in love. In the end, Apollo tricks Diana into shooting Orion and her virtue is saved — but at a cost. The moral is similar to that of Handel's *Semele:* nature to each appoints his proper sphere, and if we look outside that (in Semele's case, a human aspiring to godliness, or, in the case of Cavalli's goddesses, aspiring to the love of a half-mortal) we shall be destroyed. In the end, Jove grants Orion a place in heaven, but the damage has been done. It is a powerful tale.

Tilmouth's attitude to Leppard's reworking is that 'every generation has the right to look at the works of earlier times through its own eyes and ears... Music has always fed on its own past.' One can believe his statement that '*Orione,* revived now after more than 300 years, has been praised by critics in Santa Fe, reviled in Edinburgh, and enjoyed by audiences in both cities.' But I can hardly be expected to endore his conclusion: 'Do not read the critics. They only write for money.'

    — Nicholas Kenyon, in *The Listener* for 22 November 1984.

---

1   History being thoroughly unsentimental, however, it may be observed that, ten years later, in 1993, Venetian opera once again is perhaps "scarcely known", and thus deserves a fresh hearing via Leppard's great, pioneering versions of these works on LP. (Ed.)

APPENDIX III
DISCOGRAPHY

Ed. note: Discography is an art in itself, and a truly complete listing *ought* to include the original pressing or matrix numbers for each of the original issues — as well as (in the case of discs) those for each side of each issue — in addition to all of the reissue citations, and all of the issues by country.

The present listing cannot pretend to this degree of perfection. Nevertheless care has been taken to include comprehensive information regarding RL's more than 160 separate releases to date — and, in particular, to provide enough information to avoid confusion between any one version of a given work and some other(s) — an especially thorny problem in the case of some of the Bachs!

As a matter of statistical interest: the following list includes approx. 479 works by 108 composers. RL ranks high on the list of most-recorded classical artists.

PART 1: AS CONDUCTOR

---

    † = conducted by RL
    †/hpsd = conducted from the harpsichord by RL

ALBINONI, TOMASO (1671-1750)

- *SONATA A CINQUE* IN A, OP 2 NR 3 (ed. by RL)
  SONATA A CINQUE IN G MINOR, OP 2 NR 6 (ed by RL)
  English Chamber O†/hpsd
      LP: EMI/His Master's Voice HQS 1232 (1970/stereo); also
             issued as EMI/Classics for Pleasure Ltd CFP
             40371 (1982/stereo)
  SEE ALSO: Corelli, Vivaldi
  "The music is stimulating; the playing is expert; the conducting is lively and intelligent (Leppard leads from the keyboard)." — *Fanfare.*

- *ADAGIO*
  Scottish Chamber O†
  ALBUM TITLE: MOTO PERPETUO/MOUVEMENTS PERPÉTUELS
  Cassette: RCA/Erato MCE 71483

LP: RCA/Erato STU 71483; also as 2292-45676-2
SEE ALSO: Arensky, JS Bach, Brahms, Couperin, Lotter,
Paganini, Paradies, Rimsky-Korsakov, Strauss, Weber

ANONYMOUS

• *THE NATIONAL ANTHEM* (ed. by RL)
Tallis Chamber Choir, English Chamber O†
ALBUM TITLE: A BIRTHDAY CONCERT FOR MY GRANDMOTHER.
HRH the Prince of Wales Celebration Concert to Mark the
90th Birthday of HM Queen Elizabeth the Queen Mother.
Recorded live in the Ballroom, Buckingham Palace, 2 Aug
1990.
CD: EMI/Angel CDC 7 54164 2 (1990)
SEE ALSO: Coates, Doyle, Elgar, Gowers, Matthews, Strauss

ARENSKY, ANTON (1861-1906)

• *BASSO OSTINATO*
Scottish Chamber O†
ALBUM TITLE: MOTO PERPETUO/MOUVEMENTS PERPÉTUELS
Cassette: RCA/Erato MCE 71483
LP: RCA/Erato STU 71483; also as 2292-45676-2
SEE ALSO: Albinoni, JS Bach, Brahms, Couperin, Lotter,
Paganini, Paradies, Rimsky-Korsakov, Strauss, Weber

ARNE, THOMAS AUGUSTINE (1710-1778)

• "BLOW THOU WINTER WIND
"COME AWAY DEATH"
"THOU SOFT-FLOWING AVON"
"UNDER THE GREENWOOD TREE"
April Cantelo (s), English Chamber O†/hpsd
ALBUM TITLE: 18TH CENTURY SHAKESPEAREAN SONGS
LP: Decca/L'Oiseau-Lyre OL 50205 (1961/mono)
SEE ALSO: Chilcot, Greene, Haydn, Hook, T Linley, W Linley,
Smith, Weldon

BACH, CARL PHILIP EMANUEL (1714-1788)

• *CONCERTO* IN F FOR 4 HARPSICHORDS (arr. by RL from *Concerto* for 2 claviers & orchestra, W46)
George Malcolm, Valda Aveling, Geoffrey Parsons, Simon Preston (hpsds), English Chamber O†

ALBUM TITLE: MUSIC FOR 4 HARPSICHORDS
LP: Decca SXL 6318 (1967/stereo); reissued as Decca/
London Stereo Treasure Series STS 15075
Decca LXT 6318 (mono)
"Delightful collection... a winner." — *Records & Recording.* "The music is fine
stuff whatever its origins.... The concertos on this disc urge the legitimacy of
the art of arrangement." — Frank Dawes, *The Musical Times.*
SEE ALSO: JS Bach (album also incl. Malcolm, *Variations on a
Theme by Mozart* for 4 hpsds)

● *CONCERTO* IN B FLAT FOR OBOE, STRINGS & CONTINUO
CONCERTO IN E FLAT FOR OBOE, STRINGS & CONTINUO
Heinz Holliger (ob), English Chamber O†
LP: Philips 6500 830 (1975/stereo)
SEE ALSO: JS Bach (*Cantatas: Sinfonias*)

● *SINFONIA* IN E MINOR. WQ 177
SINFONIA IN B FLAT, WQ 182 NR 2
SINFONIA IN C, WQ 182 NR 3
SINFONIA IN B MINOR, WQ 182 NR 5
SINFONIA IN D, WQ 183 NR 1
SINFONIA IN E FLAT, WQ 183 NR 2
SINFONIA IN F, WQ 183 NR 3
SINFONIA IN G, WQ 183 NR 4
English Chamber O†/hpsd
Cassette: Philips 426 081-4 (Wq 177, 182/3, Wq 183/1, 183/2,
183/3, 183/4)(1989)
CD: Philips 426 081-2 (Wq 177, 182/3, Wq 183/1, 183/2,
183/3, 183/4)(1989)
LP: Philips SAL 3689 (WQ 177, 182/2, 182/3, 182/5 (1968)
(US/UK), also as Philips 839 741 Y (German);
Wq 177 reissued on Philips 6833 035 with JC
Bach, WF Bach, Handel, Mozart, D Scarlatti
Philips SAL 3701 (Wq 183/1, 183/2, 183/3, 183/4)
(US/UK), also as Philips 839 742 LY (German);
reissued as Philips Living Baroque 9502 013
(1980)
Philips 6500 069 (Wq 177, 182/3, Wq 183/1, 183/2)
(1968); also in 5-LP set Philips 6709 004 titled
THE BACH FAMILY — see also JC Bach, JCF Bach,
JL Bach, JS Bach, WF Bach
"I cannot recommend these records too strongly. They offer magnificent music
in superb performances, and the recording quality does full justice to com-

posers and players." — *The Gramophone.* "Leppard and the ECO do a magnificent job of capturing CPE's agitated *Sturm und Drang* with clarity, incisiveness, and a sense of pleasure." — *Fanfare.*

BACH, JOHANN (JOHN) CHRISTIAN (1735-1782)

- *CATONE IN UTICA* OVERTURE
  New Philharmonia O†
  ALBUM TITLE: 18TH CENTURY OVERTURES, VOL. II
  CD: PolyGram Special Products/Avéro verzekeringen
       434 419-2 (with JC Bach *Sinfonias* in D, B^b &
       overtures by Handel, Purcell, Rameau, A. Scar-
       latti; also incl. overtures by Laurens Van
       Rooyen, Vivaldi cond. by Vittorio Negri, Jed
       Wentz)
  LP: Philips SAL 3760 (1969)(US/UK); also as Philips
        802 901 LY (German); reissued on Philips 6833
        035 (with CPE Bach, WF Bach, Handel, Mozart,
        D Scarlatti)
  "An enjoyable disc with much orchestral brilliance from the NPO, individual
  and collective, and a spacious recorded sound." — Stanley Sadie, *The
  Gramophone.*
  SEE ALSO: Boyce, Cimarosa, Locatelli, Mozart, Rameau, A Scar-
  latti

- *CONCERTO* IN F FOR OBOE
  Heinz Holliger (ob), English Chamber O†
  Cassette: Philips 412 354-4
        CD: Philips 426 972-2
        LP: Philips 839 756 LY (German) (1969/stereo); reissued
             as Philips 426 972-1
  SEE ALSO: Fiala, Hummel

- *SINFONIA* IN D (OVERTURE TO *TEMISTOCLE*)
  SINFONIA IN G MINOR, OP 6 NR 6
  SINFONIA IN B^b, OP 9 NR 1
  SINFONIA IN B^b, OP 18 NR 2 (OVERTURE TO *LUCIO SILLA*)
  New Philharmonia O†
  CD: PolyGram Special Products/Avéro verzekeringen
       434 419-2 (*Temistocle* & *Lucio Silla* overtures,
       with JC Bach *Catone in Utica* overture & over-
       tures by Handel, Purcell, Rameau, A. Scarlatti;
       also incl. overtures by Laurens Van Rooyen,
       Vivaldi cond. by Vittorio Negri, Jed Wentz)
  LP: Philips 6500 070; also issued as Philips SAL 3685

(1968/stereo)(US/UK); also as Philips 839 713 LY
(German); also incl. in 5-LP set Philips 6709 004
titled THE BACH FAMILY — see also CPE Bach,
JCF Bach, JL Bach, JS Bach, WF Bach)
Grand Prix de l'Académie Charles Cros

BACH, JOHANN CHRISTOPH FRIEDERICH (1732-1795)

- *SINFONIA* IN E^b
  English Chamber O†
  Cassette: Philips 7300 065
       LP: Philips 6500 071 (1968); also in 5-LP set Philips 6709
              004 titled THE BACH FAMILY — see also CPE Bach,
              JC Bach, JL Bach, JS Bach, WF Bach)
  SEE ALSO: JL Bach, WF Bach

BACH, JOHANN LUDWIG (1677-1731)

- *SUITE* IN G
  English Chamber O†
  Cassette: Philips 7300 065
       LP: Philips 6500 071 (1968); also in 5-LP set Philips 6709
              004 titled THE BACH FAMILY — see also CPE Bach,
              JC Bach, JCF Bach, JS Bach, WF Bach)
  SEE ALSO: JCF Bach, WF Bach

BACH, JOHANN SEBASTIAN (1685-1750)

- *BRANDENBURG CONCERTOS* (6)
  English Chamber O†/hpsd
  2 Cassettes: Philips 420 345-4 (Concertos 1-3, BWV 1046-1048)
                 Philips 420 346-4 (Concertos 4-6, BWV 1049-1051)
                 Philips 426 345-4 (complete, with Suites 1-4)
       2 CDs: Philips (Silver Line) 420 345-2 PM (Concertos 1-3,
                 BWV 1046-1048)
                 Philips (Silver Line) 420 346-2 PM (Concertos 4-6,
                 BWV 1049-1051)
                 Philips 426 345-2 (complete, with Suites 1-4)
       2 LPs: Philips 6747 166 (complete)(1974)(individual LPs
                 numbered 6599 761 and 6599 762)

"Easily the best of the performances on modern instruments reviewed here.
The recorded sound [in the CD version] remains superb. The success of this
performance comes from the irresistible drive and impetus provided by the
strong continuo line, led by Leppard himself playing the harpsichord. The continuo bass line and harpsichord are given a prominence lacking in other versions which makes a huge difference to all six of the Concertos." — *Classic CD.*

*** "The exhilaration of the Leppard set is undeniable, even though the element of controversy remains surrounding the consistently fast tempos he adopts throughout. With sparkling solo playing (including John Wilbraham's crisp trumpet in No. 2 and a piquant recorder contribution from the late David Munrow in No. 4) there is much to enjoy here.... The remastered analogue sound is full and ample." — Edward Greenfield, Robert Layton and Ivan March, *The New Penguin Guide to Compact Discs and Cassettes* (1988).

● *CANTATA 11 ("LOBET GOTT IN SEINEN REICHEN"):* CHORALE 11

CANTATA 22 ("JESUS NAHM ZU SICH DIE ZWÖLFE"): CHORALE 5

CANTATA 135 ("ACH HERR, MICH ARMEN SÜNDER"): CHORALES 1, 6

CANTATA 140 ("WACHET AUF, RUFT UNS DIE STIMME"): CHORALES 4, 7

CANTATA 147 ("HERZ UND MUND UND TAT UND LEBEN"): CHORALE 10

CANTATA 167 ("IHR MENSCHEN, RÜHMET GOTTES LIEBE"): CHORALE 5

CANTATA 180 ("SCHMÜCKE DICH, O LIEBE SEELE"): CHORALE 1

CANTATA 192 ("NUN DANKET ALLE GOTT"): CHORALE 3

CHRISTMAS ORATORIO, BWV 248: *CANTATA 2* (SINFONIA & FNALE CHORALE), *CANTATA 4* (FINAL CHORALE), *CANTATA 6* (FINAL CHORALE0
    Michael Laird (tpt), Scottish Philharmonic Singers, Scottish Chamber O†
    ALBUM TITLE: CHORALES CÉLÈBRES
    Cassette: RCA/Erato 75089
    LP: RCA/Erato NUM 75089 (1984/digital)

● *CANTATA 12 ("WEINEN, GLAGEN, SORGEN, ZAGEN"): SINFONIA*

CANTATA 21 ("ICH HATTE VIEL BEKÜMMERNIS"): SINFONIA
    English Chamber O†
    LP: Philips 6500 830 (1975/stereo)
    SEE ALSO: CPE Bach

● *CANTATA 29: SINFONIA*
    English Chamber O†
    CD: Philips 6514 276 (1983/digital) with *Concerto 3* for 2 hpsds, BWV 1062, *Concerto* for violin, flute, hpsd & strings, BWV 1044; also issued as Poly-Gram Special Projects (Voordeeelpas Count-

down Postbank PolyGram Nederland
BI/Philips Classic) 426 867-2 (1990) — see also
Grieg, Handel (overture), Haydn (vln conc),
Mozart (sym in D), Schubert (overture)

● *CANTATA 84 ("ICH BIN VERGNÜGT MIT MEINEM GLÜCKE")*

CANTATA 52 ("FALSCHE WELT, DIR TRAU ICH NICHT")

CANTATA 209 ("NON SA CHE SIA DOLORE")
Elly Ameling (s), London Voices, English Chamber O†
    LP: Philips 6514 142 (1981/digital)

● *CANTATA 78: "WIR EILEN MIT"*

CANTATA 156: SINFONIA

CHORALE PRELUDE: "ERBARM' DICH"

CHORALE PRELUDE: "ICH RUF' ZU DIR"

SUITE 2: BADINERIE

SUITE 3: AIR
English Chamber O†
ALBUM TITLE: ALLA BAROCCA
    LP: CBS IM 37215 (1982)
    SEE ALSO: Charpentier, Gluck, Handel, Marcello, Pachelbel,
Vivaldi

● *CANTATA 80 ("EIN FESTE BURG IST UNSER GOTT")*

CANTATA 140 ("WACHET AUF, RUFT UNS DIE STIMME"
Elly Ameling (s), Linda Finnie (cn), Aldo Baldwin (t), Samuel
Ramey (b), London Voices, English Chamber O†
    Cassette: Philips 422 490-4
    CD: Philips 422 490-2
    LP: Philips 6514 097 (1981)

● *CONCERTO 1* IN D MINOR FOR HARPSICHORD, BWV 1052

CONCERTO 2 IN E FOR HARPSICHORD, BWV 1053

CONCERTO 4 IN A FOR HARPSICHORD, BWV 1055
English Chamber O†/hpsd
    Cassette: Philips 7313 002 (BWV 1053, 1055 also issued as
Philips 426 084-4 PM — with *Concerto 2* for 2
hpsds, BWV 1061, *Concerto 1* for 3 hpsds, BWV
1063, below)
    CD: Philips 422 497-2 (BWV 1052 only — with *Concerto 5*
for hpsd, BWV 1056, *Concerto 1* for 2 hpds,
BWV 1060, *Concerto 2* for 3 hpds, BWV 1064,
Concerto for 4 hpsds, BWV 1065, below)

Philips 426 084-2 PM (BWV 1053, 1055 only — with *Concerto 2* for 2 hpds, BVW 1061, *Concerto 1* for 3 hpsds, BWV 1063, below)(1989)

LP: Philips 9502 002 (1974); also in 3-LP set Philips 6747 194 titled 9 CONCERTI PER 1, 2, 3 E 4 CEMBALI ED ORCHESTRA; BWV 1052, 1053 also issued as Philips 6599 616 in 9-LP set Philips 6747 098 titled BACH ORCHESTRAL WORKS; BWV 1055 also issued on Philips 6599 617 in 9-LP set Philips 6747 098 titled BACH ORCHESTRAL WORKS)

- *CONCERTO 3* IN D FOR HARPSICHORD, BWV 1054

CONCERTO 6 IN F FOR HARPSICHORD, BWV 1057

CONCERTO 7 IN G MINOR FOR HARPSICHORD, BWV 1058
English Chamber O†/hpsd

Cassette: Philips 7300 962; also as Philips 426 448-4 (with *Concerto 3* for 2 hpsds, BWV 1062)

CD: Philips 426 448-2 PM (with *Concerto 3* for 2 hpsds, BWV 1062)(1990)

LP: Philips 9500 962 (1981)

- *CONCERTO 5* IN F MINOR FOR HARPSICHORD, BWV 1056

CONCERTO 1 IN C MINOR FOR 2 HARPSICHORDS, BWV 1060

CONCERTO 2 IN C FOR 2 HARPSICHORDS, BWV 1061
Andrew Davis (hpsd in BWV 1060-1061), English Chamber O†/hpsd

Cassette: Philips 7313 017 (BWV 1061 also issued as Philips 426 084-4 PM — with *Concerto 2* for hpsd, BWV 1053, *Concerto 4* for hpsd, BWV 1055, *Concerto 1* for 3 hpsds, BWV 1063)

CD: Philips 422 497-2 (BWV 1056, 1060 only — with *Concerto 1* for hpsd, BWV 1052, *Concerto 2 3* hpds, BWV 1064, *Concerto* for 4 hpsds, BWV 1065, below)

Philips 426 084-2 PM (BWV 1061 only — with *Concerto 2* for hpd, BVW 1053, *Concerto 4* for hpsd, BWV 1055, *Concerto 1* for 3 hpsds, BWV 1063)(1989)

LP: Philips 9502 017 (1974); also in 3-LP set Philips 6747 194 titled 9 CONCERTI PER 1, 2, 3 E 4 CEMBALI ED ORCHESTRA; BWV 1056, 1060 also issued as Philips 6599 618 in 9-LP set Philips 6747 098 titled BACH ORCHESTRAL WORKS; BWV 1061 also

issued as Philips 6599 617 in 9-LP set Philips
6747 098 titled BACH ORCHESTRAL WORKS)

• *CONCERTO 3* IN C MINOR FOR 2 HARPSICHORDS, BWV 1062
Andrew Davis (hpsd), English Chamber O†/hpsd
Cassette: Philips 7337 276
CD: Philips 426 448-2 PM (with *Concerto 3* for hpsd, BWV
1054, *Concerto 6* for hpsd, BWV 1057, *Concerto 7*
for hpsd, 1058)(1990)
LP: Philips 6514 276 (1983/digital) (with *Cantata 29:
Sinfonia* & *Concerto* for vln, flute, hpsd &
strings, BWV 1044)
"Leppard is in fine fettle here, his readings are bright and lively. The double
concerto is, of course, Bach's own remaking of his two-violin concerto, BWV
1043. The sinfonia from *Cantata a29* is an original transcription (from the E
minor Violin Sonata), one of Bach's most exhilarating inspirations." —*Fanfare.*

• *CONCERTO 1* IN D MINOR FOR 3 HARPSICHORDS, BWV 1063

CONCERTO 2 IN C FOR 3 HARPSICHORDS, BWV 1064

CONCERTO IN A MINOR FOR 4 HARPSICHORDS, BWV 1065
Andrew Davis, Philip Ledger (hpsds – all), Blandine Verlet
(hpsd in BWV 1065), English Chamber O†/hpsd
Cassette: Philips 426084-4 PM (BWV 1063 only – with *Concerto
2* for hpsds, BWV 1053, *Concerto 4* for hpsds,
BWV 1055, *Concerto 2* for 2 hpsds, BWV 1061)
CD: Philips 422 497-2 (BWV 1064, 1065 only – with
Concerto 1 for hpsd, BWV 1052, *Concerto 1* for 2
hpds, BWV 1060)
Philips 426 084-2 PM (BWV 1063 only – with *Concerto
2* for hpd, BVW 1053, *Concerto 4* for hpsd, BWV
1055, *Concerto 2* for 2 hpsds, BWV 1061)(1989)
LP: Philips (1974); also in 3-LP set Philips 6747 194
titled 9 CONCERTI PER 1, 2, 3 E 4 CEMBALI ED OR-
CHESTRA; BWV 1063 also issued as Philips 6599
617 in 9-LP set Philips 6747 098 titled BACH OR-
CHESTRAL WORKS; BWV 1064, 1065 also issued
as Philips 6599 618 in 9-LP set Philips 6747 098
titled BACH ORCHESTRAL WORKS)

• *CONCERTO* IN D FOR 3 HARPSICHORDS, BWV 1063

CONCERTO IN A MINOR FOR 4 HARPSICHORDS, BWV 1065
George Malcolm, Valda Aveling, Geoffrey Parsons, Simon Pres-
ton (hpds – BWV 1063 without Preston), English Chamber
O†
ALBUM TITLE: MUSIC FOR 4 HARPSICHORDS

LP: Decca SXL 6318 (stereo); reissued as Decca/London
Stereo Treasury Series STS 15075
Decca LXT 6318 (mono)(1967)
SEE ALSO: CPE Bach (album also incl. Malcolm, *Variations on a
Theme by Mozart* for 4 hpsds)

- *CONCERTO 1* IN A MINOR FOR VIOLIN, BWV 1041

CONCERTO 2 IN E FOR VIOLIN, BWV 1042

CONCERTO IN A MINOR FOR VIOLIN, FLUTE, HARPSICHORD
& STRINGS, BWV 1044
R. Adeney (fl), J-L Garcia (vln in BWV 1044), Arthur Grumiaux
(vln in BWV 1041-1042), English Chamber Ot/hpsd
Cassette: Philips 7337 276 (BWV 1044, with *Concerto 3* for 2
hpsds, BWV 1062—see above)
CD: Philips (Silver Line) 420 889-2 (all, with *Suite* 2 for
orchestra, BWV 1067)
LP: Philips SAL 3489 (BWV 1041-1042)(c.1969/stereo)
(US/UK), also as Philips 835 254 AY (stereo), A
02376 L (mono)(German); BWV 1041-1042 also
on Philips SAL 3660 (US/UK) & on Philips Se-
quenza 6527 120 (1982) with Haydn vln conc 1;
BWV 1044 also issued with *Cantata 29: Sinfonia*
& *Concerto 3* for 2 hpsds, BWV 1062 on Philips
6514 276 (1983/digital)
"Leppard and Grumiaux give thoroughly beautiful, graceful performances that
are enhanced by Leppard's perceptive continuo playing."—*Fanfare.*

- *PRELUDE AND CHORALE*
Scottish Chamber Ot
ALBUM TITLE: MOTO PERPETUO/MOUVEMENTS PERPÉTUELS
Cassette: RCA/Erato MCE 71483
LP: RCA/Erato STU 71483; also as 2292-45676-2
SEE ALSO: Albinoni, Arensky, Brahms, Couperin, Lotter,
Paganini, Paradies, Rimsky-Korsakov, Strauss, Weber

- *ST. MATTHEW PASSION*, BWV 244
Kristina Laki (s), Ann Murray (cn), Jon Garrison (t), David Brit-
ton (t), Benjamin Luxon (b), Hans Georg Ahrens (b),
Harald Stamm (b), NDR (North German Radio) Choir &
Knabenchor Hannover, NDR SOt/hpsd
3 LPs: EMI/Angel DSCX 3934 (1983/digital)(individual
LPs numbered DSCX 3934-1, DSCX 3934-2, DSCX
3934-3)
Grammy Nomination, 1974 (National Academy of Recording Arts & Sciences)

• *SUITE 1* FOR ORCHESTRA, BWV 1066
SUITE 2 FOR ORCHESTRA, BWV 1067
SUITE 3 FOR ORCHESTRA, BWV 1068
SUITE 4 FOR ORCHESTRA, BWV 1069
English Chamber O†/hpsd

Cassette: Philips 7505 004; also as Philips 420 888-4 (BWV 1066, 1068, 1069) & Philips 420 889-4 (BWV 1067, with *Concertos* for vln etc, BWV 1041, 1042, 1044)

CD: Philips (Silver Line) 420 888-2 (BWV 1066, 1068, 1069) Philips (Silver Line) 420 889-2 (BWV 1067, with *Concertos* for vln etc, BWV 1041, 1042, 1044 – see above)

2 LPs: Philips 6768 028 (individual LPs numbered 6542 158 and 6542 159)(1969)(US/UK), also as 839 792/93 (German); also in 5-LP set Philips 6709 004 titled THE BACH FAMILY – see also CPE Bach, JC Bach, JCF Bach, JL Bach, WF Bach; also issued as Philips 6599 612 (BWV 1066, 1069) and 6599 613 (BWV 1067, 1068) in 9-LP set Philips 6747 098 titled BACH ORCHESTRAL WORKS; BWV 1066, 1069 also issued as Philips 6500 067; BWV 1067, 1068 also issued as Philips 6500 068

"Leppard's release has the best sound, and his performance is animated andf precise, with interesting dynamic variations." — Roy Hemming, *Discovering Great Music* (1974).

BACH, WILHELM FRIEDEMANN (1710-1784)

• *CONCERTO* IN F MINOR FOR HARPSICHORD & STRINGS
SINFONIA IN F
RL (hpsd), English Chamber O†

Cassette: Philips 7300 065

LP: Philips 6500 071 (1968); also in 5-LP set Philips 6709 004 titled THE BACH FAMILY – see also CPE Bach, JC Bach, JCF Bach, JL Bach, JS Bach); hpsd concerto reissued on Philips 6833 035 (with CPE Bach, JC Bach, Handel, Mozart, D Scarlatti)

SEE ALSO: JCF Bach, JL Bach

BAX, ARNOLD (1883-1953)

- *SYMPHONY 5* IN C# MINOR
London Philharmonic O†
  LP: Lyrita SRCS 58 (1972)
  *** "The *Fifth* is considered by some critics to be Bax's finest. Dedicated to Sibelius, it was first performed in January 1934 under the Finnish master's most eloquent champion, Sir Thomas Beecham. The symphony shows Bax holding in check the purely lyrical impulse to which he could give such generous vein in favor of a grreater degree of motivic integration. In some ways this is the most symphonic of the seven, though it has the same brooding intensity and powerful atmosphere that distinguish the first three symphonies. Raymond Leppard gives a dedicated and indeed inspired account which should go far to persuade anyone who doubts the power of Bax's imagination or the strength of his symphonic instinct. The LPO are at their very best." — Edward Greenfield, Robert Layton & Ivan March, *Penguin Stereo Record Guide*, 2nd Ed. (1977).

- *SYMPHONY 7*
London Philharmonic O†
  LP: Lyrita SRCS 83 (1975), also as HNH Records HNH 4010 (US), Musical Heritage Society MHS 3618
  "The London Philharmonic plays up to its best... standard." — *Fanfare.*

BEETHOVEN, LUDWIG VAN (1770-1827)

- ARIAS —

  "AH! PERFIDO!", OP 65

  EGMONT, OP 84: "FREUDVOLL UND LEIDVOLL"

  "DIE TROMMEL GERÜHRET"

  "NO, NON TURBATI", WoO92a
  Janet Baker (s), English Chamber O†/hpsd & pno
  LP: Philips 9500 307 (1977); also issued as Philips 6597 004 & incl. in 4-LP set Philips 6767 001 titled JANET BAKER • RAYMOND LEPPARD — see also Gluck, Handel, Haydn, Mozart, Schubert
  "The Italian arias... are put across with beautiful phrasing and shading and spirit.... Leppard and the ECO provide beautifully shaped and shaded accompaniments." — Peter Branscombe, *Hi-Fi News & Record Review.* "I have never enjoyed lesser Beethoven so entirely." — *Gramophone.*
  SEE ALSO: Schubert

- *ROMANCE* IN F
  Jack Rothstein (vln), English Chamber O†, with spoken commentary "Beethoven's Deafness"
  ALBUM TITLE: MUSIC AND MEDICINE
  45 RPM: Lyntone/Merck Sharp and Dohme Intl LYN 797/798

BIBER, HEINRICH VON (1644-1704)
- *SONATA* IN A FOR 8 TRUMPETS (adapt/arr by RL)
  Wynton Marsalis (tpts), English Chamber O†
  ALBUM TITLE: BAROQUE MUSIC FOR TRUMPETS
  Casssette: CBS MYT 38482
       CD: CBS/Sony MK 42478
       LP: CBS/Sony MT 42478
  SEE ALSO: M Haydn, Pachelbel, Telemann, Vivaldi

BLOCH, ERNEST (1880-1959)
- *SUITE HEBRAIQUE*
  András Toszeghi (vla), BBC Northern SO†
       LP: ALOIV 2002 (with Berlioz *Harold in Italy* in Liszt
           vla/pno vers)

BOCCHERINI, LUIGI (1743-1805)
- *CONCERTO* IN G FOR CELLO & ORCHESTRA
  Maurice Gendron (vc), London Symphony O†
  Cassette: Philips Concert Classics 422 481-4
       CD: Philips Concert Classics 422 481-2 (digitally
           remastered)
       LP: Philips SAL 3636 (1965/stereo)(US/UK); also as
           Philips 835 358 AY (German)
  SEE ALSO: Haydn
- *6 SYMPHONIES*, OP 12 Nrs 1-6
  New Philharmonia O†
     2 CDs: Philips 438 314-2 (1993)(individual CDs numbered
           438 315-2 and 438 316-2); syms 3, 5 also reissued
           on Philips 438 377-2 (disc 2, numbered 438 379-
           2, of 1993 2-CD set titled THE BEST OF BOC-
           CHERINI which also incl. works featuring
           Maurice Gendron, Pepe Romero, Academy of
           St Martins in the Fields, I Musici, Quartetto
           Italiano)
     3 LPs: Philips 6703 034 (1972)
  "Raymond Leppard is ideally qualified to conduct Boccherini's music: his sensitivity to texture, his care over detail, his springy, balletic rhythms are precisely what this music needs. And to that his well-judged tempos may be added. I
  find these performances, which capture so well the charm, the grace and the
  vitality of the music, thoroughly enjoyable, as persuasive on Boccherini's behalf as can be imagined." — *Gramophone*. "[Leppard's] range of pulse and tempo
  is remarkable: he seizes unerringly on the individuality of each movement and

holds all Boccherini's daring explorations in a grip at once secure and affectionate." — Geoffrey Crankshaw, *Records & Recording.*

BONONCINI, ANTONIO MARIA (1697-1726)

● *POLIFEMO:* OVERTURE
New Philharmonia O†/hpsd
ALBUM TITLE: 18TH CENTURY OVERTURES
Cassette: Philips 412 406-4
LP: Philips SAL 3674 (1968)(US/UK); also as Philips 802
893 LY (German); reissued as Philips 412 406-1
"An excellent disc, in sum, music of the greatest fascination, admirably performed by the New Philharmonia, well recorded, our gratitude to Raymond Leppard and Philips." — *The Gramophone.*
SEE ALSO: Grétry, Handel, Méhul, Mozart, Pergolesi, Rameau,
Sacchini, D Scarlatti

BOYCE, WILLIAM (1711-1779)

● *CAMBRIDGE INSTALLATION ODE:* OVERTURE
New Philharmonia O†
ALBUM TITLE: 18TH CENTURY OVERTURES, VOL. II
LP: Philips SAL 3760 (1969)(US/UK); also as Philips 802
901 LY (German)
SEE ALSO: JC Bach, Cimarosa, Locatelli, Mozart, Rameau,
A Scarlatti

BRAHMS, JOHANNES (1833-1897)

● *ACADEMIC FESTIVAL OVERTURE*
Essex Youth O†
LP: Pike Films LP 007
SEE ALSO: Copland, Vivaldi

● *"O WELT, ICH MUSS DICH LASSEN"* (CHORALE)
Scottish Chamber O†
ALBUM TITLE: MOTO PERPETUO/MOUVEMENTS PERPÉTUELS
Cassette: RCA/Erato MCE 71483
LP: RCA/Erato STU 71483; also as 2292-45676-2
SEE ALSO: Albinoni, Arensky, JS Bach, Couperin, Lotter,
Paganini, Paradies, Rimsky-Korsakov, Strauss, Weber

BRITTEN, BENJAMIN (1913-1976)

- *THE YOUNG PERSON'S GUIDE TO THE ORCHESTRA (VARIA-
  TIONS AND FUGUE ON A THEME OF PURCELL), OP 34*
  Richard Baker (n), New Philharmonia O†
  Cassette: Classics for Pleasure TC-CFP 185
  LP: Classics for Pleasure CFP 185 (1971)
  ** *Penguin Stereo Record Guide*, 2nd Ed. (1977).
  SEE ALSO: Prokofiev

BYRD, WILLIAM (1543?-1623)

- MADRIGALS, ETC[1]
  Singers & insts cond. by RL, others, featuring April Cantelo (s),
  Sybil Michelow, Helen Watts (cns), Robert Tear (t), Chris-
  topher Keyte (b)
  ALBUM TITLE: MUSIC OF THE COURT HOMES AND CITIES OF
  ENGLAND, Vol 4 – MUSIC AT GREENWICH PALACE AND INGATES-
  TONE HALL
  LP: EMI/HMV HQS 1147 (1968/stereo)
  SEE ALSO: Gibbons

CAMPRA, ANDRÉ (1660-1744)

- *L'EUROPE GALANTE* (SUITE)
  English Chamber O†/hpsd
  LP: Decca/L'Oiseau Lyre SOL 302 (1968/stereo)
       Decca/L'Oiseau Lyre OL 302 (mono)
  SEE ALSO: Rameau

CAVALLI, FRANCESCO (1602-1676)

- AIRS –
  LA CALISTO: "ARDO, SOSPIRO E PIANGO"
  LA DIDONE: LAMENTO DI CASSANDRA
  L'EGISTO: LAMENTO DI CLORI
  L'ORIMONTE: "NUMI CIECHI PIÙ DI ME"
  SCIPIONE AFRICANO: "NON È, NON È CRUDEL"
  XERSE: "LA BELLEZA È UN DON FUGACE"
  Frederica von Stade (ms), Scottish Chamber O†

---

1   Titles: "Hey Ho to the Greenwood", "Lullaby, My Sweet Little Baby", "The Nightin-
    gale So Pleasant Is", "Susanna Fair", "This Day Christ Was Born".

Cassette: RCA/Erato MCE 75183
CD: RCA/Erato ECD 88100 (digital)
LP: RCA/Erato NUM 75183 (1985)
SEE ALSO: Monteverdi
**(*) "Frederica von Stade, in excellent voice, sings *Cassandra's lament* with a dignified simplicity, and she finds a similar direct eloquence for Clori's lament '*Amor, che ti diè l'alti*' from *L'Egisto*.... '*Numi ciechi più di me*—with a deliciously pointed accompaniment from Leppard and the Scottish Chamber Orchestra — really sparkles.... A most attractive program, well balanced and recorded." — Edward Greenfield, Robert Layton & Ivan March, *The New Penguin Guide to Compact Discs and Cassettes* (1988).

● AIRS —

LA DIDONE: AENEAS' FAREWELL

LAMENT OF CASSANDRA

LA DORICLEA: "OH DELLE MIE SPERANZE"

L'ORISTEO: "CAMPION DI TUA BELTÀ"

SCIPIONE AFRICANO: "AH! TRISTO SCELLERATO"

LAMENT OF SOFONISBA

STATIRA PRINCIPESSA DI PERSIA: "IN INDIA VÒ TORNAR"
Heather Harper (s), Hugues Cuénod (t), Gerald English (t),
Bath Festival Enst/hpsd
ALBUM TITLE: ITALIAN BAROQUE MUSIC
LP: EMI/HMV Records HQS 1086 (1967/stereo)
EMI/HMV HQM 1086 (mono)(HMV Baroque
Library 22)
SEE ALSO: Monteverdi

● *LA CALISTO* (Opera) (ed. Leppard)
Ileana Cotrubas, Janet Baker, James Bowman, Owen Brannigan, Hugues Cuénod, Federico Davia, Peter Gottlieb,
Ugo Trama, Glyndebourne Festival Chorus, London Philharmonic O†
2 CDs: Decca 436 216-2 (individual CDs numbered 436 217-2
and 436 218-2)
2 LPs: Decca/Argo ZNF 11/12 (1972)(individual LPs
numbered ZNF 11, ZNF 12)
***/rosette "No more perfect Glyndebourne entertainment has been devised than this freely adapted version of an opera written for Venice in the 1650s but never heard since. It is the more delectable because of the brilliant part given to the goddess Diana, taken by Janet Baker. In Leppard's version she has a dual task: portraying the chaste goddess herself but then in the same costume switching immediately to the randy Jupiter disguised as Diana, quite a different character. Add to that a bad-tempered aging nymph, hilarious portrayed by Hugues Cuénod, and parts for such singers as James Bowman that draw out

their finest qualities, and the result is magic. No one should miss Janet Baker's heartbrakingly intense singing of her tender aria '*Amara servitu*'. The recording, made at Glyndebourne, is gloriously atmospheric." — Edward Greenfield, Robert Layton & Ivan March, *Penguin Stereo Record Guide*, 2nd Ed. (1977). "*Calisto* gives us the Venetian style at its most luxurious, and Leppard responds with an at times breathtaking beauty of arrangement.... A most delightful performance of a highly picturesque work." — Ethan Mordden, *A Guide to Opera Recordings* (Oxford University Press, 1987).

- *L'ORMINDO* (opera) (Ed. Leppard)
  Isabel Garcisanz (s), Hanneke Van Bork (s), Jean Allister (cn), Jane Berbié (ms), Anne Howells (ms), Hugues Cuénod (t), John Wakefield (t), Peter-Christopher Runge (bar), Federico Davia (b), Richard Van Allen (b), London Philharmonic O†
  3 LPs: Decca/Argo (Z)NF 8-10 (individual LPs numbered
           ZNF 8, ZNF 9, ZNF 10)(1969)
  *** "We owe it above all to Raymond Leppard that the name of Francesco Cavalli has become famous again. He discovered the long-forgotten score of this fascinating opera, and subjected it to his own magical Leppardization process to produce one of the most enchanting of Glyndebourne entertainments. The gaiety of Glyndebourne is superbly caught, for wisely Argo opted to record the work on the company's home ground in Sussex, using the Organ Room for studio instead of the excessively dry-sounding opera-house proper. The sounds are nothing short of luscious, often almost Straussian in their opulence, and Leppard's array of continuo instruments constantly charms the ear." — Edward Greenfield, Robert Layton & Ivan March, *Penguin Stereo Record Guide*, 2nd Ed. (1977).

CHARPENTIER, MARC-ANTOINE (c.1636-1704)

- *MÉDÉE* (SUITE)
  English Chamber O†/hpsd
  LP: Decca/L'Oiseau Lyre SOL 300 (1967/stereo)
        Decca/L'Oiseau Lyre OL 300 (mono)
  "Altogether a very rewarding disc: splendid music, playing with feeling and style, and finely recorded." — *The Gramophone.*
  SEE ALSO: Couperin

- *TE DEUM: INTRODUCTION* (Ed. by RL)
  English Chamber O†
  ALBUM TITLE: ALLA BAROCCA
  LP: CBS IM 37215 (1982)
  SEE ALSO: JS Bach, Gluck, Handel, Marcello, Pachelbel, Vivaldi

CHILCOT, THOMAS (d.1766)

- "HARK, HARK THE LARK"
  April Cantelo (s), English Chamber O†/hpsd
  ALBUM TITLE: 18TH CENTURY SHAKESPEAREAN SONGS

LP: Decca/L'Oiseau-Lyre OL 50205 (1961/mono)
SEE ALSO: Arne, Greene, Haydn, Hook, T Linley, W Linley,
Smith, Weldon

CIMAROSA, DOMENICO (1749-1801)
● *I TRACI AMANTI:* OVERTURE
New Philharmonia O†
ALBUM TITLE: 18TH CENTURY OVERTURES, VOL. II
LP: Philips SAL 3760 (1969)(US/UK); also as Philips 802
901 LY (German)
SEE ALSO: JC Bach, Boyce, Locatelli, Mozart, Rameau, A Scarlatti

COATES, ERIC (b.20th cent)
● *ELIZABETH OF GLAMIS* (from *The Three Elizabeths*)
Tallis Chamber Choir, English Chamber O†
ALBUM TITLE: A BIRTHDAY CONCERT FOR MY GRANDMOTHER.
HRH the Prince of Wales Celebration Concert to Mark the
90th Birthday of HM Queen Elizabeth the Queen Mother.
Recorded live in the Ballroom, Buckingham Palace, 2 Aug
1990.
CD: EMI/Angel CDC 7 54164 2 (1990)
SEE ALSO: Anon, Doyle, Elgar, Gowers, Matthews, Strauss

COLLECTIONS (MISC)
¶ Singers & insts cond. by RL, others
ALBUM TITLE: MUSIC OF THE COURT HOMES AND CITIES OF
ENGLAND, Vol 1 – COMPOSERS OF CHAPEL ROYAL
LP: EMI/HMV HQS 1140
¶ Selected Madrigals etc
Soloists, English Chamber O†
ALBUM TITLE: MUSIC OF SHAKESPEARE'S TIME, VOL 1
LP: Decca/L'Oiseau Lyre

COPLAND, AARON (1900-1990)
● *RODEO: BUCKAROO HOLIDAY, CORRAL NOCTURNE,
HOE-DOWN*
Essex Youth O†
LP: Pike Films LP 007
SEE ALSO: Brahms, Vivaldi

CORELLI, ARCANGELO (1653-1713)
- *CONCERTO GROSSO* IN F, OP 6 NR 9 (ed. by RL)
  English Chamber O†/hpsd
  LP: EMI/His Master's Voice HQS 1232 (1970/stereo);
  reissued as EMI/Classics for Pleasure Ltd CFP
  40371 (1982/stereo)
  SEE ALSO: Albinoni, Vivaldi

COUPERIN, FRANÇOIS (1668-1733)
- *L'APOTHÉSE DE LULLY*
  English Chamber O†
  LP: Decca/L'Oiseau Lyre SOL 300 (1967/stereo)
  Decca/L'Oiseau Lyre OL 300 (mono)
  SEE ALSO: Charpentier
- *LES BARRICADES MYSTÉRIEUSES*
  Scottish Chamber O†
  ALBUM TITLE: MOTO PERPETUO/MOUVEMENTS PERPÉTUELS
  Cassette: RCA/Erato MCE 71483
  LP: RCA/Erato STU 71483; also as 2292-45676-2
  SEE ALSO: Albinoni, Arensky, JS Bach, Brahms, Lotter, Paganini,
  Paradies, Rimsky-Korsakov, Strauss, Weber

DESTOUCHES, ANDRÉ CARDINAL (1672-1749)
- *ISSÉ* (SUITE)
  English Chamber O†/hpsd
  LP: Decca/L'Oiseau Lyre SOL 303 (1968/stereo)
  Decca/L'Oiseau Lyre OL 303 (mono)
  SEE ALSO: Leclair

DEVIENNE, FRANÇOIS (1759-1803)
- *CONCERTO* 2 IN D FOR FLUTE
  Peter-Lukas Graf (fl), English Chamber O†
  Cassette: Claves C 501
  CD: Claves CD 50-501
  LP: Claves Cla P 501 (with Ibert)
  SEE ALSO: Ibert, Saint-Saëns

DOWLAND, JOHN (1563-1626)
- SELECTED MADRIGALS ETC
  Patricia Clark (s), Eileen Poulter (s), Mary Thomas (s),

Rosemary Phillips (cn), Wilfred Brown (t), Gerald English
(t), Christopher Keyte (b), Dolmetsch Consort†
ALBUM TITLE: MUSIC OF SHAKESPEARE'S TIME, VOL 2
LP: EMI/HMV CLP 1634 (1963)
SEE ALSO: Lassus, Morley, Tomkins, Weelkes

- VOCAL MUSIC[2]
April Cantelo (s), Janet Baker (s), Jantina Noorman (s), Wilfred
Brown (t), Granston Burgess (a), Gerald English (t), Chris-
topher Keyte (b), insts†
LP: CLP 1894 (1965)

DOYLE, PATRICK (b.20th cent)

- *THE THISTLE AND THE ROSE*
Marie McLaughlin (s), Tallis Chamber Choir, English Chamber
O†
ALBUM TITLE: A BIRTHDAY CONCERT FOR MY GRANDMOTHER.
HRH the Prince of Wales Celebration Concert to Mark the
90th Birthday of HM Queen Elizabeth the Queen Mother.
Recorded live in the Ballroom, Buckingham Palace, 2 Aug
1990.
CD: EMI/Angel CDC 7 54164 2 (1990)
SEE ALSO: Anon, Coates, Elgar, Gowers, Matthews, Strauss

DVORÁK, ANTONÍN (1841-1904)

- *LEGENDS*, OP 59 (SUITE IN 8 MOVEMENTS)
London Philharmonic O†
LP: Philips SAL 6500 188 (stereo)(US/UK); also as Philips
6500 188 LY (German)
- *SERENADE* IN E FOR STRINGS, OP 22
English Chamber O†
Cassette: Philips 7300 532 (1977)
CD: Philips (Silver Line) 420 883-2 (1988)
LP: Philips 7300 532 (1977); reissued as Philips 9500 105
"One of Raymond Leppard's first records outside his regular Baroque stamp-
ing-ground was of the Dvořák *Legends*, a delightful disc. Equally his radio per-

---

2 Titles: "Ah heart that's broken","Farewell, unkind farewell", "Fine Knacks for
Ladies", "Go Cristall teares", "If that a Sinners sighes be Angels food", "Lady if you so
spight me", "Love those beames that breede", "Psalm 51", "Psalm 100", "Say love if
ever thou didst finde", "Shall I sue", "Sorrow sorrow stay", "Tell me true love", "Up
merry Mates to Neptunes praise", "Weep you no more sad fountains", "Were every
thought an eye", "Welcome blacke night", "Where Sinne sore wounding".

formances with the BBC Northern Symphony Orchestra have regularly confirmed what a natural and warm-hearted Dvořák interpreter he is. Here again he directs a beautifully paced and crisply pointed reading of one of Dvořák's most appealing works, coupling it with an equally strong and enjoyable account of the Tchaikovsky *Serenade* in what has now become a conventional coupling." — *Gramophone.*
SEE ALSO: Tchaikovsky

ELGAR, EDWARD (1857-1934)
- *DREAM CHILDREN, OP 43*
NURSERY SUITE
THE STARLIGHT EXPRESS, OP 78: OVERTURE AND FINALE
THE WAND OF YOUTH: SUITES I & II, Opp 1A & 1B
Indianapolis Symphony O†
  CD: Koss Classics KC-1014 (1991/digital)
"What a fascinating record! These are faithful and loving performances, flamboyant in places but avoiding the Scylla of bombast on the one side and the Charybdis of sentimentality on the other. One striking feature is Leppard's attention to the dynamic markings; the contrast between loud and soft passages is exemplary, and there is a clear difference between *p* and *pp*, for instance. In 'Fairies and Giants' from the first *Wand of Youth* Suite, he saves something for the third giant at fig. 49 so that the *fff* is significantly louder than the preceding pages. (Elgar once said he loved to hear the three giants coming on one after another: he would have loved these.)
  "The orchestra plays to the manner born. There is excellent ensemble, and plenty of scope for virtuoso performances from virtually every instrument in the band, as they revel iñ the superb orchestration. Listen to the horns enjoying their fat little phrase just before fig. 3 in the 'Overture'. The recording is beautifully clear and well-balanced." — *The Elgar Society Journal,* 9/92. "British-born Raymond Leppard, now music director of the Indianapolis Symphony, has the Elgar style in his bones and elicits elegant playing throughout. The recording itself is absolutely first-class." — *Stereo Review.*

- *NURSERY SUITE: "THE WAGON (PASSES)"*
Tallis Chamber Choir, English Chamber O†
ALBUM TITLE: A BIRTHDAY CONCERT FOR MY GRANDMOTHER.
HRH the Prince of Wales Celebration Concert to Mark the 90th Birthday of HM Queen Elizabeth the Queen Mother. Recorded live in the Ballroom, Buckingham Palace, 2 Aug 1990.
  CD: EMI/Angel CDC 7 54164 2 (1990)
SEE ALSO: Anon, Coates, Doyle, Gowers, Matthews, Strauss

FARMER, JOHN (fl.1591-1601)
- "A LITTLE PRETTY BONNY LASS" (MADRIGAL)
Cambridge Univ Madrigal Soc†

ALBUM TITLE: IN PRIDE OF MAY AND OTHER MADRIGALS
LP: HMV 7EP7114 (mono)
SEE ALSO: Monteverdi, Weelkes

FASCH, JOHANN FRIEDRICH (1688-1758)

- *CONCERTO* IN D FOR TRUMPET, 2 OBOES & STRING
  ORCHESTRA
  Wynton Marsalis (tpt), English Chamber O†
  Cassette: CBS Masterworks
  CD: CBS Masterworks MK 29061 (digital)
  LP: CBS Masterworks IM 39061 (1984/digital)
  Grammy Nomination, 1985 (National Academy of Recording Arts & Sciences).
  SEE ALSO: Handel, Molter, Purcell, Torelli

FIALA, JOSEPH (1748-1816)

- *CONCERTO* IN E^b FOR ENGLISH HORN
  Heinz Holliger, English Chamber O†
  Cassette: Philips 412 354-4
  CD: Philips 426 972-2 (1990)(with Hummel; also incl.
  works by Bellini, Mollique, Moscheles, Rietz
  cond. by Eliahu Inbal)
  LP: Philips 839 756 LY (German) (1969/stereo); reissued
  as Philips 426 972-1
  SEE ALSO: JC Bach, Hummel

GIBBONS, ORLANDO (1583-1625)

- "THE SILVER SWAN"
  Singers & insts cond. by RL, others, featuring April Cantelo (s),
  Sybil Michelow, Helen Watts (cns), Robert Tear (t), Chris-
  topher Keyte (b), others
  ALBUM TITLE: MUSIC OF THE COURT HOMES AND CITIES OF
  ENGLAND, Vol 4 – MUSIC AT GREENWICH PALACE AND INGATES-
  TONE HALL
  LP: EMI/HMV HQS 1147 (1968/stereo)
  SEE ALSO: Byrd

GLUCK, CHRISTOPH WILLIBALD (1714-1787)

- ARIAS –

  ALCESTE: "DIVINITÉS DU STYX"

  ARMIDE: "LE PERFIDE RENAUD"

IPHIGÉNIE EN AULIDE: "ADIEU, CONSERVEZ DANS
VOTRE ÂME"
"VOUS ESSAYEZ EN VAIN – PAR LA CRAINTE"
IPHIGÉNIE EN TAURIDE: "NON, CET AFFREUX DEVOIR"
ORFEO ED EURIDICE: "CHE FARÒ SENZA EURIDICE"
"CHE PURO CIEL"
PARIDE ED ELENA: "LE BELLE IMMAGINI"
"DI TE SCORDARMI"
"OH, DEL MIO DOLCE ARDOR"
"SPIAGGE AMATE"
LA RECONTRE IMPRÉVUE: "BEL INCONNU"
"JE CHERCHE À VOUS FAIRE"
Janet Baker (s), English Chamber O†/hpsd
Cassette: Philips 7300 440 (1976); also as Philips 422 950-4 (1989)
    CD: Philips 422 950-2 (1989)
    LP: Philips 9500 023 (1976); also issued as Philips 6597
          003 & incl. in 4-LP set Philips 6767 001 titled
          JANET BAKER • RAYMOND LEPPARD — see also
          Beethoven, Handel, Haydn, Mozart, Schubert
"Janet Baker might have been created for just such a programme as this: her
verbal commitment, always in precise accord with her far-ranging voice, ensures that, for once, the dramatic vividness and poetic subtlety of this great
composer receive their due.... Raymond Lepaprd draws sensitve lines, has an
ear for Gluck's plangent harmonic system and shows us what a mastery of

: 595 :

colour lurks in the accompaniment to *'Che puro ciel'*. Not to be missed on any account." — *Records & Recording.*

- *ORFEO ED EURIDICE* (OPERA)
  Janet Baker (s), Elizabeth Gale, Elisabeth Speiser, Glyndebourne Festival Opera, London Philharmonic O†
  3 LPs: RCA/Erato NUM 750423 (1983/digital)(individual LPs numbered NUM 75043, NUM 75044, NUM 75045)
  "[Baker] makes the most of [her] part, in the most persuasive surroundings." — Ethan Mordden, *A Guide to Opera Recordings* (Oxford University Press, 1987).
  ¶ *"DANCE OF THE BLESSED SPIRITS"*
  English Chamber O†
  ALBUM TITLE: ALLA BAROCCA
  LP: CBS IM 37215 (1982)
  SEE ALSO: JS Bach, Charpentier, Handel, Marcello, Pachelbel, Vivaldi
  ¶ ORCHESTRAL EXCERPTS FROM THE OPERA
  Cassette: Philips 422 278-4
  CD: Philips 422 278-2
  SEE ALSO: Handel (*Serse*)

GOWERS, PATRICK (b.20th cent)

- *SUITE* FOR VIOLIN & CHAMBER ORCHESTRA
  José-Luis Garcia (vln), English Chamber O†
  ALBUM TITLE: A BIRTHDAY CONCERT FOR MY GRANDMOTHER.
  HRH the Prince of Wales Celebration Concert to Mark the 90th Birthday of HM Queen Elizabeth the Queen Mother. Recorded live in the Ballroom, Buckingham Palace, 2 Aug 1990.
  CD: EMI/Angel CDC 7 54164 2 (1990)
  SEE ALSO: Anon, Coates, Doyle, Elgar, Matthews, Strauss

GREENE, MAURICE (1695-1755)

- "ORPHEUS WITH HIS LUTE"
  April Cantelo (s), English Chamber O†/hpsd
  ALBUM TITLE: 18TH CENTURY SHAKESPEAREAN SONGS
  LP: Decca/L'Oiseau-Lyre OL 50205 (1961/mono)
  SEE ALSO: Arne, Chilcot, Haydn, Hook, T Linley, W Linley, Smith, Weldon

GRÉTRY, ANDRÉ-ERNEST-MODESTE (1741-1813)

- *LE JUGEMENT DE MIDAS:* OVERTURE
  New Philharmonia O†/hpsd

ALBUM TITLE: 18TH CENTURY OVERTURES
Cassette: Philips 412 406-4
LP: Philips SAL 3674 (1968)(US/UK); also as Philips 802 893 LY (German); reissued as Philips 412 406-1
"An excellent disc, in sum, music of the greatest fascination, admirably performed by the New Philharmonia, well recorded, our gratitude to Raymond Leppard and Philips." — *The Gramophone.*
SEE ALSO: Bononcini, Handel, Méhul, Mozart, Pergolesi, Rameau, Sacchini, D Scarlatti

● *SUITE DE BALLET* (from operas *La Caravane du Caire, Cephale et Procris, L'Epreuve villageoise*)
English Chamber O†/hpsd
LP: Decca/L'Oiseau Lyre SOL 297 (1967/stereo)
Decca/L'Oiseau Lyre OL 297 (mono)
"The performances are brilliant, and the recording first-class." — *Records & Recording.*
SEE ALSO: Rameau

GRIEG, EDVARD (1843-1907)

● *4 NORWEGIAN DANCES,* OP 35 (orch by Hans Sitt)
PEER GYNT SUITE 1, OP 46
PEER GYNT SUITE 2, OP 55
English Chamber O†
Cassette: Philips 7300 513 (1976); also as Philips 412 922-4
CD: Philips Classics 420 081-2 (with Old Norwegian Romance, op 51)
LP: Philips 9500 106; also as Philips 412 922-1
**(*) "Leppard's disc is beautifully recorded, the sound at once spacious and sparkling. The music-making is fresh and has an air of thoughtfullyness which will appeal to many.... The *Four Norwegian Dances* are splendidly done, with playing of vigor and showing a fine sense of color." — Edward Greenfield, Robert Layton & Ivan March, *Penguin Stereo Record Guide,* 2nd Ed. (1977). "As good as the best." — Lionel Markson, *Records & Recording.*

● *HOLBERG SUITE,* OP 40
LYRIC SUITE, OP 54
SIGURD JORSALFAR (suite), OP 56
English Chamber O†
Cassette: Philips 7300 833 (stereo); reissued as Philips 432 277-4 (1991)
CD: Philips 432 277-2 (1991); Holberg Suite only reissued on PolyGram Special Projects (Voordeeelpas Countdown Postbank PolyGram Nederland BI/Philips Classic) 426 867-2 (1990) — see also JS

Bach (cantata), Handel (overture), Haydn (vln
conc), Mozart (sym in D), Schubert (overture)
LP: Philips 9500 748 (1980/stereo)

**(*) "Grieg's delightful *Lyric Suite* is the finest of the performances here, very
freshly played, it has warm, transparent string texture and the closing 'March
of the dwarfs' is earthily malignant." — Edward Greenfield, Robert Layton &
Ivan March, *The Penguin Guide to Compact Discs and Cassettes Yearbook 1991*. "I
am tempted to call this disc flawless.... The program itself [is] eminently sensible." — *Fanfare*.

- *OLD NORWEGIAN ROMANCE WITH VARIATIONS*, OP 51

SYMPHONIC DANCES, OP 64
Philharmonia O†
Cassette: Philips 7337 203 (digital)
CD: Philips Classics 420 081-2 (op 51 only, with 4
Norwegian Dances, Peer Gynt Suites 1-2)
LP: Philips 6514 203 (1982/digital)
"Though Leppard's reputation [has been] that of a Baroque specialist, his forays
into the Romantic literature show him to be highly sympathetic to the 19th
century style and temperament. Enjoy." — *Fanfare*.

GUILIANI, MAURO (1781-1829)

- *CONCERTO 1* IN A FOR GUITAR, OP 30

- *CONCERTO 3* IN F FOR GUITAR, OP 70
Angel Romero (gtr), English Chamber O†
LP: EMI Records/Angel ASD 1435581(1983/digital), also
as Angel DS 37967
"Angel Romero's playing is superb.... This delightful concerto [Nr. 1]
sparkles." — *Fanfare*.

HANDEL, GEORGE FREDERIC (1685-1759)

- ARIAS —

ADMETO: "CANGIO D'ASPETTO"

ALCINA: "VERDI PRATI"

ALEXANDER BALUS: "CONVEY ME"

ATALANTA: "CARE SELVE"

CLORI TIRSI FILENO (cantata): *"LA RONDINELLA"*

OTTONE (OTHO): "VIENI, O FIGLIO", "LA SPERANZA"

PARTENOPE: "VOGLIO DIRE"

RINALDO: "LASCIA CH'IO PIANGA"

RODELINDA: "DOVE SEI"

Bernadette Greevy (cn), Academy of St. Martin-in-the-
Fields†/hpsd
    LP: Argo ZRG 501 (1966/stereo)
              Argo RG 501 (mono)
** *Penguin Stereo Record Guide,* 2nd Ed. (1977).
¶ *RODELINDA: "DOVE SEI"*
    LP: Decca SPA 448 (collection also features conductors
              Marriner, Ledger, Boult)
  2 LPs: Decca SDPA 551/2 (collection also features conductors
              Richter, Szell, Marriner, Willcocks, Boult)

● ARIAS —

BERENICE: "SI TRA I CEPPI"

FLORIDANTE: "ALMA MIA"

RADAMISTO: "PERFIDO! DI A QUELL'EMPIO TIRANNO"

RODELINDA: "SCACCIATA DAL SUO NIDO"

TOLOMEO: "CHE PIÙ SI TARDA OMAI — STILLE AMARE"
Gérard Souzay (bar), English Chamber O†/hpsd
ALBUM TITLE: BAROQUE OPERA ARIAS
    LP: Philips 835 215AY (stereo)
              Philips A02337L (mono)
1965 Grand Prix Jacques Rouché, Académie du Disque Français
    SEE ALSO: Lully, Rameau

● *ARIODANTE* (opera)
Janet Baker (ms), Edith Mathis (s), Norma Burrowes (s), David
Rendall (t), Samuel Ramey (b), James Bowman (ct),
Alexander Oliver (t), London Voices, English Chamber O†
  3 Cassettes: Philips 7699 112 (individual cassettes numbered 7300
                    734, 7300 735, 7300 736)
    CD: Philips 422 486-2 (overture only, plus overtures to
              Admeto, Alcina, Esther, Lotario, Orlando, Ottone,
              Partenope, Il pastor fido, Poro)
  4 LPs: Philips 6769 025 (1979 — individual LPs numbered
              9500 617, 9500 618, 9500 619, 9500 620)
"[Leppard's] orchestra uses modern instruments thoroughly familiar to the
players, and most of the mannerisms of both old and new [i.e. 'authentic'] performance styles are avoided; everything is expressive, as is obviously required
by this deeply felt music; the singers, well trained in the style, are given their
head, while the orchestra is handled with the utmost care and delicacy.... Further to the good, Leppard does not use the concerto grosso arrangement, necessary in Handel's day because the inferior ripieno players could not be entrusted
with the more delicate and technically difficult aria accompaniments. The
change from the cautiously thin concertino to the solid sound of the ritornels
is always a bit unsettling, even in recordings where the sound can be doctored.

Leppard has sufficient control over his excellent players to use the entire string body throughout, the result being a rounded tone with depth even in the pianissimos. Despite the known fact that before the time of Spohr, Spontini, and Weber there was no baton-wielding conductor (a practice the historicists follow religiously), it becomes increasingly evident that a performance led by a competent conductor is infinitely preferable to the *maestro al cembalo* system....[4] The orchestral playing [for this recording] is superb, airy, and pointed. In the aria accompaniments the basses use bow strokes of a mere half-inch; the two horns and the solo bassoon are outstanding; and I particularly like the way the frequent imitations between voices and the orchestra are played — as integral parts of the musical flow, instead of materializing from nowhere. The *balli*, the French dances, are delectably tossed off; note the musicianly use of ornamentation and overdotting where such things are *needed*, and not merely because the book says so.... Don't miss this great music, marvelously performed." — Paul Henry Lang, *High Fidelity Records in Review 1981.*

• *BERENICE: MINUET*

HARPSICHORD SUITE: SARABANDE

SOLOMON: ARRIVAL OF THE QUEEN OF SHEBA
English Chamber O†
ALBUM TITLE: ALLA BAROCCA
    LP: CBS IM 37215 (1982)
    SEE ALSO: JS Bach, Charpentier, Gluck, Marcello, Pachelbel, Vivaldi

• *BIRTHDAY ODE FOR QUEEN ANNE:* "ETERNAL SOURCE OF LIGHT DIVINE"

SAMSON: "LET THE BRIGHT SERAPHIM"
Edita Gruberová (s), Wynton Marsalis (tpt), English Chamber O†
Cassette: CBS Masterworks
    CD: CBS Masterworks MK 29061 (digital)
    LP: CBS Masterworks IM 39061 (1984/digital)
"The Handel arias for soprano and trumpet are rarely recorded or performed, so having them on CD is more than welcome.... Marsalis [provides] a sharp, ringing trumpet obbligato." — Larry Canale, ed., *Digital Audios: Guide to Compact Discs* (Bantam Books, 1986). Grammy Nomination, 1985 (National Academy of Recording Arts & Sciences).
    SEE ALSO: Fasch, Molter, Purcell, Torelli

---

4   Though even this might be regarded as splitting hairs... In fact, RL himself might contend that, in the end, all these matters are somewhat incidental: what matters is the *what* of a performance (does it have both relevance and coherence for its present-day auditors, for example) — less, perhaps, the *how*. (Ed.)

● CANTATAS –

"AH CRUDEL NEL PIANTO MIO" (Cantata 1)

"ARMIDA ABBANDONATA" (Cantata 13)

Janet Baker (s), English Chamber O†

 LP: EMI Records ASD 2468 (1967); also as Angel 36569 &
   SME 91670 (1969)

● CANTATAS –

"CARCO SEMPRE DI GLORIA"

"SPLENDA L'ALBA IN ORIENTE"

"TU FEDEL? TU COSTANTE?"

Helen Watts (cn), English Chamber O†

ALBUM TITLE: HANDEL – THREE ITALIAN CANTATAS

 LP: Decca/L'Oiseau-Lyre SOL 60046 (1962/stereo);
   reissued as Decca Serenata 414 053-1
   (1985/stereo); *"Tu fedel?"* also on SAWO 9945
   Decca/L'Oiseau-Lyre OL 50215 (mono)

** *Penguin Stereo Record Guide,* 2nd Ed. (1977).

● CANTATAS (ETC) –

"CRUDEL TIRANNO AMOR" (CANTATA)

"PIANGERÒ LA SORTE MIA" (ARIA FROM *JULIUS CAESAR*)

"SILETE VENTI" (MOTET)

Elly Ameling (s), English Chamber O†

Cassette: 7300 019; reissued as Philips 7310 113

 LP: Philips SAL 6500 008 (1970/stereo)(US/UK); reissued
   as Philips Festivo 6570 113

● *CANTATAS (ETC) –*

LUCREZIA (cantata)

ARIAS: *ARIODANTE: "DOPO NOTTE"*

  ATALANTA: "CARE SELVE"

  HERCULES: "WHERE SHALL I FLY?"

  JOSHUA: "O HAD I JUBAL'S LYRE"

  RODELINDA: "DOVE SEI, AMATO BENE?"

  XERXES: "OMBRA MAI FÙ"

Janet Baker (ms), English Chamber O†/hpsd

ALBUM TITLE: JANET BAKER

Cassette: Philips 7300 345; also as Philips 426 450-4 (1990)

 CD: Philips Baroque Classics 426 450-2 (1990/digitally
   remastered)

LP: Philips 6500 523 (1974); also issued as Philips 6597
001, Philips 9502 097 (1984) & incl. in 4-LP set
Philips 6767 001 titled JANET BAKER • RAYMOND
LEPPARD; see also Beethoven, Gluck, Haydn,
Mozart, Schubert

*** "Even among Janet Baker's records this Handel recital marks a special con-
tribution, ranging as it does from the pure gravity of '*Ombre mai fu*' to the passionate commitment and supreme coloratura virtuosity in '*Dopo notte*' from
Ariodante. Leppard gives sparkling support, and the whole is recorded with
natural and refined balance." —Edward Greenfield, Robert Layton & Ivan
March, *Penguin Stereo Record Guide*, 2nd Ed. (1977). "Throughout these collections [the 4-LP Philips set] Dame Janet's singing is supported with excellent
skill, sensitivity, vitality and, above all, outstanding stylistic awareness by
Raymond Leppard and the English Chamber Orchestra, while Philips' recordings strike me as models of tonal fidelity, balance and natural stereo perspec-
tives. In short, this is a superlative album celebrating a singer who is, without
question, among the greatest of the age." —*Records & Recording*. Grand Prix National du Disque Lyrique, Deutscher Schallplattenpreis, Prix Mondial de Disque.

• CANTATAS (ETC) —

LUCREZIA (cantata)

ARIAS

Ann Murray, Scottish Chamber O†
LP: EMI/Angel
SEE ALSO: Mozart (arias)

• *CONCERTO A DUE CORI 1 IN B^b, HWV 332*

CONCERTO A DUE CORI 2 IN F, HWV 333

CONCERTO A DUE CORI 3 IN F, HWV 334

English Chamber O†
Cassette: Philips 7313 021; also as Philips 422 949-4 (with
organ concs)
CD: Philips Baroque Classics 422 949-2 (1989)(with organ
concs)
LP: Philips SAL 3707 (1968)(US/UK), also as Philips 802
894 LY (German); reissued as Philips Universo
6580 212; reissued as Philips Living Baroque
9502 021

**(*) *Penguin Stereo Record Guide*, 2nd Ed. (1977). 1969 Edison Award. "One of
Leppard's best Handel efforts—the horn playing is of superlative quality. So,
too, is the oboe work, while the string consort has consistent strength of
character and pliability of phrase. Leppard has the secret of Handel to such a
degree that one wonders how it ever comes about that others often make such
heavy weather of this composer. Tempo is the essence: that, and textural
balance. Handel must never be rushed but, equally, he must never plod. The
golden mean can be elusive. Here it is the norm of performances which delight
by their eager thrust and witty character." —*Records & Recording*. "This is sunny

music.... The tunes, familiar and unfamiliar alike, are given a jaunty reading by the ECO, strings and wind sounding equally happy." — *Gramophone.*

• *CONCERTO 1* IN B^b FOR OBOE, HWV 301

CONCERTO 2 IN B^b FOR OBOE, HWV 302a

CONCERTO GROSSO IN G, OP 3 Nr 3, HWV 314

SONATA A CINQUE IN B^b FOR VIOLIN, OBOE & STRINGS, HWV 288

Heinz Holliger (ob), Kenneth Sillito (vln), English Chamber O†

Cassette: Philips 7300 450; also issued as Philips 7313 113 (c.1980)

      CD: Philips Baroque Classics 426082-2 (1989/digitally remastered)(with ob conc 3, conc grosso [Alexanderfest] in C, overture in D)

      LP: Philips 6500 240 (1971); also issued as Philips Living Baroque 9502 113 (c.1980)

** "[Holliger's] playing and that of the other artists in this recording is exquisite." — Edward Greenfield, Robert Layton & Ivan March, *Penguin Stereo Record Guide,* 2nd Ed. (1977). "The curiosity in this ablum is the inclusion of the Sonata for solo violin. The mystery is solved as the opening melody unfolds — [its] basis is a melody that Handel had written for the second oboe concerto.... [A] thoroughly enjoyable disc." — *Fanfare.*

• *CONCERTO 3* IN G MINOR FOR OBOE, HWV 287

HORNPIPE IN D, HWV 356

MUSIC FOR THE ROYAL FIREWORKS: "LA PAIX",

     "LA REJOUISSANCE"

OVERTURE TO *ALCINA*

WATER MUSIC: SUITE IN G MAJOR

Heinz Holliger (ob), English Chamber O†

      CD: Philips Baroque Classics 426082-2 (1989/digitally remastered)(ob conc 3 only, with ob concs 1-2, conc grosso op 3/3, sonata a cinque in B^b, conc grosso [Alexanderfest] in C, overture in D)

      LP: Philips 6833 200 (1971)[5]; Suite in G reissued on Philips 6833 035 (with CPE Bach, JC Bach, WF Bach, Mozart, D Scarlatti)

*** *Penguin Stereo Record Guide,* 2nd Ed. (1977).

• *CONCERTO* IN F FOR ORGAN, HWV 331

CONCERTO IN D FOR ORGAN, HWV 335a

---

5   Collection also features *I Musici,* conductors Marriner, Colin Davis.

CONCERTO IN F FOR ORGAN, HWV 335b
MUSIC FOR THE ROYAL FIREWORKS
Leslie Pearson (organ, hpsd), English Chamber O†
Cassette: Philips 7300 239; also as Philips 422 949-4 (with
               concs a due cori)
     CD: Philips Baroque Classics 422 949-2 (1989)(with
               concs
               a due cori)
     LP: Philips 6500 369 (1972)
● *CONCERTI GROSSI* (6), OP 3
CONCERTO GROSSO ("ALEXANDERFEST") IN C, HWV 318
HORNPIPE IN D
OVERTURE IN B^b
OVERTURE IN D, HWV 337/338
Leslie Pearson, John Constable (hpsds), English Chamber O†
Cassette: Philips 7313 006 (German/English); also as Philips
               Baroque Classics 422 487-4
     CD: Philips Baroque Classics 422 487-2 (op 3 complete,
               Largo from conc grosso in F); also on Philips
               Baroque Classics 426 082-2 (1989/digitally
               remastered)(HWV 318, 337/338 only, with 3 ob
               concs, conc grosso op 3/3, sonata a cinque in
               B^b); overture in B^b also on PolyGram Special
               Projects (Voordeeelpas Countdown Postbank
               PolyGram Nederland BI/Philips Classic) 426
               867-2 (1990) — see also JS Bach (cantata), Grieg,
               Haydn (vln conc), Mozart (sym in D), Schubert
               (overture)
  2 LPs: Philips 6700 050 (1971); also issued as single LP
               Philips Living Baroque 9502 006 (German/
               English)
"[Includes] welcome fillers [such as] the Overture in D, which was found in
King George III's music collection and has probably not been unearthed before
in modern times.... [Recommended] for the style and skill of the performances,
which set forth the music trimly, happily, without haste, without heaviness." —
High Fidelity Records in Review 1975.
¶ Bach Orchestra of Gewandhaus†
  2 LPs: Eterna (Op 3 & Alexanderfest — plus *Concerto grosso*
               in F, Op 3 Nr 4a)

- *12 CONCERTI GROSSI, OP 6*
  Leslie Pearson (hpsd), English Chamber O†/hpsd
  Cassettes: Philips Baroque Classics 426 465-4 (1990)
     3 CDs: Philips Baroque Classics 426 465-2 (1990)(individual
  CDs numbered Philips 426 466-2 [nrs 1-4], 426
  467-2 [nrs 5-8], 426 468-2 [nrs 9-12]
     3 LPs: Philips 8 25 900-901 (1968); also as Philips 6703 003;
  reissued as Philips Living Baroque 6768 164
  (1980/stereo)(individual LPs 6542 726 [concs 1-
  4], 6542 727 [concs 5-8], 6542 728 [concs 9-
  12])(1967); also as Philips SBAL 21 (stereo)(German)(individual LPs numbered 802 766 AY [nrs
  1-4], 802 767 [nrs 5-8], 802 768 [nrs 9-12])
  "Most highly recommended", Best Records of 1967, *Audio and Record Review.*
  "The best recommendation for these works." — *Records & Recording.* "Superb ensemble [directed] with clarity and virtuosity. Very highly recommended." —
  Fanfare.

- *MESSIAH* (oratorio)
  Felicity Palmer (s), Helen Watts (cn), Ryland Davies (t), John
  Shirley-Quirk (b), English Chamber O Choir, English
  Chamber O†
  Cassette: RCA/Erato MCE 70962-70963 (stereo)
  RCA/Erato CRL3 1426 (mono)
     2 CDs: RCA/Erato/Warner 2292 45447-2 (1990)
     3 LPs: RCA/Erato STU 70921-70922-70923 (1976)
  *** "A fine, enjoyable account.... The chorus is admirably resilient and
  luminous." — Edward Greenfield, Robert Layton & Ivan March, *The Penguin
  Guide to Compact Discs and Cassettes Yearbook 1991.*
  ¶ *MESSIAH* (excerpts)
  Cassette: Erato 71137
     LP: RCA/Erato STU 71137
  *** *The Penguin Guide to Compact Discs and Cassettes Yearbook 1991.*
  ¶ *MESSIAH: ALLELUIA*
  Chorus & ECO†
  ALBUM TITLE: LE CADEAU DE LA VIE 1980
     LP: RCA/Erato 6840 066 (sampler of current RCA/Erato
  releases)

- *MUSIC FOR THE ROYAL FIREWORKS*
  WATER MUSIC (extended suite)
  Leslie Pearson (hpsd), English Chamber O†
  Cassette: Philips 420 354-4; also as 7311 047
     CD: Philips 420 354-2 (digitally remastered)
     LP: Philips (1973/stereo)(also in 9-LP set Philips 6747 036

titled HANDEL ORCHESTRAL WORKS; reissued as
Philips Sequenza 6527 047 [1980s]; *Fireworks*
reissued on Philips Universo 6580 147, with
seven excerpts from *Water Music* — see below)
*** "Broad and spectacular interpretation of the... *Fireworks Music*." — Edward
Greenfield, Robert Layton & Ivan March, *Penguin Stereo Record Guide*, 2nd Ed.
(1977). "Splendid performances and recording." — *Gramophone*. "I still consider
Leppard's readings of these familiar but demanding scores the finest available
on disc. Listen, for example, to the clarity of the part-weaving in the fast section of the *Fireworks* Overture; and mark also that the tempo for the imposing
start is just right for the essential integration with the main section." — Geoffrey Crankshaw, *Records & Recording*.

● OVERTURES TO *ADMETO, ALCINA, ESTHER, LOTARIO,*
ORLANDO, OTTONE, PARTENOPE, PORO
English Chamber O†
Cassette: Philips 422 486-4 (all plus *Ariodante, Il pastor fido*
overtures)
CD: Philips 422 486-2 (all plus *Ariodante, Il pastor fido*
overtures); PolyGram Special Products/Avéro
verzekeringen 434 419-2 (*Admeto* overture &
overtures by JC Bach, Purcell, Rameau, A. Scar-
latti; also incl. overtures by Laurens Van
Rooyen, Vivaldi cond. by Vittorio Negri, Jed
Wentz)
LP: Philips Universo 6599 053 (1971/stereo); reissued as
Philips Living Baroque 9502 079 (1982); also in
9-LP set Philips 6747 036 titled HANDEL OR-
CHESTRAL WORKS
*** "Characteristically elegant performances from Leppard, richly recorded.
The orchestral playing is gracious and polished." — Edward Greenfield, Robert
Layton & Ivan March, *Penguin Stereo Record Guide*, 2nd Ed. (1977). "Leppard is
always good in this type of program. He leads the ECO in bright, lively perfor-
mances, notable for their enthusiasm.... Warmly recommended." — *Fanfare*.

● *IL PASTOR FIDO:* OVERTURE
New Philharmonia O†/hpsd
ALBUM TITLE: 18TH CENTURY OVERTURES
Cassette: Philips 412 486-4
CD: Philips 422 486-2 (plus overtures to *Admeto,*
Alcina, Ariodante, Esther, Lotario, Orlando,
Ottone, Partenope, Poro)
LP: Philips SAL 3674 (1968)(US/UK); also as Philips 802
893 LY (German); reissued as Philips 412 406-1
SEE ALSO: Bononcini, Grétry, Méhul, Pergolesi, Rameau, Sac-
chini, D Scarlatti

- *SAMSON* (oratorio)
  Janet Baker (s), Helen Watts (ms), Robert Tear (t), John Shirley-
  Quirk (b), Benjamin Luxon (b), Norma Burrowes (s),
  Felicity Lott (s), Philip Langridge (t), Alexander Oliver (t),
  London Voices, ECO†/hpsd
  4 LPs: RCA/Erato STU 71240 (1980 – in U.K.), also issued as
            ZL 30696 (1979 – in Germany); also as RCA ARL
            4-3635 & as Musical Heritage Society MHS
            844415
  "A recording worthy of Handel's magnificently moving oratorio.... Leppard
  rightly emphasizes the [dramatic aspects of the piece]." — *Fanfare.*

- *SERSE* (orchestral excerpts)
  Cassette: Philips 422 278-4
      CD: Philips 422 278-2
  SEE ALSO: Gluck

- *WATER MUSIC* (SUITES 1-3)
  Leslie Pearson (hpsd), English Chamber O†
  Cassette: Philips 7300 060; also as Philips 412 898-4
      LP: Philips 6500 047 (1971); reissued as Philips 9502 096
            (1984); excerpts also reissued as Philips Univer-
            so 6580 147, with *Music for the Royal Fireworks* –
            see above
  "The notes [explain] that the score comprises three distinct suites. The horn
  suite (F major) was played on the first leg of the outing; the flute suite (G major)
  was table music, played during the banquet at the destination; the trumpet
  suite (D major) accompanied the return trip.... Leppard's ensemble, of course,
  uses modern instruments. Time has neither diminished its appeal nor dulled
  its fine sound.... A delightful performance from beginning to end." — *Fanfare.*

HAYDN, FRANZ JOSEPH (1732-1809)

- *ARIANNA A NAXOS* (CANTATA)
  BERENICE CHE FAI (CANTATA)
  Janet Baker (s), English Chamber O†/hpsd
  Cassette: Philips 7300 350
      LP: Philips 6500 660 (1975); also issued as Philips 6597
            002 & incl. in 4-LP set Philips 6767 001 titled
            JANET BAKER • RAYMOND LEPPARD; see also
            Beethoven, Gluck, Handel, Mozart, Schubert
  "The Haydn/Mozart disc is full of superb singing, while the inclusion of two
  important solo cantatas by Haydn – one with orchestra, the other with
  keyboard accompaniment played by Raymond Leppard on a fortepiano – lends
  it unusual musical interest." — *Records & Recording.*
  SEE ALSO: Mozart

- ARIAS (ETC) –
  ARIA DI AGATINA ("AH, CRUDEL! POI CHÉ? LO BRAMI"),
  Hob XXXI c.5
  ARIA DI ERRISENA ("CHI VIVE AMANTE"), Hob XXIV b.13
  ARIA DI GIANNINA ("LA MOGLIE QUANDO È BUONA"),
  Hob XXIV b.18
  ARIA DI LINDORA ("SON PIETOSA, SON BONINA"), Hob XXXII
  1
  ARIA DI MERLINA ("IL MEGLIO MIO CARATTERE"), Hob XXIV
  b.17
  CANTATA ("MISERI NOI! MISERA PATRIA!"), Hob XXIV a.7
  CANTILENA PRO ADVENTU ("EIN' MAGD, EIN' DIENERIN"),
  Hob XXIII d.1
  CAVATINA DI ALCINA("SONO ALCINA"), Hob XXIV b.9
  Teresa Berganza, Scottish Chamber O†
    LP: RCA/Erato NUM 75038 (1983)
- *CONCERTO* IN C FOR CELLO
  Maurice Gendron (vc), London Symphony O†
  Cassette: Philips Concert Classics 422 481-4
       CD: Philips Concert Classics 422 481-2 (post-1980;
                digitally remastered)
       LP: Philips SAL 3636 (1965/stereo)(US/UK); also as Philips
                835 358 AY (German)
  SEE ALSO: Boccherini
- *CONCERTO* IN E^b FOR TRUMPET
  Wynton Marsalis (tpt), National Philharmonic O†
  Cassette: CBS Masterworks 37846
       CD: CBS Masterworks MK 37846 (digital); also CBS
                Masterworks MK 39310 with Yo-Yo Ma/Cho-
                lian Lin coupling as for LP
       LP: CBS Masterworks IM 37846 (1983/digital); also
                released on CBS Masterworks M 39310 with
                Concerto in D for cello (Yo-Yo Ma, vc; ECO
                cond. by José-Luis Garcia) & *Concerto 1* in C for
                vln (Cho-liang Lin, vln; Minnesota O cond. by
                Neville Marriner)

"Marsalis's tone here is full, but not crude. He employs rhythmic flexibility judiciously, but without stepping too far into the improvisational freedom common to jazz. His greatest divergence from classical restraint may be in his ability to present wide dynamic range within a single melodic phrase without misshaping the line. Raymond Leppard and the National Philharmonic provide

Marsalis with a deft and light-handed accompaniment. It's no wonder this recording won a Grammy Award." — Larry Canale, ed., *Digital Audios: Guide to Compact Discs* (Bantam Books, 1986). Grammy Award, 1984 (National Academy of Recording Arts & Sciences). ***"Marsalis is splendid.... His way with Haydn is eminently stylish, as is Leppard's lively and polished accompaniment." — Edward Greenfield, Robert Layton & Ivan March, *The New Penguin Guide to Compact Discs and Cassettes* (1988).
SEE ALSO: Hummel, L Mozart

- *CONCERTO 1* IN C FOR VIOLIN, Hob VIIa, 1

- *CONCERTO 2* IN G FOR VIOLIN, Hob VIIa, 4
  Arthur Grumiaux (vln), English Chamber O† (in conc 1), New Philharmonia O† (in conc 2)

  CD: Philips 426 977-2 (1990)(with Mozart, Schubert); conc 1 also on PolyGram Special Projects (Voordeeelpas Countdown Postbank PolyGram Nederland BI/Philips Classic) 426 867-2 (1990) — see also JS Bach (cantata), Grieg, Handel (overture), Mozart (sym in D), Schubert (overture)

  LP: Philips SAL 3660 (1964, 1967)(US/UK)(with Mozart adagio, rondo; Schubert rondo), also as Philips 802 848 LY (German); conc 1 only (with JS Bach vln concs BWV 1041-1042) reissued on Philips SAL 3489 & Philips Sequenza 6527 120

- "SHE NEVER TOLD HER LOVE"
  April Cantelo (s), English Chamber O†/hpsd
  ALBUM TITLE: 18TH CENTURY SHAKESPEAREAN SONGS
  LP: Decca/L'Oiseau-Lyre OL 50205 (1961/mono)
  SEE ALSO: Arne, Chilcot, Greene, Hook, T Linley, W Linley, Smith, Weldon

- *SYMPHONY 22 ("THE PHILOSOPHER") IN E*^{b}

SYMPHONY 39

SYMPHONY 47 ("THE PALINDROME")
  English Chamber O†
  Cassette: Philips 7300 006; sym 22 reissued as Philips 7311 096 (1981)(with *Symphony 48*)
  LP: Philips SAL 3776 (1968)(US/UK); also as 839 796 LY (German); sym 22 reissued with *Symmphony 48* on Philips 6527 096 (1981/stereo)

"A brisk yet genial performance [of] one of the most delightful of Haydn's early symphonies [Symphony 22], coupled with similarly stylish performances of Haydn's rarely played Symphonies 39 and 47." — Roy Hemming, *Discovering Music (1974).*

● *SYMPHONY 26 ("LAMENTATIONE") IN D MINOR*
SYMPHONY 34 IN D MINOR
SYMPHONY 77 IN B^b
English Chamber O†/hpsd
LP: Philips SAL 6500 084 (1970/stereo)(US/UK)

● *SYMPHONY 48 ("MARIA THERESA") IN C*
SYMPHONY 70 IN D
English Chamber O†
Cassette: Philips 7311 096 (1981)(sym 48 only, with
                Symphony 22)
LP: Philips 6500 194 (1971); sym 48 reissued with
                Symphony 22 on Philips 6527 096 (1981/stereo)

● *SYMPHONY 94 ("SURPRISE") IN G*
SYMPHONY 98 IN B-FLAT
Scottish Chamber O†
Cassette: RCA/Erato MCE 75151
LP: RCA/Erato NUM 75151 (1985)

● *SYMPHONY 94 ("SURPRISE") IN G*
SYMPHONY 103 ("DRUM ROLL") IN E-FLAT
London Philharmonic O†
LP: EMI/Classics for Pleasure CFP 40269 (1977/stereo)
                (W.D. & H.O. Wills Master Series); also issued
                as Musical Heritage Society MHS 4599

● *SYMPHONY 101 ("CLOCK") IN D*
SYMPHONY 102 IN B-FLAT
SYMPHONY 103 ("DRUM ROLL") IN E-FLAT
SYMPHONY 104 ("LONDON") IN D
Scottish Chamber O†
Cassette: RCA/Erato MCE 751412
CD: RCA/Erato ECD 88079 (digital)(Syms 101, 104)
2 LPs: RCA/Erato NUM 751412 (1985/digital)(individual LPs
                numbered NUM 75142, NUM 75143); also as 2292-
                45568-2

**(*) "These artists convey a pleasure in what they are doing.... They bring not
only geniality and high spirits to these symphonies [Nrs. 101, 104], but also
grace and considerable poetic feeling. The recording is agreeably natural and
as fresh and warm as the performances themselves. A very useful chamber-
sized alternative to the larger orchestras favored in this repertoire by DG,
Decca and Philips." —Edward Greenfield, Robert Layton & Ivan March, *The
New Guide to Compact Discs and Cassettes* (1988).

HAYDN, MICHAEL (1737-1806)

• *CONCERTO* FOR TRUMPET (adapt/arr by RL)
Wynton Marsalis (tpt), English Chamber O†
ALBUM TITLE: BAROQUE MUSIC FOR TRUMPETS
Cassette: CBS MYT 38482
    CD: CBS/Sony MK 42478
    LP: CBS/Sony MT 42478
SEE ALSO: Biber, Pachelbel, Telemann, Vivaldi

HOOK, JAMES (1746-1827)

• "THE WILLOW SONG"
April Cantelo (s), English Chamber O†/hpsd
ALBUM TITLE: 18TH CENTURY SHAKESPEAREAN SONGS
    LP: Decca/L'Oiseau-Lyre OL 50205 (1961/mono)
SEE ALSO: Arne, Chilcot, Greene, Haydn, T Linley, W Linley,
Smith, Weldon

HUMMEL, JOHANN NEPOMUK (1778-1837)

• *CONCERTO* IN E^b FOR TRUMPET
Wynton Marsalis, National Philharmonic O†
Cassette: CBS Masterworks
    CD: CBS Masterworks MK 37846
    LP: CBS Masterworks IM 37846 (1983/digital)
Grammy Award, 1985 (National Academy of Recording Arts & Sciences).
*** Edward Greenfield, Robert Layton & Ivan March, *The New Penguin Guide
to Compact Discs and Cassettes* (1988).
SEE ALSO: Haydn, L Mozart

• *ADAGIO—THEME AND VARIATIONS* IN F FOR OBOE
Heinz Holliger (ob), English Chamber O†
Cassette: Philips 412 354-4
    CD: Philips 426 972-2 (1990)(with Fiala; also incl. works
         by Bellini, Mollique, Moscheles, Rietz cond. by
         Eliahu Inbal)
    LP: Philips 839 756 LY (German) (1969/stereo); also as
         Philips 426 972-1
SEE ALSO: JC Bach, Fiala

IBERT, JACQUES (1890-1962)

• *CONCERTO* 2 FOR FLUTE
Peter-Lukas Graf (fl), English Chamber O†
Cassette: Claves C 501

CD: Claves CD 50-501
LP: Claves Cla P 501 (with Devienne)
SEE ALSO: Devienne, Saint-Saëns

LANIER, NICHOLAS (1586-1666)
- "THOUGH I AM YOUNG"
  Singers & insts cond. by RL, others, featuring April Cantelo (s),
  Helen Watts (cn), Christopher Keyte (b)
  ALBUM TITLE: MUSIC OF THE COURT HOMES AND CITIES OF
  ENGLAND, Vol 3 – MUSIC AT WHITEHALL PALACE AND WILTON
  HOUSE
  LP: EMI/HMV HQS 1146 (1968/stereo)
  SEE ALSO: Morley

LASSUS (LASSO), ORLANDUS (ROLAND DE) (1532-1594)
- SELECTED MADRIGALS ETC
  Patricia Clark (s), Eileen Poulter (s), Mary Thomas (s),
  Rosemary Phillips (cn), Wilfred Brown (t), Gerald English
  (t), Christopher Keyte (b), Dolmetsch Consort†
  ALBUM TITLE: MUSIC OF SHAKESPEARE'S TIME, VOL 2
  LP: EMI/HMV CLP 1634 (1963)
  SEE ALSO: Dowland, Morley, Tomkins, Weelkes

LECLAIR, JEAN-MARIE (1697-1764)
- *SCYLLA AND GLAUCUS* (SUITE)
  English Chamber O†/hpsd
  LP: Decca/L'Oiseau Lyre SOL 303 (1968/stereo)
  Decca/L'Oiseau Lyre OL 303 (mono)
  SEE ALSO: Destouches

LEPPARD, RAYMOND (b. 1927)
- *ALFRED THE GREAT* (FILM SCORE)
  Orig. soundtrack†
  LP: MGM Records MGMCS 8112 (1969/stereo)
- *THE HOTEL NEW HAMPSHIRE* (FILM SCORE)
  Music by Jacques Offenbach arr. by RL
  London Philharmonic O (orig. soundtrack)†
  LP: EMI/Capitol SV 12337 (1984)
- *LORD OF THE FLIES* (THEMES)
  Orig. soundtrack† & Elliot Lawrence orch

LP: AVA Records/MGM A/AS-30 (with selections from
film scores by Elmer Bernstein, others)

LINLEY (JR), THOMAS (1756-1778)
● "O BID YOUR FAITHFUL ARIEL FLY"
April Cantelo (s), English Chamber O†/hpsd
ALBUM TITLE: 18TH CENTURY SHAKESPEAREAN SONGS
    LP: Decca/L'Oiseau-Lyre OL 50205 (1961/mono)
SEE ALSO: Arne, Chilcot, Greene, Haydn, Hook, W Linley,
Smith, Weldon

LINLEY, WILLIAM (1771-1835)
● "NOW THE HUNGRY LION ROARS"
April Cantelo (s), English Chamber O†/hpsd
ALBUM TITLE: 18TH CENTURY SHAKESPEAREAN SONGS
    LP: Decca/L'Oiseau-Lyre OL 50205 (1961/mono)
SEE ALSO: Arne, Chilcot, Greene, Haydn, Hook, T Linley,
Smith, Weldon

LOCATELLI, PIETRO ANTONIO (1695-1764)
● *INTRODUTTIONE TEATRALE NR. 5*
New Philharmonia O†
ALBUM TITLE: 18TH CENTURY OVERTURES, VOL. II
    LP: Philips SAL 3760 (1969)(US/UK); also as Philips 802
901 LY (German)
SEE ALSO: JC Bach, Boyce, Cimarosa, Mozart, Rameau,
A Scarlatti

LOTTER (ANTONIO LOTTI)(1667-1740)
● *MOTO PERPETUO*
Scottish Chamber O†
ALBUM TITLE: MOTO PERPETUO/MOUVEMENTS PERPÉTUELS
Cassette: RCA/Erato MCE 71483
    LP: RCA/Erato STU 71483; also as 2292-45676-2
SEE ALSO: Albinoni, Arensky, JS Bach, Brahms, Couperin,
Paganini, Paradies, Rimsky-Korsakov, Strauss, Weber

LULLY, JEAN BAPTISTE (1632-1687)
● ARIAS —
ALCESTE: "IL FAUT PASSER TÔT OU TARD

CADMUS ET HERMIONE: "BELLE HERMIONE"
PERSÉE: "JE NE PUIS EN VOTRE MALHEUR"
Gérard Souzay (bar), English Chamber O†/hpsd
ALBUM TITLE: BAROQUE OPERA ARIAS
    LP: Philips 835 215AY (stereo)
            Philips A02337L (mono)
1965 Grand Prix Jacques Rouché, Académie du Disque Français
SEE ALSO: Handel, Rameau

- *PIÈCES DE SYMPHONIE* (from *Acis et Galathée, Amadis, Atys, Bellérophon, Persée, Phéton, Thésée*)
  English Chamber O†/hpsd
      LP: Decca/L'Oiseau SOL 301 (1968/stereo)
            Decca/L'Oiseau Lyre OL 301 (mono)

MACONCHY, ELIZABETH (b.1907)

- *ARIADNE*
  Heather Harper (s), English Chamber O†
      LP: Decca/L'Oiseau-Lyre SOL 331 (1972/stereo)
            Decca/L'Oiseau-Lyre OL 331 (mono)
  SEE ALSO: Walton

MARCELLO, ALESSANDRO (1669-1747)

- *OBOE CONCERTO: SLOW MOVEMENT*
  English Chamber O†
  ALBUM TITLE: ALLA BAROCCA
      LP: CBS IM 37215 (1982)
  SEE ALSO: JS Bach, Charpentier, Gluck, Handel, Pachelbel, Vivaldi

MATTHEWS, DAVID (b.20th cent)

- *ROMANZA* FOR CELLO & SMALL ORCHESTRA, OP 49
  Mstislav Rostropovich (vc), English Chamber O†
  ALBUM TITLE: A BIRTHDAY CONCERT FOR MY GRANDMOTHER.
  HRH the Prince of Wales Celebration Concert to Mark the 90th Birthday of HM Queen Elizabeth the Queen Mother. Recorded live in the Ballroom, Buckingham Palace, 2 Aug 1990.
      CD: EMI/Angel CDC 7 54164 2 (1990)
  SEE ALSO: Anon, Coates, Doyle, Elgar, Gowers, Strauss

MÉHUL, ÉTIENNE-NICOLAS (1763-1817)

● *LA CHASSE DU JEUNE HENRI:* OVERTURE
New Philharmonia O†/hpsd
ALBUM TITLE: 18TH CENTURY OVERTURES
Cassette: Philips 412 406-4
LP: Philips SAL 3674 (1968)(US/UK); also as Philips 802
893 LY (German); reissued as Philips 412 406-1
SEE ALSO: Bononcini, Grétry, Handel, Mozart, Pergolesi,
Rameau, Sacchini, D Scarlatti

MENDELSSOHN, FELIX (1809-1847)

● *A MIDSUMMER NIGHT'S DREAM,* OPP 21 & 61
(OVERTURE & INCIDENTAL MUSIC)
Elizabeth Gale, Ann Murray, Ensemble Vocal Féminin, London
Philharmonic O†
Cassette: RCA/Erato MCE 71090
LP: RCA/Erato STU 71090 (1977)(France/UK)

● *SYMPHONY 4 ("ITALIAN") IN A, OP 90*

SYMPHONY 5 ("REFORMATION") IN D MINOR, OP 107
English Chamber O†
Cassette: RCA Records ARK 1-2632; 8-track as ARS 1-2632
LP: RCA/Erato EPR 15533; also as STU 71064 (1977)
(France/UK); RCA Records ARL 1-2632
(1977)(US)

MERBECKE, JOHN (d. 1585?)

● "A VIRGIN AND A MOTHER"
Singers & insts cond. by RL, others, featuring April Cantelo (s),
Jeannette Sinclair (s), Helen Watts (cn), Gerald English (t),
John Noble (bar), Christopher Keyte (b)
ALBUM TITLE: MUSIC OF THE COURT HOMES AND CITIES OF
ENGLAND, Vol 2–MUSIC AT HAMPTON COURT
LP: EMI/HMV HQS 1141 (1968)
SEE ALSO: Purcell

MOLTER, JOHANN MELCHIOR (d. 1765)

● *CONCERTO 2* FOR TRUMPET & STRINGS, MWV IV.13
Wynton Marsalis (tpt), English Chamber O†
Cassette: CBS Masterworks
CD: CBS Masterworks MK 29061 (digital)

LP: CBS Masterworks IM 39061 (1984/digital)
SEE ALSO: Fasch, Handel, Purcell, Torelli

MONTEVERDI, CLAUDIO (1567-1643)

● AIRS —

L'INCORONAZIONE DI POPPEA:
ARIA DI OTTAVIA ("ADDIO ROMA")
LAMENTO DI OTTAVIA ("DISPREZZATA REGINA")
"OHIMÒ CH'IO CADO"
SCHERZI MUSICALI (1632):*"ET Ò PUR DUNQUE VERO"*
Frederica von Stade (ms), Scottish Chamber O†
Cassette: RCA/Erato MCE 75183
   CD: RCA/Erato ECD 88100 (digital)
   LP: RCA/Erato NUM 75183 (1985)
"This is an opulently realized and splendly recorded disc of pieces that are like-
ly to be unfamiliar to many vocal collectors — and could form a welcome intro-
duction to early opera. There is a great variety of construction and rhythm, and
the music is notable for its beauty of line as well as for the imaginative scoring
of Raymond Leppard's realizations.
   "Frederica von Stade is a nearly ideal interpreter for this music, her light,
warm mezzo easily accomplishes the technical demands, and she sings with
involvement, projecting a real *joie de chanter.* Highly recommended."— Larry
Canale, ed., *Digital Audios: Guide to Compact Discs* (Bantam Books, 1986).
   SEE ALSO: Cavalli

● AIRS —

L'INCORONAZIONE DI POPPEA:
ARIA DI OTTAVIA ("ADDIO ROMA")
LAMENTO DI OTTAVIA ("DISPREZZATA REGINA")
ARIADNE'S LAMENT ("LASCIATEMI MORIRE")
Janet Baker, English Chamber O†
ALBUM TITLE: MUSIC OF MONTEVERDI AND THE SCARLATTIS
   LP: EMI ASD 2615 (1970/stereo)
   SEE ALSO: A Scarlatti, D Scarlatti

● *IL BALLO DELLE INGRATE*

IL COMBATTIMENTO DI TANCREDI E CLORINDA
Heather Harper (s), Lillian Watson (s), Anne Howells (s), John
   Wakefield (t), Luigi Alva, Stafford Dean (b), Members of
   Ambrosian Singers, English Chamber O†/hpsd
Cassette: Philips Baroque Classics 426451-4 (1990/digital)
   CD: Philips Baroque Classics 426 451-2 (1990/dig remstd)
   LP: Philips 6500 457 (1971/stereo)

● MADRIGALS –

"*CHIOME D'ORO*"

"*O SIA TRANQUILLO*"

"*QUEL SGUARDO*"

"*SE VITTORIE SI BELLE*"

"*ZEFIRO TORNO*"

Heather Harper (s), Hugues Cuénod (t), Gerald English (t), Bath Festival Ens†/hpsd

ALBUM TITLE: ITALIAN BAROQUE MUSIC

   LP: EMI/HMV Records HQS 1086 (1967/stereo)
   EMI/HMV HQM 1086 (mono)(HMV Baroque
   Library 22)

   SEE ALSO: Cavalli

● MADRIGALS –

"*A QUEST' OLMO*"

"*AL LUME DELLE STELLE*"

"*COR MIO MENTRE VI MIRO*"

INTRODUCTION & BALLO FOR 5 VOICES & 2 VIOLINS

"*IO MI SON GIOVINETTA*"

LAMENTO D'ARIANNA"

"*OHIMÈ! SE TANTO AMATE*"

April Cantelo, Eileen Poulter, Helen Watts, Gerald English, Robert Tear, Christopher Keyte, English Chamber O†

   LP: EMI/HMV Records HQS 1102 (1967/stereo)(HMV
   Baroque Library 25)

● MADRIGALS (ETC) –

"*BEL PASTOR*"

"*DELLA BELLEZZA LE DOVUTE LODI*" *(BALLETTO)*

"*DOLCI MIEI SOSPIRI*"

"*FUGGE IL VERNO DEI DOLORI*"

"*GIRA IL NEMICO INSIDIOSO*"

LAMENTO DELLA NINFA

"*LIDIA SPINA DEL MIO CORE*"

"*NON COSI TOSTO IO MIRO*"

"*O RESETTA CHE ROSETTA*"

"*OHIMÈ CH'IO CADO*"

"LA PASTORELLA MIA SPIETATA"
"SI DOLCI È IL TORMENTO"
Ilse Wolf (s), Robert Tear (t), Gerald English (t), Christopher
Keyte (b), English Chamber O†
ALBUM TITLE: MUSIC BY MONTEVERDI
LP: Decca/L'Oiseau Lyre SOL 299 (1967/stereo)
Decca/L'Oiseau Lyre OL 299 (mono)
"A rare experience, and the highest praise is due to Raymond Leppard, his per-
formers, the sound engineers, and of course to L'Oiseau Lyre."—*The
Gramophone.*
¶ Reissued as GLORIES OF VENICE: MUSIC BY MONTEVERDI
Cassette: Pickwick International/Contour Red Label CCT 7534
LP: Pickwick International/Contour Red Label CC 7534
(1981/stereo)

● *MADRIGALS:* BOOKS 3 & 4 FOR 5 VOICES
Sheila Armstrong, Wendy Eathorne, Lillian Watson (s), Alfreda
Hodgson (ms), Anne Collins, Helen Watts (cn), Bernard
Dickerson, Gerald English, Ian Partridge, Robert Tear (t),
Stafford Dean, Christopher Keyte (b), Glyndebourne
Opera Chorus†
3 LPs: Philips 6703 035 (1971; individual LPs numbered
6500 338, 6500 339, 6500 340); Book 3 only reis-
sued as Philips Living Baroque 9502 008 (1979);
Book 4 only reissued as Philips Living Baroque
9502 024 (1979)
Grammy Nomination, 1974 (National Academy of Recording Arts & Sciences).
"Philips' new release is an event of major importance and cause of rejoicing.
[It] offers a rich treasury of superb music and a fascinating glimpse into the
composer's life."—*High Fidelity Records in Review 1975.* "The sound and pressing are ravishing."—*Fanfare.*

● *MADRIGALS:* BOOK 7
Sheila Armstrong, Norma Burrowes (s), Sandra Browne,
Patricia Kern (ms), Anne Collins, Alfreda Hodgson (cn),
Ryland Davies, Alexander Oliver (t), Benjamin Luxon
(bar), Robert Lloyd (b), John Alldis Choir, English Chamber O†/hpsd
3 LPs: Philips 6747 416 (1977; individual LPs numbered
6598 508, 6598 509, 6598 510)
"A virtual compendium of the new music of its time [1619].... There is much to
enjoy and treasure in this collection."—*High Fidelity Records in Review 1980.*

● *MADRIGALS:* BOOKS 8 (*"MADRIGALI GUERRIERI ET
AMOROSI"*), 9, 10 & SUPPLEMENT
Sheila Armstrong, Angela Bostock, Yvonne Fuller, Heather

Harper, Anne Howells, Lillian Watson (s), Alfred
Hodgson (ms), Anne Collins, Helen Watts (cn), Luigi Alva,
Ryland Davies, Bernard Dickerson, Alexander Oliver,
Robert Tear, John Wakefield (t), Stafford Dean, Clifford
Grant (b), members, Glyndebourne Chorus & Ambrosian
Singers, English Chamber O†/hpsd
  CD: Philips Classics 432 503-2 (Book 8 only)(1992/digitally
     remastered)
 5 LPs: Philips 6799 006 (1971)(individual
     LPs numbered 6500 197, 6500 198, 6500 199,
     6500 200, 6500 201); Book 8 only reissued as 3-
     LP set Philips 6768 175 — from which *Madrigals*
     of Love (Madrigali amorosi) further reissued as
     Philips 6500 864 and Madrigals of War (Madrigali
     guerrieri) reissued as Philips 6500 663
Grammy Nomination, 1973 (National Academy of Recording Arts & Sciences).
"[A] superb [release]." — *High Fidelity Records in Review 1973.*

- *IL RITORNO D'ULISSE IN PATRIA* (opera)
Frederica von Stade (Penelope), Ann Murray, Richard Stilwell
(Ulisse), Richard Lewis, Keith Lewis, Ugo Trama, Glyn-
debourne Festival Chorus, London Philharmonic O†
 3 LPs: Columbia M3 35910 (1979) (individual LPs numbered
    36554, 36555, 36566); also as CBS set 79332
Grammy Nomination, 1982 (National Academy of Recording Arts & Sciences).
"Frederica von Stade and Richard Stilwell hold an informal world copyright on
Penelope and Ulysses for the opulent sensitivity with which they invest their
parts." — Ethan Mordden, *A Guide to Opera Recordings* (Oxford University Press,
1987). "The whole production is on a high level." — *Fanfare.*

- *"SI CH'IO VORREI MORIRE" (MADRIGAL)*
Cambridge Univ Madrigal Soc†
ALBUM TITLE: IN PRIDE OF MAY AND OTHER MADRIGALS
  LP: His Master's Voice HMV 7EP7114 (mono)
SEE ALSO: Farmer, Weelkes

MORLEY, THOMAS (1557-1603)
- "DO YOU NOT KNOW?"
Singers & insts cond. by RL, others, featuring April Cantelo (s),
Helen Watts (cn), Christopher Keyte (b)
ALBUM TITLE: MUSIC OF THE COURT HOMES AND CITIES OF
  ENGLAND, Vol 3 — MUSIC AT WHITEHALL PALACE AND WILTON
  HOUSE
  LP: EMI/HMV HQS 1146 (1968/stereo)
SEE ALSO: Lanier

● MADRIGALS ETC
Patricia Clark (s), Eileen Poulter (s), Mary Thomas (s),
Rosemary Phillips (cn), Wilfred Brown (t), Gerald English
(t), Christopher Keyte (b), Dolmetsch Consort†
ALBUM TITLE: MUSIC OF SHAKESPEARE'S TIME, VOL 2
LP: EMI/HMV CLP 1634 (1963)
SEE ALSO: Dowland, Lassus, Tomkins, Weelkes

MOZART, LEOPOLD (1719-1787)
● *CONCERTO* IN D FOR TRUMPET
Wynton Marsalis, National Philharmonic O†
Cassette: CBS Masterworks
CD: CBS Masterworks MK 37846 (digital)
LP: CBS Masterworks IM 37846 (1983/digital)
Grammy Award, 1984 (National Academy of Recording Arts & Sciences).
SEE ALSO: Haydn, Hummel

MOZART, WOLFGANG AMADEUS (1756-1791)
● *ADAGIO* IN E FOR VIOLIN, K 261
RONDO IN C, K 373
Arthur Grumiaux, New Philharmonia O†
Cassette: Philips 426 977-4 (1990)
CD: Philips 426 977-2 (1990)
LP: Philips SAL 3660 (1967)(US/UK); also as Philips 802
848 LY (German)
*** "These two Mozart movements are far from slight; the *Adagio* is really love-

ly on Arthur Grumiaux's bow, and the *Rondo* sparkles. Excellent, stylish accompaniments." — Edward Greenfield, Robert Layton & Ivan March, *The Penguin Guide to Compact Discs and Cassettes Yearbook 1991.*
SEE ALSO: Haydn (vln concs), Schubert (rondo)

● ARIAS (ETC) —
*"A QUESTO SENO DEH VIENI — OR CHE IL CIELO A ME
TI RENDE"* (recit & aria), KV 374
*"BASTA, VINCESTI — AH, NON LASCIARMI, NÒ, BELL'IDOL
MIO"* (recit & aria), KV 486A
"EXSULTATE, JUBILATE" (MOTET), KV 165
LITANIAE, KV 243: "DULCISSIMUM CONVIVIUM"
*VESPERAE SOLENNES DE DOMINICA, KV 321: "LAUDATE
DOMINUM"*
"VOI AVETE UN COR FEDELE" (aria), KV 217
Elly Ameling (s), English Chamber O†
Cassette: Philips 7300 018; also as Philips 416 866-4
     CD: Philips Concert Classics 426 072-2 (1989)
     LP: Philips SAL 6500 006 (1979)(US/UK); also as Philips
          416 866-1

● ARIAS —
"ABENDEMPFINDUNG"
LA CLEMENZA DI TITO: "PARTO! PARTO, MA TU BEN MIO"
"DAS VEILCHEN"
Janet Baker (s), English Chamber O†/hpsd
Cassette: Philips 7300 350; also as Philips 7310 829
     LP: Philips 6500 660 (1975); also issued as Philips 6570
          829 & Philips 6597 002 & & incl. in 4-LP set
          Philips 6767 001 titled JANET BAKER ● RAYMOND
          LEPPARD; see also Beethoven, Gluck, Handel,
          Haydn, Schubert
"Leppard's support on this disc, as conductor and accompanist on the for-
tepiano, is splendid." — *Gramophone.* "Mozart's gentle and ineffable songs
'*Abendempfindung*' and '*Das Veilchen*' [are] two gems of the song literature....
One is entirely absorbed in sensuous and aesthetic pleasure.... Fine and warm-
ly recommended disc." — *High Fidelity Records in Review 1976.*
SEE ALSO: Haydn

● ARIAS (ETC) —
*ARIA DI MADAMA LUCILLA ("CHI SÀ, CHI SÀ, QUAL SIA"),
KV 582*
*ARIA DI MADAMA LUCILLA ("VADO, MA DOVE? O DEI!"),
KV 583*

LA CLEMENZA DI TITO, KV 621: *ARIA DI SESTO ("PARTO, PARTO, MA TU BEN MIO")*

"EXSULTATE, JUBILATE" (MOTET), KV 165

IDOMENEO: RECITATIVO & RONDO DI IDAMANTE ("CH'IO MI SCORDI DI TE? — NON TEMER, AMATO BENE"), KV 505

LE NOZZE DI FIGARO: ARIETTA DI SUSANNA ("UN MOTO DI GIOIA MI SENTO"), KV 579; *RONDO DI SUSANNA ("AL DESIO DI CHI T'ADORA")*, KV 577

Janet Baker (s), Scottish Chamber O†

Cassette: RCA/Erato MCE 75176
     CD: RCA/Erato ECD 88090
     LP: RCA/Erato NUM 75176 (1985/digital)

"These concert arias originated in several ways. KV 505 was set to a text from *Idomeneo;* the two Susanna arias were written to be used in *Le nozze di Figaro* by the soprano who succeeded Nancy Storace in 1789; the Madama Lucilla arias were written for Louise Villeneuve to be inserted in an opera by Martin y Soler. Janet Baker sings them as if Mozart had shaped them to her voice, as he set out to do for the singers he had in mind in the first place. The motet (*'Exsultate, jubilate'*) has been done more recklessly, ornamented with more abandon, but Baker brings maturity of expression to make up for the freedom a younger singer might enjoy. Leppard supports the singer with proper tempos from a fine chamber group." — J. F. Weber, *Fanfare.*

- ARIAS

Ann Murray, Scottish Chamber O†
     LP: EMI/Angel
SEE ALSO: Handel (cantatas etc)

- *BASTIEN UND BASTIENNE*

ARIAS —

"GIUNSE ALFIN IL MOMENTO — DEH VIENI, NON TARDAR" FOR SOPRANO (recit. & aria from *Le nozze di Figaro*)

"MENTRE TI LASCIO, OH FIGLIA" FOR BASS, K 513

"MISERO! O SOGNO — AURA, CHE INTORNO SPIRI" FOR TENOR, K 431/425B (recit. & aria)

"UN MOTO DI GIOIA MI SENTO NEL PETTO" FOR SOPRANO, K 579

Edita Gruberová (s), Vinson Cole (t), László Polgar (b), Franz Liszt CO†

Cassette: SONY 40-45855 (1990)
     CD: SONY Classical SK 45 855 (1990/digital)

*** "Leppard conducts a near-ideal performance of the eleven-year-old Mozart's charming one-acter, very well recorded. Edita Gruverová is delectably fresh and vivacious as the heroine, Vinson Cole is a sensitive and clear-voiced Bastien and László Polgar is full of fun in the buffo role of Colas. The dialogue is excellently directed, and the Liszt Chamber Orchestra of Budapest plays with dazzling precision, bringing wit to the opening with its anticipation of Beethoven's *Eroica*." — Edward Greenfield, Robert Layton & Ivan March, *The Penguin Guide to Compact Discs and Cassettes Yearbook 1991.*

● *CONCERTO* IN A FOR CLARINET, K. 622
John McCaw (cl), New Philharmonia O†
    LP: Unicorn UNS 239 (1971/stereo)
SEE ALSO: Nielsen

● *CONCERTO* IN A FOR CLARINET, K. 622

CONCERTO IN C FOR FLUTE & HARP, K. 299
Emma Johnson (cl), William Bennett (fl), Osian Ellis (hp),
   English Chamber O†
Cassette: ASV ZC DCA 532
    LP: ASV DCA 532 (1985/digital)
*** "Emma Johnson, the BBC's Young Musician of the Year in 1984, plays [the clarinet concerto] magically... Leppard and the ECO are in bouncing form, as they are too for the flute and harp concerto... the last part of the finale sends Mozart bubbling up to heaven. First-rate recording." — Edward Greenfield, Robert Layton & Ivan March, *The New Penguin Guide to Compact CDs and Cassettes* (1988).

● *CONCERT0 1* IN G FOR FLUTE, K 313

CONCERTO 2 IN D FOR FLUTE, K 314

ANDANTE IN C FOR FLUTE, K 315

RONDO IN C FOR FLUTE, K 273

RONDO IN D FOR FLUTE, K Anh 184
  ¶ Richard Adeney (fl), English Chamber O†
    LP: Classics for Pleasure CFP 40072 (Concertos 1, 2,
          Andante)(1974/stereo)
  ¶ Peter-Lukas Graf (fl), English Chamber O†
    CD: Claves CD 50-8505 (Concertos 1, 2, Andante,
          Rondo K Anh 184)(1986/digital)
    LP: Claves D 8505 (1986/digital)
  ¶ Susan Milan (fl), English Chamber O†
    CD: Chandos CHAN-8613 (Concertos 1, 2,
          Andante, Rondo K 273)(1988/digital)
    LP: Chandos ABRD 1301 (1988/digital)
  ¶ Ransom Wilson (fl), London Symphony O†
    CD: EMI/Angel CDC 7 49099 2 (Concertos 1, 2, Andante,
          Rondo K Anh 184)(1989/digital)

● *CONCERTO 1* IN B-FLAT FOR VIOLIN, K 207

CONCERTO 4 IN D FOR VIOLIN, K 218

RONDO CONCERTANTE FOR VIOLIN, K. 261A (269)

Cho-Liang Lin (vln), English Chamber O† (all cadenzas by RL)
Cassette: CBS/Sony MT 44503 (digital)
    CD: CBS/Sony MK 44503 (digital)
    LP: CBS M44503 (1987/digital)

• *CONCERTO 2 IN D FOR VIOLIN, K 211*

CONCERTO 7 IN D FOR VIOLIN, K 271A (spurious)

RONDO IN C FOR VIOLIN, K 373
Cho-Liang Lin (vln), English Chamber O†
Cassette: CBS/Sony ST 40-44913 (1990/digital)
    CD: CBS/Sony SK 44913 (1990/digital)
    LP: CBS M44913 (1987/digital)
"Sweet, elegant playing, beautifully supported by Leppard." — Edward Greenfield, Robert Layton & Ivan March, *The Penguin Guide to Compact Discs and Cassettes Yearbook 1991.*

• *CONCERTO 3 IN G FOR VIOLIN, K 216*

CONCERTO 5 IN A FOR VIOLIN, K 219

ADAGIO IN E FOR VIOLIN, K 261
Cho-Liang Lin (vln), English Chamber O†
Cassette: CBS/Sony MT 42364 (digital)
    CD: CBS/Sony MK 42364 (digital)
    LP: CBS M42364 (1987/digital)
*** "There is an element of youthful lightness running through [Lin's] performances of both concertos, though there is no lack of bite and point either.... Leppard and the ECO are the most responsive of partners, and the recording is first rate." — Edward Greenfield, Robert Layton & Ivan March, *The New Penguin Guide to Compact CDs and Cassettes* (1988). "Best Recordings of the Month / Leppard's contributions — in addition to conducting, he composed cadenzas for both the concertos and the Adagio, and he also provided the annotation — bespeak an unusual level of involvement, which is radiantly apparent in the performances themselves." — Richard Freed, *Stereo Review.*

• *LA FINTA GIARDINIERA,* K 196: OVERTURE (aka *Symphony* in D, comprising K 196 [movements 1, 2] & *Allegro,* K 121 [movement 3])
New Philharmonia O†
ALBUM TITLE: 18TH CENTURY OVERTURES, VOL. II
    LP: Philips SAL 3760 (1969)(US/UK); also as Philips 802 901 LY (German); reissued on Philips 6833 035 (with CPE Bach, JC Bach, WF Bach, Handel, Mozart, D Scarlatti)
SEE ALSO: JC Bach, Boyce, Cimarosa, Locatelli, Mozart, Rameau, A Scarlatti

- *MASS* IN C MINOR, K 427
  Ileana Cotrubas (s), Kiri te Kanawa (s), Werner Krenn (t), Hans
  Sotin (b), John Aldis Choir, New Philharmonia O†
  CD: EMI HMV C 7 47385-2; also as Angel/EMI 4AM-34710,
        CMG8-83807
  LP: EMI ASD 2959 (1974/stereo); also issued as EMI 29
        0277 1 (1985/digitally remastered)
  **(*) "The partnership of Ileana Cotrubas and Kiri te Kanawa is radiantly
  beautiful. Fine, full, clear recording."—Edward Greenfield, Robert Layton &
  Ivan March, *The New Penguin Guide to Compact Discs and Cassettes* (1988).

- *SERENADE ("EINE KLEINE NACHTMUSIK") IN G, K 525*

  6 DEUTSCHE TÄNZE, K 571

  LES PETITS RIENS, K 299B (BALLET MUSIC)
  Scottish Chamber O†
  Cassette: RCA/Erato MCE 75091
  CD: RCA/Erato ECD 88014
  LP: RCA/Erato NUM 75091 (1984)
  "A spirited and stylish performance. Recommended CD and LP."—Roy Hem-
  ming, *Discovering Great Music* (Newmarket Press, 1988). "An absolutely delight-
  ful release."—*Fanfare.*

- *SINFONIA CONCERTANTE* IN E^b, K 364

  CONCERTONE IN C, K 190
  Cho-Liang Lin (vln), Jaimes Laredo (vla in K 364, vln in K 190),
  English Chamber O†
  CD: CBS/Sony Classical SK 47693 (1992/digital)
  "Cho-Liang Lin's survey of the Mozart violin concertos with Raymond Lep-
  pard conducting has been an unfailing source of pleasure since its first install-
  ment, and this final one is a true capstone, enhanced by the participation of
  Jaime Laredo."—Richard Freed, *Stereo Review.*

- *SYMPHONY 25* IN G MINOR, K 183

  SYMPHONY 40 IN G MINOR, K 550
  Liszt O†
  CD: CBS/Sony (1993)

NIELSEN, CARL (1865-1931)
- *CONCERTO* FOR CLARINET, OP. 57
  John McCaw (cl), New Philharmonia O†
  LP: Unicorn UNS 239 (1971/stereo)
  SEE ALSO: Mozart

PACHELBEL, JOHANN (1653-1706)

- *CANON* (ed. by RL)
  English Chamber O†
  ALBUM TITLE: ALLA BAROCCA
  LP: CBS IM 37215 (1982)
  SEE ALSO: JS Bach, Charpentier, Gluck, Handel, Marcello,
  Vivaldi
- *CANON* FOR 3 TRUMPETS (adapt/arr by RL)
  Wynton Marsalis (tpts), English Chamber O†
  ALBUM TITLE: BAROQUE MUSIC FOR TRUMPETS
  Cassette: CBS MYT 38482
  CD: CBS/Sony MK 42478
  LP: CBS/Sony MT 42478
  SEE ALSO: Biber, M Haydn, Telemann, Vivaldi

PAGANINI, NICCOLÒ (1782-1840)

- *MOTO PERPETUO*
  Scottish Chamber O†
  ALBUM TITLE: MOTO PERPETUO/MOUVEMENTS PERPÉTUELS
  Cassette: RCA/Erato MCE 71483
  LP: RCA/Erato STU 71483; also as 2292-45676-2
  SEE ALSO: Albinoni, Arensky, JS Bach, Brahms, Couperin,
  Lotter, Paradies, Rimsky-Korsakov, Strauss, Weber

PARADIES, PIETRO DOMENICO (1707-1791)

- *TOCATA*
  Scottish Chamber O†
  ALBUM TITLE: MOTO PERPETUO/MOUVEMENTS PERPÉTUELS
  Cassette: RCA/Erato MCE 71483
  LP: RCA/Erato STU 71483; also as 2292-45676-2
  SEE ALSO: Albinoni, Arensky, JS Bach, Brahms, Couperin,
  Lotter, Paganini, Rimsky-Korsakov, Strauss, Weber

PERGOLESI, GIOVANNI BATTISTA (1710-1736)

- *L'OLIMPIADE:* OVERTURE
  New Philharmonia O†/hpsd
  ALBUM TITLE: 18TH CENTURY OVERTURES
  Cassette: Philips 412 406-4
  LP: Philips SAL 3674 (1968)(US/UK); also as Philips 802
           893 LY (German); reissued as Philips 412 406-1

SEE ALSO: Bononcini, Grétry, Handel, Méhul, Mozart, Rameau, Sacchini, D Scarlatti

PROKOFIEV, SERGE (1891-1953)

● *PETER AND THE WOLF, OP 67*
Richard Baker (n), New Philharmonia O†
Cassette: Classics for Pleasure TC-CFP 185
LP: Classics for Pleasure CFP 185 (1971)
** *Penguin Stereo Record Guide*, 2nd Ed. (1977).
SEE ALSO: Britten

PURCELL, HENRY (c.1659-1695)

● *ABDELEZAR* (suite)
THE GORDIAN KNOT UNTIED (suite)
THE OLD BACHELOR (suite)
SONATA IN D FOR TRUMPET AND STRINGS
English Chamber O†/hpsd
CD: CBS/Sony MDT 44644 (with Vivaldi *Four Seasons*
perf. by Zuckerman, St Paul Chamber O)
LP: CBS Masterworks 36707 (1981/digital)

● *COME YE SONS OF ART: CHACONNE & "SOUND THE TRUMPET"*
THE INDIAN QUEEN: TRUMPET OVERTURE
Edita Gruberová (s), Wynton Marsalis (tpt), English Chamber O†
Cassette: CBS Masterworks
CD: CBS Masterworks MK 29061 (digital)
LP: CBS Masterworks IM 39061 (1984/digital)
Grammy Nomination, 1985 (National Academy of Recording Arts & Sciences).
SEE ALSO: Fasch, Handel, Molter, Torelli

● *DIDO AND AENEAS* (opera)
¶ Jessye Norman (Dido), Marie McLaughlin, Thomas Allen, chorus, English Chamber O†
Cassette: Philips 416 299-4 (digital); EXCERPTS: Philips 422 893-4
CD: Philips 416 299-2 (digital); EXCERPTS: Philips 422 893-2
LP: Philips 416 299-1 (1985/digital)
"Leading the warm and transparent sonorities of the English Chamber Orchestra, Leppard lovingly projects Purcell's music without overwhelming it, in a reading that has rhythmic precision and a keen dramatic sweep. A certain risk, I suppose, was taken in casting the voluptuous-voiced Jessye Norman as Dido, but then who can deny that this is an opera built around a star soprano? Miss Norman performs the role with opulence and dignity, keeping her majestic instrument within Baroque bounds." – George Jellinek, *The New York Times*.

¶ Tatiana Troyanos, Felicity Palmer, Richard Stilwell, ECO Choir, English Chamber O†
Cassette: RCA/Erato MCE 71091
LP: RCA/Erato STU 71091 (1978); also as 2292-45263-2; also as RCA ARL 1-3021, Musical Heritage Society MHS 3810

"Tatiana Troyanos and Richard Stilwell are ideal lovers, and Felicity Palmer makes the most avid of Belindas. This is a very spirited *Dido*, sweetly embellished and always atmospheric, from sweethearts' court to helldames' cave to ship outward bound and back to court for Dido's great solo 'When I am laid in earth'.... Troyanos emphasizes [the latter's] plangent nobility, especially telling after the vitality Leppard gives to the preceding scenes." — Ethan Mordden, *A Guide to Opera Recordings* (Oxford University Press, 1987). "In my opinion the most engaging performance of the opera now available... [due to] a highly accomplished cast and the invigorating leadership of Raymond Leppard, who conducts the music with such theatrical vividness that all its power is unmistakably revealed. Under his guidance the solo singers and the chorus characterize their roles with a sense of involvement and a variety of emphasis that makes Purcell's score sound as richly human as one of Monteverdi's music dramas." — *High Fidelity Records in Review 1979*.

¶Overture
English Chamber O†
CD: PolyGram Special Products/Avéro verzekeringen 434 419-2 (see also JC Bach, Handel, Purcell, Rameau, A. Scarlatti; also incl. overtures by Laurens Van Rooyen, Vivaldi cond. by Vittorio Negri, Jed Wentz)

● "WELCOME, WELCOME GLORIOUS MORN" (ODE)
Singers & insts cond. by RL, others, featuring April Cantelo (s), Jeannette Sinclair (s), Helen Watts (cn), Gerald English (t), John Noble (bar), Christopher Keyte (b)
ALBUM TITLE: MUSIC OF THE COURT HOMES AND CITIES OF ENGLAND, Vol 2 – MUSIC AT HAMPTON COURT
LP: EMI/HMV HQS 1141 (1968)
SEE ALSO: Merbecke

RAMEAU, JEAN-PHILIPPE (1683-1764)

● ARIAS –

CASTOR ET POLLUX: "NATURE, AMOUR"
DARDANUS: "VOICI LES TRISTES LIEUX – MONSTRE AFFREUX"
HIPPOLYTE ET ARICIE: "AH! QU'ON DAIGNE DU MOINS – PUISQUE PLUTON"
Gérard Souzay, English Chamber O†/hpsd

ALBUM TITLE: BAROQUE OPERA ARIAS
LP: Philips 835215AY (stereo)
      Philips A02337L (mono)
1965 Grand Prix Jacques Rouché, Académie du Disque Français
SEE ALSO: Handel, Lully

- *DARDANUS* (opera)
  Frederica von Stade (s), Christiane Eda-Pierre (s), Georges
  Gautier (t), Michaël Devlin (bar-b), Roger Soyer (bar-b),
  José van Dam (b), Choeurs & Orchestre du Théâtre National de l'Opéra de Paris†
  2 LPs: RCA/Erato STU 71416 (individual LPs numbered
  STU 71417, STU 71418)(1981)
  "Most listeners, I suspect, will welcome [Leppard's] efforts, not only as editor,
  but as conductor, for I have never heard the Paris Opéra orchestra so supple,
  and playing with such transparency. Von Stade is particularly appealing as the
  heroine.... Recorded sound and surfaces are first rate." — *Fanfare.*

- *LES FÊTES D'HEBE:* BALLET MUSIC
  Ursula Connors (s), Ambrosian Singers, English Chamber O†
  LP: EMI ASD 3084 (1975/stereo)

- *LES PALADINS:* OVERTURE
  ZAÏS: OVERTURE
  New Philharmonia O†
  ALBUM TITLE: 18TH CENTURY OVERTURES, VOL. II
  CD: PolyGram Special Products/Avéro verzekeringen
  434 419-2 (ALBUM TITLE: OVERTURES; with
  Rameau *Pygmalion* overture; see also JC Bach,
  Handel, Purcell, A. Scarlatti; also incl. over-
  tures by Laurens Van Rooyen, Vivaldi cond. by
  Vittorio Negri, Jed Wentz)
  LP: Philips SAL 3760 (1969)(US/UK); also as Philips 802
  901 LY (German)
  SEE ALSO: JC Bach, Boyce, Cimarosa, Locatelli, Mozart, Rameau,
  A Scarlatti

- *PYGMALION:* OVERTURE
  New Philharmonia O†/hpsd
  ALBUM TITLE: 18TH CENTURY OVERTURES
  Cassette: Philips 412 406-4
  CD: PolyGram Special Products/Avéro verzekeringen
  434 419-2 (ALBUM TITLE: OVERTURES; with
  Rameau *Les Paladins* & *Zaïs* overtures; see also
  JC Bach, Handel, Purcell, A. Scarlatti; also incl.

overtures by Laurens Van Rooyen, Vivaldi
cond. by Vittorio Negri, Jed Wentz)
LP: Philips SAL 3674 (1968)(US/UK); also as Philips 802
893 LY (German); reissued as Philips 412 406-1
SEE ALSO: Bononcini, Grétry, Handel, Méhul, Mozart, Pergolesi, Sacchini, D Scarlatti

• *LA TEMPLE DE LA GLOIRE*
¶ Suite I
English Chamber O†
     LP: Decca/L'Oiseau Lyre SOL 297 (1967/stereo)
Decca/L'Oiseau Lyre OL 297 (mono)
SEE ALSO: Grétry
¶ Suite II (ed. by RL)
English Chamber O†/hpsd
     LP: Decca/L'Oiseau Lyre SOL 302 (1968/stereo)
Decca/L'Oiseau Lyre OL 302 (mono)
SEE ALSO: Campra

RIMSKY-KORSAKOV, NIKOLAI (1844-1908)

• *"THE FLIGHT OF THE BUMBLE BEE"*
Scottish Chamber O†
ALBUM TITLE: MOTO PERPETUO/MOUVEMENTS PERPÉTUELS
Cassette: RCA/Erato MCE 71483
     LP: RCA/Erato STU 71483; also as 2292-45676-2
SEE ALSO: Albinoni, Arensky, JS Bach, Brahms, Couperin,
Lotter, Paganini, Paradies, Strauss, Weber

SACCHINI, ANTONIO GASPARE (1730-1780)

• *OEIPE À COLONE:* OVERTURE
New Philharmonia O†/hpsd
ALBUM TITLE: 18TH CENTURY OVERTURES
Cassette: Philips 412 406-4
     LP: Philips SAL 3674 (1968)(US/UK); also as Philips 802
893 LY (German); reissued as Philips 412 406-1
"An excellent disc, in sum, music of the greatest fascination, admirably per-
formed by the New Philharmonia, well recorded, our gratitude to Raymond
Leppard and Philips." — *The Gramophone.*
SEE ALSO: Bononcini, Grétry, Handel, Méhul, Mozart, Per-
golesi, Rameau, D Scarlatti

SAINT-SAËNS, CAMILLE (1835-1921)

- *CONCERTO 1* IN A MINOR FOR CELLO, OP 33
  Claude Starck (vc), English Chamber O†
  CD: Claves CD 50-501
  SEE ALSO: Devienne, Ibert

SCARLATTI, ALESSANDRO (1660-1725)

- *CANTATA PASTORALE*
  Janet Baker, English Chamber O†
  ALBUM TITLE: MUSIC OF MONTEVERDI AND THE SCARLATTIS
  LP: EMI ASD 2615 (1970/stereo)
  SEE ALSO: Monteverdi, D Scarlatti
- *IL GIARDINO DI ROSE:* OVERTURE
  New Philharmonia O†
  ALBUM TITLE: 18TH CENTURY OVERTURES, VOL. II
  CD: PolyGram Special Products/Avéro verzekeringen
          434 419-2 (ALBUM TITLE: OVERTURES; see also JC
          Bach, Handel, Purcell, Rameau; also incl. over-
          tures by Laurens Van Rooyen, Vivaldi cond. by
          Vittorio Negri, Jed Wentz)
  LP: Philips SAL 3760 (1969)(US/UK); also as Philips 802
          901 LY (German)
  SEE ALSO: JC Bach, Boyce, Cimarosa, Locatelli, Mozart, Rameau

SCARLATTI, DOMENICO (1685-1757)

- *SALVE REGINA* (arr. RL)
  Janet Baker, English Chamber O†
  ALBUM TITLE: MUSIC OF MONTEVERDI AND THE SCARLATTIS
  LP: EMI ASD 2615 (1970/stereo)
  SEE ALSO: Monteverdi, A Scarlatti
- *SINFONIA* IN B^b
  New Philharmonia O†
  ALBUM TITLE: 18TH CENTURY OVERTURES
  Cassette: Philips 412 406-4
  LP: Philips SAL 3674 (1968)(US/UK); also as Philips 802
          893 LY (German); reissued as Philips 412 406-1;
          also reissued on Philips 6833 035 (with CPE
          Bach, JC Bach, WF Bach, Handel, Mozart)
  SEE ALSO: Bononcini, Grétry, Handel, Méhul, Mozart, Per-
  golesi, Rameau, Sacchini

SCHEIDT, SAMUEL (1587-1654)

- *CANZON CORNETTO*
COURANT DOLOROSA
PSALM 103
Purcell Chorus, Philip Jones Brass Ens†
ALBUM TITLE: VOICES AND BRASS
LP: Decca/Argo ZRG 576 (1969/stereo)
Decca/Argo RG 576 (mono)
SEE ALSO: Schein, Schütz

SCHEIN, JOHANN HERMANN (1586-1630)

- *ZION SPRICHT*
Purcell Chorus, Philip Jones Brass Ens†
ALBUM TITLE: VOICES AND BRASS
LP: Decca/Argo ZRG 576 (1969/stereo)
Decca/Argo RG 576 (mono)
SEE ALSO: Scheidt, Schütz

SCHUBERT, FRANZ (1797-1828)

- ARIAS —

ALFONSO UND ESTRELLA, D 732: "*KÖNNT' ICH EWIG HIER VERWEILEN*"

LAZARUS, D 689: "*SO SCHLUMMERT AUF ROSEN*"

ROSAMUNDE, D 797: "DER VOLLMOND STRAHLT"

"*ZÖGERND LEISE*", d 920 (with male chorus)
Janet Baker (s), English Chamber O Choir, English Chamber O†/pno
LP: Philips 9500 307 (1977); also issued as Philips 6597 004 & incl. in 4-LP set Philips 6767 001 titled
JANET BAKER • RAYMOND LEPPARD; see also
Beethoven, Gluck, Handel, Haydn, Mozart
"The Schubert numbers have a rapt beauty and an engaging lilt in these performances — '*Zögernd leise*' can so easily drag, but here it is crisp and fresh. The *Lazarus* aria is the biggest and finest of [the group], music that gazes out into the future (presaging *Parsifal* even at one point)." — *Hi-Fi News & Record Review.*
SEE ALSO: Beethoven

- *GRAND DUO* IN C, D. 812 (orchestration by RL)

OVERTURE IN C ("IN THE ITALIAN STYLE"), D 591

SYMPHONY 3 IN D, D 200
Indianapolis Symphony O†

CD: Koss Classics KC-2221 (1991/digital)

"Leppard's orchestra responds beautifully and the disc is filled out with a bright-eyed and elegant reading of the adorable *Symphony No. 3* and the second of two overtures in the Italian style." — *Stereo Review.* "The performance [of the *Grand Duo*], like the instrumentation, is wholly apposite, it is difficult to imagine a better one." — *Fanfare.*

- *OVERTURE* IN B^b, D 470

OVERTURE IN E MINOR, D 648

London Philharmonic O†

CD: Philips 426 978-2 (1990)(also incl. works by Beethoven, Mendelssohn, Wagner cond. by Colin Davis, Eliahu Inbal, Igor Markevitch); overture in e also on PolyGram Special Projects (Voordeeelpas Countdown Postbank PolyGram Nederland BI/Philips Classic) 426 867-2 (1990) — see also JS Bach (cantata), Grieg, Handel (overture), Haydn (vln conc), Mozart (sym in D)

LP: Philips (1972)

- *RONDO* IN A FOR VIOLIN & STRINGS, D 438

Arthur Grumiaux, New Philharmonia O†

CD: Philips 426 977-2 (1990)

LP: Philips SAL 3660 (1967)(US/UK); also as Philips 802 848 LY (German)

*** Edward Greenfield, Robert Layton & Ivan March, *The Penguin Guide to Compact Discs and Cassettes Yearbook 1991.*

SEE ALSO: Haydn (vln conc), Mozart (adagio, rondo)

- *SYMPHONY 3* IN D, D 200

SYMPHONY 6 IN C, D 589

Scottish Chamber O†

Cassette: RCA/Erato MCE 75121

LP: RCA/Erato NUM 75121 (1984)

SCHUMANN, ROBERT (1810-1856)

- *OVERTURE, SCHERZO AND FINALE, OP 52*

OVERTURE TO GENOVEVA, OP 81

SYMPHONY 1 ("SPRING") IN B^b, OP 38

Indianapolis Symphony O†

CD: Koss Classics KC-2213 (1991/digital)

"Exudes Schumanesque charm from start to finish.... Leppard, his orchestra, and Koss have achieved some of the most luminescent orchestral textures I've ever heard in a recording. The strings, the woodwinds, the brass, and the Circle Theatre acoustics collectively produce a sheen that is palpable." — Tom Aldridge, *Arts Indiana.*

SCHÜTZ, HEINRICH (1585-1672)

- *FREUE DICH*
  ICH BESCHWÖRE
  PSALM 24
  Purcell Chorus, Philip Jones Brass Enst
  ALBUM TITLE: VOICES AND BRASS
  LP: Decca/Argo ZRG 576 (1969/stereo)
  Decca/Argo RG 576 (mono)
  SEE ALSO: Scheidt, Schein

SMITH, JOHN CHRISTOPHER (1712-1795)

- "FLOWER OF THIS PURPLE DYE"
  "SIGH NO MORE, LADIES"
  "YOU SPOTTED SNAKES"
  April Cantelo (s), English Chamber Ot/hpsd
  ALBUM TITLE: 18TH CENTURY SHAKESPEAREAN SONGS
  LP: Decca/L'Oiseau-Lyre OL 50205 (1961/mono)
  SEE ALSO: Arne, Chilcot, Greene, Haydn, Hook, T Linley,
  W Linley, Weldon

STAMITZ, ANTON (1750-?1809)

- *CONCERTO* IN D FOR FLUTE
  Jean-Pierre Rampal (fl), Scottish Chamber Ot
  Cassette: RCA/Erato MCE 75039
  LP: RCA/Erato NUM 75039 (1983)
  SEE ALSO: C Stamitz, J Stamitz

STAMITZ, CARL (1745-1801)

- *CONCERTO* IN G FOR FLUTE, OP 29
  Jean-Pierre Rampal (fl), Scottish Chamber Ot
  Cassette: RCA/Erato MCE 75039
  LP: RCA/Erato NUM 75039 (1983)
  SEE ALSO: A Stamitz, J Stamitz

STAMITZ, JOHANN WENZEL ANTON (1717-1757)

- *CONCERTO* IN D FOR FLUTE
  Jean-Pierre Rampal (fl), Scottish Chamber Ot
  Cassette: RCA/Erato MCE 75039
  LP: RCA/Erato NUM 75039 (1983)

SEE ALSO: A Stamitz, C Stamitz

STRAUSS, JOHANN (1825-1899)
- *ALBION-POLKA*, OP 102
  English Chamber O†
  ALBUM TITLE: A BIRTHDAY CONCERT FOR MY GRANDMOTHER.
  HRH the Prince of Wales Celebration Concert to Mark the
  90th Birthday of HM Queen Elizabeth the Queen Mother.
  Recorded live in the Ballroom, Buckingham Palace, 2 Aug
  1990.
  CD: EMI/Angel CDC 7 54164 2 (1990)
  SEE ALSO: Anon, Coates, Doyle, Elgar, Gowers, Matthews
- *PERPETUUM MOBILE*, OP 257
  Scottish Chamber O†
  ALBUM TITLE: MOTO PERPETUO/MOUVEMENTS PERPÉTUELS
  Cassette: RCA/Erato MCE 71483
  LP: RCA/Erato STU 71483; also as 2292-45676-2
  SEE ALSO: Albinoni, Arensky, JS Bach, Brahms, Couperin,
  Lotter, Paganini, Paradies, Rimsky-Korsakov, Weber

TCHAIKOVSKY, PETER ILYICH (1840-1893)
- *SERENADE* IN C FOR STRINGS, OP 48
  English Chamber O†
  CD: Philips (Silver Line) 420 883-2 (1988)
  LP: Philips 7300 532 (1977); also as Philips 420 883-1 (1988)
  SEE ALSO: Dvořák

TELEMANN, GEORG PHILIPP (1681-1767)
- *CONCERTO* IN B^b FOR 3 TRUMPETS (adapt/arr by RL)
  CONCERTO IN D FOR 3 TRUMPETS (adapt/arr by RL)
  Wynton Marsalis (tpts), English Chamber O†
  ALBUM TITLE: BAROQUE MUSIC FOR TRUMPETS
  Cassette: CBS MYT 38482
  CD: CBS/Sony MK 42478
  LP: CBS/Sony MT 42478
  SEE ALSO: Biber, M Haydn, Pachelbel, Vivaldi

THOMSON, VIRGIL (1896-1989)
- *THE MOTHER OF US ALL* (OPERA)
  Mignon Dunn, James Atherton, Philip Booth, Sante Fe Opera†

2 CDs: New World 2-NW 288/289 (1990)
2 LPs: New World Records NW 288/289 (1977)
"This exhilarating, stirring, and touching opera, one of the six or eight works of the American musical theater that have both true artistic stature and proven popular appeal, has at last been put on records.... No one with the faintest interest in our culture should be without a copy." — *High Fidelity Records in Review 1977.*

TOMKINS, THOMAS (1572-1656)

● MADRIGALS ETC

Patricia Clark (s), Eileen Poulter (s), Mary Thomas (s), Rosemary Phillips (cn), Wilfred Brown (t), Gerald English (t), Christopher Keyte (b), Dolmetsch Consort†
ALBUM TITLE: MUSIC OF SHAKESPEARE'S TIME, VOL 2
LP: EMI/HMV CLP 1634 (1963)
SEE ALSO: Dowland, Lassus, Morley, Weelkes

TORELLI, GIUSEPPE (1658-1709)

● *SONATAS A 5* (2) FOR TRUMPET & STRINGS, TV 3, 7

Wynton Marsalis (tpt), English Chamber O†
Cassette: CBS Masterworks
CD: CBS Masterworks MK 29061 (digital)
LP: CBS Masterworks IM 39061 (1984/digital)
Grammy Nomination, 1985 (National Academy of Recording Arts & Sciences). "Wynton Marsalis's trumpet is assertive and confident in the Torelli concertos, which are bright and active, and driven by a subtle organ continuo." — Larry Canale, ed., *Digital Audios: Guide to Compact Discs* (Bantam Books, 1986).

SEE ALSO: Fasch, Handel, Molter, Purcell

VAUGHAN WILLIAMS, RALPH (1872-1958)

● *FANTASIA ON A THEME BY THOMAS TALLIS*

SYMPHONY 7 ("SINFONIA ANTARCTICA")
Roger Allam (n), Indianapolis SO†
CD: Koss Classics

VIVALDI, ANTONIO (1678-1741)

● *CONCERTO* IN D, P 175 (ed. by RL)

CONCERTO IN G MINOR, P 392 (ed. by RL)

SONATA ("AL SANTO SEPOLCRO") IN E FLAT, P 441 (ed. by RL)
English Chamber O†/hpsd
LP: EMI/His Master's Voice HQS 1232 (1970/stereo); also

issued as EMI/Classics for Pleasure Ltd CFP
40371 (1982/stereo)
SEE ALSO: Albinoni, Corelli

- *CONCERTO* IN C FOR OBOE
Essex Youth O†
    LP: Pike Films LP 007
    SEE ALSO: Brahms, Copland
- *CONCERTO* FOR 2 TRUMPETS & STRINGS, RV 537 (adapt/arr
by RL)
Wynton Marsalis (tpts), English Chamber O†
ALBUM TITLE: BAROQUE MUSIC FOR TRUMPETS
    Cassette: CBS MYT 38482
    CD: CBS/Sony MK 42478
    LP: CBS/Sony MT 42478
    SEE ALSO: Biber, M Haydn, Pachelbel, Telemann
- *CONCERTO* FOR VIOLIN, OP 3 NR 9: SLOW MOVEMENT
English Chamber O†
ALBUM TITLE: ALLA BAROCCA
    LP: CBS IM 37215 (1982)
    SEE ALSO: JS Bach, Charpentier, Gluck, Handel, Marcello,
    Pachelbel

WALTON, WILLIAM (b. 1902)

- *A SONG FOR THE LORD MAYOR'S TABLE* (song cycle)
Heather Harper (s), English Chamber O†
    LP: Decca/L'Oiseau-Lyre SOL 331 (1972/stereo)
    Decca/L'Oiseau-Lyre OL 331 (mono)
    (*) *Penguin Stereo Record Guide,* 2nd Ed. (1977).
    SEE ALSO: Maconchy

WEBER, CARL MARIA VON (1786-1826)

- *MOTO PERPETUO*
Scottish Chamber O†
ALBUM TITLE: MOTO PERPETUO/MOUVEMENTS PERPÉTUELS
    Cassette: RCA/Erato MCE 71483
    LP: RCA/Erato STU 71483; also as 2292-45676-2
    SEE ALSO: Albinoni, Arensky, JS Bach, Brahms, Couperin,
    Lotter, Paganini, Paradies, Rimsky-Korsakov, Strauss

WEELKES, THOMAS (1576-1623)

- "IN PRIDE OF MAY" (MADRIGAL)
  "ALL AT ONCE WELL MET, FAIR LADIES" (MADRIGAL)
  Cambridge Univ Madrigal Soc†
  ALBUM TITLE: IN PRIDE OF MAY AND OTHER MADRIGALS
  LP: His Master's Voice HMV 7EP7114 (mono)
  SEE ALSO: Farmer, Monteverdi

- MADRIGALS ETC
  Patricia Clark (s), Eileen Poulter (s), Mary Thomas (s),
    Rosemary Phillips (cn), Wilfred Brown (t), Gerald English
    (t), Christopher Keyte (b), Dolmetsch Consort†
  ALBUM TITLE: MUSIC OF SHAKESPEARE'S TIME, VOL 2
  LP: EMI/HMV CLP 1634 (1963)
  SEE ALSO: Dowland, Lassus, Morley, Tomkins

WELDON, JOHN (1676-1736)

- "TAKE, O TAKE THOSE LIPS AWAY"
  April Cantelo (s), English Chamber O†/hpsd
  ALBUM TITLE: 18TH CENTURY SHAKESPEAREAN SONGS
  LP: Decca/L'Oiseau-Lyre OL 50205 (1961/mono)
  SEE ALSO: Arne, Chilcot, Greene, Haydn, Hook, T Linley,
    W Linley, Smith

---

2. AS PIANIST/HARPSICHORDIST

BACH, JOHANN SEBASTIAN (1685-1750)

- *BRANDENBURG CONCERTOS* (6)
  ¶RL (hpsd for BWV 1050), London Philharmonic O: *cond.*
    Adrian Boult
  2 LPs: EMI SLS 866 (1973)
  ¶RL (hpsd), Academy of St Martin-in-the-Fields: *cond.* Neville
    Marriner
  2 LPs: Philips 6700 045 (1971)

BLAVET, MICHEL (1700-1768)

- *SONATA 2 ("LA VIBRAY")* IN F FOR FLUTE
  André Pepin (fl), RL (hpsd), Claude Viala (vc)

ALBUM TITLE: BAROQUE FLUTE SONATAS
LP: Decca SLX 6430 (1969/stereo)
SEE ALSO: Gaultier, Handel, Loeillet, Telemann, Vinci

GAULTIER, PIERRE (d. after 1638)
- *SUITE* IN G MINOR FOR FLUTE
André Pepin (fl), RL (hpsd), Claude Viala (vc)
ALBUM TITLE: BAROQUE FLUTE SONATAS
LP: Decca SLX 6430 (1969/stereo)
SEE ALSO: Blavet, Handel, Loeillet, Telemann, Vinci

HANDEL, GEORGE FRIEDRICH (1685-1759)
- *CONCERTO GROSSO* IN A, OP 6 NR 4
RL (hspd), Philharmonia O: *cond.* Otto Klemperer
10" LP: Columbia 1053
- *SONATA* IN G FOR FLUTE, OP 1 NR 5
André Pepin (fl), RL (hpsd), Claude Viala (vc)
ALBUM TITLE: BAROQUE FLUTE SONATAS
LP: Decca SLX 6430 (1969/stereo)
SEE ALSO: Blavet, Gaultier, Loeillet, Telemann, Vinci
- *SONATA 1* IN C MINOR FOR OBOE
SONATA 3 IN F FOR OBOE
SONATA 6 IN G MINOR FOR OBOE
SONATA ("FITZWILLIAM") IN B^b FOR OBOE
Marilyn Zupnik (ob), RL (hpsd), Mark Shuman (vc)
CD: ASV (Academy Sound and Vision Ltd) DCA 663
(1989/stereo)
SEE ALSO: Telemann
- *TRIO SONATA* IN G MINOR
Yehudi Menuhin, Gioconda de Vito (vlns), John Shinebourne
(vc), RL (hpsd)
LP: EMI/HMV ALP 1462
SEE ALSO: Purcell, Spohr, Viotti

LOEILLET, JEAN-BAPTISTE (1680-1730)
- *SONATA* IN F FOR FLUTE
André Pepin (fl), RL (hpsd), Claude Viala (vc)
ALBUM TITLE: BAROQUE FLUTE SONATAS
LP: Decca SLX 6430 (1969/stereo)
SEE ALSO: Blavet, Gaultier, Handel, Telemann, Vinci

MONTEVERDI, CLAUDIO (1567-1643)

- *L'INCORONAZIONE DI POPPEA* (OPERA)(RL vers — extensively cut)
  Magda Laszlo, Richard Lewis; RL (hpsd), Glyndebourne Festival Opera: *cond.* John Pritchard
  2 LPs: HMV Angel AN/SAN 126-7; set SLS 908; A/STA 91348-9; Angel set S-3644B; Seraphim set SIB 6073; EMI Angel (His Master's Voice) set SLS 5248
  "[Despite drastic cuts] here is an album which had an undeniable part in moving the Monteverdi revival forward." — *Fanfare.*

MOZART, WOLFGANG AMADEUS (1756-1791)

- *LA NOZZE DI FIGARO* (OPERA)
  Senta Jurinac, Risë Stevens, Franco Calabrese, Huegues Cuénod, Sesto Bruscantini, Graziella Sciutti, Ian Wallace, Monica Sinclair RL (hpsd), Glyndebourne Festival Opera: *cond.* Vittorio Gui
  4 LPs: HMV RLS (LP) 634 (individual LPs numbered ALPS 1312 [single-sided], 1313, 1314, 1315)

PURCELL, HENRY (1659-1695)

- *DIDO AND AENEAS* (OPERA)
  Victoria de los Angeles (Dido), Heather Harper, Patricia Johnson, Peter Glossop, Ambrosian Singers, RL (hpsd), English Chamber O: *cond.* John Barbirolli
  LP: EMI/Music for Pleasure Ltd CFP 40359 (stereo); reissued as Angel Red Line RL 32117
- *THE INDIAN QUEEN*
  RL (hpsd), Bernard Richards (vc), English Chamber O: *cond.* Charles Mackerras
  LP: Decca/L'Oiseau Lyre SOL 294 (1966)
- *TRIO SONATA ("THE GOLDEN SONATA") IN F*
  Yehudi Menuhin, Gioconda de Vito (vlns), John Shinebourne (vc), RL (hpsd)
  LP: EMI/HMV ALP 1462
  SEE ALSO: Handel, Spohr, Viotti

SPOHR, LUDWIG (LOUIS) (1784-1859)

- *DUO* IN D
  Yehudi Menuhin, Gioconda de Vito (vlns), John Shinebourne (vc), RL (hpsd)

LP: EMI/HMV ALP 1462
SEE ALSO: Handel, Purcell, Viotti

STRAVINSKY, IGOR (1882-1971)
- *PETROUCHKA* (BALLET)
  RL (pno), orch: *cond.* Effrem Kurz
  LP: RCA

TELEMANN, GEORG PHILIPP (1681-1767)
- *SONATA* IN F FOR FLUTE
  André Pepin (fl), RL (hpsd), Claude Viala (vc)
  ALBUM TITLE: BAROQUE FLUTE SONATAS
  LP: Decca SLX 6430 (1969/stereo)
  SEE ALSO: Blavet, Gaultier, Handel, Loeillet, Vinci
- *SONATA* IN G MINOR FOR OBOE (from *Tafelmusk*)
  SONATA IN G MINOR FOR OBOE
  SONATA IN A MINOR FOR OBOE
  SONATA IN B^b FOR OBOE
  SONATA IN E MINOR FOR OBOE
  Marilyn Zupnik (ob), RL (hpsd), Mark Shuman (vc)
    CD: ASV (Academy Sound and Vision Ltd) DCA 663
       (1989/stereo)
  SEE ALSO: Handel

VINCI, LEONARDO (c.1696-c.1730)
- *SONATA* IN D FOR FLUTE
  André Pepin (fl), RL (hpsd), Claude Viala (vc)
  ALBUM TITLE: BAROQUE FLUTE SONATAS
  LP: Decca SLX 6430 (1969/stereo)
  SEE ALSO: Blavet, Gaultier, Handel, Loeillet, Telemann

VIOTTI, GIOVANNI BATTISTA (1755-1824)
- *DUO* IN G, BK 2 NR 3 (Peters ed.)
  Yehudi Menuhin, Gioconda de Vito (vlns), John Shinebourne
  (vc), RL (hpsd)
    LP: EMI/HMV ALP 1462
  SEE ALSO: Handel, Purcell, Spohr

INDEX

Marx, Karl, 13
Masnadieri, I (Verdi), 348
Mass in B Minor (Bach), 7, 8
Mass (Cavalli), 316
Mass (Palestrina), 100
Masters, The (Snow), 387
Mathis der Maler (Hindemith), 377
Matoni, 328
Maurice (Forster), 383
Maw, Nicholas, *xii*, 487
Maxwell Davies, Peter, *xix*, 302, 330, 331, 334, 334
Mazarin, Cardinal, 127, 150, 152-154, 242, 295, 299
Mazeppa (Tchaikovsky), 335
Mazzenigo, Palazzo, 232
Mazzocchi brothers (Domenico, Virgilio—both composers), 146
McDonald, Gerald, 311
McEwan, Gerry, 433
McGregor, Sue, 317-323
Medici, Catherine, 219
Medici, Ferdinando de, 103
Medici, Maria de, 104
Medicis, 150
Melanto: see *Il ritorno d'Ulisse in patria*
Melide: see *L'Ormindo*
Melosio, Francesco, 129
Mendel, 19
Mendelssohn, Felix, 5, 7, 10, 106, 168, 284, 289, 292, 302, 421, 433
Ménestrière, Père, 152
Mengelberg, Willem, 364, 365
Menuhin, Yehudi, *xi*, 112, 250, 251, 329, 343, 375
Mercure galant, 35
Mercurio (Mercury): see *L'incoronazione di Poppea*
Mercury: see *La Calisto*
"Merry Waltz, A" (Klemperer), 380
Messa concertata (Cavalli), 242-244
Messel, Oliver, 168

Messiaen, Olivier, 421
Messiah (Handel), 11, 72, 269, 385
Metamorphoses (Ovid), 406
Metastasio, Pietro Antonio Domenico Bonaventura, 280
Metropolitan Opera (New York), *xiii*, 9, 174-177, 379, 435
Metropolitan Opera Encyclopedia, The (Hamilton), 143
Meyer, Karstin, 195
Meyerbeer, G, 292
Miami Opera, *xiv*
Micah: see *Samson*
Middle Ages, 13
Middleton (playwright), 175
Middleton, Dorothy, 388, 389
Middleton, Hubert, 391, 396, 397, 422, 423
Middleton, Hugh, 388, 389
Midsummer Night's Dream, A (Shakespeare), *xi*, 424, 433
Milan, 95, 127
Milanuzzi, Carlo, 241
Milhaud, Darius, 365
Mill, John Stuart, 438
Millico, Giuseppe, 39
Milton, John, 266, 435, 436
Milton Hall (Manchester), 414, 415
Minato, Nicolà, 129, 153
Minerva: see *Il ritorno d'Ulisse in patria*
Minnesota Orchestra, *xiv*
Mirinda: see *L'Ormindo*
Mirtillo: see *Il pastor fido*
Missa Solemnis (Beethoven), 11
Mitchell, Donald, 569, 570
Moeran, E.J. (Ernest John), 385
Molière (Jean Baptiste Poquelin), 151, 154, 383
Monte Carlo, 383
Monteverdi, Claudia, 97, 223
Monteverdi, Claudio, *xiii, xiv, xvi, xxi, xxiii*, 3, 4, 18, 41, 83-85, 91-

PRO/AM MUSIC RESOURCES, INC.

BIOGRAPHIES & COMPOSER STUDIES

ALKAN, REISSUE *by Ronald Smith. Vol. 1*: The Enigma. *Vol. 2*: The Music.

BEETHOVEN'S EMPIRE OF THE MIND *by John Crabbe.*

BÉLA BARTÓK: An Analysis of His Music *by Erno Lendvai.*

BÉLA BARTÓK: His Life in Pictures and Documents *by Ferenc Bónis.*

BERNARD STEVENS AND HIS MUSIC: A Symposium *edited by Bertha Stevens.*

JANÁCEK: Leaves from His Life *by Leos Janácek. Edited & transl. by Vilem & Margaret Tausky.*

JOHN FOULDS AND HIS MUSIC: An Introduction *by Malcolm MacDonald.*

LIPATTI *(Tanasescu & Bargauanu):* see PIANO, below.

LISZT AND HIS COUNTRY, 1869-1873 *by Deszo Legány.*

MASCAGNI: An Autobiography Compiled, Edited and Translated from Original Sources *by David Stivender.*

MICHAEL TIPPETT, O.M.: A Celebration *edited by Geraint Lewis. Fwd. by Peter Maxwell Davies.*

THE MUSIC OF SYZMANOWSKI *by Jim Samson.*

THE OPRICHNIK: An Opera in Four Acts by Peter Il'ich Tchaikovsky. *Transl. & notes by Philip Taylor.*

PERCY GRAINGER: The Man Behind the Music *by Eileen Dorum.*

PERCY GRAINGER: The Pictorial Biography *by Robert Simon. Fwd. by Frederick Fennell.*

RAVEL ACCORDING TO RAVEL *(Perlemuter & Jourdan-Morhange):* see PIANO, below.

RONALD STEVENSON: A Musical Biography *by Malcolm MacDonald.*

SCHUBERT'S MUSIC FOR PIANO FOUR-HANDS *(Weekly & Arganbright):* see PIANO, below.

SOMETHING ABOUT THE MUSIC 1: Landmarks of Twentieth-Century Music *by Nick Rossi.*

SOMETHING ABOUT THE MUSIC 2: Anthology of Critical Opinions *edited by Thomas P. Lewis.*

PRO/AM MUSIC RESOURCES, INC.

MAKING MUSIC GUIDES: Making Four-Track Music *by John Peel.* What Bass, 2ND ED. *by Tony Bacon & Laurence Canty.* What Drum, 2ND ED. *by Geoff Nicholls & Andy Duncan.* What's Midi, 2ND ED. *by Andy Honeybone, Julian Colbeck, Ken Campbell & Paul Colbert.*

THE MUSICAL INSTRUMENT COLLECTOR, REVISED ED. *by J. Robert Willcutt & Kenneth R. Ball.*

THE MUSICAL STAMP DATE BOOK: with an Illustrated Guide to the Collecting of Musical Stamps *by Herbert Moore.*

A MUSICIAN'S GUIDE TO COPYRIGHT AND PUBLISHING, ENLARGED ED. *by Willis Wager.*

MUSICOLOGY IN PRACTICE: Collected Essays by Denis Stevens *edited by Thomas P. Lewis.* Vol. 1: 1948-1970. Vol. 2: 1971-1990.

MY VIOLA AND I *by Lionel Tertis.*

THE NUTLEY PAPERS: A Fresh Look at the Titans of Music (humor) *by James Billings.*

PEACE SONGS *compiled & edited by John Jordan.*

PERCUSSION INSTRUMENTS AND THEIR HISTORY, REV. ED. *by James Blades.*

THE PRO/AM BOOK OF MUSIC AND MYTHOLOGY *compiled, edited & with commentaries by Thomas P. Lewis.* 3 vols.

THE PRO/AM GUIDE TO U. S. BOOKS ABOUT MUSIC: Annotated Guide to Current & Backlist Titles *edited by Thomas P. Lewis.* 2 vols.

RAYMOND LEPPARD ON MUSIC: An Anthology of Critical and Personal Writings *edited by Thomas P. Lewis.*

SKETCHES FROM MY LIFE *by Natalia Sats.*

GUITAR

THE AMP BOOK: A Guitarist's Introductory Guide to Tube Amplifiers *by Donald Brosnac.*

ANIMAL MAGNETISM FOR MUSICIANS: Making a Bass Guitar and Pickup from Scratch *by Erno Zwaan.*

ANTHOLOGY OF FLAMENCO FALSETAS *collected by Ray Mitchell.*

ANTONIO DE TORRES: Guitar Maker—His Life and Work *by José Romanillos. Fwd. by Julian Bream.*